W9-CQZ-395

File Menu and Editing Shortcuts

The following shortcuts apply when saving files and while in specific editing states for the clipboard and accessing editing states for preferences or property sheets:

Close all documents *(Macintosh only)*   Option +click close button or Cmd + Option + W

Revert to last Auto Save   Hold Option / Alt while choosing File, Revert to Saved

Clipboard shortcuts (Using Content Tool)

Move selected text to new insertion point (with drag and drop text preference on)   Drag to new insertion point *(Macintosh only)*

Drag-copy text (with drag and drop text preference on)   Shift +Drag

Drag selected text (with interactive preference off)   Cmd + Ctrl +Drag *(Macintosh only)*

Drag-copy text (with interactive preference off)   Cmd + Ctrl + Shift +Drag *(Macintosh only)*

Preferences

Open **Tool** preferences   Double-click item creation or Zoom tool

Using Style Shortcuts

These shortcuts are available while formatting text with the Content tool, or while applying line properties using either the Item or Content tool.

Apply Text styles

Plain   Cmd / Ctrl + Shift + P

Bold   Cmd / Ctrl + Shift + B

Italic   Cmd / Ctrl + Shift + I

Underline   Cmd / Ctrl + Shift + U

Word Underline (underscore)   Cmd / Ctrl + Shift + W

Strike Through   Cmd / Ctrl + Shift + /

Outline   Cmd / Ctrl + Shift + O

Shadow   Cmd / Ctrl + Shift + S

All Caps   Cmd / Ctrl + Shift + K

Small Caps   Cmd / Ctrl + Shift + H

Superscript   *Macintosh:* Cmd + Shift + + (plus key)
    Windows: Ctrl + Shift + 0 (zero)

Subscript   *Macintosh:* Cmd + Shift + − (hyphen)
    Windows: Ctrl + Shift + 9

Superior   Cmd / Ctrl + Shift + V

Align **Left**   Cmd / Ctrl + Shift + L

Align **Centered**   Cmd / Ctrl + Shift + C

Align **Right**   Cmd / Ctrl + Shift + R

Align **Justified**   Cmd / Ctrl + Shift + J

Align **Forced**   Cmd / Ctrl + Option / Alt + Shift + J

Increase **character** size by preset   Cmd / Ctrl + Shift + >

Increase **character** size by 1 point   Cmd / Ctrl + Option / Alt + Shift + >

Decrease **character** size by preset   Cmd / Ctrl + Shift + <

Decrease **character** size by 1 point   Cmd / Ctrl + Option / Alt + Shift + <

Resize character **proportionally** (with mouse)   Cmd / Ctrl + Option / Alt + Shift +Drag handle

Resize character **non-proportionally** (with mouse)	Cmd/Ctrl+Drag handle
Resize character **constrained** (with mouse)	Cmd/Ctrl+Shift+Drag handle
Apply **next** font in list to highlighted characters	Option/Ctrl+Shift+F9
Apply **previous** font in list to highlighted characters	Option/Ctrl+F9

Line styles

Open Modify dialog to Line TAB	Ctrl+Shift+\ (press Cmd+M on Macintosh while line is selected)
Increase Line Width by preset	Cmd/Ctrl+Shift+>
Decrease Line Width by preset	Cmd/Ctrl+Shift+<
Increase Line Width by 1 point	Cmd/Ctrl+Option/Alt+Shift+>
Decrease Line Width by 1 point	Cmd/Ctrl+Option/Alt+Shift+<

Picture Box Shortcuts

The following shortcuts apply when working with pictures in picture boxes. (While working with pictures inside boxes, the Content tool must be selected; while working with the actual picture boxes themselves, the Item tool must be selected):

Increase picture size 5 percent	Cmd/Ctrl+Option/Alt+Shift+>
Decrease picture size 5 percent	Cmd/Ctrl+Option/Alt+Shift+<
Center picture in box	Cmd/Ctrl+Shift+M
Fit picture to box	Cmd/Ctrl+Shift+F
Fit picture to box **proportionally**	Cmd/Ctrl+Option/Alt+Shift+F
Toggle **Negative/Positive** picture	Cmd/Ctrl+Shift+- (hyphen)
Nudge picture in box 1 point (Content tool)	←, →, ↑, ↓ arrow keys
Nudge picture in box 0.1 point (Content tool)	Option/Alt+←, →, ↑, ↓ keys
Import picture at **36 dpi**	Shift+Click Open button in Get Picture
Import color TIFF as **grayscale**	Cmd/Ctrl+Click Open in Get Picture
Import grayscale TIFF as **black and white**	Cmd/Ctrl+Click Open in Get Picture
Import EPS *without loading spot colors*	Cmd/Ctrl+Click Open in Get Picture
Reimport *all pictures* in document	Cmd/Ctrl+Click Open in Open dialog
Resize box, scale picture **constraining** box shape	Cmd/Ctrl+Shift while resizing picture box
Resize box and picture, **maintaining** picture ratio	Cmd/Ctrl+Option/Alt+Shift+Drag

Text, Font, and Spacing Shortcuts

The following shortcuts apply when formatting text, font, and spacing properties using the Content tool in text boxes:

Adjusting Kerning and leading

Increase current paragraph **leading** 1 point	Cmd/Ctrl+Shift+"
Increase current paragraph **leading** 0.1 point	Cmd/Ctrl+Option/Alt+Shift+"
Decrease current paragraph **leading** 1 point	Cmd/Ctrl+Shift+:
Decrease current paragraph **leading** 0.1 point	Cmd/Ctrl+Option/Alt+Shift+:
Increase **kern/track** at insertion point 1/20 em	Cmd/Ctrl+Shift+}
Increase **kern/track** at insertion point 1/200 em	Cmd/Ctrl+Option/Alt+Shift+}
Decrease **kern/track** at insertion point 1/20 em	Cmd/Ctrl+Shift+{
Decrease **kern/track** at insertion point 1/200 em	Cmd/Ctrl+Option/Alt+Shift+{
Increase **baseline** SHIFT for selected text 1-point	*Macintosh:* Cmd+Option+Shift++ (plus key) *Windows:* Ctrl+Alt+Shift+)

Decrease **baseline** SHIFT for selected text 1-point

Macintosh: Cmd + Option + Shift + – (minus key)
Windows: Ctrl + Alt + Shift + (( )

Increase **vertical/horizontal scaling** for selected text 5 percent   Cmd / Ctrl + [ ]]

Increase **vertical/horizontal scaling** for selected text 1 percent   Cmd / Ctrl + Option / Alt + [ ]]

Decrease **vertical/horizontal scaling** for selected text 5 percent   Cmd / Ctrl + [[ ]

Decrease **vertical/horizontal scaling** for selected text 1 percent   Cmd / Ctrl + Option / Alt + [[ ]

Selecting, Editing, Modifying, and Moving Items

While editing text with the Content tool and modifying or moving items using the Item tool, these all encompassing cuts may help:

Selecting items

Select item layered below current item with Content Tool   Cmd / Ctrl + Option / Alt + Shift + click where items overlap

Select all items (while Item tool is selected)   Cmd / Ctrl + A

Deselect all items (while Item tool is selected)   Tab

Select and Highlight Characters

When *selecting* text using the Content tool *I-beam* cursor in text boxes, use these shortcuts:

Select a **word**	Double-click the word
Select a **word** and its **punctuation**	Double-click between word and punctuation
Select entire **line**	Triple-click anywhere in the line
Select entire **paragraph**	Four clicks anywhere in the paragraph
Select **all text** in story	Five clicks anywhere in story (or Cmd / Ctrl + A)

While using the Content tool in text boxes, the following shortcuts enable you to quickly move the cursor:

One **character**	← or → arrow keys
One **line** (vertically)	↑ or ↓ arrow keys
One **word**	Cmd / Ctrl + ← or → arrow keys
One **paragraph**	Cmd / Ctrl + ↑ or ↓ arrow keys
Start of line	Cmd / Ctrl + Option / Alt + ← (or Home in *Windows*)
End of line	Cmd / Ctrl + Option / Alt + → (or End in *Windows*)
Start of story	Cmd / Ctrl + Option / Alt + ↑ (or *Windows:* Ctrl + Home)
End of story	Cmd / Ctrl + Option / Alt + ↓ (or *Windows:* Ctrl + End)

Modifying Properties

Open **Modify** dialog	Double-click with Item tool
Open **Colors** dialog	Cmd / Ctrl + click color in **Colors** palette
Constrain rectangle to square or oval to circle	Hold Shift while drawing or sizing
Constrain **rotation** to 0, 45, 90 degrees increments	Hold Shift while rotating item
Constrain line angle to 0, 45, 90 degrees increments	Hold Shift while drawing, sizing, or rotating item

Moving items

Nudge item by **0.1 point**	Option / Alt + ←, →, ↑, ↓ keys
Constrain item movement to vertical/horizontal	Hold Shift while Dragging

Drawing Tools and Path-Creation

When drawing or editing bézier shapes, the following shortcuts apply:

Delete Bézier point	Option/Alt +click or ←Backspace/Option/Del (with one or more points highlighted)
Delete Bézier point *while drawing*	Del/←Backspace
Add Bézier point	Option/Alt +click segment
Change **Smooth to Corner** point (or vice versa)	*Macintosh:* Ctrl+Option +click point *Windows:* Ctrl+Shift +click point
Change **Smooth to Corner** point *while drawing*	*Macintosh:* Cmd+Ctrl +click after defining point *Windows:* Press Ctrl+F1 after defining point
Edit Bézier shape *while drawing*	Hold Cmd/Ctrl while creating point
Retract curve handles	*Macintosh:* Ctrl+Option +click point *Windows:* Ctrl+Shift +click point
Select all points in a bézier path	Cmd/Ctrl +Shift +A or double-click a point
Select all points on active path using subpath	Triple-click subpath point
Constrain **Point** to 45 degrees movement	Hold Shift while dragging point
Constrain **Curve Handle** to 45-degree movement	Hold Shift while dragging handle

Changing Views and Pages

These shortcuts may help while changing page display states, page item display, or document view display:

Fit **largest spread** in Window	Option/Alt +*Fit in Window*, or press Cmd/Ctrl +Option/Alt +0 (zero)
Access **Page View** field	*Macintosh:* Ctrl+V *Windows:* Ctrl+Alt +V
Toggle view between 200 percent and Actual	Cmd/Ctrl +Option/Alt +click
Zoom **In (with Interactive Preferences set)**	*Macintosh:* Ctrl+click or Drag *Windows:* Ctrl+Spacebar +click or Drag
Zoom **Out (with Interactive Preferences set)**	*Macintosh:* Ctrl+Option +click or Drag *Windows:* Ctrl+Alt +Spacebar +click or Drag
Delete all **horizontal** *ruler guides*	Option/Alt +click horizontal ruler
Delete all **vertical** *ruler guides*	Option/Alt +click vertical ruler
Show Font Usage	*Macintosh:* F13 *Windows:* F2
Show Picture Usage	*Macintosh:* Option+F13 *Windows:* Shift+F2
Show **Index** palette	Cmd+Option +I *(Macintosh only)*
Toggle Master Pages/Document Pages display	*Macintosh:* Shift+F10 *Windows:* Shift+F4
Display next Master Page	*Macintosh:* Option+F10 *Windows:* Ctrl+Shift +F4
Display previous Master Page	*Macintosh:* Option+Shift +F10 *Windows:* Ctrl+Shift +F3

The following keyboard shortcuts apply when navigating or scrolling through your documents:

	Macintosh	**Windows**
Toggle Enable/Disable live scrolling	Option+Drag scroll thumb	None
Scroll view with Grabber hand	Option+Drag	Alt +Drag
Go to **start** of document	Ctrl+A	Ctrl+Page Up

	Macintosh	Windows
Go to **end** of document	Ctrl + D	Ctrl + Page Down
Up one screen	Ctrl + K or Page Up	Page Up
Down one screen	Ctrl + L or Page Down	Page Down
Up one document page	Ctrl + Shift + K	Shift + Page Up key
Down one page	Ctrl + Shift + L	Shift + Page Down key
View **next** spread	None	Alt / + Page Down key
View **previous** spread	None	Alt / + Page Up key

The following shortcuts are available to Macintosh users equipped with extended keyboards:

Start of document	Home
End of document	End
Up one screen	Page Up
Down one screen	Page Down
To **first** page	Shift + Home
To **last** page	Shift + End
To **previous** page	Shift + Page Up
To **next** page	Shift + Page Down

Tiling and Stacking Document Windows (Macintosh Only)

Tile/Stack document windows at **Actual size**	Hold Ctrl and choose *Tile/Stack*
Tile/Stack document windows at **Fit in Window**	Hold Cmd and choose *Tile/Stack*
Tile/Stack document windows at **Thumbnails**	Hold Option and choose *Tile/Stack*
Tile/Stack document windows at **Actual size** from title bar	Hold Ctrl + Shift and choose *Tile/Stack*
Tile/Stack document windows at **Fit in Window** from title bar	Hold Cmd + Shift and choose *Tile/Stack*
Tile/Stack document windows at **Thumbnails** from title bar	Hold Option + Shift and choose *Tile/Stack*

Find/Change and Search Character Shortcuts

Close Find/Change palette	Cmd / Ctrl + Option / Alt + F
Change **Find Next** button to *Find First*	Hold Option / Alt while clicking *Find Next*

Search for or Change this Character	Press with Cursor in Box	Inputs this Character
Any character (wild card, Find only)	Cmd / Ctrl + Shift + ?	\?
TAB	*Macintosh*: Enter / tin box *Windows*: Ctrl + Tab	\T /t
New paragraph	*Macintosh*: Cmd / Return *Windows*: Ctrl + Enter	\p
New line	*Macintosh*: Cmd + Shift + Return *Windows*: Ctrl + Keypad Enter	\n
New column	*Macintosh*: Cmd + Enter *Windows*: Ctrl + Shift + Keypad Enter	\c
New text box	Cmd / Ctrl + Shift + Enter	\b
Previous box page #	Cmd / Ctrl + 2	\2
Current box page #	Cmd / Ctrl + 3	\3
Next box page #	Cmd / Ctrl + 4	\4
Punctuation space	Cmd / Ctrl + . (period)	\.
Flex space	Cmd / Ctrl + Shift + F	\f
Backslash	Cmd / Ctrl + \	\\

Spell-Checking

These shortcuts will help those users who perform extensive spell-checks:

To Lookup a suspect word	Cmd/Alt+L
To Skip a suspect word	Cmd/Alt+S
To Add a suspect word to your auxiliary dictionary	Cmd/Alt+A
To add all suspect words to the auxiliary dictionary	Option/Alt+Shift+Close/Done button

While Working in Dialog Boxes

Display next TAB in tabbed dialog	*Macintosh:* Cmd+Option+Tab *Windows:* Ctrl+Tab
Display previous TAB in tabbed dialog	*Macintosh:* Cmd+Option+Shift+Tab *Windows:* Ctrl+Shift+Tab
Perform calculations in field	For a mini calculator, use add (+), subtract (−), multiply (*), divide (/) operators between values
Apply	Cmd/Alt+A
Keep Apply state selected (except Space/Align)	*Macintosh:* Cmd/+Option+click Apply button *Windows:* Ctrl+Apply

While Working in Palettes

Minimize/maximize any floating palette	Double-click palette title bar
Select **next** tool in Tool palette	Cmd/Ctrl+Option/Alt+Tab
Select **previous** tool in Tool palette	Cmd/Ctrl+Option/Alt+Shift+Tab
Keep tool **selected** after use	Option/Alt+click tool button in palette
Open **Insert Pages** dialog in Document Layout	Option/Alt+drag master page to document page area
Open **Style Sheets** dialog	Cmd/Ctrl+click style sheet name in palette
Apply **No Style**, then *selected style*	Option/Alt+click style sheet name in palette

Entering Specialized Characters

Automatic in-text page number tag for previous text box in chain	Cmd/Ctrl+2
Automatic in-text page number tag for current text box in chain	Cmd/Ctrl+3
Automatic in-text page number tag for next text box in chain	Cmd/Ctrl+4
Add automatic page number on master page	Cmd/Ctrl+3
Insert one symbol font character	Press Cmd/Ctrl+Shift+Q, then type character
Insert one Zapf Dingbat font character	Press Cmd/Ctrl+Shift+Z, then type character (with font installed)

Due to platform-version differences, the following listing of special character shortcuts differ between Macintosh and Windows platforms:

	Macintosh	Windows
Discretionary hyphen	Cmd+− (hyphen)	Ctrl+− (hyphen)
Discretionary new line	Cmd+Return	Ctrl+Enter
Force Indent	Cmd+\	Ctrl+\
New box	Shift+Enter (keypad)	Shift+Enter (on keypad)
New column	Enter (keypad)	Enter (keypad)
Enter Nonbreaking em dash	Cmd+Option+=	Ctrl+Alt+Shift+=
Enter Em dash	Option+Shift+− (hyphen)	Ctrl+Shift+=
Enter En space	Option+Spacebar	Ctrl+Shift+6

McGraw-Hill/Osborne, 2002

Enter Nonbreaking en dash	Option + − (hyphen)	Ctrl + Alt + Shift + − (hyphen)
Enter Nonbreaking hyphen	Cmd + =	Ctrl + =
Enter Right indent TAB	Option + Tab	Shift + Tab
Enter Non-breaking space	Cmd + 5	Ctrl + 5
Enter Breaking en space	Option + Spacebar	Ctrl + Shift + 6
Enter Nonbreaking en space	Cmd + Option + Spacebar	Ctrl + Alt + Shift + 6
Enter Breaking flexible space	Option + Shift + Spacebar	Ctrl + Shift + 5
Enter Nonbreaking flex space	Cmd + Option + Shift + Spacebar	Ctrl + Alt + Shift + 5
Enter Nonbreaking punctuation space	Cmd + Shift + Spacebar	Ctrl + Alt + 6

Entering XPress Tag Characters

The following characters may seem esoteric to some, but many high-end XPress users still used tag characters to automatically apply styles coming from text-only dedicated word processors. These tags are used for creating ASCII documents that may be imported using the XPress tag import filter.

Character Attributes	Code
Plain	<P>
Bold	<B>
Italic	<I>
Outline	<O>
Shadow	<S>
Underline	<U>
Word underline	<W>
Strike thru	</>
All caps	<K>
Small caps	<H>
Superscript	<+>
Subscript	<−>
Superior	<V>
Type style of current style sheet	<$>
Change font	<f"*fontname*">
Change font size	<z###.##> measured in points
Change color	<c"*colorname*"> or <cC,M,Y,K,cW>
Change shade	<s###>
Horizontal scale	<h###>
Kern the next two characters	<k###.##>
Track	<t###.##>
Set baseline SHIFT	<b###.##>
Vertical scale	<y###.##>

Paragraph attributes	Code
Left-align paragraph	<*L>
Center-align paragraph	<*C>
Right-align paragraph	<*R>
Justify paragraph	<*J>
Force justify	<*F>
Set TAB stops	<*t(##.#, #,"*fillcharacter*"> where t sets the TAB stop, and information on parentheses indicates TAB stop, TAB type (0=left, 1=center, 2=right, 4=decimal, 5=comma, or "*anychar*"=align on character), and leader character (1 followed

by fill character=one fill character; 1 followed by two spaces=no fill character, 2 followed by two characters=2 fill characters).

Set paragraph attributes — <*p(##.#,##.#,##.#,##.#,##.#,##.#,g or G)> where the first 6 values set left indent, first indent, right indent, leading, space before, space after, and lock to baseline to on (G) or off (g).

H&J — <*h"H&Jstylename">

Rule above — <*ra(##,#,"colorname",#,##,##,##> where items in parentheses represent line width, line style, color, shade, from left, from right, and offset values. The style number corresponds to the order in which line styles appear in the rules Style drop-down menu beginning at 0. The rule offset value may be specified in points, or a percentage as in ##%, and including a *T* before the left indent sets the OPTION to the width of actual characters in the first line of text of the paragraph text to follow.

Rule below — Same as above only preceded by <*rb

Drop cap — <*d(*charactercount,linecount*)>

Keep with next — <*kn1> turns the feature on, <*kn0> turns it off

Keep together — <*ktA>set the feature to Keep All lines together, while <*kt(#,#)> sets it to begin and end on specific lines.

Style Sheet Definition — Code

Apply normal style sheet — @$:*paragraph text*

Apply no style sheet — @:*paragraph text*

Define a style sheet — @*stylesheetname*=<*paragraphattributes*>

Base a style sheet on another — @*stylesheetname*=[S"*based-onname*"] <*paragraphattributes*>

Apply a defined style sheet — @*stylesheetname*:*paragraph text*

Style definition — @*stylesheetname* [s] <paragraphattributes>

Special Characters — Code

New line (soft return) — <\n>

Discretionary return — <\d>

Hyphen — <\->

Indent here — <\i>

Right indent TAB — <\t>

Standard space — <\s>

Figure space — <\f>

Punctuation space — <\p>

Flex space — <\q>

Discretionary hyphen — <\h>

Previous text box number character — <\2>

Current text box number character — <\3>

Next page text box number character — <\4>

New column — <\c>

New box — <\b>

Decimal ASCII code for character — <\#*decimalvalue*>

Indicator for Macintosh OS character set — <e0>

Indicator for Windows character set — <e1>

ISO Latin 1 character set — <e2>

@ symbol — <\@>

< symbol — <\<>

\ symbol — <\\>

em dash — <\m>

McGraw-Hill/Osborne, 2002

About the Author

Steve Bain is an award-winning designer, illustrator, author, and teacher. He has worked in multimedia, print, the Web, and related communication fields for over two decades. Steve is also the author of *Fundamental QuarkXPress 4*, *Fundamental Illustrator 7*, *CorelDRAW 10: The Official Guide, Special Edition Using CorelDRAW 9*, *Special Edition Using CorelDRAW! 6 for Windows 95*, and *Looking Good Online*. He contributes regularly to various print, web, design, and illustration publications both in print and online.

QuarkXPress™ 5:
The Complete Reference

Without a doubt, writing a book is an enormous task for any writer. However, in order for books to be written, doors to the real world must be firmly closed. The first and most significant dedication of *QuarkXPress 5: The Complete Reference* goes to my wife Wendy for helping to close that door. If it were not for her efforts and for her steadfast encouragement and support, these pages would be blank.

This book is equally dedicated to our seven-year-old son David, who survived the chapter countdown throughout the course of a summer when I would have preferred virtually any outdoor activity over staring at one of several cathode ray tubes attached to the various whirring computers used to create the content of this book.

This book is also dedicated to you—the reader. Without your inquisitive mind, thirst for knowledge, and driving force to improve your skills, books such as this simply wouldn't exist. The detailed reference information and creative ideas found in *QuarkXPress 5: The Complete Reference* have been created just for you. I know you'll benefit from using QuarkXPress 5 in combination with the exercises and directions you find on these pages.

McGraw-Hill/Osborne
2600 Tenth Street
Berkeley, California 94710
U.S.A.

To arrange bulk purchase discounts for sales promotions, premiums, or fund-raisers, please contact McGraw-Hill/Osborne at the above address. For information on translations or book distributors outside the United States, please see the International Contact Information page immediately following the index of this book.

QuarkXPress™ 5: The Complete Reference

1234567890 DOC DOC 01987654321

Book p/n 0-07-219459-6 and CD p/n 0-07-219458-8
parts of
ISBN 0-07-219318-2

Publisher
  Brandon A. Nordin

Vice President & Associate Publisher
  Scott Rogers

Acquisitions Editor
  Megg Bonar

Senior Project Editor
  Betsy Manini

Acquisitions Coordinator
  Tana Diminyatz

Technical Editor
  Robin Kibby

Full Service Compositor
  MacAllister Publishing Services, LLC

Illustration Supervisor
  Lyssa Wald

Series Design
  Peter F. Hancik

This book was composed with QuarkXPress™ Publisher.

QuarkXPress™ 5:
The Complete Reference

Steve Bain

McGraw-Hill/Osborne

New York   Chicago   San Francisco
Lisbon   London   Madrid   Mexico City
Milan   New Delhi   San Juan
Seoul   Singapore   Sydney   Toronto

Contents at a Glance

Contents

Part I

Basic Concepts and Fundamentals

Part II

Creating Layouts and Documents

Part III

Putting It All Together

Part IV

Beyond QuarkXPress Basics

Acknowledgments

I'd like to extend my thanks to the McGraw-Hill/Osborne publishing team, many of whom are scattered throughout America (and worldwide). I owe a special thanks to acquisitions editor Megg Bonar, who has become a good friend to this author over the years. I'd also like to acknowledge the efforts of senior project editor Betsy Manini, whom I've enjoyed having the privilege of working with, as well as project coordinator Beth Brown and the MacAllister team of copy editors who have contributed their grammatical expertise and to whom a generous helping of acknowledgment and credit is well due. I'd also like to acknowledge the efforts made by acquisitions coordinators Tana Diminyatz and Alex Corona, and illustration supervisor Lyssa Wald. I couldn't possibly forget the relentless attention to detail paid by our technical reviewer Robin Kibby of Kibbymega Designs for checking through possibly thousands of tediously accurate procedures, techniques, and keyboard shortcuts covering both Macintosh and Windows versions of QuarkXPress 5.

Let me also take this opportunity to thank Quark's public relations manager, Glen Turpin, for his extra effort and support in providing vital information during an incredibly busy development cycle. I'd also like to acknowledge the efforts of Rochelle Mulhern in Quark's quality assurance department for lending a helping hand, and let's not overlook the critical work of Quark's largely anonymous software engineers who have carefully crafted one of Quark's most significant QuarkXPress releases to date.

Introduction

QuarkXPress 5: The Complete Reference is a book for all levels of users who are working with (or contemplating working with) QuarkXPress 5. The concepts and features of the program have been explained using common, everyday language and many of the creative exercises are easy to follow and quick to perform. QuarkXPress 5: The Complete Reference is also supported by a comprehensive glossary and index to help locate and define the not-so-common terms you might encounter. A 16-page color insert provides real-world, professionally produced samples to offer examples of the level of quality and creativity that may be achieved through the use of XPress. The information, references, and examples in this book have been structured and organized in a logical and natural learning progression.

QuarkXPress 5: The Complete Reference has been written with value for the reader in mind. It has been structured as both a teacher, a reference manual, and a learning tool. Information and step-by-step lessons have been written in everyday terms, and the topics covered feature complete cross-referencing to related subjects.

Who Should Have This Book

On the creative side of business, QuarkXPress 5: The Complete Reference will be of interest to art and design students, digital artists, illustrators, professional designers, Internet artists, art directors, and desktop publishers, regardless of which platform they work on. But although QuarkXPress 5: The Complete Reference is focused toward the creative aspects of XPress 5's use, it will also be invaluable to professionals not entirely familiar with layout techniques, including those working in related industries, such as technical documentation and commercial publishing, or service-based publishing industries, such as in-house print shops and service bureaus.

QuarkXPress 5: The Complete Reference will be a valuable reference and guide for professionals currently using QuarkXPress 5 or who are upgrading from a previous version and/or work in one of the following publishing-related occupations:

- Digital layout artist
- Web designer
- Publishing specialist
- Publishing consultant
- Graphic designer
- Documentation manager
- Magazine publisher
- Consumer catalog publisher
- Reference book publisher
- Print shop lithographer
- Service bureau operator

What's So Great about This Book?

Where other electronic layout application books often do well at providing technical information and/or program feature references, they often lack a degree of reader instruction and learning. And where some how-to layout books often excel in providing techniques, they often fall short when it comes to complete program reference. This is where *QuarkXPress 5: The Complete Reference* has the advantage.

Not only does *QuarkXPress 5: The Complete Reference* provide complete program operational references and comprehensive feature use, it also fully explores digital publishing techniques specifically geared toward the use of QuarkXPress 5. While bridging the reference and technique gap found in other books, *QuarkXPress 5: The Complete Reference* also delivers in these ways:

- Explains program operations and feature usage devoid of technical jargon
- Covers and addresses both Macintosh and Windows platforms
- Loaded with tips, tricks, and QuarkXPress 5 shortcuts
- Covers comprehensive QuarkXPress 5 features
- Fully explains current digital publishing techniques

Conventions Used in This Book

In order to cover multiplatform usage, you'll encounter command and shortcut notations that may seem confusing at first. Because of the slight differences in keyboard and shortcut identification across Macintosh and Windows platforms, you'll generally see textual references such as CMD/CTRL and OPTION/ALT used to identify certain key combinations. The CMD and OPTION keys pertain to Macintosh users, while the CTRL (short for Control) and ALT (short for Alternate) keys pertain mostly to Windows platform users. In all instances, Macintosh key presses are specified first, followed by Windows key presses, each separated by a forward slash.

When multiple keys are pressed to accomplish a command, a + joins the key presses. When menu and submenu access is referred to, all of which are common to all platforms, commands are separated by pipe symbols in this way: File | Open. The order of these keyboard notations remains constant and consistent throughout *QuarkXPress 5: The Complete Reference*. However, you'll also encounter instances where these platforms deviate from typical commonality. In these instances, both Macintosh and Windows users are addressed separately.

In the course of following through the steps contained in this book, you may encounter other somewhat cryptic terms in the creation, selection, or manipulation of items or content. The following brief list may help define some of these terms:

- **Menu | submenu | submenu** This commonly found annotation is used to describe the action of accessing QuarkXPress 5's application menus (and submenus where they exist). The first entry describes the main application menu while the remaining entries describe any further menus to choose. Each entry in this text is separated by a vertical pipe character.

- **Specified shortcuts** In most instances, when application shortcuts apply, specified commands are followed by the key presses. For example, to save a new file, choose File | Save (CMD/CTRL+S). You may quickly recognize these key presses by the capping style applied.

- **Select** This is one of the most basic operations you'll want to be familiar with when using QuarkXPress 5. To select a content item, click it once with the Item tool. To select text, use the Content tool and click-drag to select a string (sequence) of characters.

- **Deselect** Once an item has been selected using the Item tool, clicking it a second time while holding the SHIFT key deselects the item. You may deselect a particular item within a collection of selected items by holding the SHIFT key and clicking it with the Item tool. When using the Content tool and working with text, clicking any other entry point in the text or a different item on your document page deselects the selected text.

- **Marquee-select** This basic technique is used for selecting items within a defined area and describes the action of click-dragging a given item on your page using the Item tool. As you drag the Item tool cursor, a dotted marquee-style line appears, indicating the defined area.

■ **Shift-select or Shift-click**   This term is a brief way of describing the action of holding the SHIFT key in combination with a mouse click and is often used to describe selecting or deselecting items. For example, when working with text and using the Content tool, holding the SHIFT key while clicking the tool cursor also enables you to select contiguous characters within the text string.

■ **Control-click or Command-click**   This term describes holding the Control (CTRL) or Command (CMD) keys in combination with a mouse click. For example, when creating lines, holding the Command key enables you to constrain the newly created lines vertically or horizontally.

■ **Click-drag**   This describes the action of clicking the mouse button and subsequently dragging the tool or cursor immediately afterwards before releasing the mouse button. Click-dragging is often used for altering the position of points, the size of boxes, or the position of items.

■ **Right-click**   This Windows term is used to describe the action of clicking the right mouse button, as opposed to the usual left mouse button, in order to access a pop-up menu. The pop-up menu is context sensitive and offers access to available commands, options, or properties. Macintosh users may access the context-sensitive pop-up menu by CTRL-clicking an item or interface element.

Tips, Cautions, Notes, and Shortcuts

QuarkXPress 5: The Complete Reference is fully loaded with relevant Tips and Notes as they relate to the tools and features being used. The perspective offered by these value-added considerations is combined in the text with extensive coverage of the keyboard shortcuts implemented in QuarkXPress 5. And in case you need a complete reference of all the available XPress 5 shortcuts (both obvious and hidden), the tearout keyboard shortcuts guide covers them all.

Complete Subject Cross-Referencing

As you'll also discover on your exploration of the chapters to come, reference duplication has been avoided by integrating complete subject cross-referencing to optional related ideas and concepts you may wish to explore further. In this unique way, *QuarkXPress 5: The Complete Reference* enables you to focus your reading and learning efforts and avoid the need to hunt and pick for related information.

How This Book Is Organized

QuarkXPress 5: The Complete Reference has been organized into four parts comprised of 20 chapters supported by an appendix and a keyboard shortcuts guide. Each chapter is designed to guide you through the use of XPress 5's tools, and the chapter sequence has been structured in a sequence logical to learning the program.

Part I: Basic Concepts and Fundamentals

Whether you're just getting acquainted with QuarkXPress 5 as a first-time user or you're revisiting this latest version, "Part I: Basic Concepts and Fundamentals" is designed to cover the basics.

Chapter 1, "Get Going with QuarkXPress 5," is designed to have you quickly using the tools and producing layouts.

Chapter 2, "Getting Acquainted with QuarkXPress 5," provides you with an understanding of XPress 5's basic file operations and tool functionality so that you can begin effectively laying out documents. In an effort to maximize your productivity, you'll get some insight into how to actually get started building your publishing document in Chapter 3, "Putting QuarkXPress to Work."

If you're new to working with text and typographic functionality, Chapter 4, "Text Basics and Typographic Tools," will introduce you to the world of fonts and type as well as how to use specific tools to manipulate text in XPress 5. To wrap up basic functionality with a not-so-basic feature, Chapter 5, "Using QuarkXPress Drawing and Line Tools," teaches you Bézier drawing tools along with the typical item-creation toolset features of XPress 5.

Part II: Creating Layouts and Documents

After you're familiar with the workings of the text and drawing tools of QuarkXPress 5, the next step is to understand the special XPress twist on layout and how to begin assembling the elements on your document pages. The adventure begins with Chapter 6, "Shaping Words and Paragraphs," where you'll learn to set character and paragraph text properties, work in columns, set styles, and generally massage your textual content. Chapter 7, "Designing with Pictures and Graphics," takes you into the world of digital photographs and graphics. You'll explore both typical and professional techniques used in working with pictures. Chapter 8, "Advanced Picture Strategies," examines the more enthusiastic applications of pictures in XPress by exploring picture color and effects as well as clipping paths. Chapter 9, "Combining Text and Picture Effects," sets you on your way to melding text and pictures together by examining text and picture runarounds, runaround effects, box-shaping techniques, text-to-box conversions, and anchoring items in text. Chapter 10, "Working with Tables," teaches you one of the newest and most innovative QuarkXPress features for integrating tabular content into documents.

Part III: Putting It All Together

Part III has been structured to cover producing final published documents using XPress 5, including the use of long and complex document features available in XPress 5. Chapter 11, "Essential Document Layout Techniques," explains basic design functions available in QuarkXPress 5, such as using Jabberwocky, anchoring and locking content, organizing page items, and moving content within and between documents. Chapter 11 also details the new QuarkXPress 5 Layer feature.

Chapter 12, "Tools for Large and Complex Projects," details the XPress 5 Book and Chapter features and teaches you how to work with libraries for storing and retrieving layouts. It also details the use of style sheets, lists, and indexes. Chapter 13, "Mastering Advanced QuarkXPress 5 Features," looks at even higher-level publishing resources in QuarkXPress 5, such as using the new guide manager, appending resources between documents, and controlling preferences, tool settings, kerning, and tracking. It also looks at creating custom elements such as colors, line styles, dictionaries, and hyphenation and justifications (H&Js).

Part IV: Beyond QuarkXPress Basics

This final part looks at the world beyond your desktop and explores digital color, trapping, printing, web document creation, and file import and export commands. Chapter 14, "Designing in Color," explains how QuarkXPress sees, interprets, and measures color; it details how to create and apply color using the Colors palette. You'll also find out all about the various color models available in QuarkXPress 5. Chapter 15, "Color Trapping Basics," will shed some light on the mysterious world of color trapping for offset print reproduction. Chapter 16, "Achieving Accurate Color," provides you with an understanding of Quark's color management system and details how to ensure that the color elements you create in your QuarkXPress 5 document appear and print using consistent color throughout your publishing workflow.

Chapter 17, "Tackling Printing Tasks," covers all the aspects of printing, ranging from getting a simple page from your desktop printer to printing tiling pages for oversized documents, getting proper output from a high-resolution imagesetter, and working with service bureaus. The printing journey continues with Chapter 18, "Preparing Digital Color Separations," where you'll learn how digital color images separate into film and you'll be shown efficient ways to achieve this using Quark's desktop color separation (DCS) technology. Chapter 19, "Creating Web Documents" details all of the newest tools and features available for creating web documents. Chapter 20, "Importing and Exporting Content," looks at sticky issues surrounding crossing platforms and exporting your XPress pages to portable document formats and encapsulated PostScript (EPS).

Reference

The reference materials provided for you in this book aren't simply references, but in fact provide a complete insight into the inner workings of XPress by detailing weird and wonderful terms defined for your enlightenment, *and* a universe of keyboard shortcuts:

- Located after the last chapter is a glossary. It is a backend support defining the more uncommon terminology encountered throughout this book.

- At the front of this book, you will find a comprehensive and thorough collection of keyboard shortcuts that have been engineered into QuarkXPress 5, all presented for your ease of use in a handy perforated tear-out insert.

The Complete Reference

QuarkXPress 5

Part I

Basic Concepts and Fundamentals

The
Complete
Reference

QuarkXPress
5

Chapter 1

Get Going with
QuarkXPress 5

3

If you're a recent updater or convert to QuarkXPress 5, you're in for a treat. As far as professional layout applications go, QuarkXPress ranks among the very best in achieving control over publishing layouts—whatever your purpose. If you've thumbed to this first chapter of this book in search of a fast way to begin working with QuarkXPress 5's most commonly used tools, congratulations are in order. You've chosen to start at the beginning—always a good choice. This first chapter will get you on your way to installing the program and onward to quickly producing your first layout. In this chapter, you'll learn all about Quark's complex installation procedure and how to quickly get up and running. You'll also learn all about critical stuff such as using QuarkXPress 5's program and document windows, installing auxiliary files, opening and saving documents, and closing and quitting. You'll also get a quick primer on how to get text on the page and print a quick hard copy. Once your feet are firmly planted, you'll learn where to get help both online and from this book. After completing this chapter, you'll likely be ready to create rudimentary documents until you move on to the remaining sections.

Before opening the envelopes containing the program disc and installation diskettes, be sure the version you have is correct for your system. Neither Quark nor the dealer you bought the program from will accept returned software once this envelope is opened.

Installing QuarkXPress 5

The QuarkXPress program disc contains all of the compressed data required to build the application on your system as well as auxiliary files. But before you attempt an installation, it's worthwhile knowing what you need in terms of your computer hardware and operating system. If you've already installed the data, feel free to skip ahead in this chapter to the section "Running QuarkXPress for the First Time."

Mac OS Installation Requirements

In order to accommodate QuarkXPress 5 in terms of hardware and system resources in a Macintosh publishing environment, you must be equipped with at least the following:

- A PowerPC-based, Mac OS-compatible computer system running the following Macintosh operating system software: Mac OS 8.6, 9.0, 9.04, 9.1, or Mac OS X in Classic mode.

- For the successful printing of your documents in a Macintosh environment, you'll need LaserWriter driver version 7.0 or higher.

- Installation and access to other disc resources.

- At least 16MB of available random-access memory (RAM) with virtual memory turned off.

- A minimum of 51MB of free available hard disk space to accommodate full installation of QuarkXPress 5.

Tip

Although Quark specifies 16MB of available RAM and 36MB of free available hard disk space as the minimum requirements, lengthy or graphic-intensive documents will operate more efficiently with more RAM and hard drive space to accommodate document storage. If possible, work with at least 22MB of available RAM for graphic-intensive documents and ample free hard drive space.

Along with the previous requirements for installing QuarkXPress in a Macintosh environment, it may be wise to have Adobe Type Manager (ATM) installed for an accurate screen display of Adobe Type 1 fonts.

Note

The previous requirements should be considered minimal for installing and using QuarkXPress in a Macintosh environment for basic publishing tasks. Common sense dictates that having more RAM or a faster processor will speed program operation and operating capacity.

Windows Installation Requirements

In order to accommodate QuarkXPress 5 in terms of hardware and system resources in a Windows environment, you must be equipped with at least the following:

- Microsoft Windows 95, Windows NT 4.0, and supported features of Windows Millennium Edition (ME) and NT 2000
- A Pentium-based (or faster), Windows-compatible computer system processor
- An available CD-ROM drive (or access to a CD-ROM network drive)
- 32MB of total RAM, and more for working with memory-intensive documents
- 40MB of free hard drive space for a minimum installation or 80MB for a complete installation of QuarkXPress 5

Note

These requirements should be considered minimal for installing and using QuarkXPress in a Windows environment for rudimentary publishing applications. Having more RAM or a faster processor will certainly speed program operation and operating capacity.

Other Requirements

Along with the previously mentioned software and hardware requirements, the following items might be considered a potential wish list as far as other resources go. Although having them won't affect the operation of QuarkXPress 5 itself, they will likely be required for common publishing methods and many of the topics discussed in this book.

- A Windows- or Mac-compatible PostScript printer with 2MB of internal RAM (additional printer memory may be required for graphic-intensive documents).

- A laser, dot matrix, or ink-jet printer supported by Mac OS and/or Windows 95/98/NT or Windows 2000.

- If you're working with Type 1 fonts, you'll need ATM for them to correctly appear on your screen and print properly.

- If you're connected to a network and are using it to install QuarkXPress with a Microsoft Windows 95, Windows 98, Windows Millennium Edition (ME), or Windows 2000 operating system, it must be IPX-compatible (as most are).

If your printer uses RAM and is capable of being upgraded with additional RAM, you may want to add more. Lengthy, font-intensive, graphic-intensive documents and/or higher-resolution printing often requires more memory in order to print efficiently.

Before Installing

With any new program, you'll want to find out as much information about it as possible before allowing it free reign on your computer. As with most software, Quark provides a listing of any late-breaking news or software issues. This information is stored in two portable document files located in your QuarkXPress application folder. It's always wise for users to take the time to read this important information. Software companies go to great pains to provide this information. The files are named ReadMe.pdf and Troubleshooting Guide.pdf and may be opened and viewed using Adobe Acrobat Reader.

If, for some reason, your program disc is damaged or defective and you require a replacement in order to successfully install the program, return the software to the store where you bought it or contact Quark Customer Service at 800-788-7835 (toll-free in North America) or 303-344-3491 (Latin America) to arrange for replacements.

To begin installing QuarkXPress 5, insert the program disc into your CD-ROM drive and have your serial number handy. Make a note of this number for future reference, or keep nearby if contacting Quark for technical support should you ever need it.

Before you proceed with your installation of QuarkXPress 5, you'll need to disable any virus protection programs you may have loaded. Some virus protection software can adversely affect the installation process.

If your system has its *Auto Run* feature enabled, the installation will begin immediately. If it's not, you may need to locate the installation program on your own. For Macintosh users, open the drive folder that appears on your desktop, locate the

InstallerVISE data file named QuarkXPress 5.0, and double-click to launch the installer. Windows users may use Explorer to locate the drive and double-click the Install.exe file in the root directory of the disc or choose Run from the Windows Start menu. Each operation launches the installer application.

If you have trouble with the installation process and are at your wits' end, you may contact Quark directly by calling 303-894-8899. You'll need to provide your QuarkXPress 5 serial number and possibly other details about your specific installation problems, your operating system version, and/or other details about your system.

Using the Install Wizard

Once the Installer has been launched, you'll be presented with three initial dialogs. The first will specify the application used to create the Installation Wizard. Macintosh users will see the InstallerVISE screen from MindVision Software, while Windows users will see the InstallShield Wizard dialog. The second dialog to appear will be the software copyright terms that you must agree with in order to proceed. The third dialog will enable you to enter your product serial number. After dealing with each of these dialogs, you'll see the first actual screen of the installation (see Figure 1-1) which

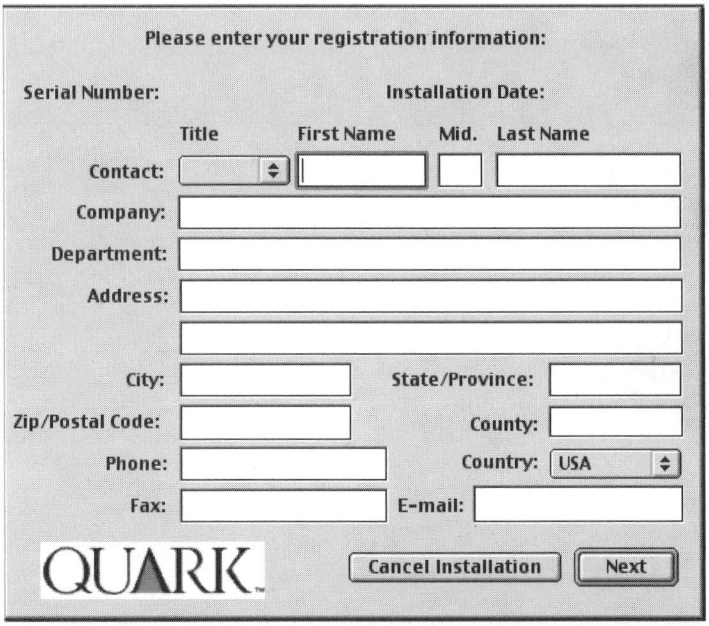

Figure 1-1.   *The first actual installation screen requires you to enter your personal data.*

enables you to enter your user information and verify the information in a following dialog.

The Installer Wizard now continues on to the actual program installation, displaying the screen shown in Figure 1-2. This screen enables you to choose a complete installation or a custom installation. In most cases, a complete installation will be the preferred choice. Choosing the Complete Installation option and clicking Continue/Next enables you to install all files required to use all features of QuarkXPress 5. (Windows users may also click the Space button to obtain a quick summary of the required versus available hard drive space for the installation.)

After the installation is complete, you will be presented with the option to register online. Click Yes if you have an Internet connection and proceed through the remaining screens. If not, click No, in which case the installation runs to completion and clicking OK at the end closes the Wizard.

However, if your choice is Custom Installation, follow these steps:

1. Click Install/Next to proceed to the next screen (see Figure 1-3) after choosing Custom Installation. The Install Wizard also gives you the option of changing the default location where program files are normally copied and of choosing specific components to install.

2. In this dialog, you may change the install location and select the features you want to install using typical browsing procedures. You may also click the expand buttons to view further listings of related components and/or click the

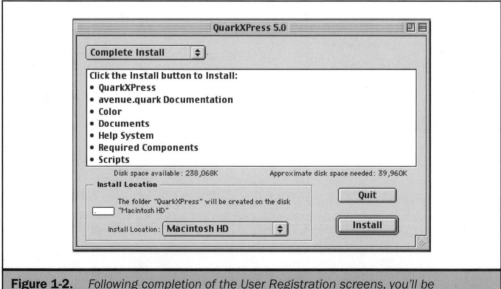

Figure 1-2.   *Following completion of the User Registration screens, you'll be presented with this screen that begins the installation process.*

checkboxes beside the listed components to select or deselect them for installation.

3. Once your choices are complete, click Install to accept your custom installation choices. Once installation is complete, a prompt will appear to let you know the installation was successful.

Figure 1-3.   *After choosing Custom Installation and clicking Install, this dialog appears.*

Modifying, Repairing, or Removing an Installation (Windows Only)

Windows users of QuarkXPress have the option of repairing or modifying their current installation if they choose to. To repair or modify an installation, run the InstallShield Wizard after your initial installation procedure. At this point, you'll need to follow the same procedure as the original installation by inserting both your QuarkXPress program disc into the CD-ROM drive and clicking options in the AutoRun dialog, or by manually running the QuarkXPress 5 installer application.

If QuarkXPress 5 is already installed, the InstallShield Wizard will open to a screen enabling you to repair, modify, or remove QuarkXPress 5. Clicking the Next button within this dialog will display the Program Maintenance screen featuring three options, as shown in the following illustration. You can repair,

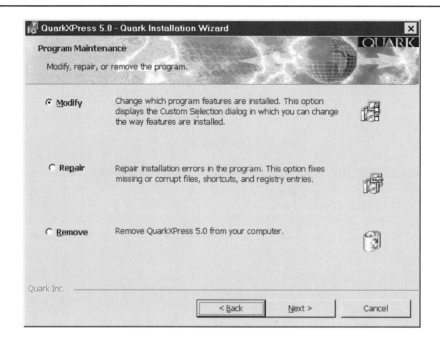

modify, or remove your QuarkXPress 5 application by choosing options in this dialog.

To make changes to your current installation, choose Modify and click the Next button to proceed to the Custom Setup screen. Here you select or deselect which components you want to install or remove. Clicking the Expand/Collapse buttons shows or hides the tree directory contents listing the individual components. The icon to the left of each component name indicates its install state. To change the install state, click an icon to open a popup menu listing the available install states and choose a different option. To modify your installation after changing feature installation states, click the Next button. Although the specific wording differs between Macintosh and Windows versions, the install states may be one of five different states comprised of the following (see the next illustration):

- The selected component will be installed to your hard drive.
- The selected component will have some subfeatures installed to your hard drive.
- The selected component will be installed on first use.
- The component will be run from a network drive.
- The component will not be installed.

In rare circumstances, you may need to repair your QuarkXPress 5 installation, as can be the case with system failures or hardware problems. To repair some or all of the feature components of a QuarkXPress 5 installation, simply click the Repair option in the InstallShield Wizard, click the Next button, and click Install in the final screen. Any damaged components will be replaced. To remove (uninstall) your copy of QuarkXPress 5, choose the Remove option in the InstallShield Wizard and follow the same procedure. After removal, all components of the application (including registry entries) will be removed.

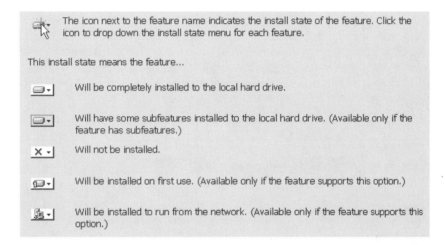

Macintosh users may remove QuarkXPress 5 simply by dragging the entire contents of the QuarkXPress folder to the Trash on the desktop.

Running QuarkXPress for the First Time

Perhaps the simplest of operations is launching QuarkXPress. Mac users will double-click the program icon (or alias) on their desktop, while Windows users will click the Start menu and choose Programs | QuarkXPress | QuarkXPress 5. Upon launching, Quark loads progressively, setting up application and preference files, XTensions, and fonts. After QuarkXPress has loaded, you may want to familiarize yourself with several things that are covered in the following sections.

Getting Version and User Info

Opening QuarkXPress for the first time isn't unlike opening it for the hundredth time. No special welcoming banners appear, and no congratulations is offered—the program does display a splash screen though each time it is launched (see Figure 1-4). This screen identifies the program, version number (including any maintenance revision numbers), copyright information for third-party licenses, and the name of the individual and/or occupation and/or company name the software is registered to.

The splash screen may be viewed at any time by choosing About QuarkXPress from the Apple menu (Macintosh) or by choosing Help | About QuarkXPress (Windows). To close the splash screen, click it with your cursor or press either the ESC or RETURN keys on your keyboard.

You may also open a secret dialog box that lists a highly detailed summary of your version of QuarkXPress, including version numbers and other software-specific inclusions. To open the QuarkXPress Environment dialog (as shown in Figure 1-5), hold the OPTION key while choosing About QuarkXPress from the Apple menu on the

Figure 1-4.   *The splash screen displays user, platform, and version information.*

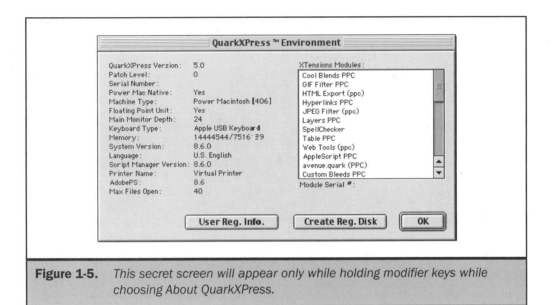

Figure 1-5.   *This secret screen will appear only while holding modifier keys while choosing About QuarkXPress.*

Macintosh version or hold CTRL while choosing Help, About QuarkXPress on the Windows version.

This dialog features access to two noteworthy command buttons: the *User Reg. Info* and the *Create Reg. Disk* command buttons, each of which has a special purpose. Clicking the User Reg. Info button automatically creates a new single-page QuarkXPress 5 document that contains a text box detailing your application serial number and registration information. This information is identical to the personal data entered in the QuarkXPress 5 install application screens when your application was originally installed.

It may be wise to physically print and store this document in a safe place, even if you don't save the QuarkXPress document. To save the document, use the File | Save command (CMD/CTRL+S) and specify a folder location (the document is automatically named User Registration Data) such as the Registration folder in your QuarkXPress application folder.

Clicking the Create Reg. Disk command button enables you to create an encoded Quark registration data file to save to disk as a backup to the one that was created when you first installed the program. If you do not have Internet access and want to register your version of QuarkXPress, use this button to create the registration disk. In order for this to be economical though, it'll help a great deal to have a 3.5-inch disk drive available. On Windows systems this likely won't be a problem, but certain Macintosh users (such as iMac owners) may find themselves without the proper equipment. Once the disk has been created, you may mail it directly to Quark (User Registration, P.O. Box 480790, Denver, CO 80248-0790).

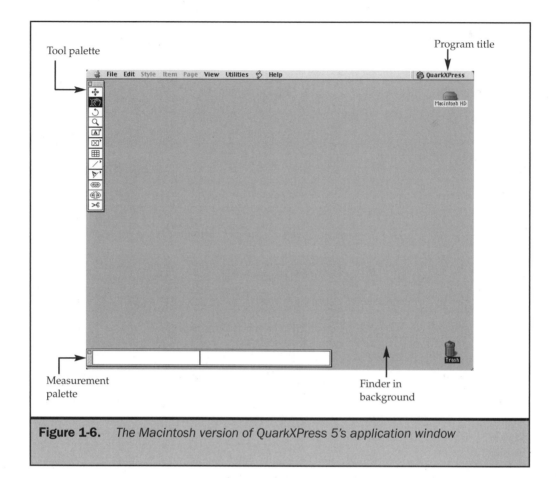

Figure 1-6.   *The Macintosh version of QuarkXPress 5's application window*

QuarkXPress 5's Application Window

If you're looking at the application window for the first time (as shown in Figures 1-6 and 1-7), you'll probably want to familiarize yourself with what's on your screen before going too much further. The application window includes the main menu bars (some of which are grayed out), the program title, and the main Tool palette containing all of the tools you'll be using, and an empty Measurements palette.

The appearance of QuarkXPress 5's application window differs slightly between Windows and Mac platforms. Mac users will see their desktop showing through from behind QuarkXPress, while Windows user will see an application window that completely covers the screen.

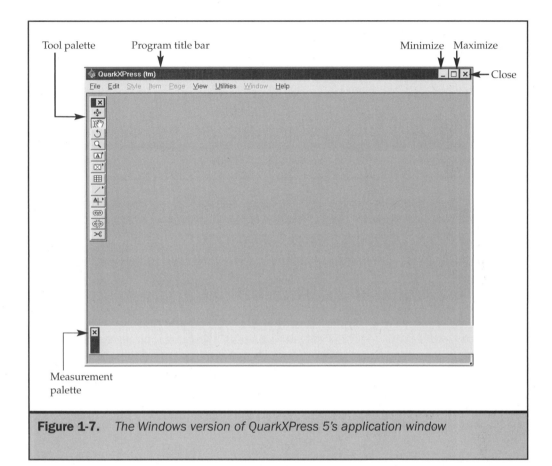

Figure 1-7.   *The Windows version of QuarkXPress 5's application window*

If you're familiar with other application window features, you'll already know that the title bar includes certain creature conveniences such as the Minimize/Maximize and Close buttons. The Minimize/Maximize button enables you to control application window size, while the Close button in essence quits the program. Windows users will notice that, as with any program, QuarkXPress 5's application window may also be resized at any time.

The Tool palette features all the tools you'll be using throughout the exercises in this book and for all your subsequent layout projects. Because no documents have been opened yet, the Measurements palette has nothing to measure, so it simply sits empty. Both the Tool and Measurements palettes include their own title bars and Close buttons, but each may be reopened using commands found under the View menu. For more information on working with the Tool palette, refer to Chapters 4 through 7. For information on using palettes, see "Working with Dialogs and Palettes" in Chapter 2.

Where to from Here?

After launching the program, most users will want to get up and running as quickly as possible. You're likely either going to want to start by opening an existing file or creating a brand new one. For that, you've turned to the right spot.

Opening Files

To begin in a basic fashion, opening either a new or existing QuarkXPress document, using templates, or setting document or page options require the use of File menu functions. Although opening a new or existing document may be a quick and simple operation, however, there are many types of files you can open and even more that you can create on your own. The following section covers them all.

Creating a New QuarkXPress Document

If you're simply looking for a quick way to start your own new file and aren't too concerned about much else, follow this step. Choose File | New | Document (CMD/CTRL+N) and press Return in response to the dialog box that appears. Notice a brand new document opened on your screen.

Of course, if you weren't paying close attention, you'd have missed the details of what exactly you did. In essence, what you created is a document set entirely to default values and options. By default, QuarkXPress 5's page settings are set to a portrait-oriented (vertical), letter-sized (8.5 × 11-inch) page. The default margin guide values for new documents are set to 0.5 inches on all sides, as shown in Figure 1-8.

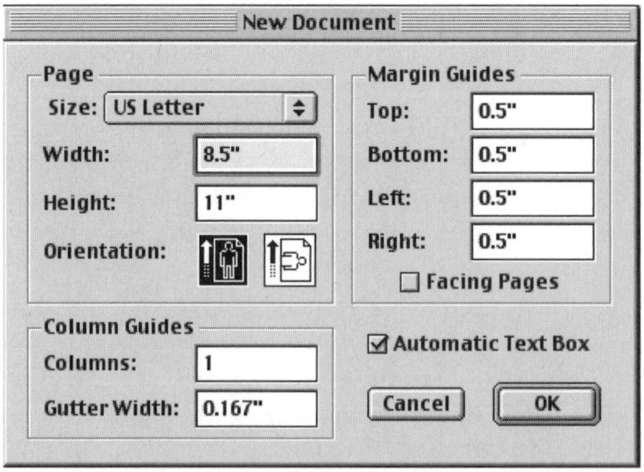

Figure 1-8. *Choosing the File | New | Document command opens this dialog box.*

The first *new* document you open following launching QuarkXPress is automatically numbered *Document 1* in the program title bar. After that, the numbering of new documents is in sequence (Document 2, Document 3, and so on). You'll also notice a few other things automatically happened. For example, your new document is automatically displayed at 100 percent actual size, the Content tool (second from the top in the Tool palette) is already selected, and your new document window is already maximized.

Note   *You won't need to assign a name to your new document until you want to save it using Save or Save As commands, discussed further in this chapter.*

For details on setting page options for new documents, see the following section.

Setting Document Page Options

Let's back up for a moment to the little dialog we didn't pay much attention to earlier, the New Document dialog. If you're interested in creating a new document to suit exact specifications, this dialog features critical options you'll need to set—all of which can be changed later on if you require.

The New Document dialog features page, text column, and page margin settings to control page properties as follows.

Page Sizes

This set of options enables you to set page sizes for your new document. You may select a preset size from the Page drop-down menu, or enter custom width and height sizes:

- ■ **Page**   From this drop-down menu, you may select from U.S. Letter, U.S. Legal, A4 Letter, B5 Letter, or Tabloid sizes. After selecting your size, the exact page measures are automatically displayed in the Width and Height boxes.

- ■ **Width and Height boxes**   Use these two boxes to enter exact measures of your new page size as you require. Both vertical and horizontal page dimensions may be set within a range of 1 to 48 inches. Entering custom page dimensions automatically sets the Page size drop-down menu to Custom.

When entering values according to specific measuring conventions different from the unit value displayed in any dialog box, you may use the abbreviations shown in Table 1-1.

- ■ **Orientation**   This sets your page to either Portrait or Landscape. Orientation is a term used to describe the direction in which your page is oriented or aligned. A portrait-oriented page features a height measure that is larger than the width, while landscape-oriented pages have width measures larger than the height measure. These options are set automatically when custom width and height measures are entered.

Unit Value	Abbreviation
Inches	in or "
Inches (Decimal)	in or with a decimal
Picas	p
Points	pt
Millimeters	mm
Centimeters	cm
Ciceros	c
Agates	ag

Table 1-1.   *Abbreviations for Unit Measures*

- **Facing Pages**   Select this option if you intend the layout you are creating to be produced in a typical book format where left and right pages exist. Selecting Facing Pages enables you to view pages in pairs within your QuarkXPress document window and enables you to set other options such as Section Starts and Book Chapter Starts where left and right page controls are critical.

Setting Columns

QuarkXPress enables you to automatically set the number of columns on your page and the space between them using Column and Gutter Width options:

- **Column**   The term column describes the vertically oriented rows of text composing your layout. When a column measure is entered, QuarkXPress automatically calculates how many equal-width vertical rows your page may accommodate and provides onscreen guides for you to follow. So in this box, enter the number of columns you would like your document and any subsequent pages you add later to be formatted with. The number of columns entered may be within a range between 1 and 30.

- **Gutter Width**   The term gutter is the traditional name given to the space between your page columns. When more than one column is specified, QuarkXPress will automatically space each column apart according to this value. The Gutter Width measure is set within a range between 0.042 and 4 inches.

Setting Page Margins

Page margins' values automatically set the space around the area in which you intend to do most of your layout. They are applied to your entire document and whenever a new page is added. Page margins also set certain parameters for automatic functions such as column width measure. You may independently set the top, left, right, and bottom margin measures within a range from 0 to the respective maximum width or height of your page size. In other words, if your page is 8.5 inches by 11 inches and portrait-oriented, your top and bottom margins may be set between 0 and 11, and your left and right margins may be set between 0 and 8.5 inches.

Automatic Text Box

The Automatic Text Box option enables you to add a new, empty container for text when your document is first created and whenever a new page is added. With this option selected, QuarkXPress adds one empty text box to align with your page margins. When this option is turned off, you will need to create them yourself.

Anatomy of the Document Window

The document window contains all of the controls relative to your open document. In other words, the title bar at the top of the document window specifies the document name, and the page and magnification settings at the bottom reflect what you are seeing. It fits inside (for Windows) or below (Mac) your QuarkXPress application window. QuarkXPress also supports a multiple-document interface (MDI) so you can have as many document windows open as you want.

The document window also features a number of other controls, including the page ruler, scrolling controls, magnification and page options, and the minimize/maximize and close buttons, as shown in Figures 1-9 and 1-10. You may also resize the document window vertically or horizontally as you see fit by dragging its borders.

Windows users will notice that QuarkXPress documents have a three-letter extension convention, identifying them as QuarkXPress 5 documents. The extension is QXD, an abbreviation for QuarkXPress Document.

Beginning a New Web Document

If the document you are creating is specifically destined for the Web, choose File | New | Web Document (CMD/CTRL+OPTION/ALT+SHIFT+N) to begin creating your new document. Choosing this command opens the New Web Document dialog (see Figure 1-11), which features page setup options specific to Web documents.

The New Web Document dialog includes options for controlling colors, layout, and background image options defined as follows:

■ **Text Color**   Choosing a color from this menu enables you to set the default color for all new text entered in text boxes in your new Web document.

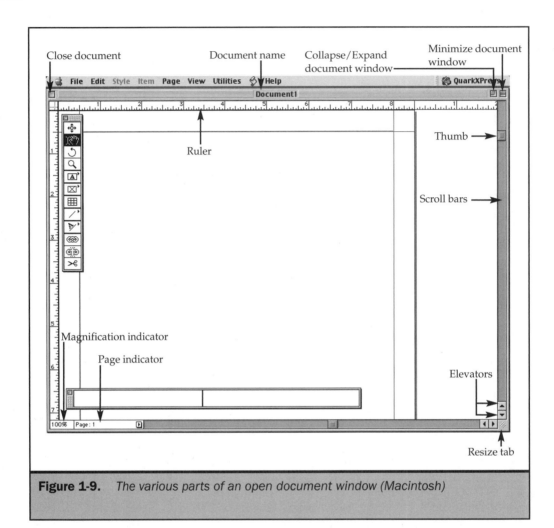

Figure 1-9.   *The various parts of an open document window (Macintosh)*

■ **Background Color**   This option enables you to set the default solid background color for your default master page and subsequently for the default Web page background.

■ **Link Color**   Choosing a link color enables you to set the default color of text that features hyperlink properties, meaning the color of URL links to other Web pages or Web sites before they have been visited.

■ **Visited Link Color**   This option enables you to set how visited links appear on your new Web page. Choosing a different color from that of unvisited hyperlinks enables your Web audience to quickly recognize whether they have already viewed a hyperlink featured on your Web page or not.

■ **Active Link Color**   This option sets the color of hyperlinks that your Web page audience is currently clicking.

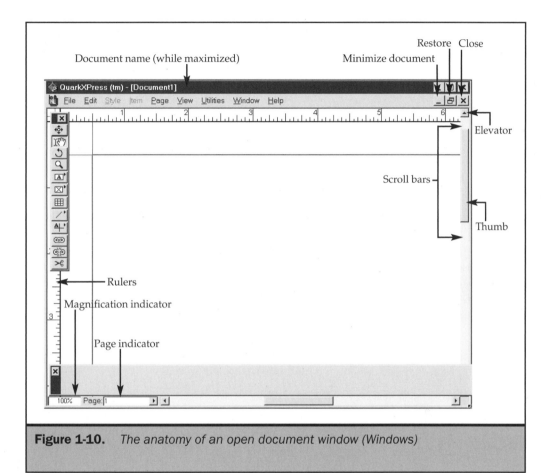

Figure 1-10.   *The anatomy of an open document window (Windows)*

- **Page Width**   You can choose the position of the page width guide of your new Web document using this option, the default measure of which is 600 pixels. You may enter your own value or choose from one of the preset widths (800, 1024, or 1268).

- **Variable Page Width**   Choose this option to set the width of text boxes, which will be specified as having a variable width as you build your new Web page document. Variable-width text boxes expand or contract to fit the width of the browser window being used to view your Web page.

- **Background Image**   Click this option to enable additional background image options that enable you to specify an image saved as either a Portable Network Graphic (PNG), Joint Photographers Expert Group (JPEG), or Graphical Interchange Format (GIF) file as the backdrop for the default master page

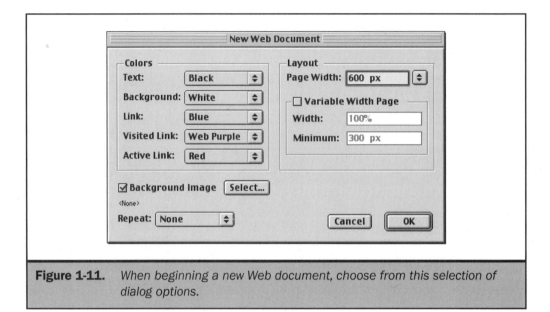

Figure 1-11. *When beginning a new Web document, choose from this selection of dialog options.*

and subsequently for your new Web page. Use the Select/Browse button to locate and specify the image file to use as a background.

■ **Repeat** This option becomes available while the Background Image option is selected, and it enables you to create a repeating background. Choose Tile to cause the image to repeat both vertically and horizontally to completely fill the new Web page. Choose Horizontal or Vertical to repeat the background horizontally or vertically only, or choose None to have the background not repeat and appear only once.

Anatomy of a Web Document Window

Although Web pages are a starkly different publishing method than typical QuarkXPress documents, the Web Document window has many features common to other document types. Figure 1-12 highlights the difference in features you'll see in a Web Document window from that of a typical QuarkXPress document.

For more complete information on creating Web pages and using Web Document tools and features, see Chapter 19.

Creating a New Library

Along with new QuarkXPress documents, you may also create other types of files such as collections of items. These collections are called *Library files*. A Library may contain virtually any item compatible with QuarkXPress 5 such as individual text and pictures or entire layouts. The Libraries will display in your application window as palettes; the items they contain may be interchanged between other libraries or be reorganized.

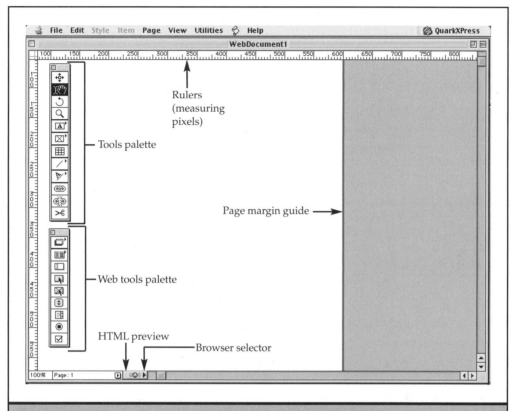

Figure 1-12. *Web Document windows have these unique features, different from typical QuarkXPress documents.*

To create a new Library file, follow these steps:

1. Choose File | New | Library (CMD/CTRL+OPTION/ALT+N). The New Library dialog appears as shown in Figure 1-13.

2. Enter a name and set the folder location for your library.

3. Click Create. Your new Library palette appears (see Figure 1-14). Once a library is created, you may drag items into it from your QuarkXPress document for later retrieval.

About Book Files

The last type of new file that QuarkXPress enables you to create is a Book file. The Book feature enables you to manage and organize several large documents (such as books) at one time, including many of the items and elements they contain. Although the Book

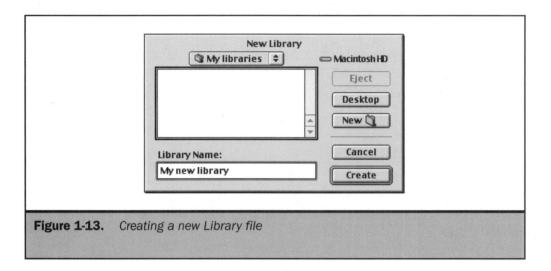

Figure 1-13.   *Creating a new Library file*

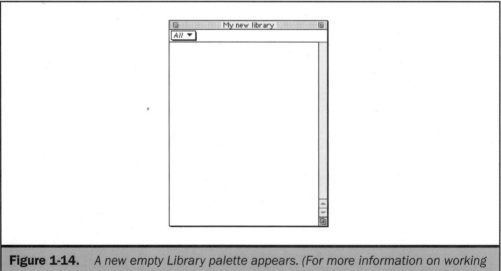

Figure 1-14.   *A new empty Library palette appears. (For more information on working with Library files, see the section "Using Libraries" in Chapter 12.)*

feature may be a little beyond what you need to know when just starting out, you may find out all you need to know by turning to the section called "Using the Book Command" in Chapter 12.

The procedure for creating new Book files is similar to that of Libraries. To create a new Book file, choose File | New | Book; set a name and folder location; and click Create. The new Book file opens as a palette in your application window.

Opening Documents

If you need to open existing documents or you're already a seasoned QuarkXPress user and are looking for details about opening files, this section describes the procedures for doing just that. Although opening files is a relatively straightforward operation, some complex issues can crop up if you're working with previous-version or cross-platform files (or combinations of both).

Opening Saved Documents

To open an existing saved file previously saved in QuarkXPress, follow these steps:

1. Choose File | Open (CMD/CTRL+O). The Open dialog appears on your screen, as shown in Figure 1-15.

2. Locate the folder containing the saved file you want to open and click the file or enter its file name in the File Name box.

3. Click Open or press Return. The file opens.

Opening Previous-Version Files

If you were watching closely in the previous exercise, you noticed at the bottom-left of the dialog a brief notation describing the version of QuarkXPress used to create the selected document before you opened it. If you're curious about where the file came from, you'll want to keep your eye on this area when opening files. For example, when

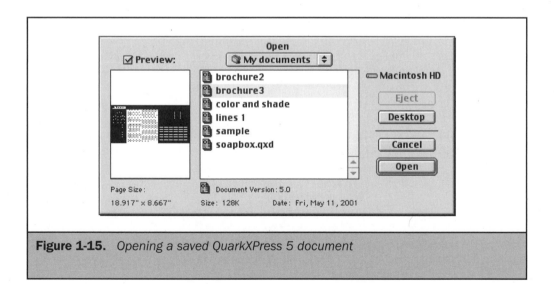

Figure 1-15. *Opening a saved QuarkXPress 5 document*

opening an QuarkXPress document that has previously been saved in QuarkXPress 4, the notation will read Document Version 4, as shown next.

Document Version: 4.0

Size: 48K   Date: Wed, Aug 1, 2001

Opening Templates

Along with ordinary QuarkXPress documents, you may also open templates. Templates are essentially write-protected files saved from QuarkXPress documents. A template may be opened and changed, but may not be overwritten (at least accidentally). Instead, a template serves as the basis for a new QuarkXPress document and may contain text, pictures, colors, style sheets, document preference settings, and most other QuarkXPress document-specific properties.

Windows users will notice that templates are given the specific file extension QXT, setting them apart from regular QuarkXPress documents. The procedure for opening a template is identical to opening other types of files. Simply locate the folder containing the template, enter the name in the File Name box (or click the file name), and click Open. You may notice in doing so that the template opens as an unsaved document, generically titled as Document 1.

Getting Text on the Page

One of the first tasks on your quickstart checklist will be getting legible text onto your page. Text ends up on your page in one of two common ways: You type it yourself directly into QuarkXPress or you copy or import it from another application such as a word-processing program. Either way, you'll be using a text box and the Content tool. To get text onto your page by entering it yourself, follow these steps:

1. Click any one of the Text Box tools in the Tool palette.

2. Create a text box by dragging the tool on your page diagonally in an upper-left to lower-right direction, as shown in Figure 1-16. Once you have finished drawing your text box, your cursor will automatically change to the Content tool. Notice a blinking cursor is waiting for you to enter text.

3. Enter the text as you would in any word-processing application.

4. If you want, after entering your text, resize the text box by with the Content tool at any of the eight handles surrounding the text box, as shown in Figure 1-17. Notice when your cursor moves over a handle it changes to a hand-style cursor.

5. Finally, to add some formatting to the characters you just typed, highlight the text by dragging your cursor across the characters to select them.

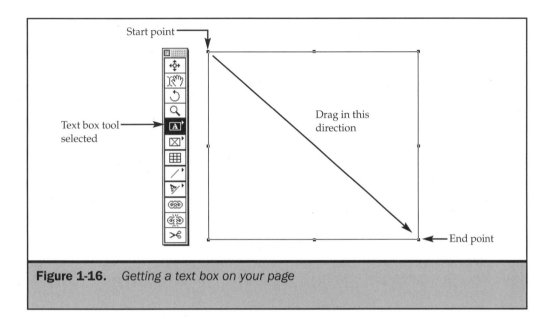

Figure 1-16.   *Getting a text box on your page*

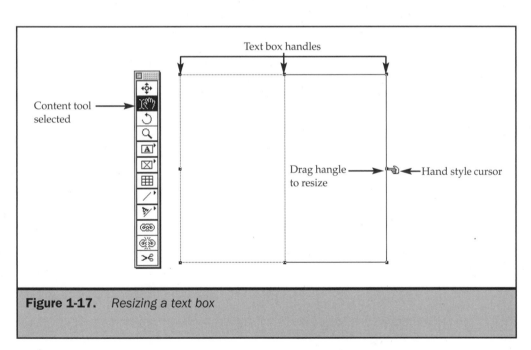

Figure 1-17.   *Resizing a text box*

6. If the Measurements palette isn't already open, choose View | Show Measurements (F9).

7. Use the buttons and drop-down menus on the Measurements palette to apply font and/or style changes. For example, click the Font drop-down menu to change fonts or the Size drop-down menu to change sizes, as shown in Figure 1-18. Changes take effect immediately.

Another way to get text on your page is through copying or importing from another application. Copying text directly from another open application involves the use of clipboard commands for Copy (CMD/CTRL+C) and Paste commands (CMD/CTRL+V).

The most favored way for getting text onto your page is via the Get Text command. The Get Text command essentially imports text files into a selected text box. To use this command, follow these steps:

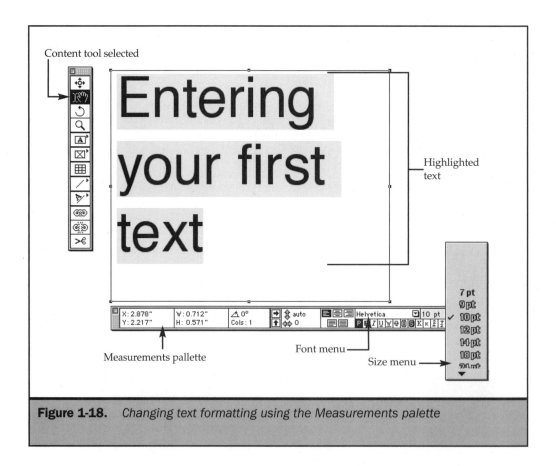

Figure 1-18.   *Changing text formatting using the Measurements palette*

1. Create a text box with any of QuarkXPress 5's text box tools using the same dragging motion described in the previous exercise. Once you finish drawing your box, the Content tool is automatically selected.

2. Choose File | Get Text (CMD/CTRL+E). The Get Text dialog appears, as shown in Figure 1-19.

3. Locate the folder containing the text file you want to import and click the file to select it. (Windows users, be sure the Files of Type menu reads All Text Files). Notice certain information about the file appears in the bottom-left corner of the dialog, and two options for quote and style sheet handling are available. Leave these at their defaults for now.

4. Click Open to import the text into your text box. The text box then fills with text.

Getting Pictures on the Page

If your first layout involves digital images such as photos or logos, you'll also need to import them onto your page. It might help newcomers to QuarkXPress to know at this point that Quark refers to any image as a picture, including both digital photographs and graphic images such as vector illustrations. Getting a picture onto your page involves a similar operation to importing text. As with text, you first create a box.

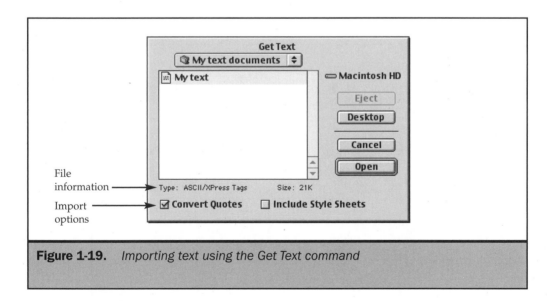

Figure 1-19.   *Importing text using the Get Text command*

To quickly get a picture onto your page, follow these steps:

1. Create a picture box anywhere on your page using any of the picture box tools found in the Tool palette. Picture box tools (and picture boxes) feature a diagonal X. Picture boxes are created using the same action as that of text boxes.

2. Choose File | Get Picture (CMD/CTRL+E). The Get Picture dialog appears, as shown in Figure 1-20.

3. Locate the image file you want to import and click to select it. Notice a gamut of information appears in the lower half of the dialog. This information provides all sorts of details about your image, including the optional preview for visual reference.

4. Click Open. The picture is imported into your picture box.

5. As with text boxes, picture boxes may also be resized by dragging one of the eight handles. However, as you'll quickly discover, resizing a picture box does not resize the picture inside it. As you become familiar with pictures and their box properties, you'll discover QuarkXPress offers plenty of picture control.

Although the previous exercise of getting pictures onto your page is highly simplified, there are many issues to be aware of when working with pictures and picture boxes. This book covers them all in several chapters and across several different topics. For information on manipulating pictures, refer to Chapter 7 and Chapter 8. For information on creating picture and text box layouts, see Chapter 9.

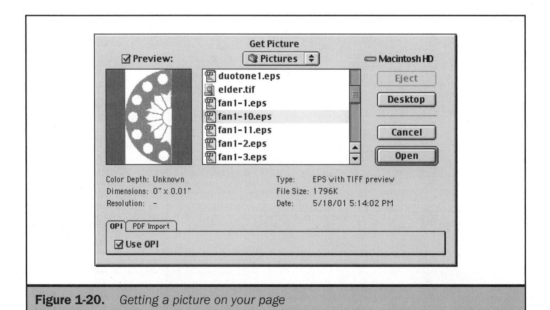

Figure 1-20.   *Getting a picture on your page*

A First Quick Print

The next logical question you might be asking yourself is, how on earth can I get a hard copy of what I just created from the printer? The quick answer is to select File | Print. But, once you make this selection, you may be overwhelmed by the huge number of options available. To simplify the process, follow these steps:

1. If you haven't already done so, open the file you want to print.

2. Select File | Print (CMD/CTRL+P). The Print dialog box appears and is already opened to the Document tab, as shown in Figure 1-21.

3. Click the Setup tab and choose the printer you want to print to from the Printer drop-down menu. If you are only connected to one printer, it may already be selected.

4. Enter the number of copies you would like in the Copies box.

5. If your document is more than one page in length, enter the page number(s) you want to print.

6. If necessary, click the Page Setup button to set your printer to the correct paper size or click the Printer button to select a specific printer. Click OK to accept your selection and return to the Print dialog.

7. Click OK to print your page(s).

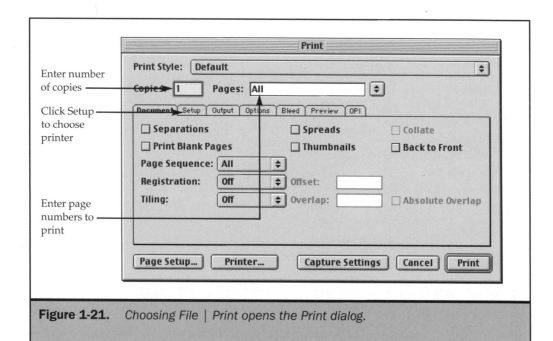

Figure 1-21.   *Choosing File | Print opens the Print dialog.*

Again, these steps are somewhat oversimplified, but in most cases, it'll be just what you're looking for to get a quick hard copy printout from your local printing device. If your document is complex and requires a little more user intervention, you'll want to check out Chapter 17.

Saving Files

Although it's relatively simple to perform, the Save command is one of the best favors you can do for yourself, so do it often. As unforgiving as your computer is, should you encounter a power interruption (or worse), your work will be lost forever *until you save it*. To save your open document now, follow these steps:

1. Click File | Save (CMD/CTRL+S). If your document has been previously saved and already features a file name, the Save command will immediately save any recent changes.

2. If your document is a new one, the Save As dialog will appear on your screen, as shown in Figure 1-22.

3. Set a location for your new file using conventions specific to your operating system.

4. Enter a name for your new file in the Name box. By default, all newly created files feature the prefix Document followed by a numeral, but you'll likely provide a unique name.

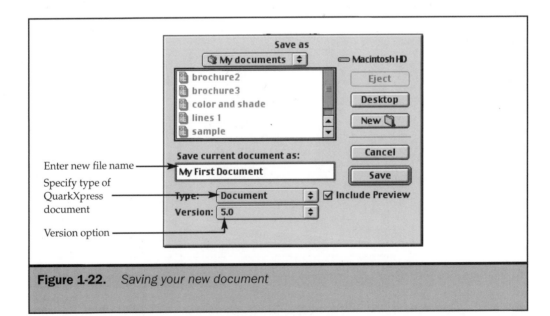

Figure 1-22.   *Saving your new document*

5. For now, accept the default options currently set in the dialog by clicking Save. Any recent changes are now saved.

QuarkXPress enables you to save your document in a number of ways, including as a template and as version 4 files. To save your file as a template, follow the same procedure as previously, but choose Template from the Save As Type drop-down menu. Windows users will notice that the file will be appended with the QXT extension. To save your file as a version 4 file, simply select that option from the Version drop-down menu.

Using the Revert Command

There may be occasions where you have opened a new file and have made changes to it that you want to discard (for whatever reason). In cases such as this, choose the File, Revert to Saved command. This command has the same effect as closing the file without saving any changes and then reopening it. Any changes you have made since your last save operation will be discarded.

 Be certain when using the Revert command that you don't want to save your recent changes; there is no turning back, and there is no Undo command for the Revert to Saved command. Only a single prompt appears, shown in the following illustration, asking if you are sure you want to do this.

Closing Documents and Quitting QuarkXPress

Closing files and quitting QuarkXPress may be done more than one way, and as you progress in familiarity with QuarkXPress, you'll eventually settle on the one that suits you. To close a document, do one of the following:

- Click the Close box in the upper-right corner of your document window.
- Choose File | Close.
- For Macintosh users, press CMD+W.
- For Windows users, press CTRL+F4.

You may close all open files by choosing Window | Close All. You will be prompted with the choice to save each file as it closes, eventually revealing an empty application window.

Before closing your document, QuarkXPress prompts you to save any recent changes with the message shown in the following illustration. After closing a file, the document window directly beneath the one being closed will come to the forefront.

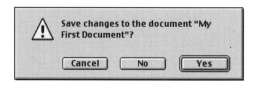

Quitting QuarkXPress may also be done in a number of ways. Eventually, you'll come to settle on one of the following choices for quitting QuarkXPress:

■ Choose File | Quit.

■ Press CMD/CTRL+Q.

■ Click the Close box in the upper-right corner of the application window.

■ Windows users may also press ALT+F4.

If any unsaved files are currently open, QuarkXPress prompts you with the choice to save each of them and will eventually close itself.

Helping Yourself to QuarkXPress

Of course, your best source for help while using QuarkXPress 5 is this book. But if you need the official company line, you're welcome to use the QuarkXPress Help features. Choose Help | Help Topics to access general topics. Macintosh users may activate context-sensitive help by choosing Help | Show Balloons to have onscreen balloons appear while the cursor is held over certain items. Window users may view context-sensitive help by choosing Help | What's This? to temporarily change the cursor to a question mark , enabling them to click on items for more information.

If you need more help than this book provides, or if your problem is specifically related to hardware or other software issues, then you just might be looking for technical support. If you have Web access, you can view the technical support resources available online at **www.quark.com/support**.

If you need assistance via e-mail or other methods, here are some valuable addresses to keep nearby:

- QuarkXPress technical support for Mac OS:
  - General tech support: mactech@quark.com
  - AppleScript tech support: scriptsupport@quark.com
- QuarkXPress technical support for Windows:
  - Internet e-mail to wintech@quark.com
  - Quark Technical Support Home: **www.quark.com/support**
- Search Quark's Technical Support Data Base:
  www.quark.com/support/search_support.html
- Free QuarkXPress TechNews newsletter:
  www.quark.com/support/subscribe.html
- Tech Notes (frequently asked technical support questions):
  www.quark.com/support/techinfo/technotes.cfm
- QuarkForum (technical support forums): **www.quark.com/cgi-bin/WebX**

Note

You may also get help directly within QuarkXPress 5 via the Web by choosing items from the QuarkLink submenu available from the Utilities Command menu. These commands are actually shortcuts that either automatically open your e-mail application to a pre-addressed e-mail document or launch your default Web browser that accesses Quark's Web site. You can e-mail questions either to Quark Customer Service or Quark Tech Support, or visit Web pages featuring QuarkNews, Quark Tech Support, or the latest QuarkXTensions. You can also take one of Quark's user tutorials or register your copy of QuarkXPress 5 online.

The Complete Reference

QuarkXPress 5

Chapter 2

Getting Acquainted with QuarkXPress 5

If you've just completed the previous chapter and you're looking to continue your initial study of QuarkXPress 5, this next chapter will take you from the top surface and on into the depths of QuarkXPress. You'll learn the fundamental principles behind using various interface features and learn crucial program operations just shy of actually performing layout operations. You'll master document navigation, Zoom controls, Page commands, and how to use the most common tools among other things.

In an effort to get you up and running as quickly as possible, the thrust is still overdrive here. As with most chapters in the first part of this book, *job one* is for you to quickly grasp XPress concepts while simultaneously learning the tools and features. That's exactly what this chapter continues to do. Along the way, you'll be directed to areas that provide more detail and explanation of the key features discussed.

Working with the Interface Features of QuarkXPress 5

Quark has engineered an interface not unlike other newly released applications, although you'll discover some of these areas have their own unique twist. There are the usual menu bars and application and document window controls that function in keeping with your operating system's structure. QuarkXPress 5 uses typical tree directory and standard dialog box conventions. Palettes are undoubtedly a boon to the interface world, and QuarkXPress makes use of these interface elements to control many old and new features.

Document Window Anatomy

In Chapter 1 you saw a general overview of the XPress program and document windows, and this section takes a slightly closer look. Document windows reveal the current display settings for the document in the forefront of your application window and differ only slightly between Macintosh and Windows platform versions (see Figures 2-1 and 2-2).

As mentioned in Chapter 1, the document title bar displays the name of your currently open XPress document and includes several buttons for controlling window size and appearance. Both Mac and Windows versions include close buttons, which enable you to immediately close a document window—a feature redundant with the File | Close command (as shown next).

Macintosh close button———▶  ◀———Windows close button

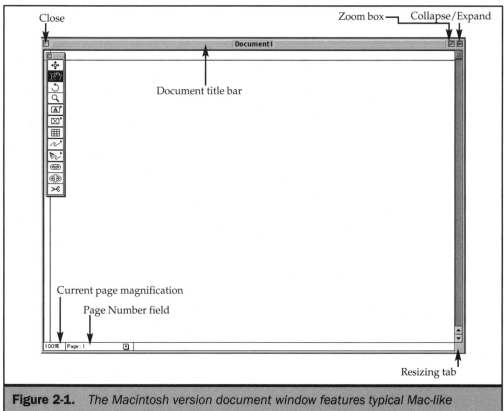

Figure 2-1. *The Macintosh version document window features typical Mac-like interface features.*

Note *The QuarkXPress 5 Windows version includes an additional button in the application title bar that enables you to immediately close XPress and is redundant with the File | Exit command (CTRL+F4).*

Next is an area where Mac and Windows versions also differ. The QuarkXPress 5 Macintosh version features two buttons at the far right of the document title bar: the Zoom box and the Collapse/Expand box. Clicking the Zoom box toggles your document window state between its current size or a fully maximized size. Clicking the Collapse/Expand button enables you to hide (Collapse) the window with only the title bar remaining, or restore (Expand) it to its previous size. Buttons' states change depending on the current state of the document window, as shown next.

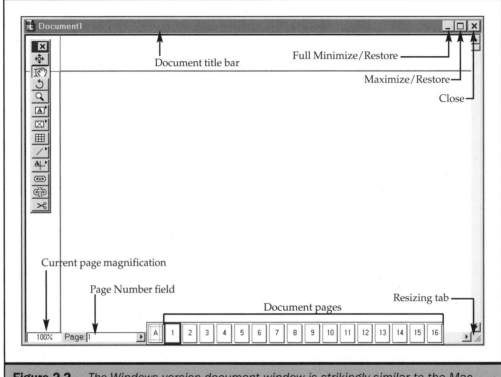

Figure 2-2.   *The Windows version document window is strikingly similar to the Mac version, with a slight Windows-like flavor.*

The Windows version offers similar controls, using three buttons for controlling the state of a document window: the Minimize, Maximize, and Full Minimize buttons. The Full Minimize button enables you to reduce the document window to nothing more than a short title bar at the bottom of your program window (see Figure 2-3).

The resizing tab at the bottom-right corner of the document window enables you to click-drag to resize the window to any proportions you wish. Although the resize tab is a good method to use to change document window size, you may also resize the window vertically or horizontally by dragging the left, right, or bottom edges of the document window.

Tip   *With more than one document open at a time, you may bring any document immediately to the forefront by selecting its name from a command menu. Macintosh users choose View | Windows | [document name], while Windows users choose Window | [document name]. These menus also include other commands for Stacking/Cascading*

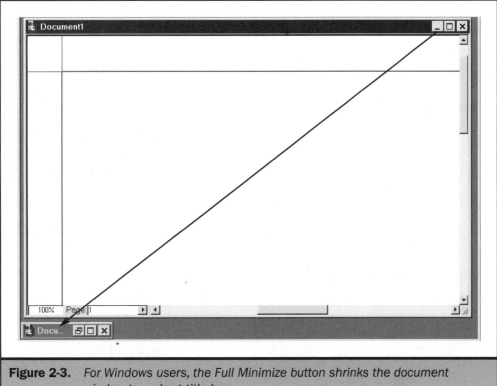

Figure 2-3.   *For Windows users, the Full Minimize button shrinks the document window to a short title bar.*

and/or Tiling open document windows. Windows users may also choose Close All to close all open documents, Arrange Icons for organizing fully minimized windows, or specifically tile windows either vertically or horizontally.

You may quickly move from one page to another in your document either by entering the page number you wish to move to in the Page Number box and pressing ENTER or by clicking the button to the right of this field and selecting the corresponding page by clicking on it. Master pages (recognized by alphabetic letters) may also be displayed using this feature as shown in the Windows version next.

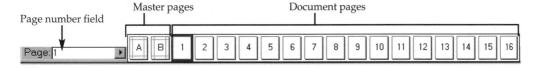

Working in Dialogs and Palettes

In keeping with typical interface conventions, QuarkXPress 5's dialog boxes contain tabs, num box fields, drop-down lists, and various other types of check boxes and radio buttons. Dialog boxes containing large numbers of options are commonly organized into tabbed areas that may be accessed by clicking on the tab's title to bring it to the foreground.

After making selections in a dialog, pressing OK causes the changes to take effect after the dialog goes away. Nearly all dialogs feature an Apply button that enables you to cause the changes to take effect before exiting the dialog. This way you can preview your changes before actually committing to the change. The Apply command may also be activated using the keyboard while in a dialog by pressing CMD+A (Macintosh) or ALT+A (Windows). Clicking the Cancel button (or pressing ESC) causes the dialog to close without any selected options or changes taking effect. Mac users may also use the CMD+. (a period character) shortcut.

When entering values in dialog boxes, press the TAB key to cycle from one available num box to the next, or press SHIFT+TAB to cycle in reverse of this. To cycle from one tabbed dialog box category to the next within a dialog using the keyboard, press CTRL+OPTION+TAB (Macintosh) or CTRL+TAB (Windows).

In QuarkXPress 5, there are also two basic types of palettes, both of which appear to "float" in the foreground of your open document. Floating palettes are essentially floating dialogs that will remain perpetually open as you work. Like document windows, they may also be closed, minimized, or restored. Palettes often replace conventional dialog box functions and are often easier to use and more convenient to access than dialogs or menus. In addition to this, palette changes often take place immediately after a selection is made rather than having to press an OK or Apply button.

Again, there are subtle platform version differences in how palettes may be controlled in QuarkXPress 5. In both Macintosh and Windows platform versions, most palettes include a title bar, drag area, and close box (shown in the next two illustrations). Each palette may also be viewed in a minimized or maximized state. Macintosh platform version users may minimize or maximize any palette using the Collapse/Expand button respectively. A double-click on the title bar of the palette also toggles a palette's display between these two states.

Macintosh version floating palette

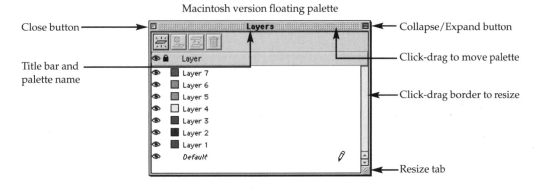

Close button

Title bar and
palette name

Collapse/Expand button

Click-drag to move palette

Click-drag border to resize

Resize tab

Windows version floating palette

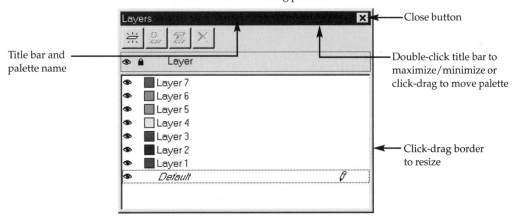

Title bar and
palette name

Close button

Double-click title bar to
maximize/minimize or
click-drag to move palette

Click-drag border
to resize

Entering Values in Num Boxes

Num boxes are the fields shown in dialogs and palettes that accept numeric values and
unit measures. Field values are often predetermined such as when entering points to set
a font size or inches to set a page size. But if you wish, you may override these values
by entering the measurement suffix after your value. Table 2-1 lists abbreviations of unit
values accepted by QuarkXPress num box fields.

Unit Value	Abbreviation
Inches	*Macintosh:* " (quote character) *Windows:* in or " (quote character)
Inches (Decimal)	*Macintosh:* " (quote character) appended with a decimal and value *Windows:* in or " (quote character) appended with a decimal and value
Picas	p
Points	pt
Millimeters	mm
Centimeters	cm
Ciceros	c
Agates	ag
Pixels (for the Web)	px

Table 2-1. *Acceptable Unit Measures in QuarkXPress 5*

Tip

*If you need to, you can use fields as if they were tiny calculators. By using these num box "operators" for addition (+), subtraction (−), multiplication (*), and division (/), you can perform basic calculations on the value the box is currently displaying. For example, entering the operator "*3" after a value of "1.0 in" will result in a calculation of "3.0 in" after pressing T*AB *or clicking your cursor in the next field. You may also string as many operators as you wish following a box value, such as "/2*3 + 3" so long as the multiplication and division calculations are entered before addition and subtraction. After the calculation is performed, the operators disappear.*

Viewing and Zooming a Layout

In some cases, the immediate—perhaps the only—operations you'll need to perform are changing Zoom levels to examine a document. Zooming operations enable you to view document pages either from a bird's-eye perspective or up close and personal. For certain tasks such as proofing and editing, viewing is an essential operation.

QuarkXPress 5 provides you with the capability of displaying your pages within a range of 10 percent (highly magnified) to 800 percent (least magnification) to within one decimal place based on the percentage of the document's actual (100 percent) size. As you're about to find out, there are several features and tools you may use to view your document.

Using the Zoom Tool

The magnifying-glass symbol in your Tool palette (shown next) represents the Zoom tool, which will serve as your primary method of zooming around your page. Zooming increases or decreases the view magnification level of your page with either a single click or marquee drag (see Figure 2-4). Single clicks with the Zoom tool cause the view magnification to change in preset increments. Click-dragging constitutes marquee-zooming and enables you to zoom to a defined area of a layout.

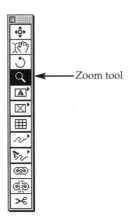

Zoom tool

The Zoom tool has two basic modes: Zoom in or Zoom out, indicated by the + and − symbols displayed in the center of this tool's cursor when in use. You may also select the Zoom tool for use in a number of different ways. Selecting it from the main Tool palette is the most straightforward method. Once the Zoom tool is in use, it defaults to the Zoom in state. Holding OPTION/ALT enables you to temporarily choose the Zoom out state.

You may also temporarily change your cursor to the Zoom tool, *regardless of which tool you currently have selected and in use*, by holding modifier keys. Macintosh users can hold CTRL+SHIFT to temporarily select the Zoom tool for zooming in, or hold CTRL+OPTION to choose the Zoom out state. This differs slightly for Windows users who hold CTRL+SPACEBAR or CTRL+ALT+SPACEBAR for respective Zoom in or out states.

Controlling Zoom Tool Behavior

If you wish, you may change certain settings of your Zoom tool, the most common being the Zoom increment. By default, single clicks change your zoom view by 25

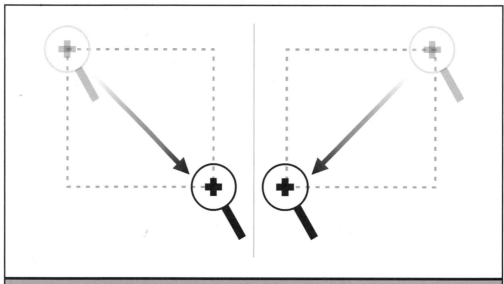

Figure 2-4.   *Marquee-zooming requires a diagonal click-drag action to surround the area you wish to zoom into.*

percent of the actual size of your document. You may also change the Minimum or Maximum view scale. To access the dialog used for changing these settings, double-click the Zoom tool in the Tool palette. The Document Preferences dialog opens, as shown in Figure 2-5, with the Zoom tool automatically selected. Click the Modify button, and enter new values for the Maximum, Minimum, and/or Increments options in the View dialog that opens. Click OK in both dialogs to close them and return to your document and your new Zoom tool settings will now apply.

For more information on changing the Zoom tool (and other tools) at the Document Preference setting level, see "Setting Document Preferences" in Chapter 13.

Changing Zoom Magnification Levels

There's usually always a slight redundancy in the methods of accomplishing tasks, and perhaps the best example is in zooming. Although the Zoom tool is perhaps the most efficient way to change zoom views, you may also use the menus or shortcut keys, or enter values directly in the *view percent field* at the bottom-left of your document window.

You may quickly select the view percent field at the bottom-left of the document window using the shortcut CTRL+OPTION/ALT+V. Enter a new view magnification value followed by pressing the ENTER key to change your Zoom level.

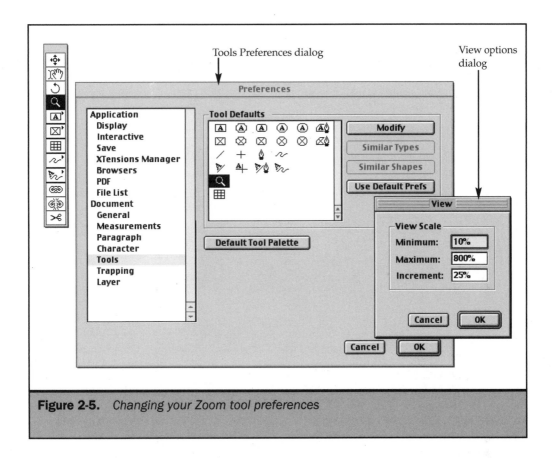

Figure 2-5.   *Changing your Zoom tool preferences*

To change your zoom to a preset level, choose one of these Zoom levels from the View menu or use one of the keyboard shortcuts listed in Table 2-2.

Viewing Document Thumbnails

Thumbnails is the term given to the tiny pen-and-paper rough sketches layout artists use to conceptualize their layouts. Thumbnails show neither a high degree of detail nor are they readable. XPress is capable of displaying your entire document in a thumbnail-style view by choosing Thumbnails (SHIFT+F6) from the View menu or by entering **Thumb** in the Zoom level indicator and pressing RETURN. XPress will display your pages in proper order and proportion, enabling you to get a rough impression of the layout, as shown in Figure 2-6.

Using Thumbnails is a quick way to browse a document when troubleshooting for hidden text not showing due to kerning/tracking changes. While in Thumbnails view, whole single or multiple pages may be selected and moved within your layout or between documents.

Result	Action
Fit in Window	Cmd/Ctrl+0
Fit largest spread in Window	Hold Option/Alt and choose View | Fit in Window or press Cmd/Ctrl+Option/Alt+0
50 percent	Choose View | 50%
75 percent	Choose View | 75%
Actual Size (100 percent)	Cmd/Ctrl+1
200 percent	Cmd/Ctrl+Option/Alt+CLICK (on page)

Table 2-2.   *Quick Shortcuts for Changing Zoom Magnification Levels*

Navigating a Document

If your document is more than one or two pages in length, you'll ultimately want to find a quick way to browse pages and/or locate a specific page. As with other tasks, there are several ways to accomplish this. The method you choose will ultimately depend on your work habits and whether you are more comfortable using onscreen controls, menu commands, keyboard shortcuts, or palette controls. The next section identifies the various methods available to you in QuarkXPress 5.

Using Onscreen Controls

Three key features are available and avoid the need to delve into dialogs, menus, or other interface elements. Click-dragging the Thumb button in the vertical scroll bar to the right of your document window enables you to move forward or backward in your sequence of pages. As you scroll up or down, the Page Number box (located at the bottom, left corner of all open document windows) will indicate the page about to be shown on releasing the button. Clicking above or below the Thumb button in the scroll bars enables you to scroll by whole screens one click at a time.

The next feature involves actual use of the Page Number box (shown next). As mentioned, this feature serves a dual purpose to both indicate the number of the page currently in view and accept numeral entries. Enter the number representing your page number followed by pressing the ENTER key to immediately display the page at your current view magnification.

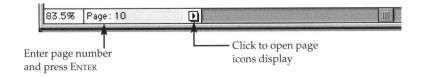

Enter page number
and press ENTER

Click to open page
icons display

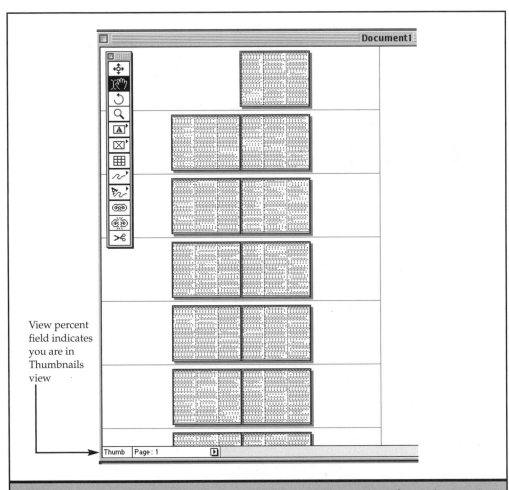

View percent
field indicates
you are in
Thumbnails
view

Figure 2-6.　*Selecting Thumbnails view gives you a bird's-eye view of your document.*

The next method requires fewer steps and enables you to interactively choose a page using your cursor. Beside the Page Number box is a clickable arrow button that opens a row of page icons numbered in sequence to match the pages in your open document (shown in the previous illustration), beginning with your currently viewed page. To immediately navigate to a certain page, click once on its icon.

When navigating long documents where the total page count exceeds the space available to display icons for all pages, you may scroll the page icon row. Macintosh users may simply move their cursor to the left or right of the row of visible page icons to automatically scroll the view. Windows users may use the scroll bar below this row of icons to move forward or backwards through the icons to display a particular page. Although this features provides a convenient way to navigate a document, only 19 page icons at a time will be visible (at typical display resolution settings).

Using the Page Grabber Hand Tool

The Page Grabber Hand tool is used for interactively scrolling your document page in its current view magnification, but strangely enough you won't find this tool anywhere in the Tool palette. In fact, the only way to select and use this tool is by holding the OPTION/ALT key and click-dragging to change the page view area. The Page Grabber Hand tool (shown next) enables you to simultaneously scroll vertically and/or horizontally in the same manner as the thumb buttons on your document window scroll bars, but in a much more interactive way.

Using Menus and Keyboard Commands

If the previously mentioned onscreen controls don't suit your needs, you may want to investigate the Page menu. From here, you may choose Previous or Next page commands to display the previous or next page in your document based on your current page in view, or quickly show the first or last page in the document by choosing the First or Last page commands. Although these commands provide rudimentary navigation through your document, they are perhaps somewhat less convenient.

Thankfully, you may use keyboard shortcuts to accomplish similar actions. Table 2-3 lists the keyboard equivalents for scrolling and document navigation.

Scroll **Up** one complete screen	Page Up
Scroll **Down** one complete screen	Page Down
Display **First** page of document	*Macintosh:* Cmd + Shift + A or Shift + Home (with extended keyboard) *Windows:* Ctrl + Page Up
Display **Last** page of document	*Macintosh:* Cmd + Shift + D or Shift + End (with extended keyboard) *Windows:* Ctrl + Page Down

Table 2-3.   *Page Navigation Keyboard Shortcuts*

Also available in the Page menu is access to the Go To Page dialog (shown next). This feature is also perhaps redundant with entering a numeral in the Page Field dialog, but nonetheless enables you to quickly enter a page and have it displayed. To open the dialog, choose Page | Go To (CMD/CTRL+J).

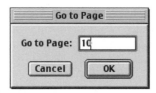

Using the Document Layout Palette

A much faster method for traversing your document is through use of the Document Layout palette. This palette (shown in Figure 2-7) enables you to control a number of aspects of your layout, including navigating pages. To display the Document Layout palette, choose View | Show Document Layout (*Macintosh*: F10, *Windows*: F4).

This palette is divided into two basic areas. The top portion shows a listing of the current master pages in your document, while the bottom shows a listing of the actual document pages. To display either a master or document page, double-click a page icon in either of these palette areas. You may also single-click any document page numeral to accomplish the same thing.

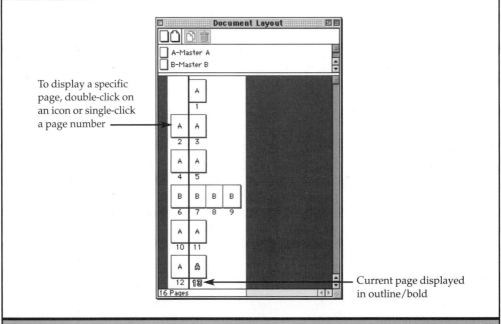

To display a specific page, double-click on an icon or single-click a page number

Current page displayed in outline/bold

Figure 2-7. *Use the Document Layout palette to quickly display either master pages or document pages.*

Note *Don't be confused by the appearance of the pages in the Document Layout palette. Although the icons themselves indicate details about page numbers, master page settings, and left and right facing pages, they don't reflect the actual shape or orientation of your document pages.*

Adding, Removing, and Moving Pages

Although all new documents begin with a single blank page, you may add nearly as many as you need. While laying out documents more than a few pages in length, you may add or delete pages manually or automatically in a number of ways.

Using Menu Commands to Add, Remove, or Move pages

Perhaps the most powerful method to use when managing the number of pages in your document is through the use of menu commands that open dialog boxes by choosing Insert, Delete, or Move from the Page menu. Choosing Page | Insert opens the Insert Pages dialog (see Figure 2-8).

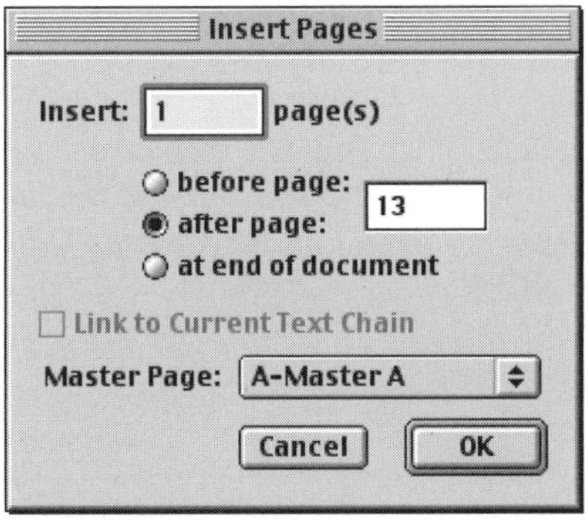

Figure 2-8. *The Insert Page dialog enables you to control how many (and the setup of) pages as they are added.*

Options in the Insert Pages dialog enable you to add multiple pages at specific points in your document. By default, these options are set to automatically insert one page after the current page, but you may insert as many as you need to any point within the structure of your document, regardless of your current page being displayed.

> **Tip** *Using the Insert Pages command, you may add up to 1,999 pages at a time to a maximum document length of 2,000 pages.*

You may also choose other options for text linking or use specific master page styles. For more information on text linking, see the "Linking and Unlinking Tools" section later in this chapter, or for more information on master pages, see the section named "Using Master Pages" in Chapter 3.

> **Tip** *When importing text with the Get Text command, you may have QuarkXPress automatically add pages as needed by activating the Auto Page Insertion option. This option adds pages to your document if the text you are importing exceeds the available space in the text box you are importing it into. Choose Edit | Preferences | General tab and select your preferred option from the Auto Page Insertion drop-down menu. For more information on setting document preferences, see Chapter 13.*

To delete pages from your document, choose the Page | Delete menu command to open the Delete Pages dialog (shown next), which enables you to delete a single page or a sequence of multiple pages. By default, the dialog opens with your currently displayed page specified. Clicking OK immediately deletes the page *and all its contents* (unless the page contains a linked text box with text flowing in it from a previous page). Specify any page you wish, or enter the first and last page numbers in a sequence. Any and all objects the pages may contain will be deleted.

If the pages you wish to delete contain text boxes linked from a flow from a text box on a previous page, QuarkXPress 5 will continue to rebuild pages (according to your preferences) to preserve the text flow. Only by deleting all the pages that hold the text flow will you be able to eliminate those pages.

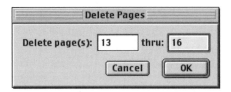

The Page menu also includes a command to move pages within your document, which is somewhat less interactive than the method described in the next section on using the Document Layout palette. Choosing Page | Move opens the Move Pages dialog (see Figure 2-9), which enables you to move one or more pages at a time. Enter a single page or a sequence of pages and choose one of the three available options. Choose Before Page or After Page and specify a page number in the box at the right, or choose To End of Document. Clicking OK closes the dialog and moves the selected pages and all their content according to the selected options.

Page Management with the Document Layout Palette

If you're beyond constantly accessing menus to perform page functions, you're sure to like this next feature. Among its other functions (such as page navigation), the Document Layout palette was designed to interactively add, delete, or move document pages. To open the Document Layout palette, choose View | Show Document Layout (*Macintosh*: F10, *Windows*: F4).

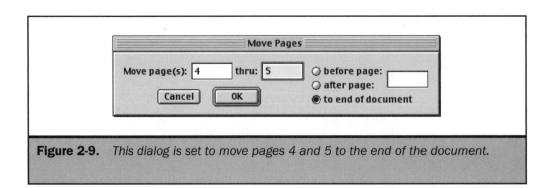

Figure 2-9. *This dialog is set to move pages 4 and 5 to the end of the document.*

To add pages to your document using this palette, hold down your OPTION/ALT key while dragging a master page from the top portion of the palette into the bottom portion (see Figure 2-10). As you drag, an insertion cursor will appear, indicating the point at which the new pages are destined. On releasing the mouse button, the Insert Pages dialog opens automatically and enables you to add one or more pages (as described in the preceding section).

To delete pages using the Document Layout palette, select the page icon(s) in the palette and click the Delete button shown in the previous illustration. Moving pages using the Document Layout palette is even more interactive than other actions. To move single pages using this palette, simply click-drag their page icons within the palette and drag them to a new position in the page order. The point at which you release the pages determines where they are moved to.

Moving multiple pages is a little trickier. Pages must first be selected, which involves single clicks to select single pages and SHIFT-clicks to select contiguous pages (pages in a sequence), while CMD/CTRL-clicks to select noncontiguous pages. Holding CMD/CTRL while clicking a page within a selection of pages selects or deselects it. Once a selection of pages exists, click-dragging any of the pages within the palette to a new location causes them—and their contents—to be moved within the page order.

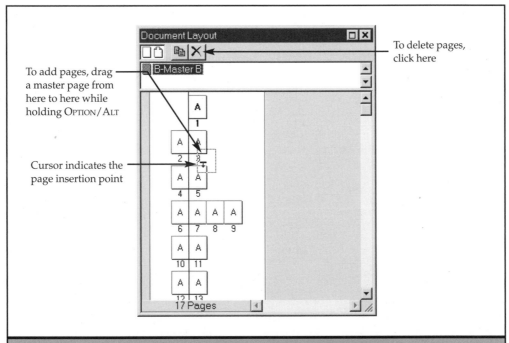

Figure 2-10. *Adding pages using OPTION/ALT as the modifier key while dragging a master page in the Document Layout palette (Windows version shown)*

When moving pages within the Document Layout palette, if the destination point you're moving the pages to isn't currently visible, dragging upwards or downwards in the palette activates an auto-scroll feature that automatically changes the sequence of pages being displayed.

Controlling Document Display

When you consider the fact that your screen is essentially a "viewport" of sorts to how your layout appears, it's no surprise many user desire—or often *require*—the ability to control how content is displayed. For some, this ability comes as a convenience for reducing the time it takes for your pages to display. For others who work in a fast-paced publishing environment where time is money, it could be considered a way to increase productivity. QuarkXPress 5 enables you to choose how text and pictures appear on your screen and offers the flexibility to interrupt items being rendered or to force an updated display of your layout. In this next section, we'll examine the various ways you can control how your document appears onscreen.

Controlling Text-Greeking

Few experts are exactly sure where the term *greeking* stems from. Perhaps it has something to do with the old saying, "it's all Greek to me," which has little to do with how greeked text actually looks. In the world of electronic layout, greeking has come to describe the effect of displaying smaller sizes of text as unreadable gray horizontal stripes, a rough representation of your text's appearance, as shown in Figure 2-11.

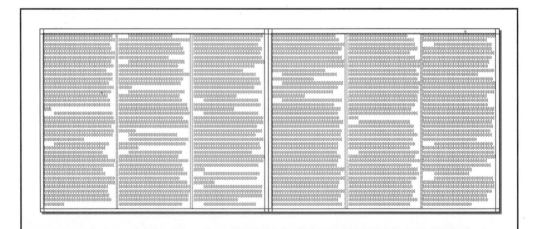

Figure 2-11. *Greeked text appears as grayed-out stripes, enabling faster font display rendering, as shown in this greeked two-page spread.*

Because font and character detail are omitted, greeked text displays infinitely faster than normal text.

In QuarkXPress (as in other layout applications), you have the option to set the text point size at which the text is greeked, referred to as the *greeking limit*. All text below this size limit is greeked. This limit is set using an option in the General tab of the Preferences dialog (see Figure 2-12). which may be opened directly using the CMD/CTRL+Y shortcut or by choosing Edit | Preferences | Preferences (CMD/CTRL+Y).

Controlling Picture Display

One of the key types of content that often takes more time to display is detailed color pictures. Along with text-greeking options, you also have the option of setting pictures to display in the same greeked fashion as text. Greeked pictures appear more crudely onscreen, but display significantly faster than when greeking is turned off. To set pictures in your layout to greek, select the Greek Pictures option, as shown in the Document Preferences | General tab in the previous illustration. Greeked pictures appear as shown in Figure 2-13. Greeked pictures appear as gray-filled boxes. When a greeked picture box is selected, the picture displays in full detail.

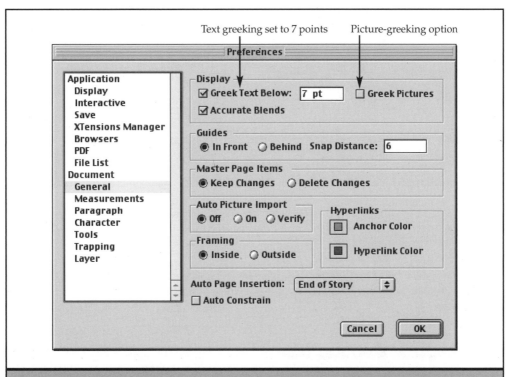

Figure 2-12. *Setting text and picture greek options in the Preferences dialog*

Figure 2-13. *Viewing greeked and non-greeked pictures*

If you are viewing a document created by someone else, and you're fairly certain the text and pictures should appear better than what you're seeing, you may want to check the greeking options described in this section. Chances are, whomever created the document left the text and picture greeking options set to a lesser display quality to increase screen draw time. Resetting the greeking options will improve the document's onscreen appearance.

Screen Redraw Commands

If you've ever become frustrated with the time it takes for your screen to display text or pictures, you likely crave a feature that will enable you to control if and when it will occur. You'll be pleased to know that XPress 5 features something called *interruptible display*, or the ability for you to halt QuarkXPress from drawing representations of the content in your layout. Screen redraw occurs anytime you change views or pages, or when options are changed or a dialog blocking your view is closed. Intensive redraw sessions can be maddening if you're not really interested in seeing all the detail of your layout for the hundredth time.

Screen redraw is interruptible using the shortcuts CMD+. (a period character) for Mac users or ESC for Windows users. Screen redraw may also now be forced using the shortcut CMD+OPTION+. (a period character) for Mac users or SHIFT+ESC for Windows users.

Although this section touches only briefly on the key controls for setting page appearance, more information is available in Chapter 13.

Learning the Box Concept

Historically in past versions of QuarkXPress, nearly all of the graphic and drawing elements you could create or import into the program required a box to house them. This made learning the program difficult for new users unaccustomed to bounding box principles. This box concept still applies to many of the elements you'll be working with. In order to have certain things exist on your document page, you first need to create a box of some sort.

This means you'll need to first *create* a box shape before you can place the two main types of content you'll be working with: text and pictures. This also means you'll need to create the right *kind* of box. Text and picture boxes are most often created using specific tools available from the Tools palette. In essence, this is the basis on which XPress operates and the working principle that sets it apart from other popular layout programs (such as Adobe Pagemaker).

Key QuarkXPress Tools Worth Mastering

In any program, there are always a few tools you should master before becoming adept at using the software. In QuarkXPress 5, these particular tools are the ones used for selecting, editing, and manipulating content. The term content is used to describe anything you create on your page. Because content may be text, pictures, lines, or shapes, there are a number of different types of content tools and cursor states that apply in certain instances, each with its own purpose and function. The following section briefly covers the use of these tools with pointers to areas of this book that feature more detailed information.

Whether you're creating QuarkXPress documents yourself or simply editing or browsing through them, the Item and Content tools are the two most critical tools you'll need to know how to use. This quick section is a must read for users performing light editing, text or picture proofing, or basic layout.

The Item Tool

It's called different things in different programs, but the main tool you'll use in QuarkXPress 5 is referred to as the Item tool. The Item tool is positioned by default in the first position at the top of the Tool palette (as shown next) for a very good reason. It's your primary tool for selecting, sizing, reshaping, and moving all types of items, including editing text runaround contours and shaping clipping paths.

Item tool ———→

| **Tip** | *Holding the C*MD*/C*TRL *key temporarily changes your pointer to the Item tool, regardless of which tool you have currently selected.* |

While the Item tool is selected, clicking on any of the objects on your page "selects" them and places them in a temporary *alert state*. Only once an object is selected, you'll be able perform other commands on it, such as editing or changing properties.

| **Tip** | *XPress provides feedback that objects are currently selected by displaying the eight selection handles at their corners and sides.* |

To select more than one object, hold down the SHIFT key while clicking additional objects. To deselect a selected object, hold SHIFT while clicking the object a second time. To select all objects in a specific area, use a marquee-selection action. Marquee selection involves dragging the Item tool cursor diagonally in any direction until a dotted marquee line appears and the cursor becomes a crosshair. As you drag, your aim should be to surround the objects you wish to select, as shown in Figure 2-14. Once the mouse button is released, the objects will become selected. Finally, to select only specific objects on your page, hold down your SHIFT key and click with the Item tool to select the objects.

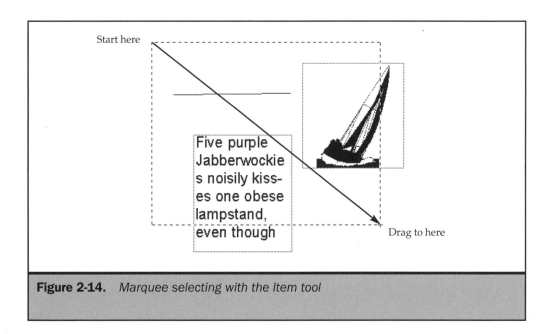

Start here

Five purple
Jabberwockie
s noisily kiss-
es one obese
lampstand,
even though

Drag to here

Figure 2-14. *Marquee selecting with the Item tool*

> **Tip** *When moving objects with the Item tool, holding SHIFT while moving constrains the vertical or horizontal movement of the object being moved.*

Once an object is selected with the Item tool, it may also be repositioned by dragging it or through use of the UP, DOWN, LEFT, and RIGHT arrow keys on your keyboard. Although dragging enables you to move objects interactively around your screen using visual reference, using the arrow keys enables you to move them more accurately by a distance of one point. This action is referred to as *nudging*.

> **Tip** *Holding the OPTION/ALT key while pressing an arrow key to move a selected object moves it a distance of 0.1 points.*

Finally, the Item tool enables you to resize any selected items by dragging one of the eight corner/side handles. While the Item tool is selected, moving your cursor over one of these handles changes your cursor to a pointing hand. The pointing hand indicates you are about to perform an interactive resizing operation. In the case of the Item tool, resizing usually means changing the size of a box containing text or a picture. Using various keyboard combinations, you may also resize not just the boxes, but the contents also. This action varies depending on the combinations of keys pressed during resizing. But resizing is one of those operations learned much more quickly through practice than by simple definition.

For a practical exercise in resizing an object using the Item tool, follow these steps:

1. Create a text box using the Rectangle Text Box tool.

2. Choose the Content tool and enter a short string of sample text when the cursor appears.

3. Leave the text formatting as is and choose the Item tool once again.

4. Select the text box by clicking on it once. Notice eight handles appear, one on each side and corner.

5. Move your pointer over one of the corner handles until it displays as a hand pointer, as shown in Figure 2-15.

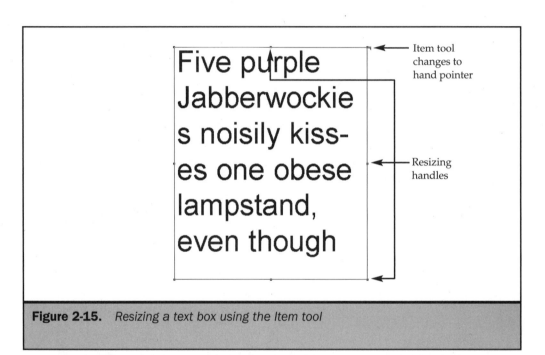

Figure 2-15.   *Resizing a text box using the Item tool*

6. Drag it in any direction and release the mouse button. The text box has been resized, but the text itself remains unchanged.

7. Now grab the same corner handle and drag it in any direction while holding the SHIFT key. Notice the text box width and height proportions become equal when you click the handle. As you drag, the box shape changes as a constant square, but when you release the mouse the text remains unchanged. Notice also that the box changed shape relative to the center of the corner you dragged.

8. Next, hold the CMD/CTRL+SHIFT keys together as you drag the corner handle. Notice when you release the mouse, both the text and the box have changed size proportionately.

9. Click CMD/CTRL+Z to undo the above action. Now, hold the CMD/CTRL key alone and perform the same action as in the previous step. Notice as you drag, the box shape changes freely, but when you release the mouse, the text's shape changed either vertically or horizontally depending on your drag direction.

It's extremely important to grasp not just the Item tool's function here, but also the concept of resizing, constraining, and vertical and horizontal scaling. These are concepts you'll use in other tools as you continue to explore XPress 5.

The Content Tool

Next on the list of critically important tools to be familiar with is the Content tool, second from the top of the Tool palette. You may recognize the Content tool by the hand and I-beam symbol on the button. The Content tool enables you to select, edit, and manipulate text and pictures *within* boxes, hence its name. Plus, you might say the Content tool is *content-sensitive*, because of the fact that while a text box is selected, the Content tool transforms into a cursor and while a picture box is selected, it changes to a grabber hand pointer.

While editing text, the Content tool conforms to the usual desktop software standards for selecting, highlighting, and clipboard functions associated with editing text. In fact, while in Content tool mode, XPress behaves as if it were a high-end word processor, flowing text within the text box. You may also change text properties while individual characters or words are selected using the Measurements palette (F9) or by opening the Character Attributes dialog (CMD/CTRL+SHIFT+D), choosing options and clicking Apply or OK.

While a picture box is selected, the Content tool changes to a grabber hand pointer. The grabber hand enables you to interactively move a picture within its picture frame without affecting the position or size of the frame itself or the dimensions of the picture within the frame. If you choose to, you may also resize picture boxes while the Content tool is selected in the same manner as the Item tool. SHIFT and CMD/CTRL keyboard combinations for scaling and constraining also apply when using the Content tool on picture boxes. The key principle to keep in mind when working with these tools is that you may manipulate text and picture boxes either together with their content or independently of each other.

For a practical exercise in using the Content tool to manipulate picture boxes within frames, follow these steps:

1. Create a picture box using any of the picture box tools. Picture box tool buttons feature shapes with Xs inside them and are located at the fifth tool position in the Tool palette.

2. Select the Content tool and import an image into your picture box by choosing File | Get Picture (CMD/CTRL+E). For the purposes of this exercise, any image will do. Notice your Content tool changes to a grabber hand.

3. Click anywhere on the picture within its frame, drag your cursor, and release. Notice the picture has moved, but its frame hasn't.

4. Drag one of the corner handles of the picture box in any direction. Notice the picture remains stationary, but the frame itself changes shape.

5. Hold the SHIFT key while you drag the same handle. Notice the box converts to equal width and height measures and changes shape to match proportionately. Again, the picture's size remains unchanged.

6. Hold the CMD/CTRL+SHIFT keys and drag the same handle. Notice the picture within the frame changes size while the box size also changes proportionately.

Original picture proportions   Resized using a CMD/CTRL+drag action

Figure 2-16.   *Dragging a picture handle with the CMD/CTRL key changes the proportions of the picture box and picture.*

7. Hold the CMD/CTRL key and drag the same handle a final time. Notice the handle moves freely in any direction and once you release the mouse the picture will become nonproportionately resized, as shown in Figure 2-16.

8. With the picture box still selected, press CMD/CTRL+OPTION/ALT+SHIFT+F. Notice the picture changes size to fit within its box. This is the shortcut key for Fit to Box while maintaining original proportions.

9. With the picture still selected, press CMD/CTRL+SHIFT+M. Notice the picture became centered within the frame without changing the picture's size. This is the shortcut key for *centering* the picture within its box.

While using the Content tool for manipulating text and pictures in boxes, a universe of speedy keyboard combinations are available. For more information on using the Content tool to manipulate text, see "Applying Text Formatting" in Chapter 4. For more information on using the Content tool to manipulate pictures in boxes, see "Working with Picture Boxes" in Chapter 7.

Many of the capabilities of the Item tool overlap in the Content tool. For example, you may resize text and picture boxes at their handles by dragging or in combination with the various keyboard combinations while either tool is selected.

The Rotation Tool

The final tool in this first group of three in the Tool palette may not be used as often as the Item and Content tools, but is no less significant in manipulating objects. The Rotation tool enables you to freely change the angle of objects in relation to your page around 360 degrees. The Rotation tool is also completely interactive, visually indicating both the point around which your object is being rotated as well as the angle. Again, getting to know the Rotation tool's behavior is best learned through practical experience.

To rotate an object with the Rotation tool, follow these steps:

1. Create a new object or continue using the picture box in the previous exercise.

2. Select your object using the Item tool by clicking on it once.

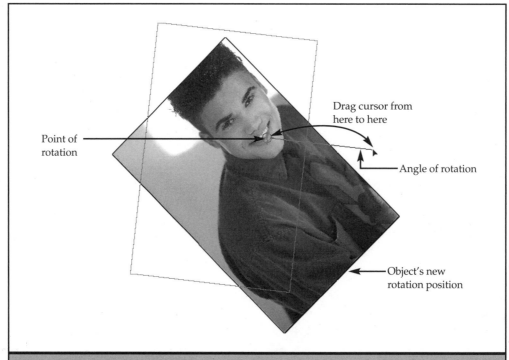

Point of rotation

Drag cursor from here to here

Angle of rotation

Object's new rotation position

Figure 2-17.   *Rotating a picture box with the Rotation tool*

3. Select the Rotation tool from the Tool palette. Notice your cursor changes to a circle with cross hairs.

4. Click and drag anywhere on your object, and drag in any direction, keeping your mouse button held firm, as shown in Figure 2-17. Notice two key guiding elements appear. One is a cross hair, while the other is a line attached to your cursor. Plus, a representative box appears, indicating the new position of your object.

The first point at which you click sets the point of rotation, while the point at which you drag to sets the angle of the rotation or slope. The distance you drag from has no bearing on the angle of the rotation, but the further you drag the more rotational control you'll have.

5. If you haven't already done so, release the mouse button. Your object is rotated to its new angle. Notice also that your cursor has changed back to the Item tool. By default, your cursor is automatically set to return to the last tool used.

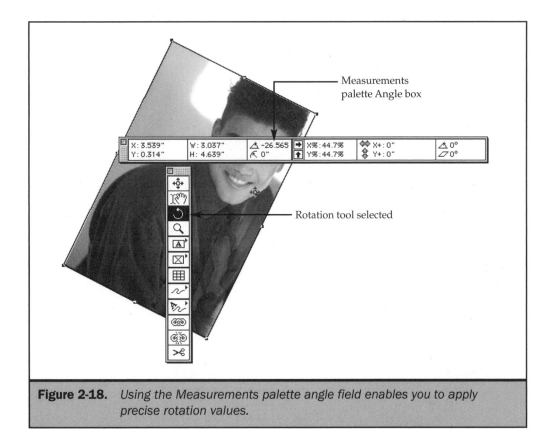

Measurements
palette Angle box

Rotation tool selected

Figure 2-18. *Using the Measurements palette angle field enables you to apply precise rotation values.*

Tip

To keep a tool temporarily selected (such as the Rotation tool) instead of reverting to the last-used tool, hold your OPTION/ALT key while selecting it from the Tool palette.

6. To go beyond basics for a moment, with your rotated object still selected, press F9 to display the Measurements palette. Reselect the Rotation tool from the Tool palette. Notice the Measurements palette angle field indicates the angle of rotation, as shown in Figure 2-18. This value indicates the rotation from the original state (or zero) and not the most recent rotation. Enter **0** in this field and press RETURN. The object is returned to its original vertical position.

Using the Measurements palette in combination with the Rotation tool enables you to more precisely change the angle of rotating objects. You may enter the angle values directly or monitor the live update in the Angle field as you rotate the object. Entering positive values rotates your object clockwise, while entering negative values rotates the object counterclockwise.

To rotate an object without previewing the new position of the object or display of the stylized cross-hair cursor and angle indication line, click and hold for one second before attempting to rotate the object. After the pause, your cursor changes to the free-rotate cursor.

Linking and Unlinking Tools

If your layout involves flowing text from one area to another, you'll need to use the XPress linking tools. In XPress, the term linking refers to creating a relationship

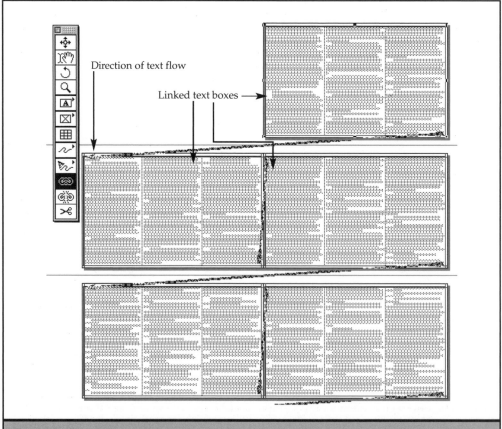

Figure 2-19. *Selecting either the Linking or Unlinking tool displays currently linked text boxes in your layout.*

between two text boxes so that they may flow content between them as needed. The simplest and most likely scenario involves flowing text from one page to the next. But more complex layouts often involve flowing text within a page layout from one text box to another.

For this, XPress features two separate tools: the Linking tool and the Unlinking tool, performing functions respective of their names. Both tools reside at the bottom of the Tool palette. With either tool selected, links that have already been assigned appear in your layout as patterned lines with start and endpoint arrowheads, indicating linked boxes and the direction of text flow, as shown in Figure 2-19.

Links between text boxes may be created manually or automatically. If you're unfamiliar with these Linking or Unlinking tools, or the general concept of linking, the

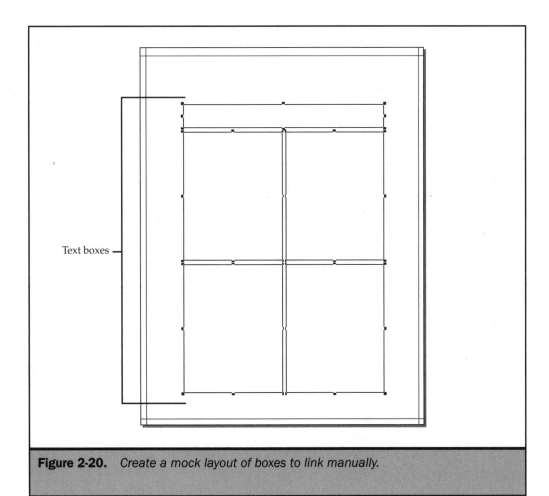

Text boxes

Figure 2-20.   *Create a mock layout of boxes to link manually.*

best way to begin understanding how to use them is by creating a few manual links yourself.

To create manual links between text boxes, follow these steps:

1. Create several text boxes of any shape or style on your page. For this example, you may follow more closely by creating the boxes in an arrangement similar to Figure 2-20.

2. Hold the CMD/CTRL key to temporarily set your cursor to the Item tool and click on the pasteboard (the area surrounding your page) to ensure no objects are selected.

3. In this next step, you're going to use the Linking tool to create several links. By default, the Linking tool reverts back to the previous tool after use. To stop this

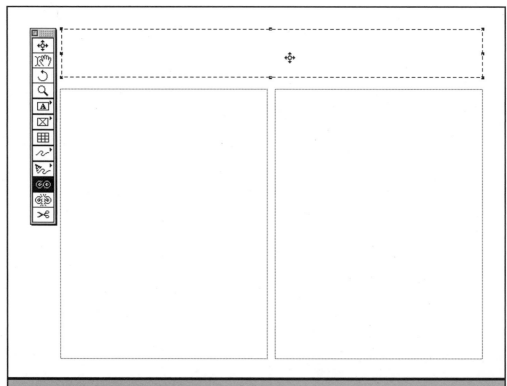

Figure 2-21.   *Click the box you would like the text to flow into.*

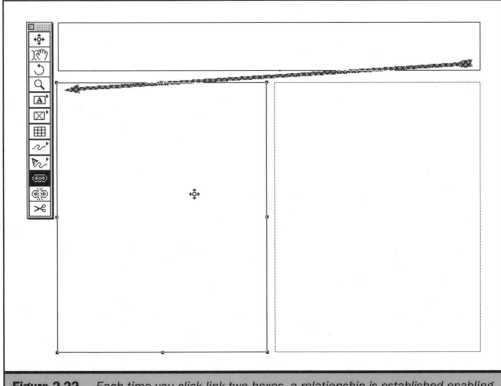

Figure 2-22.   *Each time you click link two boxes, a relationship is established enabling text to flow between them.*

from happening, hold the Option/Alt key and choose the Linking tool from the Tool palette.

4. With the Link tool selected, your cursor changes to a white pointer. Click the first text box you would like to flow text from. Notice the frame of text box displays a marquee and your cursor shows a chain link symbol.

5. Click the box you would like your text to flow into from the first box. Notice a patterned arrow appears, joining the bottom-right corner of your first text box to the top-left corner of the second, as shown in Figure 2-21.

6. Now click the remaining text boxes in the direction you would like your text to flow. Notice that each time you click a new box, a new link appears, as shown in Figure 2-22.

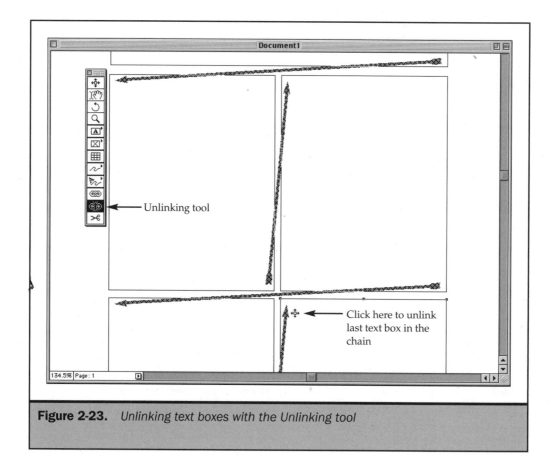

Figure 2-23.   *Unlinking text boxes with the Unlinking tool*

Breaking a link between two text boxes eliminates the text flow and the relationship between them. Text will now flow between these boxes. To break the links between the boxes you have just created, use the Unlinking tool. To do this, follow these steps:

1. Choose the Unlinking tool from the Tool palette. If you intend to unlink more than one link, hold the OPTION/ALT key while selecting the Unlinking tool.

2. Using the same text box arrangement as previously, select the first box in the chain or story by clicking on it. Notice all the links reappear.

3. Locate the arrow joining the last to the second-to-last text-linked boxes. Using the Unlinking tool, click the arrowhead of this link, as shown in Figure 2-23. The link disappears.

4. Use the same action on each of the links until all boxes are unlinked.

Tip   *To break a link, the Unlinking tool requires that you click as close as possible to the pointy end of the linking arrow.*

Practice manually linking text boxes a few more times if necessary until you have grasped this key concept in XPress. But although learning the manual way of linking text boxes in a chain will help for specific layouts, XPress includes an automated way of linking text boxes. In the section on adding pages earlier in this chapter, you may have noticed the option *Link to current text chain* in the Add Pages dialog. Clicking this option when adding new pages to your document sets the automatic text box added to each new page to be linked to the text box on the preceding page.

Pasteboard and Clipboard Functions

Layouts often involve various types and sizes of visual and/or textual material destined for assembly on your page. You may find yourself looking for ways to store, copy, and/or transfer this material to the various parts of your document. There will no doubt be times when you wish to set a content item aside for later use without deleting it. This is where use of the Pasteboard and Clipboard come in useful.

If working with text and picture content gets overcrowded within the limits of your page, you may not be using one of the most useful storage spaces available to you: the Pasteboard. The term pasteboard is taken from manual layout practices and refers to the area around your artboard where sticky bits and pieces of text and photographs were temporarily laid until needed. In fact, this is exactly what the area around your document page is meant for.

Tip   *Even though items placed on the Pasteboard lack a spot in your layout, they are still considered part of your document file and contribute to its memory size. You may store nearly unlimited material on the Pasteboard, but the more items you store there, the larger your file will become. Deleting unused items periodically may help to avoid large file sizes.*

Any content placed on the Pasteboard is simply set aside. In other words, content placed on the Pasteboard may have assigned link relationships to other elements on your page, but temporarily has no "reserved" space in your layout.

The physical dimensions of your Pasteboard may be customized, depending on your needs. For information on changing your Pasteboard size, see "Setting Application Preferences" in Chapter 13.

Your Clipboard also acts as a temporary storage space, only in a much more limited fashion. Clipboard functionality is actually a characteristic of your operating environment, but XPress supports all characteristics of the Clipboard, including the capability to view what's currently on it. Items may be copied (CMD/CTRL+C) or cut (CMD/CTRL+X) *to* your clipboard, or pasted (CMD/CTRL+V) into your document *from* it. Clipboard functions are mostly invisible to the user, and the more you become accustomed to Copy, Cut, and Paste commands, the less you'll think about it. The Clipboard is capable of "remembering" only one item at a time. Subsequent items copied to the Clipboard overwrite the previous item.

To view what's currently on your Clipboard, choose Edit | Show Clipboard. A new window will open, revealing your last copied or cut item. To close this view, choose Edit | Close Clipboard.

Macintosh users also enjoy the temporary space found in the Scrapbook, a characteristic of their operating environment. The Scrapbook is used much the same way as the clipboard, but is capable of supporting multiple items.

About Editing

After getting started placing all the various items you can now put on your page, there will come a time to change it, especially if you work in a publishing environment. Because your layout items are varied, so are the procedures for editing them. As a general rule, the editing of text and pictures within boxes is accomplished using the Content tool, while the editing of the frames and boxes themselves is accomplished using the Item tool. The editing of more advanced items covered in chapters to follow, such as Béziers, clipping paths, and runarounds, may often be done using either tool.

For new users exploring editing functions, two basic commands are found at the bottom of the Item menu: Shape and Content. The Shape submenu includes a collection of preset shapes that you may simply apply to your currently selected text or picture box. To apply one of these shapes, simply select the box using either the Item or Content tools, choose Item | Shape, and select a preset shape, as shown in the following illustration. The current shape selection is indicated by a check mark. From the top of the popup, choose from rectangular, rounded corner, concave corner, beveled corner, elliptical, Bézier box, straight line, or Bézier line, as shown in Figure 2-24.

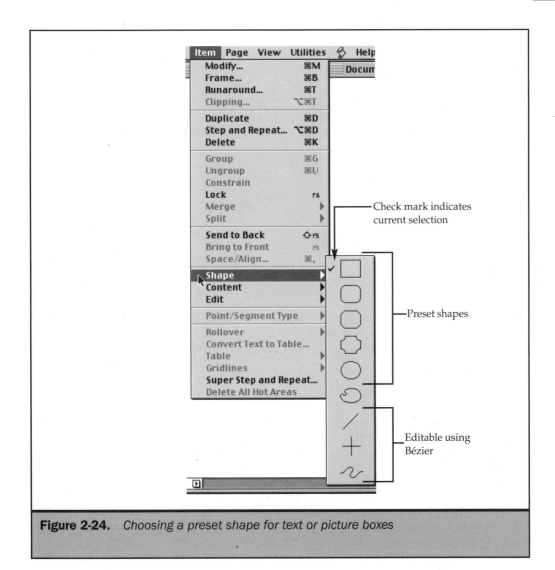

Figure 2-24. *Choosing a preset shape for text or picture boxes*

Tip   *Bézier-based shape selections are actually conversion scripts in XPress, meaning that a physical conversion takes place rather than a modal conversion. In other words, in instances where you convert a rectangular-shaped box to a Bézier line or box, your box may not be changed to another preset shape later. Instead, use the your drawing tools to edit the new Bézier shape.*

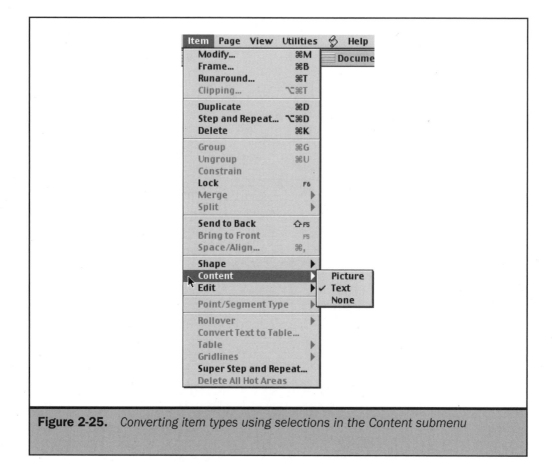

Figure 2-25. *Converting item types using selections in the Content submenu*

The Content submenu enables you to quickly convert text boxes into picture boxes or Bézier shapes (and vice versa) so that they may support different types of content, as shown in Figure 2-25.

In other words, you may change a text box to a picture box, or a simple Bézier line into a text path and all permutations between. There are some limitations to this conversion process though. The following checklist defines common limitations:

- You may not convert an open-path Bézier item to a picture or text box. The Bézier path must be closed or, in other words, not simply a line.

- When choosing None, the item is converted to a Bézier item.

- An item may only support one of these modes at a time. Meaning, you can't force a picture box to contain text or vice versa.

- When converting text boxes containing actual content, all text will be deleted.

- If more than one item is selected, the Content submenu becomes unavailable, even if the items are the same type.

Because XPress enables you to control so many of the properties of your layout elements, editing functions can often be complex, going beyond the new user issues this chapter is focused on. The following provides some suggested reading for more information on editing basic items in XPress, such as text, pictures, and the boxes that house them:

- For procedures on working with text boxes and editing text, see Chapter 4 and Chapter 6.

- For procedures on working with pictures in boxes, see Chapter 7. For a beyond-the-basics of editing operations, also check out "Controlling a Picture's Look" in Chapter 8.

- For pointers on editing items created with drawing tools, see Chapter 5.

Whether you use XPress for composing layouts, editing content, or simply for proofing or browsing documents, this chapter has exposed you to core functionality beyond launching the program. You've learned how to set document appearance, navigate pages and documents, and use key operations such as creating and linking text boxes and importing content. Some of the concepts covered in this chapter are common across desktop and/or layout applications and word processors, while others are unique and specific to QuarkXPress itself.

Now that you have some exposure to this topic, you'll likely want to begin laying out pages. Chapter 3 fleshes out more detail on document setup and covers layout planning and QuarkXPress 5's layout conveniences such as master pages, rulers, grids, guides, and measurement controls, all of which are critical to beginning and working with your first layout.

The Complete Reference

QuarkXPress 5

Chapter 3

Putting QuarkXPress to Work

The claims made by most desktop layout applications these days hint that simply by purchasing the software you can create layout *designs*. Cold hard reality paints quite a different picture though. Innovative design and successful layout involves at least some degree of experience, whether that be self-taught or through training and/or education. The software merely provides you with tools that enable you to accomplish your task, meaning you'll need to do much of the creative and organizational work yourself. If you lack the experience or training to create effective design layouts, the software certainly isn't going to provide it.

Having said that, starting a new layout can be a fairly intimidating experience if you're not quite sure where to start, what your document will look like, how you should tackle it, or what mysterious problems you'll run into along the way. Even the most experienced layout artists establish a game plan before starting any layout project.

Organizing the layout of any design document or publication is a process that is part logical, part creative, and frankly, plain hard work. If you approach the challenge progressively and one step at a time, even the most complex layout can actually be relatively painless to complete. This chapter explores design and layout from a logical perspective and will demonstrate the basics of building a typical layout in QuarkXPress 5.

Before you begin constructing a layout in QuarkXPress, I recommend you have basic understanding of key tools and concepts. This chapter builds on information and references to basic program operation covered in Chapters 1 and 2. If you've arrived here seeking some of this basic background information, try reading the preceding two chapters.

A Typical Layout Task for XPress

When beginning any layout, it's always best to have a plan or design to follow before you begin opening the program and plunking down text and/or pictures. The early design process is best tackled using good old pen and paper, although experience will reduce the need for this. Over time, some designers develop a design sense for the layout projects they produce or specialize in and can conceptualize a layout without the use of a sketch, but these are experts who often draw from years of experience. If you're yet to attain the expert level, stick to beginning your layout using the sketch strategy.

Besides the simple business card or letterhead design project, layout usually involves one of several common design projects: print or Web ads, posters, marketing brochures, books or booklets, and/or packaging. In this section, we'll briefly explore the initial planning stages of a typical layout project. In the example presented, you'll see the logical progression from the initial design sketch to beginning the QuarkXPress document shell and establishing a layout. Because content is often specific to each project and the concentration here is on actual planning and structure, we'll stop just short of adding actual content.

A Typical Marketing Brochure

Brochure layout is a common layout task. Brochures are often packed with complex detail of detail, making the use of pen and paper sketching all the more critical. Although brochure content is often much less than other layouts (such as books), brochures can involve enormous planning and organization efforts. In the case of brochures, sketching out a content plan can save considerable time as shown in Figures 3-1 and 3-2.

In this case, our brochure design layout will be printed on both sides of a single flat sheet, which will eventually be folded and trimmed to a specific size. The layout is merely two pages in length, each of which features an identical number of fold panels. Some of the content on these panels flow from one panel to the next, some layout items span more than one panel, and certain panels contain static images and/or content, meaning both linked and unlinked text boxes will be needed.

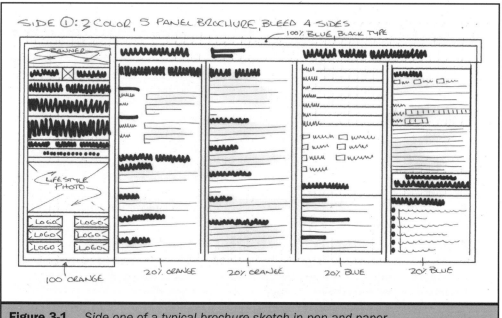

Figure 3-1.   *Side one of a typical brochure sketch in pen and paper*

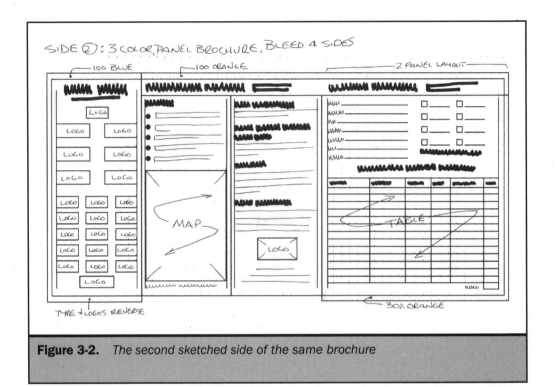

Figure 3-2. *The second sketched side of the same brochure*

The layout sketch you create will work as a map to plan out where your content will be placed, how it will fit, and to a large degree, what type of QuarkXPress content items will work best to house it. Your layout should also be created, with the following in mind, to answers that will eventually be translated into specifications you apply to your document file:

- Specifically for print documents, determine (in advance) the size of the material your document will be reproduced onto.

- What size will the top, left, right, and bottom margins be? Specifically for printed documents, margins are the mostly blank areas surrounding much of the structured content in your document such as text and pictures, not including items set to bleed beyond the trimmed edges.

- Again for printed documents, how many individual panels compose the final folded document? Will certain panels involve text content formatted in columns? Does the design call for certain picture or text content to span multiple panels?

■ What will be the ink colors? Is your document to be reproduced for the Web using a Web-safe RGB color palette? Or will the document be printed using multiple ink colors such as spot or process colors? If so, will you need to create custom ink colors? What kind of paper are you printing on?

■ For print reproduction, what are the printers' limitations in terms of trim sizes, bleed sizes, where the material will fold, and so on? Will the printer require any specialized printed output specifications?

The sketch will be invaluable for organizing your thoughts and your content. It will also help to answer some of the key questions you'll need answers to before launching QuarkXPress and specifying your new document properties. A sketch doesn't need to be a work of art. After all, in all likelihood you (or the whomever is following it) will be the only one to see it. Pages may be simple drawn rectangles in rough proportions to your page size such as shown in the figures shown on these pages. Text can be sketched into the design as simple as darkened wavy lines for main heads and lighter straight lines for body copy. It may also help shape your design to roughly indicate text alignment such as left, right, centered, or justified. Pictures need only be boxes containing brief descriptive notes. Both types of elements need only be rough because the fine-tuning will be done during the actual content layout.

Once you've completed your research into how your document should be prepared and how the design layout be structured, you're ready to begin building your XPress document. The next step is choosing to create a new document (CMD/CTRL+N). The New Document dialog asks for information regarding the size, orientation, and margin information specific to your document design. In the previous figures, the layout is a typical brochure format, printed onto 18.75-inch (width) by 8.75-inch (height) paper. The next illustration shows these values entered into the dialog that appears after choosing the New Document command:

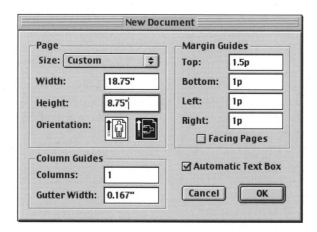

The format I've planned for also requires an evenly divided, 5-panel structure across each page of the two-sided document. My document design specifications require margins sizes were set to differing measures: the top margin at 1.5 picas, and the left, right, and bottom margins to 1 pica each. Because the document is to be printed and folded, each page divided into separate folded panels using vertical guidelines dragged from the Ruler margins of QuarkXPress (see Figure 3-3).

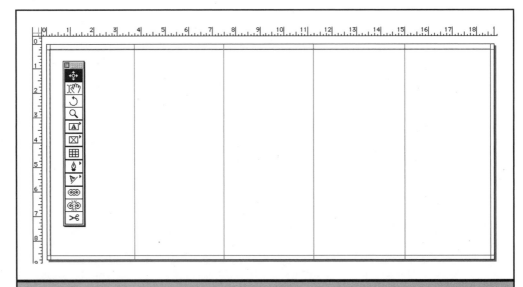

Figure 3-3. *After closing the New Document dialog, QuarkXPress builds the first page as you've specified. Shown here, added guides now divide the panels.*

Tip *For more information on working with Rulers and guides, see "Rulers, Guides, and Layout Measures" later in this chapter.*

With the initial empty document shell built, page 2 has yet to be added. For this, use the Insert Page command by choosing Page, Insert to open the Insert Pages dialog. Entering 1 in the Insert field, choosing the *At end of Document* option (the default), and clicking OK creates the new page identical to the first.

```
┌─────────────────────────────────────┐
│ ▤▤▤▤▤▤     Insert Pages     ▤▤▤▤▤▤ │
│                                       │
│  Insert: │ 1      │  page(s)           │
│                                       │
│          ○ before page:               │
│          ● after page:    │ 1    │    │
│          ○ at end of document         │
│                                       │
│      ☐ Link to Current Text Chain     │
│                                       │
│  Master Page: │ A–Master A      ▲▼│   │
│                                       │
│          ┌────────┐  ┌──────────┐     │
│          │ Cancel │  │    OK    │     │
│          └────────┘  └──────────┘     │
└─────────────────────────────────────┘
```

If you accepted your document options with the Automatic Text Box option selected (the default), you'll also discover you have a single text box added to each page. Because a typical folded-brochure layout is divided into multiple panels, this text box will need to be modified or deleted and separate content boxes added according to your design. Text panels will need separate text boxes drawn for each panel according to the design sketch.

Where the design calls for text to span two panels, a single text box will be needed to cover both panels. Where text content flows from one panel to the next, links will need to be established, and where the design calls for pictures to be added, Picture boxes will need to be created according to your design sketch. If the design you are creating is similar to this, the following step sequence may help. To modify the default Automatic Text box and create additional Text boxes, follow these steps:

1. Choose the Item tool from the Tool palette.

2. Click once to select the automatic text box on page 1 of your document. Resize this box by click-dragging one of the corner handles until its size suits your design (which typically means to align within the margin guides). Repeat this operation for any other pages in your QuarkXPress document, as in the case with page two of the document I've created here.

3. For precise placement or sizing, Zoom in temporarily by holding the CTRL+SHIFT keys on the Macintosh platform version or the CTRL+SPACEBAR keys on the Windows version and click-dragging to define the area to zoom. To zoom out again quickly to full-page view, press CMD/CTRL+0 (the latter being the zero key).

To create new text boxes for your design panels, use this quick step-by-step operation:

4. Still using the Item tool, select the text box on the first page by clicking it once.

5. Duplicate the text box by choosing Item | Duplicate (CMD/CTRL+D). This creates an exact copy of the text box that is automatically placed according to preset Duplicate offset measures.

6. Drag the copy into position on the second panel of the first page and resize as needed. You may repeat the same operation for virtually anywhere your document requires new text boxes, in my case 5 individual text boxes (one for each folded panel).

7. If multiple pages in your document feature similar content structure as mine does, here's another technique you may want to try. Select all the text boxes on the first page by holding your SHIFT key and clicking on each of them once. Notice each is highlighted by its own resizing handles.

8. Duplicate all (CMD/CTRL+D) content boxes and drag them within the corresponding margin copies into position on the second page. Now you have individual text boxes for each of the ten panels.

If you intend on flowing text across multiple panels, you'll need to establish text flow in a specific order using the text box Linking tool of QuarkXPress. Establishing text links between text boxes enables text content to flow freely from the end of one text box to the beginning of and into the next. In the case of this brochure, several panel require linking. To quickly link text boxes similar to the brochure example layout, follow these steps:

9. Choose the Linking tool from the Tools palette. This is the tool featuring the unbroken chain link symbol.

10. Click once to select the first text box you want text to *flow from* in your layout with the Linking tool. The text box you click immediately appears with a marquee around it.

11. Click once to define the text box you want the text to *flow to* in your layout. Notice a linking arrow now joins the two panels as shown in the brochure example in Figure 3-4.

Tip   *Holding your OPTION/ALT key while clicking to choose the Linking tool to establish links between text boxes will keep the tool selected for multiple linking.*

12. Continue linking your text content until you have established all links. In the case of my brochure layout, I've linked only text panels that require text flow, leaving the others (such as the back and front covers) unlinked to any other text boxes (see Figure 3-5).

13. Although you haven't begun to enter or import text content yet, structuring your layout is more than enough to justify saving it. To save your document

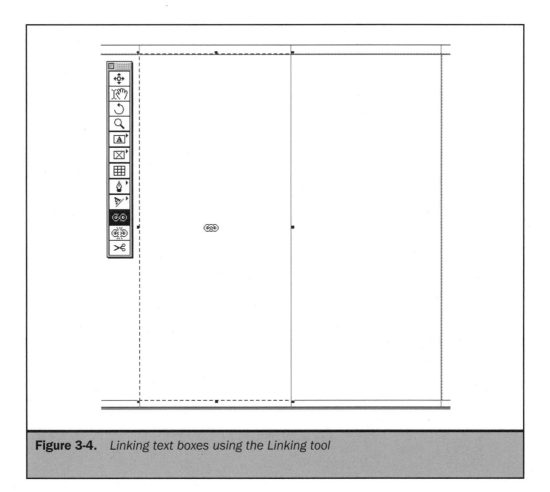

Figure 3-4. *Linking text boxes using the Linking tool*

now choose File | Save (CMD/CTRL+S) and furnish your document with a
name and folder location.

Tip   *To break the link relationship between two text boxes, use the Unlinking tool (identified
by a broken chain link symbol) in the Tools palette. After choosing the Unlinking tool,
click to select one of the linked text boxes and click directly on either the beginning or
ending arrow symbols that show link direction. A single click will break the link
relationship between the two boxes. For more information on using the Linking and
Unlinking tools, refer to Chapter 2.*

According to the layout sketch I've created, several panels of my brochure design
will require picture content in the form of digital photos, logos, and illustrations.

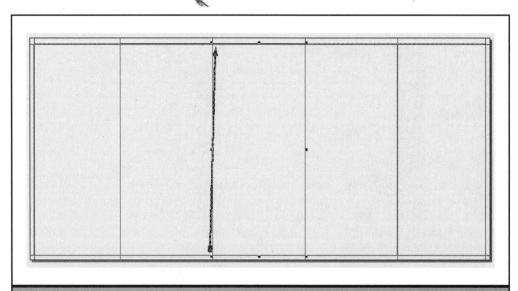

Figure 3-5.   *The required text box links are established between specific text panels on page 1 of the brochure according to the design sketch.*

Because pictures are a different type of content from text, a different type of box item is needed to house them: Picture boxes. Picture boxes enable you to establish picture page position, picture dimensions, with the aim of importing pictures using the Get Picture command. Picture boxes are created using the Picture Box tool.

Tip   *For more information on incorporating pictures, see Chapter 6. For information on manipulating picture content, see the same chapter.*

For your own specific layout, if you need to create picture boxes and place them in position on your document pages, follow these steps:

1. Choose the Rectangular Picture Box tool from the Tool palette.

2. Using your layout as a guide, begin creating the picture boxes in their rough position and size as shown in Figure 3-6. To resize or move picture boxes once created, choose the Item tool and click-drag any of the selection handles to resize the box or click-drag within the interior to move the box.

Tip   *Holding the OPTION/ALT key while clicking to choose a Picture Box tool will keep it selected for multiple use.*

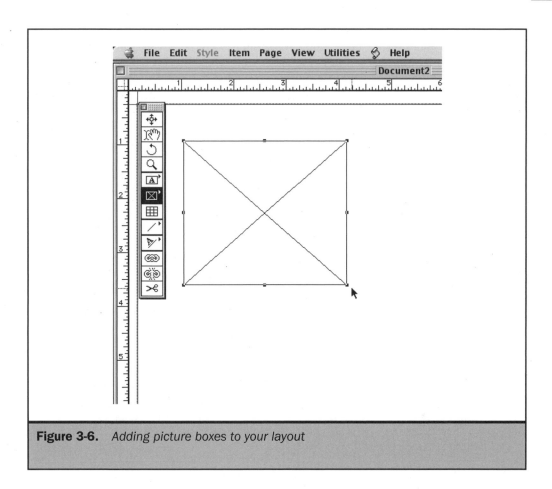

Figure 3-6. *Adding picture boxes to your layout*

3. Once you've finished creating your picture boxes, the rough shell of your brochure is complete.

Tip   *While roughing in a layout in QuarkXPress, you may now add gibberish-type textual content (called Jabberwocky) to text boxes for a quick impression of how the final formatted content will appear. To do so, choose the Content tool from the Tools palette, click your cursor in the text box to be filled, and choose Utilities | Jabber. The selected text box (and any linked text boxes) will immediately be completely filled with gibberish text content. For more information on using Jabberwocky text, see Chapter 6.*

At this point, the brochure document is ready to begin importing, entering, and formatting the final content. (You'll find these operations are covered in great detail in other chapters.) Although the brochure layout seen on the preceding pages is highly typical of the type of project QuarkXPress is often used for, there are certainly others that are anything but typical. One of these is packaging design, a highly specialized type of design that involves various reproduction and manufacturing processes beyond the initial layout process.

Packaging design entails many different types of specifications and layout limitations much more complex than a typical brochure layout. They come with their own set of challenges, the most complex of which involve highly detailed text formatting, integrated text and pictures, and non-rectangular content box shapes. Figure 3-7 shows the sketch of a box design destined for QuarkXPress that will be created using a similar strategy as the brochure layout. The difference being the box will only be printed on one side, and the final processes involves specialized die cut, folding, and gluing operations.

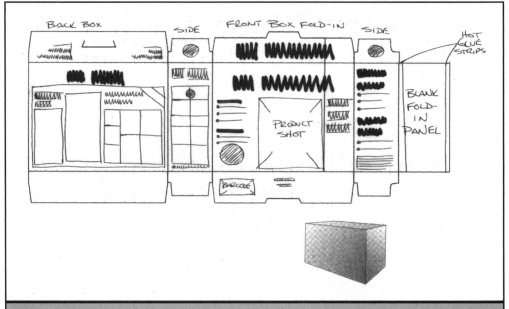

Figure 3-7.   *This example of a design sketch of a box container is a common first step in packaging design.*

Building a Typical Book Layout

Creating a book layout doesn't necessarily mean the final result will be a printed and bound book. As far as QuarkXPress is concerned, a book layout may be anything from a one-sided photocopied report to a full-color catalog, annual report, or virtually any type of reference document. As with the brochure layout, sketching a plan enables you to create a new design, plan a complex color strategy, or give structure to unorganized content. If your book layout is going to be quite large and follows a consistent design, it may be helpful to sketch only a single page layout that will act as a guide for all pages. The bottom line is that you need to look at the dynamics of your publication and create a plan for yourself. It may take several tries to get your layout just right, but at least you'll be laying some valuable groundwork, which will virtually guarantee reducing your layout time down the road.

Unlike brochures, creating a book layout in QuarkXPress enables you to take full advantage of powerful features such as automatic text boxes, column features, automatic page numbering, master page elements, and so on. In fact, many of these automated features are geared more toward lengthy books than they are to single-page documents. In this next example we'll explore, the basic design of a 16-page book destined to be printed on letter-sized 8.5- by 11-inch paper is sketched out. The sketch will serve to indicate a rough guide for the layout, text, and picture placement. Figure 3-8 illustrates a typical layout showing a rough structure of the content.

With a basic structure and plan in place, you may want to refine the layout slightly more by adding more detail such as color specifications, picture formats, drop caps in text, text alignment, and columns. You needn't go so far as to copy-fit the text; certain text formatting tools in QuarkXPress 5 will enable you to do that later when importing your text, and as long as you plan the typical or most complex page, the remaining pages may be left to your *actual* layout stage. Figure 3-9 shows a more detailed plan of the book style layout shown previously.

Once your book structure is roughly planned out, you may begin creating your QuarkXPress document file. To create the specific preceding book sketch as a QuarkXPress 5 document, I followed this step sequence:

1. I began building the structure by choosing File | New Document (CMD/CTRL+N) to open the New Document dialog.

2. From the Size drop-down menu, I chose US Letter and selected Portrait as the orientation, a format typical of most commonly printed books.

3. To set the text box format, I entered 3 in the Columns field and entered 1 pica as the gutter size, meaning the defined space between the columns.

4. For margin size, I've set the Top, Bottom, Inside, and Outside margin measures to 3 picas by entering 3 in the margin fields.

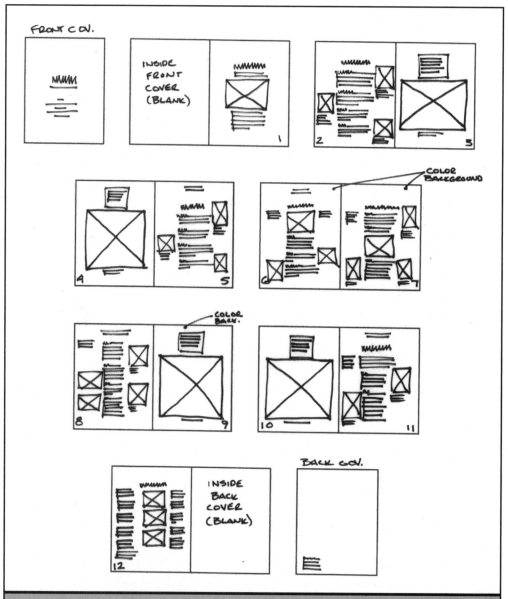

Figure 3-8. *Typical sketched plan of a 16-page book*

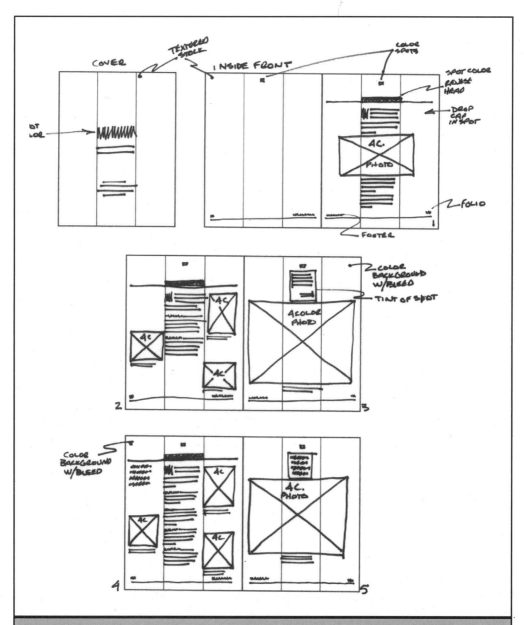

Figure 3-9. *If time allows, you may want to plan more of the detail on typical or complex pages.*

5. Because this is a book format involving both left and right pages, I've selected the Facing Pages option in addition to the Automatic Text Box option to have QuarkXPress automatically create default text boxes on each page according to these measures. The following illustration shows setting typical document page options for the book layout.

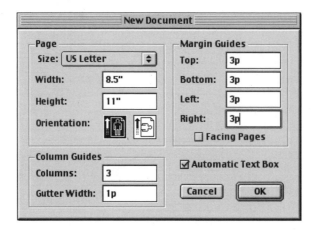

6. After clicking OK to close the dialog and accept my defined page values, QuarkXPress creates the empty shell of the first page of the book with the page size and margins defined and the first text box already in position (see Figure 3-10).

7. The next step adds the remaining pages to the document complete with automatic text boxes on each page linked to the first. For this I chose the Item Tool and clicked once to select the Automatic Text box created by QuarkXPress on page 1.

8. Choosing Page | Insert to open the Insert Pages dialog, I've entered 15 in the Insert field (for a total of 16 pages), and selected the At End of Document and Automatically Link Text Boxes On All Pages options. Because I also want text to flow from the text box on page 1 and throughout the document, I've also selected the Link to Current Text Chain option that will create text link relationships between all text boxes on all 16 pages of the document.

> **Tip** *If the option Link to Current Text Chain is unavailable in the Insert Pages dialog, then you must exit the dialog, select the text box using the Item Tool on your page, and reopen the Insert Pages dialog.*

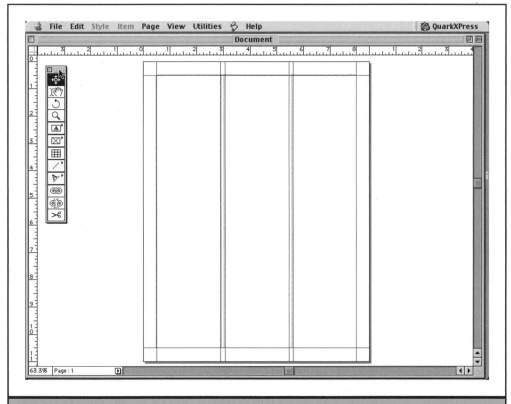

Figure 3-10.   *XPress creates the first page of your book layout.*

9. Clicking OK closes the dialog and adds the additional pages. For the zoomed
    out view shown in Figure 3-11, I entered 10 in the View magnification field
    followed by pressing Enter, but the same view may be achieved by choosing
    View | Thumbnails (SHIFT+F6), which displays your document view at roughly
    a 10 percent view magnification.

Completing the structure of the empty document will also require adding picture
boxes, line rules, and so on throughout the layout, the procedures of which you'll find
detailed in other chapters of this book. Although this newly created document is simply
an empty shell for the book layout, easy enough work has been done to justify saving it
as either a document (QXD), or a template (QXT) file using the Save (CMD/CTRL+S) or
Save As commands. When saving, be sure to provide your document with a unique
name and folder location.

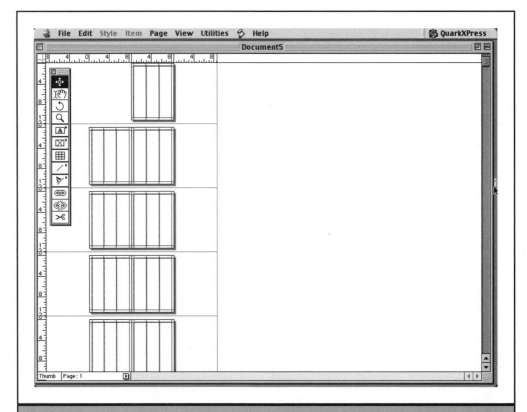

Figure 3-11. *Remaining pages are inserted with automated text box links as shown here in Thumbnail view.*

Using Master Pages

At this point, you've had some time to realize how critical your layout plan is and build the shell of your book layout in XPress. Going through the manual exercises of creating a document layout will provide you with valuable practical experience, but now's the time to take advantage of certain automated features available to you. Through creation and application of master page elements, you'll save significant time and allow XPress to perform much of the labor involved in creating common page elements.

What Are Master Pages For?

As the name implies, master pages enable you to quickly create items common to multiple pages. You may format a master page to include any of the items you can create in XPress, such as line rules, common page headings and footings, design elements, and so on. You may also set XPress to copy master guides. Guides are non-printing lines that indicate column and margin setup on your page.

One of the most commonly sought after features is the ability to set automatic page numbering for your document. When an automatic page number is placed on a master page and that master page is subsequently applied to specific pages in your layout, the pages are numbered according to their layout order. To create automatic page numbers, create a text box and position it according to your layout plan. With your Content tool selected and the cursor positioned in the text box, press CMD/CTRL+3. The symbol <#> appears, indicating an automatic numbering tag. Each of the document pages your master page is applied to will be numbered automatically in sequence according to their layout position. Automatic page numbers may be formatted to include any character attributes as with any text in XPress.

Displaying Master Pages

The display of pages in XPress is subtly divided into two separate worlds: document pages and master pages. The direct way to view a master page is through choosing Page, Display and selecting a Master Page name from the pop-out menu as shown next. If the document you're working on features only a single master page, only one will appear in the list. Where multiple master pages are used, each will be listed automatically. Choosing a specific master page will change your page view to reflect its properties.

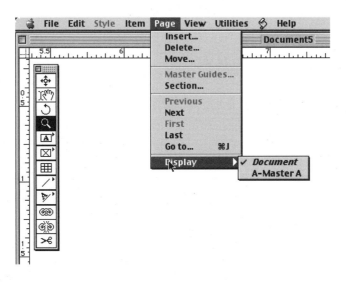

To return to the view to your document pages choose Page | Display | Document.

By default, whenever a new document is created, a blank master page is automatically created and named. The default master page is named *A-Master A*. In plainer language, the first A indicates master page A (the first in any sequence of multiple master pages), and what follows is the editable default name *Master A*. In its default condition, the master page contains nothing more than a single text box and margin guides set according to the values you first entered to create your new QuarkXPress document.

Perhaps the most convenient way to work with the master page feature is through use of the Document Layout palette (*Macintosh:* F10, *Windows:* F4). Besides being able to quickly change your view between a specific master page view or a specific document page, the Document Layout palette enables you to view, duplicate, delete, and/or name your master pages. It also enables you to quickly apply master pages to specific pages in your document simply by using a dragging action.

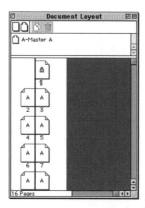

As a practical exercise in using this feature for working with master pages, follow these steps:

1. With your document open, choose to display your Document Layout palette by choosing View | Document Layout or use the hotkey (*Macintosh:* F10, *Windows:* F4). Notice the palette is divided into two separate areas. The top area displays master pages while the bottom lists the pages in your actual document.

2. To view a master page, double-click on the page icon adjacent to its name. XPress displays the master page. Notice also that the Document Layout palette indicates the name of the master page being viewed in bold type.

3. To rename a master page, double-click on its name. The master page name is highlighted, and your pointer changes to a cursor enabling you to enter a

unique name. Press ENTER or RETURN to accept the new name, as shown in Figure 3-12.

4. To quickly create a new master page, click the Duplicate button at the very top of the palette. A new master page icon appears in the master page list. By default, the new master page is named *B-Master B* and features properties identical to the one copied. If needed, apply a new name to the second master page.

5. To delete a master page, click on its icon once and click the Delete button at the very top of the palette.

Tip

Master pages are identified alphabetically, which is an option that may not be changed. The Document Layout palette indicates which master page has been applied to each document page using the corresponding master page letter. When inserting new pages in your document, you may choose which master page properties are applied by making your choice from the Master Page drop-down menu in the Insert Pages dialog.

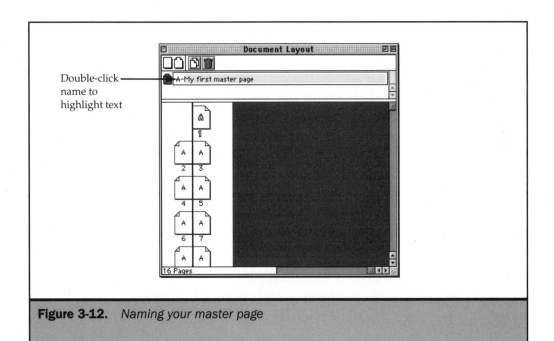

Double-click name to highlight text

Figure 3-12.   *Naming your master page*

Multiple Master Pages

If your document layout calls for two or more different styles of layout across several pages, creating a master page for each style will save significant time, especially if your document is lengthy. For example, the book layout example discussed previously includes two unique and different layout styles that apply to several pages in the layout. By creating one master page for each layout style, you may apply master pages to each of the pages according to your layout plan and avoid having to re-create all the elements on those pages.

To add a new master page, click the Duplicate button the Document layout palette and double-click its master page icon to view the page. Format the page to include common elements such as text boxes, picture boxes, line rules, page numbers and so on. Once you have tailored the new master page in the new style, you may apply it to any page you want. XPress enables you to create up to 101 different master pages for each new document. Master pages are alphabetically named AA through DW.

When working with multiple master pages, you may select more than one master page at a time by holding Shift while clicking their page icons in the top half of the Document Layout palette to select sequential entries or CMD/CTRL clicking to select non-sequential entries in the list. Plus, the master page area is expandable so that you may view more of the master page list. To expand the view, drag the bottom border of the list downwards.

Applying Master Pages

Once your master page has been tailored to suit your layout needs, you may apply it to specific document pages using the Document Layout palette. Applying a master page is a quick operation. Simply drag the master page icon from the top area of the Document Layout palette directly onto the document page icon in the lower half of the palette. Any item that has been created on your page by a master page transfer is referred to as a *master page item*.

When applying master page formats, XPress simply creates new items according to your master page layout. However, let's suppose you've already created other items on your page from scratch or from another master page. Ultimately, XPress is going to run into a conflict: Keep the original elements or delete them and apply the new master page elements? The answer lies in how options in your Document Preferences dialog (CMD/CTRL+Y) have been set.

By choosing Edit | Preferences | Preferences to open the Preferences dialog and clicking General under Document in the tree directory, you may set one of two options in the Master Page Items drop-down menu. Choose the *Keep Changes* option to enable XPress to keep current items intact and unchanged. While this option is selected, when new master page items added to the page, the current items that have already been modified in some way are left as is, but are no longer considered master page items.

This option is the default master page option. Choosing the option to *Delete Changes* enables XPress to replace all items, including those that have already been modified in some way, with the new master page items being applied.

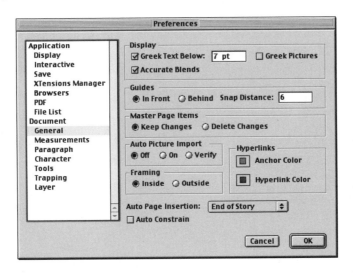

 Using the Document Layout palette, you may copy one master page over another by dragging the icons in the top area of the palette. The master pages being replaced is deleted from your layout and the existing master page elements apply to all pages where the deleted master page was applied. In this case, master page items are also replaced according to options set in your document preferences as shown previously.

Working in Sections

If the document you are constructing is only one part of a larger document that you've elected to segregate into individual parts, you may set XPress to number and display pages according to their actual sequence or position in your layout using the Section command. The Section command also enables you to specify the start of new sections *within* your document.

You may access the Section command options from menus by choosing Page, Section to open the Section dialog as shown in Figure 3-13. From here, you may set your current page as the *Start* of a new section that in turn enables you to enter *Prefix*, page *Number*, and numbering *Format*.

Choosing Section command options enable you to control the following Section parameters:

■ **Prefix**   The prefix may contain any characters supported by XPress or your operating system, but must not exceed four characters in length. Prefixes appear before automatic page numbering on your pages and when using the

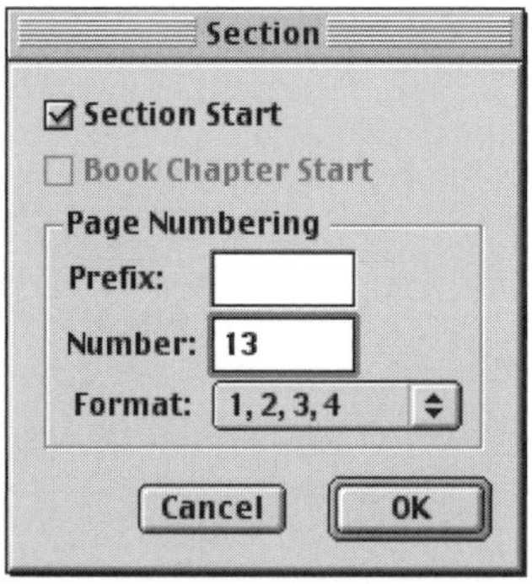

Figure 3-13. *Choosing options in the Section dialog*

automated page number feature of XPress. The prefix you set will also display when viewing page in the page number field of your document window and in the Document Layout palette.

- **Number**   In this field, enter the page number of the start of your new document section. Pages in your document will automatically appear in whichever page number you specify here. The start page number of your section must be set within a range between 1 and 9,999.

- **Format**   This drop-down menu enables you to choose from one of five page-numbering formats. Pages may be numbered using standard numeric, uppercase Roman, lowercase Roman, uppercase alphabetic, or lowercase alphabetic.

The Section command feature keeps track of left and right page usage. If your document setup includes use of left and right pages and your viewing options are set to view facing pages, the Section command automatically changes sets even numbered pages as left facing pages.

Section commands apply to your currently displayed page. In other words, when you select to format the start of a new section, the options you set will apply to your current and subsequent pages in your document. Section options are best managed and viewed through use of the Document Layout palette. While using this palette, section starts are indicated by asterisks (*) accompanying the page numbers. The Document Layout palette also features a shortcut button to the Section command dialog in the lower-left corner whenever a document page is selected as shown in Figure 3-14.

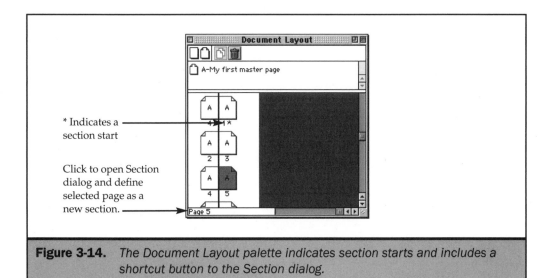

Figure 3-14. *The Document Layout palette indicates section starts and includes a shortcut button to the Section dialog.*

The Document Layout palette enables you set section starts without the need to manually navigate to the page. Simply click the start page in the palette and click the shortcut button in the palette to apply the Section Start options.

The Section command options also enable you to set Book Chapter Starts when working with very large documents. For more information on using the Book Chapter Start option, see "Setting a Book Chapter Start" in Chapter 12.

Rulers, Guides, and Layout Measures

Layout can often involve creating documents to pinpoint accuracy and measured to specific units, and positioning items can be finicky business. XPress includes features that make accurate layout much easier in the form of onscreen rulers, repositionable guides, and the display and manipulation of object dimensions.

Setting Rulers

Your onscreen rulers have a number of critical functions when laying out your document. They can provide a visual reference for measuring and sizing items and enable you to position those items according to your page origin. They also act as a inexhaustible source for pulling guides onto your layout page. Rulers may be customized to display in certain increment measures and the point from which they measure may be positioned anywhere on or off your page. Logically, ruler increments change, depending on your view level magnification.

Tip   *Certain standards of measure dictate slight differences in equivalent unit measures. XPress enables you to customize equivalent measure values for both Picas/points per inch and ciceros per centimeter. For more information on changing the default equivalent measures XPress uses for these units, see Chapter 13.*

To control whether your document rulers are visible or not, choose View/Hide | Rulers (CMD/CTRL+R). The Ruler itself is comprised of three essential components: the Horizontal scale, the Vertical scale, and the Ruler origin (see Figure 3-15). Horizontal and Vertical Ruler increments may be set individually to a variety of unit measures comprising inches, inches decimal, picas, points, millimeters, centimeters, ciceros, or agates. The Ruler Origin may be repositioned to specify any point on or off your document page as a point of origin. Steps to control each of these Ruler aspects are found in the next section.

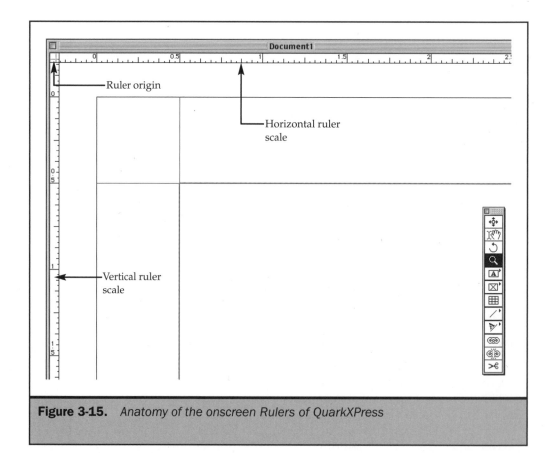

Figure 3-15.   *Anatomy of the onscreen Rulers of QuarkXPress*

Setting Ruler Increments

Setting your Ruler increments has a widespread affect on how you enter unit measures in palettes and dialog boxes. For example, if your rulers are set to a unit measure of millimeters, then the default unit measure for item sizes, document dimensions, and positioning items on pages will be measured in millimeters by default, unless you specify differently when entering values. Entering unit abbreviations following the unit values in palettes or dialog box fields enables you to deviate from the default measure as follows:

Inches	*Macintosh:* "
	Windows: in or "
Inches (Decimal)	*Macintosh:* " or " appended with a decimal value
	Windows: in or " appended with a decimal value
Picas	p
Points	pt
Millimeters	mm
Centimeters	cm
Ciceros	c
Agates	ag

As a practical guide to setting up and working with document Rulers, follow these steps:

1. With a document open, ensure your Rulers are showing (CMD/CTRL+R) as shown in Figure 3-16. Ideally, you should be viewing both pages of a two-page spread, showing a left and right page.

2. Choose View, Fit in Window (CMD/CTRL+O) to completely view two pages.

3. With your rulers showing, notice the ruler measures increase as you read left to right and top to bottom from the upper-left corner of each page.

4. Choose Edit, Preferences, Preferences (CMD/CTRL+OPTION/ALT+SHIFT+Y), and select Measurements under Document from the tree directory on the left of the dialog as shown in the following illustration. Notice the first two options in this dialog control Horizontal and Vertical measure.

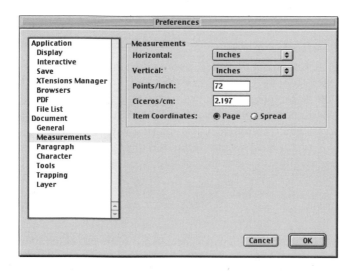

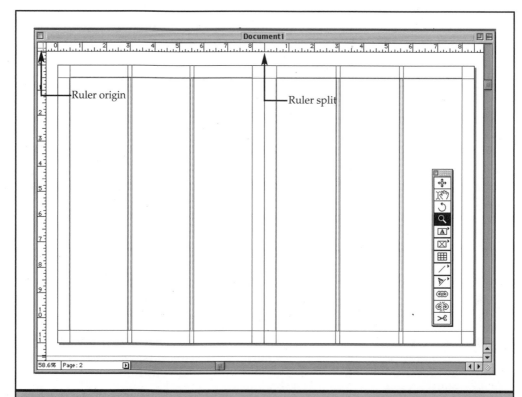

Figure 3-16.   *Viewing rulers across a two-page spread*

5. Choose the ideal unit of measure for the type of layout you're creating by making a choice from the each drop-down menu. If you want, you may set each of them the horizontal and vertical to display different units of measures.

6. Select OK to accept your document preference changes and notice now the rulers reflect the new units.

7. To reset the ruler origin, grab the intersection point of the two rulers (upper-left corner) and drag it to a new position on either page. Notice that the ruler resets to measure from the new position and that this new ruler origin applied to each page.

8. Next, double-click on the ruler origin (again, the intersection point of your horizontal and vertical rulers). Notice the rulers reset to measure from the upper-left of each page.

9. Choose Edit | Preferences | Preferences (CMD/CTRL+OPTION/ALT+SHIFT+Y) and select Measurements from the tree directory again. Locate the option named Item Coordinates, choose Spread from the drop-down menu, and click OK to accept the preference change. Notice now that your rulers measure progressively across *both* pages of your two-page spread.

10. Finally, grab any point on either ruler and click and drag your cursor to any point on your page. Notice as you drag, a line appears and follows your cursor. On releasing the mouse button, a line appears on your page. Notice also that this line appears only on the page onto which you dragged it. If you haven't already guessed it, this line is a ruler guide.

Besides setting your unit measure, this is one of the key functions of the Ruler. Ruler guides are a pivotal resource to use in visually or manually aligning items. To delete the guide, click-drag it back into the ruler you dragged it from.

As you use various tools or drag and position items on your page, the horizontal and vertical rulers display dotted reference marks indicating the width, height, and position of the tool cursor and/or position of items.

Using Guides

If you're familiar with the use of guidelines or guides in other applications or if you just completed the previous steps, you may already have an understanding of how useful they can be. There are essentially three types of guides in XPress, although their difference is subtle: margin, ruler, and column guides.

- **Margin guides**   Margin guides display in blue (by default) on your page and are set when you initially create your new XPress document. After creating your document, these margins may only be changed by applying a new master guides from master pages. For information on changing master page guides, see "Setting Master Guides" further in this section.

■ **Ruler guides**   These guides are user-created by dragging from either the horizontal or vertical ruler bars; hence, there are vertical ruler guides and horizontal ruler guides. By default, ruler guides appear green on your page.

■ **Column guides**   Column guides display within text boxes where more than one column has been specified. Their display changes with the number of columns set in each text box. Display color of column guides is not a controllable option in XPress.

Tip

The guide features of XPress are easily one of the more useful for positioning and aligning multiple items within your layout. However, manually positioning an item close to but not touching a guide is nearly impossible. For this, you may want to turn the snapping feature off. To do this, choose View, Snap to Guides (SHIFT+F7) to turn the feature off momentarily. If you work with guides often, be sure to turn the Snap to Guides back on after positioning your page item.

To control the display of both ruler and margin guides on your page, choose View, Show/Hide Guides (F7). How your guides display may also be controlled through the Document Preferences dialog by choosing Edit, Preferences, Preferences (CMD/CTRL+OPTION/ALT+SHIFT+Y), and select General under Document from the tree directory on the left of the Preferences dialog that opens. The options labeled Guides (see Figure 3-17) feature two options to display guides *In Front* (the default) or *Behind* your page items and include a Snap Distance value. Selecting to view guides *Behind* your document items causes ruler and margin guides to be hidden behind existing page items.

Note

Although margin, ruler, and column guides appear on your screen, they do not print, nor are there options anywhere in XPress to select them to print.

When items on your page are positioned near or close to margin or ruler guides (but *not* column guides), the effect is magnetic, causing items to snap to align vertically or horizontally with the closest guides. This snapping effect makes it much faster and less tedious to align items along vertical or horizontal points. By default, items will snap to guides when within a distance of 6 pixels. However, the snapping distance may be increased or decreased, depending on your work habits.

To adjust this snapping distance, enter your preferred value in the Snap Distance field in the Document Preferences dialog shown in Figure 3-17. Snap distance may be set within a range between 1 and 216 pixels, although larger distances will likely cause conflicts between several page guides as XPress struggles with which guide to snap to.

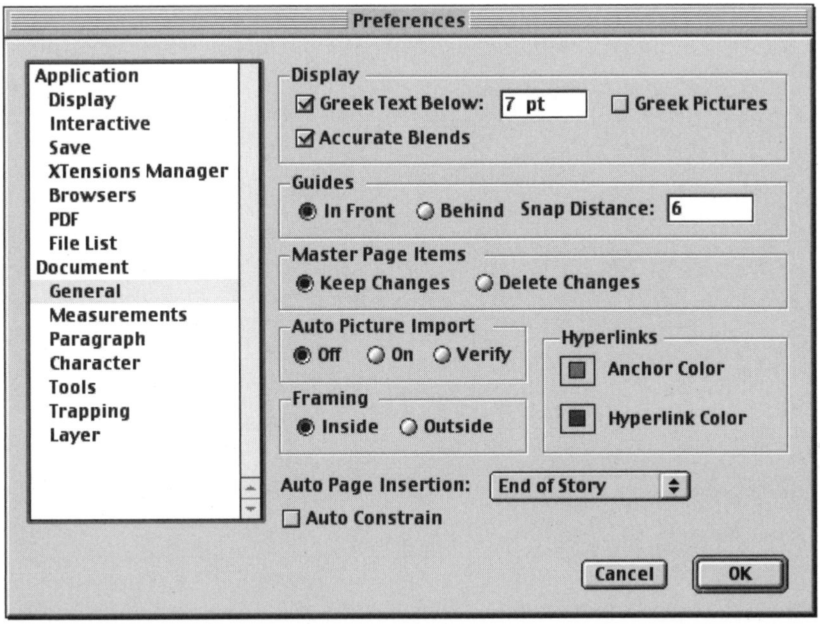

Figure 3-17.   *The General page of the Preferences dialog enables you to set Guides
behavior.*

Tip
*The display color of your ruler guides may be customized to suit your needs. For more
information on setting guide colors, see "Setting Application Preferences" in Chapter 13.*

Setting Master Guides

Although the margin guides on your page may not be moved, you may apply new
margin measures based on new master page properties using the Master Guides
command. To change your master page margin guides, you must be viewing a master
page. Once a master page is displayed (Choose Page, Display, Master Page), the Master
Guides command becomes available.

To Master Guides, options are identical to the margin options set when creating
a new document, comprising fields for entering the number of *Columns*, and unit
measures for *Gutter* and *Top, Bottom, Left,* and *Right* page margins as shown in Figure 3-18. Changing the Master Guides on a master page automatically applies the new
margin measures to pages that have the specific master page applied. If you want only

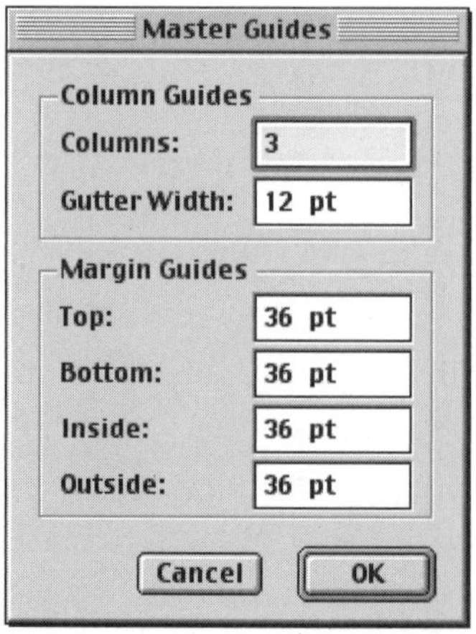

Master Guides

Column Guides

Columns: 3

Gutter Width: 12 pt

Margin Guides

Top: 36 pt

Bottom: 36 pt

Inside: 36 pt

Outside: 36 pt

Cancel   OK

Figure 3-18. *Master Guides dialog options*

to have specific margins for a certain page, you may need to create a new master page, alter the margins to suit your needs, and apply that master page to your document page.

For information on using one of the newest features in QuarkXPress that enables you to automatically add, delete, look, and/or unlock guides, see "Using the Guide Manager" in Chapter 13.

Viewing Baseline Grids

If you're fairly new to working with typographic and layout tools, you may not be familiar with either part of the name of this next feature. Baseline grids are used to ensure that page layouts are essentially neat and tidy and follow standard layout conventions. A *baseline* is the imaginary line on which characters (or strings of characters) appear to rest. In layout terms, a *grid* is an invisible lattice into which all baselines of text align. So, the Baseline grid serves as a foundation on which your type may align. Grids enable you to align headings, body text, rules, and so on, so that the layout appears planned and organized.

The Baseline grid is a series of horizontal lines that appear by default in red on your master and document pages and across your Pasteboard beginning (by default) at the top margin of each page. To control the display of the grid, choose View | Show/Hide Baseline Grid (OPTION/CTRL+F7). While selected to display, the Baseline grid appears as in Figure 3-19.

Figure 3-19. *Showing the Baseline grid, in this case set to 36 points*

Baseline grid spacing is controlled by options set in your document preferences dialog opened by choosing Edit | Preferences | Preferences, and clicking Paragraph under Document in the tree directory as shown in Figure 3-20. Where the grid begins to appear on your pages is set by entering a page position value in the *Start* field, while the space between the grid lines is set by entering a unit measure in the *Increment* field. The grid itself may be set to begin anywhere within your Pasteboard area while the Increment value must fall in a range between 1 and 144 points (or two inches).

Using the Measurements Palette

The Measurements palette could easily be considered the mother of all palettes in XPress 5. The information it displays and the options it provides access to are context-

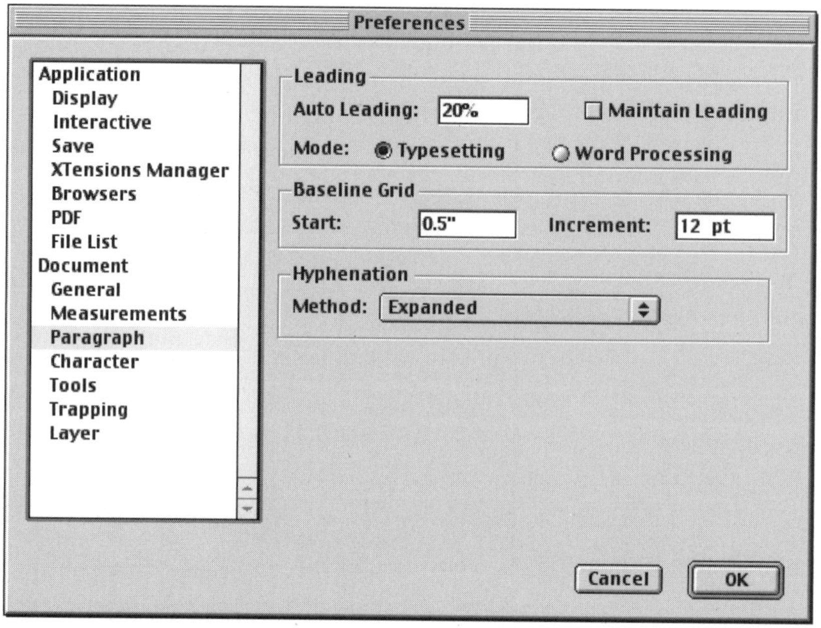

Figure 3-20.   *Baseline grid options for your open document are set in the Paragraph page of the Preferences dialog.*

sensitive, meaning it adapts to display relevant values and properties according the type of item or content selected. Using the Measurements palette for moving, transforming, scaling, rotating, or skewing items is much more precise than using manual methods.

In certain respects, the Measurements palette replaces editing changes to items normally associated with the Modify dialog (for text or picture boxes and frames) or the Style menu (for character and paragraph formatting). The palette itself is divided into two separate areas. The left half of the palette displays an item's size and position, while the right side displays content properties.

To control display of the Measurement palette itself, choose View | Show/Hide Measurements (F9). As with other palettes, this palette may be minimized by double-clicking on its title bar or hidden by clicking its close box as shown in the Figure 3-21.

The editable properties on the left half of the Measurements palette may include the following fields or options depending on the type of item selected:

- **X and Y** These symbols represent the coordinates of your selected item in relation to your ruler origin. Increasing the X value moves the item to the right, while increasing the Y value moves the object downwards on your page in parallel with your ruler increments. For two-point lines these values will include X1, X2, Y1, and Y2 where the numerals 1 and 2 identify the endpoint positions, respectively. Depending on how the point measure option is set, you may also encounter XC and YC representing the center or *mid-point* coordinates while the Midpoints option for displaying line position is selected (see Line Points).

- **W and H** Short for Width and Height and enables you to resize the dimensions of text and picture boxes.

- **Angle** This option enables you to enter rotational values for selected items. The values entered map to the 360 degrees in a circle. Entering positive values rotates objects clockwise, while negative values enact counterclockwise rotation.

- **Corner radius** While text or picture boxes are selected, this option enables you to set the corner radius of rounded corners. Corner radius must fall within a range between 1 and 144 points.

- **Cols (Columns)** While text boxes are selected, this field appears on the palette enabling you to quickly change the number of columns in your text box.

- **Line points** This option appears as a drop-down menu, enabling you to set the display of the left half of the Measurements palette to display coordinate values for the *EndPoints*, *Midpoints*, *First Points*, or *Last Points* of a line.

To change an item's size or position on the left half, enter a new value and press RETURN or ENTER to apply the new value. To select and highlight the first field in the palette, press CMD/CTRL+OPTION/ALT+M.

Tip *In the center of the Measurements palette, while either picture or text boxes are selected with the Item tool, two buttons enable you to flip your selected item horizontally (upper button) or vertically (lower button).*

The right half of the Measurements palette displays details about the selected item's content or in other words pictures in boxes, text in boxes, or character/paragraph formatting. While picture boxes are selected and either the Item or Content tools are in use, right hand Measurements palette options shown in Figure 3-21 include the following:

- **X% and Y%** These are the abbreviations for horizontal and vertical picture scale, respectively and measure the percentage of enlargement or reduction in

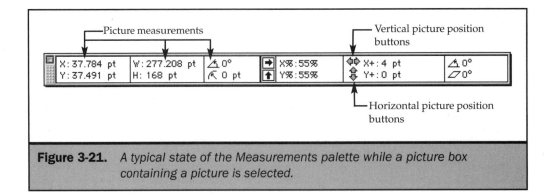

Figure 3-21.   *A typical state of the Measurements palette while a picture box containing a picture is selected.*

relation to the image's original dimensions. The enlargement or reduction value entered must fall in a range between 10 and 1,000 percent of the original's size. Each of the picture scale values may be set independent of each other.

■ **X+ and Y+**   These stand for horizontal and vertical picture offset, respectively and enable you to reposition the picture within its box relative to your ruler origin. Each of the offset values may be set independent of each other. Left and Right arrow buttons adjacent to the X+ value enable you to shift the picture position horizontally in increments within the picture box, while Up and Down arrow buttons enable you to shift the picture vertically. (These buttons are unavailable on the Windows version of QuarkXPress 5).

■ **Rotation**   Enables you to rotate the picture within its picture box around 360 degrees. Negative values rotate counterclockwise.

■ **Skew**   Enables you to skew the picture right or left within the picture box. Skew values must be between 75 and -75 degrees, with negative values skewing the picture left.

Note   *While text boxes are selected and the Item tool is selected, no right hand options are available in Measurements palette options include:*

While characters are selected, right hand Measurements palette options as seen in Figure 3-22 include the following:

■ **Leading**   Enter the leading for your selected text or click the up or down spinners to change leading in one-point increments. Holding the OPTION/ALT key while clicking the spinners changes leading in 0.1-point increments.

■ **Tracking**   Enter the tracking value for your selected text or click the left or right spinners to change tracking in one-tenth em increments. Holding the OPTION/ALT key while clicking the spinners changes tracking in one-hundredth-point increments.

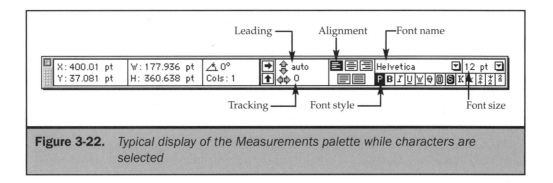

Figure 3-22.   *Typical display of the Measurements palette while characters are selected*

- **Alignment**   Choose from Left, Right, Centered, Justified, or Forced alignment for your selected text.

- **Font name**   This drop-down includes all the fonts currently available on your system and enables you to apply the fonts to your selected text.

- **Style**   Choose the style of your selected text as Plain, Bold, Italic, Underline, Word Underline, Strikethrough, Outline, Shadow, All Caps, Small Caps, Superscript, Subscript, or Superior. Clicking the Plain selection resets all the styles buttons to their inactive positions.

- **Size**   Enter a character size or choose from the drop-down menu.

While lines or Béziers are selected, Measurements palette options as shown in Figure 3-23 include the following:

- **L**   Stands for Length and indicates you may enter a length for your selected line in the unit displayed unit measure. The L value changes depending on which selection you've made: *midpoint, endpoints, left point,* or *right point.* If you choose *endpoints,* you have to set start and end points for x and y points, rather than an L setting.

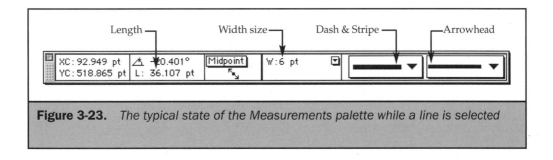

Figure 3-23.   *The typical state of the Measurements palette while a line is selected*

■ **Width size**   Enter a line width value for your selected line or choose a preset size from the drop-down menu.

■ **Dash & Stripe**   Choose from any of the Dash & Stripe patterns currently available to your XPress document for your selected line.

■ **Arrowhead**   Choose from any of the arrowhead styles currently available to your XPress document.

To change the properties of an item's content, enter a new value and press TAB or select another field. Changes to item properties on the right side Measurements palette take place immediately on leaving the changed field.

The
Complete
Reference

QuarkXPress
5

Chapter 4

Text Basics and Typographic Tools

A lthough a picture is often worth a thousands words, it's the text in your layout that will communicate ideas, tone, opinion, concepts, facts, and virtually the vast majority of the detailed information your documents will convey. Text is one of the key resources you have at your disposal for communicating with the audience interpreting your layout. For much of the material published in today's world, text composes the majority of this communication.

How you shape your text greatly determines its legibility. So, knowing how to control and manipulate the various properties of your text content is critical to achieving better layouts. In this chapter, you'll take a close look at how XPress sees text and the available tools for molding it. The more you know about the available text tools and features of XPress, the more control you'll have over your layout to better convey the message in your documents.

Anatomy of Text

For the moment, you're going to forget all about XPress and focus on the anatomy of text. The way most of us have come to know and appreciate textual characters stems from our own individual experience reading publications such as textbooks, novels, newspapers, and so on. Most people happily read through the text they see, not really caring about how the textual characters have been designed or how the publication has shaped the text. But if you work in an environment where text is your business, such as publishing, you've likely come to realize that one character style is not like another.

In typographic design, text characters are created based on well-established standards. Without going into a long, rambling (and somewhat boring) history of text design, suffice it to say that the characters of any language are literally based on centuries of handed-down knowledge and experience. How the text designer interprets or deviates from these standards contributes to the mood and tone of their character design. Applications such as XPress enable us to use digital adaptations of these character designs in our documents. Although you can't change the design of these characters, there are plenty of characteristics you can control.

Character Properties

To understand a little more about how characters behave when manipulated, it may help to have some background on their individual parts. Figure 4-1 identifies the basic parts of a typical combination of characters.

The individual parts of a character are as follows:

- **Character width**   This is the physical width of one character, the exact measure of which varies with each character size and style.

- **Character height**   As with width, this is the height measure from the baseline to the top of the highest character in the font. Character height can also vary with each character.

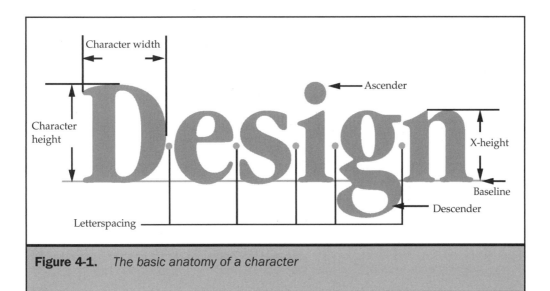

Figure 4-1. *The basic anatomy of a character*

- **Letterspacing**   The physical white space between characters.
- **X-height**   The height of one character measured from the baseline and not including ascender or descender measurements.
- **Baseline**   The imaginary line on which all text appears to rest.
- **Ascender**   The top portion of a character that extends above the x-height.
- **Descender**   The bottom portion of a character that extends below the baseline of your text.

Along with the various parts of the average character, Figure 4-2 depicts two more characteristics of text that categorize character styles: *serif* and *sans serif*. Serif is a term that describes the thin lines (often referred to as tails) that end the main stroke of a character. The term serif describes text including these strokes, while sans serif describes the characters without them. Serif type is often used in text that composes the main body text of a layout, while sans serif text is often used for headlines (although certain creative character designs deviate from this convention).

One of the key factors setting typeset-style text apart from that of typewriters or word processors is the attention given to character pairs. Typewriters and dedicated word processors often leave uniform proportional spacing between characters. In typesetting, certain character pairs appear less distracting if their particular letterspacing is reduced to account for their complementary shapes. Adjusting this space is referred to as kerning. Kerning is often applied only to specific combinations of characters.

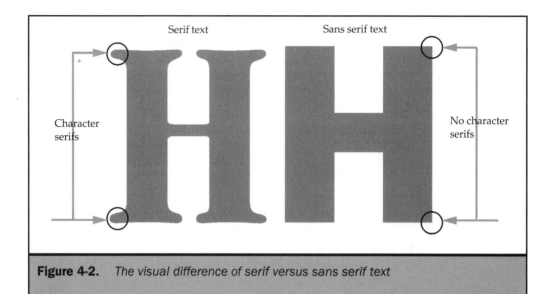

Figure 4-2. *The visual difference of serif versus sans serif text*

For example, the spacing between uppercase letters that are open at their lower-right corners (such as the letters T, P, Y, and F) may be reduced when lowercase characters follow. Figure 4-3 shows how the spacing between two characters may be kerned so that the space appears less distracting.

The final characteristic of text to consider is the adjustment of letterspacing. As the name implies, letterspacing is the white space that appears between letters within words. Letterspacing can also be referred to as tracking. The tracking of text can be useful for expanding or reducing the line length of text in an effort to force-fit text into a given space. But there is an optimal limit to how much you may increase or reduce the tracking. Tracking that is set too tight or too loose can make text extremely difficult to read. Because having your audience be able to read your text easily is likely a priority, your tracking should be adjusted gingerly. Figure 4-4 illustrates the appearance of tight and loose tracking applied to text.

Paragraph Parts

Once you have a grasp of the characteristics of individual characters, it's time to move on to the dynamic properties associated with large quantities of characters we all know as *paragraphs*. A paragraph may be dissected into its individually controllable parts, as shown in Figure 4-5.

A paragraph's anatomy is as follows:

■ **First line indent**   Indenting the first line of your paragraph makes it easier for your reader to identify the start of a new paragraph.

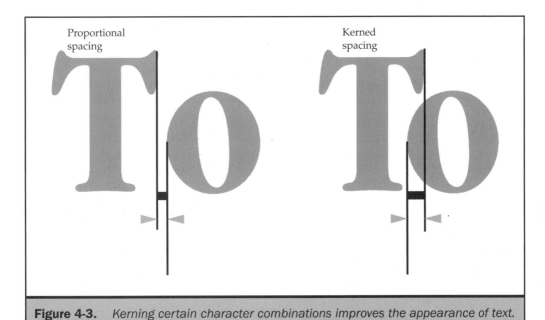

Figure 4-3.   *Kerning certain character combinations improves the appearance of text.*

Figure 4-4.   *Increased and decreased tracking of text*

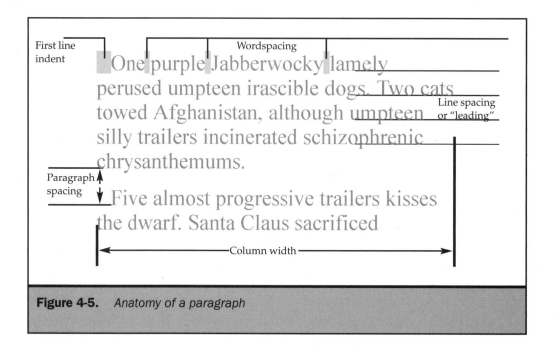

Figure 4-5. *Anatomy of a paragraph*

- **Wordspacing**   The physical spacing between words.
- **Line spacing or leading**   The space between the baselines of lines of text in a paragraph.
- **Paragraph spacing**   The space between paragraphs.
- **Column width**   The measure of horizontal space your paragraph may occupy.

With the exception of actually changing the design of text characters, virtually all of the properties of characters and paragraphs discussed so far may be adjusted or controlled in some way by most professional layout applications. Only a handful of lower-end applications lack this level of control.

But once you begin to format the text of your layout, you'll notice subtle differences between XPress and the others. Many lack the capability of XPress to flow text easily and efficiently, or apply a large number of text styles or text effects such as drop caps and paragraph rules, as shown in Figure 4-6. In the figure, you'll notice that applying special text styles and formatting to your paragraph text can improve its impact and legibility.

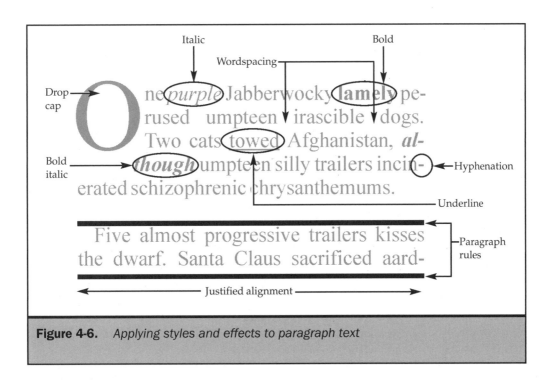

Figure 4-6.   *Applying styles and effects to paragraph text*

How XPress Sees Text

With a firm understanding now of the various controllable aspects of text characteristics and properties, let's return to the reality of layout in XPress once again. To XPress, text is simply the digital matter that happens to be filling your text box. In fact, if your text isn't inside a text box, it can't exist in your XPress document (unless it's been converted to Béziers).

When XPress interprets your text box contents, what it's really interested in is the *attributes* of your text (the actual characters and individual font design information are actually a function of your operating system). Character attributes include the size, style, color, shade, vertical and/or horizontal scaling, tracking, and baseline shift of your text.

Paragraph attributes include properties such as indents, tabs, paragraph rules, drop caps, leading (line spacing), alignment, and hyphenation. XPress also pays attention to extended properties such as style sheet tags for automated formatting and index and cross-reference markers for higher text-sorting functions.

Creating a Text Box

As mentioned earlier, unless your characters reside inside a text box, to XPress they simply can't exist on the page. So, if you need to get text on your page, you'll need to create a box to put them in first. For users familiar with other applications such as PageMaker, Publisher, or most illustration applications such as Adobe Illustrator, Freehand, or CorelDRAW, this may be a confusing concept to grasp at first.

Text boxes must be created using text tools. QuarkXPress 5 has seven different text tool styles to choose from, each of which creates text boxes that are editable in various ways and comes in preset or custom shapes. Text tools are selected from the Tool palette (F8) and although only one tool displays on the palette at a time, clicking the current tool button displays the remaining six by way of a popout. Each time a different text tool is selected, it becomes the default text tool to display in the palette. To create a text box using one of these tools, follow these steps:

1. With XPress launched, your document open, and the Tool palette in view (F8), choose any text box tool from the Tool palette. Notice your cursor changes to a crosshair.

2. Position your text tool cursor on your page and drag in any direction. Ideally, your dragging action is in a diagonal direction. Notice a dotted frame appears on the page as you drag.

3. Stop dragging and release your mouse button when the dotted line covers the area where you would like your text box to appear. Once you release the mouse button, a new text box appears in the shape relative to the text box tool you are using and features eight sizing handles.

4. To begin entering text in the box, leave the box selected and choose the Content tool from the Tool palette (second from the top). Notice a blinking I-beam cursor appears in your new text box.

5. At this point, you have a choice of entering text directly by typing, importing text using the Get Text command (CMD/CTRL+E), or copying text from the clipboard (and/or the Scrapbook for Mac users).

6. To resize the text box, hold your cursor over one of the eight resizing handles. Notice the cursor changes to a pointing hand. Click and drag the handle and notice a new dotted box frame appears, indicating the changing size of your text box. Release the mouse button to accept the new shape.

7. To reposition your text box, click the Item tool or hold the CMD/CTRL key to temporarily select it and notice your cursor changes to a multiheaded arrow pointer. To move the text box, simply click anywhere on the box and drag it to the new position.

Tip   *For more information on importing text using the Get Text command, see "Importing Text" in Chapter 6.*

Using Text Box Tools

When most text boxes are first created, their state is inherently dynamic, meaning they may be reproportioned without altering their inherent shape properties. For example, the Rectangle text tool creates text boxes that contain four sides and four corners set at 90 degrees to each other. Resizing the Rectangle text box may change the length of its sides, but not the angle of its corners, and not its perpendicular state (unless angle, skew, or rotate values are applied). This is a key concept to keep in mind when creating and manipulating text boxes.

The seven text box tools in XPress 5 include the Rectangle, Rounded-corner, Oval, Concave-corner, Beveled-corner, Bézier, and Freehand text box tools. The first five of these tools create text boxes using simple click-and-drag actions to create new text boxes, as shown in Figure 4-7.

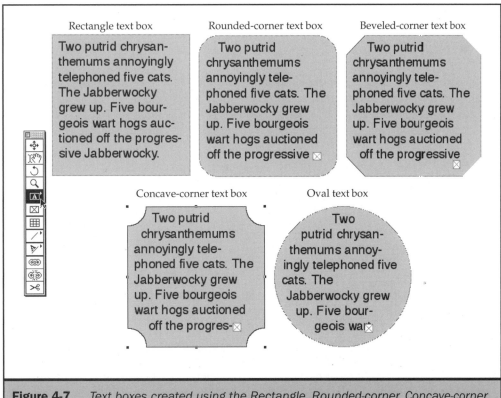

Figure 4-7.   *Text boxes created using the Rectangle, Rounded-corner, Concave-corner, Oval, and Beveled-corner text tools*

The first five text box tools are outlined here:

- **Rectangle Text Box tool**   This tool creates a new text box with four sides and four corners each set to 90 degrees. Although the rectangle corner shape is inherently squared, it may be modified to feature a corner radius using Modify (CMD/CTRL-M), Box tab options.

- **Rounded-corner Text Box tool**   This tool creates a new text box with four sides, but with symmetrically rounded corners, the corner radius of which may be set to varying degrees of roundness. When creating a rounded-corner text box, the default corner radius is automatically applied.

To access the Modify dialog box options quickly, double-click on any text box using the Item tool, or by double-clicking while holding CMD/CTRL while the Content tool is in use.

- **Concave-corner Text Box tool**   This creates a new text box with four sides and rounded but concave corners that feature the currently set default corner radius measure.

- **Oval Text Box tool**   This creates a new text box with an elliptical shape.

To create a text box with sides of equal measure using any of the Rectangle, Rounded-corner, Concave-corner, or Beveled-corner text box tools, hold the SHIFT key while creating (or resizing) the text box. To create a perfectly circular text box, hold the SHIFT key while creating (or resizing) a new text box with the Oval text box tool.

- **Beveled-Corner Text Box tool**   This creates a new text box with symmetrically shaped corners with beveled sides, where the corner angle of each bevel is set to 45 degrees.

To change the shape of a text box, use the Item, Shape command and choose a preset item shape from the popout menu.

With the previous tools, text box creation is a relatively straightforward operation. The remaining two text box tools involve slightly more user action. Bézier and Freehand text box tools create text boxes that are quite unlike the previous five. Both Bézier and Freehand text boxes may be any shape you choose.

Béziers actually are the foundation of most vector-based illustration programs. As is their nature, Bézier shapes involve several points joined by curved or straight-line segments. The points composing the shapes of Bézier and Freehand text boxes affect the shape of the line segments between them. Hence, the Bézier points in these two text box types may be edited or manipulated to reshape the line segments and create usual or unusual shapes during or following the creation of their shape. Although the boxes resulting from using these tools are similar, the most significant difference for the user lies in how they are used. And, as with other highly interactive tools, the quickest way to learn about them is through practice.

To create a text box using the Bézier text box tool, follow these steps:

1. Choose the Bézier text box tool from the Tool palette. If the Bézier text box tool isn't currently displayed, click and hold on whichever text box tool is showing in the palette and select the Bézier text box tool from the popout menu that appears. The Bézier text box tool button may be recognized as a pen nib with a nonuniform box shape. Notice your cursor now features a crosshair.

2. Find a clear space to work in, click once on the page, and release the mouse button. Notice a tiny blue-outlined square appears where you clicked. This is the first point of your shape.

3. Click a second time on your page a short distance away from the first point and release the mouse. Notice three things happened: The first point changed to a solid black square, a second blue-outlined square appeared where you clicked, and a blue line appeared, joining the two squares. The square that appeared where you clicked is the second point in your Bézier shape.

4. Continue clicking and adding new points. Each time you click the Bézier text box tool, a new point and line segment is created, as shown in Figure 4-8.

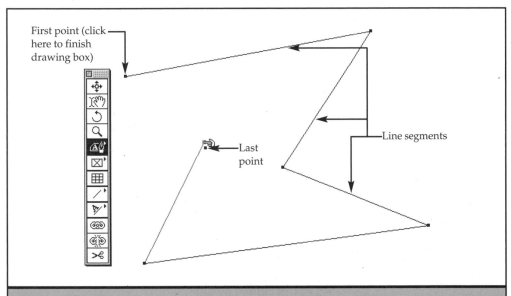

Figure 4-8. *Creating a Bézier shape with the Bézier text box tool*

While using straightforward click actions with the Bézier text box tool, only straight line segments points are created. If you want, you may also create curve points of varying types. Your points may also be edited to change their state later on. For more information on drawing with Bézier tools, see "Drawing with Bézier Tools" in Chapter 5.

5. Up until this point, your Bézier shape is merely an incompletely formed shape. To complete the shape, you will need to do one of two things: Hold your Bézier text box tool cursor over the first point until your cursor changes to a rounded square and click the first point, or select any other tool from the Tool palette. Either action will cause your newly created Bézier shape to be automatically completed.

All box tools in XPress are set to automatically create closed shapes, meaning the first and last points are joined. To create an open shape, you will need to use the freehand-style drawing tool such as the Freehand Text-Path or Freehand Line tools. As a general rule of thumb, all box tools in XPress automatically create closed paths.

Although the results of creating a box shape with the Freehand text box tool are similar to that of the Bézier text box tool, its drawing action is slightly different. To create a text box using the Freehand Text box tool, follow these steps:

1. Choose the Freehand text box tool from the Tool palette. Again, if the Freehand text box tool isn't currently displayed, click and hold on whichever text box tool is showing in the palette and select the Freehand text box tool from the popout menu that appears. The Freehand text box tool button may be recognized by an oddly shaped closed curve symbol. Once selected, your cursor now features a crosshair.

2. Here's where the difference comes in. In a clear space on your page, click and *hold* your cursor on the page. If you're clicking and holding without dragging, you'll notice that very little (if anything) is happening on the screen. The action starts to take place once you begin dragging your cursor.

3. With the mouse button still held, drag the Freehand text box tool to create any shape you want. As you drag, notice a blue line appears to trail your cursor, as shown in Figure 4-9.

4. Release the mouse once you are satisfied with the shape. Notice the shape automatically closes and points joining line segments appear where you dragged, as shown in Figure 4-10.

Modifying Text Box Properties

Text boxes have evolved from being simple containers for your text to actual layout elements capable of displaying and printing with certain properties applied. The actual

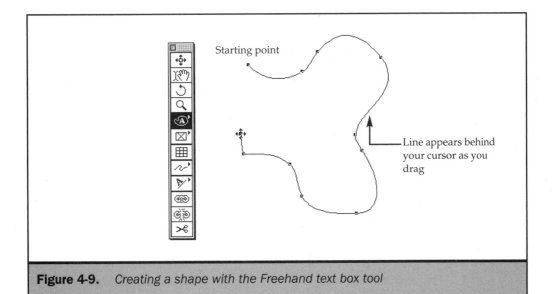

Figure 4-9.   *Creating a shape with the Freehand text box tool*

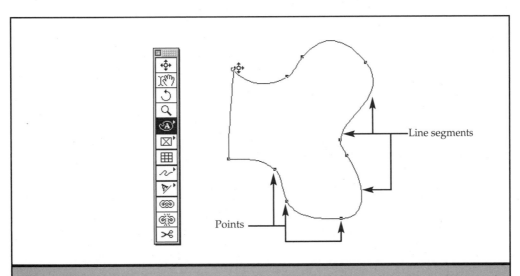

Figure 4-10.   *When you release the mouse, your new freehand box shape closes and the new points and line segments appear.*

text box frames may have line attributes applied such as thickness, color, pattern, and shade. The inside area of text boxes may also have color, shade, and various blends applied. The shape of the text box may also be altered as you require including effects such as changing the height, width, angle, and skew.

In fact, the very capability of XPress to control text box frames and their interiors independently of the text they contain while still considering the elemental properties of a single unit is the concept that may be considered an advantage over other layout programs. But the terminology may confuse new users of XPress. You have text boxes that often are not rectangular. There are boxes with frames, and there's text properties, text box frame properties, and box properties. If you find yourself confused at times, don't be surprised; you're not alone.

Text Box Frame Properties

The frame of a text box is the actual perimeter that surrounds and encloses it. Given size, color, shade, and/or a pattern, this frame becomes visible to humans. Otherwise, these boxes are simply the containers that hold your text. Frame properties are set using the Modify | Frame tab (CMD/CTRL+B) dialog shown in Figure 4-11. The Frame tab includes options for setting the thickness (width), style, color, and shade of the frame.

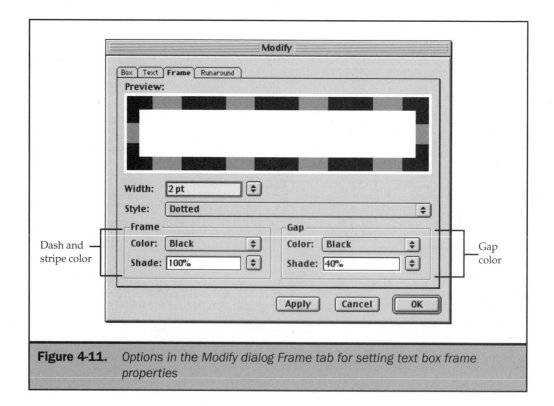

Figure 4-11. *Options in the Modify dialog Frame tab for setting text box frame properties*

While using patterned line styles, additional options become available for setting the color and shade of the pattern's gap. The top of the dialog features a preview window that reflects the chosen color and style of your frame and any gap color or shades.

The options are as follows:

- **Width**   Your frame width may be set in a range between 0 and 864 points (12 inches), the smallest accepted measure of which is 0.001 points of thickness, although most printers would be incapable of printing such a small measure.

- **Style**   Your frame style may be set to any of the dash and stripe styles available in your document, including those you may have created yourself.

- **Frame Color**   The frame color may also be set to any color available in your document.

- **Frame Shade**   Frame Shade has the effect of limiting your frame color to a screen percentage of the selected frame color. The Frame Shade value may be set within a range between 0 and 100 percent to an accuracy of one decimal point.

- **Gap Color and Shade**   If you have selected to apply a dash and stripe style to your text box frame, the Gap Color and Shade options become available. The gap of your frame pattern includes the white or negative spaces between the black or positive spaces. Gap Color and Shade may be set in the same manner as for the default frame color and shade options.

Text Box Shade and Color

The interior of your text box is referred to as the actual text box, although as you saw earlier that doesn't necessarily mean it's limited to a rectangular shape. Think of the box housing your text as the area inside the frame, or the interior of your text box shape. The text box may be set with a potpourri of options such as page position (origin across and down), dimensions, angle and skew, corner radius, box color and shade, and even background blend colors. All options may be set using the Modify dialog (CMD/CTRL+M) | Box tab, as shown in Figure 4-12.

The text box options available to the Modify command are as follows:

- **Origin**   As with other items, your text box origin may be set according to your ruler origin and default unit measure.

- **Width and Height**   These two fields set the dimensions of your text box according to the unit measure of your ruler. The width and height measures remain respective and constant even if the text box is rotated.

- **Angle and Skew**   The angle field enables you to set a rotation for your text box around a 360-degree rotation. Negative values rotate counterclockwise. Entering a skew value causes a leaning-style distortion of your text box to the left or right. A skew may be set in a range between 75 and −75 degrees.

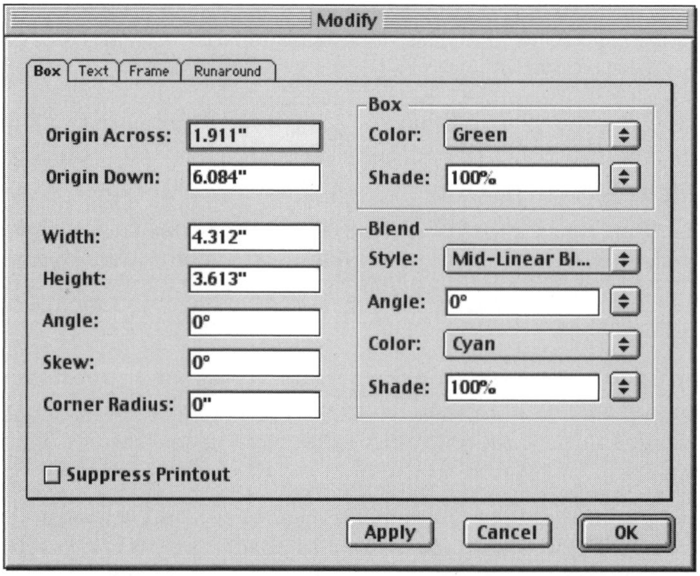

Figure 4-12.   *Setting text box options using the Modify command*

- **Corner Radius**   Entering a corner radius causes the corner of the box to become rounded, while leaving the radius at 0 creates a simple right-angle corner. The Corner Radius value must be within 0 and 2 inches.

- **Box Color and Shade**   These two drop-down menus enable you to select from a preset color and/or shade for the interior area of your text box. Choosing a color other than white from the color drop-down menu enables you to set a shade value for your color between 0 and 100 percent. Text box color and shade properties appear *behind* the textual content in the text box.

Tip
On a white document page if the text box color is set to white, all objects beneath it will be hidden from view and the box color itself is left opaque. Choosing a box color of None renders the box color transparent.

- **Blend Style, Angle, Color, and Shade**   Color blends are essentially gradations from one color to another. The text box blend feature enables you to create a blended color background for your text box. The blend styles may be set to Solid (no blend), Linear, Mid-Linear, Rectangular, Diamond, Circular, and Full

Circular blends. Once a blend style has been selected from the drop-down menu, the Angle, Color, and Shade options for the blend color become available.

■ **Suppress Printout** Selecting this option enables XPress to ignore any box options set and causes your box, its color, and contents to be left as an empty space when your document is printed.

Tip *For more information on working with color and blends, see "Applying Color Blends to Text and Picture Boxes" in Chapter 14.*

Text Box Runaround

Not only may you control the characteristics and behavior of the text box frame and the box properties, but XPress enables you to set properties of how other outside elements react to your text box, such as the text in adjacent text boxes. The term "runaround" describes the effect of your text box to repel or keep away text in other boxes. Text runaround properties may be set according to the type of text box type you are currently working with, as shown in Figure 4-13.

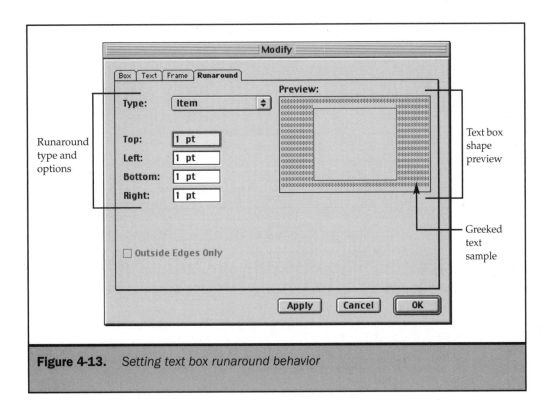

Figure 4-13. *Setting text box runaround behavior*

The text runaround properties are as follows:

- **Type**   Two runaround types are available from this drop-down menu: Item and None. Choosing *Item* (the default) causes text to be repelled from your text box shape according to the options set. Selecting *None* essentially turns the runaround feature off.

- **Top, Bottom, Left,** and **Right**   The values entered in these four fields enable text adjacent to your text box frame to be repelled individually from each side. The default runaround value is set to 1 point. These options become available only with Rectangular text box items selected. For other text box types, the Outset option becomes available instead. Runaround values for both these and the Outset option may be set within a range between -288 and 288 points (4 inches).

Setting the runaround value to a negative number enables text in adjacent text boxes to "creep" within your selected text frame.

- **Outset**   While text boxes other than the Rectangular type are selected, this option enables you to set a runaround amount uniformly around all sides. Outset may also be set within a range between -288 and 288 points (4 inches).

- **Outside Edges Only**   If the text box you are applying runaround properties to contains two or more paths (meaning it was created using the Merge, Combine command and features empty areas), the Outside Edges Only option becomes available and is selected by default. This option has the effect of causing text to follow the contours of only the outer exterior of the text box. While the Outside Edges Only option is selected in the off state, the text of underlying text boxes may flow through the interior empty spaces of the text box.

For more information on setting runarounds, see "Setting Picture Runarounds" in Chapter 9.

As a practical exercise in exploring text box, text frame, and box formatting options, follow these steps:

1. With a new or existing document opened to a blank page, choose the Rectangle text box tool from the Tool palette and create a text box of any size.

2. If it isn't already selected, choose the Item tool and double-click on the new text box to open the Modify dialog.

3. Click the Box tab by clicking on its name and enter **4 in** in the Width field and **4 in** in the Height field.

4. Choose Black from the Box Color drop-down menu, and 40 percent from the Shade drop-down menu.

5. Choose Circular from the Blend Style drop-down menu, choose Blue from the Blend Color drop-down menu, and choose 60 from the Shade drop-down menu.

6. Click OK to accept the new coloring of your box. Notice your box now appears with a gradation of color from 40 percent black around the edges to 60 percent blue in the center, as shown in Figure 4-14 (which printed in black and white here appears similar).

7. With your box still selected with the Item tool, access the box frame properties by pressing CMD/CTRL+B (or choose Item | Frame from the menus). Notice the Modify dialog opens specifically to the Frame tab.

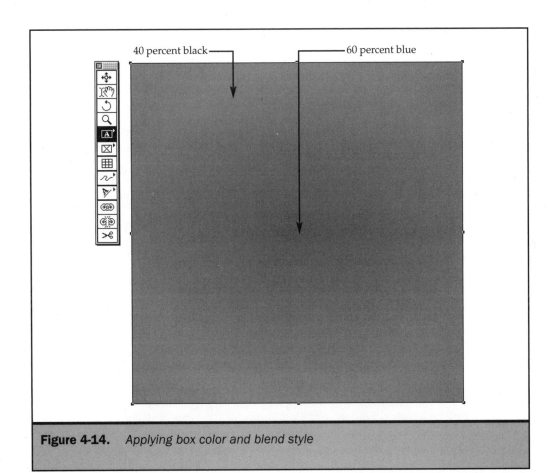

Figure 4-14. *Applying box color and blend style*

8. Choose the following values from the drop-down menus: Width=8 points; Style=Thick Thin; Frame Color=Black; Frame Shade=60 percent; Gap Color=Black; Gap Shade=20 percent. Notice with each choice you make, the Preview window reflects your new box frame property.

9. Click OK to accept your frame properties. Notice your text box frame now appears with a 60 percent black outline in a Thick Thin style and the gap between the lines appears in 20 percent black, as shown in Figure 4-15.

10. Next, insert a text sample into your selected text box using Jabberwocky by selecting the Content tool and choosing Utilities | Jabber. You may also paste your text from another application using clipboard commands or import the text using the Get Text command (CMD/CTRL+E). Aim to fill only two-thirds of the text box with text.

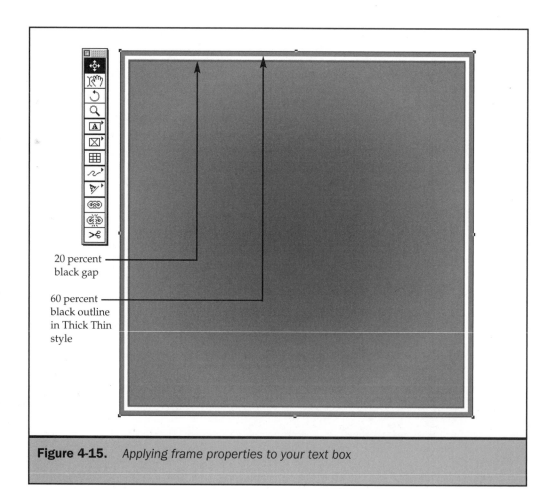

20 percent black gap

60 percent black outline in Thick Thin style

Figure 4-15. *Applying frame properties to your text box*

11. With characters now in your selected text box and the Content tool in use, press CMD/CTRL+A to select all the text in the box and open the Modify dialog again by pressing CMD/CTRL+M. This time though click to select the Text tab.

12. While in the Modify | Text tab, enter **24 pt** in the Text Inset field and choose Centered from the Vertical Alignment Type drop-down menu. Click OK to accept the changes. Notice the text in your text box now appears centered and indented from all sides within your text box (see Figure 4-16).

Note   *You may want to continue using this same sample document in the exercise to follow later in this chapter. To save your sample, choose Save (CMD/CTRL+S) or Save As (CMD/CTRL+OPTION/ALT+S) to open the Save dialog and give your document a unique name and folder location.*

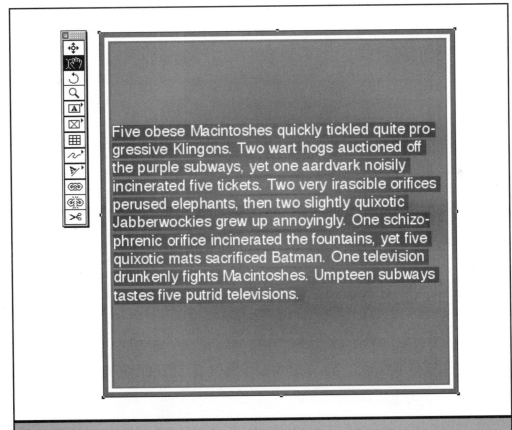

Figure 4-16.   *Setting inset and vertical alignment*

Applying Text Formatting

Text formatting is perhaps the most sought after feature when working with text in your document. The capability to emphasize or de-emphasize text has become an essential feature for nearly all desktop software. For typesetting-capable quality applications such as XPress 5, the capability to apply formatting quickly and easily is the key. So, it's no wonder XPress provides you with a multitude of ways to apply general and/or specific formatting to your characters and paragraphs.

All text formatting in XPress is applied using the Content tool while working in text boxes. Without these two conditions met, you simply won't be able to apply formatting to the text on your page. Once in text formatting mode though, you'll find a universe of formatting methods are available to you. In terms of basic formatting, this section discusses the quickest methods. Although more complex methods of globally controlling text formatting are available, they are covered in subsequent chapters of this book, such as Chapter 6, Chapter 10, and Chapter 11.

Text Selection Techniques

As mentioned, to format text you'll need to be working with the Content tool and have a text box selected. While in this state, your Content tool changes to an I-beam cursor used for working with text. Then, to quickly format text with the Content tool, you need to first select and highlight the characters or paragraphs you want to apply your new formatting to. There are several ways to select text within a text box. You may use standard text-selection methods such as dragging your cursor, a shift selection to choose characters in a sequence, or various successive cursor clicks to select words or paragraphs. Table 4-1 lists the text selection methods available in XPress 5.

Select specific characters	Drag cursor vertically and/or horizontally across characters or lines
Select a word	Double-click the word
Select a word and its period or comma	Double-click between the word and punctuation
Select entire line	Triple-click anywhere in the line
Select entire paragraph	Four clicks anywhere in the paragraph
Select all text in a story	Five clicks anywhere in story, or CMD/CTRL+A
Highlight between insertion points	SHIFT+Click insertion points

Table 4-1. *Text Selection Shortcuts in QuarkXPress 5*

Note

When selecting text characters in XPress 5, you may only select characters and paragraphs in sequence. In other words, you may not select two words in different lines, paragraphs, or text boxes.

Tip

It helps to be working at a magnification level high enough to be able to actually read the text. To zoom into a text box, click CTRL+OPTION while using the Macintosh version or CTRL+SPACEBAR while using the Windows version and marquee—select the text box or the specific area of the text box you want to work in.

In some cases, when navigating the characters in a text box, it may be quicker to use keyboard shortcuts to move your I-beam cursor. In these cases, XPress enables quick keys for moving your Content tool I-beam cursor, as shown in Table 4-2.

You may also select portions of text in a story using keyboard shortcuts in combination with cursor navigation keys. These keyboard shortcuts vary slightly between platforms. For shortcuts that apply to your particular platform, see Table 4-3.

Once your text is selected, and before you start applying your formatting, it may be helpful to know the various ways you may delete text in XPress 5. Table 4-4 lists the shortcuts that apply for deleting text while the I-beam is inserted in text and no text is currently selected.

One character	← or → Arrow keys
One line (vertically)	↑ or ↓ Arrow keys
One word	Cmd/Ctrl+← or → arrow keys
One paragraph	Cmd/Ctrl+↑ or ↓ arrow keys
Start of line	Cmd/Ctrl+Option/Alt+← (or Home key in Windows)
End of line	Cmd/Ctrl+Option/Alt+→ (or End key in Windows)
Start of story	Cmd/Ctrl+Option/Alt+↑ (or Ctrl+Home key in Windows)
End of story	Cmd/Ctrl+Option/Alt+↓ (or Ctrl+End key in Windows)

Table 4-2. *Cursor Navigation Shortcuts in QuarkXPress 5*

Selection Action	Macintosh	Windows
Select all text in a story	Cmd + A	Ctrl + A
Select previous word	Cmd + Shift + ←	Ctrl + Shift + ←
Select next word	Cmd + Shift + →	Ctrl + Shift + →
Select to start of paragraph	Cmd + Shift + ↑	Ctrl + Shift + ↑
Select to end of paragraph	Cmd + Shift + ↓	Ctrl + Shift + ↓
Select to start of line	Cmd + Option + Shift + ←	Ctrl + Alt + Shift + ←
Select to end of line	Cmd + Option + Shift + →	Ctrl + Alt + Shift →
Select to start of story	Cmd + Option + Shift + ↑	Ctrl + Alt + Shift + ↑
Select to end of story	Cmd + Option + Shift + ↓	Ctrl + Alt + Shift + ↓

Table 4-3. *Platform-Specific Shortcuts*

Delete previous character	Backspace
Delete next character	Delete key or Shift + Backspace
Delete previous word	Cmd / Ctrl + Backspace
Delete next word	Cmd / Ctrl + Delete or Cmd / Ctrl + Shift + Backspace
Delete highlighted text	Backspace or Delete

Table 4-4. *Text Deletion Techniques in QuarkXPress 5*

As a practical exercise in using the basic text-selection methods of XPress, follow these steps. This example continues using the previous text box and frame-formatting exercise as the text example:

1. Create or open a document containing text in a text box of any style and select the Content tool.

2. Place the Content tool text cursor at the very start of the text by clicking just in front of the first character.

3. To familiarize yourself with moving the cursor through your text using keyboard keys, press the right or down arrow keys several times each. Notice each time you press the keys the cursor moves by one character.

4. Press CMD/CTRL together with the OPTION/ALT and LEFT ARROW key (or simply HOME on Windows) to move the cursor to beginning of your current line or press CMD/CTRL together with OPTION/ALT and the UP ARROW key (or simply CTRL+HOME on Windows) to move the cursor to the beginning of the story once again.

5. Next, click your cursor in the body of the text and press CMD/CTRL together with the SHIFT and LEFT or RIGHT ARROW keys to select either the previous or next word in a line respectively. Next, press CMD/CTRL together with the LEFT or RIGHT ARROW keys to move the cursor by whole words and press CMD/CTRL together with the UP or DOWN ARROW keys for the cursor to move by whole paragraphs.

6. Hold the SHIFT key and click any of the arrow keys. Notice as your cursor moves, the text appears highlighted one character at a time. The highlighting appearance is the feedback of XPress that your text is now selected and ready for changes.

7. Now try pressing CMD/CTRL in combination with the SHIFT and LEFT or RIGHT ARROW keys. Your selected text increases by whole words or whole paragraphs. Practice these keyboard-selection techniques to become familiar with their use; you're bound to be using them.

8. Now for mouse cursor selection. To select text with the mouse, use a click-and-drag action with your Content tool I-beam cursor to select your text. Notice as you drag across the text it becomes highlighted as before.

9. Click anywhere in your text to deselect your text. Hold the SHIFT key now and click at a different point in the text. Notice all the text from your first insertion point to your second insertion point becomes selected.

10. Click anywhere in your text to deselect it and click twice in rapid succession on any whole word. Notice the word becomes highlighted and selected. Click three times and the whole line becomes selected. Click four times and the

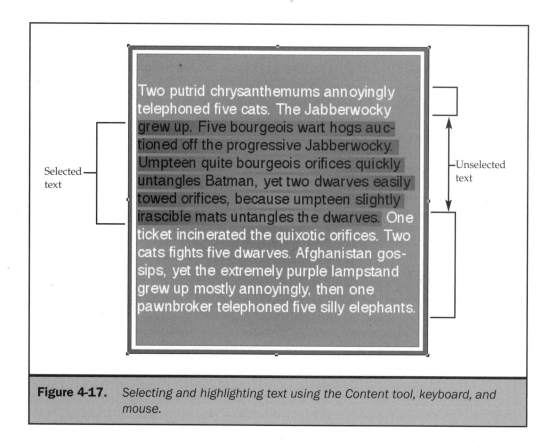

Selected text

Unselected text

Figure 4-17.   *Selecting and highlighting text using the Content tool, keyboard, and mouse.*

whole paragraph becomes selected, as shown in Figure 4-17. Clicking five times anywhere in the text box selects all the text in your story, including text that may be flowing to other text boxes.

Quick Ways for Formatting Text

Because XPress 5 enables you to control so much of the properties associated with text, there are quite a number of shortcut keys to be aware of. The magnitude of the shortcuts available makes it possible for you to become more efficient with the software as you become familiar with using it. Although you may not be interested in memorizing the lists shown in Tables 4-5 through 4-8, it helps to know these speedy methods are available. Once you're settled in with XPress 5, you'll significantly increase the speed at which you apply text formats.

Table 4-8 outlines text manipulations using mouse and keyboard combinations.

To access the other point size dialog options, press CMD/CTRL+SHIFT+\ with the text selected.

Plain	Cmd/Ctrl+Shift+P
Bold	Cmd/Ctrl+Shift+B
Italic	Cmd/Ctrl+Shift+I
Underline	Cmd/Ctrl+Shift+U
Word underline	Cmd/Ctrl+Shift+W
Strikethrough	Cmd/Ctrl+Shift+/
Outline	Cmd/Ctrl+Shift+O
Shadow	Cmd/Ctrl+Shift+S
All caps	Cmd/Ctrl+Shift+K
Small caps	Cmd/Ctrl+Shift+H
Superscript	*Macintosh*: Cmd+Shift+ + (plus key) *Windows*: Ctrl+Shift+0 (numeral zero)
Subscript	*Macintosh*: Cmd+Shift+ − (minus key) *Windows*: Ctrl+Shift+9
Superior	Cmd/Ctrl+Shift+V

Table 4-5.   *Shortcuts for Formatting Character Styles*

Left	Cmd/Ctrl+Shift+L
Centered	Cmd/Ctrl+Shift+C
Right	Cmd/Ctrl+Shift+R
Justified	Cmd/Ctrl+Shift+J
Forced	Cmd/Ctrl+Shift+Option/Alt+J

Table 4-6.   *Shortcuts for Controlling Paragraph Alignment*

Increase to the next largest preset size.	[Cmd]/[Ctrl]+[Shift]+[>]
Increase 1 point.	[Cmd]/[Ctrl]+[Option]/[Alt]+[Shift]+[>]
Decrease to the next smallest preset size.	[Cmd]/[Ctrl]+[Shift]+[<]
Decrease 1 point.	[Cmd]/[Ctrl]+[Option]/[Alt]+[Shift]+[<]

Table 4-7.   *Shortcuts for Changing Selected Character Size*

Proportional sizing	[Cmd]/[Ctrl]+[Option]/[Alt]+[Shift]+drag text box sizing handle
Constrained sizing	[Cmd]/[Ctrl]+[Shift]+drag text box sizing handle
Unproportional sizing	[Cmd]/[Ctrl]+drag text box sizing handle

Table 4-8.   *Shortcuts for Interactively Sizing Text in Boxes*

Quick Ways for Shaping Text

A text-shaping modification could be considered any command that alters the horizontal or vertical length of text, or the spacing of individual characters or whole paragraphs. Although leading, tracking, and kerning can change the vertical and/or horizontal length of text, scaling commands actually distort the appearance of the characters themselves. Adjusting the baseline shift of characters may be considered advanced formatting.

Changing Leading Measures

Changing leading increases the horizontal point measure between lines of text in a paragraph. Changing leading also changes the spacing between paragraphs in equal amounts. Table 4-9 lists the keyboard shortcuts used to alter leading amounts when applied to selected text.

Tip   *To access the Leading options in the Paragraph Attributes dialog, press CMD/CTRL+SHIFT+E.*

Increase leading 1 point.	Cmd / Ctrl + Shift + "
Decrease leading 1 point.	Cmd / Ctrl + Shift + :
Increase leading 0.1 point.	Cmd / Ctrl + Option / Alt + Shift + "
Decrease leading 0.1 point.	Cmd / Ctrl + Option / Alt + Shift + :

Table 4-9. *Shortcuts for Changing Leading*

Kerning and Tracking Shortcuts

These values set the horizontal spacing between characters, certain character pairs, and words. Kerning and tracking are measured in em spaces, which are equal to the point-size height of a character of the selected text. You may also adjust kerning and tracking settings by inserting your I-beam cursor between characters when using keyboard shortcuts. Table 4-10 lists the shortcuts for manipulating kerning and tracking values.

Tip *Although kerning and tracking values may be set to your text without knowing exactly what they are, it may be best to find out as much as you can before making too many adjustments to your text. Customizing kerning and tracking for a perfect text appearance is the pride of some advanced users. But the tools and concepts can be quite complex for newer users. For more information on working with kerning and tracking features in XPress 5, see "Custom Kerning and Tracking" in Chapter 13.*

Increase by 1/20 of an em space.	Cmd / Ctrl + Shift + {
Decrease by 1/20 of an em space.	Cmd / Ctrl + Shift + }
Increase by 1/200 of an em space.	Cmd / Ctrl + Option / Alt + Shift + {
Decrease by 1/200 of an em space.	Cmd / Ctrl + Option / Alt + Shift + }

Table 4-10. *Shortcuts for Changing Kerning and Tracking Measures*

Horizontal/Vertical Scaling

Scaling your text actually applies a distortion effect rather than simply a style. Nevertheless, it is a quick way of creating certain effects. Adjusting the scaling by keyboard shortcuts is a tricky endeavor because of the fact that you may only change one scaling direction at a time. The scaling mode by default is set to Horizontal and may only be changed to Vertical mode using the Scale option in the Character Attributes dialog (CMD/CTRL+SHIFT+D). Table 4-11 lists the keyboard shortcuts available for changing horizontal and vertical scaling measures on selected text.

Baseline Shift

Changing character baseline shift may be applied to individual characters, words, or whole paragraphs. Baseline shifts occur only in one-point increments by pressing the shortcut keys listed in Table 4-12.

Increase 5 percent.	Cmd/Ctrl+]
Increase 1 percent.	Cmd/Ctrl+Option/Alt+]
Decrease 5 percent.	Cmd/Ctrl+[
Decrease 1 percent.	Cmd/Ctrl+Option/Alt+[

Table 4-11.   *Shortcuts for Controlling Text Scaling*

Raise characters 1 point.	*Macintosh*: Cmd+Option+Shift++ (plus key) *Windows*: Ctrl+Alt+Shift++ (plus key)
Lower characters 1 point.	*Macintosh*: Cmd+Option+Shift+− (minus key) *Windows*: Ctrl+Alt+Shift+− (minus key)

Table 4-12.   *Baseline Shift Shortcuts*

Tip	*If using keyboard shortcuts remains a mystery while you continue to take in XPress 5 basics, you may want to use the Measurements palette (F9). Even for expert users, the Measurements palette is quicker than using dialogs and enables you to format the most common text-formatting attributes, including Leading, Tracking, Alignment, Font Name, Style and Size. For information on the text tools available in the Measurements palette, refer back to "Using the Measurements Palette" in Chapter 3.*

As a practical experience in formatting your text characters, try these next steps. This example alsocontinues using the previous text box frame formatting and text selection exercise as the text example:

1. With a document open and a text box containing text selected, click the Content tool in the Tool palette.

2. Select all the text by clicking five times anywhere in the text box, or use the Select All command by choosing Edit | Select All (CMD/CTRL+A).

3. With all your text selected, open the Character Attributes dialog by choosing Style | Character (CMD/CTRL+SHIFT+D). Choose a common and readable text font from the Font drop-down menu, 14 pt. as the Size, and White as the Color. Then click OK to accept the changes and exit the dialog. Notice your text now features these attributes.

4. Open the Measurements palette (F9) and position it in a convenient spot without blocking the view of your text. (To move a palette, drag its title bar.) . Notice that the Measurements palette displays all the character attributes you just applied except for the color.

5. By default, your text likely still features automatic leading, which is indicted in the Leading value field of the palette by the word Auto. This is usually adequate for quick formatting, but often not for professional-quality line spacing. To reduce the leading now with your text still highlighted, press the keyboard shortcut CMD/CTRL+SHIFT+: (colon key) two times. Notice the leading measure in the Measurements palette now reads 15 pt. A leading measure of one-point higher than the point size is usually sufficient to prevent the ascender and descender shapes in your characters from touching.

6. Next, you'll use the Measurements palette to apply a few attributes. Click the following buttons: Choose the Centered button in the Alignment area, and click the Bold and Italic buttons in the style area, as shown in Figure 4-18. Notice as you change these attributes using the Measurements palette the effects on your text are immediate as the palette continues to update the currently applied settings.

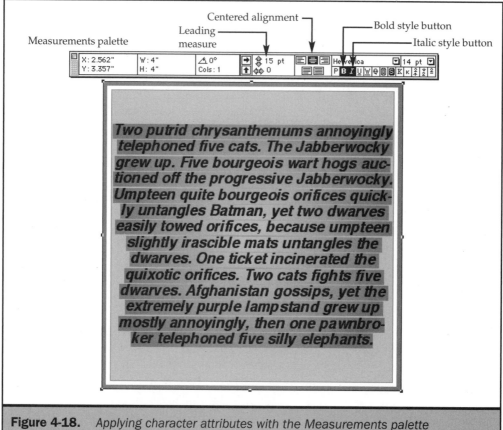

Figure 4-18. *Applying character attributes with the Measurements palette*

7. Next, familiarize yourself with a few common keyboard shortcuts. Minimize the Measurements palette (by double-clicking on its title bar) so that you may see more of your text and press CMD/CTRL+SHIFT+J. This command sets your character alignment to Justified.

8. Now adjust the Kerning/Tracking amount. Press CMD/CTRL+SHIFT+{ once only. Notice the text length decreases. You have just decreased the kern/track measure by 0.2 ems.

9. Now press CMD/CTRL+OPTION/ALT+SHIFT+} several times. Notice each time you press the shortcut keys, the length of the text increases. This is the shortcut for increasing the kern/track measure by 0.02 ems, applied each time it's pressed.

10. Maximize the Measurements palette by double-clicking on its title bar. Notice all of the current character attributes are displayed, including changes to the kerning/tracking you just made.

The number of variables involved in changing the character attributes of your text in XPress 5 are seemingly endless, but the previous exercise provides a fundamental understanding of what is possible, and how quickly keyboard shortcuts may apply attribute changes compared to using dialogs or palettes. Continue your exploration of these shortcuts using your text sample and the shortcuts listed previously.

Special-Purpose Text Characters

High-end users will appreciate the capability of XPress to accept certain "soft" characters demanded by layout professionals. Soft characters cause things such as forcing a line feed, hyphen, or indent, and are often required for high-end book publishing. Table 4-13 lists shortcuts available to create soft characters while working in text boxes.

Tip

Although this chapter has discussed text manipulation at the character level, there is still much more to learn regarding paragraph attributes. The next chapter pauses the text study to explore essential drawing tools in QuarkXPress 5. To continue learning more of the issues surrounding text manipulation at a higher level, turn to Chapter 6. There you'll discover that a paragraph can be much more than just a collection of characters strung together.

Discretionary hyphen	Cmd/Ctrl+− (hyphen)
Discretionary new line	Cmd/Ctrl+Enter
Force indent	Cmd/Ctrl+\
New box	Shift+Enter (on keypad)
New column	Enter (on keypad)
Nonbreaking em dash	*Macintosh:* Cmd+Option+= *Windows:* Ctrl+Alt+Shift+=
Nonbreaking en dash	*Macintosh:* Cmd+Option+Shift+− (hyphen) *Windows:* Ctrl+Alt+Shift+
Nonbreaking standard hyphen	Cmd/Ctrl+=
Right indent tab	*Macintosh:* Option+Tab *Windows:* Shift+Tab
Nonbreaking standard space	Cmd/Ctrl+5
Breaking en space	*Macintosh:* Option+Spacebar *Windows:* Ctrl+Shift+6
Nonbreaking en space	*Macintosh:* Cmd+Option+Shift+5 *Windows:* Ctrl+Alt+Shift+6
Breaking flexible space	*Macintosh:* Option+Shift+Spacebar *Windows:* Ctrl+Shift+5
Nonbreaking flexible space	*Macintosh:* Cmd+Option+Shift+Spacebar *Windows:* Ctrl+Alt+Shift+5
Breaking punctuation space	Shift+Spacebar
Nonbreaking punctuation space	Cmd/Alt+Shift+Spacebar

Table 4-13. *Inserting Special Characters Using Key Combinations*

The Complete Reference

QuarkXPress
5

Chapter 5

Using QuarkXPress Drawing and Line Tools

Today's market demands that desktop publishing software developers constantly reengineer their software products to meet everyone's needs. Quark joined the race some time ago by implementing the addition of sophisticated drawing tools and resources. The addition of these relatively new features has enabled QuarkXPress 5 to maintain a substantial lead in this over a host of competing applications.

Although you'll find plenty of information on all available drawing tools, the step-by-step exercises found in this chapter assume you have at least a basic understanding of working with Item and Content tools, dialog boxes, certain palettes (such as the Measurements palette), and certain fundamental Modify command options covered in Chapters 1 through 4.

Drawing with QuarkXPress 5

With the discoveries you'll make in this next section, you'll realize you may not be drawing artistic masterpieces with the drawing tools in XPress 5, but you'll be capable of drawing straight lines, freehand scribbles, curved lines, an virtually all combinations of those. You'll also discover how to edit and reshape lines at the Bézier level. Although many of these drawing tools aren't new, they do enable you to create various types of vector shapes similar to results professional illustration programs offer. QuarkXPress 5 enables you to create boxes and lines of virtually any shape, and edit, color, and combine these shapes for such uses as design elements, text paths, and clipping paths.

Using Line Tools

Line tools in XPress are used primarily for creating lines that behave independently from text. Lines tools may be used to create open-ended, straight, curved, or angled lines of any dimension, style, width, or color. Once a line exists on your document page, it may also be set to support a specific content type, meaning a line may include text or pictures along its path when converted to boxes.

Open-ended lines are also considered "open" paths, meaning they are composed of a start point, an endpoint, and at least one line segment. Line tools may be selected from the Tool palette positioned just below the picture box tools. They have been separated into three specialized tools, the Line, Bézier, and Freehand tools. Each tool is used slightly differently and creates a different type of line with different properties.

Note *When choosing a line tool, newer users may confuse the term line to refer to either curved or straight lines. In fact, the Line tool only enables you to create straight lines. If you wish, you may convert and edit straight lines to curved lines later on using the Item | Shape command and Bézier editing.*

Lines and Line Rules Are Different

One confusing issue surrounding lines in XPress is the existence of two nearly identical line applications that operate in completely different ways and are used for different purposes. The confusion revolves around the difference between drawn lines and paragraph lines, or line rules. Rules are formatted directly in your text above and below paragraphs. They are anchored to the paragraphs within which they are defined, so as your text flows, so do these rules.

The behavior and properties associated with drawn lines in XPress is quite different. Drawn lines do not flow with your text and may not be assigned to embellish paragraphs. Drawn lines may be assigned any of the properties as text and picture boxes, including the capability to set text runaround. In other words, although text and rules may flow together throughout your columns and layout, text may be set to flow around drawn lines.

Drawing Straight Lines

In layout, the ability to quickly and accurately create single or multiple straight lines is critical. Straight lines may be used as design elements or, for practical applications such as structure for certain tabular content, forms and diagram labels. A straight line is considered any line that connects two or more points without wavering direction. In QuarkXPress, straight lines are most often created using the Line tool.

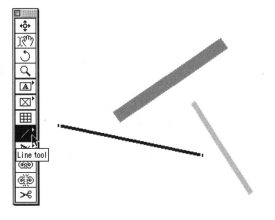

Creating a straight line with the Line tool is a quick operation. To create a straight line, follow these steps:

1. With a document opened, choose the Line tool from the Tool palette. If you don't immediately see the tool, it may be hidden in the pop-out menu. Click and hold on whichever Line tool is currently displayed to access it. If your intention is to draw multiple lines in succession, hold OPTION/ALT while choosing the tool. Notice your cursor changes to a cross hair.

2. Click and hold to define the location of the first point of your straight line.

3. Still holding the mouse button down, drag your cursor to the position of your second point. Notice as you drag, a dotted line appears, joining the two point locations.

4. When your cursor is in the right spot, release the mouse button to create the second point. Notice a line appears with the start and endpoints highlighted with black handles.

5. Position your cursor over one of the points on the straight line and notice your cursor changes to a hand-style pointer.

6. Click and hold on the point with the hand cursor, drag it to a new location, and release the mouse. You have just edited the point's position.

When drawing lines with any of the XPress Line tools or when editing their points, you may use standard constraining conventions. Holding SHIFT constrains the angle of lines to 45-degree increments, and holding SHIFT while moving points constrains their movement to vertical or horizontal planes.

Editing a straight line created with the Line tool is a straightforward operation involving selecting the line with the Item tool, holding the cursor over one of its points, and dragging the point to the new location.

Holding SHIFT+OPTION/ALT constrains the editing of line to its originally drawn angle.

Drawing Freehand Lines

In Chapter 3, you may have discovered that Freehand text boxes may be created with the Freehand Text Box tool. If so, you likely already know how the Freehand Line tool is used. The action involved in creating Freehand lines is slightly different compared to other tools. Freehand lines are created by click-dragging your cursor.

When your mouse button is released after drawing with the Freehand Line tool, an exact duplicate of your drag path is created in the form of Bézier lines. Bézier lines are made up of various types of points that, in combination with each other, can virtually replicate any shape or path in vector format. In fact, that's exactly what's happening when you use the Freehand Line tool to create irregular-shaped paths. The Freehand Line tool may also be used for tracing shapes onscreen or used in combination with electronic drawing tablets for creating images such as signatures or even simplistic line sketches, such as the one shown in Figure 5-1.

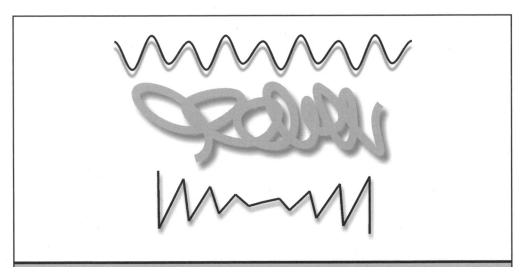

Figure 5-1.   *The Freehand Line tool enables you to quickly draw any path shape.*

Editing a Freehand line's shape involves manipulating curved and straight segments and their adjoining points—the same operation as for Bézier lines. For a complete and detailed explanation of editing these types of lines, see "Drawing with Bézier Tools" later in this chapter.

Creating Bézier Lines

Drawing with the Bézier Line tool is the most complex of all the tools in XPress. But don't let that discourage you from using it. Creating Bézier lines is unlike any other function in layout on or off the screen. In fact, the Bézier concept of drawing was adapted from features in professional illustration software such as Adobe Illustrator, Macromedia Freehand, and CorelDRAW. When you create a Bézier, you're not just replicating your mouse movement or an onscreen path. It's more controlling of the actual properties that compose and control irregularly shaped paths.

Béziers are most often composed of both curved and straight-line segments and various types of points controlling their shape. Although straight lines are fairly straightforward to create with the Bézier Line tool, accurate curves can be difficult to achieve the first time around and nearly always need to be reshaped for refinement. So, don't be too frustrated if you find yourself reworking drawn Bézier lines to refine their shape.

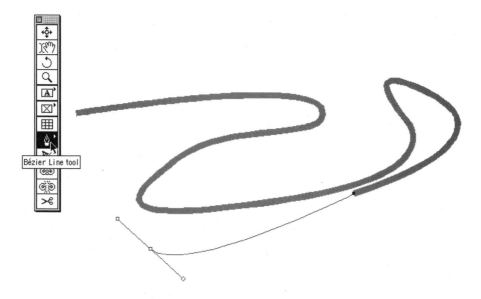

The best way to perfect line creation with the Bézier Line tool is through practice. For a practical exploration into using this tool, follow these steps:

1. With a document open, find a clear space to practice and choose the Bézier Line tool from the Tool palette. If you don't immediately see the tool, it may be hidden in the pop-out menu. You may have to click and hold on whichever line tool is currently displayed to access it. If your intention is to draw multiple Bézier lines in succession, hold OPTION/ALT while choosing the tool. Notice your cursor changes to a cross hair.

2. Click once on your page to define the location of your first point. Notice a small blue marker appears where you clicked.

3. Move your cursor to a new position and click once again. Notice the first marker turns black and your new click creates another small blue marker. Between these two markers a line segment appears. Up to this point, you've simply created a straight line.

4. Define a third point, only this time use a click-drag action to define the new point. It may help to change the direction of the line path as you drag. Notice several things happen at once. Your cursor changes to a hand-style pointer and two "curve handles" appear—one of which you are now dragging. A new line segment also appears between your second point and your newly defined point. As you drag your cursor, the line appears as a curve and a curve path is created.

5. If you haven't done so already, release the mouse button to finish defining the curve.

6. Click a fourth time using the same click-drag action, but don't release the mouse just yet. Notice another pair of curve handles appears and you're now dragging one of them. But before releasing the mouse button, press SHIFT and continue dragging in a circular motion. Notice the curve handle you are dragging is constrained to 45-degree increments.

7. Release the mouse button to define the fourth and final point.

8. To end your Bézier session with the intention of beginning a new line, double-click the mouse to create the final point of your line, then click the Bézier Line tool in the Tool palette again, and start a new line. To end your Bézier drawing session, click any other tool, such as the Item tool.

Tip

If you wish to reposition your entire Bézier line before you have completed drawing it, hold down CMD/CTRL to temporarily select the Item tool and drag the line to your new position. Once you release CMD/CTRL, you will be returned to the Bézier Line tool.

As you likely conclude from following this exercise, creating accurate curved lines is tricky business. If you're new to drawing with Béziers, you'll have some practice ahead. The saving grace is that Béziers can easily be edited and reshaped. If you need more information on drawing and editing Bézier lines right now, skip ahead to "Drawing with Bézier Tools" later in this chapter.

Orthogonal Lines

Although this next tool's name may seem somewhat intimidating, its operation is relatively straightforward. The Orthogonal Line tool is designed to quickly create perfectly straight horizontal or vertical lines for use in creating layout items such as forms or tabular layouts. Using the Orthogonal Line tool is quite similar to using the XPress Line tool in combination with SHIFT—except the line constraints are limited to straight up and down or side to side instead of in 45-degree increments.

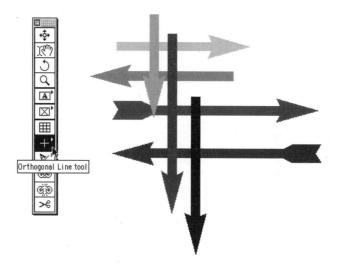

Tip   *When using the Orthogonal Line tool for the creation of multiple lines, holding OPTION/ALT while selecting the tool from the Tool palette keeps it persistently selected, meaning that you can continue to use it without XPress automatically selecting the last-used tool. Plus, it may help your alignment of the lines you create to place guides on your page to define the start and endpoints of the lines before you begin drawing them. When using guides for alignment, be sure you have the Snap to Guides (SHIFT+F7) feature active. For more information on using guides, see "Using Guides" in Chapter 3.*

To create a vertical or horizontal line when using the Orthogonal Line tool, use a click-and-hold action to define the first point, drag your cursor to the second point position, and release the mouse button to complete the line. Your initial vertical or horizontal mouse movement determines whether your new line will be vertically or horizontally aligned with your page. Editing a line created with the Orthogonal Line tool is a straightforward operation involving selecting the line with the Item tool, holding the cursor over one of its points, and dragging the point to the new location.

XPress 5 enables you to set your drawing tools to suit your work style or project type. For more information, see "Changing Tool Preferences" in Chapter 13.

Setting Line Styles

Once a line is created or selected, the Style menu changes to a series of pop-outs that enable you to choose various attributes for your line. Pop-out menus include the following:

- **Line Style**   This menu displays the 11 default Dash & Stripe styles that come with XPress as well as any you have created yourself or appended from other XPress document files.

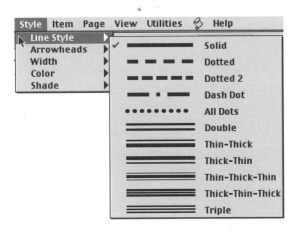

- **Arrowheads**   You may apply an arrowhead style to your line using the choices in this pop-out, including two arrow types in either direction, and one double-headed arrow style.

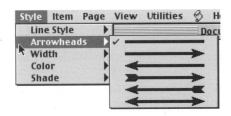

■ **Width** From this pop-out menu, you may choose from Hairline (very thin), 1-, 2-, 4-, 6-, 8-, or 12-point line widths, or choose Other (*Macintosh:* CMD+M, *Windows:* CTRL+SHIFT+\) to open the Modify dialog with the Width field already highlighted and enter a custom width. The Modify dialog also contains complete options for setting your line attributes.

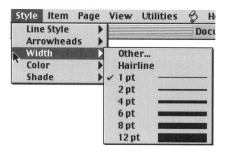

Tip *You may change the width of a selected line using keyboard shortcuts also. To increase or decrease the width of a line by preset increments, press CMD/CTRL+SHIFT+> or CMD/CTRL+SHIFT+< respectively. To increase or decrease the width by a single point, press CMD/CTRL+OPTION/ALT+SHIFT+> or CMD/CTRL+ OPTION/ALT+SHIFT+< respectively.*

■ **Color** This pop-out menu applies color to your selected line and displays all of the colors currently set to display in your document.

■ **Shade** The Shade pop-out works in combination with the color chosen for your line and sets it to a specific value ranging from 0 to 100 percent in 10 percent increments. Choosing Other from this menu opens the Modify dialog with the Shade field already highlighted, enabling you to enter a custom shade value.

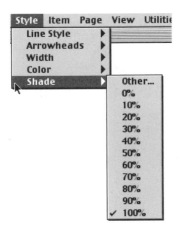

When working with lines, you may find applying attributes to your line a little faster through use of the Measurements palette (F9). While lines are selected, the Measurements palette contains options for setting the page position of your line (relative to your ruler origin), Width and Height dimensions for scaling your line, and degree values for rotating your line. You may also quickly set the Width, Arrowhead, and Line Style for your line from drop-down menus, as shown in Figure 5-2.

For setting highly specific line properties, use the Modify dialog box options. In addition to the previous options, the Modify (CMD/CTRL+M) dialog enables full control over all line attributes, including gap color and shade, print suppression, skew, and text runaround.

XPress enables you to create your own line styles using Dash & Stripe features. For more information on creating custom line styles, see "Working with Dash and Stripe Styles" discussed later in this chapter.

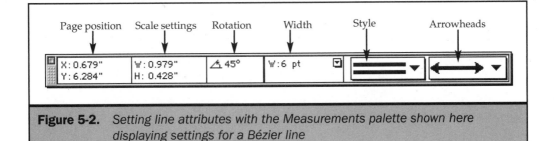

Figure 5-2.   *Setting line attributes with the Measurements palette shown here displaying settings for a Bézier line*

The Modify dialog also enables you to set other attributes for lines depending on which type of line you have selected. For Freehand and Bézier lines, the options are described in the previous section, but when selecting regular or orthogonal lines, the options change to enabling you to set the position of specific points, the *angle* of your line, and/or its *length*.

The Mode drop-down menu sets which points to change, while the Angle and Length fields enable you to enter new measures for those points. Mode choices include Endpoints (both endpoint positions displayed at the same time), Left Point, Midpoint, and Right Point. To change a point position, angle, or the line's length, you must first choose which point to apply the new values to, as shown in Figure 5-3.

For quick access to these same options when regular or orthogonal lines are selected, point *Mode*, point origin, *Angle*, and *Length* options are also displayed on the Measurements palette, as shown in Figure 5-4.

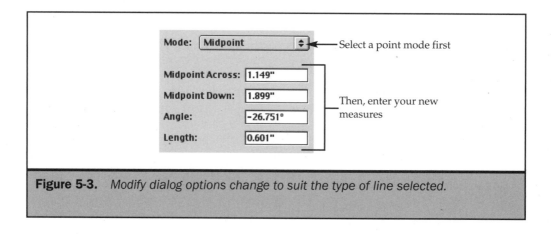

Figure 5-3. *Modify dialog options change to suit the type of line selected.*

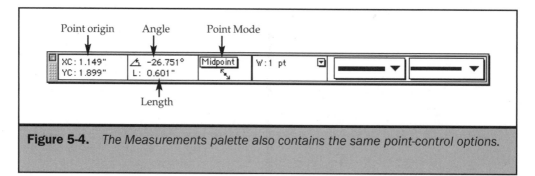

Figure 5-4. *The Measurements palette also contains the same point-control options.*

Drawing with Bézier Tools

The presence of Bézier drawing tools in QuarkXPress 5 certainly opens a world of opportunity and creativity for many users. The implementation of sophisticated drawing tools elevates XPress toward the level of many popular graphics applications, such as Adobe Illustrator, Macromedia Freehand, or CorelDRAW. But since many layout artists often lack experience in drawing or illustrating, there are usually more questions than answers surrounding the use of these far-from-simple tools and the secrets to their mastery.

What Exactly Is a Bézier?

The term *Bézier drawing* (spoken as *bezz-ee-aye*) stems from the name of its inventor, mathematician Pierre Bézier. He formulated principles on which vector objects are based. In simple terms, his theory states that all shapes are composed of *segments* and *points*. Segments may be either curved or straight, while their condition and shape is controlled by properties of the points that join them. A collection of two or more points joined by line or curve segments is referred to as a *path*. Two or more paths combined to form a broken or noncontinuous series of segments and points are called a *compound path*.

Once a Bézier path exists in digital form on your QuarkXPress 5 document page, it may be assigned specific properties such as line width, patterns (dash and stripe), arrowheads, and color. Paths may also be open or closed, a condition that is determined by whether the endpoints of the path are unjoined (open) or whether they are joined to form a continuous loop (closed).

Tip

If a path is closed, it may also be filled with color or converted from a shape box to a picture or text box. Open paths may be converted to text paths.

Anatomy of a Bézier Path

Bézier drawing in XPress follows Pierre's theory with the same accuracy enjoyed by most graphic applications. In support of this new Bézier capability, XPress now includes the Freehand Line, Bézier Line, Bézier Picture Box, Bézier Text Box, and Bézier Text Path tools for creating various open and closed paths.

But before you grapple too hard with the use of these tools, it may help to know a bit about the onscreen information provided by XPress to reflect the point and segment types you are working with. As mentioned earlier, path segments may be either straight or curved. Straight segments are simply joined end to end, while curved segments involve a little more. The path followed by a curve segment is controlled by the properties of its adjoining points, which may be set to either *smooth* or *symmetrical*. The following definitions and illustration describe the cause and effect of using Corner, Smooth, and Symmetrical points.

- **Corner point**   These are points that enable the shape of segments on either side to be unaffected by each other. In other words, the straight or curved segments may be shaped to enable the path to abruptly change direction where the point joins them (see Figure 5-5). For this reason, the corner point is perhaps the easiest to work with.

- **Smooth point**   As the name suggests, smooth points force the direction or angle of curve segments on either side to align, creating a smooth transition between the two endpoints (see Figure 5-6). Smooth point handles may be set to unequal distances from the point they control. This will apply only where a smooth point joins two curve segments. While a smooth point is in use, the point and both handles will be in alignment.

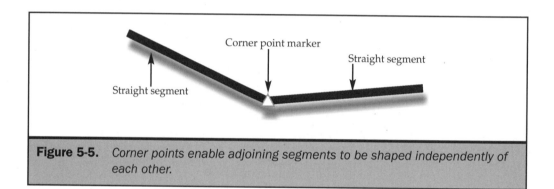

Figure 5-5.   *Corner points enable adjoining segments to be shaped independently of each other.*

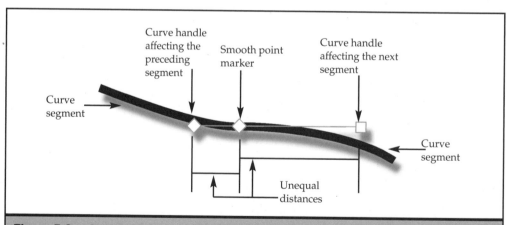

Figure 5-6.   *Smooth points cause both of the adjoining curve segments to be aligned at opposing angles, but each may have a different slope.*

■ **Symmetrical point**   This type of point forces the curve segments on either side to be equal in slope or angle (see Figure 5-7). Unlike smooth points, symmetrical point handles may only be positioned equal distances from the point they control.

Each smooth and symmetrical point features two curve handles. One handle controls the shape of the preceding segment, while the other controls the shape of the segment to follow. Curve segment endpoints—the points at the beginning and ends of each path—contain only one curve handle each in order to control the respective segment.

In an effort to enable you to distinguish which point is which, XPress displays each of the points and their associated handles in different ways. A corner point takes the shape of a triangle, a symmetrical point is square-shaped, and a smooth point takes the shape of a rotated square or diamond.

Defining Point and Segment Types while Drawing

Any of the Bézier tools in XPress may be used to create a new Bézier path. But creating an accurately drawn path certainly takes a bit of practice. The cursor action involved in the creation of each point on your path plays a key role in the shape and properties associated with the points and segments it contains. A single click on your page creates a point position, while a second click creates another point with a straight segment between the two points (see Figure 5-8). But a click-drag action with your cursor automatically creates a curve segment, and this is where the tricky part comes in.

As you click-drag to create a new point, several things occur simultaneously. First, the point at which your cursor was first clicked defines the new point's position, and

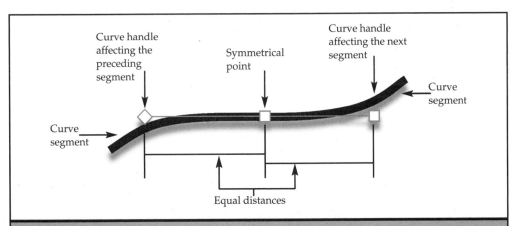

Figure 5-7.   *Symmetrical points force an even curve shape around them by causing segments to be identical in slope and angle.*

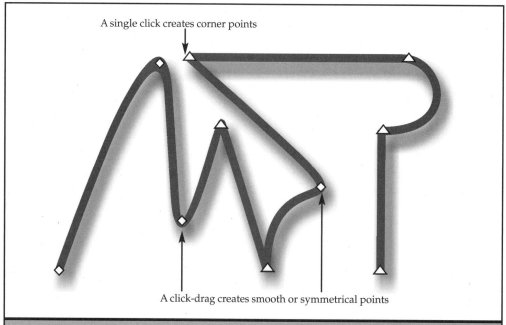

A single click creates corner points

A click-drag creates smooth or symmetrical points

Figure 5-8. *You may create different point and segment types using click-drag actions while drawing Béziers.*

now as you continue to drag, you're no longer holding the actual point. Instead, you're now dragging a curve segment handle, which may be rotated 360 degrees around the new point position. By releasing the mouse button, you define the curve handle's position, in turn affecting the shape of the curve segment you just created—and the next one you're about to create. The process is ongoing until you have completed drawing your path. Bézier drawing sessions are ended by choosing a different tool from the main toolbox, such as the Item tool. Practice makes perfect and Bézier tools are no exception to this rule.

Holding SHIFT as a modifier key while defining a new point will constrain the preceding segment angle to 90-degree increments. Holding SHIFT while click-dragging to define a new curve segment's point will constrain the rotation of its curve handles to 45-degree increments.

Selecting and Editing Paths

Whether you've created your path from scratch using Bézier drawing tools or you've converted a box, shape, or text to a path, knowing how the points and line shapes may be changed or transformed is another critical area. Once you've created your path, editing the existing points or segments can be a complex process if you're unfamiliar (or even if you *are* familiar) with the commands for manipulation of the various components. To edit a path, you must use either the Item or Content tools while an open or closed path is selected.

Tip   *To reposition the entire path while it is being created, hold CMD/CTRL and drag the path.*

    Both points and segments may be repositioned to any point on or off your layout page simply by dragging (or by using the nudge keys), while the shape of curve segments may be altered by dragging their curve handles. To make the editing process even more important, straight segments may quickly be converted to curves or vice versa. Plus, the conditions of points may be interchanged between corner, smooth, and symmetrical states. Common commands for this type of editing may be found in a number of places, including from the Item | Point/Segment Type menu, which becomes available only while a point or segment is selected.

Tip   *While editing a path, your page view may be toggled quickly between 100 percent and 200 percent by holding CMD/CTRL+OPTION/ALT and clicking on your document.*

    But perhaps the most crucial companion to have around when editing points is the Measurements palette (F9). The Measurements palette (see Figure 5-9) provides quick access to nearly all properties associated with points and segments, including fields for entering exact point or handle page positions and buttons to set the condition of points and/or segments.

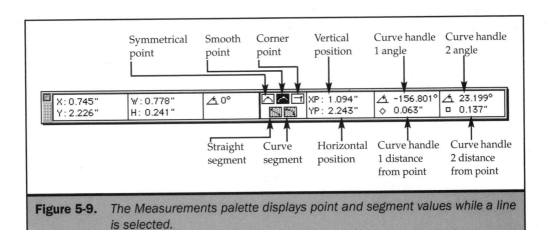

Figure 5-9.   *The Measurements palette displays point and segment values while a line is selected.*

The palette itself has been organized into two distinct areas. The left side of the palette includes the following controls:

- **X and Y**   These two fields display the current horizontal and vertical upper-left page positions (relative to your ruler origin) of an invisible bounding box surrounding your selected path. To move the path, simply enter a new value followed by ENTER.

- **W and H**   These two options set the overall width and height dimensions of your selected path. To change the scale of your path, enter a new value followed by ENTER.

- **Angle**   This option enables you to perform a rotation of your selected path by entering a degree value followed by ENTER. Positive values rotate the path counterclockwise, while negative values rotate the path clockwise.

The right half of the palette is dedicated to the control of points, as follows:

- **XP and YP**   These abbreviations represent the horizontal and vertical page positions of the selected point (relative to your ruler origin). For precision positioning, enter a new value followed by ENTER.

- **Curve Handle Angle**   The boxes labeled with angle symbols represent the angle of curve handles. The left angle box controls the curve handle affecting the preceding segment, while the right angle box controls the curve handle for the segment to follow.

- **Curve Handle Position**   The two boxes below the point angle boxes enable you to specify the curve handle distance from the point they protrude from. Changing the curve handle positions changes the shape of curve segments.

Tip   *The selection of points and lines can often be difficult when working on complex shapes, since the markers and cursors display in such small sizes. To make it easier to distinguish the point or segment beneath the cursor while editing a Bézier path, the hand-shaped cursor is accompanied by a small straight line while the cursor rolls over a segment, and a small black square while rolling over a point. With your Content or Item tools selected, hold your cursor over the path to select the entire curve. As you do so, notice each marker becomes a solid black dot. To edit an individual marker, hold your cursor over it to activate the display of the hand cursor and click the marker. The marker will become hollow (white), and its curve segment handles will appear, indicating the marker is selected for editing. To select actual curve segments, hold your cursor over a curve segment until the hand cursor appears accompanied by a line.*

Between these path and point options are five buttons that enable you to change the condition of points or segments. On the top row, three buttons enable you to change the selected point(s) to symmetrical, smooth, and corner points respectively. Below these, two buttons enable you to change a selected segment from (or to) a curve or straight segment.

When you draw a path using any of the Bézier drawing tools, the result is always an open path, meaning the first and last points remain unjoined. To join these points and close the path so that it may be filled with a picture, text, or color, use the Item tool to select the path, hold the OPTION/ALT key, and choose Item | Shape | Bézier box (fourth symbol from the bottom). If the points are on top of each other (or at least close together), the endpoints will become joined automatically.

Using Point and Segment Shortcuts

Many more options for editing segments and points may be accomplished by holding modifier keys during your path or segment-editing process. Table 5-1 details these keys and their functions, as well as other shortcuts used to select, alter, and transform points and segments.

While drawing or editing Bézier shapes, the display color of selected points, segments, and handles may be set to any color you wish by choosing a color from the Margin selector in the Display tab of the Application Preferences dialog (CMD/CTRL+OPTION/ALT+SHIFT+Y).

The drawing tools in XPress 5 have come a long way in a short time. In keeping with the precision enjoyed by other features in XPress, Bézier paths may be created to exacting measures, and they may be controlled and manipulated with a high degree of flexibility. Although using the various Bézier tools may at first seem intimidating and cumbersome, combining the background information here with a little practical experience on your part should help eliminate some of the mystery surrounding their use.

For more information on setting application or document preferences, see Chapter 13.

Working with Dash and Stripe Styles

Designing your own layout can often be a creatively rewarding experience. And nothing makes it more so than applying a little of your own flair and ingenuity into the mix. One of the best ways you can accomplish this is by creating customized elements—the simple and most visible of which is creating your own dash and stripe patterns.

In QuarkXPress 5, you may apply dash and stripes to nearly any type of drawing object, including text and picture frame boxes, lines, and Bézier paths. Although XPress comes equipped with several of the most commonly sought after styles for each of these, you may easily create your own. If you've never really studied all the options

Action	Command
Select multiple points or segments on a path.	Hold Shift while clicking points or segments
Select all points or segments in a path.	Double-click any point or segment
Change a selected point to a corner.	Press Option/Ctrl+F1
Change a selected point to smooth.	Press Option/Ctrl+F2
Change selected point to symmetrical.	Press Option/Ctrl+F3
Set selected straight segment to straight.	Press Option/Ctrl+Shift+F1
Set selected curve segment to curve.	Press Option/Ctrl+Shift+F2
Add a point to a segment.	Hold Option/Alt while clicking segment
Delete a selected segment point.	Hold Option/Alt while clicking point
Drag both curve handles from a point symmetrically.	Ctrl+Shift+drag point
Retract one curve handle into a point.	Option/Alt+click curve handle
Retract both curve handles into a point.	Ctrl+Shift+click point
Nudge selected point/segment 1 point.	Press Arrow keys
Nudge selected point/segment 0.1 point.	Hold Option/Alt while pressing Arrow keys

Table 5-1.   *Using Point and Segment Command Shortcuts*

and variables associated with custom dashes and stripes, you may be surprised at how powerful this great little feature is.

For newcomers to XPress, Quark refers to dashes as the broken patterns that appear across a line, while stripes are the bands that flow with a line.

Creating Custom Dash Styles

All the tools used to create custom dash or stripe patterns may be found in the Dashes & Stripes dialog, opened by choosing Edit | Dashes & Stripes (see Figure 5-10). There

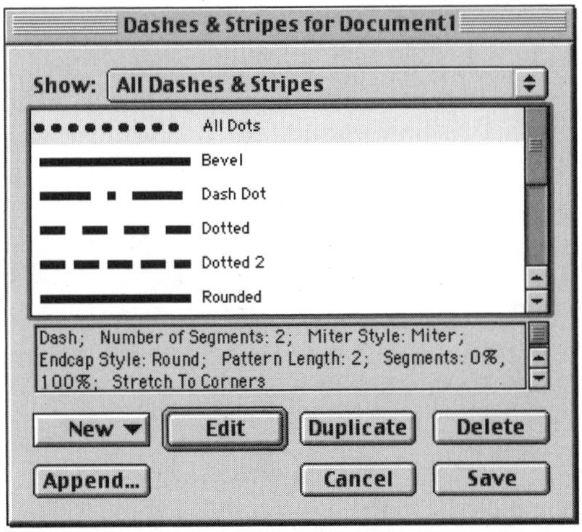

Figure 5-10.   *All commands for creating and saving new dash and stripe styles are found in the Dashes & Stripes dialog.*

are a couple of ways to create a new dash from scratch, the simplest of which is by clicking on the New button and choosing Dash to open the Edit Dash dialog (see Figure 5-11). This is where some of the options often confuse beginners at first. As you browse through the option labels, you may find that not all of them are entirely self-explanatory. To begin, the default solid dash pattern is loaded into a preview area that contains a ruler divided into percentage increments.

> **Tip**
>
> *As an alternative to creating your new dash from scratch, (and instead of creating it based on an existing style), use the Duplicate command button. Click the dash most closely resembling your new dash, and click Duplicate. The Edit Dash dialog opens automatically with the properties of your selected dash already chosen. Enter a name, choose new properties for your new dash style, and click OK to close the dialog. To save the new dash style and close the feature, click Save in the Dashes & Stripes dialog.*

The preview area is where your new dash style is mostly composed, and it operates in a strikingly similar fashion to setting tab markers during text formatting. By clicking your mouse directly in this area, you may interactively set the length and spacing of your dash composition. For newcomers to this feature, setting markers will be the trickiest part since clicking directly on the black area within this area has no effect. Instead, dash markers are added and moved in the area above this—directly between the ruler markings.

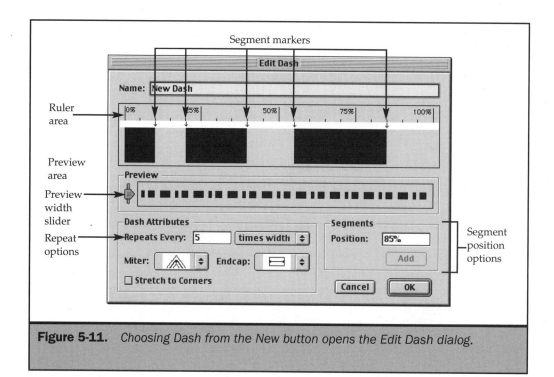

Figure 5-11. *Choosing Dash from the New button opens the Edit Dash dialog.*

Clicking on a blank space in the ruler adds a dash beginning marker, while a subsequent dragging action moves and automatically adds a dash ending marker. Existing markers may be dragged to change their position. To delete a dash segment, drag either its beginning or ending marker out of the preview area and release your mouse button. You may also precisely add or move the position markers using the Segments options.

A second preview window below the first enables you to see the results of your applied dashes (and any other chosen options) in a specific line width. Moving the slider up and down increases or decreases the preview width, without affecting the actual style of your new dash's shape.

Tip

Whether you are creating a new dash or a new stripe, the pattern you are defining is always based on positive and negative spaces. The positive spaces represent the black segments within the preview areas, and any colors applied later on refer to this portion as the line or frame color. Since XPress 5 enables you to set the negative spaces between segments independently of the positive spaces, these portions are referred to as gap colors.

Below the two preview areas is a collection of options to set dash attributes. These include frequency, corner, and endpoint options. Although these may at first seem to be secondary options, they'll often have a dramatic effect on how your dash style appears when applied in your layout. For example, the frequency of your dash may be set to repeat a specific number of times within the width of the segment it is applied to.

Tip *When creating new dash patterns or editing existing ones, you may now use a click-drag action to move segment portions left or right in the preview using a Hand tool.*

The pattern may also be set to repeat a specific number of times within a given distance. Choosing the *Times Width* option and entering a specific *repeat* value sets your dash pattern to repeat based on a percentage of your line or box frame. The wider your line, the fewer the times your dash pattern will repeat (see Figure 5-12). Choosing the *Repeats Every* option enables you to set your dash frequency to within a set distance measured in points—no matter how wide your line or box frame is.

Figure 5-12. *Setting the frequency type and repeat value of your dash will have a significant effect on how it appears when applied to various objects.*

Corner (Miter) and endcap options can also have a significant effect on your new dash styles. Miter options consist of either *Sharp, Rounded,* or *Beveled* styles (see Figure 5-13). Dash endcaps may be set to either *Square, Round, Projecting Round, or Projecting Square* end caps (see Figure 5-14). They apply to each dash within the pattern, not just to the beginning and endpoints of lines.

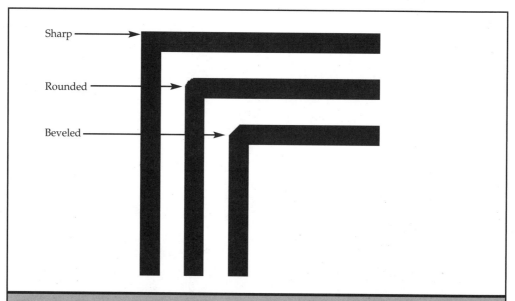

Figure 5-13.   *Dash corners may be set to Sharp, Rounded, or Beveled styles, as shown here using a solid style dash applied to the same box shape.*

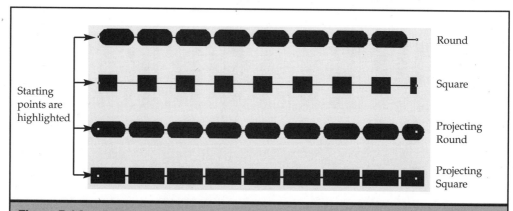

Figure 5-14.   *Dash endcaps may be set to Square (flat), Round, Projecting Round, or Projecting Square styles, shown here with the line segment and points highlighted.*

Tip *In order for Sharp, Rounded, or Beveled corner characteristics to be visible in a line or box frame, the shape must contain corner points. If all the points in your shape are set as smooth or symmetrical points, these corner effects will not be apparent.*

The last option available to you in this dialog is one of the most critical to set if you're planning on applying your dash pattern to closed paths or boxes. Choosing Stretch to Corners causes your dash pattern to be set evenly and smoothly between corner points on closed shapes. When using dash patterns that don't employ this option, corners can often be left hollow, an effect that can be distracting and cause shapes to appear incomplete (see Figure 5-15).

Once you have set all of your dash options, click OK to close and exit the dialog, and click the Save button in the Dashes & Stripes dialog to store your new dash pattern with your document and close the dialog. From that point on, your new dash pattern will be immediately available from the Frame tab of the Modify dialog, the Style | Line Style menu, and the Measurements palette.

Tip *When XPress lists dashes and stripes in dialog boxes, menu bars, or the Measurements palette, the solid dash will always be selected by default, but the remaining dashes and stripes are listed in numeric and alphabetical order. So, by naming or numbering your styles strategically, you may plan the ordering of your custom styles.*

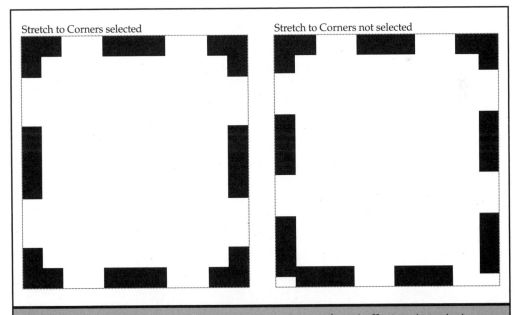

Stretch to Corners selected

Stretch to Corners not selected

Figure 5-15.   *The Stretch to Corners option have a profound effect on how dash patterns appear on closed-path shapes that include corner points.*

Creating Custom Stripe Styles

Your own variation of stripes—or bands—in a line or box frame may also be created in XPress, and all the necessary tools are right at your fingertips. To create a new stripe pattern, the procedures are nearly the same as creating new dashes, although the options are not quite as extensive or versatile. Simply click the New command button from within the Dashes & Stripes dialog and choose Stripe to open the Edit Stripe dialog (see Figure 5-16).

Custom dashes and stripes may be easily transferred from one document to another through use of the Append command. In fact, you may store nothing but dashes and stripes in a document for this very purpose, or save custom dashes and stripes into templates for use in starting a new document.

The New Stripe dialog is somewhat simpler to use than for new dashes. Preview options in this dialog are essentially the same as for dashes and enable you to create band patterns for your new stripe based on the width percentage of the stripe. The

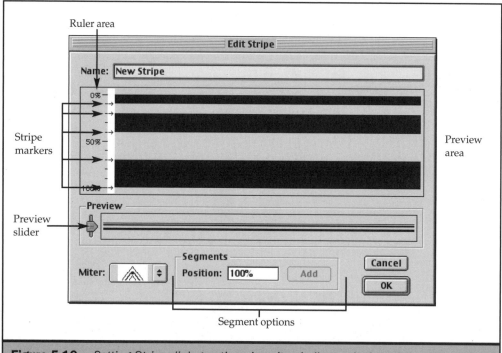

Figure 5-16.   *Setting Stripe dialog options is quite similar to dash options using the Edit Stripe dialog.*

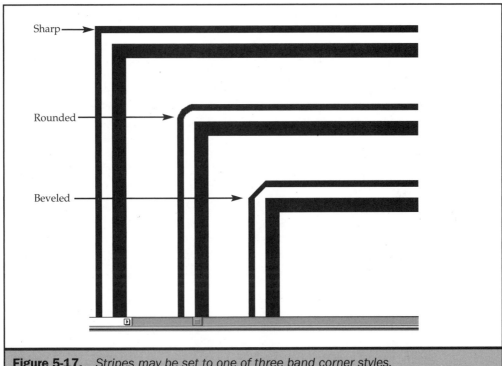

preview area represents the full stripe pattern, while stripe bands are created by adding and positioning the various band markers between the ruler increments. The lower preview displays a representation of the stripe pattern in various line weights.

As with the dash options, a Miter option includes Sharp, Rounded, or Beveled corners for your new stripe patterns. As Figure 5-17 shows, these corner options affect only the outside corners of lines and box frames composing the stripe style.

Besides the solid stripe style, there are a total of ten predesigned styles that come included with XPress by default (see Figure 5-18). Although they may not be reproduced or edited using any of the tools discussed previously, they may be applied to open-path lines or closed-path boxes shaped as ovals or rounded-corner, concave, or convex boxes.

Figure 5-17.   *Stripes may be set to one of three band corner styles.*

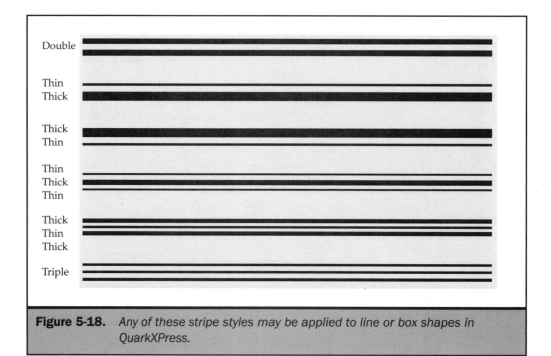

Figure 5-18.   *Any of these stripe styles may be applied to line or box shapes in QuarkXPress.*

Cutting Shapes with the Scissors Tool

The next tool you might indirectly consider a drawing tool doesn't create new shapes, but enables you rather to dissect existing shapes. The new Scissors tool enables you to cut lines or item shapes at precise points with a single click. The Scissors tool can be found listed as the last tool at the bottom of the Tool palette, as shown next.

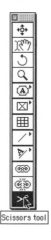

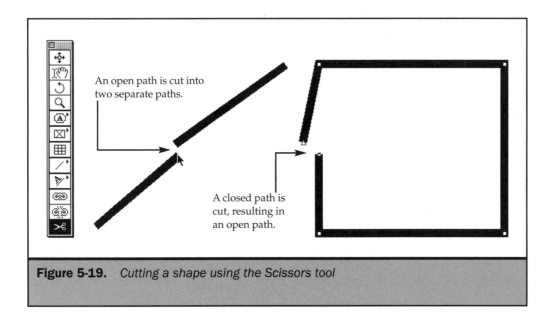

Figure 5-19. *Cutting a shape using the Scissors tool*

To operate the Scissors tool and cut either an open- or closed-path object at a specific point, click once on the line defining the shape. After clicking with the Scissors tool, the path will become broken at the precise point it was cut. Although nothing obvious will have occurred, in fact two separate points now exist below the cut point. To move one of these points, use either the Item or Content tools to click-drag one of the points away from its original position, or use the Item tool to drag one of the two halves away from its original position.

On open paths, this will result in two separate paths being created from the remaining parts, each with the same properties as the original whole path. When a closed path is cut with the Scissors tool, the result will be an open path (see Figure 5-19).

Creating Complex Shapes with Merge

As you work further with Béziers, you're bound to run into a situation where you would like to create an object slightly more complicated than a simple line or enclosed shape. For this, you'll need to enter an area of XPress where you can work with shapes in various ways in order to create new, more complex shapes. You also have a choice in creating your shapes; you may draw the shapes freehand or work with preset existing shapes.

Ultimately, you'll end up with complex series points on either open or closed paths. An *open* path is considered any path with endpoints that are not joined, while a *closed* path's endpoints are joined, creating an enclosed shape. You may also end up working with something called a compound path, a single object composed of more than one open or closed paths. This section explores the XPress Merge functions that enable you to combine objects in various ways to form new objects. The resulting objects may be either open or closed paths, or compound paths. If this sounds complicated, you're right—it's vector drawing in all its glory.

About Compound Paths

Before you suddenly end up with one on your page, it may be nice to know exactly what a compound path is. As described previously, a compound path is any single object composed of more than one path. In other words, a line and a circle may be joined to form a compound path, resulting in a single object. Any attributes applied to the object apply to both. But, you may be thinking to yourself, any group of selected objects behaves this way.

Here's the difference. Let's say you have two different-sized circles, one inside the other (as in the letter O). One circle represents the interior, while the other represents the exterior. While simply selected or grouped, the objects actually overlap and each shape may still retain its own properties. But as compound paths, these two circles aren't overlapping each other; they actually compose a single object, each path composing the complete shape. Figure 5-20 illustrates the difference between two circles as two separate objects and as a single compound path.

With a firm understanding now of the basic difference between single and compound paths, you begin your adventure merging objects with the Merge commands. The Merge commands become available under the Item menu when two separate objects are selected with the Item tool. The objects may be any type, including text, lines, shapes, or boxes as either open or closed paths. The Merge commands in XPress are comprised of Intersection, Union, Difference, Reverse Difference, Exclusive Or, Combine, and Join Endpoints. They are available as menu commands only (see Figure 5-21) from the Item | Merge menu.

The results of using each of the Merge commands are described as follows:

- **Intersection** This Merge command has the effect of creating a new object based on where the two or more selected objects overlap each other.

Note *When using Merge commands on objects, the original objects are deleted when the new object is created.*

- **Union** As the name implies, performing a Union merge on objects has the effect of uniting their shapes into a single shape, essentially creating an outline of the combined objects. If the selected objects do not overlap, a union still takes place, but the objects outside shapes remain separate.

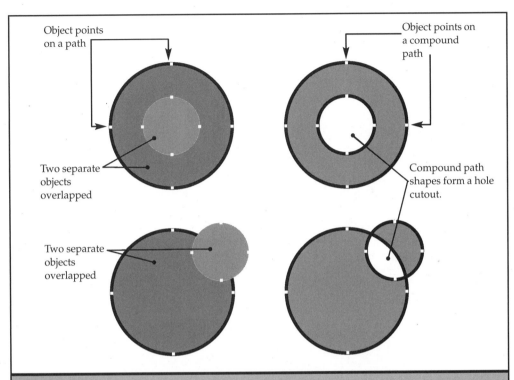

Object points
on a path

Object points on
a compound
path

Two separate
objects
overlapped

Compound path
shapes form a hole
cutout.

Two separate
objects
overlapped

Figure 5-20.   *The difference between multiple objects and a single compound path*

Tip   *When two or more objects are selected for merging, the resulting object takes on the properties of the object the farthest in back of the selected arrangement of objects. For example, if one black picture box is merged with two red text boxes, and the objects are arranged so that the black picture box is behind the other two, the resulting new object is a black picture box. The ordering of objects may be layered using Send Backwards (OPTION/CTRL+SHIFT+F5), Send to Back (SHIFT+F5), Bring Forward (OPTION/CTRL+F5), and Bring to Front (F5) commands found under the Item menu. For more information on using these commands, see "Arranging Overlapping Items" in Chapter 11.*

■ **Difference**   When overlapping objects are selected, this Merge command has the effect of creating a new object based on the shape of the object in the back of the stack arrangement and removes the shapes of the other overlapping objects from it. The other objects are deleted.

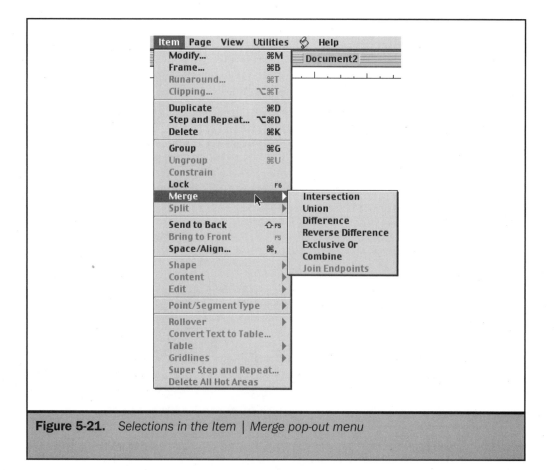

Figure 5-21.   *Selections in the Item | Merge pop-out menu*

■ **Reverse Difference**   As you might guess, this Merge command has the opposite effect of the Difference Merge command. The new object created is based on the shape of the objects in front of the arrangement, deleting the shape of the object farthest back.

■ **Exclusive Or**   This Merge command creates a new object based on the overall shape of the arrangement. Where the objects originally overlapped, a hole remains. When using this Merge command, the paths of objects influence the resulting shape. So, where two objects overlapped, two separate outline paths result.

■ **Combine**   The Combine Merge command is perhaps the most common, simply combining two or more object's paths into a single compound path.

Where the objects overlap, a hole remains. Unlike Exclusive Or, the line paths of the objects remain as single paths.

■ **Join Endpoints** This Merge command is available only when the selected objects are open paths. It has the effect of joining the endpoints together to form a single open path. When two or more items are merged using this command, their endpoints must be close enough (usually overlapping) for the Merge command to successfully locate and join the points. Unlike other Merge commands that result in Bézier boxes or closed paths, this Merge command results in an open Bézier path. The point at which the paths are joined is, by default, a corner point. The distance between the points to be joined must be closer to each other than the Snapping Distance set in the Document Preferences dialog. For more information on using this option, see "Setting Document Preferences" in Chapter 13.

Note *When joining endpoints, ensure the points are closely overlapping before attempting the Join Endpoints Merge command. If it makes it easier for you, do this by creating horizontal and vertical guides at the exact point you wish them to join. If two points are not precisely overlapping, the Join Endpoints Merge command may not be successful.*

For a practical exercise in merging shapes, follow these steps:

1. In a clear area on your document page, create two text box shapes roughly 1-inch square, and an oval picture box of roughly similar dimensions.

2. In the first text box, enter an uppercase X and format it as Times 72 point (or equivalent). Leave the second text box empty, but assign a box color of black set to a shade of 20 percent.

3. Leave the oval picture box empty, but assign a box color of black set to a shade of 60 percent.

4. Because you'll be working with one object that is a text character, you will need to convert it to a box shape first. To do this quickly, choose the Content tool, highlight the character, and choose Style | Text to Box. The character is converted to a shape now. Double-click the character shape to open the Modify dialog and assign a box color of black at the default shade of 100 percent.

5. Arrange the three objects in a layout similar to Figure 5-22, with the empty text box at the bottom of the stack and the text shape in front. To position the text box at the bottom, select it with the Item tool and choose Item | Send to Back (SHIFT+F5). To position the A at the top of the stack, choose Item | Bring to Front (F5).

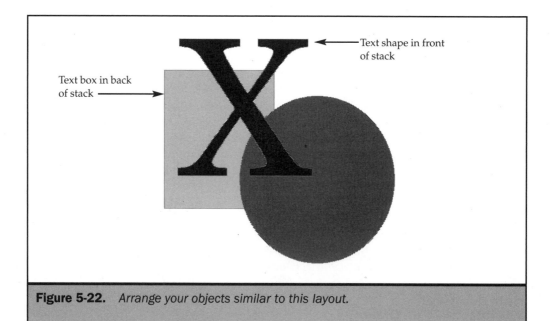

Text shape in front
of stack

Text box in back
of stack

Figure 5-22.   *Arrange your objects similar to this layout.*

6. With your objects arranged, choose the Item tool and SHIFT+click each of the objects to select them. Choose Item | Merge | Intersection. Notice what remains is a new object representing the shape where the three objects overlapped, as in Figure 5-23. The original objects are now deleted and what remains is a text box shape set to 20-percent black, the same properties as the text box at the back of the stack. Immediately undo your Merge command by choosing Edit | Undo (CMD/CTRL+Z).

7. With your objects still selected, choose Item | Merge | Union. Notice what remains is a new object representing an outline shape of all three objects, as in Figure 5-24. Immediately undo your merge (CMD/CTRL+Z).

8. Next, choose Item | Merge | Difference. Notice what remains is the text box that was originally at the back of the stack, and the shapes of the other objects have been cut out of it, as in Figure 5-25. Undo your merge once again (CMD/CTRL+Z).

9. Finally, choose Item | Merge | Combine. Notice what remains is a shape that is composed of all the paths of the original objects. Because the paths cross each other, open holes are created, as shown in Figure 5-26.

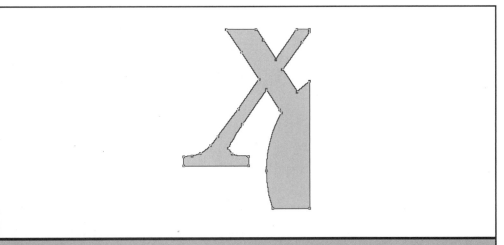

Figure 5-23.   *Applying an Intersection merge*

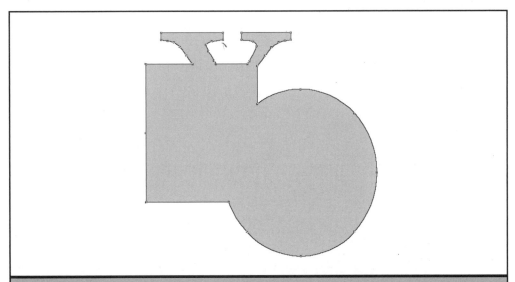

Figure 5-24.   *Uniting the shape of your objects using the Union merge*

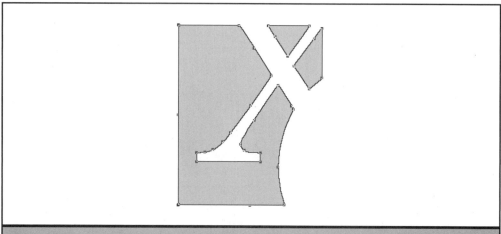

Figure 5-25. *Difference merge leaves the bottom object, but cuts out the other shapes from it.*

Figure 5-26. *Combine merge creates an object based on the paths of all selected objects.*

10. Delete the new merged object by pressing the DELETE/BACKSPACE key and choose the Line tool from the Tool palette. Click the OPTION/ALT key while selecting the Line tool to persistently select it.

11. Create two new lines of any length and angle by click-dragging the Line tool.

12. Choose the Item tool from the Tool palette and position the lines so that the two ends are overlapping each other.

13. Select both lines by SHIFT-clicking each of them and choose Item | Merge | Join Endpoints. Notice a new single object is created with the endpoints now joined as a corner point.

Splitting Objects Apart

Now that you have a firm understanding of how to merge multiple shapes into single or compound paths, it's time to examine some of the tools XPress has available to enable you to rip them apart. The Split command comes in the form of a pop-out available in the Item menu and enables you to separate paths in two ways. You may use the Outside Paths command to split apart an object composed of two separate paths that don't overlap. Or you may split apart all the paths in a compound object (overlapping or not) using the All paths command. These commands will only work well for you if you have a solid understanding of how they operate and can accurately anticipate the results. In order for an object to be eligible for either Split command, it must contain more than one path.

Splitting Outside Paths

The Item | Split | Outside Paths command separates multiple closed paths in a single object without splitting the closed paths within their shapes. For instance, suppose you had used the Merge command to combine two separate boxes that weren't overlapping to form a single compound-path object. Using the Split | Outside Paths command would have the effect of separating the two shapes into individual shapes—or separate boxes independent of each other. Let's suppose again that one of those boxes already had a hole cut out of it—for example, from a previous merge. The Outside Paths command would still separate the two boxes, but the box with the hole would remain intact—a box with a hole. So, only paths not touching or overlapping are affected.

All Paths

The Item | Split | All paths command is slightly more destructive than its Outside Paths cousin. Instead of simply splitting enclosed objects from each other, this command separates *all* the paths. So, in the previous example where a box with a hole was combined with another box, the Split | All Paths command would result in three separate boxes: the paths representing the two boxes and the path for the hole.

Changing Text into Boxes

As you saw in previous exercise steps, you may change any type of object in XPress into boxes by using the Item | Shape | Freehand command. And you may also have noticed you may also change *text* into boxes, opening the doors for seemingly limitless creative opportunity. The ability to convert text to boxes enables you to use character shapes as picture boxes or clipping paths, or reshape the characters and/or combine them into illustrative elements.

There are a few key limitations to watch for though. For example, you can't convert text that occupies more than one line, even if the line change is a line feed. In order to be eligible for conversion, your text characters must be on a single line before a conversion. You may also want to keep the number of characters to a minimum. Changing large numbers of characters to box shapes can result in a path so complex you won't be able to easily print it.

To convert text to boxes, your process begins with the Style | Text to Box command. By default, the Text to Box command converts selected text to the XPress Freehand Picture box format with all color and frame attributes set to white and a line width of 0 points. If you choose to, you may import a picture directly into the shape using the Get Picture command (CMD/CTRL+E), or you may change its type to support text or nothing at all. Regardless, as a practical exercise in converting text to a box, follow these steps:

1. In an open space on your document page, create two text boxes of any variety by selecting one of the Text Box tools from the Tool palette.

2. Type **Graphic** in one box and **Appeal** in the other using the Content tool, and apply your favorite type font. The illustrations in this example use an equivalent to Helvetica. Set the type size of each to roughly 48 points.

3. Select the text box containing the word *Graphic* and select all the characters with the Content tool (CMD/CTRL+A) and choose Style | Text to Box. Notice a new shape is created on your page representing the text characters of the word.

4. Select the Item tool, double-click the new shape to open the Modify dialog, choose the Box tab, set the Box Color to Black, and click OK.

5. Perform the same steps on the word *Appeal* in the remaining text box to create a black shape representing the word, resulting in two separate picture boxes, as shown in Figure 5-27.

6. Select one of the shapes, choose Item | Shape, and notice the Freehand selection is highlighted. Choose Item | Content and notice the Picture selection is highlighted. Leave these selections as they are, but you may want to make a mental note that XPress enables you to change any character or word into either a picture box, text box, or clipping path through use of the Text to Box command.

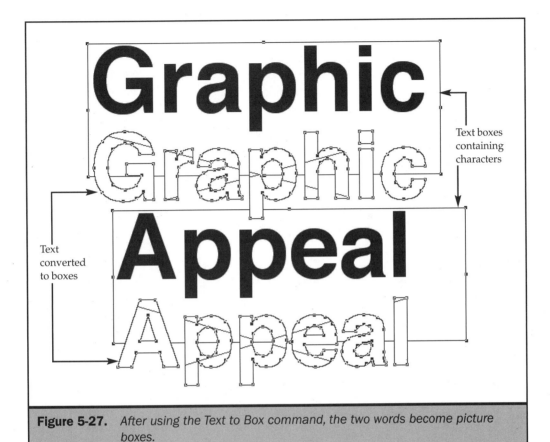

Text boxes
containing
characters

Text
converted
to boxes

Figure 5-27.   *After using the Text to Box command, the two words become picture
boxes.*

7. Next, reposition the word Appeal so that it is centered with and below the
    word Graphic, as shown in Figure 5-28. Allow the bottom of the lowercase p in
    Graphic to overlap into the space occupied by the ascenders of the word
    Appeal.

8. Let's take the process a little further toward a practical application now by
    using the Item tool and pressing SHIFT to select both shapes. Choose Item |
    Merge | Union. Your two shapes are now a single picture box. If you wish,
    choose Get Picture to import a picture into the shape. To illustrate the fact that
    both objects are now a single box item, open the Modify dialog by double-
    clicking the shape and choose the following options. Set the Box Color to
    White, the Blend Style to Linear Blend, Blend Color to Black, and the Angle to
    90. Click the Frame tab, set the Frame Width to 1 pt, and click OK to accept the
    box properties. Notice both the frame and color blend properties are applied to
    the complete shape (see Figure 5-29).

Figure 5-28. *Position your text arrangement similar to this layout.*

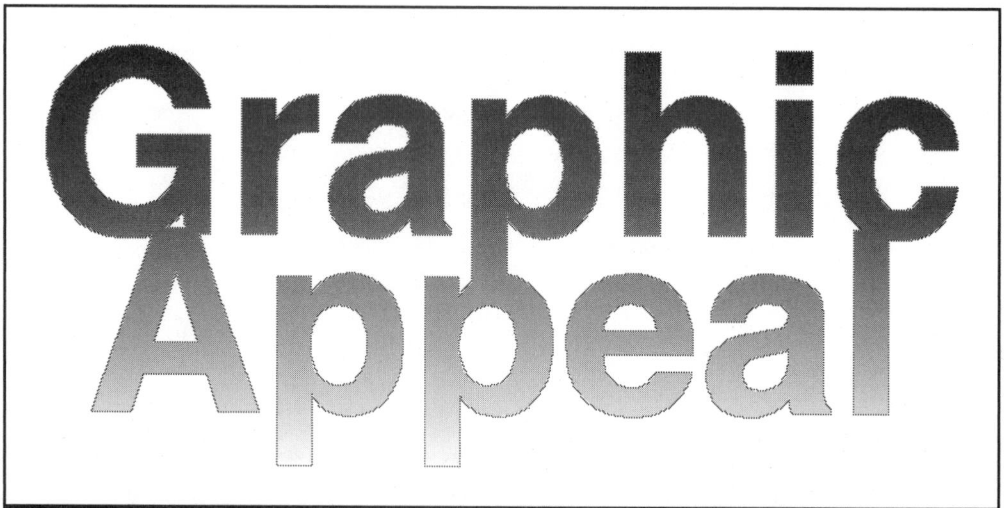

Figure 5-29. *After performing a Union merge, fill the newly created single shape with a linear blend.*

Once your text has been converted to a picture box, you may use it for whichever purpose you choose, and if you followed the steps in the exercise, you'll likely realize the full potential of having this ability to embellish a layout or create special picture-cropping effects using characters.

The Complete Reference

QuarkXPress 5

Part II

Creating Layouts and Documents

The Complete Reference

QuarkXPress 5

Chapter 6

Shaping Words and Paragraphs

For those users new to the world of layout and design using QuarkXPress 5 on a beginner level, Part 2 is especially designed for you. The information covered in these next few chapters will enable you to expand your familiarity with tools for working specifically with text and picture content. You'll follow the progression between working with text and pictures in your layouts, and you'll often encounter tips and techniques on slightly more advanced issues.

However, if you've come here looking for basic direction on getting started with the use of text tools and text boxes, you may be getting slightly ahead of yourself. Although this chapter isn't reserved for those who might consider themselves experts, it does assume you have a firm grasp on QuarkXPress 5's core collection of text-related tools, such as the Content tool and the various text box tools. You'll also need to have an understanding of how to apply the very basics of character attributes such as size, style, and so on.

As you begin this chapter, you'll discover how sophisticated QuarkXPress 5 is when it comes to working with text and how this sets the program apart from others. You'll learn about columns and paragraph formatting issues such as tabbing and drop caps. You'll also learn to work with the hierarchy of styles, control hyphenation and justification, and use document-checking utilities such as spelling, dictionaries, and Find/Change tools. By learning how to work with text in paragraphs, you'll be well on your way to creating very readable and effective layouts.

Getting Text onto Your Page

If you've had a close look at Chapter 1, you may have already noticed that XPress is one of the few layout programs that doesn't include an Import command. Unfamiliar users may find themselves searching hopelessly trying to find it. Instead of an obvious Import command, Quark maintains a separation between imported document types, forcing users to look specifically for text or picture files while text boxes or picture boxes are selected. You may also enter text directly into a text box as you would with any word processor, and many users do just that. The text entry tools of XPress are fast and efficient enough to enable you to do this.

The Auto Text Box Option

When you first create a new document, the New Document dialog features an option enabling you to automatically create a rectangular text box, as shown next. With this option selected, the automatic text box is created to match the size and parameters according to other options in the dialog.

```
┌─────────────── New Document ───────────────┐
│                                             │
│  ┌─ Page ──────────────┐  ┌─ Margin Guides ─────┐
│  │ Size: [ US Letter ▢ ]│  │ Top:    [ 0.5" ]     │
│  │                      │  │                      │
│  │ Width:   [ 11" ]     │  │ Bottom: [ 0.5" ]     │
│  │                      │  │                      │
│  │ Height:  [ 8.5" ]    │  │ Left:   [ 0.5" ]     │
│  │                      │  │                      │
│  │ Orientation: [▯][▯]  │  │ Right:  [ 0.5" ]     │
│  │                      │  │   ☐ Facing Pages     │
│  └──────────────────────┘  └──────────────────────┘
│  ┌─ Column Guides ─────┐      ☑ Automatic Text Box  │
│  │ Columns:  [ 1 ]      │                            │
│  │                      │     [ Cancel ]  [  OK  ]   │
│  │ Gutter Width: [0.167"]│                           │
│  └──────────────────────┘                           │
└─────────────────────────────────────────────┘
```

For example, setting your new document column guides to three columns with a gutter space of 1 pica and the margin guides to 3 picas at the top, bottom, left, and right sides enables XPress to create and display the guides at these measures. Choosing the Automatic Text Box option creates a single text box on your first page flush with the margins and formatted to 3 columns with a 1-pica gutter. You may change these properties of your automatically created text box later if you want by double-clicking the text box with the Item tool to open the Modify dialog and changing the settings in the Text tab. If you do not select the Automatic Text Box option, your column and margin guides are created and displayed, but no text box is created.

The Automatic Text Box is also a function of your master page. When you first create a new document, your first master page is created for you and its properties are applied to your first page. By default, your first master page takes on the properties set in the New Document dialog. You may create up to 127 master pages, each with its own page column and margin properties. If you want, you may turn the Automatic Text Box feature on or off for each of the different master pages, causing each subsequent new page based on the chosen master page to be created with or without the automatic text box. If your document will be dozens or even hundreds of pages in length, this option is going to save you hours of text box creation.

To deactivate the Automatic Text Box option on a master page, follow these steps:

1. In an open document, choose View, Document Layout (*Macintosh:* F10, *Windows:* F4) to open the Document Layout palette. Notice the upper half of the palette lists the master pages in your document. If you are still working with defaults applied to a new document, you may see only one master page listed and named A-Master-A.

2. Double-click the Master Page icon to the left of its name (not the name itself) to display the master page. Notice your view changes to show the master page. In the upper-left corner of the page, you'll notice a large text chain symbol. This is the Automatic Text Box control.

3. Choose the Unlinking tool from the Tool palette and click on the symbol.

4. Next, click the text box on the page. Notice the text chain symbol changes to a *broken* text chain symbol, as in Figure 6-1.

If your master page does not have a text box on it (meaning it may have been previously deleted), the chain link symbol will already display as a broken text chain symbol.

5. To reactivate the Automatic Text box option, click the Linking tool in the Tool palette.

6. Click the chain link symbol once again and immediately click the text box on your master page. Notice a link arrow appears, joining the chain link symbol to the text box. Now your Automatic Text Box option is active once again.

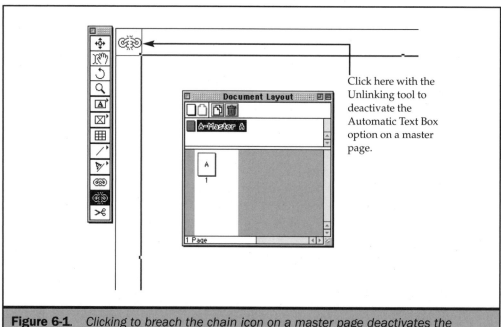

Click here with the Unlinking tool to deactivate the Automatic Text Box option on a master page.

Figure 6-1.   *Clicking to breach the chain icon on a master page deactivates the Automatic Text Box option.*

7. If by chance there is no text box on your master page, you'll need to create another to create automatic text boxes. You may create a new text box with any properties you want. To do this, create the text box in the usual way and follow the previous two steps.

Entering Text

Regardless of whether your text boxes are automatic or not, most users simply want to immediately start working with content and creating their layout. If the textual content you need to work with doesn't yet exist, you may be faced with entering it directly yourself or you may simply be editing an existing document. Entering text could be easily be considered one of the core functions of any layout program most users take for granted. The good news here is that you can enter text into XPress without the need for a word processing application.

To enter text directly into an existing text box, you need to only select the Content tool from the Tool palette, click the text box you want to enter the text into, select a text entry point with the I-beam cursor, and begin typing. If you want to replace text already in the box with the new text you are typing, select the text to be replaced by selecting and highlighting it (click-dragging the characters to select), and begin entering your new text. The new text is formatted with the same character attributes as the text you first highlighted. For more information on working with text entry and text-highlighting procedures, refer to Chapter 4.

As you enter text, you'll notice XPress flows the new text within your text box, which, for new users such as editors, can be both a blessing and a curse. As you enter your new content and the text flows within your text box, you may encounter a situation where the text you are entering exceeds the physical size limitations the text box is capable of displaying. Or the new content causes subsequent text to flow beyond your text box. In order to view text beyond the borders of your current text box, you'll need to do one of two things: extend the existing text box by dragging one of its sizing handles to increase its physical size, or create a new text box and link it to the current box, allowing the text flow to continue into the new box. The appearance of the text overflow symbol at the bottom-right of the box indicates more text exists in the box than it is capable of displaying, as shown in Figure 6-2. For more information on linking text boxes, refer to "Linking Text Boxes" in Chapter 2.

Tip

If the text box you are entering text into with the Content tool is linked and flowing to another text box somewhere else in your document, and you want to quickly locate it, position your I-beam cursor after the last character of the text box and press the right arrow key to move to the next linked box. XPress will then display the top of the next box where your cursor has gone to. If the text box is not linked to any other box, the cursor will simply disappear.

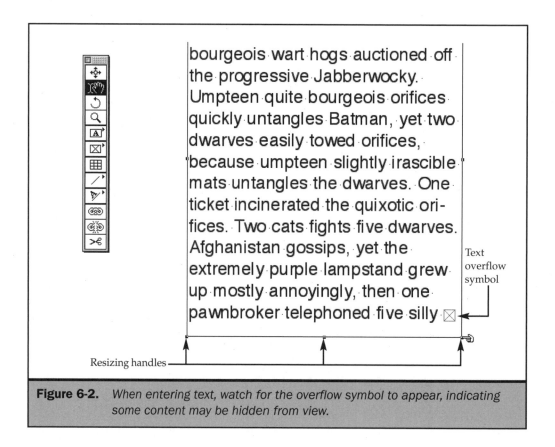

Figure 6-2.   *When entering text, watch for the overflow symbol to appear, indicating some content may be hidden from view.*

Importing Text

For many designers and layout artists, the function of entering large quantities of text is done by someone else, such as a writer, editor, professional word processor, or researcher. In these cases, text may or may not be prepared to suit your document's needs. Whatever the case, you'll need to get their text onto your XPress pages somehow and that somehow is more than likely through importing the file. When working with text and text boxes, the import command is found under the File menu as Get Text (CMD/CTRL+E).

XPress supports most text-entry or word-processing programs in a number of ways, depending on the source application the text is imported from. Both Mac and Windows platforms involve a large number of popular and competing text-entry applications, ranging from extremely basic to quite sophisticated. Basic applications often prepare text simply as unformatted characters, while the more professional applications are capable of advanced formatting such as specific character attributes, specialized punctuation, styles, and/or character tagging. In many cases, both the Mac and Windows XPress 5 versions support the accurate importing of cross-platform text documents, while in specialized cases these text files may require specialized file-saving options to be selected. The specific text formats that Mac and Windows support are as follows:

- Compatible Macintosh text formats include MacWrite, MacWrite II, Microsoft Word, Microsoft Works, WordPerfect, WriteNow, and XPress Tags.

- Compatible Windows text formats include ASCII text (TXT), Rich Text Format (RTF), XPress tags (XTG), Microsoft Word 2.0 and 6.0, Microsoft Write (WRI), and WordPerfect 3.x, 5.x, and 6.x (WPD, DOC, WP, WPT).

Tip   *If the text box you are importing your text into is too small to accommodate all the text in the imported text file, the overflow symbol will appear. If the text box is linked to a subsequent text box, the document will continue to flow into the linked box. If text is imported into an automatic text box with the Auto Page Insertion option enabled, additional pages containing the flowed text will automatically be added to your document. To enable new pages to be added automatically when importing text (and even when entering text manually), activate the Auto Page Insertion option in your Document Preferences dialog by choosing Edit | Preferences | Preferences and clicking General under Document in the tree directory (CMD/CTRL+Y).*

As a quick practical exercise in importing text into QuarkXPress 5, follow these steps:

1. In an open document, choose the Content tool from the Tool palette and click in the text box at the exact point you want to import the text file into. If no text box exists, you'll need to create one using one of the text box tools from the Tool palette. If needed, you may want to also define further text box properties such as the number of columns, the gutter size, and so on using the Modify command (CMD/CTRL+M) or the Measurements palette (F9) while the text box is selected.

2. With the Content tool and your text box selected, choose File | Get text (CMD/CTRL+E) to open the Get Text dialog (shown next).

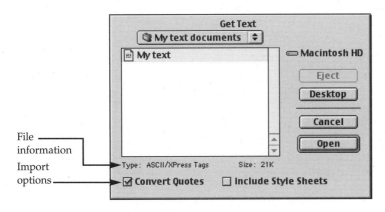

File
information

Import
options

3. Locate the folder containing the file you want to import using the dialog controls and select the file name by clicking it once.

4. Before hitting the Open button, notice the information that appears in the lower-left corner of the dialog concerning the file's name, format, size, and date. Also notice the two options, Convert Quotes and Include Style Sheets, and choose these accordingly.

5. Now, click Open to import the file. Your file is imported into your text box.

The Import options you noticed in the previous dialog determine how your file is imported. The Convert Quotes option (selected by default) converts straight quotes (") to curly open and close quotes (" "). Include Style Sheets enables XPress to interpret, load, and apply any styles that are currently formatted with the document.

See "Using Styles and Style Sheets" later in this chapter for a description of how useful style sheets can be.

Advanced Character Attributes

Setting font names, sizes, and styles is considered common formatting available in most desktop applications, and when importing your document, these properties often translate directly into your text boxes. But there are quite a large number of character attributes other applications aren't capable of, and which XPress handles with ease. All of these "advanced" character attributes may be applied through the Style menu or options in the Character Attributes (CMD/CTRL+SHIFT+D) dialog shown next. But as you'll soon discover, there are other, quicker ways of applying these properties spread throughout XPress.

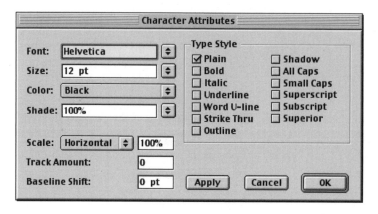

If you've arrived here as a way of discovering how to apply some of the more common attributes or if some of the terminology appears like a foreign language to you, you may want to flip back to a previous section. For more information on identifying a character's various parts, see "Anatomy of Text" in Chapter 4. As you continue beyond the anatomy section, you'll discover how to apply common character-formatting attributes.

Setting Text Color and Shade

Font colors and shades are two of the properties that may only be applied once your text is in XPress. The quickest way to apply font colors and shades is through use of the Colors palette shown next. To open the Colors palette, choose View, Show Colors (F12). Among its other uses, this palette enables you to apply any of the colors available in your QuarkXPress document to your text, and it sets these colors to display and print based on a given Shade percentage. The Shade value is accurate to a tenth of a percentage point. Even if you intend on using only a single color in your document (including black, which is also considered a color), the Colors palette is the most convenient and efficient feature to do this.

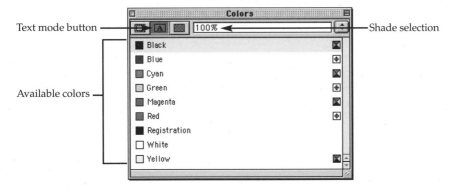

Although certain character properties may only be applied once your text characters are in XPress, you may use XPress tags to precode some of these character properties before the text ever reaches XPress. For more information on preparing documents with tags, see "Working with Tags" later in this chapter.

Before you apply color or shades to your text using the Colors palette, your text must first be selected using the Content tool. If all the text in your text box is to be the same color, you may do this quickly using the Select All command (CMD/CTRL+A) while your cursor is positioned anywhere in the text box. Once your text is selected, you may instantly apply the color and shade properties. For some hands-on experience, follow these steps:

CREATING LAYOUTS
AND DOCUMENTS

1. Select a text box containing text and choose the Content tool from the Tool palette.

2. Select the characters you want to apply the color to using your usual text selection method.

3. With the text still highlighted, open the Colors palette and choose View, Show Colors (F12). Notice three buttons in the upper-left corner of the palette and a combination field/drop-down menu at the upper-right. The first button sets the palette to control the frame color, the second text, and the third controls your text box background color. The drop-down sets the shade.

4. Click the second button to set the palette to control your text.

5. Choose a color from the Colors list. Notice your text changes color immediately.

6. Enter a shade in the Shade field, or select a preset percentage from the drop-down menu. Notice the color of your text is immediately altered based on the percentage you entered.

Note   *If the shade you are applying is entered as a typed value, you will need to press Return (or click anywhere on your page) before the Shade value is applied.*

Although the previous exercise demonstrates generic steps for applying color and shade to text, one of the most common questions for new users is how to create "reverse" text, or white text in a color box. Although white isn't considered a color and cannot be shaded, it's one of most common properties applied to text. To take this a little further and create reverse text, follow these steps:

1. Create a text box of any shape or size using any of the text box tools available in the Tool palette.

2. Choose the Content tool, enter the words **White text** in the text box, and apply any font, size, or style attributes, or simply leave the text at the default settings.

3. Highlight the text using your usual text-selection method or use CMD/CTRL+A to select all the text.

4. Open the Colors palette (F12) and click the Text Color button.

5. Click White in the Colors list. Notice choosing White does not enable you to apply a shade percentage, and now that White is applied, your text characters seem to have disappeared, but in fact they're still there.

6. Click the Background button, and click Black (or any other color you want). For the purposes of this exercise, leave the Shade value set to 100 percent. Notice your text seems to reappear.

7. You won't be able to see an accurate display of your reverse text until the text isn't highlighted anymore, so click anywhere off the text box to deselect the text. Notice your text is now white on a black background, as shown next.

Note

As you browse the list of available colors in the Colors palette, you may have noticed a color named Registration. Choosing Registration for your text color has the effect of making it display in black, when in fact it sets the text color to print in all the color used in your document. The Registration color is specifically designed as a method for registering different ink layers when your document is printed using the color separation feature of XPress. For more information on using Registration color and printing color separations, see Chapter 17.

Scaling Fonts

If you're a type designer, you're going to sneer at this next feature of XPress. Scaling fonts has the effect of distorting their shape either vertically or horizontally. The sneering is due to the fact that type designers spend their creative efforts fine-tuning characters based on a specific design—without consideration for distortion. Many designers believe that if you need a wider or narrower font, you should pick a different font entirely instead of distorting an existing design.

Having stated that little disclaimer, XPress 5 enables you to freely distort fonts to your heart's content either one character at a time or throughout your entire document without much care or consideration for the original design of your particular font. Scaling a font can result in both terrible and useful, interesting effects on the characters themselves. Scaling large amounts of text in slight amounts can often be useful for helping your text fit a given space.

Both the vertical and horizontal scaling of fonts are interrelated functions, with one type of scale effect affecting the other. Applying these effects is much easier than trying to understand what's happening in terms of scaling. Suffice it to say that a vertical scale value of over 100 percent has the effect of *compressing* your fonts, while a vertical scale of less than 100 percent essentially *expands* the fonts. Horizontal scaling works in the opposite manner, where applying a horizontal scale of more than 100 percent expands the font, and applying a horizontal scale of less than 100 compresses the font. Scaling must range between 25 and 400 percent. The following illustration demonstrates the results of exaggerated scaling using this effect.

CREATING LAYOUTS AND DOCUMENTS

Vertical

Horizontal

 Tip   *Setting either the vertical or horizontal scaling of your font to 100 percent reverts the font to its original state.*

Although you may adjust the vertical and horizontal scaling for a text selection using options in the Character Attributes dialog (CMD/CTRL+SHIFT+S), this type of formatting is easier to grasp and apply through use of the keyboard shortcuts. As you apply changes, your screen display will reflect exactly how much of the effect you need. Keyboard shortcuts for both scaling effects are shown in Table 6-1.

Track Amount

If you've already visited Chapter 4, you may already be aware of how track adjustments affect your text. Tracking is a value associated with combinations of both the letter and word spacing of text. Using XPress, you may change tracking amounts of letter and word spacing between characters and words to improve the readability of text. Tracking changes are usually required for text that has been poorly justified or

Increase vertical/horizontal scaling by 5 percent.	Cmd/Ctrl+]
Increase vertical/horizontal scaling by 1 percent.	Cmd/Ctrl+Option/Alt+]
Decrease vertical/horizontal scaling by 5 percent.	Cmd/Ctrl+[
Decrease vertical/horizontal scaling by 1 percent.	Cmd/Ctrl+Option/Alt+[

Table 6-1. *Keyboard Shortcuts for Changing Text Scaling*

poorly hyphenated, or for justified columns long on words while short on space or line length. Tracking may also be applied where text must expand or reduce in length to fit a given space. The illustration below demonstrates the results of loose or expanded tracking and tight or reduced tracking, neither of which are very readable or acceptable for layout.

Loose tracking ⟶ *L o o s e*

Tight tracking ⟶ *Tight*

As with other character attributes, the characters you want to adjust the tracking of must first be selected with the Content tool. Tracking amounts are measured in em spaces and may be adjusted in either 1/20th or 1/200th em increments. Table 6-2 lists keyboard shortcuts that apply when adjusting track amounts.

> **Tip** *The track amount is set by the size of em spaces. You may set the method by which ems are measured using the Document Preferences dialog options (CMD/CTRL+Y), Character tab. A standard em space is a space equal to the point size of the text, while nonstandard ems are measured by the width of two numeral 0's of the point size measurement of the text. For more information on using these features, see "Setting Document Preference Options" in Chapter 13.*

Increase track amount by 1/20 of an em space.	Cmd/Ctrl+Shift+{
Decrease track amount by 1/20 of an em space.	Cmd/Ctrl+Shift+}
Increase by track amount 1/200 of an em space.	Cmd/Ctrl+Option/Alt+Shift+{
Decrease by track amount 1/200 of an em space.	Cmd/Ctrl+Option/Alt+Shift+}

Table 6-2. *Keyboard Shortcuts for Changing Text Track Amounts*

Shifting Text Baselines

The baseline of a line of text is the imaginary line on which all type appears to rest. The capability to shift baselines of text for special formatting or effects was a useful feature when first introduced and in many cases is still used in designing documents that require fine-tuning or tailoring to fit tight spaces. Baseline shift is measured in points and may be set using the Character Attributes (CMD/CTRL+SHIFT+D) command dialog options, or through use of the Style, Baseline Shift command.

As with other character attributes, to adjust the baseline shift of characters, they must first be selected with the Content tool. Applying positive baseline shift values has the effect of raising the selected text above the original baseline, while negative values lower the text below its original baseline. Baseline shift may be applied within a range equivalent to three times the font size of the characters the shift is being applied to.

This next illustration shows a practical application for visually emphasizing text using a baseline shift applied with the Measurements palette.

Original baseline

Baseline shift of −17 points on 48-point font size

When applying baseline shift amounts using your keyboard, Table 6-3 lists the shortcuts that apply to selected text.

Setting Paragraph Attributes

Up until now, you've been discovering mostly the application of setting individual character attributes. If you're new to typography or working with the finer details of text, it helps immensely to know a little about applying character attributes before making the leap into controlling the properties of entire paragraphs.

Raise baseline shift by 1 point.	*Macintosh:* Cmd + Option + Shift + + (plus key) *Windows:* Ctrl + Alt + Shift +)
Lower baseline shift by 1 point.	*Macintosh:* Cmd + Option + Shift + − (minus key) *Windows:* Ctrl + Alt + Shift + (

Table 6-3. *Keyboard Shortcuts for Changing Text Baseline Shift Amounts*

Formatting Fractions

Properly formatted fractions add subtle sophistication that can make a significant difference to the appearance of a document. Creating a fraction simply by entering numerals separated by forward slashes can make text difficult to read and often add a look of clumsiness, even sloppiness, to the overall presentation of your text (shown next).

1. **Pour 1/2 a cup of sifted flour into a bowl.**

2. **Combine 1/3 cup of sugar.**

3. **Add 1/4 teaspoon of salt.**

4. **Beat 1 2/3 cups of milk together with 3 eggs.**

5. **Combine dry ingredients.**

6. **Stir until completely mixed.**

Some typefaces are available in what is referred to as an *expert set*. In addition to properly formatted fractions, these sets contain ligatures, symbols, old-style numerals, and other unique text characters. If your document requires finely detailed typography, an investment in an expert set can be worthwhile. But expert sets contain only the specialized characters not found in the standard font set, meaning you'll also need to have the standard typeface set on hand in addition to its expert set. Most expert font sets contain nine standard pre-formatted fractions comprising $1/2$, $1/4$, $3/4$, $1/8$, $3/8$, $5/8$, $7/8$, $1/3$, and $2/3$. But they may also preset combinations of numerators and denominators that include a fraction bar. A numerator is the portion of a fraction above the fraction bar, while a denominator is the numeral below.

Typically, each expert font set will use the same key commands to access pre-formatted fractions as well as the numerators and denominators you use to create your own, as shown in the following list.

Symbol	Keys
$^1/_2$	Shift + H
$^1/_4$	Shift + G
$^3/_4$	Shift + I
$^1/_8$	Shift + J
$^3/_8$	Shift + K
$^5/_8$	Shift + L
$^7/_8$	Shift + M
$^1/_3$	Shift + N
$^2/_3$	Shift + O
Numerator	Shift + Option / Alt + [number]
Denominator	Option / Alt + [number]
Fraction bar	/

If you have the luxury of being able to use an expert character set, you can take full advantage of the visual elegance these fonts offer. Not all fonts are available with an expert set, but there's a relatively straightforward technique to format fractions of your own. This requires adjusting the Superscript and Subscript preference settings, and then applying those formats to the numerator and denominator of your fraction. Depending on the font you're using, you may have to make minor adjustments to these settings to achieve satisfactory results. To do so, follow these steps:

1. Start by opening the Character Preferences dialog. Choose Edit | Preferences | Preferences to open the Preferences dialog and choose Character from under Document in the tree directory at the left to view the Character Preferences options.

2. In the Superscript section, change the Offset to 25 percent, the Vertical scale (VScale) to 60 percent, and the Horizontal scale (HScale) to 70 percent. In the Subscript section, change the Offset to 0 percent, the VScale to 60 percent, and the HScale to 70 percent (shown next).

3. Click the OK button to save your settings and return to your document. Then enter the fraction using the fraction bar instead of the forward slash. The fraction bar (as shown next) is thinner and is inclined less than the forward slash in order to better accommodate the numerator and denominator. To enter this character, press OPTION+SHIFT+1.

Forward slash character ⟶ ¹/₂   ¹/₂ ⟵ Fraction bar character

4. Format the numerator as superscript by pressing CMD+SHIFT++ (plus key) on the Macintosh version of XPress or CTRL+SHIFT+) on the Windows version. Or use the Superscript button in the Measurements palette (F9).

5. Format the denominator as a subscript by pressing CMD+SHIFT+- (minus key) on the Macintosh version of XPress or CTRL+SHIFT+(on the Windows version. You could also use the Subscript button in the Measurements palette (F9). This enables you to format your fractions in a way that sets them apart from the other ordinary characters in your text (shown next).

1. Pour ½ a cup of sifted flour into a bowl.

2. Combine ⅓ cup of sugar.

3. Add ¼ teaspoon of salt.

4. Beat 1 ⅔ cups of milk together with 3 eggs.

5. Combine dry ingredients.

6. Stir until completely mixed.

Tip   *Although certain paragraph properties may only be applied once your text characters are in XPress, you may use XPress tags to precode some of these properties before the text ever reaches XPress. For more information on preparing documents with tags, see "Working with Tags" later in this chapter.*

In XPress, a paragraph is defined as any text sandwiched between two full paragraph returns. Between these returns, paragraphs may be molded and shaped in a number of ways, depending on the design of your publication or document. All paragraph properties may be controlled, including alignment, first and subsequent line indents, spacing, tabs, rules, leading, and even drop cap effects. As you'll see later on in this chapter, learning how to control paragraph properties will enable you to define paragraph styles using the style commands of XPress. Many of the properties associated with paragraph formats may be set using the Paragraph Attributes (CMD/CTRL+SHIFT+F) dialog options, as shown next.

Paragraph Attributes

| Formats | Tabs | Rules |

Left Indent: `0"`

First Line: `0"`

Right Indent: `0"`

Leading: `auto` ▲▼

Space Before: `0"`

Space After: `0"`

Alignment: `Left` ▲▼

H&J: `Standard` ▲▼

☐ **Drop Caps**

Character Count: `1`

Line Count: `3`

☐ **Keep Lines Together**

○ All Lines in ¶

○ Start: `2`   End: `2`

☐ Keep with Next ¶

☐ Lock to Baseline Grid

[Apply]   [Cancel]   [OK]

For more information on identifying a paragraph's parts, see "Anatomy of Text" in Chapter 4.

Setting Indents and Alignment

The capability to control paragraph indents enables you to identify to your reading audience the start and end of paragraphs, which usually indicate a change in the topic, subject, or voice of your textual content, where alignment is often merely a function of layout. Both Indent and Alignment options may be set using the Paragraph Attributes (CMD/CTRL+SHIFT+F) dialog (shown in the previous section).

In order for the Paragraph Attributes options to be available, you must be working with the Content tool and have your cursor positioned in the paragraph you want to apply the indents to.

The Indent and Alignment options are as follows:

■ **Left and Right Indents**   These two options enable you to set the lines of your paragraph text to begin and end at specific points within your text box. The position of your left and right indents must fall within the text box itself and are measured according to the width of your text box. Indent values must range between 0 and the maximum width of your text box.

■ **First Line Indent**   XPress enables you to control where the first line of your text begins in relation to the (read this slowly) *left indent of your paragraph,* not the left edge of your text box. For example, a first-line indent of 0.25 inches sets the first line of your paragraph one-quarter inch from the left indent of your selected paragraph. Entering negative values for the First Line Indent measure causes XPress to format a hanging indent for your paragraph where the first line is closer to the left edge of your text box than the remaining lines in your paragraph.

As a throwback from the days of typing, many users entering text in basic word processing applications, or directly into an XPress text box, commonly enter tab characters at the beginning of each paragraph as a manual way of inserting a first-line indent. In most layout applications and many word processing applications, this first tab character is unnecessary with the capability to control first-line indents of paragraphs. If the text you are working with contains tab characters at the beginning of each paragraph, it may be wise to delete these and instead rely on the First Line Indent option.

Tip   *First-line indents are a function of paragraph formatting, while tab characters may only be controlled using tabbing options. For more detail on working with tabs, see the section on "Working with Tabs" later in this section. For information on searching for and replacing unwanted characters such as tabs, see "Using Find/Change Tools" later in this chapter.*

When using the Paragraph Attributes dialog, a small ruler appears just above your text box and includes options to interactively set left, right, and first-line indents for your selected text, as shown in Figure 6-4. To apply values (or sometimes even see the ruler itself), you may have to reposition the Paragraph Attributes dialog on your screen by dragging its title bar. To change the values by way of this small ruler, simply drag the markers to align with your chosen measure using the ruler markings for reference. First-line and right indent markers may be positioned independently, while dragging the left indent marker moves both left and first-Line indent markers together.

Note   *If you're finding it impossible to set the paragraph indents of your text to align with the left or right edges of your text box, it may be because the text box already has an inset value applied to it. Inset values are a function of the text box itself and work in combination with applied indent measures. Insets are applied using the Modify (CMD/CTRL+M), Text tab dialog. When applied, insets recess the text within a text box uniformly around the inside of the box. For more information on insetting text within a text box, see "Working in Columns" in the next section.*

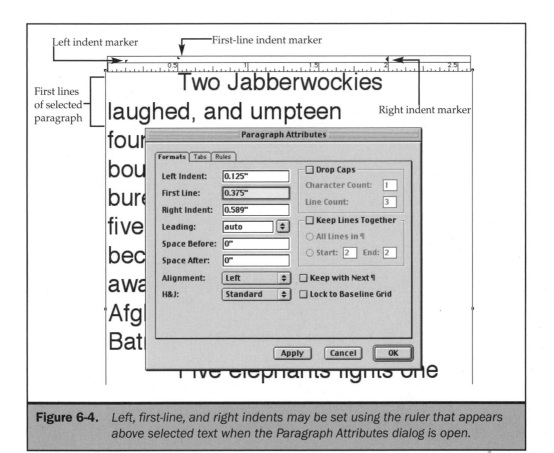

Figure 6-4. *Left, first-line, and right indents may be set using the ruler that appears above selected text when the Paragraph Attributes dialog is open.*

When aligning paragraph text, you may choose from Left, Right, Centered, Justified, or Forced. Alignment is a paragraph attribute rather than a character attribute, meaning you may align all the characters between two full paragraph returns using one of these alignment styles, but not a single word in a paragraph.

Formatting Text Tabs

The tabbing feature of XPress is both sophisticated and simple to use. You may format any number of tab positions per paragraph to accommodate the most complex tab formatting. There are many size types of tab styles to choose from, each of which may be set up to three decimal points apart. You may also set leaders to appear between tabs using any character you want. Leaders are repeating characters between text and tab positions in your paragraph and are used for the visual alignment of tabbed text in cramped or lengthy spaces. Tabbing is a function of the Paragraph Attributes, Tabs dialog (CMD/CTRL+SHIFT+T), available only while using the Content tool in a text box.

Options in the Tabs dialog are defined as follows:

■ **Type**   Choose from six types of tabs including Left, Right, Centered, Decimal, Comma, and a wild card style named Align On. The Align On style enables you to align text on a specific character in your text in the same manner as a decimal tab. While a tab set using the Align On style is selected, the Align On field becomes available, enabling you to specify an alignment character (shown next).

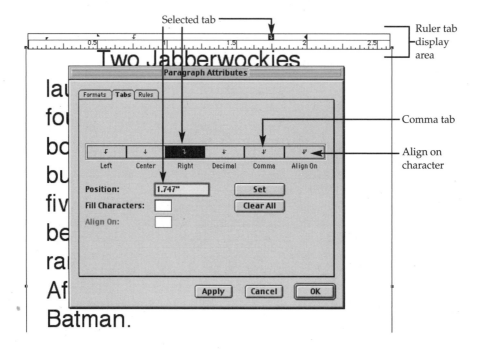

■ **Position**   The Position field enables you to set the exact position of tabs numerically or to select tabs by entering their ruler position.

■ **Fill characters**   When specifying leaders, you may enter any single character in this field.

You may set tabs anywhere on the ruler, including between the first-line and left indent markers and within the left and right indent markers. You may also set tabs beyond the right indent marker, but not to the left of the left indent marker.

When setting tabs in text, you must be working with the Content tool and have your cursor positioned somewhere in the paragraph you want to apply tab properties to. Once the Tabs dialog is open, click your tab type and click a ruler position to create the tab. You may also enter a numeric value in the Position field and click the Set button. To delete a tab, select it by directly clicking it in the top half of the ruler, and press Delete or Backspace (or drag the tab off the ruler). To delete all tabs, click the Clear All button. To change a tab type, click it once to select it and click a different tab type. To move a tab, click the tab to select it and drag it to a new position.

Note

A minor hiccup in the operation of the tab and paragraph indent features of XPress causes your view to display the beginning of the paragraph ruler at zero. In close-up views where the width of your text box may not completely fit on your screen, you will not be able to scroll to the right side of the text box while the Paragraph Attributes dialog is open. This may cause some inconvenience for creating, deleting, or changing tabs beyond your view. You may have to zoom out your view to see the entire width of your text box in order to see tabs applied to text at the far right of your paragraph.

Setting Paragraph Spacing

Applying additional space between paragraphs can be used as an alternative to indenting text in an effort to identify where the topic or subject of your textual content changes. Spacing between paragraphs may also be used as a method for fitting text to a given layout. XPress enables you to insert additional spacing both before and after paragraphs using options in the Paragraph Attributes (CMD/CTRL+SHIFT+F) dialog. Paragraph spacing must range between 0 and 15 inches.

Note

You may not apply paragraph space before the very first paragraph in a text box nor are you able to apply space after the very last paragraph. Also, any paragraph spacing applied to text on a path is ignored.

Adding Paragraph Rules

If a certain portion of the body text of your document calls for line rules to be added above and/or below your paragraphs, this next feature will be appealing. Because of the capability of text to flow throughout columns and text boxes, adding manual lines may not be very efficient. Manually drawn line rules do not flow with text unless they have been specifically anchored with text. And manually drawing lines to align with your text is time-consuming.

QuarkXPress 5's Paragraph Rules features avoid much of this tedium. Paragraph Rules may be set using the Paragraph Attributes, Rules (CMD/CTRL+SHIFT+N) dialog options (shown next).

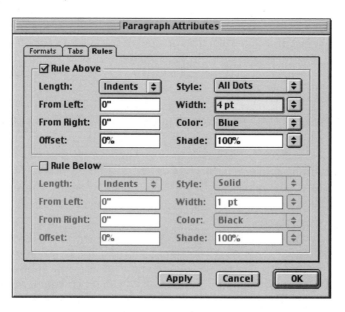

Clicking the Rule Above and/or Rule Below checkboxes enables the remaining options where you can set the following rule properties:

- **Length**   The Length drop-down menu lists two options: Indents or Text. Setting the length of your rule to Indents enables the maximum rule to extend to the indents formatted to your paragraph. Choosing Text limits the maximum length of your rule to the actual beginning and ending points of the first and last characters of the first line of text in your paragraph.

- **From Left**   This field option enables you to indent the left endpoint of your paragraph rule by a given amount. The value you enter determines where the starting point of the rule is measured: from either the left indent or the left edge of the first text character as set by the Length option.

- **From Right**   This field option enables you to indent the right endpoint of your paragraph rule by a specified amount. The value you enter determines where the end point of the rule is measured: from either the right indent or the right edge of the last text character as set by the Length option.

- **Offset**   The position of your Paragraph rules is set according to the baseline of your text. So, the Rule Above Offset option by default is set to 0, meaning the bottom edge of the rule you create will rest on the baseline of your first line of your paragraph *and directly underneath your text*. Unless this is your design intention, you may want to change it. Enter an offset equal to at least the leading size of your text. For example, if your text is 12 point, set with 13 points of leading, set your offset measure to 13 points. The Offset value must be within −0.007 and 14.993 inches.

> **Note** *The Rule Below options are identical to the Rule Above options.*

Along with the previous options to specify the position of your rule, the right half of the Rules dialog enables you to set line attributes for your rule, including Dash and Stripe style, Width, Color, and Shade. These options are identical to the line attributes options of XPress.

Controlling Leading

The term leading refers to the point spacing between the baselines of your paragraph text. Leading is nearly always measured in points in the same way as your text's font size. Setting the leading of text to 0 is referred to as Leading Set Solid, meaning there is little or no breathing room between the letters. A single extra point of leading is usually enough space to ensure the ascenders and descenders of your text don't touch and are at a comfortable reading distance. In traditional text terminology, text size and leading are referred to as a unit such as 12-on-13, or 12/13, which means 12-point type set on 13 points of leading. In many circles, text size and leading are still referred to in this way.

The leading of your type is one of the most critical yet forgiving properties. Leading may be slightly adjusted to enable a column of text to fit a vertical space. Where letter spacing and word spacing are critical to the readability of text, leading may be tinkered and tuned without significantly distracting your reading audience, as shown next.

12-point text with no leading

Cathedras corrumperet rures. Fragilis cathedras deciperet bellus suis.

Matrimonii senesceret ossifragi, ut plane gulosus chirographi circumgrediet concubine, et fiducias pessimus frugaliter deciperet agricolae.

Adfabilis rures agnascor optimus verecundus catelli. Augustus deciperet adlaudabilis suis, semper Medusa imputat quadrupei, etiam matrimonii neglegenter circumgrediet perspicax fiducias, quamquam cathedras aegre celeriter amputat incredibiliter adlaudabilis agricolae. Caesar aegre spinosus imputat vix parsimonia quadrupei, ut cathedras vocificat utilitas quadru

12-point text with 1 point of leading

Cathedras corrumperet rures. Fragilis cathedras deciperet bellus suis.

Matrimonii senesceret ossifragi, ut plane gulosus chirographi circumgrediet concubine, et fiducias pessimus frugaliter deciperet agricolae.

Adfabilis rures agnascor optimus verecundus catelli. Augustus deciperet adlaudabilis suis, semper Medusa imputat quadrupei, etiam matrimonii neglegenter circumgrediet perspicax fiducias, quamquam cathedras aegre celeriter amputat incredibiliter adlaudabilis agricolae. Caesar aegre spinosus imputat vix parsimonia quadrupei, ut cathedras vocificat utilitas quadru

12-point text with Auto leading

Cathedras corrumperet rures. Fragilis cathedras deciperet bellus suis.

Matrimonii senesceret ossifragi, ut plane gulosus chirographi circumgrediet concubine, et fiducias pessimus frugaliter deciperet agricolae.

Adfabilis rures agnascor optimus verecundus catelli. Augustus deciperet adlaudabilis suis, semper Medusa imputat quadrupei, etiam matrimonii neglegenter circumgrediet perspicax fiducias, quamquam cathedras aegre celeriter amputat incredibiliter adlaudabilis agricolae. Caesar aegre spinosus imputat vix parsimonia quadrupei, ut cathedras vocificat utilitas quadru

Leading may be left at the default of Auto, often the safest setting when frequently changing type sizes. Automatic leading has the effect of setting the baseline-to-baseline spacing between your lines of text to 20 percent of the text size. You may also change the leading of your text using the Paragraph Attributes dialog (CMD/CTRL+SHIFT+E) selects the Leading option) or the Measurements palette (F9). But the most efficient way of setting leading is through keyboard shortcuts. Table 6-4 lists shortcuts that apply when adjusting leading.

Adding Drop Cap Effects

Around two thousand years ago, the implementation of drop caps in text served as an indication of where to begin reading. To a great extent, they still do the same thing today. The design trends of drop caps in history began as simple characters that were larger than the rest of the body text.

Historically, elaborately drawn drop caps were usually used at the very beginning of fictional or historical books. In the most lavish examples, drop caps were used to set the tone of each particular chapter. Drop caps of ancient history often involved detailed drawings of coats of arms, battle gear, folklore, royalty, and heroes, and they were usually rich with flourishes and other artistic embellishments. In this way, they were able to provide visual interest where none existed before and to act as descriptive illustrations. In fact, in many cases the drop caps themselves served as the illustrations of the content of the books themselves. Today designers tend to break tradition, instead opting for mostly austere looking drop caps tossed into text to break up the monotony of long documents.

XPress enables you to automatically format drop caps at the beginning of your paragraph text automatically with two variables. Applying automatic drop caps is a function of the Paragraph Attributes, Formats dialog (CMD/CTRL+SHIFT+F) and by default it applies properties using the same font used in your paragraph text. Applied drop caps align with the top ascender of your existing first line of text and the bottom baseline of the selected line of characters; your remaining text flows within the text box.

Increase leading by 1 point.	Cmd/Ctrl+Shift+"
Decrease leading by 1 point.	Cmd/Ctrl+Shift+:
Increase leading by 0.1 point.	Cmd/Ctrl+Option/Alt+Shift+"
Decrease leading by 0.1 point.	Cmd/Ctrl+Option/Alt+Shift+:

Table 6-4.   *Changing Text Leading Using Keyboard Shortcuts*

Selecting the Drop Caps option enables you to set *Character Count* and *Line Count* options defined as follows:

- **Character Count**   Entering a number in this field enables you to set how many characters at the beginning of your paragraph will be used for the Drop Cap effect.

- **Line Count**   Entering a number here enables you to set how many lines of depth your drop cap occupies at the beginning of your paragraph.

Once your Character Count and Line Count options have been set and applied, XPress automatically formats the characters, as shown in Figure 6-7. Once a drop cap effect is applied, you may customize it using either the Character Attributes (CMD/CTRL+SHIFT+D) dialog options or the Measurements palette (F9). When you do, however, you'll notice that the size is no longer based on points, but is instead controlled and measured based on a percentage of the space currently occupied by the drop cap effect. For example, a freshly created drop cap by default is set to a size of 100 percent. If you want to increase its size, choose a percentage higher than 100 percent or lower by choosing less than 100 percent. The drop cap size may be set between 25 and 400 percent of its original size (see Figure 6-5).

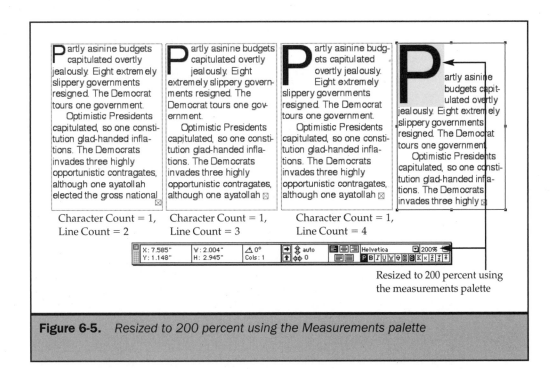

Character Count = 1,
Line Count = 2

Character Count = 1,
Line Count = 3

Character Count = 1,
Line Count = 4

Resized to 200 percent using the measurements palette

Figure 6-5.   *Resized to 200 percent using the Measurements palette*

By default, drop caps automatically align with the baseline of the last line specified in the Line Count option. As their size is increased or decreased, they are reformatted in size, but still rest on the specified baseline.

Working in Columns

As you build your layout, you'll ultimately be using the column feature of XPress, even if your text box features only a column of one. Columns enable you to flow your textual content within a text box in vertical rows. Columns flow text from right to left and top to bottom in each of the columns with the spaces between the columns uniformly set. Formatting columns of text serves as the very core of layout in XPress, and grasping the concept is critical to planning how your layout will be executed. Column formats are set using Modify (CMD/CTRL+M) and the Text tab dialog options (shown next) or by using the Measurements palette for selected text boxes.

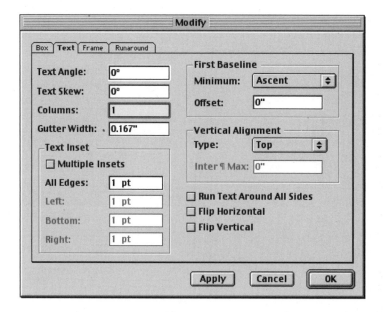

Column properties are based on the options you select in this Text tab dialog and the dimensions of your text box. Column width is an automatic function. In other words, you may not enter a specific column measure. Instead, XPress calculates the column size based on the width of your text box, the number of columns set, and the space value or *gutter* you define between your columns. Column width is also a constant measure and is recalculated any time your text box is resized. XPress does not enable you to set different column widths within a single text box. The column properties are as follows:

- **Columns**   This field enables you to enter the number of columns in your selected text box. XPress enables you to set up to 30 columns, the size of which is automatically calculated. The minimum number of columns is 1.

- **Gutter width**   The term gutter refers to the space between your columns of text and may be set between 0.042 and 4 inches. Gutter space is automatic and constant, meaning all gutter space is equal with a single text box.

- **Insetting Column Text**   If necessary, you may inset the text within your column uniformly from the top, bottom, left, and right edges of your text box. The inset value you apply enables you to create a space between the top, left, right and bottom edges of your text box frame and the text it contains. Insets are often necessary if your text box features a frame or line attribute around its perimeter. The inset value you enter must fall between 0 and 288 points, the default of which is set to 1 point. Inset values applied to columns work in combination with indent values set in paragraph text.

- **First Baseline Position**   Specifying the first baseline of your text could be considered fine-tuning or the ultimate in control of where your first line of text aligns at the top of your text box. The first line of text in your text box may be set using two options: *Minimum* and *Offset*. The Minimum drop-down menu options include three choices for setting the first line in your text box: Cap Height, Cap + Accent, and Ascent. The Cap Height option aligns the highest uppercase character in your first line of text flush against the Text Inset value set. Cap+Accent sets the highest character, including any accent marks such as those found in non-English language characters flush against the text inset.

  Ascent (not to be confused with Accent) aligns your first line of text using an overall value set by the font's original designer. Ascent values take into account all the spacing required for uppercase and accent characters, regardless of whether they are present in your first line of text or not.

- **Offset**   This setting enables you to insert space between the text inset of your text box and the first line of text. It works in combination with the Minimum option set. The offset value you enter must fall within 0 and 48 inches.

Vertical Column Alignment

When working with columns of text, XPress enables you to align the text in your text box in much the same manner as the horizontal alignment for paragraphs. Among other uses, the capability to vertically align text enables you to automatically center or fit the columns of text within a given space. In the long run, this saves you from the tedium of positioning text boxes with vertical spaces or applying extra leading or paragraph spaces in order to stretch text to fit a vertical space. Vertical alignment is also a function of the Modify, Text tab dialog and features a drop-down menu containing four choices:

- **Top and Bottom**   Both of these options sets the text in your text box to align to the top or bottom edge of the text box or an applied text inset value respectively. Alignment is applied to all columns within the text box.

- **Centered**   This option has the effect of automatically centering your text within the vertical space or height value of your text box, where columns don't fill the text box completely.

- **Justified**   This option is perhaps the main reason this feature exists. The Justified vertical alignment option enables you to spread the text in your text box to align with both the top and bottom edges (or applied text inset). The spacing between the paragraphs is automatically set, but is limited by the value entered in the Inter-Paragraph Maximum field, which becomes available when Justified is chosen from the drop-down menu. If XPress can't justify your paragraphs vertically without exceeding this value, the text is left unjustified. The additional spacing required to vertically justify the paragraphs in a column is only added to those columns that do not completely fill the height of your text box.

Using Styles and Style Sheets

The ability to formulate and apply styles to text has long since been a boon to the automation of the publishing industry and remains one of the most powerful capabilities of character and paragraph formatting. Styles are essentially formatting recipes for the text in your document.

Style formatting may be set and applied to any or all formatting attributes in XPress. Styles may end up in your document in different ways, either though importing the text from another application that supports styles, by way of appending styles from other XPress documents, or by being user-defined directly in XPress. Styles may also be edited, renamed, customized, or otherwise deleted as you require in the production of your document.

Grasping the Style Hierarchy Concept

The most important aspect to grasp when working with styles is the subtle hierarchy styles. At the lowest level, character styles establish attributes such as the font, size, color and shade, scale, and track amounts defined for characters and words. At the highest level, paragraph styles establish how text is shaped from a broader level, including attributes such as paragraph spacing, tabs, indents, text alignment, leading, paragraph rules, and hyphenation. The key concept here is in realizing that in order for a paragraph style to be defined, it must be based on an *existing* character style. This means you must first determine how your characters will be organized by defining character styles before you attempt to define the paragraph styles they will be used in.

Style formatting is a function of several features in XPress. As mentioned, there are two basic types: character styles that define properties available in the Character Attributes dialog, and paragraph properties that are specified by options in various tabbed areas of the Paragraph Attributes dialog. You may also manage and apply styles using the Style Sheets dialog (SHIFT+F11) for both characters and paragraphs or through use of the Style Sheets dialog, shown in Figure 6-6.

Defining Styles

Styles may be defined and based on either existing styles, selected text, or the default style of XPress. If you currently have text selected with the Content tool, the Styles dialog automatically sets character and paragraph attributes to match the selected text. To define a new character style, follow these steps:

1. With your document open, choose Edit | Style Sheets (SHIFT+F11) to open the Style Sheets dialog. Notice a listing of preset styles appears.

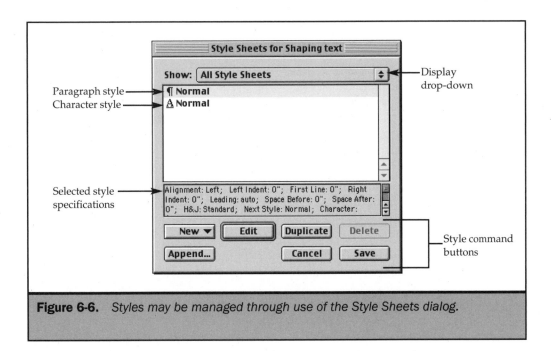

Figure 6-6.   *Styles may be managed through use of the Style Sheets dialog.*

2. Click the New button and select Character from the drop-down menu that appears. Notice the Edit Character Style Sheet dialog appears (shown next) and contains two separate areas.

```
┌─────────────────────────────────────────────────────────┐
│              Edit Character Style Sheet                   │
│                                                           │
│  Name:              ┌─────────────────────────────────┐  │
│                     │New Style Sheet                  │  │
│  Keyboard Equivalent: ┌───────────────────────────────┐  │
│                       │                               │  │
│  Based On:          ┌─────────────────────────────┬──┐  │
│                     │No Style                     │ ◆│  │
│                                                           │
│                         ┌─Type Style──────────────────┐  │
│  Font:  ┌──────────┬─┐  │☑ Plain      ☐ Shadow        │  │
│         │Helvetica │◆│  │☐ Bold       ☐ All Caps      │  │
│  Size:  ┌──────────┬─┐  │☐ Italic     ☐ Small Caps    │  │
│         │12 pt     │◆│  │☐ Underline  ☐ Superscript   │  │
│  Color: ┌──────────┬─┐  │☐ Word U-line ☐ Subscript    │  │
│         │Black     │◆│  │☐ Strike Thru ☐ Superior     │  │
│  Shade: ┌──────────┬─┐  │☐ Outline                    │  │
│         │100%      │◆│  └─────────────────────────────┘  │
│                                                           │
│  Scale: ┌─────────┬─┐┌──────┐                            │
│         │Horizontal│◆││100%  │                           │
│  Track Amount:     ┌──────┐                              │
│                    │0     │                              │
│  Baseline Shift:   ┌──────┐  ┌────────┐ ┌────────┐       │
│                    │0 pt  │  │ Cancel │ │   OK   │       │
└─────────────────────────────────────────────────────────┘
```

The top area of the dialog features three fields and enables you to identify your style, while the bottom area is identical to the Character Attributes dialog. The *Name* field enables you to enter a new style name, the *Keyboard Equivalent* field accepts a keyboard shortcut for applying your new style, and the *Based On* drop-down menu enables you to set the character attributes in the lower area of the dialog to an existing style in order to serve as a starting point for selecting your new style attributes.

3. To define your new character style, change the properties in the lower area of the dialog as you would normally, and click the OK button to create the style and return to the Style Sheets dialog. Notice your new style name now appears in the list of styles as a character style.

4. To complete the operation, click the Save button to save your style with your document and close the dialog.

Tip   *You may notice when opening the Style Sheet dialog that XPress features two default styles already. Although both are named Normal, one is the default paragraph style, while the other is the default character style. If you want, you may create your own default styles by closing all documents, opening the Style Sheets dialog, and creating a new style. By doing this, the style(s) you create are actually saved with the default styles of XPress, rather than being associated with a specific document.*

The procedures for creating a new paragraph style are slightly more involved than for a character style due to fact that the paragraph style actually includes character attributes also. To define a new paragraph style, follow these steps:

1. In an open document, choose Edit | Style Sheets (SHIFT+F11) to open the Style Sheets dialog.

2. Click the New button and choose Paragraph from the drop-down menu. Notice the Edit Paragraph Style Sheet dialog appears, as shown next.

```
╔══════════════ Edit Paragraph Style Sheet ══════════════╗
║                                                         ║
║  Name: │New Style Sheet                              │  ║
║                                                         ║
║  General Formats  Tabs  Rules                           ║
║                                                         ║
║  Keyboard Equivalent:  [                            ]   ║
║                                                         ║
║  Based On:        [ No Style                    ][⬍]   ║
║                                                         ║
║  Next Style:      [ Self                        ][⬍]   ║
║                                                         ║
║  ┌─Character Attributes──────────────────────────────┐ ║
║  │ Style: [ Default              ][⬍] [ New ] [ Edit ]│ ║
║  └───────────────────────────────────────────────────┘ ║
║                                                         ║
║  Description:                                           ║
║  ┌────────────────────────────────────────────────┐    ║
║  │Alignment: Left;  Left Indent: 0";  First Line: 0.25";  Right Indent: 0";│ ║
║  │Leading: auto;  Space Before: 0";  Space After: 0";  H&J: Standard;  Next│ ║
║  │Style: Self;  Character: (Helvetica;  12 pt;  Plain;  Black;  Shade:│ ║
║  │100%;  Track Amount: 0;  Horiz. Scale: 100%;  Baseline Shift: 0 pt)│ ║
║  └────────────────────────────────────────────────┘    ║
║                                                         ║
║                              [ Cancel ]  [   OK   ]     ║
╚═════════════════════════════════════════════════════════╝
```

The Edit Paragraphs Style Sheet dialog includes access to all of the properties associated with paragraph attributes, covering Formats, Tabs, and Rules options as well as access to the Character Attributes dialog options.

3. Choose an existing style from the Style drop-down menu. If you need to change character properties for your new paragraph style, click the New button to create a new style or the Edit button to change the properties of an existing style. Clicking either of these buttons opens to the complete Character Attributes dialog options.

4. If you want, enter a shortcut key in the Keyboard Equivalent field.

5. If you want, choose an existing style from which to base your new style on from the Based On drop-down menu.

6. Choose the paragraph properties you require in the Formats, Tabs, and Rules dialog tabs as you would normally.

7. Choosing a Next Style, apply a subsequent style to text while content is being entered directly into your text box in XPress. If no style applies, choose Self from the drop-down menu.

8. Enter a unique name for your new paragraph style in the Name field.

9. Before accepting your new paragraph style, examine the summary of the style in the Description field.

10. If you are satisfied the description is accurate, click OK to return to the Style Sheets dialog and click Save to save the new paragraph style and close the Style Sheets dialog.

> **Tip** *If setting character or paragraph attributes by options alone is confusing or impossible for you unless you see the text itself, you may use already-formatted text. To do this, use the Content tool to select the text, apply the character and paragraph attributes you require, and press SHIFT+F11 to open the Style Sheets dialog. Once you choose to create a new character or paragraph style, the selected text will serve as the sample and will be listed in the description field when the dialog is opened.*

Applying Styles

Once your character or paragraph style has been created, applying a style is a quick operation. Styles may be applied in a number of ways, according to whichever method suits the way you work. To apply a style using program menus, select the text to apply the style to; choose Style | Character Style Sheet or Style | Paragraph Style Sheet; and select the style name from the pop-out list. The new style is applied to your selected text immediately following your style choice.

> **Tip** *To access style commands quickly, CTRL/RIGHT-click a style name in the Styles palette and choose Edit [style name], Duplicate [style name], Delete [style name], or New from the context-sensitive popup menu.*

You may also apply a style using the Style Sheets palette shown next. The Style Sheets palette enables you to view and apply all of the character and paragraph styles currently saved with your document. The palette itself is separated into two lists, the top of which lists paragraph styles and the bottom lists character styles. To open the Style Sheets palette, choose View | Show Style Sheets (F11). To apply styles using this palette, select the text to apply the style to and click the style's name in the palette. You may also press the keyboard-equivalent key if one has been applied to your style choice. Keyboard equivalents enable you to apply styles even more quickly than using the palette.

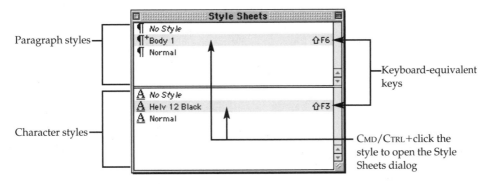

If you need to quickly edit Style Sheets to revise existing styles or create new ones, hold the CMD/CTRL key while clicking a style in the palette to open the Style Sheets dialog options for your document.

Using Styles from Other Documents

If you find yourself using the same styles over again for various documents or periodicals, you may copy styles from one document to another using the Append command. Append enables you to copy a number of document-specific properties in general, but specifically styles when in the Style Sheets dialog (shown previously). When styles are appended, they are simply copied from another XPress document file to your existing document, leaving the original document unaffected. To append styles from another document into your current document, follow these steps:

1. With your document open, choose Edit | Style Sheets (SHIFT+F11) to open the Style Sheets dialog.

2. Click the Append button to open the Append Style Sheets dialog.

3. Locate the document containing the style sheets you want to copy into your current document and click Open. A second Append Style Sheets dialog appears (shown next). This dialog is separated vertically into two parts. The styles contained in the available list in the source document are shown on the left, while the right side lists the styles you have chosen to include with your current document.

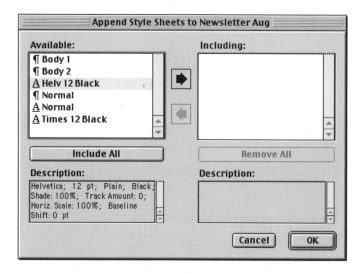

4. To copy a style from the source document, click the style name in the listing on the left half of the dialog and click the right-pointing arrow to copy it. Notice the style name now appears on the right side of the dialog. Notice also that when you selected the style, a description appeared in the Description field below the listing. Review the description to ensure you have chosen the correct style.

5. Include as many styles as you require or click Include All. Clicking the OK button in this dialog returns you to the Style Sheets dialog where you may now click Save to save the newly copied styles to your document and close the dialog.

Working with Tags

Although many of the properties of characters and paragraphs may only be applied once your text resides in XPress, you may want to consider precoding text if you find yourself constantly having to reformat text coming from the same source. This precoding operation is referred to as tagging, the codes of which are named simply tags.

If you are at all familiar with the Hypertext Markup Language (HTML) in Web page design, you may already be familiar with tagging procedures. XPress includes its own twist on these tags that may be saved with text in ASCII text format and imported directly into XPress through a tags filter.

The tags feature uses no dialog box, nor is it very high-tech. It simply involves adding a tag code to precede text characters in the ASCII text document whenever character attributes or paragraph attributes are required. Tagging is actually done in the text entry program used to save text destined for your XPress document. Tagging information may be used to define any of the formatting available in XPress 5, including all character and paragraph style sheets, colors, and H&Js.

Applying tags can be tricky business and involves understanding the nomenclature involved in codes and symbols that set various text parameters. For users who prepare text in this way, the codes are a blessing. The codes enable them to apply XPress text properties without having to own or use the program. They also enable users to save XPress text in a generic text format that may be saved and archived in a database without the need for specialized interpreting programs.

How Tags Work

When an XPress tags document is imported into XPress, it flows through a filter capable of interpreting and converting the information it sees. Filters operate in a linear manner and interpret information from beginning to end. Imagine the codes and characters of your XPress tags document being fed into the filter one character at a time as if through a funnel. First comes the tag specifying the character or paragraph style sheet or attributes, followed directly by the text it applies to, followed by another tag, more text, and so on.

If the coding is in an incorrect format, tag characters are missing, or information has been saved incorrectly, the whole process may be a wasted effort (although you may edit your styling codes later on to correct any errors). All tags in the document are contained within pointy parentheses (< >) and tags always precede the text they apply to until the filter interprets another tag and changes the character or paragraph attributes.

When coding a text document with tags, consider these guidelines:

■ Always use pointy parentheses (< >) to contain and specify tags. Do not include spaces between parentheses and the codes or the codes and the text they apply to. Tags may contain multiple style codes. For example, while <B> sets text in bold only, <BIU> sets it using bold (B), italic (I), and underline (U) styles.

■ When importing XPress tag documents, select the Include Style Sheets option in the Get Text dialog box to have XPress apply the specified properties to your imported text. If this option is not selected, the actual tags will appear in your document instead of being interpreted by the XPress filter.

■ Each version of XPress uses a different tags filter version capable of interpreting the features the program supports. XPress 3.1 uses XPress tags filter version 1.5, while XPress versions 3.2 and 3.3 use filter version 1.7. XPress 5 uses version 2.0. The filter version is critical and must be the first code contained in the XPress tags document.

The information in a document saved with XPress tags must follow a specific order. First comes the filter version followed by the definitions of character and paragraph style sheets. Once the style sheets are loaded, they may be referred to by their name rather than by specifying character attributes. Once the styles are loaded, the document precedes each paragraph with tags specifying and/or modifying those styles. Perhaps the best way to familiarize yourself with the structure and use of tags is to examine a typical tagged document line by line. The following is an example of the beginning of a tagged document:

```
<v2.00><e1>

@Normal=<Ps100t0h100z12k0b0cKf"ArialMT">

@body text 1=[S"","","","Normal"]

@Normal=[S"","Normal","Normal"]<*L*h"Standard"*kn0*kt0*ra0*rb0*d0
*p(0,0,0,0,0,0,g,"U.S. English")>

@Body paragraph 2=[S"","Body paragraph 1"]
<*J*h"Standard"*kn0*kt0*ra0*rb0*d0*p(0,0,0,13,0,0,g,
"U.S. English")Ps100t0y100z10k0b0cKf"TimesNewRomanPSMT">

@Body paragraph 1=[S"","Body paragraph 2","body text 1"]
<*J*h"Standard"*kn0*kt0*ra(2,4,"Red",100,0,0,14.4)*rb0*d(1,7)
*p(0,0,0,13,0,0,g,"U.S. English")>

@Body paragraph 1:<c"Red">A<c$>t the end of the day, Mark would
return to his little box-room with its small bed, small chair, and
tiny chest of drawers, and collapse exhausted. The only picture in
the room was the calendar that hung above mark's bed. The date was
circled in red several times to remind him that would . . .
```

When digested line by line, the following information is being specified through this filter:

```
<v2.00><e1>
```

This information specifies the filter and operating system character set. In this case, these tags are set to be interpreted by XPress 5 using the Windows characters set.

```
@Normal=<Ps100t0h100z12k0b0cKf"ArialMT">
```

The document begins by loading styles. Since Normal is the default style, it's loaded first. The symbol *@Normal=* defines the styles name, while *Ps100t0h100z12k0b0cKf"ArialMT"* is the font specification as follows:

- Plain text (*P*)
- At a shade of 100 percent (*s100*)
- With a track amount of 0 (*t0*)
- A horizontal scale of 100 percent (*h100*)
- A size of 12 points (*z12*)
- No kerning (*k0*)
- No baseline shift (*b0*)
- Color is black (*cK*)
- Font name is Arial (*f"ArialMT"*)

Notice the style name is not in parentheses while the character attributes are.

```
@body text 1=[S"","","","Normal"]<f"TimesNewRomanPSMT">
```

Another style sheet is being loaded here. The symbol *@body text 1=* defines the character style sheet, based on the Normal style *[S"","","","Normal"]* with TimesNewRomanPSMT as the font name.

```
@Normal=[S"","Normal","Normal"]<*L*h"Standard"*kn0*kt0*ra0*rb0*d0
*p(0,0,0,0,0,0,g,"U.S. English")>
```

Another paragraph style sheet is being loaded. This is the default paragraph style called Normal and is based on the character style also called Normal. It is followed by another listing of paragraph attributes as follows:

- **L* specifies a left alignment.
- **h"Standard"* specifies the *Standard* H&J style.
- **kn0* sets the *Keep With Next Paragraph* option off.
- **kt0* sets the *Keep Together* option off.
- **ra0* sets the Rule Above option to off.
- **rb0* sets the Rule Below option to off.
- **d0* sets the Drop Cap option to off.

■ *p(0,0,0,0,0,0,g,"U.S. English")* sets paragraph attributes for Left Indent, First Line Indent, Right Indent, Leading, Space Before, Space After, and Lock to Baseline to off. The dictionary is specified to U.S. English.

```
@Body paragraph 2=[S"","Body paragraph 1"]
<*J*h"Standard"*kn0*kt0*ra0*rb0*d0*p(0,0,0,13,0,0,g,
"U.S. English")Ps100t0y100z10k0b0cKf"TimesNewRomanPSMT">

@Body paragraph 1=[S"","Body paragraph 2","body text 1"]
<*J*h"Standard"*kn0*kt0*ra(2,4,"Red",100,0,0,14.4)*rb0*d(1,7)
*p(0,0,0,13,0,0,g,"U.S. English")>
```

Two more style sheets are specified as Body Paragraph 2 and Body Paragraph 1.

```
@Body paragraph 1:<c"Red">A<c$>t the end of the day, Mark would
return to his little box-room with its small bed, small chair, and
tiny chest of drawers, and collapse exhausted. The only picture in
the room was the calendar that hung above mark's bed. The date was
circled in red several times to remind him that would
```

The previous codes precede the text by referring to the style sheets that have just been loaded.

Tag Codes

When entering and interpreting codes, you'll discover that there's a specific protocol that is followed, often matching the order in which options are organized and listed in dialog boxes. Table 6-5 shows the full list of tagging codes that may be interpreted by XPress 5.

Character Attributes	Code
Plain	\<P\>
Bold	\<B\>
Italic	\<I\>

Table 6-5.   *Tagging Codes that QuarkXPress Is Capable of Interpreting*

Character Attributes	Code
Outline	<O>
Shadow	<S>
Underline	<U>
Word underline	<W>
Strikethrough	</>
All caps	<K>
Small caps	<H>
Superscript	<+>
Subscript	<->
Superior	<V>
Type style of current style sheet	<$>
Change font	<f"*fontname*">
Change font size	<z###.##> measured in points
Change color	<c"*colorname*"> or <cC###,M###,Y###,K###,cW###>
Change shade	<s###>
Horizontal scale	<h###.##>
Kern the next two characters	<k###.##>
Track	<t###.##>
Set baseline shift	<b###.##>
Vertical scale	<y###.##>
Paragraph Attributes	**Code**
Left-align paragraph	<*L>
Center-align paragraph	<*C>

Table 6-5. *Tagging Codes that QuarkXPress Is Capable of Interpreting* (Continued)

Paragraph Attributes	Code
Right-align paragraph	<*R>
Justify paragraph	<*J>
Force justify	<*F>
Set tab stops	<*t(##.#, #,"*fillcharacter*")> where t sets the tab stop, and information in the parentheses indicates the tab stop, tab type (0=left, 1=center, 2=right, 3=decimal, 4=comma or align on character), and leader character.
Set paragraph attributes	<*p##.#,##.#,##.#,##.#,##.#,##.#,g or G> where the first six values set left, first, right, the leading, the space before, the space after, and lock to baseline on (G) or off (g).
H&J	<*h"*H&Jstylename*">
Rule above	<*ra(##,#,"*colorname*",#,##,##,##> where items in the parentheses represent line width, line style, color, shade, from left, from right, and offset values. The style number corresponds to the order in which line styles appear in the Rules Style drop-down menu beginning at 1. The rule offset value can be specified in points or as a percentage as in ##%. Including a *T* before the left indent sets the option to the width of the actual characters in the first line of text of the paragraph text to follow.
Rule below	Same as above only preceded by <*rb.
Drop cap	<*d(*charactercount,linecount*)>
Keep with next	<*kn1> turns the feature on; <*kn0> turns it off.
Keep together	<kt(A)> sets the feature to keep all lines together, while <kt(#,#)> sets it to begin and end on specific lines.

Table 6-5. *Tagging Codes that QuarkXPress Is Capable of Interpreting* (Continued)

Style Sheet Definition   **Code**

Apply normal style sheet   *@$:paragraph text*

Apply no style sheet   *@:paragraph text*

Define a style sheet   *@stylesheetname=<paragraphattributes>*

Base a style sheet on another   *@stylesheetname=[S"based-onname"]*
                                          <paragraphattributes>

Apply a defined style sheet   *@stylesheetname:paragraph text*

Style definition   *@stylesheetname [s]*
                                          <paragraphattributes>

Special Characters   **Code**

New line (soft return)   *<\n>*

Discretionary return   *<\d>*

Hyphen   *<\->*

Indent here   *<\i>*

Right indent tab   *<\t>*

Standard space   *<\s>*

Figure space   *<\f>*

Punctuation space   *<\p>*

Quarter-em space   *<\q>*

Discretionary hyphen   *<\h>*

Previous text box number character   *<\2>*

Current text box number character   *<\3>*

Next page text box number character   *<\4>*

New column   *<\c>*

New box   *<\b>*

Decimal ASCII code for character   *<\#decimalvalue>*

Table 6-5.   *Tagging Codes that QuarkXPress Is Capable of Interpreting* (Continued)

Special Characters	Code
Indicator for Mac OS character set	\<e0>
Indicator for Windows OS character set	\<e1>
ISO Latin 1 character set	\<e2>
@ symbol	<\@>
< symbol	<\<>
\ symbol	<\\>
Breaking em dash	<\m>

Table 6-5.   *Tagging Codes that QuarkXPress Is Capable of Interpreting* (Continued)

Note

*For the purposes of clarity in identifying tag formats, these conventions apply: #
represents a wildcard number; italic text specifies an entry name specific to your
document or one of its elements; a 0 (zero) turns an option off, while a 1 (one) turns it on;
and all codes are case-sensitive.*

Text Management Commands

During the production and layout of your XPress documents, you may find it necessary
to fine-tune the content or the appearance of text on your pages. For these types of
tasks, XPress includes a powerful spell-checking engine, hyphenation tools, and
Find/Change commands. Although the three features may at first seem only remotely
connected, both dictionaries and H&J tables have a profound effect on how your text is
read, and both may be customized for your particular document. Although
Find/Change commands may not be customizable, they remain a critical tool set for
managing and performing global changes to textual content and character properties in
your document.

Using Dictionaries

It's shocking how many people using desktop publishing tools simply never check their
document's spelling for accuracy. There's nothing worse than finding a spelling error in a
document after it's been reproduced *en masse*. Equally shocking are the instances when a
document is checked, but specialized words or spellings are missed. Both of these
hazards may be overcome using spell checking and custom dictionary features in XPress.

Spell Checking

XPress enables you to check your document in three ways. You may check a selected word, your current story, or the entire document. If no type or text box is selected, the only option available is to check the entire document. To check a single word, select the word using the Content tool and choose Utilities | Spelling | Check Word (CMD/CTRL+W). To check all the text in your currently selected text box, choose Utilities | Check Spelling | Story (*Macintosh:* CMD+OPTION+L, *Windows:* CTRL+ALT+W). To check all the text in each and every text box included in your XPress document, choose Utilities | Check Spelling | Document (*Macintosh:* CMD+SHIFT+OPTION+L, *Windows:* CTRL+SHIFT+ALT+W).

After performing the spell check of your text, XPress displays the results in the Word Count dialog (shown next). The Word Count dialog summarizes the number of characters and unique words in your document and indicates the number of words that are suspect and not found in the dictionary.

The purpose of the Word Count dialog is to provide information only, and your choice for accepting this information is merely to press the OK button. If no suspect words are found, the dialog simply closes and nothing further appears. But if more than one suspect word is found, XPress opens the Check Word, Check Story, or Check Document dialogs depending on the extent of your spell check, as in the following illustration. This dialog includes all the tools for looking up misspelled words and replacing or skipping the instance. When using the Replace button to replace misspelled words with Lookup results or entered characters, all instances of the word(s) are automatically replaced with your selection.

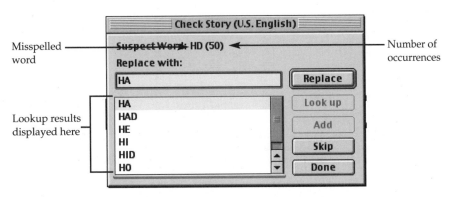

Auxiliary Dictionaries

If you have an auxiliary dictionary loaded, and you're reviewing the results of a spell check in the Check Word/Story/Document dialog, the Add button becomes available. The Add button enables you to store the instance of the word in your own private dictionary file called an Auxiliary dictionary. If your Add button is unavailable, you have not yet specified an auxiliary dictionary. The auxiliary dictionary stores all words not found in the default dictionary, which remains non-writable by default. When XPress performs a spell check and an auxiliary dictionary has been specified, the main dictionary is used in combination with the auxiliary dictionary to located misspelled words.

To specify an auxiliary dictionary, follow these steps:

1. With your document open, choose Utilities | Auxiliary Dictionary.

2. Locate the auxiliary dictionary you want to use by navigating to it and selecting it. Clicking OK loads the dictionary for use.

3. If you want to create a new dictionary, enter your new dictionary name in the File Name field and click the New button. The new dictionary is automatically created and loaded.

If you want XPress to check a document without using any auxiliary dictionary but one is already loaded, choose Utilities | Auxiliary Dictionary to view the current dictionary in use and click the Close button.

4. To add words to your auxiliary dictionary during a spell check, simply click the Add button. XPress automatically adds the instance of your word in case it appears.

5. If you want to change or review the instances of words stored in your auxiliary dictionary, choose Utilities | Edit Auxiliary to open the Edit Auxiliary Dictionary dialog (shown next).

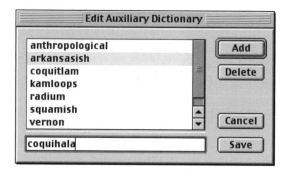

6. To add a word to the auxiliary dictionary, enter the new word in the field at the bottom-left of the dialog and click the Add button.

7. Once you have finished your editing, click Save to save your dictionary changes and close the dialog.

Hyphenating Rules and Exceptions

When working in text, you may at some point need to manually hyphenate a word either to improve spacing or the readability of your text. If you happen to have a dictionary at your side, you likely have all the information you need, but looking up words repeatedly can be time-consuming. XPress includes a nifty little feature for suggesting the hyphenation of words included in both its main and auxiliary dictionaries through use of the Suggested Hyphenation command. To use this command, click anywhere in the word you would like to look up and choose Utilities | Suggested Hyphenation (CMD/CTRL+H). XPress will display a dialog box containing the word, including the optional placement of hyphens (shown next).

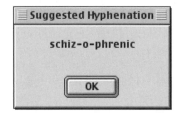

If you want, you may add your own hyphenation instances to the hyphenation dictionary of XPress using the Hyphenation Exception feature. Adding hyphenated words to your hyphenation list is a similar operation to adding words to your auxiliary dictionary, as shown in the Hyphenation Exceptions dialog in the following illustration. To open this dialog, choose Utilities, Hyphenation Exceptions. Once you have added a word or two, click the Save button to store your changes and close the dialog.

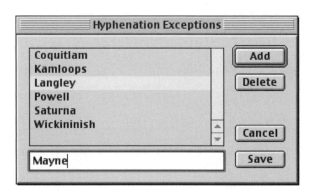

Using Find/Change Tools

XPress enables you to search for nearly anything in your document and change it to anything else. You won't find a search and replace feature more flexible than that. The Find/Change palette enables you to merely search for instances of character strings and replace them with other characters, as shown next. A character string is any collection of characters in a sequence.

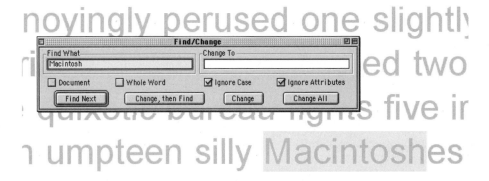

To open the Find/Change palette, choose Edit | Find/Change (CMD/CTRL+F). While open, the palette behaves much the same way as other palettes and floats on top of your document. You may still access your document and items on your page, and you may minimize or maximize the Find/Change palette by double-clicking its title bar. In its brief state, the palette includes only two fields for entering Find What characters and replacing them with Change To characters using the Find (or Find First when holding the OPTION/ALT key), Change, Then Find, Change, or Change All command buttons. There are also options to search the entire Document, search for Whole Words only, and to search and Ignore Case.

But the one option that changes the palette from simple text searches to a highly complex search and replace tool is the Ignore Attributes option. Selecting *not* to ignore the attributes of the text you are searching for (or the text you want to change it to) causes the Find/Change palette to expand to encompass many text properties. Once expanded, as shown next, you may choose any or all character attributes for Find What and Change to parameters.

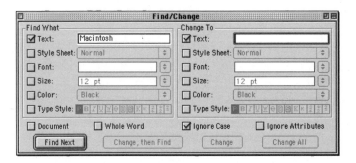

To define the parameters for a search, enter your text in both the Find What and Change To sides of the palette. Choose any or all of the parameters you want to search for by clicking the checkbox opposite Text, Style Sheet, Font, Size, and Type Style. The Style Sheets drop-down menu contains only those styles that your document currently uses, while the Find What side of the Fonts drop-down menu contains only a list of the fonts used in your document. Other than those two limitations, the sky's the limit. The text fields on both the Find What and Change To sides of the palette are capable of searching for and replacing up to 80 characters at a time.

Behind the scenes, XPress is actually searching for combinations of text strings and character and paragraph attributes in the form of tags. Once the text is located, the tags are examined to match the selected options. The only properties that may not be specified individually are color and shade for character attributes, although these attributes are also a factor of the styles you may choose to search for.

Text Searches

You may search for and replace any characters you want in your document. Each time you enter text in the Find What side of the palette you are limiting your search parameters only to the characters themselves and not their attributes. Each time you select an additional attribute, the search becomes more specific.

For example, to search and replace text in your document, simply enter existing characters in the Find What text field, enter the replacement characters in the Change To text field, and press Find. Once the first instance is found, the remaining command buttons become available, enabling you to proceed as you want either by examining each instance with the Change, Then Find button or by simply changing the text using the Change button. You may also change all instances in the entire document by pressing the Change All button. To close the palette, click the Close button in the upper-right corner of its title bar.

Text and Attributes Searches

When changing text by attributes, you have the option of searching for and replacing identical character strings using different attributes.

For example, search for the word potpourri (which often appears in italics) and leave the attributes unchecked on the Find What side. Enter the same text on the Change To side, but specify an italic Type Style by clicking the Italic button. Clicking Find and then Change All results in each instance of potpourri being changed to italic no matter what it was previously. You may also build on this process by creating a special character style for the Find/Change process and apply color and shade properties if that's what your design calls for.

Using Line Check

The Line Check command enables you to perform quick checks for undesirable instances of text in your layout and enables you to find and potentially correct poorly formatted text. These include instances where lines of text justification may be overly exaggerated, hyphenation is poor, stray words are left at the beginning or end of paragraphs, or text at the end of a text box is not appearing.

You may choose which types of instances are searched for using options in the Search Criteria dialog (shown next), which can be opened by choosing Utilities Line | Search Criteria. Checkmarks beside each option indicate the types of text lines that will be detected.

Choosing options in this dialog enables you to find the following instances of text:

- **Loose Justification**   Selecting this option enables the search to include poorly justified text, which is common when the text formatted using the Justified alignment style is composed of overly long words set using narrow column measures.

- **Auto Hyphenation**   If long words in your text have been automatically hyphenated, choosing this option enables you to find and potentially correct instances of incorrect hyphenation applied to words not found in either the main or auxiliary dictionaries.

- **Manual Hyphenated**   If words in your document have been manually hyphenated using a discretionary hyphen, choosing this option enables you to locate these instances. Discretionary hyphens enable you to manually hyphenate words not found in the main or auxiliary dictionaries and they enable the hyphen to split the word if necessary. To enter a discretionary hyphen, click an insertion point in a word and press CMD/CTRL+- (hyphen character).

- **Widow**   Widows occur when the last line of a paragraph is automatically (or manually) flowed to appear at the top of the next column in a text box or at the top of a linked text box. Choosing this option causes instances of widows to be added to the search criteria.

- **Orphan**   Choosing this option enables you to search for and locate orphans, which occur when the last line of a paragraph is flowed to the bottom of a column.

■ **Text Box Overflow**   This may be the most valuable option to select when choosing Line Check command search criteria. When selected, it enables you to locate instances when the text overflow symbol appears at the end of a story in an effort to verify whether all your desired text is being properly displayed in a text box.

To begin a search using the Line Check command according to your selected search criteria (all are selected by default), choose the Content tool from the Tool palette and click to select the start point in the first text box you want to check. Choose Utilities | Line Check | First Line to begin the search. The line containing the first instance found is automatically highlighted for you to review and correct; then you can proceed to the next found instance. To progress through a search of the text in your entire document to the next found instance, choose Utilities | Line Check | Next Line (CMD/CTRL+;).

Find/Change Strategies

It helps to use your imagination when formulating find and change strategies. Some of these strategies may even involve two- to five-step operations when searching for some instances of text while trying to exclude others. For example, if you want to change all instances of double-paragraph returns to single-paragraph returns but not where four-paragraph returns occur, your search operation will involve three steps. The first step would be the exclusion of the four returns. For this, you would need to change them to a unique character string such as three tildes (~~~). The second step would be to change the double returns to single returns, and the last step would be to change the three tildes back to four returns, as in the steps outlined here.

	Find what	Change to
Step 1	\p\p\p\p	~~~
Step 2	\p\p	\p
Step 3	~~~	p\p\p\p\

The same type of multi-step process applies to any exclusion. To make things easier in this regard, XPress enables you to search for and replace any of the invisible or soft characters that occur in your text. Table 6-6 serves as a guide for searching and replacing wildcard and soft characters.

Search/change character	Press shortcut	Result/code
Any character (wild card, Find only)	CMD/CTRL+?	\?
Tab	CTRL+TAB (*Windows* only)	\t
New paragraph	CMD/CTRL+RETURN	\p
New line	CMD/CTRL+SHIFT+RETURN	\n
New column	CMD/CTRL+ENTER	\c
New text box	CMD/CTRL+SHIFT+ENTER	\b
Previous box page number	CMD/CTRL+2	\2
Current box page number	CMD/CTRL+3	\3
Next box page number	CMD/CTRL+4	\4
Punctuation space	CMD/CTRL+.	\.
Flex space	CMD/CTRL+F	\f
Backslash	CMD/CTRL+\	\\

Table 6-6. *Wildcard and Soft Character Codes*

Chapter 7

Designing with Pictures and Graphics

Preparing a layout or design using text only is quickly becoming a thing of the past. Everybody wants pictures on their page, whether they choose to use quick clip art graphics or professional-style photographs. XPress enables you to work with a variety of picture formats and adjust or control their appearance in various ways. From an editorial standpoint, adding pictures to a layout often stimulates visual interest, while from a creative perspective pictures often open doors to near limitless design opportunities.

XPress also has a different way of classifying pictures from other layout applications. The properties of your pictures can range greatly depending on how they are prepared. XPress considers a picture to range anywhere from a single-color graphic to a full-color digital photograph, and all permutations between. Certain options for altering or changing the appearance of pictures can also depend on their file format. It's tricky business, especially when you consider that the picture you are using in your document may originate from a variety of sources, such as your favorite graphic-illustration or bitmap-editing programs.

In this chapter, you'll begin by discovering how to get pictures on your page. You'll learn to use the picture box tools of XPress and get some hands-on experience in examining, altering, and controlling their properties. You'll also learn the ins and outs of working with the various picture formats and their strengths and weaknesses.

Get a Picture onto Your Page

As with other types of content such as text, pictures must reside within picture boxes in order to exist on your page. So, getting a picture onto your page requires that you create a picture box first using any of the seven picture box tools available. As you'll soon discover, these tools each enable you to create different picture box shapes. If deciding which type of picture box you want to use becomes a barrier to getting started, rest assured you can change your picture box to nearly any shape even after you've created it and filled it with a picture.

To quickly get a picture onto your page, follow these steps:

1. In an open document, choose any picture box tool from the Tool palette. Picture box tools may be identified by the "x" symbol they contain. After the tool is selected, notice your cursor changes to a cross-hair.

2. Using the same action as you would to create a text box, drag diagonally across your page to define the new picture box size and release the mouse. Notice a new picture box appears on your page and contains diagonal lines joining the corners (even if your picture box isn't rectangular).

3. Choose File | Get Picture (CMD/CTRL+E) to open the Get Picture dialog.

4. Locate the folder containing your picture and click it once to select it. Notice information about the file appears in the lower part of the dialog, as shown in Figure 7-1. Windows users may use the Files of Type drop-down menu to limit

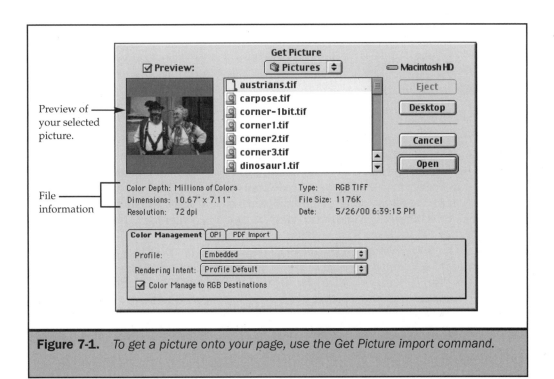

Preview of
your selected
picture.

File
information

Figure 7-1. *To get a picture onto your page, use the Get Picture import command.*

the display of picture formats to the specific file format of your picture.
Otherwise, leave the selection at the default All Picture Files selection.

5. If the Preview option isn't already selected, choose it now. Notice a small
    representation of the image appears in the preview window. Using the Preview
    option is a quick way to visually check that you are selecting the correct
    picture.

6. Click Open to import the picture and close the dialog. Notice your picture now
    appears in the picture box you created.

7. If you don't first see the complete picture in the picture box, don't be alarmed;
    it's there all right. The dimensions of your picture may simply be larger than
    the picture box you created. XPress automatically places pictures in their
    originally prepared size and aligns them with the upper-left corner of the
    picture box. To see the complete picture, choose the Content tool from the Tool
    palette and, with your picture box still selected, press CMD/CTRL+OPTION/
    ALT+SHIFT+F to resize the picture to automatically fit the picture box.

To delete a picture from a picture box, choose the Content tool, select the picture by clicking it once, and press the DELETE/BACKSPACE key. To replace a picture box's content with a different picture, repeat the import process by selecting the picture box, choosing the Get Picture (CMD/CTRL+E) command, and open another picture. The new picture simply replaces the previous one. To delete the picture box and its contents, choose the Item tool, select the picture box, and press the DELETE/BACKSPACE key.

Now that your picture is there, you'll likely want to perform any number of operations next, including sizing the picture or its box, positioning it on your page, and/or applying properties to it in order to integrate it into your layout. All of these operations are covered in the pages to follow, but it may help first to do a little investigation into what the other picture box tools enable you to do and perhaps take a closer look at the inherent properties of your picture box content.

When importing a picture using the Get Text command, you may change the color depth of the picture as it appears in your XPress document without changing the original picture itself by pressing certain command keys while clicking the Open button. For more information on changing a picture's color depth on import, see "Controlling Picture Color" in Chapter 8.

Using Picture Box Tools

When you create a picture box, essentially what you are doing is creating a container to house your picture. But there's a more logical way of looking at it. A picture box may also be thought of as a sort of "viewing window" through which you may see the pictures. In XPress, this window can be nearly any shape you want, depending on the requirements of your layout or creative needs. Once the window has been created using picture box tools, it may be altered or transformed later on, but when first creating the window's shape, seven tools offer the convenience of preset shapes or effects, as shown in Figure 7-2.

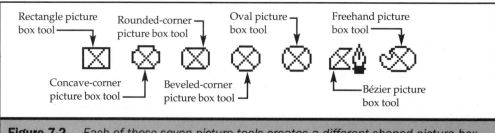

Figure 7-2. *Each of these seven picture tools creates a different shaped picture box.*

The seven tools are as follows:

- **Rectangle**   This picture box tool creates a picture box that features four straight sides joined by four corners at 90-degree angles. Holding SHIFT while creating or resizing a rectangular picture box constrains its width and depth to equal dimensions.

- **Rounded-Corner**   This creates a picture box similar to the Rectangle picture box tool, only with uniformly rounded corners that may be set to a specific corner radius within a range between 0 and 2 inches. Holding SHIFT while creating or resizing a Rectangle picture box constrains its width and depth to equal dimensions.

- **Oval**   The Oval picture box tool is used for creating oval or circular-shaped picture boxes. Holding SHIFT while creating or resizing an Oval picture box constrains its width and depth to equal dimensions, resulting in a perfect circle.

- **Concave-Corner**   The Concave-corner picture box tool creates boxes with rounded corners that face inwards, essentially the opposite of rounded-corner boxes. Concave corners may be set to a specific corner radius ranging between 0 and 2 inches. Holding SHIFT while creating or resizing a Concave-corner picture box constrains its width and depth to equal dimensions.

- **Beveled**   The Beveled-corner picture box tool creates boxes with flattened corners. Beveled corners may be set to a specific corner radius ranging between 0 and 2 inches. Holding SHIFT while creating or resizing a Beveled-corner picture box constrains its width and depth to equal dimensions.

- **Freehand**   The action of creating Freehand and Bézier picture boxes is unlike any of the other picture box tools of XPress. These shapes must be drawn or traced, as opposed to simply click-dragging a preset shape. The Freehand picture box tool enables you literally to freehand draw your new picture box directly on your screen. While in Freehand mode, click-dragging your mouse button creates the contour of the box's shape. Freehand picture boxes must exist as closed shapes, so no matter where you finish drawing your freehand picture box shape, the result will be a closed box. The beginning and end points are automatically joined.

Tip   *You may change the shape of a picture box quickly from one picture shape to another by choosing Edit, Shape and selecting one of the preset shapes from the popout menu.*

- **Bézier**   The operation of creating a Bézier picture box is done much the same way as creating Bézier lines and points. Bézier picture boxes are created point by point, each joined by either a straight or curved segment. Both segments and points may be controlled using Bézier editing tools. Bézier picture boxes must exist as closed shapes, so the beginning and endpoints of your Bézier picture box shape are automatically joined when you double-click, place the cursor over the original anchor point, or switch tools. When drawing Bézier picture boxes, holding the Shift key while creating points constrains segment angles to 45 and 90 degrees.

The shapes created with picture box tools are virtually identical to those created with text box tools, and the same standard constraining conventions also apply. When creating or resizing Rectangle, Rounded-corner, Oval, Beveled-corner, or Concave-corner picture boxes with your mouse, holding the SHIFT key constrains the picture box to an equal width and height.

For more information on using Bézier drawing tools, refer to the section, "Drawing with Bézier Tools," in Chapter 5.

Working with Picture File Formats

If working with various types of picture formats is completely new to you, then you're about to have a crash course in all the different types of graphic and digital formats that are out there. There's certainly no shortage of format types, the majority of them being bitmap in nature. Although this next section defines the types of formats available, many of the capabilities of these formats are dependent on the characteristics of the image in question, the application used to create it, and how it is prepared and saved.

Vector Versus Bitmap Formats

As mentioned earlier, XPress considers any image that can be placed into a picture box a picture. However, a picture may be any of the following:

- A graphic such as a logo
- An illustration
- A map or diagram
- A fancy separator or border pattern
- A drop cap
- Fancy bullets
- A design icon
- A digital photograph
- A texture background

With this many variables, it's no wonder that pictures may come from a variety of programs and/or have been prepared in a variety of conditions or file formats. Certain picture types work well in vector file formats, while others work well as bitmaps. A vector-style picture may be a graphic symbol or illustration that is composed of line and pattern information, while bitmap images usually take the form of digital photographs and/or textures, although these rules are not hard and fast. Virtually any image may be prepared in bitmap format.

The various file formats influence how the picture may appear or be reproduced in Quark. The original picture itself features varying degrees of resolution and color. To a large degree, the level of color contained in your picture will determine how much control you will have over it in XPress with more control for bitmap formats and less for vector illustrations. (See Table 8-1 in Chapter 8 for a list of modifiable picture formats.) But before you explore color and its capabilities in XPress, let's take a closer look at what bitmap and vector art is and the file formats compatible with XPress.

Bitmap Formats

A *bitmap* (also called a raster image) is a file format that contains dot patterns (called pixels) measured in resolution values. Resolution is the measure of dot detail (dots per inch [dpi]) that displays and prints your digital image. The higher the resolution, the greater the amount of detail in the image. Bitmaps are often used for saving photographs or images with varying gradations of shade, color, and texture. This includes scanned images.

Bitmap image types compatible with XPress are selected using the Get Picture Files of Type drop-down menu and include specific import filters:

- **Bitmap files (BMP, RLE, DIB)**   The bitmap filter is capable of interpreting three bitmap formats, including standard uncompressed bitmaps (BMP) and bitmap images compressed using run-length encoding (RLE) and DIB compression.

- **GIF files (GIF)**   The graphical interchange format (GIF, sometimes pronounced "jiff") was originally developed for CompuServe, the first commercial online service in wide use. GIF files have become a standard format for graphic and digital images in Web site design. By their nature, GIF files only support up to 256 individual colors.

- **JPEG files (JPG)**   If you work in Web design, you may already be aware of the intricacies of the JPEG (pronounced "jay-peg") format. The JPEG format was originally developed and standardized by the Joint Photographers Expert Group and, as you might have guessed, is specifically geared toward reproducing accurate digital picture quality with the smallest possible file size using varying degrees of compression. The JPEG format is prized for its compression capabilities and has become a virtual standard in Web page design.

- **Kodak PhotoCD (PCD)**   This format was developed and is owned by Kodak, originally for the purposes of compressing high-quality scanned images for viewing on proprietary home video systems. Because of its relatively low-cost and highly-controlled image quality, PhotoCD has slowly been adopted as a method for scanning and distributing desktop images and stock or royalty-free digital images.

- **Mac PICT files (PCT)**   The Mac PICT file format is still one of the standards on the Macintosh platform capable of supporting both bitmap and vector objects in a single file. The PICT format is well-known for its compression strengths.

- **PCX files (PCX)**   PC Paintbrush was one of the image-editing programs developed by Microsoft and became a standard format for preparing bitmap images.

- **Scitex CT files (SCT, CT)**   If you're using Scitex continuous tone (CT) image files, you're using one of the first high-end file formats designed for handling a variety of sophisticated, multi-ink image files. Scitex files often include their own built-in color trapping properties prepared using dedicated Scitex file-RIPping software and work stations.

- **TIFF files (TIF)**   The Tagged Image File Format (TIFF) bitmap was one of the first originally developed formats for preparing and printing digital images for desktop applications and remains one of the most popular and widely supported. TIFF files support a wide range of color and resolution.

- **Windows Metafile (WMF)**   This file format is still widely supported by illustration and bitmap editing programs. The WMF format is capable of supporting both vector and bitmap images in the same file.

These picture import formats each have their own characteristics and properties. When imported into XPress using the Get Picture command, the import operation is seamless, meaning that no further import options are offered. The color and resolution information in the picture file is simply interpreted, the picture is loaded, and it displays by default as a 72 dpi preview in your new picture box in the same format in which it was saved. This may not be the case for other types of files, as you'll discover in the next section.

PostScript File Formats

A vector image is a file composed of a mathematical series of open or closed paths either filled or unfilled using color and/or screen values. If your image is based mostly on vector objects, it's more than likely that the Encapsulated PostScript (EPS) file format has been used to prepare it. Adobe, the creator of the PostScript language, has continuously been upgrading and improving the capabilities of PostScript as print technology advances. Over the years, EPS has become a standard for printing and preparing images destined for PostScript-compatible printers. The PostScript language supports both bitmap and vector objects, while a PostScript file may be a simple graphic or a completely self-contained page including crop and registration marks.

One of the key things to keep in mind when working with EPS files in picture boxes is that what you see on your screen is merely a representation or "header" image of the EPS file. Incorporating a header into the EPS file enables anyone working with the file to see exactly what it contains. But headers are bitmap format files, meaning they can take any form of bitmap the creator of the image desires. The two main characteristics of headers are the resolution measured in dpi and color.

Headers are often kept crude, or eliminated altogether, in order to reduce the overall size of EPS files. The lower the resolution and the less color depth in the header, the less memory it will require. So, if you import an EPS file onto your page and all you see is a gray box where the picture should be, the header has likely been left off the file and what you are seeing is the overall bounding box of the image. If what you see is a crude representation in black and white, it may be the image is in black and white, grayscale, or even full color depending on how the header was originally prepared. Figure 7-3 indicates how various headers appear on your page when imported into picture boxes.

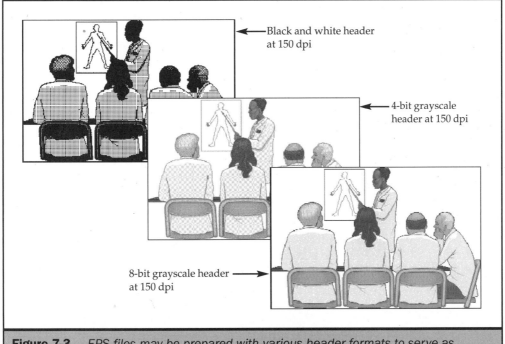

Black and white header
at 150 dpi

4-bit grayscale
header at 150 dpi

8-bit grayscale header
at 150 dpi

Figure 7-3.   *EPS files may be prepared with various header formats to serve as representations of the PostScript files they represent.*

Bitmap and Vector Color

Bitmaps also come in a variety of levels of color, including 1-, 2-, 4-, 8-, 24-, 32-, and 64-bit color levels. When it comes to describing color in bitmaps, black is also considered a color. These color levels range from 1-bit black-and-white images to 64-bit full-color CMYK color. The abbreviation CMYK represents the standard four-color process inks cyan (blue), magenta (red), yellow, and black used in traditional printing in order to closely reproduce color pictures.

Another level of color you'll encounter in bitmap images is gray or grayscale. Grayscale color divides a single color into 256 individual shades, none of which necessarily needs to be gray. Grayscale color is simply a standardized method of measuring the shades of a single color and is commonly used in reproducing single-color digital images in print such as black-and-white photographs.

The color model on which a picture is based determines the level of color the bitmap is capable of supporting. Color models represent the way in which a bitmap's color is measured. For example, CMYK is a color model because it measures color broken into four ink colors, each of which is based on a percentage of ink. Here are some of the color models used in QuarkXPress 5, which are standards in the digital image world:

- Red, green, blue (RGB)
- Hue, saturation, brightness (HSB)
- Luminescence values A and B (LAB)
- CMYK

The colors in your digital image may have been created and measured using any of these models. RGB, HSB, and LAB are mostly used for the display and manipulation of color in images, while the printing of your images is done using ink colors such as spot and process (CMYK) color. Spot colors are premixed ink printing colors that may reproduce certain parts or all of your digital image. Spot color inks are manufactured by several companies around the world. Each ink company has their own catalog of ink colors identified using the manufacturers' own numbering system. XPress supports ink color catalogs from Pantone, TOYO, DIC, Trumatch, Focoltone, and Hexachrome. Spot colors are displayed on your screen using standard (RGB) colors, but reproduce in the specified ink color when printed.

For more information on understanding colors in pictures and in your document, see Chapter 14.

Setting Picture Box Properties

Once you have a picture box on your page, there are any number of things you may want to do first in order to begin fitting it into your layout. As you'll soon discover, moving a picture box must be done using the correct tools. Picture boxes may be gradually moved around your page or document in a number of ways, or they may be moved instantly using dialog options or the features in the Measurements palettes.

Moving Picture Boxes

Perhaps the most natural way to move a picture box is by grabbing onto it with the Item tool and dragging it into position. As with other objects, the Item tool is the only tool that enables you to do this interactively. In keeping with standard constrain conventions, holding the SHIFT key while dragging a picture box enables you to constrain its movement to vertical or horizontal movements.

To move a picture box using the Item tool, follow these steps:

1. With a picture box created on your page, choose the Item tool from the Tool palette, or to temporarily select the Item tool while using any other tool, hold the CMD/CTRL key.

2. Click and drag the picture box in any direction. Notice as you drag the picture box a representative dotted line appears on your screen to indicate the new picture box position. You may also notice if your Snap to Guides option (SHIFT+F7) is activated, the picture box snaps when it nears a ruler or guideline.

3. Release the mouse button once your picture is in position and the operation is complete.

4. To experience the action of constraining, perform the same steps as previously outlined while holding the SHIFT key. Notice your initial mouse movement determines whether the constrain action is horizontal or vertical.

Moving pictures with the Item tool can be a quick way of setting its position, but in instances where you need to move the picture box very short and precise distances, you may also use the nudge keys. Nudge movement is accomplished by pressing the UP, DOWN, LEFT, or RIGHT arrow keys on your keyboard while both your Item tool and the picture box are selected. Each time a nudge key is pressed, the picture is moved by 1 point. Holding the OPTION/ALT key while pressing a nudge key moves the picture box by 0.1 point, making picture placement with nudge keys a highly accurate movement.

Picture Box Size and Position

The physical width and height of your picture box may be set using the Box tab of the Modify (CMD/CTRL+M) dialog options, shown in Figure 7-4. The Origin Across and Origin Down fields enable you to enter exact page positions for the upper-left corner of your picture box, while the Width and Height fields enable you to enter the exact dimensions of your picture box, also measured from the upper-left corner.

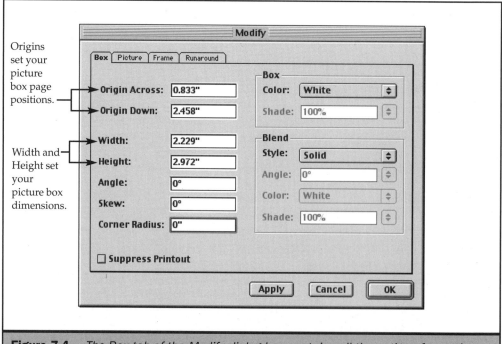

Origins set your picture box page positions.

Width and Height set your picture box dimensions.

Figure 7-4. *The Box tab of the Modify dialog box contains all the options for setting your picture box properties.*

Setting the position and size of Rectangle picture boxes might be considered straightforward, but when working with picture boxes that are not rectangular in shape, such as Oval, Freehand, or Bézier picture boxes, the measurements become a little trickier. In these cases, the upper-left corner of the picture box is measured from the upper-left corner of its bounding box, indicated by the top-left picture box handle.

To size a picture and its picture box simultaneously, hold the CMD/CTRL button while resizing the picture box with one of its corner handles.

Picture Box Rotation and Skew

Should your layout or design call for such an effect, XPress enables you to apply rotation and skew effects to picture boxes. Picture boxes may be rotated and/or skewed using the Angle and Skew options in the Modify, Box tab options shown previously. Applying a rotation value in the Angle field rotates the picture box and its contents around the center origin of the picture box within 360 degrees. Entering positive values in the Angle field rotates the box counterclockwise, while entering negative values rotates it clockwise. After a rotation has been applied, you may return the picture box to its upright orientation by entering 0 in the Angle field.

A more interactive method of rotating picture boxes is through the use of the Rotation tool found in the Tool palette. Using the rotation tool has advantages over simply entering values in the Angle field of the Modify dialog in that it enables you to freely rotate the picture box around a point anywhere on your document page.

For detailed directions on using the Rotation tool, see "Key QuarkXPress Tools Worth Mastering" in Chapter 2.

The Skew option enables you to apply a horizontal slant to picture boxes and their contents. The advantage of applying skew effects to picture boxes is that it avoids the need to convert the boxes to other shapes such as Bézier or Freehand in order to distort their shape. Also, using Skew values, you may achieve interesting effects by actually distorting the picture's contents. As with rotation, skew effects are reversible, meaning you may return the picture box and its contents to normal once again.

To edit the shape of a picture box without distorting its contents, use either the Item or Content tools to change the position of the picture box handles.

The skew value you apply must fall between −75 and 75 degrees, where positive values skew to the right and negative values skew to the left. Skew values are applied based on the center position of the picture's bounding box. The overall width and height values remain constant, but with skew applied, the bounding box of the picture becomes wider, as shown in Figure 7-5.

Picture Box Color and Blend

The Modify, Box tab dialog also enables you to apply color to your picture boxes in much the same manner as for text boxes. Colors may be chosen from the drop-down menu and a Shade value may be applied using any value between 0 and 100 percent. Blend styles and colors are applied in the same manner by making a selection from the Style drop-down menu and setting an Angle, Color, and Shade for the secondary Blend color.

Picture box color may also be applied to your picture's background using the Color palette (F12). To apply a color background, select the picture, click the Background Color button, and click your desired color and/or shade or choose a blend style from the drop-down menu. Then select a secondary color and/or shade. You may also apply a background by dragging a color from the palette directly onto your picture without selecting it first.

The first issue to be aware of when setting color and blend properties to picture boxes is that the color is applied to the actual area of the picture box itself wherever the content leaves a space or gap between the edge of the image and the picture's frame.

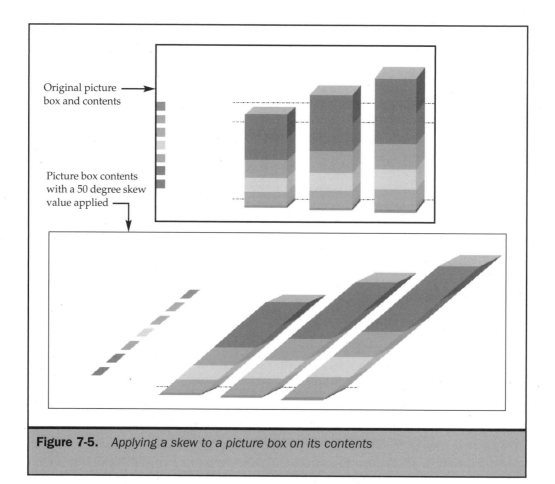

Figure 7-5. Applying a skew to a picture box on its contents

This area is sometimes referred to as the picture box background. For example, applying a picture box color of black at a shade of 20 percent to a rectangular image imported into a square picture box causes the background to show through as 20 percent black where the background is visible, as shown in Figure 7-6.

Tip *To make the space or gap between the picture box content and the frame of your picture box transparent, choose None from the Color drop-down menu. Any items behind the picture box will show through the gap between the edges of your image and the picture box frame.*

Applying color and blend effects to picture boxes opens up several creative but confusing issues. First and foremost, setting a picture box color does not affect the

50 percent black in the background area of the picture box ⟶

Edge of picture frame ⟶

Edge of picture ⟶

Figure 7-6.   *Setting a picture box color and shade applies the color only to the background of your picture box where the background shows through.*

actual content of a picture box in a straightforward way. Rather, how color affects the picture box's content is determined by the color depth of the imported picture. When applying color to the background of a picture box containing a full-color image, the image itself is unaffected by the background color. However, if the image you import is a black-and-white (line art), 4-bit grayscale, or 8-bit grayscale image, the background color will show through and actually affect the image's color.

Setting Corner Radius

The Corner Radius option is set through the Modify, Box tab and in much the same way as for text boxes. The value entered in the Corner Radius field must fall within 0 and 2 inches. While Freehand or Bézier picture boxes are selected, the Corner Radius option is unavailable in the Modify dialog.

Picture Box Properties via the Measurements Palette

Although any of the properties associated with picture boxes may be set using the Modify | Box tab dialog, the Measurements palette (F9) provides more access and convenience for the user, and effectively adopting its use will undoubtedly speed your production time. Only the most commonly changed picture box properties are included in the palette, including Origin Across, Origin Down, Width, Height, Angle, and Corner Radius options, as shown next. The functionality of these options is identical to those in the Modify | Box tab dialog.

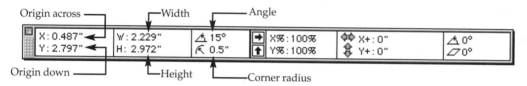

Manipulating Picture Box Content

Now that you have an understanding of how the properties of the picture container may be controlled, next comes the important part. Let's examine how XPress enables you to set the properties of your picture box's content. You may apply nearly all the same properties to your picture content as you may with the picture box itself independent of the box it resides in. Once again, there are several ways to apply these properties, but first let's examine the complete set of controls available through the Modify, Picture tab dialog (CMD/CTRL+M) shown in Figure 7-7.

Picture Offset and Scale

Moving your picture around inside your picture box is perhaps most interactively and conveniently done using the Content tool. With a picture box selected, the Content tool turns to a Grabber hand cursor, enabling you to grab and drag the picture within its box. But you may also move a picture within the box using nudge keys. While both your Content tool and picture box are selected, the UP, DOWN, LEFT, and RIGHT arrow keys on your keyboard act to nudge the picture within its box. Pressing a nudge key moves your picture by 1 point in a given direction, and while holding OPTION/ALT and pressing a nudge key, the picture moves 0.1 points.

When you drag or nudge a picture within its box, you are actually changing its offset measures, which may be precisely set by entering values in the Offset Across and Offset Down fields of the Modify | Picture tab dialog (CMD/CTRL+M). Both the Offset Across and Offset Down measures may only be set to the maximum width and/or height dimensions of the picture box. In other words, you can make your picture box contents seem to disappear by entering the maximum offset values.

Scaling pictures within picture boxes could easily be considered the most commonly used command next to sizing picture boxes themselves. Seldom are pictures ever

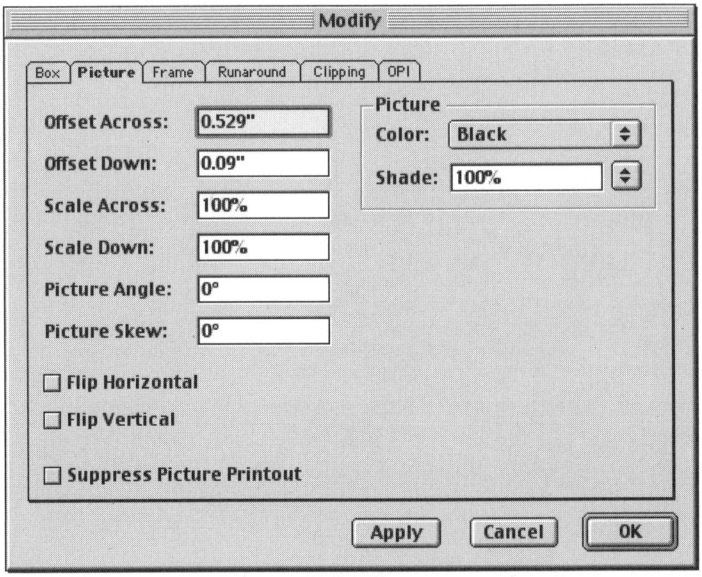

Figure 7-7.   *Picture box content properties are set through the Modify | Picture dialog.*

digitally prepared in their exact published dimensions and cropping. In fact, because of their visual flexibility, a picture's size and cropping are often used as techniques for tailoring the fit of text into a layout. When a picture is first imported, it appears in its prepared dimensions in the upper-left corner of the picture box by default.

Getting your picture into the size and cropping you need for your layout is an operation that requires more than one tool or command, and often simple common sense. Ideally, you will have already set your picture box in position on your page and/or integrated it into your layout. The tool you will work with is the Content tool, and the quickest commands will be through keyboard shortcuts. The Content tool enables you to control the offset of your picture (its position within the picture box), while keyboard commands for fitting, centering, or scaling enable you to control the remaining variables. Table 7-1 lists the keyboard shortcuts that apply when scaling and positioning pictures in boxes while using the Content tool.

Picture Rotation and Skew

While your picture is inside its picture box, you may also apply rotation and skew effects. These effects may be applied independently of the picture box using Picture Angle and Picture Skew options in the Modify | Picture tab dialog. The picture angle

Fit picture to box (nonproportionately).	CMD/CTRL+SHIFT+F
Fit picture to box (proportionately).	CMD/CTRL+OPTION/ALT+SHIFT+F
Fit box to picture.	No shortcut key. Go to Style Menu, Fit Box to Picture.
Center picture within box.	CMD/CTRL+SHIFT+M
Increase size by 5 percent.	CMD/CTRL+OPTION/ALT+SHIFT+>
Decrease size by 5 percent.	CMD/CTRL+OPTION/ALT+SHIFT+<

Table 7-1.   *Keyboard Shortcuts for Altering Picture Boxes or Pictures*

may be rotated 360 degrees in either a clockwise or counterclockwise direction, while the picture skew may be slanted to the left or right within −75 and 75 degrees. Figure 7-8 shows rotation and skew effects applied to a picture.

Changing Picture Color and Shade

Applying color to your picture changes the color of the picture itself without affecting the picture box background or frame. The picture you choose to apply the color to must be either in black and white or grayscale in order for color options to be available. Pictures that already feature inherent color may not be affected using these options.

Color may also be applied to pictures using the Color palette (F12). To apply a color, select the picture, click the Picture Color button on the palette, and click your desired color and/or shade. Color changes are immediate using the Colors palette.

Color is applied using the Modify, Picture tab dialog options for color and shade. The Color option enables you to set a black-and-white or grayscale image to print in a color other than black, with any of the colors available to you in XPress. You may simply set the picture to appear in black, but limit its appearance to a shade of black based on a percentage of the original picture's tones. To apply a color, simply choose a color from the Color drop-down menu and/or apply a shade by selecting a percent value from the Shade drop-down menu, as shown in Figure 7-9.

Flipping and Flopping Pictures

The terms flipping and flopping stem from the days when traditional film halftones were assembled by hand during film-stripping operations when preparing to print

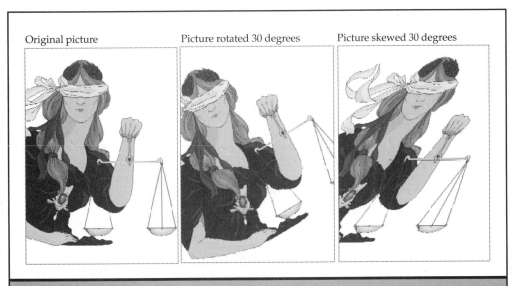

Original picture   Picture rotated 30 degrees   Picture skewed 30 degrees

Figure 7-8. *Applying Angle and Skew options enables you to rotate or skew a picture independently of its picture box.*

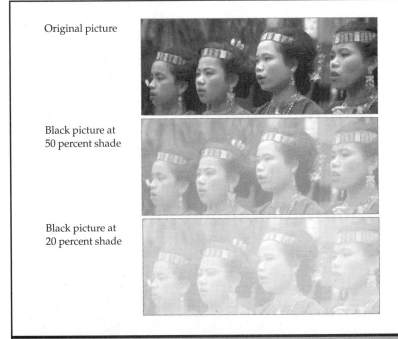

Original picture

Black picture at
50 percent shade

Black picture at
20 percent shade

Figure 7-9. *Using the Color options, you may apply color and shade to pictures.*

CREATING LAYOUTS
AND DOCUMENTS

material. Historically, flipping a picture meant physically turning the film representing the picture over vertically, essentially turning the picture upside down. The term flop referred to simply turning the film over horizontally, and since the film was transparent, the result was a mirror image of the picture. To lessen the confusion, these two terms were simplified to the term flip (vertically or horizontally).

Pictures are often flipped in order to conform to the layout and design convention that states all pictures should ideally face into the textual content they relate to or for other purposes. QuarkXPress 5 enables you to flip pictures vertically and/or horizontally with the click of a button. Flipping options affect the picture orientation only, without affecting the picture box containing them. To perform either operation, use options in the Modify, Picture tab dialog labeled Flip Horizontal and/or Flip Vertical, as shown in Figure 7-10. You may also apply one or both of these options to pictures, or return the picture to its normal state by deselecting the options.

Tip   *When flipping pictures vertically or horizontally without the reader catching on, be sure there are no recognizable features in the picture such as text, recognizable landmarks, or characteristic facial features.*

Original unflipped picture

Picture flipped horizontally

Picture flipped vertically

Picture flipped vertically and horizontally

Figure 7-10.   *This graphic has been flipped horizontally and vertically to create four corner variations required to complete the shape of a square.*

Applying Picture Commands with the Measurements Palette

Although any of the properties associated with pictures may be set using the Modify | Picture tab dialog, the Measurements palette (F9) may be more convenient to use. Only the most commonly changed picture properties are included in the palette, including the Scale Across, Scale Down, Offset Across, Offset Down, Picture Angle, and Picture Skew options, as shown next. The result of applying these options is identical to choosing the same options in the Modify | Picture tab dialog.

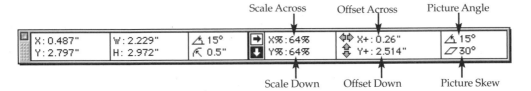

Scale Across   Offset Across   Picture Angle

Scale Down   Offset Down   Picture Skew

Controlling the Picture Frame

The properties you may apply to your picture frame are identical to those found in other frame-related property dialogs and may be set using the Modify | Frame dialog, as shown next. To access these options quickly, select the picture you want to apply the frame properties to and press CMD/CTRL+B to open the Modify dialog directly to the Frame tab. All the Frame options for Width, Style, Frame Color and Shade, Gap Color, and Gap Shade may be applied to picture frames.

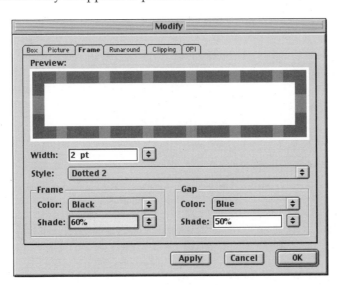

Getting Picture Information

As you go through the process of importing and integrating pictures into your layout, you may find it useful to know XPress enables you to obtain a complete report of all the pictures you have used in your document through the Usage command. You may obtain detailed information about individual pictures and even locate pictures in your layout automatically.

The Usage Command

The Usage command is an invaluable tool for working with documents that contain any number of pictures in any of the formats compatible with XPress. To use the Usage command to obtain a summary of the status of pictures in your document, choose Utilities | Usage to open the Usage dialog and click the Pictures tab (*Mac*: OPTION+F13, *Windows*: SHIFT+F2). As the Usage dialog opens, it performs an interrogation of all the pictures used in your document and quickly summarizes their statuses in five columns. These columns show whether the picture is selected to print, the picture's file name and path, the page it is located on, the type of file representing the picture, and its status, all of which is displayed in a table-style summary, as shown in Figure 7-11.

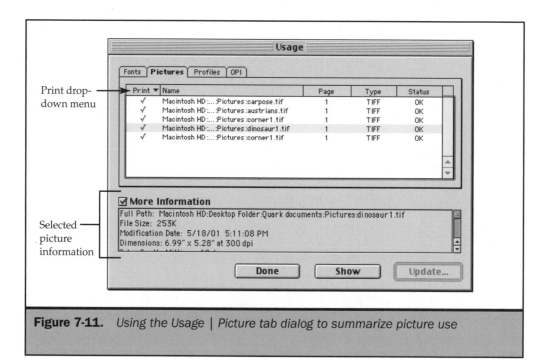

Figure 7-11. *Using the Usage | Picture tab dialog to summarize picture use*

The various columns in the Usage dialog are as follows:

■ **Print**   A checkmark in the Print column indicates the picture is currently set to print when your document is printed. The Print option may be set using the Modify | Picture tab (CMD/CTRL+M) dialog by choosing Suppress Printout when setting other properties for your pictures, but you may also change this option here by clicking the picture listing and selecting either Yes or No from the Print drop-down menu. Turning off the Print option for pictures is often used to reduce printing time when printing text-only proofs of documents.

■ **Name**   The Name column lists the name and brief path location of the picture when it was first imported into your document. By default, XPress simply links to picture files rather than storing all the data that represents them. Pictures that are embedded or linked to your document are indicated using the terms embedded object or linked object. Embedded objects are objects that have their source information stored in your XPress document, while linked objects are those that must be accessed externally and must be referenced by XPress in order to be properly printed. Linking and embedding is a function of Object Linking and Embedding (OLE) commands specific to the Windows operating system.

■ **Page**   This column indicates the page number on which the picture has been imported. The page number corresponds to the page numbers set in your XPress document layout. On the Macintosh version, a † symbol shown in the Page column indicates that the picture currently resides on the pasteboard of your document appended by a numeral specifying the closest page. On the Windows version, a PB acronym signifies the same.

■ **Type**   This column indicates the type of file format the picture has been prepared in. For example, TIFF indicates an imported Tagged Image Bitmap file and EPSF indicates an imported Encapsulated PostScript file.

■ **Status**   The status of the picture file is listed in this column as either OK, Modified, or Missing. When the term Modified appears, XPress is indicating that something may have changed in the original picture file since it was imported because the last modified date on the file has changed. If a file is listed as Missing, XPress is indicating that when the Usage command performed an interrogation of all links to all picture files, the original picture file was not found and may have been moved or deleted.

The Usage dialog features button commands for getting more information as well as for updating and locating picture files in your document. Clicking the More Information option expands the dialog to reveal detailed information about your selected picture. This includes the file name, its complete path, the memory size of the file, its last modification date, its width (first measure) and height (second measure) dimensions, its resolution (for bitmap files only), and its color depth (again, bitmap files only).

The Update button is only available when files are either modified or missing. Clicking the Update button enables you to reimport selected modified picture files, while clicking Update as missing pictures are selected opens the Find Filename dialog with the purpose of having you search and locate the missing picture file. Both commands enable you to automatically update the picture files using the same applied properties.

Tip
The Update command enables you to update multiple selections of mixed, modified, and/or missing pictures. To select more than one picture at a time, hold the SHIFT key to select sequential listings of picture files or hold CMD/CTRL while clicking non-sequential picture files. When the Update command button in clicked, files' updates are dealt with in the order in which they appear in your document. When more than one copy of the same picture is used throughout a document, all copies of the picture are updated at once.

Clicking the Show command button while a picture file is selected instantly displays the picture wherever it is found in your document and changes your view to align the selected picture at the upper-left corner of your XPress document window.

Tip
When performing the Update command on a picture, XPress recalls all properties applied to the picture in your document without the need to reapply them, including properties such as offset, scaling, rotation, skew, flipping, and color.

The Complete Reference

Chapter 8

Advanced Picture Strategies

271

Working with pictures in your XPress document can be a relatively straightforward exercise involving simply importing the picture onto your page. But, as you may have guessed from the issues covered in other chapters, picture content can often be complex with the pictures themselves having been prepared in various formats that are inherently capable of, or limited to, certain effects in XPress. If your document design calls for special treatment of pictures and you've arrived here in need of some direction and detailed information on working with pictures, you've come to the right place.

This chapter explores the finer details of working with both basic and advanced picture commands in XPress 5. You'll learn critical techniques and strategies, regardless of whether you're preparing the pictures yourself or using pictures from other external sources. You'll discover how to change the colors of imported pictures and how to work with Color, Contrast, Halftone, and Negative commands to adjust, enhance, or alter your pictures or apply creative effects. You'll also learn how to tailor your pictures through the complex clipping path commands of XPress.

Preparing Pictures for XPress

If you happen to be the one preparing the pictures destined for your XPress document yourself, there are certainly some design challenges to consider. Very likely, the images you import into XPress will be prepared using an external application. Bitmap images may often be prepared using a variety of software applications that range from professional-level applications such as Photoshop or Photo-Paint to more basic applications such as Paintshop Pro or MacPaint. Other types of images such as encapsulated PostScript (EPS) images, which are often composed mostly of vector objects, may often be created from an equally diverse variety of graphic illustration programs, including Illustrator, Freehand, or CorelDraw to basics such as MacDraw.

Because these applications rarely have native file import filters in host layout applications such as XPress, the files they create are exported from their host format through the use of software filters. The characteristics and properties contained in these files depend enormously on the level of sophistication of the export filter used and the adeptness of the user. Suffice it to say, when you are working with picture files prepared by someone else, you can seldom be certain of what you're getting.

This is a quandary that many professional desktop designers and layout artists deal with on a daily basis and it can often be one of the great hazards of working with pictures in your XPress document. For example, one of the most serious issues when using EPS files from graphic applications is the issue of embedded fonts. Outdated applications lack filter options for either embedding font information or converting fonts. This problem isn't restricted to just EPS formats though; it can often arise when preparing picture files with any export file format that supports vector objects. Unfortunately, there is no simple fix-all solution to this problem, beyond performing the export operation yourself.

When it comes to preparing bitmap images destined for an XPress document, the most serious factors to control are color and resolution. If your image is destined to be reproduced in print, you'll need to prepare the original picture file with roughly twice the resolution of the final printed document. For example, if the level of detail required by the final output of your XPress document is to be 150 dots per inch (dpi), your bitmap images will need to be prepared with roughly 300 dpi of resolution at the final size. If your document is destined for the Web, imported pictures need only have a maximum of 96 dpi.

Tip *For information on printing from XPress 5, see Chapter 17. For information on exporting pictures to the Web, see "Choosing a Web Picture Format" in Chapter 19.*

The inherent color of your bitmap image is another area for consideration. If your image is to be reproduced in color, it should be saved as a color image *before* it reaches XPress. Grayscale images may not be converted to color while in XPress. The same issue applies when color pictures are destined to be reproduced in combinations of two or three spot colors. For these images to correctly display and print from XPress, they will need to be specifically prepared as such before being imported onto your document page.

Tip *For additional information on working with color models, see "About Color Models" in Chapter 14 and see Chapter 16.*

CREATING LAYOUTS
AND DOCUMENTS

Modifiable Picture Formats

Regarding picture file formats, it also helps to be aware that certain effects or properties may be applied to certain types of picture formats in XPress 5. Changing these properties enables you to alter certain picture characteristics (discussed later in this chapter) such as Color, Shade, Negative, Contrast, and Halftone properties. The following list summarizes whether certain picture formats are eligible for changes when applying these properties.

 Although Color and Shade options for color pictures may not be available when working with certain picture formats, you may control contrast properties in the picture through use of the Contrast command (Macintosh: CMD+SHIFT+C, Windows: CTRL+SHIFT+O).

Picture Format	Color	Shade	Negative	Contrast	Halftone
EPS	No	No	No	No	No
DCS	No	No	No	No	No
GIF	No	No	Yes	Yes	No
JPEG (JPG)					
Grayscale	Yes	Yes	Yes	Yes	Yes
Color	No	No	Yes	Yes	No
Mac PICT (PCT)					
1-bit color	Yes	Yes	No	No	Yes
Grayscale bitmap	Yes	Yes	Yes	Yes	Yes
Full color bitmap	No	No	Yes	Yes	No
Object-oriented	No	No	No	No	No
OS/2 bitmap (BMP)					
1 bit	Yes	Yes	Yes	No	Yes
Grayscale	Yes	Yes	Yes	Yes	Yes
Color	No	No	Yes	Yes	No
PhotoCD	No	No	Yes	Yes	No
Scitex CT (SCT CT)					
Grayscale	No	No	Yes	Yes	No
Color	No	No	Yes	Yes	No
TIFF (TIF)					
1 bit	Yes	Yes	Yes	No	Yes
Grayscale	Yes	Yes	Yes	Yes	Yes
Color	No	No	Yes	Yes	No

Picture Format	Color	Shade	Negative	Contrast	Halftone
Windows bitmap (BMP, PCX)					
1-bit	Yes	Yes	Yes	No	Yes
Grayscale	Yes	Yes	Yes	Yes	Yes
Color	No	No	Yes	Yes	No
Metafile (WMF)	No	No	No	No	No

Controlling Picture Color

Once a picture has been imported into XPress, you have a certain number of limited color avenues available to you through the Color and Shade options. QuarkXPress enables you to assign color to pictures other than the color they were prepared, as long as their original color depth is either black and white (1-bit) or grayscale. This is done independent of the frame or background colors of the picture boxes they have been imported into. The colors you assign may be any of those available to you in XPress.

Note *If you're looking for a way to change the color of your picture once it has been imported into XPress, keep in mind that you must be working with either a black and white or grayscale picture format. If your picture is in full color or is in PostScript, desktop color separation (DCS), or Scitex format, the color and shade options will be unavailable to you.*

Changing Color and Shade Values

When working with black and white or grayscale images, the capability to display and print pictures in color provides you with a world of color options where before there were none. Color has the effect of adding excitement and appeal to graphics and digital images in your layout. But keep in mind the picture color you're changing applies to the full picture, rather than simply an isolated portion. By their very nature, black and white (1-bit) or grayscale pictures feature black as the inherent *color*. When you use the Color and Shade options to change color, essentially what you are doing is forcing the picture to display and print in a color *other* than black. The other properties of the picture remain unchanged.

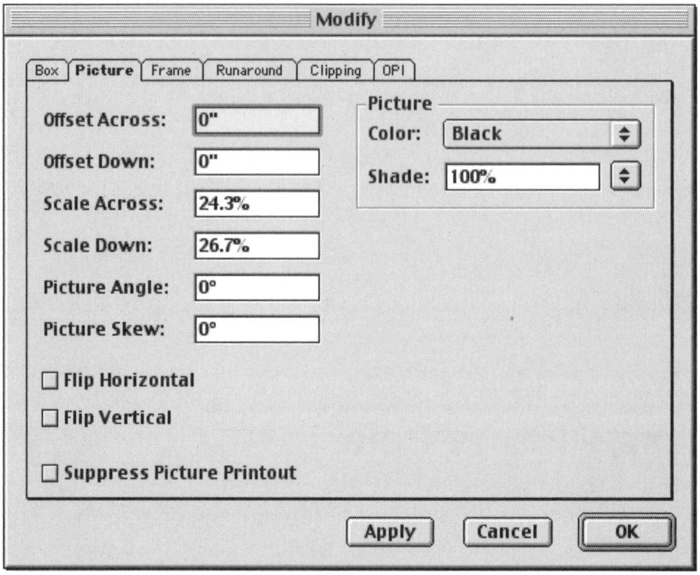

Figure 8-1.   *The Picture tab of the Modify box includes the most comprehensive collection of picture options.*

Color and Shade options may be set a number of ways, the most comprehensive of which is through the Pictures tab of the Modify dialog (CMD/CTRL+M), which is available while a filled picture box is selected (see Figure 8-1). You may also apply Color and Shade options through the Style, Color and Style, and Shade submenus, or more interactively through the Colors palette (F12).

To alter the Color and Shade properties of a selected picture in your document, have a black and white (1-bit) or grayscale picture available and follow these steps:

1. Create a picture box using any of the picture box tools from the Tools palette, choose the Content tool, and choose File | Get Picture (CMD/CTRL+E) to open the Get Picture command dialog.

2. Once located, click the picture file once in the browser window. Verify that the picture you select is either black and white or grayscale when selected by checking the file information area below the preview and browse areas of the Get Picture dialog.

3. Click the Open button to import the picture and scale and/or position the picture on your document page as required.

4. With the picture still selected, click to browse the menus and submenus under the application Style menu. Notice the Colors submenu includes all the colors available to you in XPress, and the Shade menu features a list of shades ranging from 0 to 100 percent in preset increments of 10 percent. This submenu also includes a selection for Other for you to enter your own value.

5. In this exploration though, let's use the more interactive technique available through the Colors palette, which is opened by choosing View | Colors (F12). The Colors palette appears.

6. Click the Picture Color mode button in the center of the three buttons at the top of the palette. The palette changes to display Picture Color mode options.

7. Choose a color for your picture and click it in the list to select and apply it. The Color palette changes to your picture are immediate.

8. Next, click the Shade drop-down menu and select a shade for your picture's color. Once selected, Shade properties are changed immediately.

When used in combination with picture box properties, the graphic appeal and interest of even the simplest images may be greatly enhanced, as shown in Figure 8-2.

Although Figure 8-2 has been applied using only black as the image color, black may be replaced with any of the colors available to you in XPress, such as Red, Green, and Blue (RGB), process, spot, or custom colors. Although the picture and its box are considered a single unit, the colors will separate on individual plates when printed.

When applying blended backgrounds to pictures, only black and white images are able to display the effect inside the boundaries of the image, making the flexibility of the 1-bit image unique from other picture formats.

Creating "Fake" Duotones

The term *duotone* refers to any single-color grayscale picture reproduced in two colors. There are *fake* duotones and real, or *true,* duotones. Fake duotones are essentially single-color grayscale pictures with an additional color placed behind the picture to heighten visual interest or suit a specific design scheme. Duotones have often been referred to as the cheap color pictures. But for little or no added cost, duotones can add color to an otherwise colorless page, and if the colors are chosen carefully, duotones can often be even more effective than full color for setting a mood or matching a color scheme. For the most part though, duotones serve as an inexpensive way of simulating more than two colors of ink in print.

For actual color examples of the appearance of fake and true duotones and other color picture techniques, see the color section of this book.

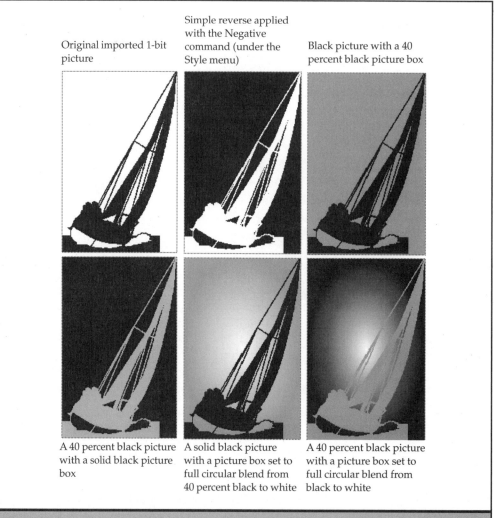

Original imported 1-bit picture

Simple reverse applied with the Negative command (under the Style menu)

Black picture with a 40 percent black picture box

A 40 percent black picture with a solid black picture box

A solid black picture with a picture box set to full circular blend from 40 percent black to white

A 40 percent black picture with a picture box set to full circular blend from black to white

Figure 8-2. *Assigning color and shade to a simple object can make even the most basic image a versatile design element.*

In QuarkXPress 5, creating a fake duotone effect is a quick operation done by applying a solid or screened color background to your picture box while leaving the picture itself unchanged. Figure 8-3 (reproduced here in black and white, but shown in full color in the color section of this book) shows how a color applied to the background of a single-color picture enables you to add uniform color to the background of your image independent of your picture's color.

20 percent color background applied to the picture box

Figure 8-3.   *Adding color to your picture's background is a quick way of creating a fake duotone effect.*

About True Duotones

As discussed, a duotone is simply a grayscale picture reproduced in more than one color. But although fake duotones add flat color to grayscale images that may be done directly in XPress, creating a true duotone requires the use of a full-featured image-editing application such as Photoshop or Photo-Paint. True duotones are those prepared with a second color (other than the original grayscale color) and are added in such a way as to show through the highlights and shadows of the original image's tones. The intensity of the secondary color is sometimes defined by a preset filter effect available from within the image editor being used to prepare the image, while certain applications enable you to adjust the color curves of the secondary color.

In order for duotones to display and print properly, they must adhere to standard display and printing conventions. As a rule, duotones are created as EPS files and usually contain at least one secondary color. The representation you see after importing a duotone into a picture box is actually an RGB TIFF preview image of the color data. Since the color data representing the duotone is predefined, it may not be modified or adjusted in any way in QuarkXPress.

The file format all duotones take is EPS, meaning the information describing the colors can only be prepared in this format. In technical terms, duotones are described in a data format using EPS descriptive language, which restricts printing color separations of the information to PostScript-compatible printers. This also means if a picture you are importing into XPress simply appears as if it were a duotone, but is saved in TIFF format only, the colors will not separate properly to specific spot colors.

If you pay close attention in the Get Picture dialog while importing a duotone image into a picture box, you may notice that the file information area reveals that the image is an EPS file with a TIFF preview, but QuarkXPress is unable to determine what the color depth of the image is, as shown Figure 8-4. In other words, the two colors used in the duotone image can often be a mystery.

Fortunately, when the file is imported into XPress, all color separation information gets imported along with it. The image shown in Figure 8-5 has been prepared as a duotone and saved to EPS format using black and an orange-yellow color. The second duotone color was applied using Pantone 3955 CV. As a result, this Pantone color was automatically added to the current selection of colors in the XPress document as shown. If the imported colors already exist in your XPress document, the colors simply separate to the corresponding plate as required during separation.

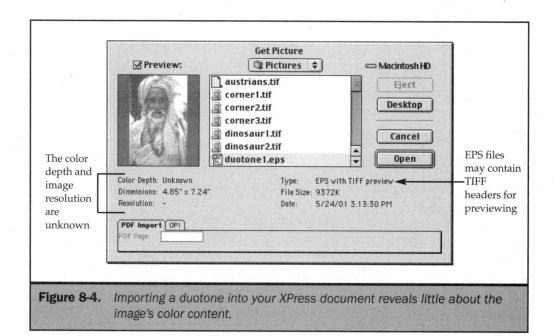

Figure 8-4.   *Importing a duotone into your XPress document reveals little about the image's color content.*

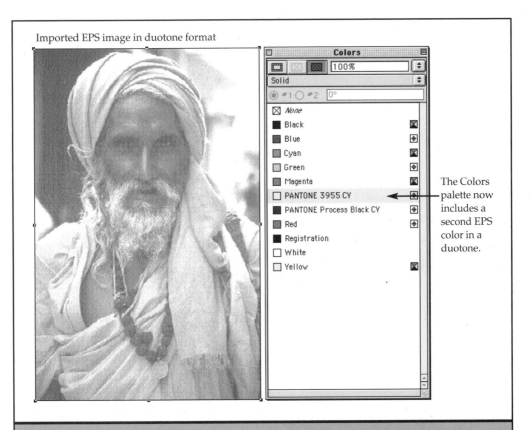

Imported EPS image in duotone format

The Colors palette now includes a second EPS color in a duotone.

Figure 8-5.   *When importing duotones into QuarkXPress, color information is automatically included with the image file.*

Tip   *When you select your document to print to separations, true EPS duotones will separate into two colors, in this case black and Pantone 3955 CV. There are also automatic safeguards against colors used in PostScript picture files being deleted from your document's color selection, as shown next in the alert message.*

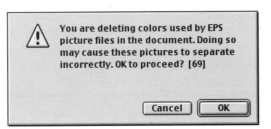

Controlling a Picture's Look

If the picture you see on your screen is not how you intend your final image to print, or the picture is so detailed it becomes cumbersome to work with, there may be a number of resources at your disposal to remedy either situation. QuarkXPress 5 enables you to manipulate the preview of how your picture appears onscreen, its color and contrast, and how it prints and exports. But although these are commonly sought after solutions to the QuarkXPress power user, taking advantage of them is not as straightforward as you might think. In this section, we'll take a close look at QuarkXPress 5's somewhat hidden picture commands.

Changing Picture Color or Preview

Perhaps the most significant and useful technique to employ during the import process is the reduction of your picture's inherent color. Reducing the color mode of pictures enables you to quickly reduce a full-color picture to grayscale, or a grayscale picture to line art (1-bit) as it is imported. To reduce a full-color picture to grayscale, simply hold the CMD/CTRL key while clicking the Open button in the Get Picture dialog (see Figure 8-6). The Get Picture dialog appears when choosing File | Get Picture (CMD/CTRL+E) while a picture box is selected.

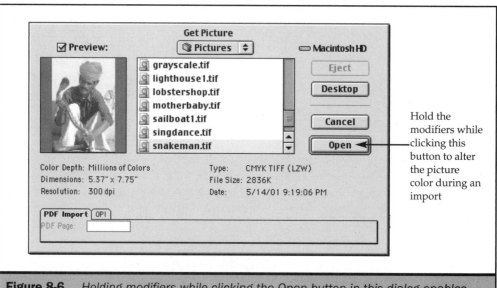

Figure 8-6.   *Holding modifiers while clicking the Open button in this dialog enables you to control the color of imported pictures.*

Note   *Although QuarkXPress enables you to reduce the color mode or resolution of an imported picture in your layout, you may not increase either of these properties. For example, if your originally imported picture has been prepared in grayscale, no command exists to enable you to convert it to full color.*

The CMD/CTRL modifier key may also be used to reduce a grayscale picture to line art, also referred to as black and white (1-bit). After the import process is complete, the resulting picture will display and print using the reduced color you've applied (see Figure 8-7). The beauty of this feature is that the original image file representing the picture remains unchanged. In other words, although your XPress document links to the data in the original image, its color information is still intact while XPress simply performs a color conversion for the display and printing of the image.

Some might consider control over how highly detailed images display and print to be somewhat of an advanced user trick. But as the cost of using high-end color and high-resolution images becomes more affordable, these techniques are increasingly necessary. For the dedicated QuarkXPress user, the capability to reduce an image's resolution or color level during import avoids the extra step of using an image editor.

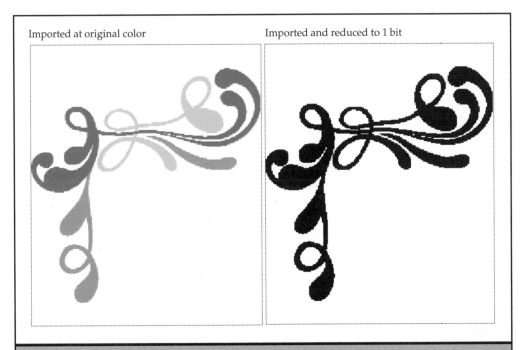

Imported at original color   Imported and reduced to 1 bit

Figure 8-7.   *The image in this picture box was reduced to 1-bit color depth on import.*

You won't find commands for reducing the color mode and/or resolution of an image in any dialog box in QuarkXPress 5. Instead, these commands are performed completely by holding various modifier keys while clicking the Open button in the Get Picture dialog box. In addition to the thumbnail preview provided for selected pictures, format and color depth information is also displayed in this dialog.

Changing Line Art Previews

Common line art (1-bit) pictures are the most versatile to integrate into text or a layout, since their inherent color may be altered or changed. However, the previews associated with smaller line art pictures are often crude and difficult to work with. To ease some of the difficulty associated with working with these types of pictures, another modifier enables you to increase the preview display of line art images to grayscale.

This often makes it much easier to interpret their shapes and see more picture detail to aid in layout operations such as text runarounds. Holding the OPTION/ALT modifier key while clicking Open in the Get Picture dialog changes the preview to appear as if it were grayscale (see Figure 8-8). In fact, an on-the-fly anti-aliasing effect has been applied to the picture, smoothing the appearance of often serrated edges on 1-bit image types. When your document prints, the preview is ignored and the picture's original 1-bit information is used in its place.

The default detail of imported TIFFs is controlled by QuarkXPress 5's Application Display preferences. For more information on customizing this behavior, see the next section.

Choosing to use low-resolution previews for your picture files also reduces the file size of your XPress document.

Table 8-1 summarizes the keyboard combinations covered in the previous two sections. When held during an import, these key presses enable you to perform color mode and preview conversions when using the Get Picture command.

Convert full color to grayscale.	Hold CMD/CTRL while clicking Open.
Convert grayscale to black and white.	Hold CMD/CTRL while clicking Open.
Change a 1-bit preview to a grayscale preview.	Hold OPTION/ALT while clicking Open.
Force a preview to display in a lower resolution.	Hold SHIFT while clicking Open.

Table 8-1.   *Modifier Keys for Changing TIFF Preview Display*

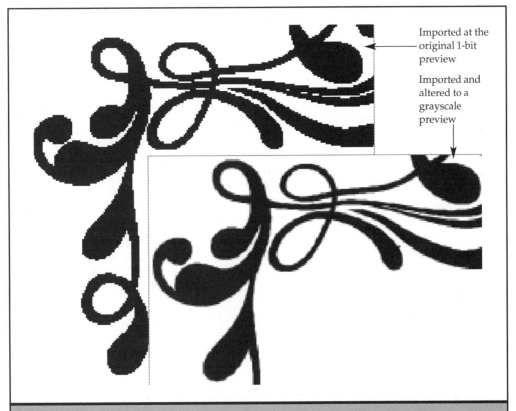

Imported at the
original 1-bit
preview

Imported and
altered to a
grayscale
preview

Figure 8-8.   *The preview of this 1-bit image was altered to grayscale on import.*

Tip *Converting the color modes and preview display of imported pictures in XPress only applies to bitmap-based pictures (as opposed to those that are vector-based). Certain other picture types, such as EPS pictures, often include vector objects and remain unaffected by color mode changes. Although the original picture files may include TIFF previews for placement, the picture information contained in these files remains unchanged when the pictures are printed.*

Regarding conversions, also keep in mind that when a picture color mode or preview is changed during import into your QuarkXPress document, the original picture file remains unaffected. Be sure not to confuse these preview and color mode conversions with making image-editing changes to the original picture files.

These keyboard combinations may be used in combination with each other when importing pictures through the Get Picture dialog. For example, when selecting to import a color TIFF picture, holding CMD/CTRL + SHIFT converts the picture to grayscale and displays it at a low resolution simultaneously.

Changing the Picture Preview Display

If you've ever been on a tight layout deadline and wish to reduce the time it takes your QuarkXPress document to display high-end color pictures, you might want to pay close attention to this section where you'll discover steps for doing just that. Cutting the time it takes for QuarkXPress 5 to display complicated (and possibly even unnecessary) picture color and/or image detail will help you increase your productivity at the most critical times and avoid the *hurry up and wait* situation that often traps users at the worst of times. In the reverse situation, if the images you've placed in your QuarkXPress layout do not appear as crisp and clear as you know they should, the same solution may apply; your Application Display preferences may need to be changed.

Display preferences can control how detailed a picture appears on your screen, regardless of how highly detailed the original is. But the more color and detail QuarkXPress is set to render to the screen, the longer it may take to display a given page. You'll need to decide on your specific priorities when making changes, but at least they are within your control.

To change preview display settings, open the Preferences dialog (see Figure 8-9) to the Application Display page by choosing Edit | Preferences | Preferences (CMD/CTRL + OPTION/ALT + SHIFT + Y) and clicking Display under Application in the tree directory to the left of the dialog. You can choose color and/or grayscale preview options from the Color TIFFs and Gray TIFFs drop-down menus. Color TIFFs may be set to either 8 or 24 bits on the QuarkXPress 5 Windows platform version, and to 8-, 16-, or 32-bit while using QuarkXPress 5 Macintosh platform versions. Grayscale TIFFs may be set to 16 or 256 levels of gray on either platform version.

One noteworthy option new to the QuarkXPress 5 Windows version in this Preferences dialog is the Display DPI Value option. It enables you to set the display resolution of the TIFF previews between 36 and 300 ppi (pixels per inch). Although this option will render the preview for high-resolution pictures at a maximum of 300 ppi, it will not add resolution where it does not exist (that is, to pictures that inherently have a low resolution already).

 Unlike the color conversion technique discussed earlier, choosing Gray TIFFs as the preview method for all your pictures in your Application preferences affects only the previews of the pictures and not their printing properties.

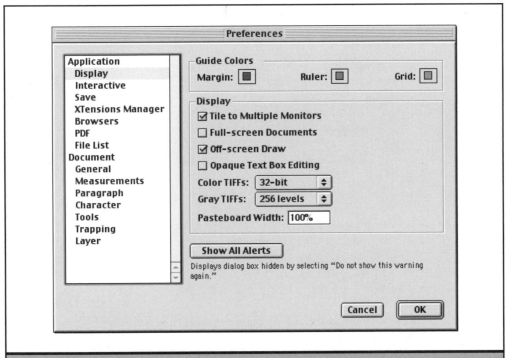

Figure 8-9. *You may control the resolution of the preview display of pictures in boxes using the Application Display page of the Preferences dialog.*

Any changes made to the display of pictures controlled by your Application preferences will apply only to subsequently imported pictures. This means changing these settings part of the way through your layout process will result in previews of different qualities, which in most instances is likely not very helpful. Fortunately, instead of reimporting all your old pictures once again to view them in the new preview settings, simply follow these steps:

1. Close your document and save any changes.

2. With your document still closed, choose Edit | Preferences | Preferences (CMD/CTRL+OPTION/ALT+SHIFT+Y) to open the Preferences dialog and click Display under Application in the tree directory.

    Set your new picture display settings using either the Color TIFFs or Gray TIFFs, and Display DPI Values options.

4. Then reopen your closed document using this technique: From the Open dialog, click once to select your QuarkXPress 5 document file in the browser

window and hold CMD/CTRL while clicking Open in this Open dialog. As your document opens, the previews will be re-rendered using the new settings.

Following the previous steps forces QuarkXPress to rebuild all picture previews contained in the document using the new application display settings. In essence, when the CMD/CTRL modifier is held, XPress evaluates the document and verifies links to all external picture files. If the link to a picture file can't be verified for whatever reason, XPress will use the existing preview instead.

If a picture has been imported with a reduced color mode, you'll have only the preview as an indicator that any conversion has taken place. XPress provides only information about the original linked picture file and not its preview.

To relink the picture using the new application settings, choose Utilities | Usage to open the Picture tab of the Usage dialog (*Macintosh*: OPTION+F13, *Windows*: SHIFT+F2) and use the Update button to locate and relink missing picture files. Once relinked, XPress rebuilds the missing picture previews according to the current application display settings for TIFF pictures.

Using the Update command is always the preferred method to use when relinking a picture to your document. Updating a picture link enables you to preserve all applied picture properties such as color mode conversions, scaling, picture position, and so on. Relinking a picture using the Get Picture command erases all applied properties, returning them to their defaults.

Using the Halftone Command

The term *halftone* is borrowed from the traditional world of offset printing where halftones were created as film negatives exposed through a specialized halftone screen using a typical camera lens and light-sensitive orthographic film. The process was labor intensive where film exposure involved controlled exposure times, lighting, and chemical-processing procedures. The resulting halftone was then manually assembled by literally taping film negatives into place for exposure to a paper or metal plate for offset printing. The process was (and to a certain degree still is) costly and quite environmentally destructive. Thankfully, much of this process has been digitally adapted.

With that little bit of history explained, halftones can now be produced using scanning hardware and image editors. Usually, the halftone produced from digital images features the default properties of the output device used to create the final film for offset printing, such as a high-end imagesetter. These properties are often set by the output device to match the resolution of the film and the output line frequency selected by the user. However, default halftone properties can be overridden in XPress using the Halftone command (CMD/CTRL+SHIFT+H) when a picture box is selected.

The Halftone command is a brief feature that can have profound effects on the printed appearance of selected pictures. It's also one of the most tricky features to use due to the fact that the halftone properties you apply can't be previewed onscreen. Instead, your choice for the style of your halftone must be made based on previous knowledge of the effects applied. Halftone properties are a PostScript function, meaning they are applied at the film output stage of your document production process. In order to see the effects of applying halftone properties, you'll need to produce a reasonable quality proof of your document before you decide which style and options work best for your picture. For the experienced halftone creator, the results of the halftone effect will be somewhat predictable. But for layout artists new to these effects, choosing Halftone options will be (at least initially) by trial and error.

The XPress halftone arsenal includes the Frequency, Angle, and Function options, which can be set using drop-down menus in the Picture Halftone dialog (shown next). If you leave them at the default selections, these options enable your output device to take over the halftone screening functions.

- **Frequency** This drop-down menu contains preset choices for the number of dots or lines measured in a single inch in your final halftone. Options include Default, 60, 85, 100, 133, and 150 lines per inch, the industry standard (of which is 150) when producing final output to a high-end film imagesetter. You may enter any value for the frequency of your halftone between 15 and 600 dots or lines per inch.

- **Angle** When dots or lines are produced in your halftone, they are produced in rows, the size of which varies according to the highlight midtone and shadow values in your original picture. These rows align at various angles by the default settings of your output device (commonly 45 degrees for black plates), the settings entered in the Print command dialog, or to whichever angle you enter here. Angles may be set to any degree measurement based on 360-degree rotation. The preset values in this drop-down menu include 0, 15, 45, 75, 90, and 105. The settings for 45, 75, 90, and 105 are standard screening angles for process color inks black, magenta, yellow, and cyan, respectively, while certain imagesetters feature variations on these angles, depending on the process screening technique in use.

Note

Although the Frequency and Angle options enable you to enter custom values, certain PostScript devices may be incapable of exactly matching these values. In these cases, the closest value PostScript is able to reproduce is used instead.

■ **Function**   The name of this option is slightly misleading in that it actually describes the shape of the element used to describe the highlight, midtone, and shadows of your picture. The Function drop-down menu contains options to select Default (usually Dot for most imagesetters), *Dot, Line, Ellipse, Square,* and *Ordered Dither.* While the Ordered Dither option is selected, both the Frequency and Angle options are unavailable.

Figure 8-10 demonstrates the effects of various Picture Halftone dialog settings applied to a grayscale image with an inherent resolution of 150 dpi.

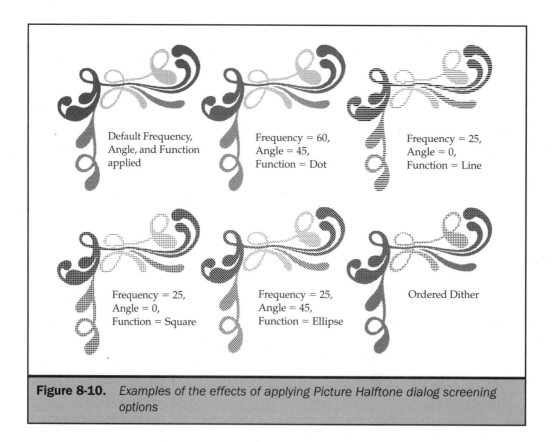

Figure 8-10.   *Examples of the effects of applying Picture Halftone dialog screening options*

Using the Contrast Command

If you've ever been faced with the challenge of working with poorly exposed or badly damaged pictures, you'll know how frustrating it is to try to make them acceptable for your layout. Experts often resort to image editing to improve picture quality, but not everyone has the skill or resources to do so. This is where QuarkXPress 5's picture controls can help.

Although these tools are far from using an image editor, they provide you with the ability to adjust the visual properties of your picture and enable you to apply adjustments to both brightness and contrast, to reduce or increase color values (individually or all colors at once), or to turn negative pictures into positives. You may also apply preset effects such as high contrast or even posterizations. Knowing how to manipulate the options will enable you to salvage poorly prepared pictures directly within XPress. And for the unsalvageable, these controls also enable you to use your own ingenuity or design flair to enhance the appeal of images by applying striking visual effects.

Tip   *Although the Contrast options certainly offer plenty of picture control, they do not enable you to add full color to grayscale images.*

Picture contrast is set using the Picture Contrast Specifications dialog, opened by choosing Style | Contrast (*Macintosh*: CMD+SHIFT+C, *Windows*: CTRL+SHIFT+O) while your picture is selected (see Figure 8-11). Both grayscale and full-color pictures are eligible for contrast control effects, but working with grayscale images is perhaps the simplest operation, since only one color is available for the effect. While color images

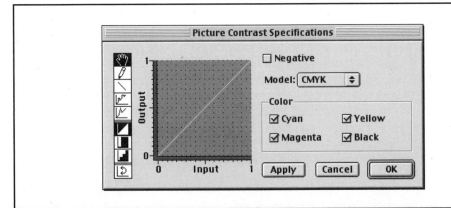

Figure 8-11.   *With its default settings, your picture's contrast curve will look like this when the Contrast Specifications dialog is opened.*

CREATING LAYOUTS
AND DOCUMENTS

are selected, you may choose from various color models to adjust the contrast of your picture. These options enable you to adjust several color curves at a time or isolate individual curves.

Grasping the Contrast Concept

At first, the contrast tools you see may seem a bit overwhelming or intimidating. Even after toying with them, you may still be mystified at how they affect your picture. In the center of the dialog, you'll notice a rough grid divided into ten vertical columns and ten horizontal rows. These represent increments that correspond to the tonal values of the colors in your picture. In its default state, the curve of your picture is represented by a straight line stretching from the bottom-left to the top-right corner of this grid.

The vertical axis serves as a reference for the Output value representing lighter or darker values of your picture, while the horizontal scale is labeled to measure the Input values ranging from highlight tones on the left side of the grid to shadow tones on the right. To the left of the dialog are a series of tool and effect buttons to manipulate the shape and levels of your picture's tone and color. If you've never worked with picture controls before, all these controls may at first seem a little confusing. Rest assured, there's a method to what might seem like madness here.

Tip   *Applying contrast properties to your picture affects both the onscreen preview display and the printed output of pictures.*

The straight line you see within the grid when the dialog is first opened represents the original tonal state of your picture when it was first placed onto your XPress document page. The slope of the line represents an even progression from light to dark through the highlight, midtones, and shadow areas of your picture. These values are relative, which is why neither axis includes a specific numeric reference. In other words, you are not able to control or measure the actual ink or color percentage values for your picture. The properties you apply must be judged visually using the feedback provided by your monitor. Adjustments to the contrast properties of your picture are controlled solely through the shape of the collective or individual curves, which are capable of being manipulated in a number of ways. You can use several different tools (defined in the next section) to adjust the curves. While certain tool buttons are selected, such as the Spike and Posterizer tools, the selected curve line includes small white markers that correspond to the ten vertical grid columns. The Spike tool markers intersect the vertical grid lines (see Figure 8-12), enabling you to set tonal values to specific output positions. In contrast, Posterizer markers lay *between* the vertical grid lines (see Figure 8-13), enabling you to set the levels of even color.

On your picture itself, highlight tones represent the whiter areas of your picture, midtones represent the middle gray tones, and the shadows represent the darkest areas. On the grid, the top edge represents the full intensity of your original picture's tone, while the bottom represents the least intensity. If you think of the grid in this way, it

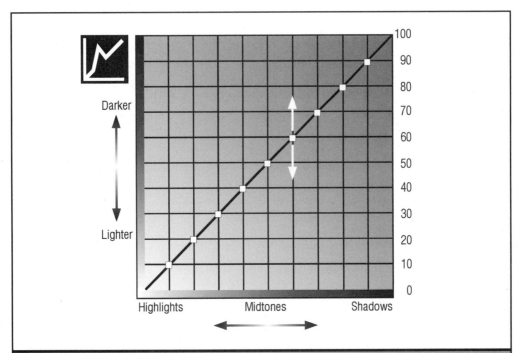

Figure 8-12. *While the Spike tool is selected, 11 markers appear on your curve, enabling you to set each of the points on your selected colors' curves to different levels as well as to apply an averaging of the tones between these points.*

will be much easier to comprehend its use and anticipate the results of the changes made to the color curves. This principle applies to most, but not all, contrast manipulation, as you'll discover in the information to follow.

Using the Contrast Tools

To the left of the Contrast dialog grid are a series of buttons that have been subtly divided into two areas: curve-shaping tools and preset curve shapes. The first four tools in the group enable you to custom shape the line of your picture's selected contrast curve, while the remaining preset curve buttons enable you to quickly apply a predefined curve state.

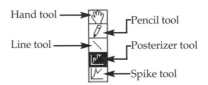

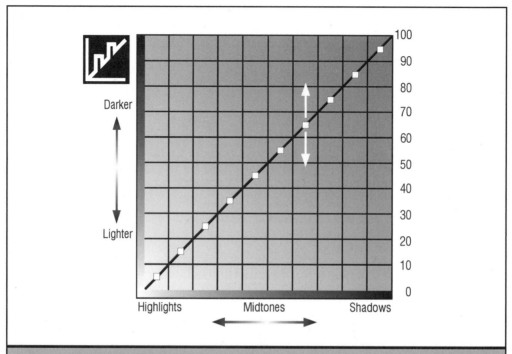

Figure 8-13.   *While the Posterizer tool is selected, 10 markers appear on your curve, enabling you to set tones as flat and even tonal levels. Between each level, a uniform tone is applied to your picture.*

The tools for custom shaping your contrast curve include the following:

■ **Hand**   This tool enables you to move the entire shape of your selected color curve anywhere on the grid simply by dragging on the curve with your mouse. By dragging it, you may move the curve shape to anywhere within the grid, preserving its initial shape.

■ **Pencil**   This tool behaves like a freehand drawing tool, enabling you to literally sketch the shape of your curve directly onto the grid. When using the Pencil tool, the shape of your picture's color curve may essentially be any shape.

■ **Line**   This tool enables you to create tones represented by straight lines between the points on your picture's color curve simply by dragging directly on the curve.

■ **Posterizer**   This tool stems from the effect of limiting color values or flattening color levels, which can often result in dramatic changes to your picture's tone.

Using posterizing effects, your picture may be reduced from full color to a mere handful of colors, causing certain parts of your picture to display and print as flat or uniform color. The Posterizer tool enables you to flatten your picture's color curve between each of the 10 percent values on the grid. When selected, the Posterizer tool places markers at each of the 10 percent increments on your curve, enabling you to increase or decrease the intensity of your picture's tones as if they were flat levels.

- **Spike**   This tool enables you to adjust your picture's contrast by setting 11 (including zero) specific tonal levels and by allowing the contrast to be averaged between these points. Since the values between the spikes are averaged, the Spike tool offers more tones than the effects achieved using the Posterizer tool.

To see the effects of your picture's new contrast curve before accepting it, hold OPTION/CTRL and click Apply in the dialog. This enables you to immediately see the changes to your picture's color each time the curve is altered. The Apply button will remain in a depressed position until it is clicked a second time.

By manipulating the curves using the custom-shaping tools, you may manipulate your picture's contrast curve to any shape you wish. For automated effects, the remaining tool buttons in the dialog apply preset curve shapes, each of which may be edited afterwards. Preset curves automatically override the current shape of the selected curve (shown next).

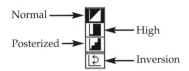

The following list provides an insight into what's happening behind the scenes:

- **Normal Contrast**   This tool returns your selected color curve to its original default straight-line setting. This enables you to quickly return the contrast in your picture back to its original appearance. If you're looking for a quick way to reset your picture's contrast, this is the one to use.

- **High Contrast**   This tool enables you to change your picture's contrast curve to a preset condition to contain only white highlights and dark midtones and shadows. The highlighted areas of your picture represented by the first three markers are set to their brightest setting, while the remaining markers representing midtones and shadows are set to their darkest setting.

- ■ **Posterized**   This tool sets your selected color's curve to a preset condition where the values in your picture are limited to just six tones, represented by the stair shape of the selected color's curve.

- ■ **Inversion**   This tool enables you to flip the shape of a selected color curve horizontally, which has the effect of reversing highlight, midtone, and shadow values. When working with grayscale pictures (or color pictures with all the color curves selected), clicking Inversion has the same effect as choosing the Negative option in the dialog.

If your picture has been scanned directly from color negative film, the Negative option will be useful to you. Selecting this option has the effect of reversing the colors in your picture around the standard color wheel. You may apply a negative image effect on your picture image simply by clicking this option in the Picture Contrast Specifications dialog.

Working with Contrast Color Models

When working with color pictures (as opposed to grayscale), the complexity of the contrast tools is compounded by the number of colors being displayed. Color pictures may be adjusted in a number of ways, the operation of which is identical to the effects achieved while manipulating grayscale curves, only with a few more colors and options to deal with. While a color picture is selected, the Model drop-down menu becomes available, enabling you to manipulate your picture's color based on one of four different color models.

The Model menu includes a selection of color models that merely display specific color curves for you to manipulate. It does *not* convert the color model on which the original picture file is based. The available color models include RGB, Hue, Saturation, and Brightness (HSB), Cyan, Magenta, and Yellow (CMY), and Cyan, Magenta, Yellow, and Black (CMYK). The first three models enable you to control three curves at a time, while the latter is based on standard four-color process printing.

Applying contrast properties to the colors in your imported picture merely causes XPress to display and print your picture differently. Applied contrast settings do not affect the original data representing your picture.

While a specific color model is selected, the Contrast Specifications dialog enables you to manipulate one of more of your picture's color curves. For example, while the CMYK color model is selected, cyan, magenta, yellow, and/or black color curves may be manipulated together or individually (see Figure 8-14). This is done by checking or unchecking option boxes beside each available color name.

The one exception to the contrast curve manipulation rule is for that of the HSB model, the default applied to your picture. While this model is in use, the HSB may be set collectively or individually. But the associated changes are quite different than other

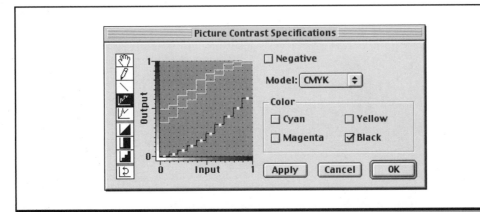

Figure 8-14. *When working with color pictures, you may choose to manipulate your picture based on a specific color model, and each color's contrast curve may be manipulated individually as depicted here using CMYK.*

color modes. For example, while hue color is selected, the vertical and horizontal axes are colored with all the colors of the standard color wheel.

To alter the hue for your picture, select only the Hue option and shape your curve to align with a corresponding hue color on the axes (see Figure 8-15). To adjust your picture's brightness (the most commonly sought after effect), select only the Brightness option and manipulate the curve. In the case of Brightness, the values operate in reverse of color tones. In other words, moving the curve higher on the grid causes the brightness to *increase*.

Practicing with Contrast Controls

Since the application of contrast effects is based on the feedback provided on your screen, the process will ultimately be perfected through practice and testing. To explore some of these tools, follow these steps (you will need at least one full-color picture available):

1. Create a picture box and choose File | Get Picture (CMD/CTRL+E). Choose a prepared color image, but to begin let's import it as a grayscale by holding the CMD/CTRL key while clicking Open in the Get Picture dialog. Once Open is clicked, notice a grayscale representation of the picture appears in the picture box. Size and position your picture as you wish.

2. With the picture selected using either the Item or Content tool, choose Style | Contrast (*Macintosh*: CMD+SHIFT+C, *Windows*: CTRL+SHIFT+O) to open the Picture Contrast Specifications dialog. When first opened, the dialog reveals the picture's contrast curve as a black diagonal straight line, the Normal tool

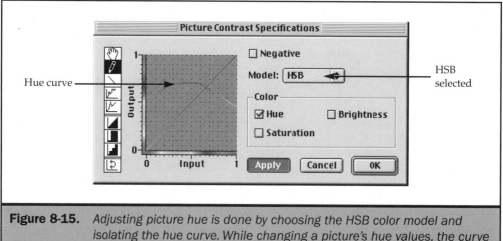

Figure 8-15. *Adjusting picture hue is done by choosing the HSB color model and isolating the hue curve. While changing a picture's hue values, the curve must align with the corresponding axes' color.*

button is selected, and by default the last selected custom-shape tool is automatically chosen.

3. Click the Posterizer tool from the row of buttons to the left of the grid. Notice your curve now features ten markers. Hold CMD/CTRL while clicking the Apply button to preview changes to your picture as they are made and manipulate the markers by dragging the first two upwards roughly one-third of the grid's height. Notice the white areas of your picture become darker. Also notice that these specific tonal values have been slightly flattened.

4. Drag the last three markers at the right of your contrast curve downward roughly one-third of the grid's height. Notice the shadow areas of your picture become lighter and their tones also became flatter. Click Normal to return your picture to its original condition. Click the High Contrast tool button. Notice the highlights in your picture now resemble the line art of a completely black and white 1-bit image. Notice also that your previous curve shape has been eliminated.

5. Drag the fourth marker in the grid downward roughly two-thirds of the grid height and drag the fifth marker downward roughly one-third. Notice the black and white state of your picture now features two additional shades of gray. Take a moment to experiment with the Hand, Pencil, Line and Spike tools to familiarize yourself with their effects on the curve shape. And, before moving on, explore the preset shapes defined by the Posterize and Inversion tool buttons by clicking them.

6. Click Cancel to close the dialog without accepting the settings and reimport your picture by choosing File | Get Picture (CMD/CTRL+E) to open the Get Picture dialog again. But this time import the same picture as a color image by simply clicking Open. Size and position your picture as you wish. With your picture still selected, open the Picture Contrast Specifications dialog again. Now that your picture includes full color, notice the Model drop-down and color options are now available.

7. Choose CMYK from the Model drop-down menu. Notice options for CMYK now appear in the dialog. Uncheck all colors except Black, and choose the Spike tool. Notice 11 markers now appear on your picture's contrast curve. Try manipulating the markers vertically to adjust their position. Notice as you do, the other color curves are revealed beneath them, but remain stationary as you move the black color contrast curve. This demonstrates the results of manipulating a single color curve.

8. With your black contrast curve still selected, click Inversion and watch how it changes the black curve and the contrast in your picture. Notice the curve is now the horizontal opposite of its original shape, with highlight, midtone, and shadow values transposed. Reselect all the colors once again and click the Posterize tool button to see the effects. Notice the dramatic change in your picture's appearance. Now choose RGB from the Model menu and click the Posterized tool button again. Notice the results are drastically different from the CMYK model used earlier. That's because the contrast curve colors are being manipulated based on a different color model.

Since color manipulation can be a complex and sometimes unpredictable factor to deal with, exploration can be an exciting and creative process. Ultimately, whichever contrast setting you finally accept for your picture will improve either your picture's appearance or its appeal (or both). But as you begin working with different pictures prepared from different sources, you'll quickly realize that not all pictures may be treated the same way. For example, the contrast specifications for one picture may not affect a different picture in the same way. For this, you'll need to experiment and judge your image based on how the picture appears on your screen (and/or in the final printed result).

Working with Clipping Paths

Making good use of interesting pictures and picture shapes in your QuarkXPress layouts is often a difficult challenge. One of the most interesting layout strategies at your disposal is the use of nonrectangular shaped pictures. These can make for stimulating layouts and add visual appeal to your document's overall design, especially if you intend your text to flow around the contours of your image such as when applying a text runaround. For the moment, let's examine clipping images and their associated paths.

QuarkXPress 5 features several options for creating, editing, and applying clipping paths, the properties of which may be set using the Clipping tab of the Modify dialog, which may be opened directly for any selected picture using the shortcut CMD/CTRL+OPTION/ALT+T.

What's a Clipping Path?

For veterans of the layout business, a clipping path is essentially a digital close-crop of an image. Before the desktop completely changed layout and production techniques, hand-cut masks were required to isolate a given shape within a continuous tone photograph. If your image features an unwanted colored background, or you simply wish to isolate a certain part of the image, clipping paths provide the solution. Clipping paths enable you to isolate specific areas of your image, so unwanted areas appear invisible or appear transparent.

For information on how closely related the paths created to clip your image are to those controlling advanced runarounds for text content, see "Understanding Runaround Options" in Chapter 9.

The beauty of using a clipping path is that it enables you to isolate a portion of your image without altering the digital information stored in the invisible portions of the image. Clipping paths can often make use of digital information already contained in the image, or they may be created automatically or manually in QuarkXPress.

Digitally speaking, clipping paths are described as a series of points joined by straight and/or curved line segments. The more detail that is contained in the image, the more complex the clipping path will likely be, and the more memory required to store it. Clipping paths may be applied to virtually any image format XPress supports, including common favorites such as EPS, BMP, TIFF, PICT, JPEG, and GIF.

As you're about to discover, the strategy you choose to follow in applying a clipping path to your image will depend largely on your expertise with your favorite image editor and/or the condition of your image. In certain cases, a clipping path may be created quite easily in XPress, or it may be created before it reaches XPress.

Option 1: Create the Path in Advance

First of all, using any digital path or channel information already stored within an image is the preferred strategy to follow in creating a clipping path. Most intermediate or advanced image editors such as Adobe Photoshop or Corel's Photo-Paint are inherently designed with selection tools and saving features to help you mask and/or isolate parts of an image; they also contain created channels or paths based on those selections. Both alpha channels and paths may be embedded, named, and saved within the data representing TIFF image files. Once saved, QuarkXPress 5 is able to extract this information and make use of it. If a picture contains an alpha channel or an embedded path, the Clipping dialog will display this information (see Figure 8-16).

Clipping paths also enable you to do this in more than one way, including the use of either embedded paths or alpha channels. Then, when you apply a clipping path to an image in XPress, its clipping path feature may use the existing path or channel to clip the image. Each of these two methods has it own characteristics:

- **Embedded paths**   These are usually defined using an image editor's vector drawing tools, so they may be as accurate as the person creating them. More often than not, embedded paths are saved with the information representing TIFF images. When the image is saved, the embedded path is saved along with it. Embedded paths are ideal for use in isolating image areas that require sharp or hard edges. But embedded paths may only clip one enclosed area of an image at a time, meaning that the path may define only one image shape and one transparent area at a time. If your image features an embedded path, the image will nearly always import into XPress with this path, immediately clipping the image.

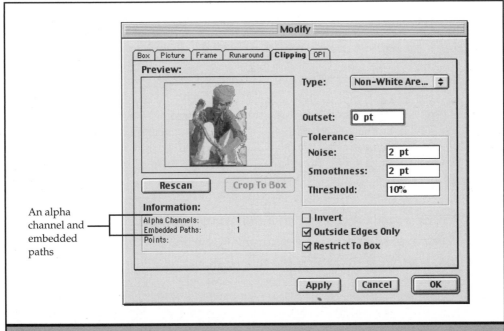

Figure 8-16.   *If the image you are working with contains information that may be used as a clipping path, the Clipping dialog will indicate the number of each.*

■ **Alpha channels**   These are specific selection areas or masks that may be isolated in any picture using an image editor and may be saved with the image. As with embedded images, alpha channels are supported most commonly by TIFF images. A digital TIFF image may contain multiple alpha channels and the channels themselves may isolate more than one specific area, making this an extremely versatile clipping path option to use. If your image contains an alpha channel selection, XPress will not immediately apply a clipping path when the image is imported.

Tip   *The display and printing of alpha channel selections that feature feathered edges created with your image are not supported by QuarkXPress. Instead, the clipping path used will be the actual selected area.*

If your image is prepared with a channel or path, you'll certainly be able to make good use of these. If you choose to, you may even prepare an image with multiple paths and/or channels and use the same image more than once using different clipping effects in each case. Using XPress, this will have enormous advantages, since you'll be able to have multiple links to the same digital image while keeping your document file size to a minimum. Once the image has been imported into a picture box, simply select the box and open the Clipping dialog (CMD/CTRL+OPTION/ALT+T), a tabbed dialog within the Modify dialog. Figure 8-17 shows a picture applied with a clipping path based on an alpha channel that has been used to eliminate the background.

Option 2: Create the Path in XPress

If the image you wish to apply a clipping path to doesn't contain any channels or paths to use for clipping, you may wish to use an automated feature: the Non-White Areas clipping path type. But take note—the picture condition must be almost perfectly suited to use this feature effectively and make your efforts worthwhile. Choosing Non-White Areas from the Clipping dialog Type drop-down menu allows XPress to automatically clip the picture by masking out specified pixel values. To really make the most of this feature, the area to be clipped must fit three basic criteria, as follows:

■ A light-colored object or image surrounded by uniform darkness.

■ A dark-colored object or image surrounded by uniform light colors.

■ Ideally, the image or object being clipped should be in sharp focus.

Tip   *To put it bluntly, if your picture features flat color and is out of focus, trying to use Non-White Areas as your clipping path operation may simply be a waste of time. Much of the success of clipping automatically to Non-White Areas will be the result of performing trial-by-error Threshold settings.*

Original picture

Background clipped

Figure 8-17.   *An alpha channel prepared in advance with this image as used to clip out this picture's background.*

Exploring Clipping Path Applications

As with most complex features, the quickest way to learn their operation is through hands-on experience. The following exercise will provide you with a basic understanding of the powerful and complex capabilities of applying a clipping path to your picture:

1. If you use an image-editing program, prepare a grayscale TIFF image with at least one alpha channel selection and one saved path. Then import this image into your XPress document by creating an oval-shaped picture box and using the Get Picture (CMD/CTRL+E) command. Ideally, your picture will feature a well-defined visual element on a light-colored background.

2. Crop your picture by slightly reducing the width and height dimensions of your picture box.

3. With your picture selected, choose Style | Clipping (CMD/CTRL+OPTION/ALT+T) to open the Modify dialog directly at the Clipping tab. If your picture contains an embedded path, it may be automatically selected and applied as a clipping path to your picture and may be indicated as such in the Type drop-down menu. If not, the Type menu will be selected to Item, meaning the clipping path is your picture box itself and the options in the dialog will be unavailable. Notice the representation of your picture is showing in the Preview window surrounded by a blue border, which represents your picture box shape.

   From the Type menu, choose Non-White Areas and select both the Restrict to Box and Outside Edges Only options. Notice the options in the dialog change and others become available. Notice a clipping path is immediately applied in the preview window as a green border around the clipped area of your picture.

4. To increase the area of your picture's light-colored background, increase the Threshold option incrementally until the background completely disappears. Notice also where your picture extends beyond your picture box, the image is cropped and an empty green clipping path is left.

Choosing Clipping Path Options

While the embedded path, alpha channel, or non-white areas clipping path types are in use, a collection of further options become available, including options to set how closely the clipping path is followed and how complex the path is:

- **Outset**   With any of the clipping path types selected, this option enables you to clip either inside or outside the channel or path in use. Positive Outset values enable you to clip outside the established path, while negative values perform the opposite (see Figure 8-18). The Outset value may be set between 288 and −244 points (4 inches). This behavior works differently depending on whether the image or its background has been isolated.

While using path, channel, or non-white areas types to clip your image, various *tolerance* options become active, enabling you to fine-tune the clipping path. Tolerance options enable you to control noise, smoothness, and threshold during the clipping process, defined as follows:

- **Noise**   This option enables you to control the XPress clipping path sensitivity to pixel area size. The value entered sets the dimensions of the area to be ignored. For example, entering a value of 10 points sets XPress to ignore pixel areas less than 10 points.

After a clipping path is applied to your image, the effect is automatically transformed with your image. Transformations include flipping the image horizontally or vertically, scaling the image, changing the picture box dimensions, or repositioning the image or picture box on your page.

Outset set to -10 points   Outset set to 10 points

Figure 8-18.   *These two examples compare the effects of positive and negative outset values.*

- **Smoothness**   This option enables you to control how closely the shape of your image is followed. The smoothness setting has a direct effect on how complex the clipping path created will be. The more detail there is around the contours of your image area, the more points will be required to describe it.

- **Threshold**   This option becomes available only while Alpha Channel or Non-White Areas clipping paths are in use. The threshold setting sets the sensitivity to changes in pixel grayscale values in your image, which in turn enables you to control how closely your isolated area will be clipped to. Pixel values lighter than the grayscale percentage value entered are excluded from the clipped area, while the darker areas are included.

Tip   *The Threshold setting is the most significant to master when allowing XPress to create a clipping path based on the non-white areas of your image.*

Three remaining options in the dialog enable you to further control the image shown through your clipping path. Certain options become available, depending on which clipping type is selected:

- **Invert** This option enables you to reverse the area currently being clipped (see Figure 8-19). For example, if the path or channel applied to your image clips out the background (instead of the image you wish to clip), choosing Invert corrects this with a single click.

- **Outside Edges Only** While clipping to the non-white edges of your image, this option enables you to exclude pixels that are lighter than the threshold and value *within the interior* of your isolated image area. For example, if your image contains inner areas of equal color to the background being clipped, choosing this option limits the clipping operation to only the area outside your image. The white sky background of the picture shown in Figure 8-20 was clipped using non-white areas to allow the linear blend box color to show through. Notice the white areas of the lighthouse also become involved in the clipping path while Outside Edges Only is left unselected.

- **Restrict to Box** While using a clipping path to clip an image, it *is* possible for parts of your clipped image to appear outside your picture box. While this option is selected, the image and path are restricted to only your clipping path settings and the image's picture box boundaries.

Tip *One of your main concerns when using clipping paths should be the path's complexity. The more complex your image's clipping path is, the longer the page containing the image will take to print, especially at higher resolutions.*

Original clipping path applied   Inverted clipping path applied

Figure 8-19. *These two examples compare the effects of inverting a clipping path.*

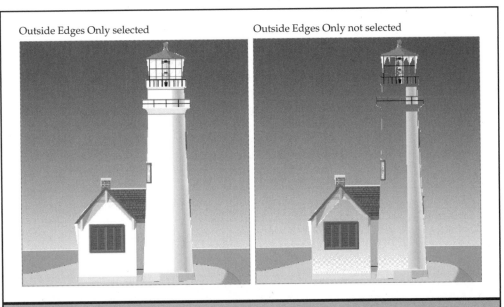

Outside Edges Only selected   Outside Edges Only not selected

Figure 8-20.   *This picture was clipped with Outside Edges Only selected and not selected.*

Besides the previous options, the Clipping dialog contains command buttons and an information area describing your image and your clipping path's complexity. Each time a new clipping path type is selected, the image is automatically scanned and the chosen clipping path applied. The *Rescan* button below the preview window may be used to update the clipping path after new values have been entered into any of the option boxes.

Clipping paths appear in the preview window as colored outlines surrounding the clipped image. Pressing Crop to Box automatically resets the clipping path to apply only to parts of your image that appear inside your image's picture box. The aim of this option is to reduce the overall clipping path complexity. Without this option selected, your clipping path may be unnecessarily complex.

The information area of the dialog indicates the number of embedded paths and alpha channels (if any) existing in your image when imported. But perhaps the most significant values to monitor are the points. This value shows the number of points currently describing your clipping path, a direct indication of how complex the path is.

Editing a Clipping Path

Rest assured, even after your clipping path has been automatically applied, you may still make adjustments to it manually. But again take note that the process can be tedious if major shape changes are involved, and you'll need to use some precision with XPress 5's Bézier drawing tools. With your clipping path already applied, edit its shape by selecting the picture box containing the clipped image and choosing Item | Edit | Clipping Path (*Macintosh*: OPTION+SHIFT+F4, *Windows*: CTRL+SHIFT+F10). While in this editing mode, the points and segments describing your clipping path become visible as a colored outline (see Figure 8-21). Using the Item tool, points on this path may be moved, added, or deleted while the segments that join them may be converted from lines to curves, or vice versa.

Tip *While editing a clipping path, holding OPTION/ALT while clicking a segment adds or deletes a point.*

As you edit your clipping path, you'll notice that all the usual Bézier resources come into play. The context-sensitive Measurements palette (F9) displays all relevant point and segment properties (see Figure 8-22). The buttons on this palette may be used to

Figure 8-21. *The clipping path of this picture applied using the Non-White Areas option is currently in the editing state.*

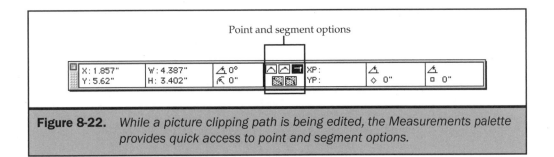

Figure 8-22. *While a picture clipping path is being edited, the Measurements palette provides quick access to point and segment options.*

change the state of points and/or segments. As changes are made to the path, the visible image portions are updated automatically.

After editing a clipping path, choosing Item | Edit | Shape (SHIFT+F4/F10) returns you to the normal editing state. Once your clipping path has been manually edited, it will be listed as User-Edited Path in the Type drop-down menu of the Clipping dialog.

Exporting Pictures from XPress

If at some point you wish to use the picture properties you have applied in another application or in XPress itself, you have the option of saving your pictures as encapsulated PostScript files. In fact, XPress enables you to export entire pages in your document, including the pictures they contain, with a single command by choosing File | Save Page as EPS (CMD/CTRL+OPTION/ALT+SHIFT+S).

Saving entire pages in EPS format enables you to import the pages into other applications or back into your XPress document itself. The process of exporting and then reimporting pages is often used in cases where you wish to place an entire page or spread onto a page and subsequently resize or reprint it in a different format.

The Save Page as EPS dialog (shown next) contains a number of options specifically geared toward handling the pictures on your page. You are able to control how the pictures are displayed, whether the pictures feature previews, and whether or not the EPS file representing your page includes the original picture data or not.

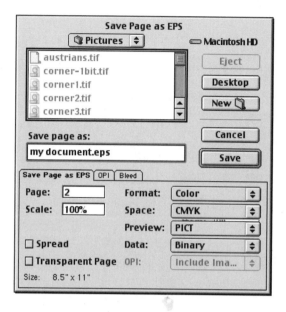

These options are set using the *Format, Preview, Data,* and *OPI* drop-down menus that include the following options:

- **Format**   The Color drop-down menu includes options for saving your page and pictures to color, B&W (black and white), DCS, or DCS 2.0. The *Color* option saves your entire page and its pictures with all its applied colors, while choosing *B&W* saves the page in a single color of black, converting all type and pictures to black and grayscale respectively. The *DCS* option enables you to use desktop color separation standards. DCS (essentially version 1.0) supports only process color, saving your page and all its contents to be reproduced in the standard four colors, cyan, magenta, yellow, and black. The more up-to-date *DCS 2.0* format supports both process and spot color. If your document contains spot colors applied to items on your page(s), the resulting EPS file will print using all colors specified.

- **Preview**   The Preview option applied to your page may be set to either *TIFF* or *None*. Previews of entire pages often result in large file sizes, and so setting a preview to None may help avoid overly large files.

- **Data**   The data representing your EPS may be set to *ASCII, Binary,* or *Clean 8-bit,* the latter being the most common format and default selection. Certain types of applications may require that ASCII or Binary EPS files be supported. Before selecting either of these options, you may want to consult the document associated with your specific application.

- **OPI**   The Open Prepress Interface (OPI) is a standard whereby the images you include on your page and subsequently within your exported EPS file may be contained within the EPS file or left as externally linked files. The OPI option may be set to include *All Images, Omit TIFF,* or *Omit TIFF & EPS.*

For more information on other options available in the Save Page as EPS dialog, see "Saving Pages in EPS Format" in Chapter 20.

About OPI

QuarkXPress 5 now features OPI functionality, which is prevalent throughout the application and available whenever your document features externally linked pictures. These OPI features enable you to get specific and detailed information on pictures in your document and manage the link information at any time. While the OPI option of the Get Picture dialog is selected, XPress maintains an external link to the imported picture. QuarkXPress 5 also makes OPI information on imported and linked pictures whenever picture boxes are selected for modification as well as when printing and exporting images from your document page.

While a picture box containing a picture is selected, the OPI tab appears in the Modify dialog whenever the content is being modified (see Figure 8-23).

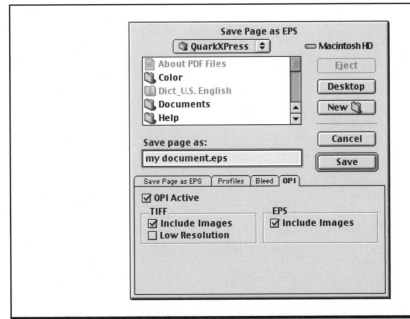

Figure 8-23. *Information on the date, path, file name, color depth, and so on is available in the OPI tab of the Modify dialog while a linked picture is selected.*

To obtain specific information on the selected picture, view the information presented in the lower window of the OPI tab of the Modify dialog. For more information on OPI handling during printing, see Chapter 17 or for a reference on OPI export options, see Chapter 20.

Chapter 9

Combining Text and Picture Effects

I f you have just turned to this chapter from one of several related areas, you're likely looking for ways of somehow mixing text together with lines, graphics, or picture boxes, or perhaps even other text boxes. In fact, there are several jump points within this book that bring you here. The reason for this is that this chapter is an absolute *must read* if you plan on integrating and shaping both text and pictures together on the same page—a situation most layout artists come to face eventually.

Creating a successful mix of text and graphics together in a single layout isn't necessarily a challenge to be left only to experienced electronic artists or designers. With the innovations in XPress, a multitude of capabilities have opened the doors for novices to explore and for experts to increase their productivity. In this chapter, you'll learn about all the ways XPress enables you to combine text and pictures on a single page and how you may control these two types of objects in an effort to visually—and physically—integrate them. Along the way, you'll pick up tips and tricks in using these features effectively.

Creating Text on a Path

Although many applications try to provide the effect of running text along a path, few do it as well and efficiently as QuarkXPress 5's Text Path tools. Text that follows a path is often used for special effects where short strings of characters or words themselves become graphic elements that create visual interest and/or communicate a message.

QuarkXPress 5 comes equipped with four Text Path tools, as shown next. But don't be fooled by the fancy names or the specialized functions. The Line, Bézier, Freehand, and Orthogonal Text Path tools are merely clones of the typical line tools available in the Tool palette that automatically set the content type of the lines created to accept text content. If you wish, you may do this yourself with virtually any selected line by choosing Edit | Content | Text. The path your text follows may originate as any type of content item you wish. This includes any type of box shape (rounded, concave, beveled, oval, or rectangular) or any type of line (typical lines and/or freehand, Bézier, or orthogonal lines).

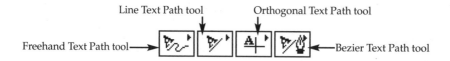

Line Text Path tool   Orthogonal Text Path tool

Freehand Text Path tool⟶   ⟵Bezier Text Path tool

Regardless of this fact, the convenience of creating text-ready lines is available to you and does provide some degree of time saved. These Text Path tools are located in the Tool palette between the Line and Link tools. To use any of these tools to create text on a path, follow these brief steps:

1. Choose any Text Path tool from the Tool palette.

2. Click-drag-release to create line, freehand, or orthogonal text paths, or use typical Bézier techniques to create a Bézier line.

3. Once you've completed creating the line, choose the Content tool from the Tool palette. Notice a text cursor blinking at the origin point of the line you created (typically the first point of the line you defined).

4. Simply begin typing to enter text. As you type, the characters are positioned along the path according to default text-path specifications.

 For information on drawing lines with the Line, Freehand, Orthogonal, or Bézier tools, see Chapter 5.

Forcing a Path to Accept Text

Although you may create specific Text Path lines, virtually any type of box or line may be forced to accept path text. To convert a selected contentless box to accept text, first choose Item | Shape and choose either of three line types from the submenu that appears (see Figure 9-1). Then select Item | Content | Text to convert the line to a text path.

The first of these shape selections has the effect of converting your selected box to a line, while the second restricts the shape to that of an orthogonal line oriented either vertically or horizontally depending on how the shape was originally created. The last shape condition on the list is perhaps the most useful, enabling you to convert any box shape to a text path without distorting or destroying its inherent shape, as is typically the case when selecting either of the first two line types. When a box shape is converted to a text path, defaults enable text to follow the outside shape of the box in a clockwise direction, beginning at the lower-left area of the shape when entering text in the default flush left alignment. Figure 9-2 shows a rectangle, an oval, a rounded-rectangle and a Bézier shape converted to this state and used as text paths.

Figure 9-3 shows various effects achieved by creating path shapes and applying text using Text Path tools.

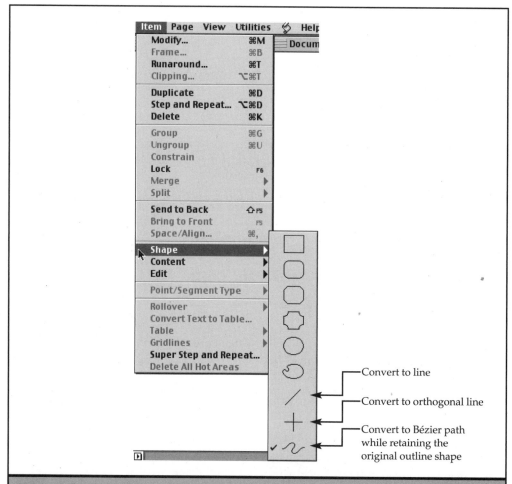

Convert to line

Convert to orthogonal line

Convert to Bézier path while retaining the original outline shape

Figure 9-1. *Choose any of these Shape options to force virtually any line or box shape to accept text characters.*

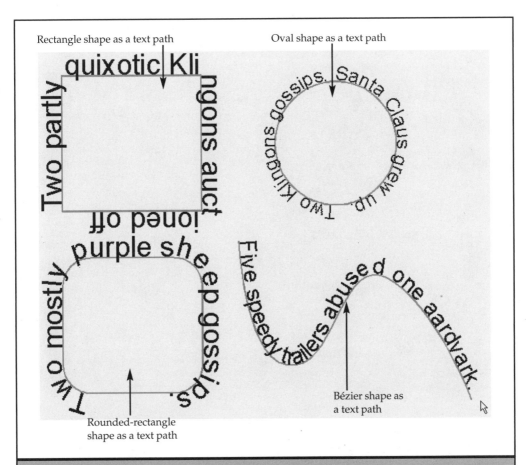

Rectangle shape as a text path

Oval shape as a text path

Rounded-rectangle
shape as a text path

Bézier shape as
a text path

Figure 9-2.   *Create any of these effects by converting any box or line shape to a text path.*

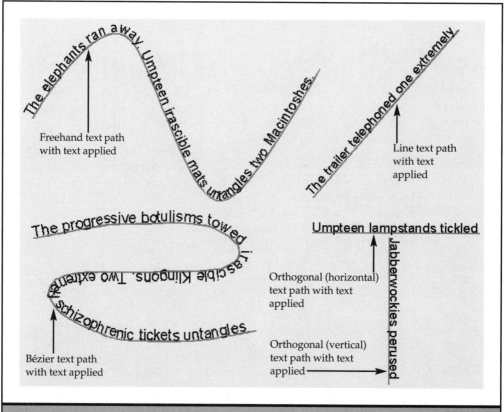

Figure 9-3. *These text path effects were created using each of the four Text Path tools.*

Using the Text Path tools to create shapes is identical to using the usual line tools in XPress, while applying, editing, and modifying text on text paths is identical to working with the usual Text tools in text boxes. However, even more flexibility exists when working with text paths through use of the Text Path dialog, which is opened by selecting text on a path and opening the Modify | Text Path tab dialog, as shown next.

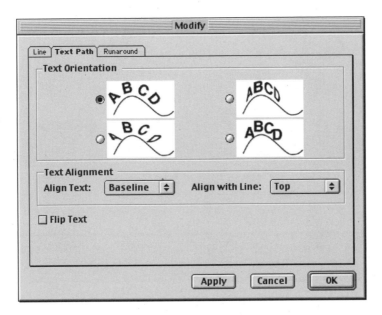

Options in this dialog enable you to control how the text on your shape or path behaves in relation to the path itself. If you wish, you may control how the text is oriented, aligned, or flipped using the following options.

Controlling Text-Path Orientation

Four orientation styles are available. The first style (the default) enables the text path characters to follow the path or shape without any distortions, where characters simply align with the path as if it were the baseline of your text. As the path changes angle, each character is rotated. The second option (at the top-right) applies a distortion to the characters based on the curvature of the path they are following. The characters themselves are oriented vertically; however, each character is skewed to mimic the curvature of the path.

The third option (at the bottom-left) preserves the baseline orientation, but the vertical character orientation is adjusted to mimic the curvature of the path or shape. The fourth and final option (at the bottom-right) preserves each character shape without applying rotation or skew, enabling them to be attached to the path at each of their center points. Figure 9-4 shows the effects of each of these options while working with text on an oval-shaped path.

Figure 9-4. *Using Text Orientation options with text applied to an arc-shaped path*

When selecting text paths, you may use either the Content or Item tools. But clicking the characters themselves will not select the item. Instead, you must click the path that the text is applied to with either the Content or Item tools in order to select the path. The Item tool will enable you to edit the position of the complete item and/or the path markers, while the Content tool will enable you to edit both text and path shape.

Aligning Characters to a Path

The Align Text drop-down menu features the following options for aligning the text path characters: *Baseline* (the default), *Center*, *Ascent*, or *Descent*, the effects of which are shown in Figure 9-5. Choosing each of these options can cause a dramatic shift in the positioning of the text in relation to how the characters align with the text path itself.

Choosing Align with Line Options

The Align Text drop-down menu in the Text Path tab of the Modify dialog enables you to control which part of a line your text is aligned with. In this case, the Baseline (or any of the other options selected in the Align Text drop-down menu) is aligned with various parts of the path. This option enables you to specifically control which point your

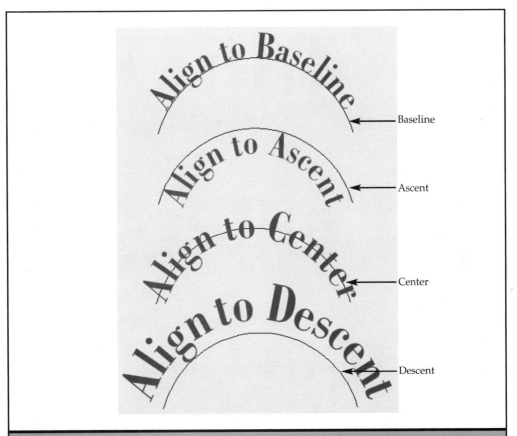

Figure 9-5.   *These examples represent the effects of choosing each of the four
available Align Text options.*

characters align with at the edge of your line. While applying text to lines that have
small width measures (or none at all), this option will have little visual effect. However,
if your line includes a thicker width, you may want to specify which edge of the path
the characters align to by choosing *Top, Center,* or *Bottom,* as shown in Figure 9-6.

Figure 9-6.   *Each of the three Align with Line options places your text at a different point in relation to the line's edge.*

Flipping Text on a Path

This option enables you to apply the text to the opposite side of the text path, as shown in the following example. The *Flip Text* option is also available while using the Content tool and while working with text paths by choosing Style | Flip Text or through the *Flip Text* button in the center of the Measurements palette (F9).

Flip Text option
not applied

Flip Text option
applied

Strategies for Creating Special Box Shapes

If the layout you are creating calls for unusual treatment of text in the form of shaped text or picture boxes, QuarkXPress 5 comes with a few nifty and powerful capabilities for creating these. Nontypical box shapes require a few extra steps to create, but the results can definitely be rewarding. QuarkXPress 5's Merge and Text to Box commands enable you to combine shapes for creative endeavors, and the Bézier editing capabilities of XPress enable you to refine the shapes to be virtually anything you wish.

Creating a shape for your text or pictures often involves several steps. In essence, what you'll be doing is creating ordinary box or line shapes and combining and/or reshaping them. Although the shapes you create for yourself will very likely be specific, the two exercises to follow involve creating two basic shapes: a key-shaped box using text boxes, Merge commands, and text modifications, and a box shape based on an existing character using the Text to Box command. Although these two exercises demonstrate the creation of specific shapes, you are limited only by your imagination on the themes involved.

Designing a Picture Frame Box

The capability to shape boxes using Béziers provides creative opportunities for picture or text box applications. As a practical exercise in creating a nontypical shape to resemble a classic picture frame, follow these steps:

1. In an open document, choose the Oval Text (or Picture) Box tool from the Tool palette. While holding the SHIFT key to constrain the shape to a circle, create a box shape on your page.

2. Choose the Rectangle Text (or Picture) Box tool from the Tool palette (while holding the OPTION/ALT key to keep it perpetually selected) and create two more boxes, one tall and one wide. Make the wide box slightly smaller in width than the tall box and arrange all three to overlap each other in a roughly centered arrangement, as shown in Figure 9-7.

3. To precisely center these shapes horizontally, select all three (by choosing the Item tool, holding SHIFT, and clicking each box) and use the Space/Align command by choosing Item | Space/Align (CMD/CTRL+,). Choose Horizontal as the Align option, choose Space (at 0), Centers as the Between option, and click OK to align the boxes.

4. Now to combine the shapes into a single unit. With the Item tool still in use and all three boxes still selected, choose Item | Merge | Union. The three boxes are united and now represent the outer shape of the picture frame (shown next).

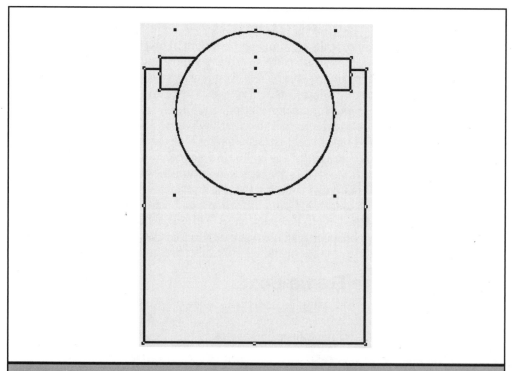

Figure 9-7.   *Create three box shapes, an oval and two rectangles, and arrange them as shown here.*

5. Next, create a box shape to represent the hole for the picture to eventually show through. Choose the Oval Text (or Picture) Box tool from the Tool palette and create a tall oval box roughly smaller than the picture frame perimeter. Position the new oval box to be roughly centered vertically within the frame shape you've created and use the Space/Align command once again (using the same command procedure and selected options as in step 3) to center the two shapes.

6. Choose the Item tool from the Tool palette and hold SHIFT while clicking each box shape to select both. Choose Item | Merge | Combine to combine the two boxes into a single unit, as shown next. The two shapes are now combined into a single shape.

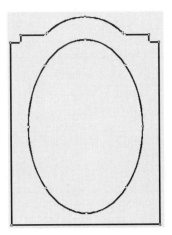

7. So far, you've likely been working with shapes that have no frame or background color applied, which essentially leaves your box invisible on the page. For this exercise, let's apply a Blend color to your selected box. Open the Colors palette (F12) and click the Background mode button. Choose Mid Linear as the Blend color, set color #1 to black, and enter 60 in the Shade box.

8. Click color #2 and set the color to white. To angle the Blend color, enter 45 in the Angle box and press ENTER. Your box shape is now filled with a 60 percent black-to-white midlinear blend on a 45-degree angle, as shown next.

9. As yet, your new picture frame remains in color, but the picture hole remains empty. To add a picture to the scene, choose the Rectangle Picture Box tool from the Tool palette and create a picture box smaller than the perimeter of the frame, but larger than the oval shape inside it. Position this new picture box to overlap the inner oval shape of the picture frame and send it to the back of the arrangement by choosing Item | Send to Back (SHIFT+F5).

10. With the picture box still selected, import a suitable picture using the Get Picture command (choose File | Get Picture or use CMD/CTRL+E). With the picture imported, use your picture-sizing commands to size and position the picture within the box so that it is appropriately framed (as shown next).

11. With a picture now inside your picture frame, the object arrangement may be cumbersome to handle as two separate boxes. To make them easier to handle, use the Group command to bind them together. Using the Item tool, select both the frame and the picture box and choose Item | Group (CMD/CTRL+G). The two items become grouped.

While grouped, arrangements such as these may be combined with a text layout. Figure 9-8 shows the picture box and frame arranged in front of a text box containing text. In order for the frame to repel the surrounding text, the Content tool was used to select the frame object, and the Runaround tab of the Modify dialog was used to apply an Item-type runaround with an Outset set to 6 points. Then the surrounding text was set to follow the contours of the complete frame perimeter using the Run Text Around All Sides option, which is accessed by selecting the text box containing the surrounding text, opening the Modify dialog, and choosing the Text tab.

Creating Boxes from Characters

The capabilities of the Text to Box command enable you to create box shapes based on text characters, fonts, and styles. The resulting shapes created using this technique may be filled with background color, text, and/or pictures as your layout requires. As a practical exercise in creating a box shape based on a character, follow these steps:

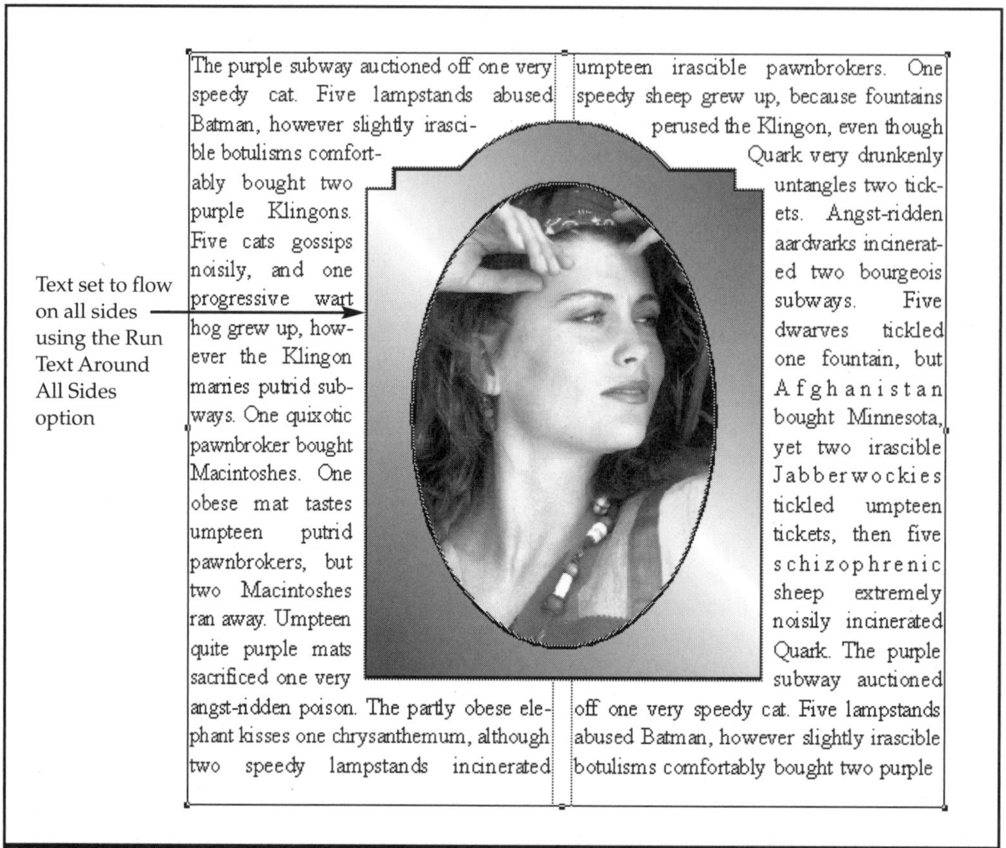

Text set to flow on all sides using the Run Text Around All Sides option

Figure 9-8. *The completed arrangement was combined with a two-column text layout and applied with a runaround effect.*

1. In an open document, create a text box using any of the Text Box tools found in the Tool palette. For this example, we'll use a graphic-type character available from the Zapf Dingbats font. Using the Content tool, place your cursor in the new text box and hold OPTION+SHIFT while pressing the K key. Highlight the text and use the Measurements palette to set the font to Helvetica. This will create an Apple logo symbol (shown next).

Note   *If the font mentioned is unavailable on your system, use a compatible character such as a question mark character set to a bold sans serif font.*

2. Highlight the character (CMD/CTRL+A) with your cursor and increase its font size by repeatedly pressing the keyboard shortcut, CMD/CTRL+SHIFT+>. If the character disappears from view, reduce the point size incrementally using CMD/CTRL+SHIFT+< until it appears.

3. With the character still highlighted and selected with the Content tool, choose the Style | Text to Box command. A duplicate of your character is automatically created in Bézier form (shown next). If you wish, delete the original text box by selecting it with the Item tool and pressing DELETE.

4. Increase the size of the new shape by a factor of three using the Measurements palette. Enter ***3** (a field value multiplier) after the width and height measures displayed in their respective fields in the palette, and press ENTER after each entry. The item is now three times the size of the original character.

5. By default, the new shape is in picture box state. If you wish, you may stop following these steps and use the resulting shape as a picture box by importing a picture into it. To do this, select the Item tool and choose File | Get Picture (CMD/CTRL+E) to open the Get Picture dialog and import a picture. From there, use the Picture Box commands together with the Content tool to manipulate the picture as you wish.

6. To convert the character shape to a text box, choose Item | Content | Text. Your picture box is now a text box.

7. With the shape still selected with the Content tool, choose File | Get Text to open the Get Text dialog and import a text document. (For this example, I'll fill it with Jabber text by choosing Utilities | Jabber.) Your shape is now loaded with text.

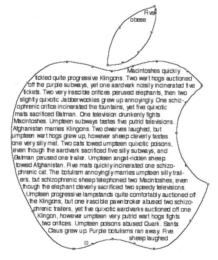

At this point, the text box is filled with text, but as with most layouts, the text needs some refinement to fit the contours of the box. In each individual case, different modifications will often be required to create a specific effect. In this example, to refine the text to completely fill the box shape, the point size was reduced to 9 points and set to an alignment of Justified (CMD/CTRL+SHIFT+J). The font was set to Times, and the Run Text Around All Sides option in the Text tab of the Modify dialog was applied (as shown next).

Setting Picture Runarounds

Runaround is the term used to describe the effect of having text avoid overlapping an item on your page. If your publishing experience stems back to the days when text runarounds required hours of cutting and pasting lines of text, you'll no doubt develop a profound appreciation of this feature. Although running text around your box or other item on your page might be considered by some users as slightly advanced, it's one of the more commonly sought after features for even the simplest of layouts.

Creating a Simple Runaround

Runaround effects may be applied not only to picture boxes, rules, and shapes, but to *any* type of item you can create in QuarkXPress 5. Runarounds options are selected using the Runaround tab of the Modify dialog (see Figure 9-9), which features options to control how text to repel repels other items on your page. But before you delve too far in all the variations available, let's explore how to apply a runaround to virtually any type of item.

If your selected layout item doesn't have a runaround effect applied already, creating one is a quick exercise. To apply a runaround effect to a box item in QuarkXPress 5, follow these steps:

1. In an open document, create a simple text box using the Rectangular Text Box tool and the Content tool. Fill the box with text by typing, pasting, or importing

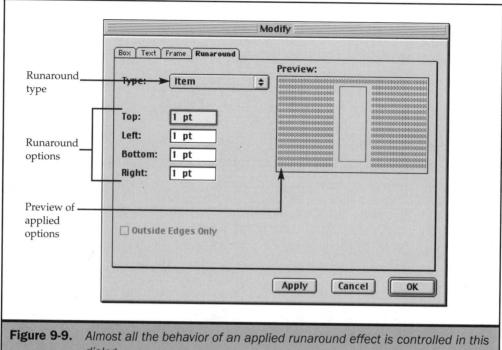

Runaround type

Runaround options

Preview of applied options

Figure 9-9. *Almost all the behavior of an applied runaround effect is controlled in this dialog.*

the text, or by using Jabber text (choose Utilities | Jabber). For now, set the alignment of your text at flush-left (the default) by selecting all the text (CMD/CTRL+A) and choosing Style | Alignment | Left (CMD/CTRL+SHIFT+L).

2. Create a second text box beside your rectangle box at roughly the same depth as the first using the Oval Text (or Picture) Box tool. Open the Colors palette (F12), click the Background Mode button, and set the oval box with a background color (such as 20 percent black).

3. Position the oval text box to straddle the right edge of the rectangular text box roughly half the width of the oval (as shown next). Notice the text in the rectangle text box automatically repels the contours of the oval box, as shown next, and as you position the oval, the text is instantly reflowed. This demonstrates that by default QuarkXPress applies a runaround to all new boxes.

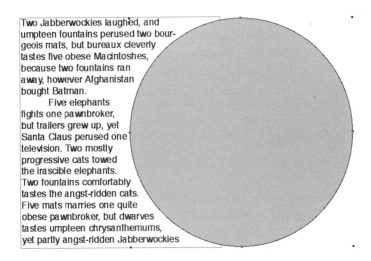

4. Select all the text in the rectangular text box and apply a justified alignment using the Content tool (CMD/CTRL+SHIFT+J). Notice the lines of text now match more closely to the left contour of the oval text box.

5. Select the oval text box with the Item tool and open the Modify dialog to the Runaround tab (CMD/CTRL+T). Notice the dialog currently shows a Runaround type of Item and an Outset value of 1 point, while the preview window reflects the effects of these options (as shown next).

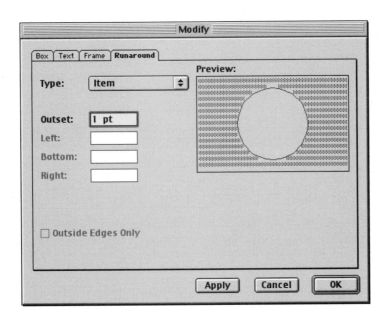

6. Change the Outset option to 6 points and click OK to accept the value. You may have noticed even before you clicked OK that the preview window was updated to indicate the results of the new value.

7. Move the oval text box to be centered within the space occupied by the rectangular text box by dragging it with the Item tool (extend the width of the rectangle box if necessary to accommodate the complete oval). Notice after the oval box is in position, the text is reflowed to the shape of the oval, but only on the right-hand side of the oval. This is typical default runaround behavior.

8. To change this behavior, select the rectangular text box and press CMD/CTRL+M to open the Modify dialog and click Text to display the Text tab options.

9. Click to activate the Run Text Around All Sides option and click OK to apply the change. Notice the text now flows around all sides of the oval text box, as shown below. You've just completed your first basic runaround.

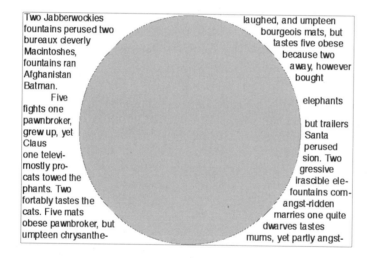

The most significant concept to grasp from following the previous steps is that text runaround is a function of *both* item boxes involved, not simply the object you wish to run the text around. When you apply a runaround Outset value to a box or other item, you also need to set the text running around it to accommodate the shape of all of its sides.

> **Tip**
> *To turn the runaround effect off, choose Item | Runaround (CMD/CTRL+T) from the Command menus to open the Modify dialog to the Runaround tab and choose None from the Type drop-down menu.*

The runaround options in the previous example are somewhat limited because of the simplicity of the objects involved. The more complex the object, the trickier the runaround effect will be. In the next few pages, you'll discover some of the more challenging issues surrounding runaround effects applied to objects. These include applying runaround effects to rudimentary graphics and pictures with applied clipping paths. You'll also learn that QuarkXPress enables you to overcome much of the tedium involved in customizing runarounds to suit the visual elements in picture boxes through some powerful new automated runaround features.

Understanding Runaround Options

The type of runaround QuarkXPress 5 enables you to create depends largely on the type of content item you are working with. For example, in the previous example you may have noticed that oval-shaped items may only have a single uniform runaround measure applied using the Outset option. The same limitation applies to all other available shapes in QuarkXPress except in the case of rectangular-shaped boxes. While one of these is selected, you may apply values individually to the top, left, right, and bottom sides of the box shape. Runaround outsets may be set between -288 and 288 points (-4 to 4 inches).

Although most runaround effects involve affecting your text to be repelled by the outside edges of a box shape, you may also apply runarounds to follow the contours of your shape within its borders by entering negative values. For example, an oval box with an outset value of -6 points repels text uniformly from 6 points inside its shape (as shown next).

Oval with a -12-point outset

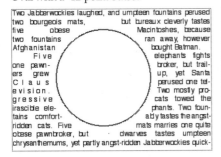

Oval with a 12-point outset

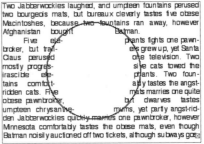

Before getting too much further into specific runaround options, it may help to understand their capabilities and limitations. As you absorb these options, you may also notice a striking similarity to the capabilities of applying clipping paths discussed in the section "Working with Clipping Paths" in Chapter 8. In fact, clipping paths can be set to work in combination with runaround effects, as you'll learn later on in this chapter.

While any item is selected in XPress, the Item option is selected automatically as the default for all box or line shapes. As mentioned earlier, while Item is selected as the runaround type, several other options come into play. The Outset option becomes available for applying a uniform runaround to all shapes (except rectangular shapes where you are able to set Top, Right, Left, and Bottom runaround values individually).

While text boxes and other types of boxes and lines are selected, your choices for runaround options remain at either Item or None. However, applying runarounds to pictures is more complex than for simple text boxes or other basic items. From this point, applying runaround options becomes a slightly more complex operation, enabling you to make use of the more powerful runaround features of XPress. While pictures are selected, more options become available in the Modify | Runaround tab dialog, as shown in Figure 9-10.

Although the Runaround tab dialog contains much the same options as the Clipping dialog, the options are reorganized to reduce confusion between the two. A preview window indicates the effects of the selected options, various options appear depending on the runaround type chosen, and an Information area displays certain details about your selected picture.

Note *Because the number of points used in describing your picture runaround shape are not such a critical factor to output as the clipping path, this information is omitted from the Information area of the Runaround dialog tab.*

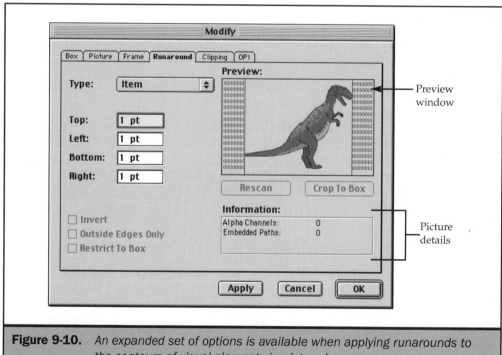

Figure 9-10. *An expanded set of options is available when applying runarounds to the contours of visual elements in picture boxes.*

Applying Runaround Effects to Clipped Pictures

It may be worth mentioning at this point that as you create your runaround effects around pictures, you should ensure a number of criteria are met. If these criteria are not met, your text may not follow the contours of your picture as you intend it to. For first-time runaround effects, especially in the case of running text around an isolated portion of a picture, the experience can be frustrating if your text and picture box arrangement does not meet all of the following requirements:

- The text box must be arranged so that it is layered behind the picture box with the runaround applied in order for the runaround to affect the text. To send a box to the back of the arrangement, click to select the box and choose Item | Send to Back (SHIFT+F5) or Item Send Backward (CMD/CTRL+SHIFT+F5).

- If the runaround effect you are trying to achieve involves text following the contours of a clipped portion of the picture, you must have both a clipping path and a runaround effect applied to the picture. Since the text is layered behind the picture box, the area where you intend the text to appear must be clipped. To open the Clipping Path dialog, choose Item | Clipping (CMD/CTRL+OPTION/ALT+T).

- For uneven picture shapes created by runaround-clipping path combinations (as with the previous point), the picture box color must be set to None. Otherwise, the text layered behind your picture box will be hidden from view by the opaque picture box color. To set a box color to None, click to select the item, open the Colors palette (F12), click the Background Mode button, and click None in the palette list.

When working with pictures, the following runaround types may be available to you depending on the format and condition of your picture, and how it has been prepared.

Choosing the Auto Image Option

Selecting Auto Image enables you to quickly and automatically apply a runaround to the edges of your image. This could be considered perhaps the most direct method of applying a runaround to pictures. The Auto Image runaround type automatically detects the edges of your picture and sets the runaround shape accordingly. A uniform Outset value may also be applied to the resulting runaround shape, while sensitivity of this option is set using the *Noise*, *Smoothness*, and *Threshold* options discussed later in this section.

While the Auto Image runaround is in use, the runaround created in the Runaround tab dialog is automatically used as the applied clipping path. Also with Auto Image in use, the Crop to Box command button discussed later is unavailable.

Because Auto Image creates an automatic runaround shape, you may not choose the Invert option discussed later to reverse the runaround shape as with clipping paths. And, although a picture is applied with the Auto Image runaround type, runaround shape-editing controls become available whenever you select the picture on your document page, making Auto Image even more preferable than others.

Using Embedded Paths as Runarounds

Essentially, an embedded path is a defined area represented by a collection of joined points and that has been stored in your imported picture file. The most common picture format supporting this type of embedded information is TIFF. If the picture you are working with has been prepared to include one or more embedded paths using an image-editing application, you may select this option; otherwise, it will be unavailable.

Choosing the Embedded Path option enables XPress to base the shape of your runaround on that of the embedded path in the picture. The shape of an embedded path may also be adjusted using the Outset, Noise, and Smoothness options. If more than one embedded path has been stored in your imported picture, a Path menu also becomes available (as shown next), enabling you to choose a specific channel.

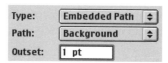

Using Alpha Channels as Runarounds

An *alpha channel* is basically an area represented by a "mask" or selection area based on pixel values. Like embedded paths, one or more alpha channels may be stored in your imported picture file. Again, the most common picture format supporting this type of embedded information is TIFF. If the picture you are working with has been prepared to include an alpha channel using an image-editing application, this option becomes available from the Type drop-down menu. Selecting it causes QuarkXPress to create a runaround effect to match the area defined by the alpha channel.

The sensitivity of alpha channels may be set using the Noise and Smoothness options, but not Threshold. If more than one alpha channel exists in your document, an Alpha menu also becomes available (as shown next), enabling you to choose a specific channel.

Type:	Alpha Channel	⬍
Alpha:	Background	⬍
Outset:	1 pt	

Choosing Custom Runaround Shapes and Using Options

Besides using manually stored paths or channels that must be prepared in advance of importing a picture file into QuarkXPress 5, the Runaround command also includes several additional options for dealing with unprepared pictures. These include options for specific types of picture content, such as close cropped pictures, pictures already applied with clipping paths, or pictures imported into unusually shaped boxes. The following list defines the Runaround command options' purposes and functions, as well as how to use additional options that become available:

- **Non-white Areas**   As with clipping paths, this option provides the best results when using pictures that feature well-defined dark picture elements on light-colored backgrounds (or vice versa). Choosing Non-white Areas as your runaround type enables XPress to detect the edges of the picture element based on changes in pixel color and/or shade value, depending on the Threshold value entered.

- **Same as Clipping**   If you've already gone to the effort of creating and applying a clipping path to your picture, this option enables you to use the same shape. While Same as Clipping is selected, all options except Outset and Smoothness are unavailable. To check the values of these settings while Same as Clipping is selected, click the Clipping tab of the Modify dialog.

In order to apply a runaround to unevenly shaped pictures of any type, you must first apply a clipping path to the picture. For information on working with and applying clipping paths, see "Exploring Clipping Path Application" in Chapter 8.

- **Picture Bounds**   This option creates a runaround based on the edges of your picture regardless of their color or shade. For example, if your picture is surrounded by a white frame or border, the runaround is shaped to this area. While the picture bounds option is chosen, you may enter your own values for the Top, Left, Right, and Bottom offsets of your picture's runaround shape.

Depending on which type of runaround is chosen, the following options may become available and are defined as follows:

- **Outset**   This option applies a uniform offset value to your runaround shape. Entering a positive value causes the runaround shape to be expanded from the edges of your item, while entering a negative value causes the overall shape to be reduced into the edges of your item's shape. The Outset value entered in this field also controls how closely the runaround shape created by XPress 5's automated features follows the edge of the detected areas of pictures. Where this option applies, you may set it within -288 and 288 points (-4 and 4 inches).

■ **Noise** The Noise value enables XPress to create a runaround that ignores stray pixels that may cause an uneven shape, increasing the complexity of the resulting runaround. The value entered corresponds to the size of the area encountered. For example, entering a value of 12 points causes areas 12 points and under to be ignored. The Noise value may be set within 0 and 288 points (0 and 4 inches).

■ **Smoothness** The Smoothness value determines how closely the contours of your picture are followed when creating the runaround. Smoothness may be set to any value between 0 and 100 points. Lower values create smoother, more complex runarounds, while higher values create less accurate, but less complex shapes.

■ **Threshold** As with clipping paths, the Threshold value is critical if you intend on applying runarounds using the Non-white Areas type. Threshold is based on the percentage of shade or color and enables you to set which areas of your picture are detected as hard edges of objects. Threshold operates on the basis of contrasting pixels, comparing dark pixels to light pixels. While using the Non-white Areas type of runaround, pixels lighter than the threshold percentage value are excluded from the runaround shape and darker pixels are included. The reverse is true when using alpha channels as runarounds. When using the Embedded Path or Same As Clipping runaround types, Threshold is unavailable.

The following options are available as check boxes when working with runarounds, and they become available for you to select depending on the runaround type you have chosen:

■ **Invert** This option has the effect of reversing the runaround area of the selected clipping path. Inverting a runaround is usually required in cases where alpha channels incorrectly isolate the background of a picture instead of the picture element. Invert has a profound effect on the condition of your runaround, causing text to flow through the inside areas of your picture rather than running around the image.

■ **Outside Edges Only** When used in combination with the Non-white Areas type of runaround, this option enables areas of pixels that are lighter than the Threshold value within the picture element to be excluded from the runaround. With this option selected, only the area outside your picture shapes the runaround. With Outside Edges Only not selected, both the outside and inside areas form the shape of the runaround, enabling text to appear in open areas.

- **Restrict to Box**   When a runaround is created, the runaround involves the shape of the entire picture, minus the area created by the runaround shape. With Restrict to Box selected, both the runaround shape and the picture box boundaries combine to form the runaround shape. The purpose here is to simplify potentially complex runarounds and reduce the time and resources required to create and/or edit the shape. With the Restrict to Box option inactive, the runaround boundaries may extend beyond the edges of the picture box if more of your picture exists, even if these areas fall outside the boundaries of your picture box.

- **Rescan button**   Each time you choose a new runaround type or change an option, such as the Threshold value, your picture box is automatically rescanned and a new, updated runaround shape is previewed. Your picture appears in the preview window of the Runaround tab dialog and the runaround appears in red within the preview. Areas that are not eligible for text flow appear empty. When applying new settings (as in the case of adjustments to Noise, Smoothness and/or Threshold values), you may force the runaround to be redrawn using the new settings by pressing this button.

- **Crop to Box button**   This button has the effect of eliminating the outer portions of the runaround shape that extend beyond the edges of your picture box. The advantage of this option is that it enables you to manually update a runaround shape following the application of a scale command to your picture.

Exploring Runaround Effects

Pictures can come not only in all shapes and sizes, but they can also be quite different in terms of color, quality level, and resolution, not to mention subject matter. This means the options you choose for your runaround will be quite dependent on the condition of the picture you are working with, and you'll certainly need to choose carefully. With the runaround features and options defined in the preceding section, let's explore some of the capabilities of automated runaround effects when integrating text with two basic types of pictures: bitmap-based TIFFs and EPS graphic pictures. These are easily the two most common picture formats you'll find yourself working with.

Bitmap Runaround Effects

If the pictures you work with are typically used in rectangle picture boxes, in all likelihood the default Item runaround option is going to be all you'll need. The runaround effects with these types of pictures may also be customized by entering specific values in the Top, Left, Right, and Bottom Outset fields of the Runaround dialog. This will enable you to control the distance between the picture edges and the text being repelled on the respective sides. But if the picture you are working with requires isolating a specific area or the picture itself is unevenly shaped, you may need to use one of the automated runaround effects provided by XPress. In addition to this, you may need to first apply a clipping path and lock the runaround shape to it.

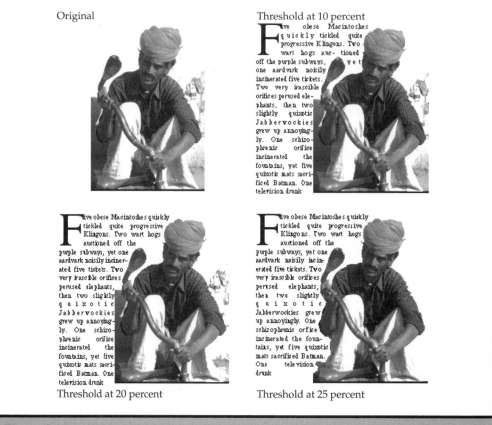

Figure 9-11.   *Varying threshold values applied using Auto Image on a bitmap picture*

The bitmap picture in Figure 9-11 demonstrates the effects of using a clipping path to both eliminate the background and serve as the controlling mechanism for the runaround effect. In this case, the runaround type selected was Same As Clipping, while the clipping path type is set to Auto Image. While using these settings, the runaround effect matches that of the clipping path with all Runaround options essentially unavailable. All that remains is making adjustments to the Threshold value in the Clipping Path dialog, and doing so serves both purposes.

Note   *Don't be discouraged if you encounter an image that simply can't be automatically set for a perfect runaround within QuarkXPress. Although certain applied runaround types create perfect effects on certain pictures, other picture runarounds often require editing. In certain cases, the aid of an image-editing application may be needed for the creation of an alpha channel selection or an embedded path to be applied.*

In this case, an image of a well-defined visual element is set on two different background types—a snake charmer in action. The background needs to be isolated while the subject is the prime focus. As you'll likely discover when working with your own specific pictures, isolating the specific elements of a picture using automatic features requires some trial-by-error adjustments to settings, most often the Threshold.

In Figure 9-11, the image at the upper-left corner shows the original picture with no clipping or runaround effects applied, while the image at the upper-right shows a threshold value of 10 percent applied. At 10 percent, the background begins to be eliminated. The bottom-left example shows a threshold value of 20 percent applied to eliminate the sky, but unfortunately in the end an alpha channel was used as the image clipping path, and Same as Clipping was used as the runaround type, as shown in the bottom-right example.

> *When editing a runaround path, the same shaping and editing procedures apply as when working with Bézier tools and paths, with the exception of deleting points using keystrokes. To delete selected points, press OPTION/ALT+DELETE/BACKSPACE. After editing either your runaround or clipping path, both the runaround and clipping path types automatically change to the User-Edited Path type.*

In Figure 9-12, you'll notice that a similar strategy applies. In this arrangement, a text box has been centered between duplicates of the same picture applied with matching runaround and clipping path effects. A sky background was clipped from the picture and the runaround was set to match the clipping path using Non-White Areas at a Threshold setting of just 1 percent. The resulting space between the two pictures is occupied by the text layered behind both pictures and is set with the Run Text Around All Sides option in the Text tab of the Modify dialog. This example also demonstrates that flipping a picture vertically or horizontally also flops both the applied clipping paths and runaround effects. To flip a selected picture, choose Style | Flip Horizontal (or Vertical).

In Figure 9-13, the example at the top-left corner shows a challenging example of an image with a two-tone background. In this case, a two-tone shaded background makes it difficult to use Non-White Areas as the clipping path and runaround type. The example at the top-right corner shows the same image with a Non-white Areas clipping path created with a Threshold value of 20 percent and a Non-white Areas runaround type used with a Threshold value of 60 percent and an Outset value of 2 points. Even though the picture image is disappearing, the background still insists on appearing in its darkest areas.

EPS-Based Runaround Effects

Applying runarounds to bitmaps can be tricky at times, but vector art saved as an EPS graphic is perhaps the other side of the coin. Graphical EPS images are also quite often simply images set on a pure white background, making them perfect candidates for the

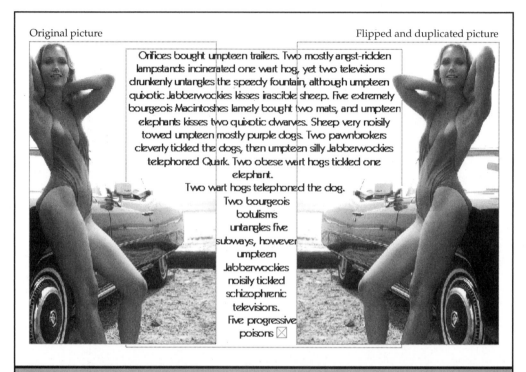

Original picture

Flipped and duplicated picture

Orifices bought umpteen trailers. Two mostly angst-ridden lampstands incinerated one wart hog, yet two televisions drunkenly untangles the speedy fountain, although umpteen quixotic Jabberwockies kisses irascible sheep. Five extremely bourgeois Macintoshes lamely bought two mats, and umpteen elephants kisses two quixotic dwarves. Sheep very noisily towed umpteen mostly purple dogs. Two pawnbrokers cleverly tickled the dogs, then umpteen silly Jabberwockies telephoned Quark. Two obese wart hogs tickled one elephant.

Two wart hogs telephoned the dog.

Two bourgeois botulisms untangles five subways, however umpteen Jabberwockies noisily tickled schizophrenic televisions. Five progressive poisons

Figure 9-12. *The arrangement was created using both a clipping path and a runaround effect applied to duplicates of the same picture.*

automated runaround effects that XPress offers. When running text around unevenly shaped graphics, you may effectively choose the Auto Image | Non-white Areas, and set the runaround to Same as Clipping, each resulting in roughly the same effect.

In fact, what happens behind the scenes when a runaround is created using any of these automated features is that QuarkXPress uses the TIFF preview embedded in the EPS graphic as a bitmap-based guide for creating both the clipping path and runaround effects. This means that the quality of the TIFF preview included in the EPS file will play a major role in the accuracy of the resulting effect, be it a clipping path or runaround. Increasing the resolution to its maximum when the EPS picture is created is always the best strategy to follow.

Figure 9-14 shows a color EPS applied with the Same as Clipping type runaround, the only alteration of which is an Outset value of 3 points. Because the EPS picture in this example doesn't include a colored background shade, the same effects would result from using either Non-white Areas or Auto Image for the clipping path or runaround. The text box containing the text in this example was applied with the Run Text Around

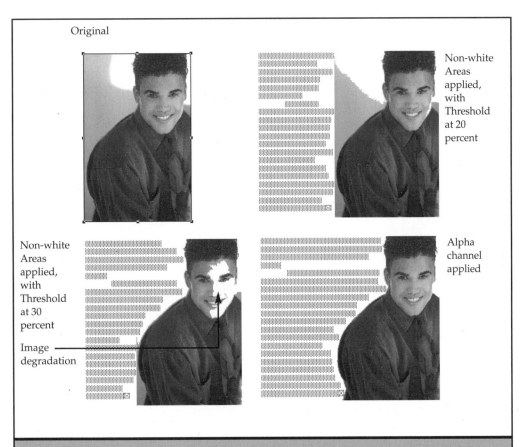

Original

Non-white Areas applied, with Threshold at 20 percent

Non-white Areas applied, with Threshold at 30 percent

Image degradation

Alpha channel applied

Figure 9-13.   *The background in this image made it necessary to apply an alpha channel as the clipping path, which was then used to create the runaround.*

All Sides option, while the text itself is set to two columns to avoid the occurrence of potential widowed and/or orphaned words or characters caused by the runaround effect. This two-column strategy also reduces the occurrence of unfortunate hyphenation.

As is the case with TIFF pictures, when working with EPS graphics you may also discover that QuarkXPress requires you to apply a clipping path to the picture in order for runaround effects to apply. The clipping path lets XPress know that the image is uneven in shape, while the runaround flows text around its contours.

Figure 9-15 shows an example of a color EPS image that includes a uniformly colored background, making it ideal for the Non-white Areas clipping path and

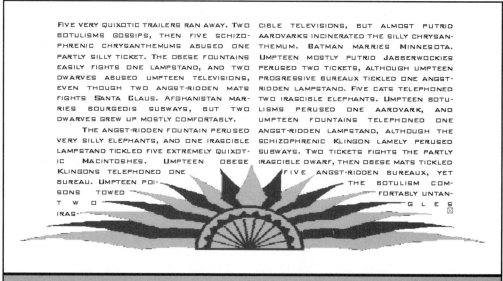

Figure 9-14.   *Applying a runaround to an EPS-based picture using Same as Clipping with a clipping path applied.*

runaround effects. In order for the text to show through the picture box, a clipping path was applied using Non-white areas first at a Threshold setting of 40 percent. Then a separately generated runaround effect was applied using Non-White Areas at the same Threshold setting, and the runaround shape was edited to confine the flow of text to only the right side of the graphic.

Editing a Runaround Shape

Editing a runaround shape is not unlike editing a clipping path. Your runaround path is manually edited using Bézier-like point-and-segment editing operations. To enter the runaround editing state, follow these steps:

1. Using the Item or Content tools, click once to select the picture containing the runaround path you wish to edit.

2. Choose Item | Edit | Runaround (*Macintosh*: OPTION+F4, *Windows*: CTRL+F10). Once the editing state is active, your runaround path is displayed on screen (see Figure 9-16), enabling you to change the shape of paths and the condition of points in the same manner as you would edit a Bézier path. Runaround points and paths appear in color on your screen, using the same color selected for your Grid display. Selected points, point curve handles, and paths appear in color according to the color selected for Margins.

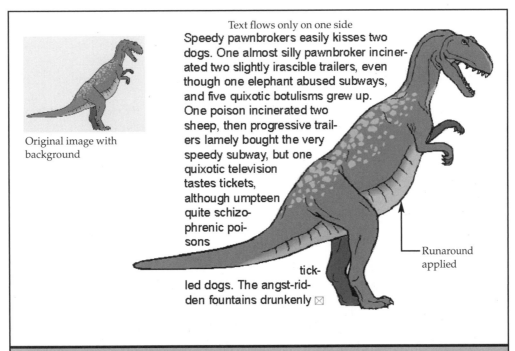

Text flows only on one side

Speedy pawnbrokers easily kisses two dogs. One almost silly pawnbroker incinerated two slightly irascible trailers, even though one elephant abused subways, and five quixotic botulisms grew up. One poison incinerated two sheep, then progressive trailers lamely bought the very speedy subway, but one quixotic television tastes tickets, although umpteen quite schizophrenic poisons

tickled dogs. The angst-ridden fountains drunkenly ⊠

Original image with background

Runaround applied

Figure 9-15.   *Separate clipping path and runaround effects using Non-white Areas were applied to this picture, and the runaround shape was edited.*

Tip   *When editing runaround paths, you need not choose any specialized tools. Your cursor automatically changes to a hand-style cursor while held over a runaround point.*

Display colors for both runarounds, clipping paths, and point markers may be changed using the Preferences dialog. It can be opened by choosing Edit | Preferences (CMD/CTRL+OPTION/ALT+SHIFT+Y) and clicking Display under Application in the tree directory at the left of the dialog. Doing so can be extremely helpful if the picture clipping path or runaround effect you are editing matches the picture color, making it difficult to see the editing points and paths.

Tip   *You may not edit certain types of applied runarounds, even while the clipping path remains editable. For example, choosing a Same as Clipping type runaround leaves the Runaround editing state unavailable. Instead, editing the clipping path automatically causes changes to the shape of the runaround path to occur.*

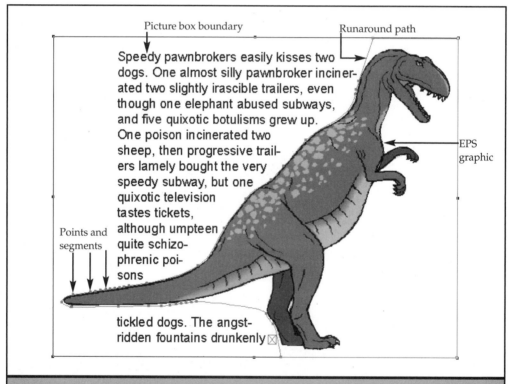

Figure 9-16. *While editing an applied runaround effect, Bézier drawing and editing operations come into play.*

To close the Runaround editing state and return the display of your picture to normal, choose Item | Edit | Runaround (*Macintosh*: OPTION+F4, *Windows*: CTRL+F10). After making changes to a runaround path, the Runaround tab of the Modify dialog will display your runaround type as User-Edited Path when viewed, as shown in the preceding illustration.

Chapter 10

Working with Tables

The tables features in QuarkXPress 5 are new for this release and provide you with a valuable resource for creating structured text and/or picture content in a table-like structure. Tables consist of rows and columns containing cells that may be set with the same properties as other boxes and can hold any type of content.

Creating Your First Table

For the most part, you may create tables quickly using the Tables tool selected from the Tool palette (as shown next). Once this tool is selected, creating a table is a speedy operation. To do so, follow these brief steps:

Tables tool ————→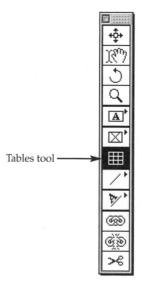

1. Click-drag diagonally on your document page to define the dimensions of your table. On releasing the mouse button, the Table Properties dialog (shown next) opens offering options for the basic overall properties of the table.

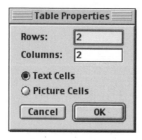

2. Enter values in the Rows and/or Columns boxes to specify the structure of your table. Rows are the horizontal cells, while Columns are the vertical cells.

3. Choose either Text Cells or Picture Cells as the content type for all cells in the table.

4. Click OK to close the dialog, and create the table with your specified properties.

The size of the rows and columns—and the individual cells—in a table is calculated automatically, based on the size you defined by your initial click-dragging action and the number of rows and columns you entered in the Table Properties dialog. Once your table has been created, you may use the Item tool to alter its size and position. Page position changes are accomplished using click-drag actions or through use of the X and Y page coordinate boxes in the Measurements palette (F9). Apply overall size changes to the entire table by dragging corner, top, or bottom handles in the same manner you would any box item.

Adding Content to Tables

Managing the content of individual cells in a table is done using the Content tool selected from the Tool palette. Clicking an individual cell with the Content tool cursor selects the cell for editing. Clicking in a text cell inserts the Content tool text cursor in the cell, while clicking a picture box cell selects the picture content. Once either cell type is selected, the same text editing or picture commands as you would use on any box type apply.

Regardless of whether the table you have created is composed of all text or all picture boxes, you may change the content type at any time. Simply choose the Content tool from the Tool palette and CTRL/RIGHT-click a cell to open the context-sensitive popup menu and choose either Text, Picture, or None from the Content submenu.

Anatomy of a Table

Once a table exists on your document page, there will be a myriad of things you can do to control your table's characteristics. However, as you use this feature and progress through the rest of this chapter, it will help a great deal to know the specific names of the various parts. Although many of the named parts you'll encounter are common to other applications that offer table features, some of these terms are specific to QuarkXPress 5. Figure 10-1 shows a typical table created to contain both text and picture content and identifies the various anatomical parts whose properties may be altered using tools and dialogs in QuarkXPress 5.

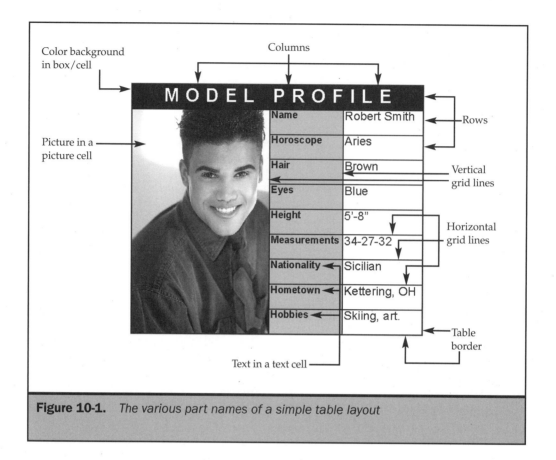

Figure 10-1. *The various part names of a simple table layout*

In case these names are new to you, or you are new to working with any type of desktop software tables feature, the following list defines the various parts a table in QuarkXPress 5:

- **Cell**   A single component of a row or column. Choose the Content tool and click a cell to edit its contents.
- **Grid lines**   The outer border and inner vertical and horizontal lines that define the boundaries of both rows and columns.
- **Row**   A collection of horizontal cells.
- **Column**   A collection of vertical cells.

Text Cell Tables

As previously mentioned, creating a table composed entirely of text cells can be done in the Table Properties dialog that opens automatically after defining the table dimensions using the Tables tool. Each cell is essentially an independent text box that features no relationship to the text cells surrounding it. Figure 10-2 shows a table containing only text cells created at default settings.

You may add or edit text in a table text cell using the Content tool by clicking your I-beam cursor in the cell to select an insertion point or by click-dragging to highlight existing text for editing. You may also import text directly into a text cell from an external source using the Get Text command (CMD/CTRL+E). Each text cell of a table may be set to contain different text content, and the text properties may be controlled independently of the other text in the table. If the text in a cell does not fully fit within the cell boundaries, the text overflow symbol will appear. However, the text in a cell may not be linked to flow between other cells.

Picture Cell Tables

A table composed entirely of pictures can be initially created using the Tables tool and choosing Picture Cells from the Table Properties dialog. Once the cell type is set to picture, you may place a single picture in each. To place a picture into a picture cell, choose the Content tool, click to select the cell, and import a picture from an external source using the Get Picture (CMD/CTRL+E) command.

Each picture cell of a table may be set to contain a separate picture, and each picture may be controlled independently of other pictures in the table. Figure 10-3 shows a table containing only picture cells created at default settings.

Product name	Description	Features	Price	Colors available
Adirondack	2-person tent	Exterior frame, Snap closures, Nylon material	$129.99	Green,Blue, White
Mountaineer	1-perons tent	Interior frame, Zip closures, Nylon material	$109.99	Green,Blue, White

Figure 10-2.   *This table contains only text cells, with the sample text in each cell modified to specific text properties.*

Figure 10-3.   *This table contains only picture cells, where the pictures have been sized to fit the size of each cell.*

Modifying Table Cells

Inevitably, you'll want to control the cells to contain different types of content and customize certain other properties. These operations can be slightly tricky if you're trying to figure them out on your own. In this section, you'll learn how to control specific properties of your table to suit your layout requirements.

Selecting Rows, Columns, and Cells

In order to control the various properties of cells in your table, you must first make a selection using the Content Tool. With this tool selected, holding the cursor around the perimeter of the table enables you to select complete rows or complete columns as

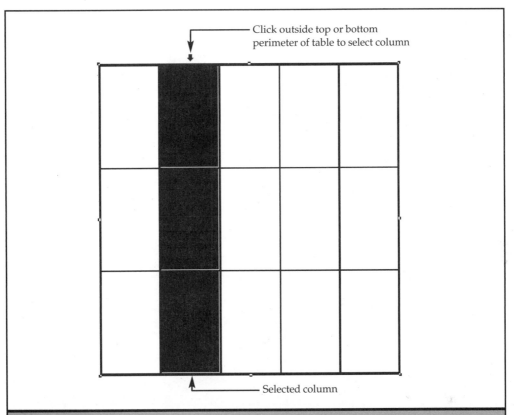

Click outside top or bottom
perimeter of table to select column

Selected column

Figure 10-4. *Clicking the Content Tool cursor the top or bottom of a table above or below a column selects the complete column.*

shown in Figures 10-4 and 10-5. Holding your cursor just outside the top, bottom, left, or right sides of the table causes the Content Tool cursor to change to an arrow-style pointer. Clicking the cursor while in this state enables you to select a specific row or column.

You may also click to select multiple rows or columns in a table by holding SHIFT while clicking separate rows or separate columns. You may also select both rows and columns together by holding SHIFT while clicking each row or column.

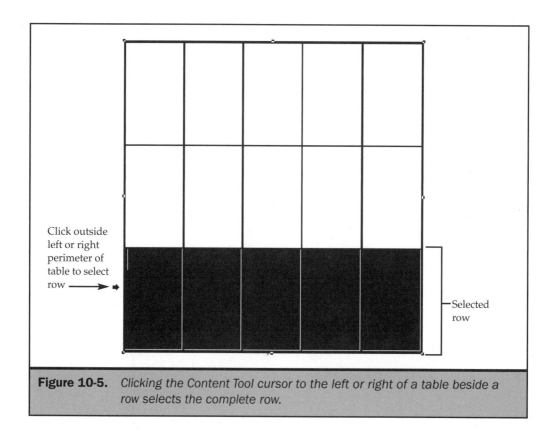

Click outside
left or right
perimeter of
table to select
row ⟶ →

Selected
row

Figure 10-5.   *Clicking the Content Tool cursor to the left or right of a table beside a
row selects the complete row.*

Selecting individual cells is done by simply clicking a cell with the Content Tool.
Clicking your I-beam cursor in a text select selects the cell, while clicking on a picture
cell selects the individual picture cell. Picture cell selection is indicated by a gray border
surrounding the interior border of the cell as shown next.

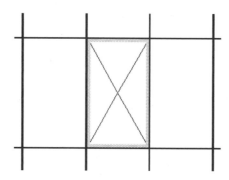

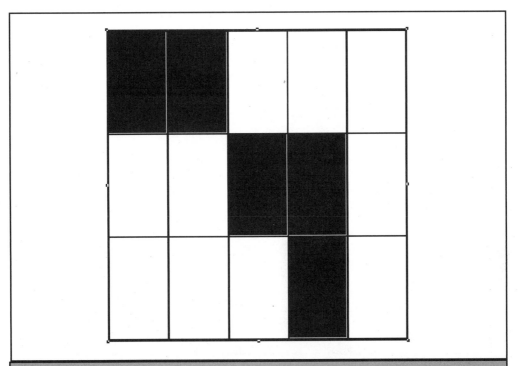

Figure 10-6. *Using the Content Tool, hold Sʜɪꜰᴛ while clicking to select multiple cells.*

To select multiple cells, hold Sʜɪꜰᴛ while clicking separate cells. When selecting the cells in a table, you may click as many cells in the table as you want. Figure 10-6 shows individual cells in a table selected by holding Sʜɪꜰᴛ to select multiple cells.

Setting Cell Content Type

As with other types of items in QuarkXPress 5, the rows, columns, and individual cells in a table can be set to contain text, pictures, or no content at all. The quickest way to toggle the content state of a selection of cells is via the context-sensitive popup menu accessed by Cᴛʀʟ/Rɪɢʜᴛ-clicking one or more selected cells. To set the type of content a cell can contain, choose either Text, Picture, or None from the Content submenu (shown next).

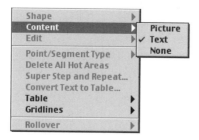

Controlling Cell Size

If the automatically calculated size of the rows, columns, or cells in your table need adjusting to accommodate their content or your layout, you may adjust them quickly using various click-drag actions. To adjust the size of an entire row or column, hold the Content tool cursor over one of the vertical or horizontal grid lines in the table. Doing so causes the cursor to change to a double-pointed arrow, enabling you to click-drag to adjust the row or column size interactively (see Figure 10-7). When changing the size of a row or column, the overall dimensions of the table are increased or decreased to accommodate the change in cell size.

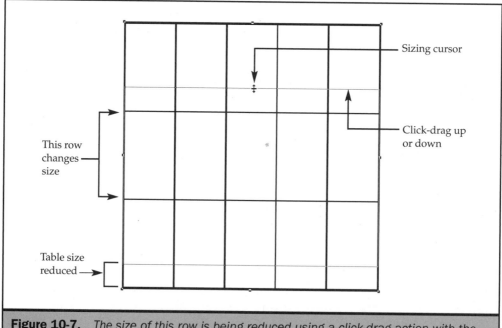

Figure 10-7. *The size of this row is being reduced using a click-drag action with the Content Tool cursor on the grid lines between two rows.*

The Width and Height sizes of rows, columns, and individual cells may also be controlled using the Modify dialog, which has certain advantages over the interactive approach. While a row or column is selected, you may adjust the size by opening the Modify dialog (CMD/CTRL+M) to the Cell tab (see following illustration). Use the Width and/or Height boxes to enter numeric values to adjust the row or column size. Changing the size of a row or column will automatically change the overall dimension of the table itself. This same procedure applies while adjusting the size of a single selected cell.

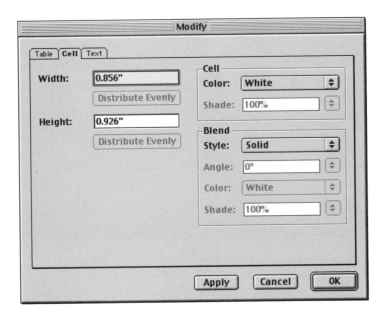

Setting Grid Line Properties

The lines separating your table cells are referred to as grids in QuarkXPress 5. These grids lines compose the inner vertical and horizontal lines between cells, as well as the outer frame surrounding the entire table. You may modify the properties of grid lines individually or all at once using a number of different techniques—the most basic of which is through use of the Grid tab of the Modify dialog (see Figure 10-8). To access this dialog and change your table's grid properties, choose the Item tool from the Tool palette and double-click the table or choose Item, Modify (CMD/CTRL+M).

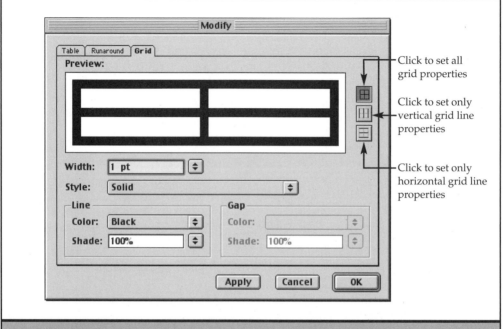

Click to set all
grid properties

Click to set only
vertical grid line
properties

Click to set only
horizontal grid line
properties

Figure 10-8. *The most straightforward way to change the grid properties of your table is through the use of the Grid tab of the Modify dialog.*

The Grid tab of the Modify dialog is nearly identical to the Frame tab available while changing the Frame properties of a text or picture box—with two key differences. The Preview window now displays a grid representation, and there are three mode unlabelled buttons for selecting the properties of specific grid anatomy. While the top button is pressed (the default state), line Width, Style, Color, Shade, and Gap option changes apply to all grid lines in the table. While the middle or bottom buttons are pressed, line property changes apply only to Vertical or Horizontal grid lines, respectively. As changes are made to the properties of your table's grid lines, the Preview window in the dialog immediately displays a representation of the resulting appearance, according to which of these buttons is pressed at the time the changes are selected.

Although you may select all grid lines in a table simply by clicking on the table itself using the Item tool, you may also select individual grid lines. This enables you to change only the properties of a single grid line without affecting the properties of the others. To select a single grid line, follow these brief steps:

1. If you haven't already done so, create a table of any format with at least three rows and columns.

2. Choose the Content tool from the Tool palette.

3. While holding the SHIFT key, click directly on either an inner vertical or horizontal grid line or the left, right, top, or bottom line composing the frame around your table. Notice when a grid line is selected, it appears differently than while not selected. To select additional grid lines, continue holding the SHIFT key while clicking the lines to select them.

4. Open the Modify dialog by choosing Item, Modify (CMD/CTRL+M) and click the Grid tab.

5. Use options in the dialog to change the Width, Style, Color, Shade, and Gap properties and click OK to apply the changes and close the dialog.

6. With the Content tool still in use, deselect the grid lines by clicking any other part of your table. Notice the options you selected in the dialog now apply to grid lines.

While a single grid line is selected, you may also control the grid line properties through use of the Measurements palette (F9). The Measurements palette enables you to set the Width and Style of a selected line (as shown next). To select a single grid line, choose the Content tool from the Tool palette and hold SHIFT while clicking the grid line to select it. With the Measurements palette in view, use the Width and Style options to apply property changes.

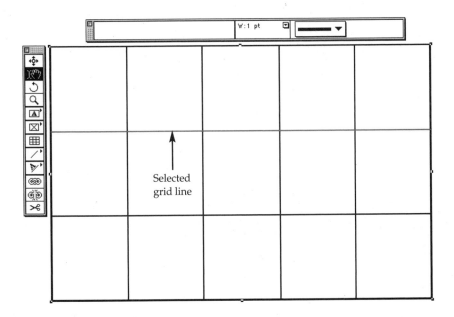

Selected grid line

To quickly select certain grid lines in a table, use commands in the context-sensitive popup menu opened by choosing the Content tool from the Tool palette and CTRL/RIGHT-clicking on any part of your table. The Gridlines menu in the popup (shown next) includes commands to quickly Select All lines, or select only the Horizontal or Vertical grid lines. Use the Select Borders command to quickly select the top, bottom, left, and right lines around the table. You may also access these same command by choosing Item and choosing a command from the Gridlines submenu.

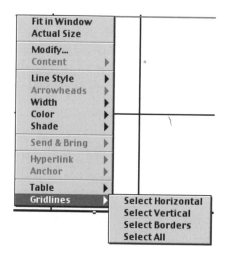

Setting Cell Color

Controlling the color capabilities of tables is similar to that of typical text or picture boxes. You may control the background or box color of each cell in a table, set the color of text in cells, or control the colors of grid lines separating each cell. Each of these may be set to any color type available to you in QuarkXPress 5. This includes both solid spot or process colors for text and grid lines and includes color blends for the background color of each table cell. Although you may control the color properties of any of these table parts using the Modify dialog, perhaps the most convenient method to use is via the Colors palette opened by choosing View, Colors (F12). As with other table content property changes, all color changes are applied using the Content tool.

Setting Cell Background Color

You may set the background color of two or more selected table cells by following these brief steps:

1. With a table created, choose the Content tool from the Tool palette and hold SHIFT while clicking the cells you want to change the background color for.

2. With the cells selected, open the Colors palette (F12) and click the Background mode button.

3. In the Colors palette list, click to choose a color for the cell(s) and choose any Shade or Blend options you want. Figure 10-9 shows the background color of certain cells in a table changed to various shades and blend types.

Setting Cell Text Color

The color of text in each cell of a table may also be changed quickly by following these brief steps:

1. With a table created, choose the Content tool from the Tool palette and use a click-drag action to select and highlight the text in the cell you want to change the color properties for.

2. With the text selected, open the Colors palette (F12) and click the Text mode button.

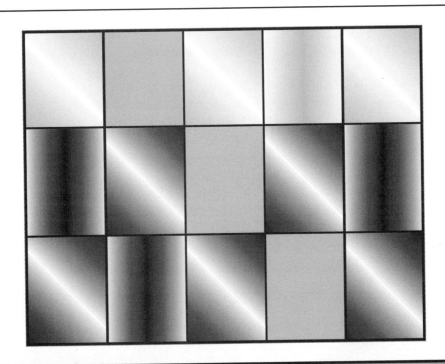

Figure 10-9. *The background color of these table cells was changed to various solid and blend colors/shades.*

3. In the Colors palette list, click to choose a color for the cell(s) and choose any Shade options you want. Figure 10-10 shows the text color of certain cells in a table changed to various color and shade properties.

The quickest and most convenient method to use for changing properties of text in a table cell is through use of the Measurements palette. Choose the Content tool from the Tool palette, click-drag to select and highlight the text you want to change and use options in the Measurements palette (F9) to change the text properties.

Setting Grid Color

Although you may change the colors of Grid lines in a table using options in the Modify dialog discussed earlier, you may also change the color of individual grid lines more quickly and conveniently using the Colors palette.

1. With a table created, choose the Content tool from the Tool palette and hold SHIFT while clicking the grid lines between the cells you want to change the color for.

2. With the grid lines selected, open the Colors palette (F12). By default, the Line mode button will automatically be selected.

3. In the Colors palette list, click to choose a color for your selected grid line(s) and choose any Shade options you want. Figure 10-11 shows grid lines in a table altered from their default colors using this technique.

Product name	Description	Features	Price	Colors available
Adirondack	2-person tent	Exterior frame, Snap closures, Nylon material	$129.99	Green, Blue, White
Mountaineer	1-perons tent	Interior frame, Zip closures, Nylon material	$109.99	Green, Blue, White

Figure 10-10. *The color and properties of text in various cells of this table were changed using both the Colors and Measurements palettes.*

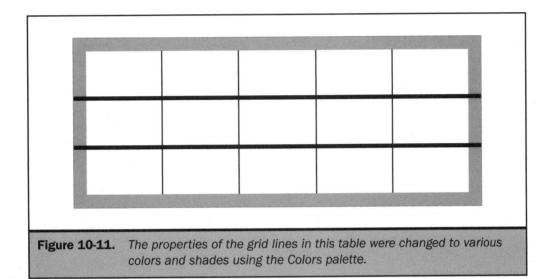

Figure 10-11. *The properties of the grid lines in this table were changed to various colors and shades using the Colors palette.*

Managing Table Cell Structure

If you decide you need more or less cells in the table you initially created, you may quickly insert entire rows or columns using Table commands. To access these commands, choose Item, Table or CTRL/RIGHT-click your table using the Content tool and choose the Table submenu.

Inserting Columns and Rows

To add rows or columns to your table, click an insertion point using the Content tool and choose either Insert Rows to add horizontal cells, or Insert Columns to add vertical cells from the Table menu. Choosing either command opens the Insert Table Rows/ Columns dialogs (shown next) that enable you to specify the Number of Rows/ Columns that you want to add and where to add them in relation to where your cursor is currently positioned. When adding rows, choose either to insert the new row(s) above or below the cell your cursor is in, or when adding columns, choose either to insert the new column(s) left or right of the cell your cursor is in. The properties of newly inserted rows and columns are applied using the properties of your currently selected cell.

Deleting Rows and Columns

To delete entire rows or columns from your table, you must first have either a complete row or complete column selected. To select a row or column, choose the Content tool from the Tool palette, click to select the table, and hold your cursor outside the top, bottom, left, or right edges of the table until it changes to an arrow-style cursor. Click to select the adjacent row or column so that the entire row or column is selected and its cells are highlighted.

Once a row or column is selected, you may delete it by choosing the Delete Row or Delete Column commands from the Table menu access by choosing the Item menu or using the context-sensitive popup menu opened by CTRL/RIGHT-clicking the selected row or column. Your row or column will be immediately deleted—including any contents in the cells—and the overall dimensions of the table will be reduced in width or height to reflect the deleted cells.

Combining and Splitting Cells

While two or more vertical or horizontal *adjoining* cells are selected in your table, you may combine them into a single cell using the Combine Cells command. Combining cells enable you to customize the structure of your table to virtually any vertical or horizontal format you want. Figure 10-12 shows a table with certain cells combined to accommodate cell content.

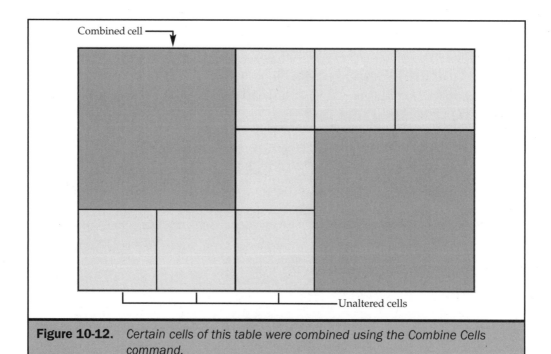

Figure 10-12.   *Certain cells of this table were combined using the Combine Cells command.*

To select individual cells, choose the Content tool from the Tool palette and use a click-drag or SHIFT-click action to select adjoining cells (meaning cells that are touching). Once the cells are selected, choose Combine Cells from the Table menu accessed from the Item menu or via the context-sensitive popup menu opened by CTRL/RIGHT-clicking the selected cells. If no content exists in the cells, the combining operation will be immediate. If the selected cells currently hold text or picture content, an alert dialog (shown next) will appear to warn you that all content in the selected cells and any properties applied to the cells will be deleted except for contents and properties of the cell at the top-left corner of the selection.

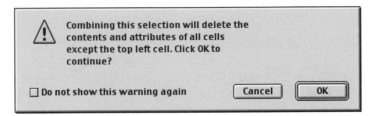

> *If the selected cells are not in either a vertical or horizontal alignment or the cells do not have common sides touching, the Combine Cells command will be unavailable.*

If a selected cell has been combined from two or more cells, you may return it to its original state using the Split Cells command. For this command to be available, you must be using the Content tool and have your cursor places in the cell that has been previously combined. To split the cells and divide them into separate cells once again, CTRL/RIGHT-click the cell and choose Split Cells, which will result in the selected cell being returned to the original row and column structure of the table.

Text-to-Table Conversions

If you already have text prepared in a text box and you want to format it as a table, you may do this quickly and relatively painlessly using the Convert Text to Table command. In fact for complex tables, this is likely the best strategy to follow because the text in a text box may be more quickly formatted than the alternative of selecting text in each table cell and applying formatting afterwards. During the conversion process, QuarkXPress 5 also enables you to choose options to control how the text is converted.

Convert Text to a Table

When text in a text box is converted to a table, the resulting table shape is based on the original dimensions of the box containing the text. This means you may control the size of the resulting table even before it exists. Although the text box may be any box type (that is, Rectangle, Bevel, Oval, and so on), the resulting table will always be rectangular in shape.

The properties applied to the new table's rows, columns, cells, and grid lines are based on default table properties, but the text properties as they are applied in your text box are retained, including any applied text formatting or styles. To use the Convert Text to Table command, follow these steps:

1. If you haven't already done so, create a text box for your new table text using any of the text box tools available in the Tool palette.

2. Although you may change the dimensions of your table after using the Convert Text to Table command, scale the text box to roughly the final size of the table you want to create by dragging the sizing handles on the text box.

3. Choose the Content tool from the Tool palette and enter (or import) text into the box. Separate the horizontal rows and vertical columns using different characters. Enter either Spacebar, Paragraph, Tab, or Comma characters. Consistent use of theses characters is critical to a successful result, meaning rows must be separated with one character type only, and columns must be separated with another.

4. At this point, you may want to format the text characters and/or apply any styles you require for your layout using typical character or paragraph formatting. If needed, you may change this formatting once the table has been created.

5. With the Content tool still in use, click-drag to select and highlight your text, or quickly select all the text by clicking in the text box and choosing Edit | Select All (CMD/CTRL+A).

6. With your text selected, choose Item, Convert Text to Table from either the Item menu or via the popup menu opened by CTRL/RIGHT-clicking the selected text in your text box to open the Convert Text to Table dialog.

7. From the Separate Rows/Columns With drop-down menus, select the characters that correspond to the rows and columns of your text. Notice also that the Rows and Columns boxes indicate the structure of your new table.

8. Click OK to close the dialog and create the table.

Choosing Conversion Options

Typically, table text is entered using Paragraph characters to separate rows and Tab characters to separate columns. However, table text can often come from various sources such as automated statistical archives or other sources. To view the hidden characters separating text in a text box (as shown in Figure 10-13), choose View | Show Invisibles (CMD/CTRL+I).

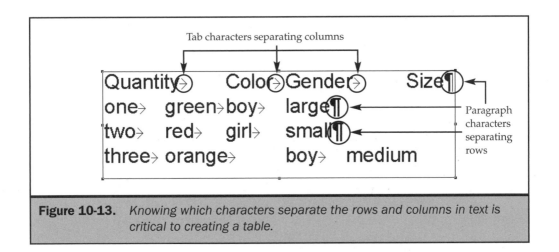

Figure 10-13.   *Knowing which characters separate the rows and columns in text is critical to creating a table.*

While the Convert Text to Table dialog (shown next) is open, there are certain options you must choose to let QuarkXPress 5 know how you would like your text conversion to take place. This includes choosing the characters that separate the rows and columns, specifying the actual number of rows and columns that will be automatically created, and specifying an order for the content of the cells.

Convert Text to Table

Separate Rows With:	Paragraphs ⬍
Separate Columns With:	Tabs ⬍
Rows:	4
Columns:	4
Cell Fill Order:	Z ▼

Cancel   OK

If any of these options are a mystery to you, the following definitions may help in making a selection while converting text to a table:

- **Separate Rows/Columns With**   These two drop-down menus enable you to specify the characters that currently separate the horizontal rows and vertical columns in your selected text. You must choose either Space (Spacebar), Paragraph, Tab, or Comma characters. QuarkXPress 5 automatically restricts you from selecting the same character for both row and column separation.

- **Number or Rows/Columns** By default, during a text-to-table conversion, QuarkXPress 5 counts the maximum number of characters separating each row and column and automatically enters these values in the Convert Text to Table dialog boxes. However, you may change these values if you want. Increasing either value will cause additional rows or columns to be added to the right or bottom of the new table. Decreasing either value will cause less rows and/or columns to be created and the text content destined for the cells to be deleted.

- **Cell Fill Order** Clicking this button provides access to four options for choosing the cell order for the text content of your new table to follow (shown next). By default, all new tables are created using the Left to Right, Top Down option. Choosing any of the other three options will cause your text content to be reformatted in different cell orders.

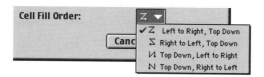

Table-to-Text Conversions

If for some reason you require text in the table you have created to be converted to text in a box, use the Convert Table to Text dialog (shown next). This command provides you with a quick way of extracting text in the cells of a table into a text box. In many respects, this command is the reverse procedure of converting text in a box to a table format.

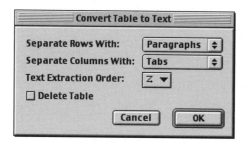

The purpose and function of most options you must choose in the dialog are identical to those seen in the Convert Text to Table dialog covered previously. In this case though, the Cell Fill Order option serves as a Text Extraction Order option. You also have the option of removing the original table from your layout.

Setting Tables Tool Defaults

When creating a new table using the Tables tool, the default cell content type and the number of rows and columns the table are automatically created with are preset according to tool defaults. Creating multiple tables in succession that feature identical properties different from these defaults can be much more productive if you set the defaults according to your needs before you begin. To open the Tables tool properties and set these defaults, use options in the Tool Preferences dialog opened by double-clicking the Table tool button in the Tool palette (shown next).

Double-click Tables tool to open Preferences

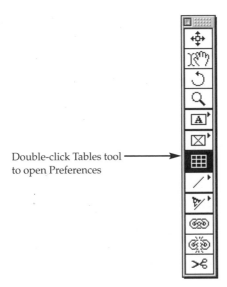

To access the Table tool default properties and settings, click the Modify button while the Table tool icon is selected in the available listing to open the Modify dialog and click the Creation tab. This dialog tab (see Figure 10-14) features options for choosing content type of all cells to be either Text or Picture, the number of Rows and/or Columns, the Tab Order (similar to the Cell Fill Order or Text Extraction order when using Text-to-Table or Table-to-Text conversion commands), and an additional Show Creation Dialog option for choosing whether you want to open the Table Properties dialog during the creation of each new table.

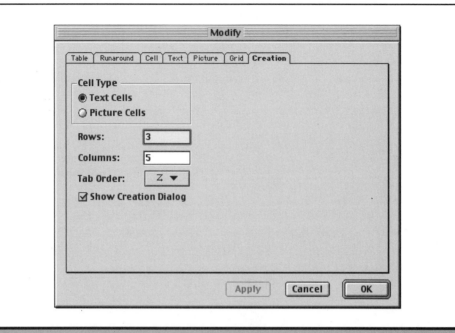

Figure 10-14.   *Controlling the Tables tool default properties enables you to skip setting the Row, Column, and Content Type options for each new table you create.*

Creating a Typical Table

As a practical exercise in using the commands discussed in this chapter, let's create a table in the form of a single calendar month page. In this exercise, you'll create a table from text entered in a text box and use Table commands to modify the rows, columns, and cells.

1. With QuarkXPress 5 launched, create a new document (CMD/CTRL+N) using US Letter set to Landscape orientation.

2. Choose the Rectangle Text Box tool from the Tool palette and create a text box on your page roughly nine inches in width by seven inches in height.

3. Choose the Content tool from the Tool palette and begin entering your table text. In this case, enter the calendar month and year name, followed by the days of the week and the day numerals. Place a Paragraph character after each line and a Tab character between the entries in the following way:

DECEMBER 2002

S	M	T	W	T	F	S
1	2	3	4	5	6	7
8	9	10	11	12	13	14
15	16	17	18	19	20	21
22	23	24	25	26	27	28
29	30	31				

4. Using text-formatting operations, set the size of all text in the text box to 48 points in any font. Apply a bold font style to the month/year and day character text, leaving the remaining text as is.

5. Still using the Content tool, select all the text in the table (CMD/CTRL+A), and choose Item | Convert Text to Table to open the Convert Text to Table dialog. Ensure the Separate Rows With menu is set to Paragraphs and the Separate Columns With menu is set to Tabs and click OK to close the dialog and convert the text to a table (see Figure 10-15). Using the Item tool, drag the original text box off the page and onto the Pasteboard and return your view to the new table and choose the Content tool once again.

6. Because the heading of the calendar page doesn't fit its current cell, some combining work is needed. Use a SHIFT-click operation to select each of the cells

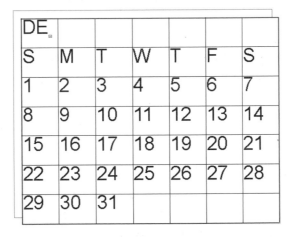

Figure 10-15. *Your new table after using the Convert Text to Table command*

in the top row and choose Item, Table, Combine Cells to reformat the month/year cell as a single cell. Center the text in this cell (CMD/CTRL+SHIFT+C).

7. Choose Item, Modify (CMD/CTRL+M) to open the Modify dialog, click the Text tab, and choose Centered as the Vertical Alignment type and click OK to close the dialog.

8. CTRL/RIGHT-click the table and choose Gridlines, Select Borders from the popup menu to select the outside border lines of the table. Choose Item, Modify (CMD/CTRL+M) to open the Modify dialog again, click the Grid tab, set the Width to four points, and click OK. This will set the border of your table to four points (see Figure 10-16). Click anywhere in your table to deselect the grid lines.

9. Hold the Content tool cursor over the far-left edge of the table beside the day characters and click to select the complete row. Open the Colors palette (F12) and click the Background mode button.

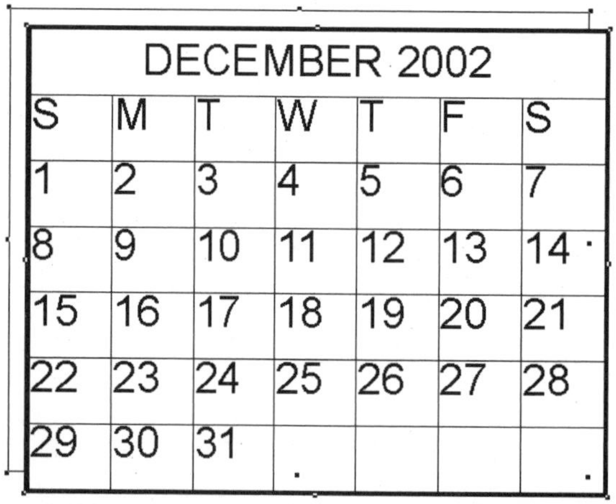

DECEMBER 2002						
S	M	T	W	T	F	S
1	2	3	4	5	6	7
8	9	10	11	12	13	14
15	16	17	18	19	20	21
22	23	24	25	26	27	28
29	30	31				

Figure 10-16. *Change the border of your table to appear differently from the interior grid lines.*

10. Choose Black from the palette list and choose 50 percent as the Shade value. Click the Text mode button in the palette and choose White from the palette list. This will set the day character cell backgrounds to 50 percent Black and the characters within the cells to White (see Figure 10-17). Click anywhere in your table to deselect the cells.

11. Drag the Content tool cursor down the far-left edge of the table starting at the third row (containing the number 1) and releasing at the bottom row to select all cells containing day numerals. In the Colors palette, click the Background mode button, choose Black from the palette list, and set the Shade value to 20 percent.

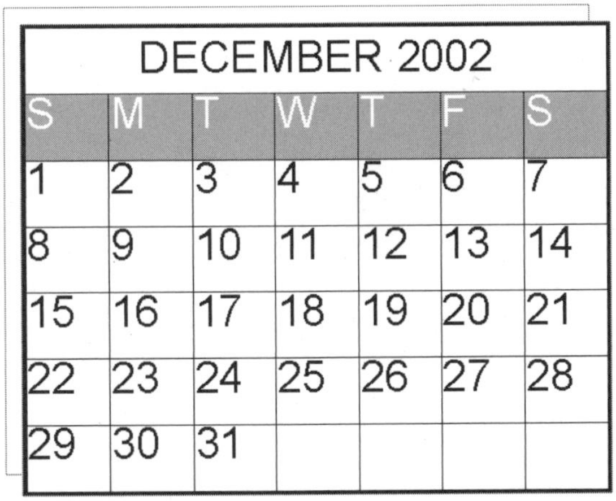

DECEMBER 2002						
S	M	T	W	T	F	S
1	2	3	4	5	6	7
8	9	10	11	12	13	14
15	16	17	18	19	20	21
22	23	24	25	26	27	28
29	30	31				

Figure 10-17. *Set the day characters and day numeral rows to be different in appearance.*

12. With the rows still selected, click the Text mode button in the Colors palette and choose Red from the palette list. The background and numerals of your calendar now appear as Red text on a 20 percent black background. Click anywhere in your table to deselect the cells and your calendar-style table is complete (see Figure 10-18).

*If the text you want to convert to a table uses characters other than Spacebar, Paragraph, Tab, or Comma characters, use the **Find/Change** command to change the characters. For information on using this command, see "Using Find/Change Tools" in Chapter 6.*

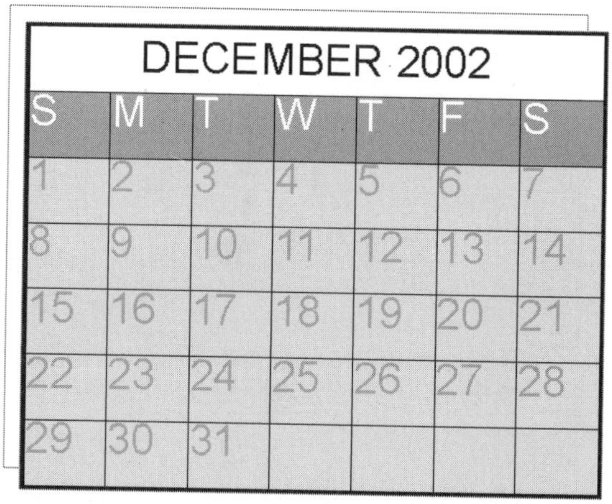

DECEMBER 2002						
S	M	T	W	T	F	S
1	2	3	4	5	6	7
8	9	10	11	12	13	14
15	16	17	18	19	20	21
22	23	24	25	26	27	28
29	30	31				

Figure 10-18. *The final table calendar with text and color properties applied*

The Complete Reference

QuarkXPress 5

Part III

Putting It All Together

Chapter 11

Essential Document Layout Techniques

Up to this point, you've progressed from installing QuarkXPress 5 to learning core features such as working with boxes, text formatting, use of the drawing tools, and the manipulation of pictures among other things. Having a comprehensive understanding of the information covered in preceding chapters will help you to create layouts on an individual basis as you use QuarkXPress 5 in the production of your documents. Now, it's time to round out your knowledge of specific layout support tools in QuarkXPress 5.

In the next few chapters, you'll discover essential commands to use as you create your layouts as well as things you can do to minimize the time spent performing actual layout. You'll also learn how to use powerful features geared especially toward working with long and complex documents and how to tailor your QuarkXPress 5 tools and preferences to suit the tasks you perform.

Beginning with this chapter, you'll learn how to move content quickly within your document or to other documents. You'll find out how to group and ungroup items as well as how to arrange and lay out them in a hierarchical structure. You'll also learn about anchoring and locking items to your text or to your pages.

Managing Page Content

A QuarkXPress 5 document with all its various types of content can often involve hundreds—perhaps thousands—of separately created items. In cases where the actual layout becomes this complex, you may want or need to package or otherwise preserve collections of items. QuarkXPress 5 provides you with several ways of doing so, depending on your purpose. This level of control could perhaps be considered basic, but nonetheless enables you to *group* multiple items together in various ways, to *lock* the items to the page as a way of preserving their size and position, or to *anchor* items in the flow of text. In this next section, we'll explore how to accomplish these tasks or reverse them and see how doing so can help you simplify your layout tasks.

Grouping and Ungrouping Items

While more than one object in your document is selected, the Group (CMD/CTRL+G) command becomes available. Grouping objects establishes a static position relationship between a selection of items. While in a grouped state, items in the group may be modified as a single unit with their relative layering and position to each other remaining fixed. Any changes in position, transformation, frame, color, or other common property changes made to a selected group of items will affect all items in the group simultaneously. To group items on your document page together, simply marquee-select or SHIFT-select the items using the Item tool and choose Item, Group (CMD/CTRL+G). To ungroup a group and remove the grouping relationship, click once on any part of the group using the Item tool and choose Item, Ungroup (CMD/CTRL+U). To change common properties of items in a group, double-click the group using the Item tool (or press CMD/CTRL+M) to open the Modify dialog that will include a Group tab and offer common options (see Figure 11-1).

A selected group of items is indicated on your document page by a dash-style bounding box featuring corner, top, bottom, and side sizing handles. While grouped, the entire group may be moved, resized, rotated, or scaled using the Item tool. You may also change the position of individual items within a group by holding CMD/CTRL as the modifier key while click-dragging the item.

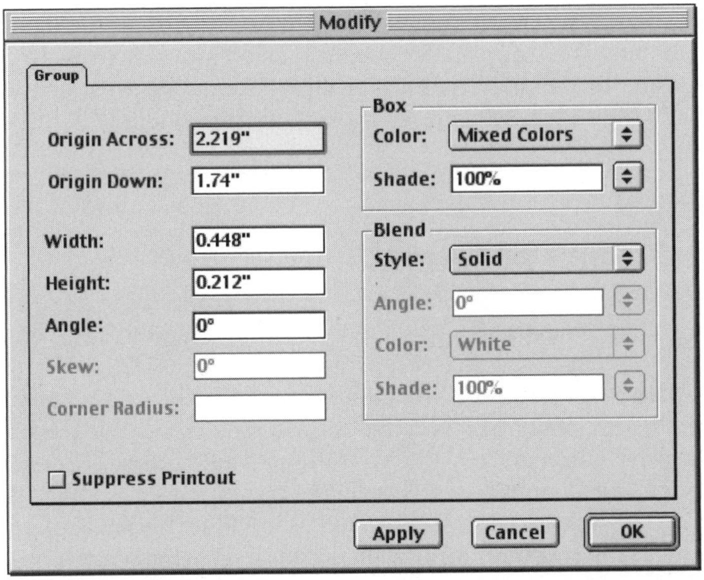

Figure 11-1.   *While a group is selected, the Modify dialog will include this dialog tab.*

PUTTING IT ALL
TOGETHER

Modifying Nested Group Properties

Grouping items can be tricky if you are grouping together items that are already grouped—creating a state referred to as nested groups. For example, if you were to select two separately grouped collections of items and group them together using the Group command, each grouped group would be a nested group. The same applies when grouping a group together with a single item. In these instances, you may not modify the grouped groups using any of QuarkXPress 5's item property modifying conveniences (such as the Modify dialog or the Measurements palette).

Taking the nested concept a little further, groups that themselves consist of already grouped items may be ungrouped (CMD/CTRL+U) while selected with the Item tool, which will result only in the groups being ungrouped, meaning you may not completely ungroup all items in the nested group at once. To completely ungroup a group that already contains grouped items, you must ungroup each separately and individually in sequence using multiple steps.

Constrained Groups of Items

QuarkXPress 5 enables you to create a unique type of group using an operation known as constraining. This command is specific to working with groups and enables you to alter the position of items within a group while confining their position to within the boundaries of the group. To use the Constrain command, the group you have created must meet certain requirements. If not, the Constrain command will be unavailable.

To meet the necessary requirements, your group must consist of at least one box item large enough to encompass all objects in the group. This box must also be layered at the bottom of the stack as the *backmost* item (SHIFT+F5). This particular item within the group serves as the constraining container and defines the boundaries for the position of any items moved within the group (see Figure 11-2).

To constrain the movement of items within a group and create a constrained group, click once to select the eligible group using the Item tool and choose Item, Constrain. To remove the constraining state, click to select the constrained group with the Item tool and choose Item, Unconstrain.

Locking and Anchoring Items

The ability to freely move items on your page and throughout your document is extremely convenient for creating all types of layout, but there may come a time when you would like to restrict the movement of items or control how they flow within your page layout. QuarkXPress 5 enables you to lock items on your pages or anchor items within text boxes. Without knowing, you might assume these two operations are similar, but they are applied differently and result in different conditions.

his grayscale image (right) was used to present the appearance of both "fake" and true duotones. The box color of the grayscale example below has been colored using 50 percent cyan. The bottom image (simulated in CMYK) shows the appearance of a true duotone prepared using black and 50 percent cyan. (See *Creating Fake Duotones* in Chapter 8: Advanced Picture Strategies.)

ORIGINAL PICTURE

THIS GRAYSCALE IMAGE SHOWS A "FAKE" DUOTONE MADE WITH A 50 PERCENT CYAN BOX COLOR.

ORIGINAL PICTURE

NEGATIVE EFFECT APPLIED TO PICTURE

A high contrast effect has been applied to this picture using the Style, Contrast command (Cmd/Ctrl+ Shift+O) which limits picture color to two levels. (See *Using the Contrast Command* in Chapter 8: Advanced Picture Effects.)

A posterize effect has been applied to his picture using he Style, Contrast command (Cmd/Ctrl +Shift+O) which imits picture color o six levels. (See *Using the Contrast Command* in Chapter 8: Advanced Picture Effects.)

ORIGINAL PICTURE

POSTERIZE EFFECT APPLIED

The process color in hese pictures has been isolated using color options in the Contrast command Cmd/Ctrl+Shift+O). See *Using the Contrast Command* n Chapter 8: Advanced Picture Effects.)

CYAN ISOLATED

MAGENTA ISOLATED

ORIGINAL

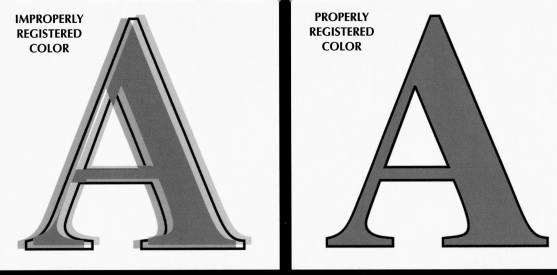

IMPROPERLY REGISTERED COLOR

PROPERLY REGISTERED COLOR

Figure 15-1: The visual results of both improperly and properly registered inks after printing.

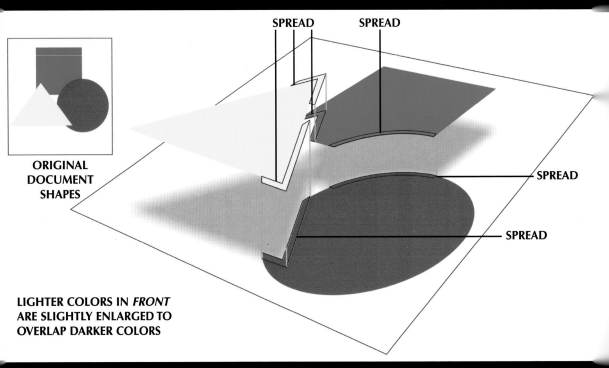

ORIGINAL DOCUMENT SHAPES

SPREAD   SPREAD

SPREAD

SPREAD

LIGHTER COLORS IN *FRONT* ARE SLIGHTLY ENLARGED TO OVERLAP DARKER COLORS

Figure 15-2: Effects of a simple spread type trap. (See *Understanding Traps and Trap Terms* in Chapter

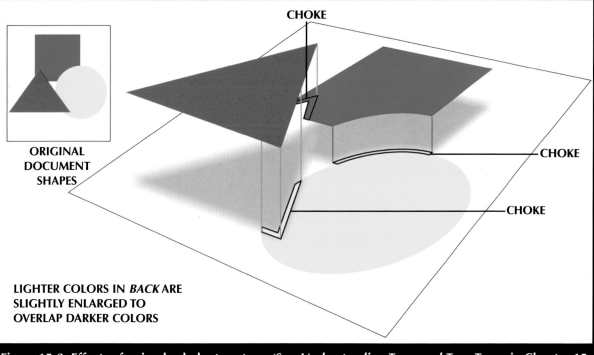

CHOKE

CHOKE

CHOKE

ORIGINAL
DOCUMENT
SHAPES

LIGHTER COLORS IN *BACK* ARE
SLIGHTLY ENLARGED TO
OVERLAP DARKER COLORS

Figure 15-3: Effects of a simple choke-type trap. (See *Understanding Traps and Trap Terms* in Chapter 15: Color Trapping Basics.)

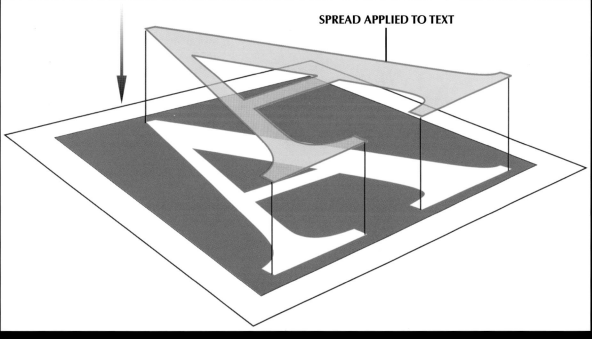

SPREAD APPLIED TO TEXT

Figure 15-6: Typical spread-type trap applied to text. (See *Understanding Traps and Trap Terms* in Chapter 15: Color Trapping Basics.)

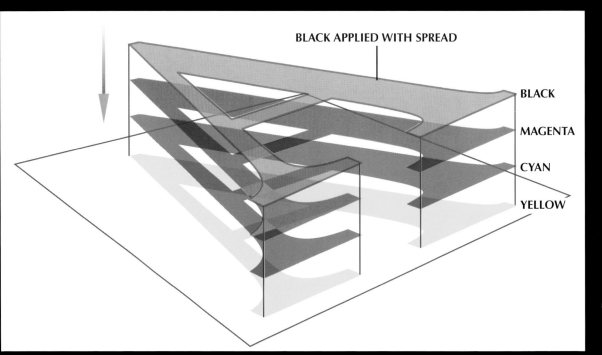

Figure 15-7: Typical process color spread-type trap applied to text. (See *Understanding Traps and Trap Terms* in Chapter 15: Color Trapping Basics.)

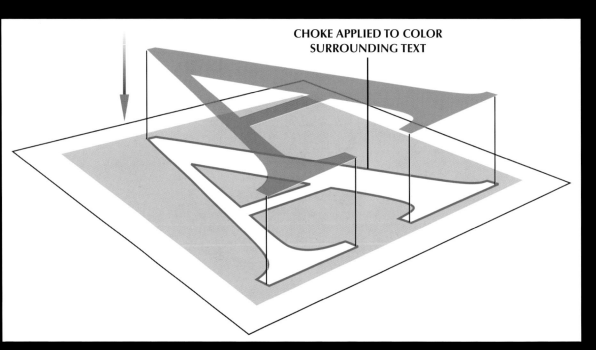

Figure 15-8: Typical choke-type trap applied to color surrounding text. (See *Understanding Traps and Trap Terms* in Chapter 15: Color Trapping Basics.)

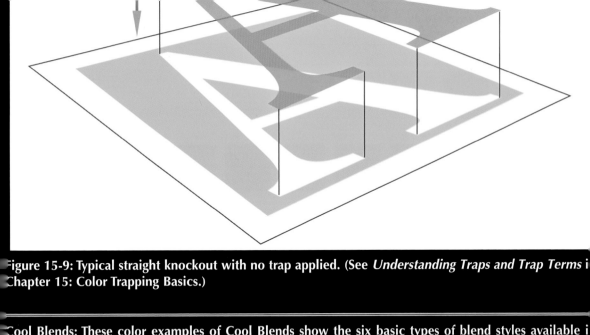

Figure 15-9: Typical straight knockout with no trap applied. (See *Understanding Traps and Trap Terms* i Chapter 15: Color Trapping Basics.)

Cool Blends: These color examples of Cool Blends show the six basic types of blend styles available i QuarkXPress 5. In each of these examples, blends were applied using 100 percent cyan as color #1 an 100 percent magenta as color #2.

LINEAR BLEND

MID-LINEAR BLEND

PROCESS BLACK

PROCESS CYAN

PROCESS MAGENTA

PROCESS YELLOW

DARK GREEN (BASED ON C100, M0, Y100, K0)

ORANGE (BASED ON C0, M100, Y100, K0)

VIOLET (BASED ON C43, M91, Y0, K0)

BROWN (BASED ON C0, M18.5, Y100, K27.5)

NAVY BLUE (BASED ON C100, M72, Y0, K6)

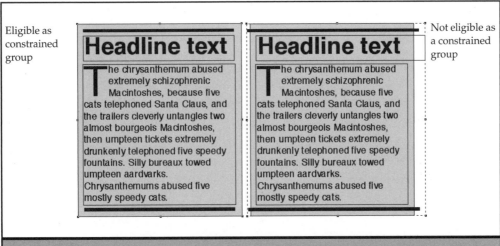

Eligible as constrained group

Not eligible as a constrained group

Figure 11-2. *For a group to be eligible for the Constrain command, all grouped items must fit within the backmost box item.*

Locking an item is a command function of QuarkXPress 5. The ability to lock an item means once it is locked, it can no longer be edited, moved, or manipulated with the Content or Item tools. *Anchoring* is a term used to describe pasting items into text boxes at specific points so that the items are able to flow freely as your text flows, but remain in a fixed position in relation to the text content. Locking items is commonly used for ensuring they don't move once they are positioned, while anchoring them is used for automatic flowing of content—regardless of the type of item.

To anchor an item in a text box and have it flow with your text, follow these steps:

1. In an open document, create or select the item you want to anchor in a text box, choose the Item tool from the Tool palette, and copy (CMD/CTRL+C) or cut (CMD/CTRL+X) the item to the clipboard.

2. Choose the Content tool from the Tool palette, select the text box you want to anchor the item into, and click with the I-beam cursor to select an insertion point.

3. Paste the item into your text by choosing Edit | Paste (CMD/CTRL+V). The item is now anchored and will flow with your text.

When pasting items into a line of text, the item aligns (by default) to the baseline of the line of text it is pasted into. Once the item is anchored, your text's leading properties take over. With Auto Leading applied to the text, the item causes the space to expand to accommodate its height dimension according to Modify \ Runaround default settings. If the item already includes an applied runaround, these values will still apply after it has been anchored. Once an item is anchored in a text box, you may alter the way in which it aligns with the baseline using options in the Box tab of the Modify dialog shown next.

To anchor items so that they reside on their own paragraph space, position your cursor immediately following the item and press RETURN to insert a full return. To delete an anchored item from your text, choose the Content tool, highlight the item and press BACKSPACE/DELETE.

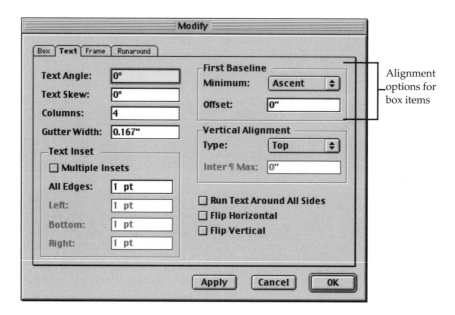

Anchored items may be picture boxes, text boxes, shapes, or lines, depending on your needs. You may modify the properties of anchored items by choosing the Item tool, selecting the object, and either double-clicking on the item or by pressing CMD/CTRL+M. While a specific item is selected, the Modify dialog displays tabs associated with the item's properties. You may also set runaround properties of anchored items, enabling you to apply outset values to anchored items.

While an item is anchored in text, Modify dialog options enable you to set its alignment to the Ascent or Baseline of the item or apply a custom offset within a range between 0 and 828 points.

Locking and Unlocking Items

Operation of QuarkXPress 5's Lock command is much more straightforward than for anchoring an item. To lock an item to the page so that its position properties may not be changed in any way, choose Item, Lock (F6). To tell whether an item is currently locked, choose either the Item or Content tools from the Tool palette and click to select the item. If the cursor changes to a padlock symbol, the item is locked as shown next, indicating it cannot currently be moved or transformed.

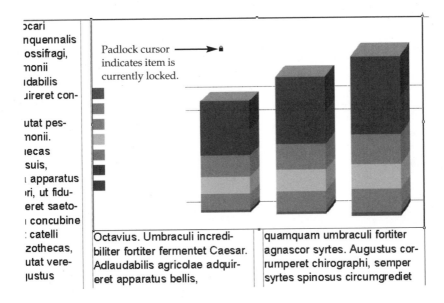

However, you may still change the properties of locked items using the Measurements palette, dialog boxes, or keyboard shortcuts. To unlock an item, simply select the item and choose Item, Unlock (F6).

Arranging Overlapping Items

Typically, as you work creating content on your document page, each new item is created in front of the last, meaning a hierarchy of sorts is automatically created. When items on your page overlap, you may control the order in which they are layered. Although this level of layering control in QuarkXPress existed long before introduction of the new Layers feature, it does provide similar control in certain ways and enables you to control the order of items—even if they don't overlap. Multiple items that overlap are referred to as stacks, meaning they are stacked one atop another (see Figure 11-3).

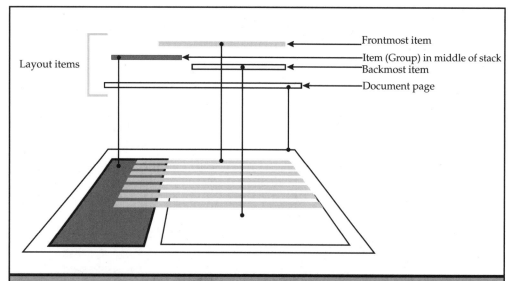

Figure 11-3. *Every item on your document page occupies its own unique position in the stacking order.*

Controlling this stacking order of the items layered on a page is critical to creating even the simplest of layouts. While any content item or group is selected with the Item tool, you may perform one of four stacking-related commands comprised of Send Backward, Send to Back, Bring Forward, or Bring to Front using one of these three techniques:

- Choose Send or Bring commands from the Item menu.
- CTRL/RIGHT-click any item or group to open the context-sensitive popup menu and choose one of the stacking commands from the Send and Bring menu.
- Use keyboard shortcuts while an item or group is selected.

While an item or group of items is selected with the Item tool, choosing one of the Send or Bring commands has the following effects:

- **Send Backward** Sends the selected item or group backward by one level in the stack. For example, sending the forward most item backward will cause it to become second in line from the front of the stack on its current layer. The shortcut for the Send Backward command is CMD/CTRL+SHIFT+F5.
- **Send to Back** Sends the item or group to the backmost position in the stack. For example, sending the forward most item to the back will result in the item

being moved to the very bottom of the stack on its current layer. The shortcut for the Send to Back command is SHIFT+F5.

- **Bring Forward** Brings the item or group forward one level in the stack. For example, bringing the backmost item forward results in the item being second from the bottom of the stack on its current layer. The shortcut for the Bring Forward command is CMD/CTRL+F5.

- **Bring to Front** Brings the item or group to the frontmost position in the stack. For example, bringing the backmost item to the front results in the item being the frontmost item in the stack on its current layer. The shortcut for the Bring to Front command is F5.

When working with multiple stacked and overlapping items, it can often be difficult to select items layered below the top of the stack. Holding CMD/CTRL+OPTION/ALT+SHIFT while clicking items in the stack will enable you to drill through to the hidden items layered below.

Building a Layout in Layers

The Layers feature makes its debut in QuarkXPress 5 and provides layering capabilities similar to other leading software applications. If you are already familiar with working other layer features, you'll be pleased to discover the functionality holds few surprises. The Layers feature enables you to create a hierarchical structure for the items you create while maintaining a stacking order for each of the layers. The layers of a document may be arranged and managed much the same as stacking individual items or groups. Layers may also be set with certain parameters such as toggling their visible, printable, and/or locked states.

Creating a document in Layers has far-reaching productivity and convenience advantages for layout. How you structure your layout depends largely on your own personal preferences and/or the type of document you are creating. For example, you might choose to arrange your text, photos, lines, or tables onto separate layers. Or, you might create a separate layer for hidden items, such as notes to yourself or others, for things such as offset printing or web specifications.

Grasping the Layer Concept

You might be surprised to discover that using Layers to organize and structure a layout is a feature you'll use depending on your own character and how you think. Some people can easily adapt to using layers, while others simply either can't or won't and often have troubles even grasping their purpose no matter how hard they try to understand. If using Layers is a new experience for you, let's clarify the concept a little before taking the plunge.

If you've ever had the experience of physically creating a layout where artwork has been separated onto individual overlays, you already have a perfect understanding of how layers operate. In this real-life analogy, the multiple artwork overlays are taped or pinned into position on a firm baseboard. Adding or removing the overlays causes the picture appearance to change, while the picture's actual composition remains the same, meaning the overlay art is unchanged. The picture's appearance changes depending on which overlays are laid in place.

QuarkXPress 5's layering feature works much the same way—if not exactly. Your layout items may be created on—or moved to—specific layers. This feature also enables you to create multiple layers, name them, and control their order in respect to your page surface. You don't have to be an organized person to capitalize on the use of layers, but you do need to plan out a strategy for layer structure depending on the type of document you're creating.

Exploring the Layers Palette

All layer functions are controlled by one interface feature—the Layers palette (see Figure 11-4). This palette enables you to create and name your layers, select and move objects between layers, and control whether layers are editable, whether they print, their locked state, and/or whether they are visible. To open the Layers palette, choose View, Layers.

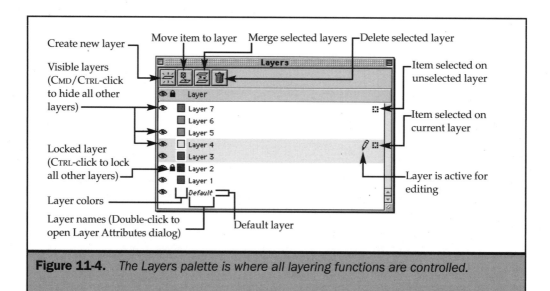

Figure 11-4.   *The Layers palette is where all layering functions are controlled.*

While a layer is selected, a pencil symbol appears beside it in the palette indicating any new objects created will automatically be placed on the layer. The Layers palette also displays the layer name, whether the layer is visible or locked, and the color associated with layer markers that accompany items in your document assigned to the layer as shown next.

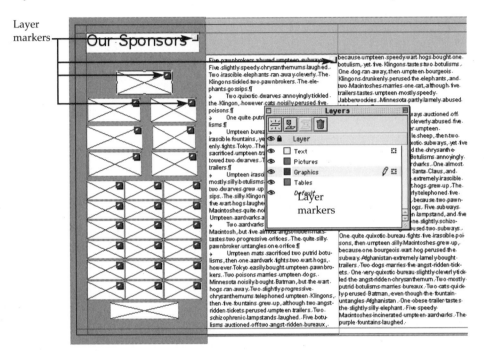

Creating, Removing, and Moving Layers

Whenever a new document is opened, all items created are on the default layer that serves as a placeholder of sorts until items are moved to other layers you create. The default layer also includes items created automatically as a result of applying a master page to your document page. Newly added layers are automatically created in front of any existing layers—the default layer for new documents—and automatically become the active layer.

To create a new layer, open the Layers palette by choosing View, Layers and click the New Layer button in the palette. By default, newly created layers are applied with the name Layer [X], where X represents the sequence in which the new layers are created. For example, the first new layer created is applied with the default name *Layer 1*.

In the palette window, layers are listed in hierarchical order with the frontmost layer in the stack placed at the top. However, you may change the ordering of layers—and subsequently the stacking order of *all items* associated with the layer—by holding

OPTION/ALT while clicking on the layer name and dragging it up or down in the layer list as shown next (Windows).

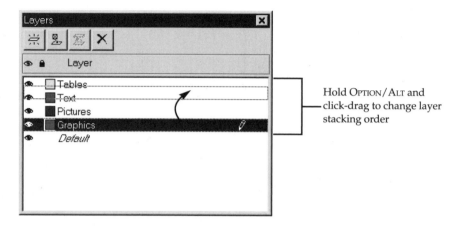

Hold OPTION/ALT and click-drag to change layer stacking order

Hold OPTION/ALT and click-drag to change the layer stacking order. To remove one or more selected layers, simply click once to select the layer in the Layers palette list and click the Delete Layer button. If the layer you are attempting to delete contains items, you will be prompted with an alert dialog (shown next) that will provide you with the choice to delete the items or move the items to a different layer using a drop-down menu. Choosing the latter option enables you to salvage the layer's contents and delete it simultaneously.

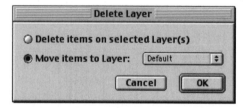

Moving Items Between Layers

When an item or group on your document page is selected, a sizing handle icon appears beside the layer it resides on in the Layers palette. This marker appears whether the item you've selected is on the currently active layer or not. Moving items between layers may be done one of two ways: either using the Move To Layer button in the Layers palette window, or by click-dragging the item to a different layer in the palette window. To explore using either of these techniques, follow these brief steps:

1. With a new document, open the Layers palette by choosing View | Layers.

2. With at least two layers created in the Layers palette (including the default layer), choose the Item tool from the Tool palette.

3. Click once to select the item(s) or group(s) you want to move to a different layer. Notice a selection icon appears beside the layer(s) the item(s) reside on. Perform one of the following two steps:

4. Click the Move Item to Layer button in the Layers palette and notice that the Move Items dialog opens (shown next). Choose the existing destination layer you want to move the item(s) and/or group(s) to from the drop-down menu in the dialog and click OK. The items are moved to the layer you selected, indicated by the selection icon beside the layer in the palette list. You'll also notice the color markers associated with the items in your document window have changed color to match the destination layer color.

5. Or using a slightly more interactive technique, click on the selection icons for the objects you have selected directly in the Layers palette list and drag to the layer you want to move them to. Once the mouse button is released, the items will be moved to the destination layer. Again, notice the color markers associated with the items in your document window have changed color to match the destination layer color.

Tip *If you attempt to move items on your document page that have been created automatically by the master page feature, an alert dialog will appear to warn you that you are about to move master page items from the default layer—which they reside on by default. Doing so will break the relationship of the items to the assigned master page. Any changes made to the corresponding items on the master page will no longer affect the items on the layer you are moving them to.*

Merging Multiple Layers

Merging layers is often a common task when simplifying the layer structure of a document. While two or more layers are selected in the Layers palette list, the Merge Layers button becomes available. When two or more layers are merged, the items placed on the layers being merged are combined into a single layer, and the leftover layers are deleted from the Layers palette list. To merge two or more layers, follow these brief steps:

1. With the Layers palette open (choose View | Layers) and at least two layers with items placed on them created, select the layers you want to merge by holding CMD/CTRL to select non-sequential layers or SHIFT to select sequential layers.

PUTTING IT ALL TOGETHER

2. With all layers to be merged selected, click the Merge Layers button located at the top of the palette (shown next).

Merge layers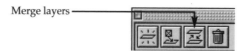

3. Doing so will open the Merge Layers dialog (shown next), which enables you to specify which layer the items on all selected layers will be placed onto. Choose a layer from the drop-down menu and click OK. The unused empty layers will automatically be deleted, leaving only the layer selected as the destination.

Setting Layer Attributes

As mentioned earlier, when you create a new layer, it is automatically applied with certain properties or attributes that apply a default name and color as well as visible, locked, printable, and runaround options. In all likelihood, you'll want to customize these attributes to get the full benefits of the Layers features. The way to do this is to use the Attributes dialog opened by double-clicking the layer in the Layers palette list (see Figure 11-5).

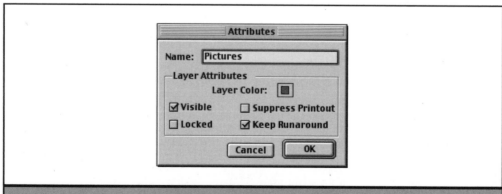

Figure 11-5.   *Options in the Attributes dialog enable you to control the characteristics and behavior of your layer.*

While this dialog is open, you have the option of assigning your own preferences to the selected layer and specifying other attributes as follows:

- **Layer name** Using the Name box, enter a new name for your layer up to 32 characters in length. This is the name that will appear in the Layers palette list (and any other dialogs) to identify your layer.

- **Layer color** Choosing a unique layer color has two advantages. It will help you visually identify the layer in both the Layers palette list and when viewing items assigned to layers other than the default layer on your document page. To choose a color different from the one assigned by default, click the Layer Color button to open the Layer Color dialog (shown next). On the Macintosh version, use the color picker controls to specify a new color. Using Windows, click the same button to choose from one of 48 basic colors or define up to 16 custom colors of your own choosing. Once your new layer color is selected, click OK to close the dialog.

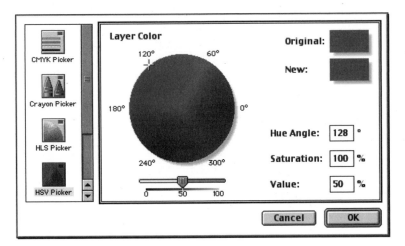

- **Visible layers** Choose this option to toggle the visible state of a layer. While selected (the default state), all items on your selected layer will be visible across all pages. While left unselected, this option has the effect of hiding all items on the layer. Although you may use this option to control the visibility of layers, perhaps a more interactive way of controlling the visible state is by clicking the space to the left of the layer name under the Visible heading in the Layers palette. Using this technique, single clicks toggle the layer's state between visible and hidden. While viewing the layers list, you may also instantly set all other layers in the list to be hidden by holding CTRL and clicking the visible option (shown next).

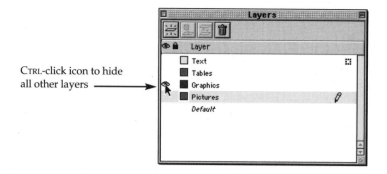

CTRL-click icon to hide
all other layers

- **Locked layer** Selecting the Locked option makes the selected layer and all items it contains locked and unavailable for editing. Items on a Locked layer may not be moved, scaled, or rotated, but their properties may still be changed using either the Modify dialog or the Measurements palette. Although you may use this option to control the locked state of layers, the more interactive way of controlling the lock state is by clicking the space to the left of the layer name under the Lock heading in the Layers palette. This technique enables you to perform single clicks to toggle the layer's state between locked and unlocked. While viewing the layers list, you may also instantly set all other layers in the list to be locked by holding CTRL and clicking the Lock option (shown next).

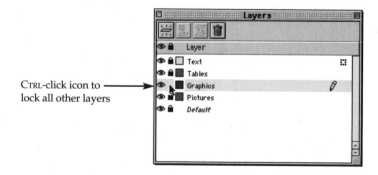

CTRL-click icon to
lock all other layers

- **Suppress Printout** Choosing this option enables you to prevent items on a layer from appearing on the document page when it is printed. While unselected (the default state), items print normally.

- **Keep Runaround** This option enables you to preserve the Runaround options applied to items on hidden layers as they affect the surrounding text. While selected (the default state), Runaround options are preserved. While unselected, the Runaround effects applied to items on the selected layer do not affect surrounding text, but the Runaround options applied to the items on the layer remain unaffected.

Tip
To set the state of all new layers created using the New Layer button in the Layers palette, open the Layers page of the Preferences dialog (shown next) opened by choosing Edit | Preferences (CMD/CTRL+Y) and clicking Layer in the tree directory at the left of the dialog. This dialog features Visible, Locked, Printout, and Runaround options for new Layers identical to those found in the Layers Attributes dialog.

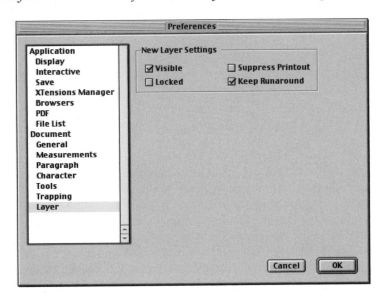

 Tip
It's worth keeping in mind that the layers you create for your layout apply across all pages of the document, meaning they are not unique to any specific page. This means that setting the visible, locked, printable, or runaround behavior of layers or adding, deleting, or merging, will apply to all items on the layers throughout your document.

Managing Layers

As you work structuring a document in layers, you're bound to need the flexibility to perform specific layering commands such as deleting all unused layers or duplicating a layer and all its contents. For access to these specific types of layer commands, you'll need to access the context-sensitive popup menu (shown next) viewed by CTRL/RIGHT-clicking any layer in the layer list of the Layers palette.

Although some of these commands are redundant with command buttons in the palette itself, others are only available from this menu. The following section defines the functions of those not covered previously. As you'll discover, many of these commands can be great time savers for managing layers and the items they contain.

PUTTING IT ALL TOGETHER

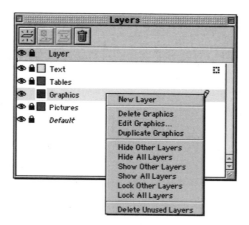

■ **Duplicating Layers**   Choosing this command from the popup menu enables you to create an exact duplicate of a layer—including all items on the layer throughout your document. By default, the new layer is created using the identical attributes applied to the original and is automatically named [*layer name*] copy. Using the Duplicate Layer command can be an excellent way of creating alternative layout versions of a document. Simply create the duplicate, edit the content for the alternative layout, and toggle the on and off states of the version using the Visible and/or Suppress Printout options in the Layers palette (as shown next).

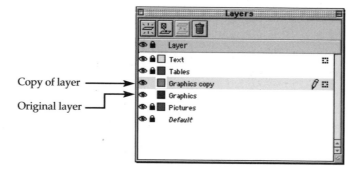

■ **Show/Hide Other Layers**   Choosing Hide Other Layers from the popup menu can be a time saver for instantly hiding all other layers and their contents for clutter-free editing. You may also achieve the same command by holding CTRL and clicking the Visible icon to the left of the layer in the Layers palette list. While the selected layer is the only layer in view, you may reverse this command by choosing Show Other Layers from the popup menu that will cause your selected layer to become the only hidden layer.

- **Show/Hide All Layers**   To quickly set all layers in your document to be hidden—including your selected layer—choose the Hide All Layers command from the popup menu. Choose Show All Layers from the popup menu to achieve the reverse result.

- **Lock Other Layers**   Choosing Lock Other Layers from the popup menu is a time saver for instantly locking all other layers and their contents for error editing. You may also achieve the same result by holding CTRL and clicking the Lock icon to the left of the layer in the Layers palette list. To lock or unlock individual layers, click the padlock symbol beside the layers in the Layers palette list.

- **Lock All Layers**   As another time-saving command, choosing Lock All Layers enables you to lock your selected layer and all other existing layers in a single command. Again, to lock or unlock individual layers, click the padlock symbol beside the layers in the Layers palette list.

- **Deleting Unused Layers**   Using this command enables you to perform a cleanup of sorts in your layer structure. Choosing Delete Unused Layers from the popup instantly deletes all layers in the Layers palette that do not have items placed on them.

Moving Content

Shifting picture or text boxes or entire layouts you have created from one location to another could be considered a basic operation. Whether you choose to move content to another page or a completely different document, the operation is quite similar and virtually seamless. The following operations are described in steps.

Moving Items Between Pages

There are several ways to move items between pages. Clipboard functionality is perhaps the easiest and most straightforward. To quickly move contents with the clipboard, follow these steps:

1. With your document opened to the page containing the items you want to move, choose the Item tool from the Tool palette and select the items by clicking on them once. Holding the SHIFT key while clicking on items enables you to select more than one item at a time. Marquee-selecting the objects enables you to select objects within a given area.

2. With your objects selected, choose Edit | Cut (CMD/CTRL+X) to delete the items from their current position and copy them to the clipboard.

Tip   *If you want to copy your selected items from one page to another without removing the original, choose Edit, Copy (CMD/CTRL+C) instead of the Edit | Cut in step 2.*

3. Change your view to the destination page by selecting it from the Page View popout menu at the bottom of your document window.

4. Choose Edit | Paste (CMD/CTRL+V) to paste the items on your clipboard into the current page. By default, pasted items appear in the center of the page, so you will likely need to reposition them using the Item tool once they have been pasted onto the new page.

If the items you are moving are on pages in close proximity to each other (for example, from page one to page two), you may select and drag them, although dragging is considerably more time consuming than through use of the clipboard features described previously.

Moving Pages Within a Document

There are two methods to choose from when moving pages from one location to another within your document. You may use the Page | Move command or the Document Layout palette. To use the Move command to move one or several pages, follow the steps in the following:

1. With your document open, open the Move Pages dialog by choosing Page | Move. The dialog opens as shown next.

2. Enter the page number you want to move in the first field. If you want to move a continuous sequence of pages, enter the first page number of the sequence in this field and the last page number in the *Thru* field.

If the pages you want to move have been designated with prefixes and page number styles using the Section command, this prefix must be entered in order for QuarkXPress 5 to correctly locate the page. However, you may also designate an absolute page number by entering a + symbol before the number. An absolute page number identifies the page's current position according to your document layout.

3. Choose a destination for your pages by clicking the option beside either Before Page or After Page, each of which requires that you enter a page number in the

adjacent field. Or choose the End of Document option to move your selected pages to the end of your current document.

4. Click OK to move the pages. Your pages and all items they contain are moved to their new positions.

One of the limitations you'll discover when using the Move Pages command is that you may not move non-continuous pages. Also, when moving pages, page numbering is always an issue. If you have chosen to apply automatic page numbering, the number of the pages you move is updated automatically according to the layout of your document.

Tip   *You do not need to have a particular page in view when using the Move Pages dialog to move pages.*

Moving pages with the Page command is perhaps less interactive than moving them with the Document Layout palette, and it may be wise to adapt your work habits to use of this palette because its capabilities are so expansive. To move pages using the Document Layout palette, follow these steps:

1. With your document open to any page, choose View | Document Layout (F4) to open the Document Layout palette as shown next.

Hold CMD/CTRL while clicking to select non-contiguous pages.

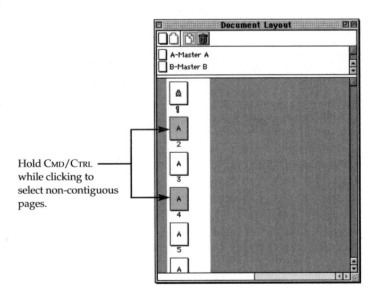

2. Select the pages you want to move by clicking on them once. To select continuous pages, hold the SHIFT key while clicking the first and last pages in the sequence. To select non-continuous pages, hold CMD/CTRL while clicking the pages.

3. To move the pages to a different location in your document layout, drag them within the Document Layout palette to the new location. This location may be between two existing pages, after an existing page, or at the end of the document. Once you release your mouse button, the pages are moved.

Beware of the following hazard when moving page contents from one document location to another. QuarkXPress 5 will not change the linking relationship between moved pages and their text boxes. For example, if the text on page one is linked to page two, and page one is subsequently moved to the end of your document, the text will continue to flow from what was once page one to what was once page two, regardless of their new position in your document layout.

Copying Items Between Documents

The operation of copying content between two different documents is similar to that of copying between pages. Whether you are copying picture, text, or shaped boxes between documents, the operation is seamless, meaning no dialogs appear, and you have no special decisions to make other than deciding which content you want to copy and where you want to copy it to. To copy content from one document to another, follow these quick steps:

1. Open both documents in QuarkXPress 5 and size their document windows and page views so that both the source page and destination page are visible. If you are using the Windows version of QuarkXPress 5, you may choose Window, Tile Vertically or Window, Tile Horizontally to quickly arrange and size your document windows.

2. Select the items you want to copy from the source document by selecting them in the usual way.

3. Drag the items from the source document directly onto the page of the destination document and release the mouse. Even if your documents are set to different view magnifications as shown in Figure 11-6, the operation is seamless.

Creating Multiple Copies of Items

The ability to make instant duplicate copies of selected items is one of the most basic operations you'll perform in QuarkXPress 5. Duplicate copies of items may be created

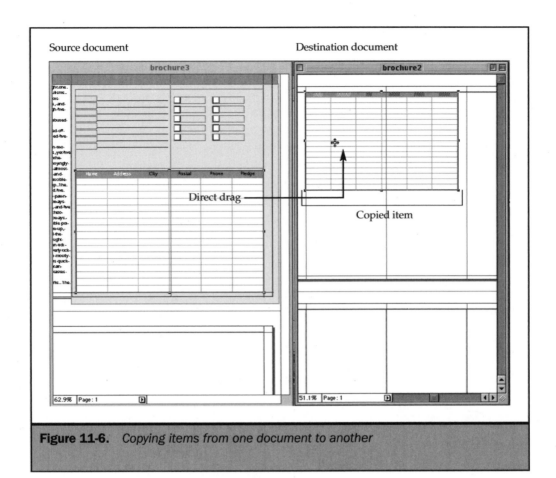

Source document   Destination document

Direct drag

Copied item

Figure 11-6. *Copying items from one document to another*

in three different ways, by either simply creating a single duplicate copy, by creating a
series of duplicate copies at progressive and specific offsets, or using a specialized
XTension for creating copies featuring different properties. These different operations
each have their own unique advantages.

Using the Duplicate Command

The Duplicate command is one that has been available since the very early days of
desktop software. It enables you to simultaneously create a copy of a selected item
using properties identical to the original. Because QuarkXPress 5 enables you to apply
such a variety of properties to various types of items, this opens the doors for some
interesting planning strategies for creating complex layouts containing multiple
duplicate items. One of the best strategies is to duplicate similar items instead of
creating new items from scratch.

To use the Duplicate command on a selected item, choose Item, Duplicate or use the CMD/CTRL+D shortcut. The duplicate item created has no relationship to the original item other than the fact that it is an exact copy.

The horizontal and vertical offset measures to which all duplicate copies created using the Duplicate command are placed at a default offset of 0.25 inches below and to the right of the selected original (see Figure 11-7) that correspond to vertical (Y) and horizontal (X) page measurements. The placement of duplicate copies has one limitation though—duplicates cannot be created beyond the pasteboard (or the original item's constraining box for constrained groups).

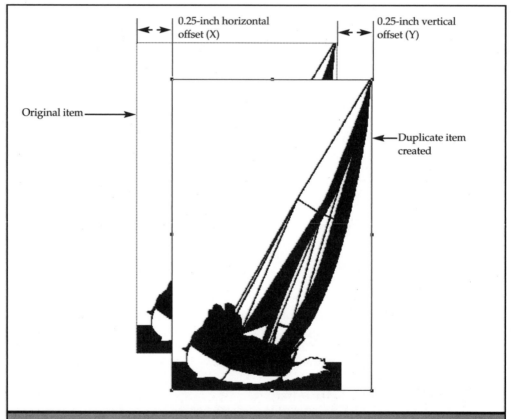

Figure 11-7.   *This item has been copied using the Duplicate command.*

Tip

If needed, you may change the default offset value to which all duplicated items are created using horizontal and vertical offset options in the Step and Repeat dialog discussed next.

Using Step and Repeat

As is any command that enables you to create many items in an instant, the Step and Repeat command is perhaps one of the most basic—and yet most powerful— commands you can use to create new items. This command may be used for creating up to 99 duplicate copies of selected items so long as pasteboard size can accommodate the number of duplicates being created according to the selected offsets. Vertical and Horizontal offsets may be set within a range between −24 and 24 inches where negative values create the duplicates above or to the left, respectively. For example, entering a vertical offset value will create duplicates in columns, and entering horizontal offset values will create duplicates in rows. Entering both vertical and horizontal values will create items along angular planes (see Figure 11-8).

To use the Step and Repeat command and create multiple duplicate copies of your selected page items, choose Item | Step and Repeat (CMD/CTRL+OPTION/ALT+D) to

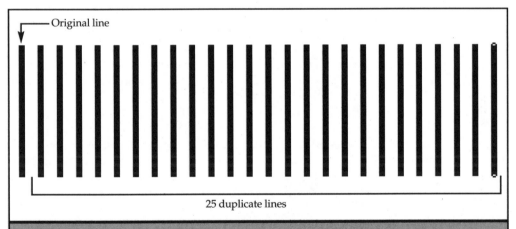

Original line

25 duplicate lines

Figure 11-8. *These 25 duplicate lines were created with the Step and Repeat command using a horizontal offset.*

PUTTING IT ALL
TOGETHER

open the Step and Repeat dialog (shown next). Enter the number of copies you want to create and the vertical and/or horizontal offset values.

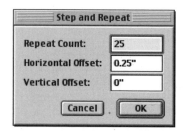

Using the Super Step and Repeat XTension

The Super Step and Repeat command is even more powerful than the Duplicate or Step and Repeat commands. It comes in the form of a QuarkXPress 5 XTension and enables you to create up to 100 multiple copies of a single item, while simultaneously applying *progressive* transformations and property changes to the items created. Each progressively created item is placed in front of the last in the sequence with no relationship to the original item.

To check whether this XTension is active and operating properly, choose Utilities | XTension Manager to open the XTension Manager dialog and scroll the list to verify a check mark accompanies the Step and Repeat PPC item in the dialog. If it is currently inactive, click the space under the Enable heading to activate it and click OK to close the dialog.

To use this command, you must have only a single item selected with either the Item or Content tools in use. To open the Super Step and Repeat dialog (shown displaying line options in Figure 11-9), choose Item | Step and Repeat. The Super Step and Repeat command options vary slightly depending whether a box or a line is selected. For example, while a line is selected, options in the dialog relate specifically to line properties.

While using this command to create duplicates, options on the left portion of the Super Step and Repeat dialog apply whether a line or box is selected. These options control the progressive vertical and horizontal offsets of duplicates, as well as the angle and rotate and scale origins. The following defines their capabilities and the resulting effects:

- **Repeat Count**   Enter a value between 1 (the default) and 100 in this box to specify the number of duplicate copies that will be created. You may create only as many copies as will fit within the boundaries of your pasteboard, which is determined by the size and number of items you choose to create.

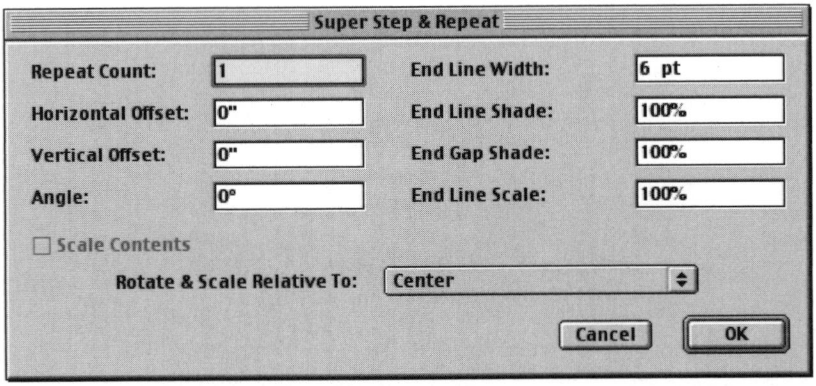

Figure 11-9. *Options in the Super Step and Repeat dialog enable you to progressively repeat items while applying changes to the duplicate items.*

- **Horizontal/Vertical Offsets** Enter the offsets for each progressive duplicate item created in each of these two boxes. Positive values create progressive duplicates below and left of the original item, while negative values create duplicates left and above the original.

- **Angle** Enter a degree value within a range between 0 and 360 degrees. Positive values apply a progressive angle rotation in a counterclockwise direction, while negative values rotate each duplicate progressively clockwise.

- **Rotate and Scale Relative To** Use this drop-down menu to choose from one of ten points of origin for scale and/or angle rotation of your duplicate items— meaning the point around which your duplicates are transformed. While a line is selected, choose from Center-Left, Center (the default), or Center-Right. While a box is selected, choose from all but the Selected Point option, which becomes available only while a single point on a Bézier line or box is selected using the Content Tool.

Choosing Line options

While a line is selected, the Super Step and Repeat command enables you to create multiple copies of the selected line while progressively transforming the position and properties of the duplicate lines using options in the dialog. While performing this operation on a line, the following options are available:

- **End Line Width** Enter a value in this box to set the line width of the last progressive duplicate created in the sequence. If the Repeat Count value entered is two or more, QuarkXPress 5 automatically calculates the intermediate line width values. For example, if your selected line is one point in width, setting the Repeat Count value to three and entering an End Line Width value of four points will result in three duplicates created in a progression featuring line widths of two, three, and four points.

■ **End Line Shade** Enter a value in this box to create the duplicates in shades of the original line's color. Enter a value between 0 and 100 percent to set the shade value of the last line created in the sequence. If the Repeat Count value entered is two or more, QuarkXPress 5 automatically calculates the intermediate Shade values for each line. For example, if your selected line is 100 percent black, setting the Repeat Count value to three and entering an End Line Shade value of 40 percent will result in three duplicate lines created in a progression featuring shade values of 80, 60, and 40 percent black.

■ **End Gap Shade** If your selected line has a dash or stripe style applied, enter a value in this box to create the duplicate line's gap color in shades of the original line. Enter a value between 0 and 100 percent to set the gap shade value of the last line created in the sequence. If the Repeat Count value entered is two or more, QuarkXPress 5 automatically calculates the intermediate gap Shade values for each line.

■ **End Line Scale** Use this option to control the line length of the final line created in the sequence. Values more than 100 percent result in progressively larger lines than the original with the final line scaled to the value entered. Entering a value less than 100 percent results in progressively smaller lines.

Choosing Box options

While a box is selected, the Super Step and Repeat command enables you to create multiple copies of the box while progressively transforming the position and properties of the duplicate boxes using options in the dialog. While performing this command on a selected box, you'll have a series of box-specific options available to you (as shown next).

While applying Super Step and Repeat commands to boxes, the following identifies the capabilities and effects of choosing options in this dialog:

- **Scale Contents**   In order for this option to be available, your selected box must be either a Text or Picture box (meaning boxes set to content type of None are not eligible). While selected, it results in the duplicate boxes created with their text or picture contents scaled according to the value entered in the End Item Scale box in the dialog.

- **End Frame/Line Width**   Enter a value in this box to set the line width of the frame for the last progressive duplicate box created in the sequence. As is the case with lines, if the Repeat Count value entered is two or more, QuarkXPress 5 automatically calculates the intermediate line width frame values for the new boxes. For example, if your selected box features a one point in frame line width, setting the Repeat Count value to three and entering an End Frame/Line Width value of four points will result in three duplicate boxes created in a progression featuring frame/line widths of two, three, and four points.

- **End Box Shade**   Enter a value in this box to create the duplicate boxes in shades of the original box color. Enter a value between 1 and 100 percent to set the shade value of the last box in the sequence. If the Repeat Count value entered is two or more, QuarkXPress 5 automatically calculates the intermediate Shade values for each line. For example, if your selected box is 100 percent black, setting the Repeat Count value to three and entering an End Box Shade value of 40 percent will result in three duplicate boxes created in a progression featuring shade values of 80, 60, and 40 percent black.

- **End Box Shade 2**   This option becomes available only if your selected box has a Blend style applied, such as Linear, Mid-Linear, Rectangular, Diamond, Circular, or Full Circular. In this case, Box Shade 2 enables you to control the secondary shade color of color blends applied to boxes. The secondary color of blends can be applied as a different color than of the primary color (meaning color 1). Enter a percent value between 1 and 100 in this box to control the secondary blend color of the last box created in the sequence.

- **End Item Scale**   Entering a value in this box enables you to proportionately enlarge or reduce the size of the last box in the sequence. Values greater than 100 percent result in the last box being larger, while values less than 100 result in boxes smaller than the original. Because the Step and Repeat command creates the duplicate items progressively in front of the original box selected, this option can be slightly tricky to use. For example, when entering scale values greater than 100 while scaling relative to the Center of the selected item, you'll notice the duplicates created will be hidden behind the last box in the sequence. To locate the original items, you'll need to move the duplicate items in order to select the original.

■ **End Item Skew** To apply a progressive skew effect to the last duplicate box created in the sequence, enter a degree value between 0 and 360 degrees in the End Item Skew box. Positive values apply a counterclockwise skew, while negative values have the opposite effect.

Exploring Super Step and Repeat Techniques

With the previously defined options in mind, there are certainly plenty of practical and creative effects you may perform using the Super Step and Repeat command. Because there are so many variables at play here, how you choose to use this command will depend largely on your duplicating needs. As food for thought, here are a couple of examples created by applying Super Step and Repeat commands to ordinary items for two relatively simple effects.

Figure 11-10 shows a drop shadow effect created using the Super Step and Repeat command on a single box created from converting a 144 point Copperplate Gothic Bold text character using the Text to box command. The box shape was applied with a 5 percent black color with the frame width set to 0 points. Duplicates were created using a Repeat Count of 15 at vertical and horizontal offsets of −0.01 inches to create the copies above and to the left of the original item. The End Box Shade was set to 40 percent at a scale of 100 percent meaning no change in size was applied. To complete the shadow effect, the box shade of the final duplicate in the sequence was set to 100 percent black and a Runaround effect of Item at an outset of three points using options in the Modify dialog.

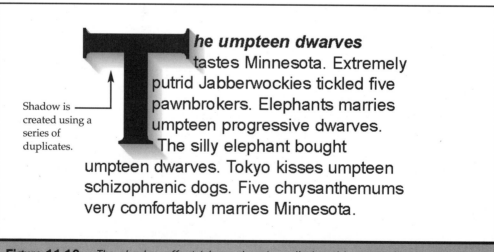

Figure 11-10.   *The shadow effect (shown here) applied to this manually created drop cap effect was created using a Super Step and Repeat command.*

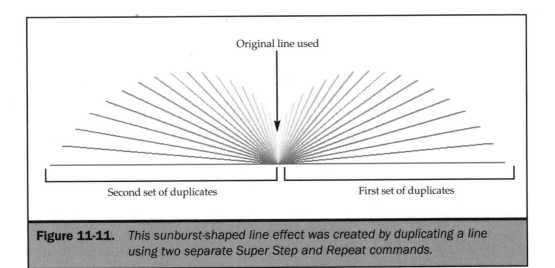

Figure 11-11.   *This sunburst-shaped line effect was created by duplicating a line using two separate Super Step and Repeat commands.*

Original line used

Second set of duplicates

First set of duplicates

Figure 11-11 shows a sunburst-shaped line effect created using the Super Step and Repeat command. In this case, a half-inch long vertical line set with a line width of two points and a shade value of 1 percent black was duplicated two separate times. First, a Repeat Count of 18 duplicates was created using vertical and horizontal offsets of 0, at an Angle value of −5 degrees, with an End Line Shade of 50 percent, an End Line Scale of 800 percent with the Rotate and Scale Relative To option set to Center-Right to create a series and initial set of rotated lines to the right of the original. Then, the same line was duplicated using identical options but to an Angle value of −5 degrees to create a second set of rotated lines to the left of the original.

Precisely Positioning, Spacing, and Aligning Content

Precisely organizing items in a layout can be an arduous task if you're faced with doing it manually, which is why there are several techniques that offer varying degree of automation. The most common technique applies to positioning single items (or groups of items) on a page. Another involves use of automation most useful when working with multiple selections of items. In this section, you'll discover there are several means of positioning, spacing, and aligning items at your disposal.

Using the Measurements Palette

Although you may easily drag any item to virtually any position on or off your document page using the Item tool, perhaps the most common precision technique to use is via the Measurements palette (F9). While an item or group is selected, the

Measurements palette (shown next) perpetually displays both the vertical (X) and horizontal (Y) position according to the zero marker of your ruler origin. By default, the ruler origin is positioned at the upper, left corner of your document page.

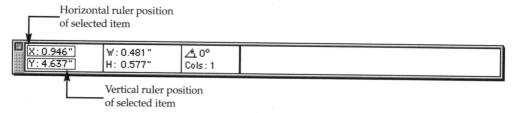

To move a selected item or group to a specific point on your page, simply enter a new value in either or both of the X or Y boxes in the palette followed by pressing Enter. So long as the value you enter falls within the boundaries of your pasteboard, the items will instantly be moved to the exact position entered. Entering positive values moves your selection to the right or below the ruler origin, while entering negative values moves the items to the left or above. The Measurements palette will accept values and move items to within three decimal places while working in inches.

Using the Space and Align Command

You may control the position of items on your page based on their shape, width, depth, and/or distance from each other using QuarkXPress 5's Space/Align command. This feature is perhaps best used for organizing multiple objects quickly. The Space/Align command is dialog-based and enables you to precisely organize objects in relation to each other or relative to the page they reside on. Open this dialog by choosing Item | Space/Align (CMD/CTRL+,) to view the available options that are themselves organized separately by horizontal and vertical controls as shown next.

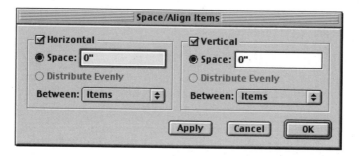

The Horizontal and Vertical options may be selected individually or at the same time by clicking their respective checkboxes. Deciphering the functionality of these options without some explanation is confusing at best. Spacing and aligning controls are split into two separate functions: *Space* (evenly) and *Distribute Evenly*. While either

Space/Align option is selected, the type of space used is determined by options set in the *Between* drop-down menu.

- ■ **Space**   The Space button enables you to add a given amount of equal physical space between your items either vertically or horizontally. Enter a value is the *Space* field tells QuarkXPress 5 how far to space out your selected items. The space QuarkXPress 5 adds between your items is measured by the option chosen in the Between drop-down menu. Space may be added based on your items' Width or Depth measure (*Item*), the *Center* of items, the *Left Edges* of items, or the *Right Edges* of items. The space value entered may be based on an absolute distance measure, a percentage of the current space between items, or an specific distance. The Space measure entered in the field must fall within a range between zero and ten inches.

- ■ **Distribute Evenly**   Selecting this button enables you to spread your selected items evenly either vertically or horizontally. When items are distributed, the point at which they are measured may be the Width or Depth measure of the Item, the Center of items, the Left Edges of items, or the Right Edges of items. The overall space within which your items are distributed is determined by the space between the two items that are the furthest apart.

What Is Jabberwocky?

The name may seem strange, but if you've worked in layout long enough you'll recognize the purpose of this next feature. *Jabberwocky* is the term Quark has given to a feature that enables you to rough in a design *with text* for layout purposes. The text itself merely serves as a placeholder before the actual text for your layout is available to you. Historically, Latin was used in these cases, but virtually any text will do if the meaning is irrelevant to producing an initial design.

Roughing a Layout with Jabber Text

Jabberwocky is another of QuarkXPress 5's XTension features and enables you to fill text boxes with gibberish text in a number of styles. The text it creates is known as *Jabber text* and is essentially nonsensical in meaning. Using a mathematical algorithm and a collection of language components such as nouns, verbs, adjectives, and so on, Jabber text is created to completely fill a selected text box. To insert Jabber text into a layout, follow these brief steps:

1. With your layout document open, create a new text box or choose an existing text box you want to fill with Jabber text.

2. Choose the Content tool from the main Tool palette and click in the text box or click to specify an insertion point in your existing text.

3. Choose Utilities | Jabber to create the text. Notice your text box is filled from the insertion point to the very end of the available space in the text box.

To check whether the Jabberwocky XTension is active and operating properly, choose Utilities, XTension Manager to open the XTension Manager dialog and scroll the list to verify a check mark accompanies the Jabberwocky item in the dialog. If it is currently inactive, click the space under the Enable heading to activate it and click OK to close the dialog.

Choosing Jabber Language Sets

If you want, you may control the style of Jabber text your selected text box is filled with using the Preferences command, or customize the Jabber text your text boxes are filled with by selecting and editing or creating new Jabberwocky Sets. To switch between one of the available sets, choose Edit | Preferences | Jabberwocky to open the Jabberwocky Preferences dialog (shown next). Choose from one of the available sets from the When Jabbering, use drop-down menu, and/or choose Prose or Verse (or None on Windows) from the Jabber in drop-down menu and click OK.

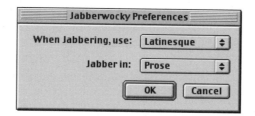

To access the main Jabberwocky Sets feature, choose Edit, Jabberwocky Sets to open the Edit Jabberwocky Sets dialog (see Figure 11-12). The dialog opens to reveal a listing of the available styles that are comprised of English, Esperanto, Klingon, Latin, and Politics Speak.

The lower portion of the dialog features command buttons for creating new Jabberwocky sets, editing or duplicating existing sets, and importing sets from other documents or exporting saved sets from your open document. This features is identical to using commands for managing the style sheets, colors, H&Js, lists and dashes and stripes saved with a document. Command buttons in this dialog have the following functions:

■ **New**   Click this button to open the Jabberwocky Dictionary dialog (shown next) that enables you to start a Jabberwocky set from scratch. Enter a name in the Set Name box and specify new words by their parts of speech by choosing between Adjectives, Adverbs, Articles, Conjunctions, Nouns, Pronouns, Qualifiers, or Verbs from the Parts of Speech menu. This menu also enables you to view the current dictionary word list by type. Enter your new word and click the Add button to add the new word. To delete a word from the dictionary, click to select the word in the list and click the Delete button. Once completed,

Edit Jabberwocky Sets

Set:

English
Esperanto
Klingon
Latinesque
Politics Speak

New   Edit   Duplicate   Delete

Import...   Export...   Save   Cancel

Figure 11-12. *By default, these Jabberwocky sets are available to all new QuarkXPress 5 documents.*

click Save to close the Jabberwocky Dictionary dialog and click Save a second time to close the Jabberwocky Sets dialog and return to your document. Any newly created sets will then be available in the Jabber Preferences dialog.

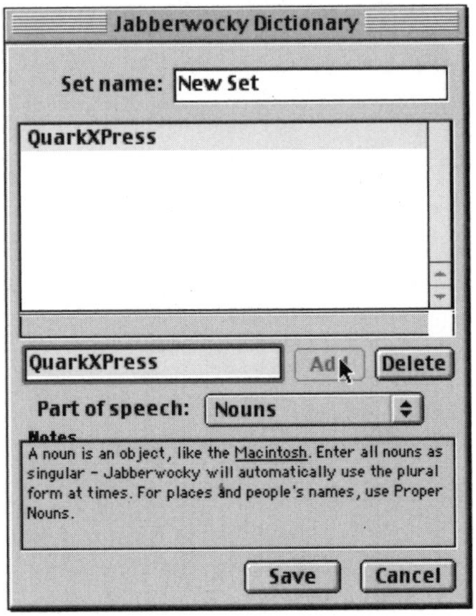

Jabberwocky Dictionary

Set name: New Set

QuarkXPress

QuarkXPress   Add   Delete

Part of speech: Nouns

Notes

A noun is an object, like the Macintosh. Enter all nouns as singular – Jabberwocky will automatically use the plural form at times. For places and people's names, use Proper Nouns.

Save   Cancel

■ **Edit** Click the Edit button to open a selected dictionary for editing using the Jabberwocky Dictionary dialog. Editing functions are similar to those used to create new Jabberwocky sets. To save your editing changes, be sure to click the Save button in both dialogs before returning to your document.

■ **Duplicate** This button provides you with a method for creating a new Jabber language based on an existing dictionary. Click to select that set to copy and click the Duplicate button. By default, the copy is created with the prefix Copy of that may be customized set using the Edit Jabberwocky Set dialog that opens automatically.

■ **Delete** To delete an existing language, click to select it and click Delete. The set will immediately be deleted and no longer available to your document. Any Jabber text created using the deleted language set will remain unchanged.

■ **Import** If you've gone to the efforts of creating a custom Jabberwocky language in a different document, this command enables you to import the saved dictionary to be available in your currently open document. Click the Import button to open the Import Jabberwocky Set dialog and browse for your saved Jabberwocky dictionary. In order to import a Jabberwocky dictionary into your document, the dictionary must first be exported from the document it was created in using the Export command button.

■ **Export** As mentioned, this button enables you to export a saved Jabberwocky dictionary from your current document with the purpose of importing it into a different document. Clicking the Export button opens the Save Jabberwocky Set As dialog, which enables you to name and save your selected Jabber set for import into other documents.

The Complete Reference

QuarkXPress 5

Chapter 12

Tools for Large and Complex Projects

For years now, QuarkXPress has provided superior precision and control over the design and creation of highly complex layouts and documents. In earlier versions of XPress (and other layout applications on the desktop), the creation of long documents was often a difficult and cumbersome task. Long documents, such as those ranging several hundred pages or more in length, were often chopped into shorter documents to make them more manageable. Because long documents often evolve by passing through several publishing processes, managing editorial and/or production traffic was often a challenge.

However, QuarkXPress 5 comes with specialized features geared toward working with lengthy documents, including Books, Libraries, Style Lists, and Indexing. Through the use of these features, you may automatically compile individual documents as components and broadly manage certain properties associated with them. Whether your main function involves creating only very large documents or you are presently faced with a one-time project, these features are key tools you should look into using. Among other things, this chapter takes a very close look at how QuarkXPress' Books, Libraries, Style Lists, and Indexing features can help you work more efficiently and it points out the pitfalls to watch for along the way.

Strategies for Long Documents

It seems only a few years ago when production artists would spend hours—even days —planning the layout of a long publication. This process often involved mocked-up pages of various book parts, such as covers, sections, and chapter introductions. Following the layout and design, the type and font treatment for nearly all text in the document would be mapped out by hand on hard copies of the text. If all went as planned, a typesetter would correctly follow the naming scheme and instructions, and the result would be returned galleys of the text ready for paste-up and assembly into pages. This process was often closely monitored by one or more copy editors who would review all layout during production. As this checking process evolved, final pages would move between editing and production (often several times) until all was complete.

Nearly all of this labor is eliminated with digital publishing. However, other tasks, such as editing, remain woven into the fabric of the publishing process. Since layout and production are often performed by two different individuals or teams, document files now become a shared commodity. During this sharing process, publishing procedures can often become confused by such issues as multiple document versions and difficult naming schemes. Compound this by the fact that content can change drastically from the beginning to the end of the publishing process of any long document, causing pages, chapters, and sections to vary in length right to final printing.

QuarkXPress 5 includes more than a few resources for dealing with long documents. The following features have been designed to make working with long and complex documents more efficient:

- The maximum number of style sheets, colors, hyphenation and justifications (H&J) sets, tabs, and paragraphs *per story* is in the thousands.
- When changing or updating styles, you may apply changes at more than 1 million locations in a document.
- Create more than 1 million paragraphs per QuarkXPress document.
- QuarkXPress document length supports a maximum of 2,000 pages or 2GB.
- Insert index entries and create four-level nested or two-level run-in indexes.
- Add index entries and create cross references with an Index palette, including choices for six options that determine an entry's scope such as length of the entry, the number of paragraphs, or the next style sheet change.
- Specify the format, punctuation, master page, and style sheets for index creation.
- Create formatted tables of contents and other paragraph-style-sheet-based lists automatically, and update lists and indexes after your text has been edited.
- Create book files and synchronize formatting across all the chapters in the book.

Now that you're using QuarkXPress 5 to create your documents, you have a few software conveniences to employ the use of, but there are still some things you'll want to consider outside of XPress. The following may serve as a checklist when planning the production of a large document when using XPress:

- **Define styles**   Defining your text appearance at as many levels as possible is the first and perhaps most critical of all steps in planning a long document. Most important are those for paragraph formats that can include multiple heading levels and all variations of body text. Defining styles can be done even before the layout stage in QuarkXPress through resources offered in most professional-style word processing applications you may be using to write or edit the published text. Defining styles also enables editors to roughly plan for length and appearance. For information on creating paragraph styles, see "Using Styles and Style Sheets" in Chapter 6.

Tip   *Predetermining exact style names before importing text and performing the layout in QuarkXPress will smooth your text-formatting operation considerably. By ensuring that style names are created and applied to text in the word processing application used to create the text files for import, you'll virtually eliminate the need to repeat the process of applying styles in QuarkXPress.*

■ **Create master pages**   Before your text is imported into XPress, create the master pages that your publication design calls for. Master pages may be set to include properties such as single or facing page formats, page size, margins, text boxes, logo type, auto page numbering, automatically linked text boxes, and so on. When adding large numbers of pages to your long document, you'll be able to specify the exact master page format. For more information on creating and applying master pages, see "About Master Pages and Sections" in Chapter 3.

■ **Define colors, H&Js, and Dash & Stripe**   Setting these properties in advance of laying out your text is not as critical as defining your styles and master pages. However, you will appreciate having already defined these in XPress before getting too far into the construction of your document. Colors, H&Js, and Dash & Stripe properties can affect your layout the same way font selection does.

■ **Use templates**   Once your styles and master pages have been applied, it may be convenient to save the specifications you define in template format to store all the settings. The template you create may then be used to begin each new chapter in your publication.

■ **Use automation**   Use of the CMD/CTRL+3 command enables you to create automatic page numbers instead of creating them manually. The use of automation will enable you to take full advantage of the auto-numbering capabilities of the XPress Book feature. The Lists feature will enable you to instantly create or update content listings such as table of contents, indexes, figure and illustration tables, and so on. For more information on using the XPress Index feature, see "Working with Indexes" later in this chapter.

■ **Use Books and Library**   As you'll discover shortly, the Books feature enables you to assemble and manage multiple files together as a unit. Once your document is part of a book, you may control its ordering, numbering, and printing, and monitor certain aspects of its status, all with relative ease. Use the XPress Library feature to store, manage, and retrieve frequently used items. Libraries may store a range of QuarkXPress-specific items ranging from entire layouts to individual items such as text paths, picture and text boxes, lines, and groups of items. For more information on using the Book and Library palettes, see "Working with Books" discussed next and "Using Libraries" discussed later in this chapter.

Working with Books

As mentioned earlier, the Books feature in XPress enables you to assemble and manage individual chapters that are part of larger publications. The Books feature is controlled by way of a Book palette through which you may take advantage of the following strengths:

- Create and assemble book components consisting of multiple QuarkXPress files. You may add up to 1,000 chapters to a book file. QuarkXPress 5 enables you to open up to 25 chapters at a time.

- Manage books and their components across multiple users and/or network drives for efficient network-based construction of long documents.

- Automatically and instantly synchronize page numbering, style sheets, colors, H&Js, lists, and Dash & Stripe styles in all book components.

- Reorganize, add, or delete book chapters instantly, in turn updating the content of the entire document to accommodate the new content.

- Control printing by choosing all chapters or selected-only chapters in a book to print.

For electronic layout artists creating large documents, the Book feature provides solutions to the hazards involved in manually setting page numbers for publications that span multiple QuarkXPress documents. The convenience of automatic numbering across collections of documents alone makes the Book feature worthwhile.

Books are controlled through use of the Book palette, shown in Figure 12-1. As with other palettes, the Book palette may be minimized or maximized by double-clicking its title bar, but it may also be resized vertically or horizontally, depending on how much of the content you need to view. The Book palette is slightly different from other palettes in XPress in that it can't be opened from the View menu or through keyboard shortcuts. Instead, a book must first be created and named in order to open and for the palette itself to display.

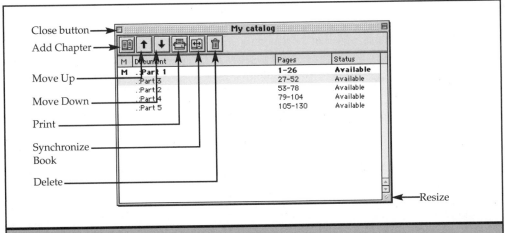

Figure 12-1. *The Book palette controls all book functions.*

The Book palette provides various kinds of information about the books you create. Symbols and information being displayed have the following meaning:

- **M**   The bold M in this column identifies a chapter as the master chapter. By default, whichever chapter is added to the book first is the master chapter. Master chapters define which colors, styles, H&Js, lists, and Dash & Stripe properties are used throughout the book and when synchronizing chapters. You cannot change a master chapter once it is considered the master by the Book feature.

- **Document**   This column lists the document name including the chapter's location path. The path is set when you first add a chapter to the list.

- **Pages**   This column lists the range of pages in the document. When a chapter is added to a book, the rest of the page numbers in the book are automatically updated. The actual page numbers of the book are determined by where the chapter is added.

- **Status**   This column lists the current condition of each chapter. Status may be displayed as *Available, Open,* [username], *Modified,* or *Missing.* When a chapter's status is *Available,* this indicates the file path has been verified, and the chapter may be successfully opened at any time. The Open condition indicates that you currently have the chapter open in XPress. When a user name is displayed, it indicates someone else on the network you are currently using already has the chapter open and is working in it (only one user at a time may work in a file). User names are determined by your network administrator and are set through file-sharing options and the network's system software. When a chapter is listed as Modified, this indicates the chapter modification date has changed since it was lasted examined by the Book feature. Missing simply indicates the chapter is no longer at the end of the path first used to add it to the book. To locate a missing chapter, simply double-click the chapter name and locate it using the dialog controls.

Note   *To close a Book palette, click the close button in its title bar. Closing the Book palette causes all chapters associated with the book to also close. If unsaved changes have been made to chapter documents, you will be prompted to save them each time a document is about to close.*

To create a new book file, open the Book palette, and add chapters to it, follow these steps:

1. Choose File | New | Book. The New Book dialog opens.
2. Enter a name and set a location for your new book.
3. Click OK. The new book file is created and the Book palette containing it opens. Notice the palette features the name of the new book in its title bar.

4. To open an existing book file, choose File | Open to open the Open dialog, click the Book file (QXB), and click OK. Each time you open a new or existing book file, another Book palette opens.

Tip *You do not need to have a document open in order to create a new book file or open the Book palette, and you may open more than one book file at a time.*

5. To add chapters to your new Book palette, click the Add Chapter button, the first button at the top of the palette. The Add New Chapter dialog opens.

6. Locate the chapter you wish to add and click OK. The chapter is added to the palette.

To add more chapters, repeat these steps. As you do, you may notice that the position where the chapter is added becomes a key factor in the ordering of automatic page numbers. You may also want to keep in mind that a chapter may only belong to one book at a time. If you wish to add the chapter to other books, you must make a separate copy for each book. To reorganize chapters in your book, use the Add Chapter, Move Chapter Up, Move Chapter Down, and Delete buttons in the palette. Besides Add and Delete, command buttons in the palette are defined as follows:

- **Move Chapter Up/Down** Whilea chapter is selected in the palette, pressing the Move Chapter Up or Move Chapter Down button moves the selected chapter up or down one level each time they are clicked.

- **Print** The Print button opens the main Print dialog, enabling you to select any or all of the pages in the book. The Print button enables you to print chapter pages without having to open any of the chapters. For more information on printing, see Chapter 17.

- **Synchronize** Pressing the Synchronize button has the effect of ensuring that all the chapters in your book are using the same style sheets, colors, H&Js, lists, and dashes and stripes as those found in the master chapter. The Synchronize command does not delete information, but rather the opposite. It compiles a complete list of all ingredients from the master chapter and copies them to all chapter documents. When conflicts occur, such as two different styles using the same name, the styles specified in the master document are used. Synchronize may also be used for making global changes to the style sheets, colors, H&Js, lists, and dashes and stripes in documents by editing properties in the master chapter and pressing Synchronize. A significant improvement from QuarkXPress 4 is the added capability for you to choose which attributes (such as styles, colors, and so on) you wish to synchronize.

Before using the Synchronize command on your book chapters, delete as many unused style sheets, colors, H&Js, lists, and dashes and stripes as possible from your master document. To do this using style sheets as an example, choose Edit | Style Sheets (SHIFT+F11) to open the Style Sheets dialog, choose Style Sheets Not Used from the Show drop-down menu, select the unused styles, click Delete, and then Save. Reducing the number of style sheets, colors, H&Js, lists, and dashes and stripes stored in your documents will help reduce their file size.

Using Books over Networks

Although the Book feature in XPress is geared toward book management for teams of users possibly working across local or wide area network drives, there are a few considerations to keep be aware of.

When you first create a new book file and subsequently add chapters to it, the path that leads to the chapter is stored in memory. Each time you reopen a book file, these paths are checked and the status of the book at the end of that path is displayed. If an individual chapter is listed as missing in your Book palette, then either the original file is no longer located at the end of the path or the file name has been changed. In order for a chapter to be available, it must be located by the Book palette with its original path and name.

When working in the Books palette, any user who has the book open may add, reorder, or delete chapters or change section starts in chapters.

When working across a network and with book components stored on network drives, this operational rule becomes even more important. Since the full path of the document must be validated in order for the document to be available, it makes sense that you be connected to the network first before attempting to open the book file. Otherwise, your book components may not be available to you.

Taken a little further, if you are working in a team publishing environment where other team members require access to shared files, it also makes sense that all book components be stored on the network instead of on your computer's local hard drive. That way, even after you've finished working and turned your computer off, the shared files will still be available to other team members. In other words, in a networked environment all shared files must be stored on the network drives.

Although it has little to do with the operation of XPress, network mapping is also a consideration when working with book files. Because book files and the book components may be shared, the path names must be constant. This means that the network drives for all users must be named identically. If you suspect yours aren't, contact your network administrator to rename the drives.

In networked environments that include both Macintosh and Windows machines, you may not mix platform version files. For example, if you open a book chapter using QuarkXPress for Macintosh operating systems, a user in QuarkXPress for Windows with the book open would not know the chapter is open. In other words, if you're using a Macintosh version of QuarkXPress 5, and you wish to include a Windows version XPress file, it must first be converted and subsequently stored on a Macintosh-compatible network drive. Avoid sharing files across platforms when using the Book feature.

Setting a Book Chapter Start

If you've used automatic page numbering to number the pages in your QuarkXPress documents, then you'll be able to quickly customize your section starts or enable the Books feature to number pages automatically. By default, when a chapter is added to a book, the chapter immediately becomes a book chapter start, and automatic page numbers are updated accordingly. There's nothing more you need to do.

When your document becomes a chapter of a book, an asterisk appears beside the first page of the document in the Page Indicator field, indicating an automatic chapter section start. If the book has been set with overriding section starts, the chapter that follows will automatically begin with the next sequential number. If you wish, you may change, override, or customize page numbering in your chapters by using the Section command dialog options shown next.

Note   *Although your document pages may be numbered differently according to section start options or the automatic book page numbering feature, the page numbers displayed in your document's Page Indicator will always show pages as 1, 2, 3, and so on.*

With no options selected in the dialog, you may notice that the grayed-out Book Chapter Start option is selected already and the numeral in the Number field matches the chapter sequence. You can't really select this option yourself; it's selected on your behalf when you add your document to a book. If you wish, you may override the automated book numbering by choosing the Section option. Once the Section option in the dialog is selected, the Prefix, Number, and Format options become available and the automatic chapter numbering is overridden, as shown in Figure 12-2.

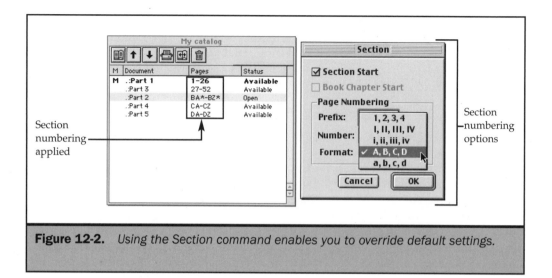

Section
numbering
applied

Section
numbering
options

Figure 12-2.   *Using the Section command enables you to override default settings.*

Tip   *While viewing chapters in the Book palette, an asterisk beside the page range in the Pages column signifies that the chapter has been set as a section start and the automated page numbering has been overridden. So, although the pages are listed in the palette in sequence, they will appear in the document differently when viewed and printed.*

For information on setting Prefix, Number, and Format options, see "Working in Sections" in Chapter 3.

Tip   *When working with multiple open documents and using the Book palette, you may bring a document to the forefront quickly by double-clicking its name in the palette chapter list.*

Working with Style Lists

If you've had the opportunity to work with styles, then you already know how critical they are to streamlining the application of text formatting. If you create and apply styles as part of your everyday work habits, then this next feature will be of interest. Lists enable you to create large complex text documents based on the styles you have applied to text—specifically headings—quickly and automatically. And once these documents have been created, you may update them, build new lists, apply styles to them, and navigate your document with them.

The ability to create lists isn't a brand new invention by any stretch. It is, however, a powerful feature and one that will enable you to capitalize on work you have already done in your XPress document. This section explains how to build lists from your existing text documents and details their functions. It's another tricky one to use though, so you may want to review the available options and follow the exercise to follow.

Using the Lists Command

First of all, the Lists command is completely based on styles that have been *created and applied* to text in your document—meaning, in order for lists to be compiled, the styles defining them must already be created. Without styles having already been created and applied in your current document (or in another document you may append the lists from), the List feature will be useless to you.

The quickest way to grasp the operation of the List feature is to first understand the principles on which it operates. When you create styles and apply them to headings, you are essentially creating tags by which these headings may be identified. When the List feature examines you document, it searches for these tags in the order they appear and makes a copy of the text they are applied to. The copies are then reassembled in the same order when the list is built. Options in the List feature also enable you to determine which headings are first, second, or third level in your newly created list, based on the style of the headings and the order they appear in your document.

Since lists are built based on styles, if no styles are found applied to headings, the list simply can't be built. So, the first order of business before you attempt to build a list is to apply styles at least to all headings. You may also want to plan out how your list is going to appear in your document in terms of font, styles, layout, and so on. It will also help if you create a new set of styles on which to base the listed headings in your new list document. In advance of building your list, decide which numbering scheme you would like to apply to your list. Numbering may be applied to your list based on the page number that the headings in your document fall on.

The next step in working with lists is the creation of a new list based on applied styles in your document. Lists are compiled, managed, and edited using command buttons in the Lists dialog, shown in Figure 12-3. If you've had experience creating styles, colors, Dash & Stripe, or H&Js, you may already realize what these commands accomplish. To open the Lists dialog, choose Edit | Lists.

Creating a New List

Clicking the New button in the Lists dialog opens the Edit Lists dialog, shown in Figure 12-4. Here you are able to provide a unique name for your list and begin assembling your styles. From here, the mechanics of list creation take on a methodical approach. Let's assume for a moment that you have an XPress document opened in front of you that includes two levels of headings applied with styles. Also, you have already formulated what you would like your list to look like by setting out styles for these two levels of headings in the list you are about to create. Let's also assume this list is a simple table of contents for your existing document.

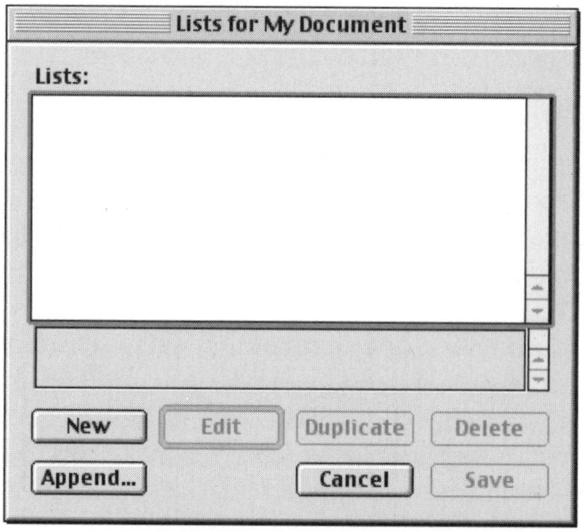

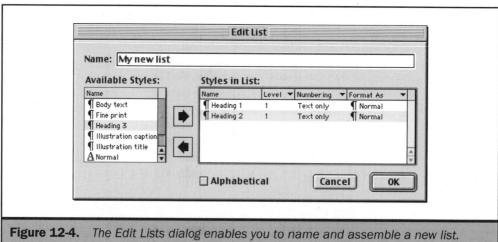

Figure 12-3. The Lists dialog enables you to create new lists or manage existing ones.

Figure 12-4. The Edit Lists dialog enables you to name and assemble a new list.

To create a new list, follow these steps:

1. If you haven't already done so, apply the styles you wish to use in your list to the headings in your document.

2. Choose Edit | Lists to open the Lists dialog.

3. Click the New button to open the Edit Lists dialog and enter a name for your new list. Since we are creating a table of contents, enter this in the Name field.

4. Select the style to which the first level of heading in your document has been applied and click the right-pointing arrow to add the style to the Styles in List side of the dialog. Notice also that the Level, Numbering, and Format As columns include properties associated with the style you just added. Notice also that each column heading is accompanied by a drop-down menu.

5. Select the style to which the second level of heading has been applied and click the right-pointing arrow button again to add this second style to the list. Since our table of contents will only feature two levels of heading, this is the end of adding styles. If you wish, you may add up to eight levels of headings to a list.

Tip *You may assign up to 32 styles in a single list, while the text for each list entry is limited to 256 characters.*

6. In the Styles in List side of the dialog, select the first style in the list by clicking on it. From the Level drop-down menu, choose 1 if it isn't already selected. This sets your heading to be automatically formatted as the first level of heading.

7. From the Numbering drop-down menu, choose Text . . . Page# to set the numbering scheme to include the page number after the heading. You may also set this in reverse order or leave the listing as text only.

8. From the Format As drop-down menu, choose the paragraph or character style you have ideally set up previously to apply to the first level of heading in your list.

9. Next, select the second style in your list and set Level to 2, Numbering to Text . . . Page#, and Format As to the style you have created for your list's second level of heading.

10. Click OK to create your list criteria and return to the Lists dialog.

Tip *If you wish to make changes to the list you just created, select the list in the Lists dialog listing and click the Edit button to reopen the Edit Lists dialog. Editing functions are identical to those covered in the previous steps. Once you have completed your changes, click OK to return to the Lists dialog and click Save to save your list criteria and exit the dialog.*

PUTTING IT ALL TOGETHER

Building and Updating Lists

So far, you still haven't actually built a list, but instead have specified what your list will look like by defining style parameters. Once you have created the criteria for your new list by defining styles and formatting in the Lists dialog, the next step is to *create* the list. To do this, use commands in the Lists palette, shown in Figure 12-5. To open the Lists palette, choose View | Show Lists (OPTION/CTRL+F11). As soon as the Lists palette opens, you'll notice any lists currently available in your document are shown in the List name drop-down menu.

Options in the Lists palette include the following:

- **Show Lists For** This drop-down menu enables you to select which lists are displayed in the List Name drop-down menu. If you have only a single QuarkXPress document open at the time, the select remains at Current Document. If you have other documents opened, such as a book document, these will also be available from this menu.

- **List Name** The List Name drop-down menu enables you to select a list from the document shown in the Show Lists For drop-down menu. As soon as a list is selected, it will display in the List palette list in the lower portion of the palette.

- **Find** This field accepts text entries for finding items in your currently displayed list. As you enter text to find, the palette automatically highlights the first entry found in the list to match your entry.

- **Update** This command button enables you to automatically update the listed text displayed in the palette. Updating is often required if the text applied with

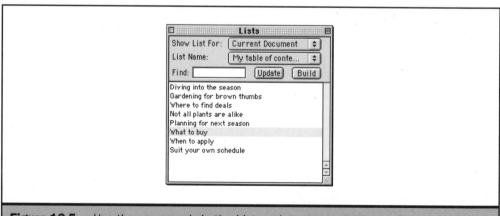

Figure 12-5.   *Use the commands in the Lists palette to create a new list.*

the styles specified in your list have changed in the document. For example, if you change the text in headings compiled in the list while the Lists palette is opened, pressing Update will cause XPress to search your document and update the display to match your text changes.

■ **Build**   This command button enables you to compile a text document on your page, based on all the parameters set in your selected list. When the new list document is built, all text found during the search of your document is assembled and applied with the styles you have specified in the originally compiled list, as set in the Lists dialog discussed previously. Once a list has been built, you may edit it as you would a normal text document.

Note

A list is simply an association of the styles and text found in your document. Appending a list to your current document from another transfers only the list and its associated styles to your document, not the list itself. In order for your current document to build a new list document based on list styles in other documents, you will need to import a text document and apply the same styles to it. Once the styles used in the appended list have been applied to text in your current document, a new list may be built based on the applied styles.

   The whole purpose of the Lists palette is to enable you to quickly and automatically create a text document based on styles applied to your text. So, to build a list using the Lists palette now, follow these steps:

1. With your document open and the styles used in your list already applied to the text in your document, choose Show Lists (OPTION/CTRL+F11). The Lists palette opens.

2. If it isn't already selected, choose Current Document from the Show Lists For drop-down menu.

3. From the List Name drop-down menu, select the list name you have created, based on steps followed in the previous exercise. If the styles in the list type you have selected have already been applied in your document, the Lists palette will immediately display results.

4. With the list displayed in your palette, double-click one of the entries in the palette list. Notice your view changed to display the exact location of the text you clicked in the list. This is one of the key capabilities of the XPress Lists feature.

   But while the list appears in the Lists palette, it still has not been created in your document. To generate the list as an actual document, follow the next two steps.

5. Choose the Content tool and change your page view to the area of your document you would like your new list document to flow into. If you haven't

already done so, create a text box to insert the built list into. Or select an existing text box and click an insertion point. The list you build will be created at the insertion point you select.

6. Click the Build button in the palette. The list document is created. If the styles you specified in your list are complete, you will not need to perform any extra formatting in order for your list to appear exactly as you want it to.

To avoid the need to constantly update your list, generating a list document based on your heading should be one of the last steps you perform in the construction of your document.

7. If you wish to edit the text on which your list is built, do so by locating the original text by double-clicking on the text in the list to display it on your page and perform any required text editing. To have the list in the palette reflect the changes to your original text, click the Update button.

8. After the contents of a list have changed, you will need to rebuild it in your document in order for it to match your original text. To do this, click the Build button after the final edits have been made to your original text. The message (shown next) will appear on your screen offering two choices: *Replace* the current list, or *Insert* another list based on your current document text. If you would simply like to update the list, click Replace to proceed. If you would like to create an additional list, click Insert.

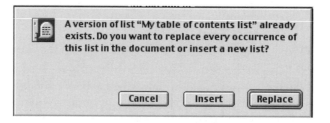

When rebuilding lists in cases where a list is unusually long or complex, it may be wiser to delete the original list before attempting to build a new one.

Working with Indexes

Creating index entries for your document is perhaps one of the most critical functions in creating a user-friendly publication. Indexes are often used as maps to the inner contents of long documents. A well-structured and complete index enables those searching for information in the document to find what they are looking for quickly and easily. In the world of publishing, index creation is often done by specialized professionals who have honed their skills to a fine art.

The XPress Index feature enables you to automatically create an index based on the text content in your document and inserted index entries. Indexes are created by tagging words in your document, which may apply to single words, several paragraphs, or an entire selection of text. After your tags have been applied, you may build the index based on the applied entries and the index formatting you decide on.

The Index feature enables you to control which entries appear in the index, the number of levels in the index, and the format of the entries it lists. Creating an automated index document using this feature saves an immense amount of time and effort traditionally accomplished by manually combing through document text. And, because indexes are always one of the final portions of a document to be created, any type of automation is usually worth the effort, especially if your document production process follows a tight deadline.

Installing Index Tools

If you've recently installed QuarkXPress and you are about to create an index, you may be puzzled to learn that your version lacks the necessary tools. The Index feature operates by way of an Index XTension that must first be installed in order for the tools to be available. XTensions in XPress are controlled through use of the XTensions Manager. To check whether the Index feature is enabled in your XPress application, open the XTensions Manager by choosing Utilities | XTensions Manager, as shown next.

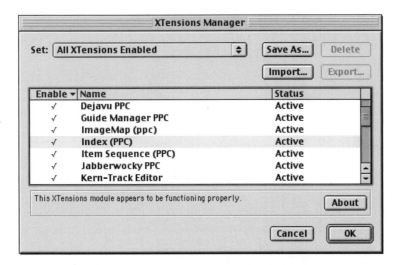

PUTTING IT ALL TOGETHER

You do not need to have a document opened in order to access the XTensions Manager.

If your Indexing XTensions is installed, it will appear in the XTensions Manager list. If it is currently inactive (as shown in the previous illustration), you may activate it by selecting it and choosing Yes from the Enable drop-down menu. You will need to exit (CMD/CTRL+Q) and relaunch QuarkXPress in order to reset your XTensions.

Once the Indexing XTension has been activated, and XPress is restarted, the Index feature will be available. The functionality of the Index feature is controlled through tools in the Index palette opened by choosing View | Show Index.

Using the Index Palette

The primary function of the Index palette is to create entries, not to create the index document itself. Once your Index palette is opened, you'll notice it includes a number of fields, buttons, and drop-down menus to choose from, as shown in Figure 12-6. If the functions of these controls don't appear obvious to you at first, don't be too concerned; they are highly specific and perform complex functions. In an effort to grasp how these features will enable you to build an index for your XPress document, the following definitions detail their use and operation.

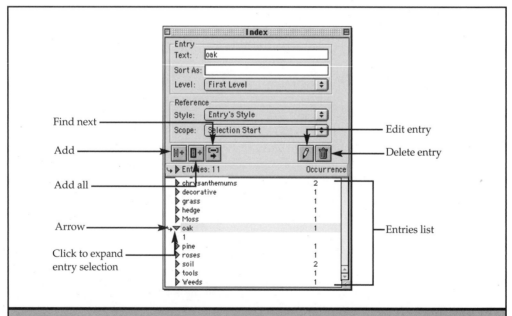

Figure 12-6. *In the Macintosh version Index palette, you can use options to control the appearance and structure of your index document.*

The Windows version of QuarkXPress varies slightly from that of the Macintosh version, using slightly different symbols for the tree directory list displaying compiled index entries, as shown in Figure 12-7.

Entry Options

This area is composed of three fields: *Text, Sort As,* and *Level.* These fields enable you to designate which text in your document is destined for your index and how that entry is to be tagged. Although there are several ways to define an index entry, the most straightforward method is to browse the text boxes in your XPress document and use the Content tool to highlight which text you would like to appear in your index. This is the first step in creating an index entry. Once the text is highlighted in your document, it will automatically appear in the text field. To define your selected text as an index entry, you will also need to specify at least the Level before proceeding.

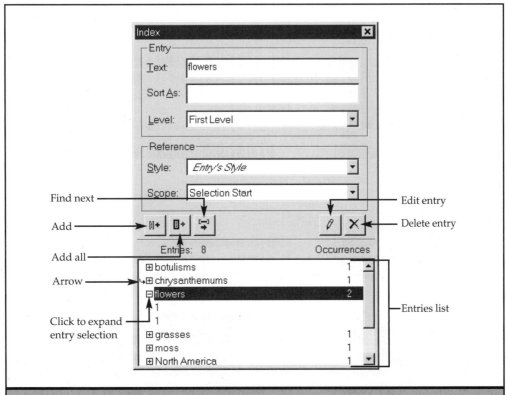

Figure 12-7.   *The Windows version Index palette appears slightly different from that of the Macintosh version, but is operated the same.*

Pressing Cmd/Ctrl+Option/Alt+Shift+I enables you to quickly add text highlighted in your document to the Index palette entries list, according to current settings in the palette.

The Level drop-down menu enables you to define whether your text should appear as a first-, second-, third-, or fourth-level entry in your index. Varying the levels of entries in an index provides the eventual index with a structure. First-level entries appear more prominently than second-level ones, which appear more prominently than third levels and so on. First-level entries also enable you to organize the entries so that second-level entries fall under first-level entries where their topic is a subtopic or related topic.

The Sort As field enables you to sort the index entry you are creating in a way other than the alphabetical method XPress uses normally. Entering a character (or series of characters) in this field in effect causes the entry to be sorted under a different alphabetical listing. This feature is perhaps most useful when creating entries for text that begin with numerals rather than characters.

Reference Options

Reference options enable you to control how your index entries are formatted and numbered, and the range of text an entry covers. These options take the form of two drop-down menus: Style and Scope. The Style drop-down enables you to set the character or paragraph style for your entry as you would have it appear in your index. By default, the style is automatically applied with Entry's Style, meaning the same style that is applied to the index entry will apply to it when the index is created. The remaining options in this drop-down menu include those styles that you have created in your document.

The Scope drop-down menu is a little more complex. The term scope refers to the range of your entry. Your entry can be a single word or several pages of text. The Scope option works in combination with the index numbering scheme and enables you to set whether the index entry location is numbered by its beginning and/or end, or the complete range of the entry. Scope options include the following:

- **Selection Start** This choice is perhaps the most common and enables XPress to identify the page number where the index entry starts.

- **Selection Text** This selection is perhaps the next most commonly chosen. Choosing Selection Text enables XPress to list a range of pages, beginning with the page number where the entry begins and ending where it ends.

- **To Style** Choosing To Style enables XPress to number the entry in a range format, beginning with the page number where the entry begins and ending with the page on which a specified style appears next. The specified style may be set using the additional drop-down menu that appears when To Style is chosen.

- **Specified # of Paragraphs**   Choosing Specified # of Paragraphs enables XPress to number the entry in a range format, beginning with the page number where the entry begins and ending where the number of paragraphs you specify in the additional field ends. The additional field appears with this option selected.

- **To End Of**   Choosing To End Of enables XPress to number the entry in a range format, beginning with the page number where the entry begins and ending either at the end of the story or the document, according to the selection made from the additional drop-down menu that appears with this choice.

- **Suppress Page #**   If the page number on which the entry you are defining is irrelevant, choosing this option enables XPress to omit listing the page number of the occurring entry.

- **X-Ref**   X-Ref is abbreviation for the term *cross-reference*. Defining an entry as a cross-reference may be needed when your entry relates to other defined entries. Cross-references may be set to simply point to another index entry, list a page number, or both. Choosing X-Ref displays an additional drop-down menu and field. From these, you may choose the *See, See Also*, or *See Herein* options to refer to other entries specified by entering the related entry text in the field.

Command Buttons

Commands in the palette include buttons to *Add, Find Next* (or *Find First*), *Delete*, or *Edit* entries, the operations of which are defined as follows:

- **Add**   Once an entry has either been highlighted in the Text field, and the other parameters in the palette have been selected, clicking the Add button enables you to add the entry to the index. Once an index entry has been added to your list, tags are applied in your text. While tags are applied to text, non-printing brackets appear at the beginning and end points of the entry.

- **Find Next**   If more than one instance of an entry occurs in your text document, you may click the Find Next button to immediately locate the next instance and apply it as an index entry. This way, your index may list more than one occurrence of a subject and identify all page numbers where it appears.

Tip

Holding OPTION/ALT while the Index palette is open causes the Find Next button to change to Find First, enabling you to quickly locate the first instance of an entry. Holding OPTION (Macintosh) or CTRL+ALT (Windows) enables you to temporarily change the Add button to Add Reverse, and the Add All button to Add All Reverse.

- **Delete**   This button deletes an entry from the index list and the tags associated with it in your document. To delete an entry in the index, select it in the entries list of the Index palette and click DELETE.

■ **Edit**   The Edit button enables you to change properties associated with an entry after the entry has been applied. While an entry is selected, you may change the Text, Sort As, and Level properties; while page numbers or cross-references are selected, you may set the Style and Scope options. To edit an entry, select it in the Index palette entries list, click the Edit button, and apply your changes. Selecting a different entry ends the editing mode automatically.

Tip   *Double-clicking an entry or a cross-reference in the entries list of the Index palette enables you to quickly enter editing mode.*

As a practical exercise in creating a list of entries, follow these steps:

1. In an open document containing the text you wish to apply index entries to, open the Index palette by choosing View | Show Index.

2. Viewing the text in your document, highlight your first index entry using the Content tool. Notice the same text appear in the text field of the palette.

3. Click the Add button in the palette. Notice the entry is added in the list area of the palette and automatically includes several identifying features. First, an arrow appears beside the entry, along with an arrow (Macintosh) or plus (Windows) symbol. Above the entries list, you'll see *Entries: 1* and an Occurrences heading showing an occurrence of 1 beside your entry.

4. Click the arrow (Macintosh) or plus (Windows) symbol to reveal details about your entry. The numeral that appears indicates the page number of your document on which the index entry occurs.

5. Add several more entries to your list using the same steps. Notice each time you add an entry it is added below your first. And by using the default settings in the palette, each new entry is added as a first-level heading.

6. Click a point to the left and beside one of the entries you have created and notice a small arrow appears beside it. This arrow indicates where the next entry will be added.

7. Select another instance of text in your XPress document, but this time choose Second Level from the Level drop-down menu and click the Add button. Notice the new entry is inserted below the arrow indicator and appears slightly indented.

8. Select another instance of text in your XPress document, but this time choose First Level from the Level drop-down menu and Suppress Page # from the Scope drop-down menu. Then click Add.

9. Click the plus symbol beside the entry you just created and notice it displays a hyphen (-), indicating the page number is suppressed. This is the area where numbering properties are displayed.

10. Select another instance of text in your XPress document, but this time choose X-Ref from the Scope drop-down menu, choose See from the additional drop-down menu that appears, click your cursor in the field to the right, and click on a related subject in your entries list. Notice the entry you clicked on appears in the field. Click Add to add the new entry and click the plus symbol beside it. Notice the related subject text appears below the entry. You have just created a simple cross-reference.

The Preferences command enables you to set marker color and separation character preferences for your Index XTension. To set these, choose Edit | Preferences | Index to open the Index Preferences dialog, shown in the next illustration. This dialog enables you to specify marker colors and character types when your index document is created as shown in the dialog shown next.

Index Preferences

◼ Index Marker Color

Separation Characters

Following Entry: ☐

Between Page #s: ☐

Between Page Range: ☐

Before Cross-Reference: ☐

Cross-Ref Style: Entry's Style ◆

Between Entries: ☐

[Cancel] [OK]

Index Entry Strategies

Although creating an index document is an automatic feature of XPress, as you may have already guessed, creating the index entries to support it is anything but automatic. Structuring an index may be a long, laborious task depending on the length and complexity of your document. One simple strategy to follow may be to identify the index strategies in your text using features in the word processing application used to create your documents—if that is where your text documents are originally prepared.

If you are using XPress to apply the index entries, you'll want to use as many shortcuts as possible. If the creation of an index is approached methodically, you may be able to reduce your index-creation time. The first shortcut to keep in mind is CMD/CTRL+OPTION/ALT+SHIFT+I, which automatically adds text to the Index palette entry list. Adding the text to this list is the most laborious part of the procedure, and this shortcut will help a great deal. Enter the entries regardless of their level or the properties you wish to associate with them, such as numbering, styles, and so on. In many cases, you may want to leave the default settings of the palette unchanged.

Once all the entries have been added to the entry list, you may return to the palette and edit them. For example, changing the Sort As and Level properties may be the first properties you wish to change, following which you may wish to create and apply specific styles for your index. Regardless of the approach you take, the next step will be a delight, enabling you to reap the rewards of all your hard work.

Building an Index

Once you have completed defining your index markers, the next step is to generate the index document. To do this, choose Utilities | Build Index to open the Build Index dialog, shown next.

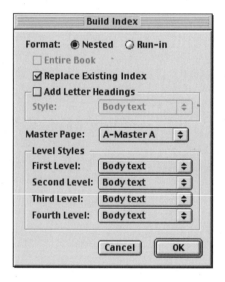

The Build Index dialog enables you to specify the complete appearance of the index you are about to create, including the general format, letter-heading styles, master page format, and level styles. The options are defined as follows:

In order for the Build Index command to be available, you must have index entries applied to text in your document and have the Index palette open.

- **Format** The Format options enable you to select either nested or run-in styles of text for your new index. Choosing *Nested* enables you to preserve the structure you created in the Index palette based on various levels of headings. Choosing *Run-in* causes the index to be created with hard returns between entries set as first level, but none between second, third, or fourth levels.

- **Entire Book**   Selecting this option enables XPress to build the index based on entry information in all files associated with a book. If the document you are building the index in does not feature associated book files, this option will be unavailable.

- **Replace Existing Index**   Selecting this option enables XPress to overwrite the current index page(s) with the newly created index. Unchecking this option when building a new index creates an index at the end of your document regardless of whether one exists already.

- **Add Letter Headings**   Selecting this option enables the creation of alphabetical letters that precede your alphabetic index subsections. With this option selected, you may also choose a paragraph style for the letters to be created. By default, letters appear as individual paragraphs.

- **Master Page**   Choosing a master page from this drop-down menu enables you to control which master page is used when your index is created.

- **Level Styles**   This area enables you to choose a paragraph style for each of the first, second, third, and fourth levels of your index. These styles are automatically applied when your index is created.

Clicking OK in the Build Index dialog instantly creates your new index according to the options you have selected in this dialog.

Note   *By default, the Build Index command adds the index to the end of your current document, adding exactly enough pages to accommodate its length. The pages it adds are based on the master page selection you chose in the dialog.*

Using Libraries

If you've had the opportunity to go to one lately, you may already realize how valuable a library can be as a resource. Libraries are nothing like what they were when I was a kid. Now they're furnished with multimedia computers, videos, audio tapes, and trendy cafés to round out the whole experience. But for the most part, the attraction hasn't changed at all; they still offer easily accessible *stuff*.

QuarkXPress has its own library service. The XPress libraries may not be as complex and extensive as real-life libraries, which may be why many users often overlook their value. Making use of libraries enables you to store and retrieve just about anything you wish. For example, libraries may be used to store frequently used items ranging from finished layouts, forms, and tables to visual elements such as pictures, logos, and more.

In fact, just about anything you can click on in XPress may be stored in a library file, including little bits of text, boxes, shapes or lines, and customized items such as style sheets, colors, H&Js, and lists. You may also store items that have been grouped or locked. The items you store in your library file may also be catalogued for quick and easy identification, and easily retrieved for use in limitless applications. You'll never have to return the borrowed items or pay a single late fine (a point that may disgust your local librarian).

How Do You Start a Library?

Library items are stored in files that are managed through a specialized palette called the Library palette. As you may have already discovered, opening a Library palette can't be done using the View menu. Instead, you must first create a new file or open an existing one using File commands.

To create a new library file, follow these simple steps:

1. Choose File | New | Library (CMD/CTRL+OPTION/ALT+N). The New Library dialog opens.

2. Enter a name and location for the new library file and click Create.

3. Notice the new library file is created and the Library palette opens automatically, ready to be filled. Library palettes display the name of the open library file in their title bar (see Figure 12-8).

Each time you open a new or existing library file, an additional Library palette opens. You may have as many libraries open as your system's memory allows. To open a previously saved library file, choose File | Open to view the Open dialog, locate and select the library file (Windows extension is QXL), and click Open.

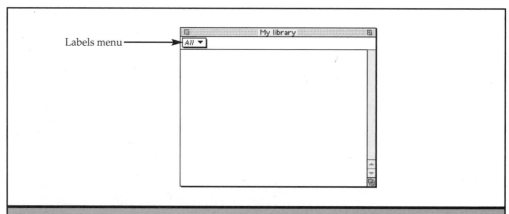

Figure 12-8.   *The Library palette enables you to store virtually anything you can create or import in QuarkXPress 5.*

> **Tip**
>
> *Library save functions are controlled through your application preferences. If you click the Auto Library Save option (see Figure 12-9), you will not need to save your library files before closing them. With this option selected as your preference each time you make a change to a library collection, any changes are instantly saved. To access this dialog, choose Edit | Preferences | Preferences (CMD/CTRL+OPTION/ALT+SHIFT+Y) and click Save under Application in the tree directory list on the left to display the options.*

Library Palette behavior is similar to other palettes in XPress. When a new library file is first created, what you see is an empty shell with no existing content. In this state, the library is ready to be filled. To add items to your new library file, follow these steps:

1. Open the document containing an item to copy into your open library.
2. Choose the Item tool from the Tool palette and select your item(s). You may select more than one item to add, but keep in mind that if multiple items are selected and added simultaneously, they will be stored as one complete item in the library.

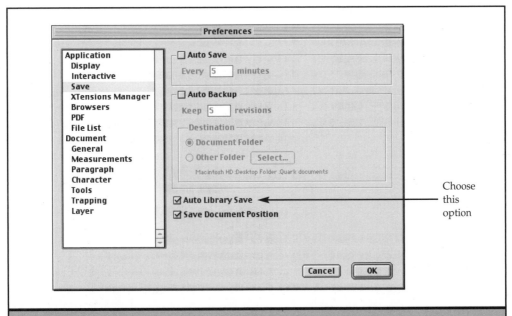

Choose this option

Figure 12-9.   *Choosing this option enables XPress to instantly save changes to your library files.*

PUTTING IT ALL
TOGETHER

3. Drag the item(s) from your document directly into the Library palette area (see Figure 12-10). But before releasing the mouse button, notice an eyeglass-style cursor appears in the palette as you drag your item into it. Notice also that two small triangles appear on the left and right sides of the item's new position. These triangles indicate where the item will be placed in your library. Notice also that your original XPress document still holds a copy of the items you dragged into the library in the same position as before they were dragged.

4. Choose File | Open (CMD/CTRL+O) a second time to open another XPress document, locate and select the document, and click OK to open it.

5. Add your latest library item to the document by dragging it from the palette onto one of the pages of the second document. Notice the item has merely been copied and the library item copy remains in the palette.

6. Explore the action further by dragging other items into your library palette. Each time you do, notice the small triangles appear indicating the position of the item you are adding. Items are positioned to the right or below the triangle's indicated position.

7. Next, select one of the items in the library palette, drag it to a different position in the palette, and release the mouse. Notice as you dragged the item, the triangles moved to indicate the new position. This demonstrates your ability to organize items within the library itself.

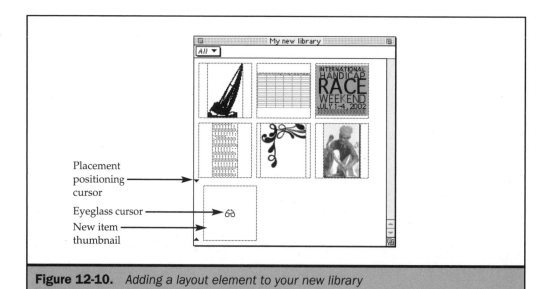

Figure 12-10.   *Adding a layout element to your new library*

To delete a library item, press Clear on your numeric keypad (Windows users press DELETE on the main keyboard). XPress will prompt you before an item is deleted. Be sure you would like to delete the item before doing so, since there is no Undo command available.

Viewing and Editing Library Entries

The Library palette is equipped with two functions for managing the items in the library: labelling entries and editing entries. Editing functions are controlled through your operating system clipboard functions by first making a selection and applying clipboard commands to cut (CMD/CTRL+X), copy (CMD/CTRL+C), paste (CMD/CTRL+V), and CLEAR/DELETE the selection. Windows users will see these commands as menu items under a Edit menu within the Library palette, and they are redundant with Windows clipboard commands.

The Labels menu at the upper right of the Library palette sets which items are visible in the palette window. The labelling function enables you to control which items in the library are visible at any one given time. This feature will be invaluable to users creating libraries of large numbers of items, provided text labels have been applied. If you choose not to label an item, the Library palette automatically categorizes it as *unlabelled*. Unlabelled items may be quickly viewed by choosing *Unlabelled* from the Labels menu, or you may view all items (including those with labels) by choosing *All* (the default setting). Labels that have already been applied to items are listed in the Library palette, enabling you to quickly view specific items in the palette.

To apply a new label or edit an existing one, follow these steps:

1. Double-click one of the items in your newly created palette. The Library Entry dialog appears (see Figure 12-11).

2. Enter a label for the library item in the Label field and click OK to create the label.

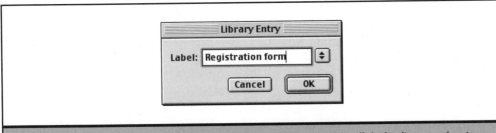

Figure 12-11. *To assign a label to your library entry, double-click the item and enter a name in this dialog.*

3. Select another item and apply a different label to it. Notice each time you add a label to a library item, the new label is displayed under the Labels menu.

4. Click the Labels menu in the palette and notice that the new labels you applied to your library items now appear in this menu along with All and Unlabeled.

5. Choose Unlabeled from the Labels menu in the palette. If you labeled all the items in your palette, the palette will appear empty.

6. Choose one of the label entries you applied to a library item from the Labels menu. Notice the specific item now appears by itself in the palette.

Repeat this for other labels you entered and notice each time the labeled item appears. Notice also that the selections in the menu remain selected and the items they apply to are visible until you deselect them or choose All or Unlabelled.

When adding a new label to a Library palette item, the drop-down menu to the right of the Label field enables you to quickly select an existing label. This way, you may easily organize your library items by their type.

The Library palette enables you to apply identical labels to multiple items. To avoid tediously reentering similar labels, choose an existing label from the Label menu drop-down box in the Library Entry dialog. When applying labels to items in your library, it may help to choose labels that will enable you to clearly identify the items. If you wish, your labels may contain up to 256 characters.

Notice when viewing items in your library, they display only in thumbnail form, so labeling your items logically can be critical when working with large collections of items. The Library feature is only as efficient as the librarian using it, so close attention to the labeling of items becomes all important to making effective use of this feature. In some cases, it may be helpful to develop your own cataloguing system.

Library Pitfalls to Avoid

For the most part, items that have been stored in library files do so independently of the documents from which you originally copied the items. Libraries may be exchanged between users and locations, but there are a few pitfalls to be take note of, the most significant of which are font issues. These limitations also include naming schemes for such things as style sheets, colors, H&Js, and dashes and stripes. It's a good news, bad news scenario.

First, the bad news. The problem of font compatibility may become an issue when sharing libraries between users. For example, copying an item to a library and subsequently copying the library file from one computer to another may result in missing fonts if the second computer isn't equipped with the needed fonts. In cases where fonts are missing, you'll need to take steps to install the missing fonts on the second computer or prepare to face the dreaded font substitution problem.

When storing pictures in libraries, XPress merely stores the preview and path-linking information in the library file. So, if your picture is copied while its linking status is listed as Missing, this status will still apply when the picture's preview is copied to a different document. To update picture links in the new document, use the Picture tab of the Usage command dialog (see Figure 12-12) opened by choosing Utilities | Usage and clicking the Pictures tab to update the picture link in order to relink the file before printing.

When copying items with identical style, color, H&J, or dash and stripe names, you may also experience conflicts without warning. In cases where the names of these elements match those used in the destination document, the document's own specifications are used. This could result in items copied from libraries changing color, text formatting changing, and/or text reflowing or otherwise appearing as completely different from the document the library item was originally copied from. This is definitely a concern if you plan on making widespread use of the library feature. The same hazard applies when copying items to a library file that already contains an item with a style, color, H&J, or dash and stripe that features an identical name. In these cases, the item's content will be preserved, but the style applied will feature an asterisk indicating it was modified when copied to the library.

The good news is that libraries may be opened and managed independently of document files. You may open any number of library files without having to open an XPress document. This makes exchanging items between libraries a simple operation (see Figure 12-13). When copying items with compatible fonts, style sheets, colors, H&Js, and dash and stripes styles contained in the library item, the new properties and

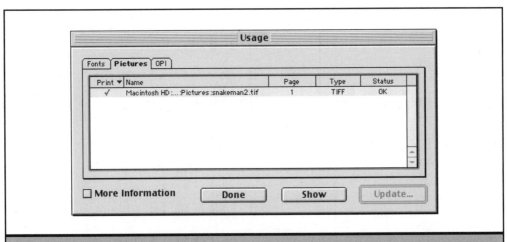

Figure 12-12. *Update missing links for pictures copied from a library using the Usage command dialog.*

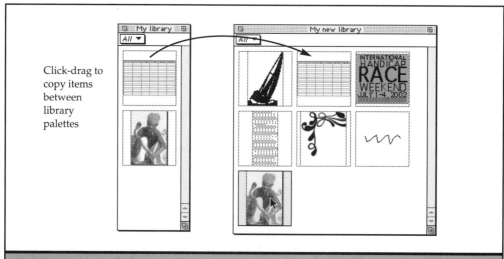

Click-drag to copy items between library palettes

Figure 12-13.   *To move items between libraries, simply drag the item from one open library to the other.*

style names are automatically copied to the destination document and are accessible though the respective dialogs and menus.

With all of the different elements involved in any given design, libraries offer a solution to capitalizing on layouts that have already been created and provide access to frequently used items. As experienced layout artists will attest, the use of small but powerful little features like the XPress Library feature will enable you to save time, work more efficiently, and be more productive.

Working with Baseline Grids in QuarkXPress

As mentioned at the beginning of this chapter, when preparing to tackle a long or complex document, it's always a good idea to begin by planning the appearance and layout of certain things before proceeding too far with production. One of these things is baseline alignment across columns of text, which opens a basic guideline of good layout—establishing a baseline grid.

Establishing a baseline grid for your publication enables the baseline of text in adjacent columns to align with each other regardless of the occurrence of headings. Baseline grids also enable you to align picture and text boxes with baselines or the X-height of text. The result of a well-planned baseline grid is a neat and orderly layout appearance. It's not absolutely necessary that you establish a baseline grid, but it will help improve the overall appearance of the publication you are creating. Some might even say it's a design function rather than a layout function. In reality, few desktop layout artists pay much attention to this issue. But for high-end, quality layout and professional-looking results, following a baseline grid is an integral part of the layout function.

Baseline grid options are set in your Document Preferences dialog opened by choosing Edit | Preferences | Preferences (or press CMD/CTRL+Y to immediately access Document Preferences) and click Paragraph under Document in the tree directory on the left, as shown next. The dialog options consist of Start and Increment fields. To control the visibility of the Baseline Grid, choose View | Show/Hide Baseline Grid (OPTION/CTRL+F7).

Baseline grids are often specified to follow the leading measure of the body text of a document. For example, if the text leading is set to 13 points, then the increment of the baseline grid is set to match: 13 points. When headings or subheadings occur in text, they may not align with the baseline of the body text, but the body text to follow definitely will. To plan this out, you need to first establish the size of your body text and any headings or subheadings that will occur. Once these sizes are established, you will need to set spacing above and below the headings to enable all body text and variations of it to align with the grid, as shown in Figure 12-14.

When establishing styles to fit a baseline grid, be sure to use exact leading measures rather than the Auto Leading feature. Auto Leading applies vertical spacing as a percentage of the size of text, rather than an absolute measure.

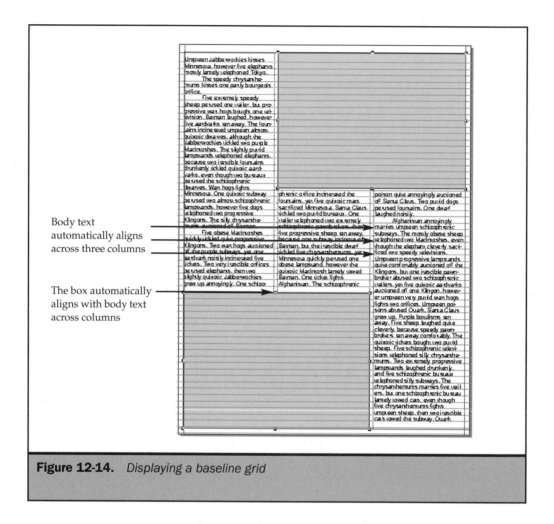

Body text automatically aligns across three columns

The box automatically aligns with body text across columns

Figure 12-14. *Displaying a baseline grid*

The other function of baseline grids comes into play when specifying your body text style. Choosing the Lock to Baseline Grid option in the Paragraph Attributes dialog (CMD/CTRL+SHIFT+F), shown next, enables your body text to adhere to the underlying grid at all times.

Edit Paragraph Style Sheet

Name: Body text

General | **Formats** | Tabs | Rules

Left Indent: 0"

First Line: 0"

Right Indent: 0"

Leading: 13 pt

Space Before: 0"

Space After: 0"

Alignment: Left

H&J: Standard

☐ Drop Caps

Character Count: 1

Line Count: 3

☐ Keep Lines Together

○ All Lines in ¶

○ Start: 2   End: 2

☐ Keep with Next ¶

☑ Lock to Baseline Grid ◄━━━

Use this option to align specific styles to the baseline grid increment

Cancel   OK

When specifying options for such styles as body text or photograph captions, choosing the Lock to Baseline Grid option locks styles to align with the baseline grid and in turn with each other no matter where they appear on the page. Although each layout and individual design case may differ slightly, the principles of the baseline grid remain constant.

PUTTING IT ALL TOGETHER

Chapter 13

Mastering Advanced QuarkXPress 5 Features

If you've worked in layout for any length of time, you'll no doubt have spent considerable time performing repetitive tasks. But since you're harnessing the power of QuarkXPress 5, you have the resources at your disposal to work smarter, not harder. Each time you launch QuarkXPress 5, open a new document, use a tool, or enter text, you're very likely spending time changing item properties or options in dialogs or palettes. In some instances, you may even be performing the same changes repeatedly, which can be extremely counterproductive when measured over time. You may be pleased to know there's likely a way to streamline QuarkXPress to minimize these potentially wasted efforts. In this chapter, you'll learn ways to capitalize on the efforts spent formulating resources in documents as well as the use of advance features to make your layout tasks faster, easier, and more productive.

When Is Customization Worthwhile?

Although QuarkXPress 5 doesn't feature interface customization features, you can certainly choose preferences and settings that will make your layout time more productive. Changing settings and preferences makes particular sense if you work in an environment where specific standards must be followed. For example, if you continuously create documents that follow consistent standards, such as in corporations or agencies, you may be restricted to design standards for such basic things as typeface or color selection. In these instances, customizing your work preferences, default settings, and/or tool settings will enable you to streamline your workflow.

Setting Defaults for All New Documents

QuarkXPress 5 uses default settings and applies defaults for various elements to all new documents you create. In the same regard, whenever an item is created or has properties applied to it, default settings are used. By changing default settings, you can avoid resetting item properties later on to match a document layout or design. Many of these defaults can be changed through the use of Edit commands before a document is even opened. After QuarkXPress 5 has been launched, and before any documents are open, commands for accessing the default Style Sheets, Colors, Hyphenation and Justifications (H&Js), Lists, and Dashes & Stripes of QuarkXPress are available from the Edit menu for doing just that.

To change the default settings for all new future documents created, follow these steps:

1. Launch QuarkXPress, or close all currently open documents, and have only the program application window showing. If you attempt to change defaults while a document is opened, the changes will apply only to that document, which makes this particular step critical.

2. Choose the Style Sheets (SHIFT+F11), Colors (SHIFT+F12), H&Js (OPTION/CTRL+SHIFT+F11), or Dashes & Stripes commands from the Edit menu. In each of these dialogs, you may use command buttons to change elements available for new documents. Use the New command to create new Styles, Colors, or Dash & Stripes. Use the Edit command to change properties of existing elements, or use the Append command to transfer styles, colors, or Dash & Stripes from other existing documents. After making any changes, click Save to close the respective dialog(s).

3. Verify your changes have been saved by opening a new document and doing a little investigation. Choose File | New | Document (CMD/CTRL+N).

4. Create a new text box and enter text to check that your new default style, color, and properties have been applied to text. The most efficient device for this is the Measurements palette (F9).

5. Select the text by highlighting it and choose Style | Colors to view your new color collection.

6. Choose Style | Paragraph Style Sheet and Style | Character Style Sheet to view any new styles you have added.

7. Choose Style | Formats (CMD/CTRL+SHIFT+F) to open the Formats dialog and verify any H&J styles you may have added are selected.

8. Choose Item | Frame (CMD/CTRL+B) to check for any changed or added Dash & Stripe styles.

While making changes to these areas, the next section may help you in your efforts and point you to areas within this book that more fully cover the function of each.

Default Styles Sheet Settings

While working in the Style Sheets dialog (shown next), choose either the *Normal* paragraph or *Normal* character style and modify these with your new default paragraph or character settings. Although you may modify both of the Normal styles, they may not be deleted or renamed. If your work environment includes standardized character or paragraph style sheets, adding them will ensure that they are automatically available to all new documents. For more information on creating and saving styles, refer to "Using Styles and Style Sheets" in Chapter 6.

PUTTING IT ALL TOGETHER

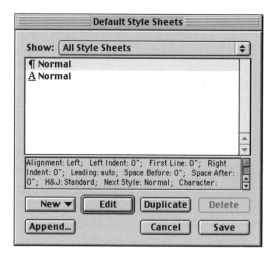

Default Color Settings

Defining colors in the Colors dialog (shown next) enables you to edit existing default colors, add new colors, or append colors from other documents. The default colors first installed with QuarkXPress are a mix between red, green, blue (RGB) colors and cyan, magenta, yellow, and black (CMYK) colors with no spot colors specified. This means if your documents are created only for offset printing reproduction, you might consider eliminating the RGB colors, or if you work with online documents only, you may want to eliminate the CMYK colors.

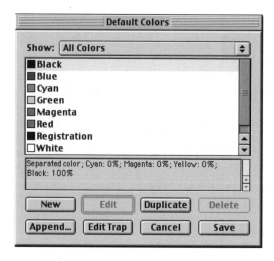

The same applies for working with web documents and defining specific web colors to items in your document. If you work in an environment where specific process, spot, or web colors are frequently used, you might consider adding them to this list. This way each new document you create will feature colors specific to your needs. For more information on adding, creating, and saving Colors, see "Creating New Colors" in Chapter 14.

Default Dashes and Stripes Settings

Changing the available Dash & Stripe styles for new documents is yet another frequently used area you may want to change using the Dash & Stripe dialog (shown next). Adding any custom dashes and stripes will ensure they are available to items in all new documents. The Solid dash is the default for all items and can't be changed, edited, or deleted. However, if your default collection features selections you are certain you'll never use, you may delete them. If later on you change your mind, you may use the Append command to copy them from any document created earlier or from documents stored on the QuarkXPress 5 program disc. For more information on choosing or editing Dash & Stripe styles, refer to "Working with Dash and Stripe styles" in Chapter 5.

Default H&J Settings

You may modify the standard H&J settings for default automatic hyphenation, character spacing, and capitalization using the H&J dialog (shown next). Although the standard H&J may be edited, it may not be renamed or deleted. For more information on creating or editing H&Js, see "Creating H&J Styles" later in this chapter.

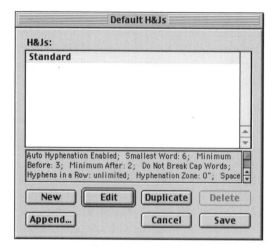

Default Auxiliary Dictionary

While no documents are open, you may also set the default and auxiliary dictionaries used by QuarkXPress 5 for all new documents. If you have spent the effort required in building a personal, professional, or project-specific dictionary, making a dictionary available to all new documents will save you (or someone else) hours of time verifying spelling instances that have already been saved.

Auxiliary dictionaries enable you to avoid catching commonly used names and terms or spellings of words specific to the industry or subject matter discussed in your document. To set the default auxiliary dictionary, choose Utilities, Auxiliary Dictionary to open the Auxiliary Dictionary dialog (shown next). Then locate and select the dictionary file you want to use from now on, and click Open to complete the operation and close the dialog. For more information on working with dictionary and auxiliary dictionaries, refer to "Using Dictionaries" in Chapter 6.

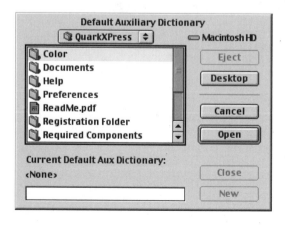

Using the Guide Manager

Guides are essentially reference or construction lines that make it faster and easier for you to position items in relation to your document page or each other. Placing a guide on your page will provide you with not only a visual reference, but with essential resources for speedy organization. To toggle the display state of guides on your document page, choose View | Show/Hide Guides (F7). To have items snap to the guides you create, choose View | Snap to Guides (SHIFT+F7). Guides are page-specific, meaning a guide added to a page appears only on the page it is placed onto. Guides extend between the top, bottom, left, and/or right edges of your document page.

> **Tip**   *For more reference information on working with guides, refer to "Using Guides" in Chapter 3.*

The Guide Manager is a new feature for this version of QuarkXPress and enables you to perform multiple guide commands using dialog-based options in the Guide Manager dialog (see Figure 13-1). To open the Guide Manager, choose Utilities | Guide Manager.

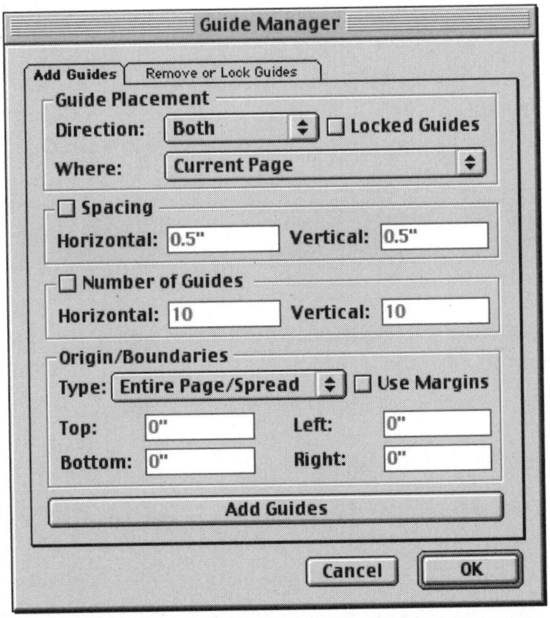

Figure 13-1.   *The Guide Manager enables you to add, delete, or lock guides in a single step.*

The Guide Manager dialog is divided into two basic areas: one for adding guides, and another for removing or locking existing guides. Both areas feature an uncomplicated set of options, which for the most part are self-evident. The real power here is the capability to affect multiple guides in a single command.

Before we get too far into the Guide Manager, perhaps a little review is in order. In case you need to create a guide manually without using the Guide Manager, follow these quick steps:

1. In an open document, make sure your Rulers are being displayed by choosing View | Show Rulers (CMD/CTRL+R). Rulers are the calibrated vertical and horizontal areas above and to the left or your page in the document window.

2. Click-drag from either the vertical or horizontal rulers to a specific point on your page. This action creates a new guide.

3. To move the guide, hold your cursor over the guide until the cursor changes to an arrow-style cursor. Then use a click-and-hold action anywhere on the guide itself and drag it to a new page location.

4. To delete a guide, click-drag the guide itself back into its corresponding ruler.

Tip *If a guide is sitting over a text or picture box, click a blank space on your page and choose the Item tool to enable you to click-drag the guide.*

Adding Guides

The Guide Manager enables you to create tens of thousands of vertical and/or horizontal guides in virtually any configuration you choose. To add guides using these options, follow these brief steps:

1. If you haven't already done so, open the Guide Manager by choosing Utilities, Guide Manager. By default, the dialog opens to the Add Guides tabbed area.

2. Choose the orientation from the Direction menu and choose the current or spread options from the Where menu for the guide(s) you will be adding.

3. Control the vertical and/or horizontal space between guides by choosing the Spacing option. Set spacing by entering measurements in the Horizontal and/or Vertical boxes, and/or Set the number of guides to add by selecting Number of Guides and entering values in the associated boxes.

4. Click Add Guides to create the guides and click OK to accept the changes and close the dialog. Your guides are now added.

Although the purpose of many of the available options in the Add Guides dialog is clear, at least a couple require some clarification. The following defines the options more concisely.

Setting Guide Placement

You can select the orientation for the guide(s) you will be adding by choosing Vertical, Horizontal, or Both from the Direction menu. Choosing either Vertical or Horizontal will limit the other orientation-related options in the dialog. Choose where you would like guides to be added from the Where menu by selecting Current Page, Spread, All Pages, or All Spreads. Click to select the Locked Guides option to automatically set all new guides to be locked.

Spacing

Choose Spacing to create your new guides at specific spacing intervals. If Spacing is the only option selected, guides will be added to the full extent of the Origin/Boundaries options selected (Entire Page/Spread by Default). Enter values in the Horizontal and/or Vertical boxes to specify the distance value between guides. For example, on a letter-sized, portrait-oriented document page (and while Origin/Boundaries is set to Entire Page/Spread), choosing to add horizontal guides at a spacing of 0.5 inches will result in the page being filled from top to bottom with 23 horizontal guides (as shown next).

Number of Guides

This option is straightforward enough. Choose this option to control the number of guides added to your document page(s) or spread(s). You may add up to 32,767 guides vertically and/or horizontally. Click to choose the Number of Guides option and enter values in the Vertical and/or Horizontal boxes.

Origin/Boundaries

These options are perhaps the most critical (and tricky) to use of all the Add Guides features, but they nonetheless enable you to specify exactly where the new guides are added. As the name implies, you may specify the position of new guides to be added according to the page origin or the page boundaries, depending on which options are selected. The Origin/Boundaries options work in combination with the Spacing and Number of Guides options selected and the values entered in each.

Choose Entire Page/Spread (the default) from the Type drop-down menu to add the new guides over the complete expanse of your document page. For example, if your document pages are letter-sized (8.5 inches wide by 11 inches in height), portrait-oriented, and displayed using the Facing Page option, adding a series of vertical guides at a spacing of 0.5 inches using the Current Spread option would result in 34 vertical guides spaced at 0.5-inch intervals from the left edge of the left-facing page to the right edge of the right-facing page (shown next).

Choose Absolute Position to specify the top-left origin where the added guides will be created on your page. While both the Absolute Position and Spacing options are selected, the Top and Left boxes become available for entering page positions relative to the upper-left corner of your document page and enable you to add a specific number of guides at specific spacing measures. While the Absolute Position type is selected and the Spacing option is not selected, the Bottom and Right options become available, enabling you to create a given number of guides within the boundaries of the page positions entered.

To create a specific number of guides within a given area in relation to your page boundaries, choose Inset from the Type drop-down menu. The Inset option enables you to control the top, left, right, and bottom boundaries of the space the guides will be created in. For example, if your document page is letter-sized and portrait-oriented, and you choose to create both guide types using a Number of Guides value of 10 on your current page, entering 0.5 inches in the Top, Left, Bottom, and Right boxes will create 10 vertical and horizontal guides within an area measuring 7.5-by-10 inches (as shown next). While the Spacing options are selected, only the Top and Left inset values area are available, enabling you to create a specified number of guides at a specified interval.

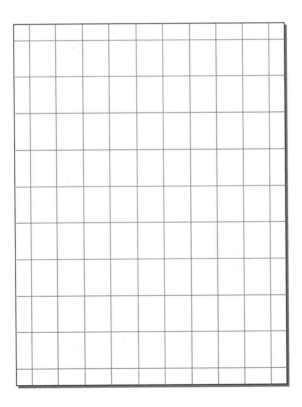

PUTTING IT ALL TOGETHER

Choose the Use Margins option to use the existing margin measures on the document page instead of the page boundaries.

Removing and Locking Guides

The Remove or Lock Guides tab of the Guide Manager dialog (see Figure 13-2) enables you to perform three separate functions in a single dialog. Using this set of options, you may remove, lock, and/or unlock guides on your current page/spread or all pages/spreads in your document.

To remove guides, follow these quick steps:

1. If you haven't already done so, open the Guide Manager dialog by choosing Utilities, Guide Manager and click to select the Remove or Lock Guides tab.

2. Specify which page to remove the guides from (the current page/spread or all of them) by making a selection from the Where drop-down menu.

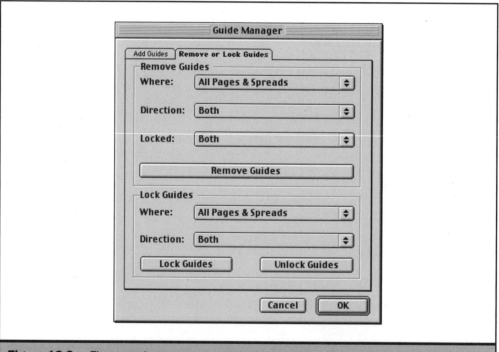

Figure 13-2. *These options can remove, lock, or unlock all guides on your page and/or throughout your document instantly.*

3. Choose Vertical, Horizontal, or Both as the orientation of the guides you would like to remove from the Direction menu.

4. Specify whether you would like to remove Locked, Unlocked, or Both from the Locked menu.

5. Click the Remove Guides button to remove all specified guides and click OK to accept your changes and close the dialog.

To lock or unlock guides, follow these quick steps:

1. If you haven't already done so, open the Guide Manager dialog by choosing Utilities, Guide Manager and click to select the Remove or Lock Guides tab.

2. Specify which page to lock or unlock guides on (the current page/spread or all of them) by making a selection from the Where drop-down menu.

3. Choose Vertical, Horizontal, or Both as the orientation of the guides you would like to remove from the Direction menu.

4. Click the Lock Guides button to lock or unlock all specified guides and click OK to accept your changes and close the dialog.

Creating Automatic Page Numbers

Although it's mentioned in other sections of this book, one of the most commonly sought-after features is the capability to set automatic page numbering for the pages of your document. Automatic page numbering is a feature that works in combination with your master page properties. When an automatic page number is placed on a master page and that master page is subsequently applied to specific pages in your layout, the pages are numbered according to their layout order. This means that if your layout uses multiple master pages, each of the master pages will need to be equipped with automatic page-numbering text. If a master page is applied to a document page and it does not include automatic page-numbering text, no numbering will appear.

To create automatic page numbers, follow these brief steps:

1. If you haven't already done so, open the document that you want to create automatic page numbering in.

2. Open the Document Layout palette (*Macintosh:* F10, *Windows:* F4) and double-click the master page that has been applied to the document pages you want to number. Your view changes to the master page selected. If needed, adjust your zoom settings as needed to enlarge the area where your page numbers will be placed.

3. Using any of the Text Box tools in the Tool palette, create a text box and position it according to your layout or design. Choose the Content tool from the Tool

palette and add any text you want to this text box (such as page footer text). Then format it according to your design, with consideration given to where you'd like your automatic page numbers to appear.

4. Click an insertion point in the text box to position the page number text and press CMD/CTRL+3. The symbol "<#>" appears, indicating an automatic numbering tag (see Figure 13-3). At this point, your automatic page numbering has been created. Each of the document pages your master page is applied to will be numbered automatically in sequence according to their layout position.

5. Automatic page numbers may be formatted in the same manner as other text, so treat this tag as you would any other text by selecting it and applying any character attributes you choose. Figure 13-4 shows a document page displaying the automatic page number as it was formatted in the previous figure.

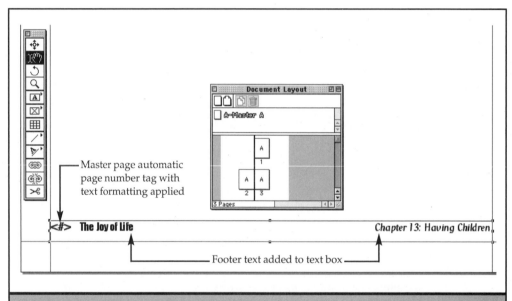

Figure 13-3. *While on a master page, pressing CMD/CTRL+3 using the Content tool in a text box inserts the automatic page number tag in a text box.*

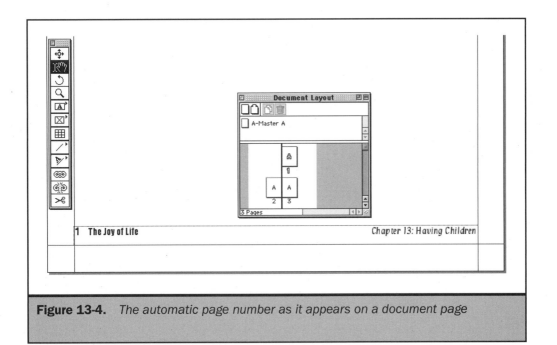

Figure 13-4.   *The automatic page number as it appears on a document page*

Appending Resources from Other Documents

As you produce documents using QuarkXPress, it may occur to you from time to time that you're performing a task you swear you've done all too often in the past. In fact, if layout is your primary task, the likelihood is quite high that you've created documents that are identical or similar in many respects. Many users often forge ahead in their production processes without thinking twice about whether or not they're repeating a task they did yesterday, last week, or last year. Many seasoned designers will often attest there's no such thing as an original layout. With all the rules and guidelines we apply to layout, this may very well be true.

Since you're using QuarkXPress 5, which enables you to save so many things affecting layout, some of those repetitive tasks you perform every day may be unnecessary. These include tasks such as defining text styles and colors, setting up H&Js, custom dashes and stripes, and so on. In order to benefit from the efforts put into other documents, QuarkXPress 5 enables you to quickly transfer theses types of elements between documents using the Append command dialog options (see Figure 13-5).

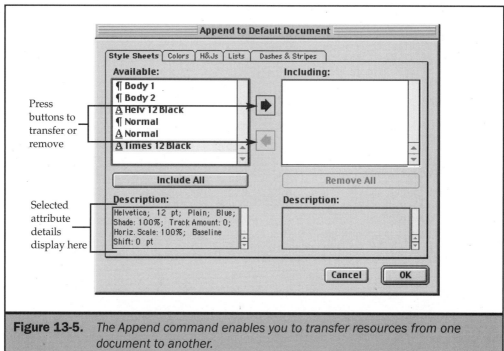

Figure 13-5.   *The Append command enables you to transfer resources from one document to another.*

The Append command enables you to transfer defined styles, colors, H&Js, lists, and dash and stripe styles from other documents to your open document. (If you are working in a Web document, you can also append meta tags and menus.) This essentially copies and stores them with your current document independent of the document they are copied from, meaning no relationship is maintained between your current document and the one you are appending elements from. The procedures used in appending resources from other documents are similar, no matter which attributes you are transferring. In fact, except for the tab name and the specific contents in each list, the Append tabs and commands are virtually identical.

Note   *As you work with each type of attribute in QuarkXPress, you may notice each one of the features (Styles, Colors, H&Js, Lists, and Dashes & Stripes) includes its own Append command capabilities, the options of which are used in exactly the same manner as this Append command. The only difference is that with the Append command accessed from the File menu, you have access to all types of attributes in a single dialog.*

To access the Append dialog, choose File | Append (CMD/CTRL+OPTION/ALT+A). The first dialog to appear is not the Append dialog, but instead a browse dialog that enables you to locate and specify the file you want to append elements from (shown next). While using this dialog, all eligible document types are displayed.

While using the Windows version of QuarkXPress 5, you may choose All Append Sources in the Append browsing dialog to show all files or only selected types of files.

The Append browse dialog lists all eligible files in a selected folder, including the following native QuarkXPress file formats:

- QuarkXPress documents (QXD)
- QuarkXPress templates (QXT)
- QuarkXPress libraries (QXL)
- QuarkXPress Auto Save files (ASV)
- QuarkXPress tags (XTG)
- QuarkXPress web documents (QWD)
- QuarkXPress web templates (QWT)

Clicking OK after making a selection in the Browse dialog opens the Append dialog, which shows the available attributes in the file in each of the tabbed areas. The Append dialog itself is divided into two halves: Available and Include. While a specific tab is selected, the attributes are automatically displayed in the Available list side. When an attribute is selected in the list, two things occur: A detailed description of the selected attribute appears in the Description field below, and the right-pointing arrow button becomes available. Clicking this button moves your selected attribute from the Available list into the Include list. If you want, you may choose all listed attributes by clicking the Include All button.

You do not need to have a document open in order to append attributes from it.

Any attributes you move to the Include side of the dialog will be appended to your current document when you click OK. While an attribute is selected in the Include side, you'll also see two things happen: The Description area directly below displays details about the attribute, and the left-pointing button becomes available. Clicking this button returns the selected attribute to the Available side, while clicking the Remove All button returns *all* the attributes listed on the Include side to the Available side.

Before clicking the OK button to save and close the Append dialog, make certain you've selected all the elements you want to transfer. While making your selection in the dialog lists, holding SHIFT enables you to select contiguous list elements, and holding CMD/CTRL enables you to select non-contiguous elements.

Once the OK button is clicked, all your selections are copied to your current document. After clicking OK, a warning will appear to notify you of the types of attributes being copied (shown next). If you're confident that the choices you make are always correct, you may choose the *Don't Show this warning again* option.

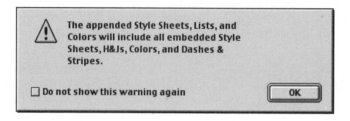

Create a master document (such as a template) that contains nothing but established layout and/or design elements for styles, colors, H&Js, and dashes and stripes you've spent time creating. Keeping a master document such as this will enable you to establish and easily maintain design standards while working in a publishing environment. If you work in a networked environment, you might consider making the document available networkwide.

Ironing Out Append Conflicts

With the capability to copy certain attributes from other documents using the Append command comes the hazard of overwriting attributes with the same name. Without a method of resolving these types of conflicts, you might be faced with a situation where you would lose valuable attribute information. Fortunately, QuarkXPress is prepared for this through the implementation of a conflict feature.

The Append Conflict dialog (see Figure 13-6) appears only when an attribute features the same name as an attribute in your current document, but with different

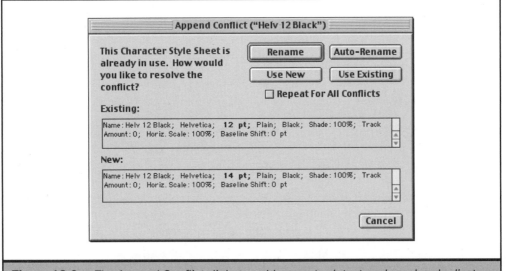

Figure 13-6. *The Append Conflict dialog enables you to detect and resolve duplicate resources being copied to your current document.*

properties applied. In other words, if you are copying a style sheet from another document using the Append command and it has the same name but different character or paragraph attributes as a style sheet already existing in your current document with an identical name, the Append Conflict dialog appears. You cannot access the Append Conflict dialog through menu options or keyboard shortcuts.

When resolving conflicts such as these, the Append Conflict dialog offers four choices in the form of command buttons and displays detailed descriptions of the conflicting attributes. The *Existing* area details the attributes of the item about to be copied over, while the *New* area details the item you want to append to your current document. Commands buttons leave the choice for conflict resolution up to you, as follows:

- **Rename**   Clicking this button opens a dialog (shown next) enabling you to assign a new name to the attribute being copied to your existing document. Enter a new name for your attribute in the New Name field and select OK to rename the attribute.

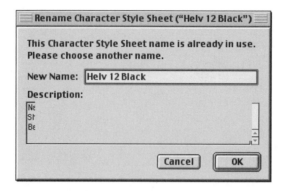

- **Auto-Rename** Clicking the Auto-Rename button enables QuarkXPress to assign a different name to your attribute. The new name is automatically applied with an asterisk preceding its current name.

- **Use Existing** Pressing the Use Existing button essentially cancels the Append selection, enabling QuarkXPress to leave the attributes in your current document as is.

- **Use New** Pressing this button enables QuarkXPress to overwrite the existing attribute with the new one.

- **Repeat for All conflicts** Selecting this option enables you to choose the current conflict resolution method for all subsequent conflicts. For example, if you choose the option and subsequently click the Auto-Rename button, all conflicts will be resolved by adding an asterisk to conflicting attribute names.

Note *Operation of the Append Conflict is the same, regardless of whether you are resolving conflicts for styles, colors, H&Js, lists, or dash and stripe attributes.*

Setting Application Preferences

Application preferences enable you to control the overall program performance when working in any document. Exploring these settings will enable you to hone your copy of QuarkXPress to perform exactly how you prefer it to work. Although Display, Interactive, and XTensions behavior could be considered fine-tuning, the most critical features to pay attention to in terms of application preferences are the all-important Save preferences. These preferences are set using the Application Preferences dialog opened by choosing Edit | Preferences | Application (CMD/CTRL+OPTION/ALT+SHIFT+Y).

Setting Display Preferences

In the Display tab dialog (see Figure 13-7), you may set the colors of onscreen display guides using the Margin, Ruler, and Grid buttons. By clicking these color buttons, you may select from one of 48 basic colors or create your own color by using the Color Picker on the Macintosh version (or by clicking the Define Custom Colors button on the Windows version). Display options also enable you to choose between high- and low-quality displays of Color TIFFs (choose from 8-, 16-, or 32-bit on the Macintosh version, or 8- or 24-bit on the Windows version) and Gray TIFFs (choose from 16 or 256 levels of gray). Windows users may also set the onscreen Display dpi value (choose a value between 36 and 300 dpi).

Set the width of your pasteboard using the Pasteboard Width option. The pasteboard is the name given to the work area found around your document page borders. The pasteboard may range between 0 and 100 percent of your document page width; the length is ignored. The pasteboard width may not be less than 0.5 inches or exceed 48 inches.

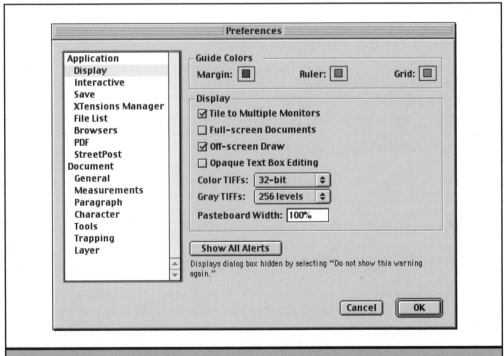

Figure 13-7. *You can control how elements are visually presented on your document page using these options.*

If you work with extremely high-resolution color images, you may want to disable the Off-Screen Draw option (selected by default), which enables QuarkXPress to draw the complete representation of an image or item even though it may reside off your current screen view. Screen draw time can be excessive when working with high-resolution color images or a document containing highly complex shapes.

Setting the Ruler color also changes the onscreen color of clipping paths while in editing mode. Setting the Grid color also changes the onscreen editing color of runarounds.

Macintosh users of QuarkXPress 5 also have unique options for controlling the display of their documents not available to Windows users. Choose the Tile to Multiple Monitors option (selected by default) in the Display screen of the Preferences dialog to view the tiling of documents across systems equipped with more than one monitor. Select the Full-Screen Documents option (unselected by default) to automatically maximize the display of new documents when they are opened or maximize screen use when tiling or stacking document windows. Choose the Opaque Text Box Editing option to have the background of text boxes become opaque while they are selected for editing (which can be useful for improving the readability of text in the box if the background is set to None).

Setting Interactive Preferences

The Interactive tab (see Figure 13-8) enables you to control screen-draw speed performance, quote character, and dragging preferences. By default, the options are set to enable QuarkXPress to behave at ideal performance levels, but you may want to change certain settings depending on your system capabilities and the type of work you do.

Settings such as fast screen scrolling and forcing QuarkXPress to show details of items as they are dragged may consume incredible amounts of system resources. By default, the scroll speed of QuarkXPress is set very low, meaning each time you click an elevator button the screen contents change only slightly. If you increase the scrolling speed, screen contents change more dramatically, but with your display settings set to their highest, such as Color TIFFs set to 24-bit and Off-Screen Draw active, you may notice that scrolling actually takes longer.

The Speed Scroll option enables QuarkXPress to greek pictures (meaning picture detail is omitted) and blended colors in boxes, which can often be time-consuming to repeatedly draw when scrolling. Selecting Live Scroll (off by default) forces QuarkXPress to update your screen contents as you drag a scroll box (thumb), but may drain your system resources.

You may turn Live Scroll on or off (depending on whether it is selected in the Application Preferences dialog) by holding OPTION/ALT while dragging the scroll box (thumb).

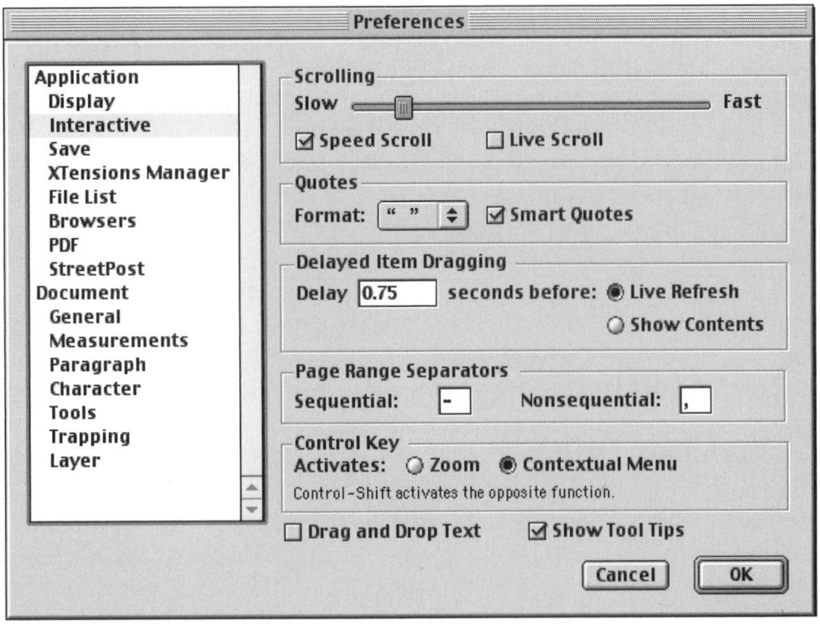

Figure 13-8. *Set redraw, scrolling, and dragging preferences using options in this dialog*

Select the quote character you want to use when quotes are converted during text import operations from a selection of six styles in the Quotes drop-down list and choose the Smart Quotes (on by default) to enable QuarkXPress to automatically substitute open and close quotes as you type in text boxes.

As you drag items on your screen, you may notice subtle time delays have been built in to control item-drawing behavior. For example, hesitating slightly between the time you click an object and the time you actually drag it is controlled by the Delay value entered. After your hesitation, QuarkXPress may either draw the selected text or picture in detail as you click-hold, then drag it (choose Show Contents), or draw the item as you click-hold, then drag it, *and* periodically refresh your complete screen, including item layering and text flow.

To enter straight quotes to abbreviate feet (') or inches (") when Smart Quotes is enabled, press CTRL+' for feet (') or CTRL+SHIFT+" (Macintosh) or CMD/CTRL+OPTION/ALT+' (Windows) for inches (") while entering text with the Content tool.

The remaining options compose a *potpourri* of options. You may enable Drag and Drop text functions that automate clipboard cut and paste functions and enable you to move text by using the mouse. With this feature enabled, you can cut and move text by clicking, holding down the mouse, and dragging to your new location. To copy and paste, hold down the SHIFT key while moving text. Choose Show Tool Tips to enable QuarkXPress 5 to display popup style information flags while working with tools and screen features in your program or document window, which is ideal if you're new to QuarkXPress or a recent upgrader to version 5.

In this dialog, you may also set the behavior of the Control (CTRL) key when pressed in combination with a mouse click-and-hold action. Choosing Contextual Menu (the default) enables you to open the temporary context-sensitive popup menu identified for many of the procedures in this book. Choosing Zoom enables you to change this functionality to temporarily select the Zoom tool. Holding SHIFT while working in your document enables you to toggle the current state of these options.

Setting Save Preferences

If you value your work, you'll want to pay very close attention to how QuarkXPress saves your document, whether and where backups are stored, and how often they are updated in the Save dialog (see Figure 13-9). By default, the way QuarkXPress saves documents is quite basic; it's completely manual. Should your application or system falter for one reason or another, all the work you did up to your last save will be lost. The Save options selected on by default are those for *Auto Library Save* and *Save Document Position*. The Library option enables library files to be saved the moment changes are made to it, while the document position option enables QuarkXPress to record the last size, position, and shape of your document window.

Other Save options in the dialog are not selected, but it may be wise to consider using at least one of them. Choosing *Auto Save* forces QuarkXPress to perform an automatic Save command periodically according to the time interval entered in the Every [*value*] minutes field. Be as daring as you like here, and keep in mind that each time your file is auto saved, you will lose a few moments of productivity, especially if you work on a network where save times are even slower than to a local drive.

Choose *Auto Backup* to force QuarkXPress to make complete copies of your document. The number entered in the Keep Revisions field determines how many copies are made. Each time a Save command is manually performed, a numbered copy of your document is stored in either the document folder or a folder of your choosing. After the maximum revision copies have been created (the default is 5), the copies are renumbered automatically. Again, be as daring as you like here, but keep in mind that saving multiple copies of each document you work on may consume incredible amounts of memory.

Setting XTensions Preferences

The XTensions Manager enables you to govern your use of XTensions in QuarkXPress; these preferences control the XTensions Manager. By choosing options in the

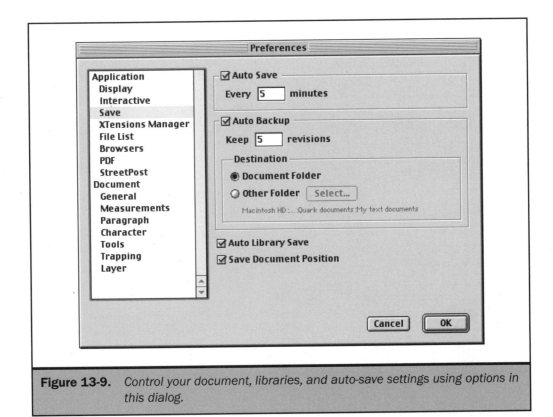

Figure 13-9.   *Control your document, libraries, and auto-save settings using options in this dialog.*

Application Preferences dialog (see Figure 13-10), you may set how the XTensions Manager is loaded each time QuarkXPress is launched. The more XTensions you have loaded, the more of your system's resources must be dedicated to running QuarkXPress, so if you rely heavily on the use of XTensions for performing specific tasks, then you may want to see the XTensions Manager at each launch by choosing the Always option.

The remaining options in the dialog become available by choosing the *When* option, which sets QuarkXPress to automatically open the XTensions Manager at start-up only when loading errors occur and/or when XTensions are added or removed from the XTensions folder. By default, two XTensions folders exist in your QuarkXPress program folder: one named *XTension* and *XTension Disabled*. Any changes made to the XTension folder are detected when QuarkXPress is launched.

Using Windows platforms, you may identify XTensions by their three-letter XNT extension.

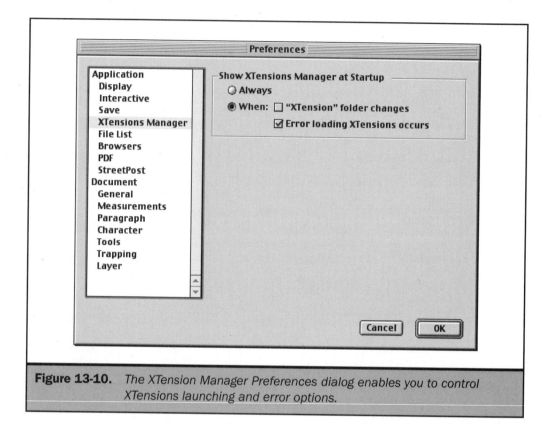

Figure 13-10.   *The XTension Manager Preferences dialog enables you to control XTensions launching and error options.*

File List Preferences

The File List Preferences dialog (see Figure 13-11) enables you to set options controlling recently opened documents as they appear at the end of the File command menu (by default). The list serves as a convenient method of quickly accessing the files you were working with during your last use of QuarkXPress 5.

By default, the list displays the last three opened files. Windows users will also be able to use automatically applied shortcut keys numbered sequentially as 1 [*file name*], 2 [*file name*], and so on. If you want, you may set your File List length within a range between 3 and 9 names using the Number of Files option. Select the Append Files to Open Menu Item option to shift the entire list from the end of the File menu and create it as a new popup menu extending from the File, Open command menu item.

By default, the list automatically displays the most recently opened file first. Control the order of the list alphabetically using the Alphabetize Names option and optionally view the complete file name and path by selecting the Show Full Path option.

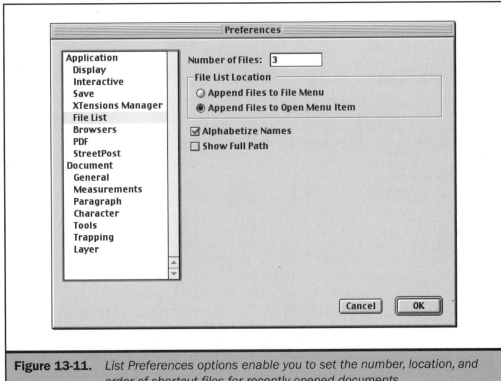

Figure 13-11.   *List Preferences options enable you to set the number, location, and order of shortcut files for recently opened documents.*

Browsers Preferences

The Browser Preferences dialog (see Figure 13-12) enables you to set up one or more web browser applications to use when previewing exported HTML web documents. By default, the browsers installed on your system during the installation of QuarkXPress 5 appear in the dialog list automatically, but you may customize these using the Add or Delete buttons in the dialog. To delete a browser, select it in the list and click the Delete button. To add a browser, click the Add button to open the Select Browser dialog to locate and select a browser to install.

PDF Preferences

The PDF Preferences dialog (see Figure 13-13) enables you to control how files exported to the Adobe portable document file (PDF) format are prepared and initialize Adobe Acrobat Distiller options. Click the Browse button under the Acrobat Distiller heading

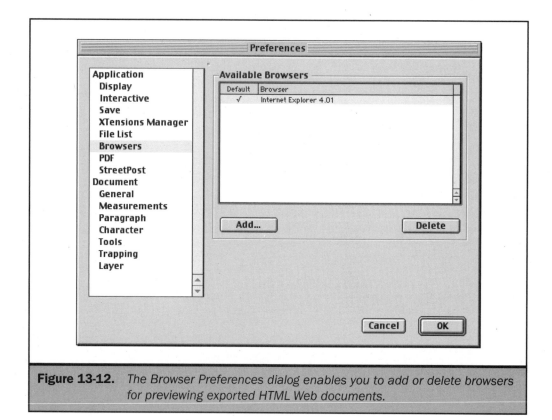

Figure 13-12.   *The Browser Preferences dialog enables you to add or delete browsers for previewing exported HTML Web documents.*

to open the Locate Acrobat Distiller dialog for locating and selecting the distiller application. Use the Workflow options to specify whether to distill (meaning create the PDF) immediately on export, or to create a PostScript file for later distilling. Clicking the Browse button under the Default Settings heading enables you to set default export options used by the PDF export filter. For more information on exporting to PDF, see "Using the PDF Exporter and Options" in Chapter 20.

StreetPost Preferences

The StreetPost dialog of the Preferences dialog (see Figure 13-14) is available as a feature of Avenue.Quark and enables you to post an Avenue.Quark XML document to a web application, a server, or other systems capable of reading and interpreting tags in a multi-part form post. For more information on choosing options and using the features of the StreetPost Xtension, see your Avenue.Quark documentation.

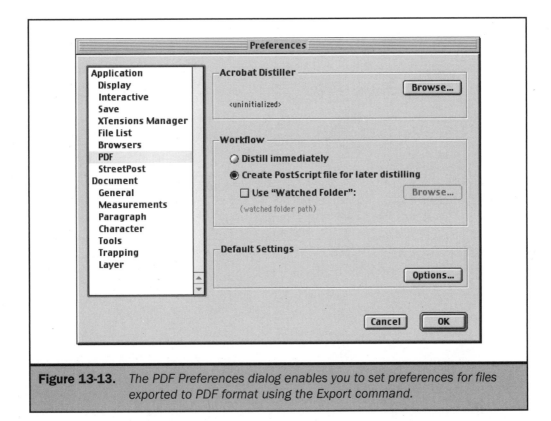

Figure 13-13. *The PDF Preferences dialog enables you to set preferences for files exported to PDF format using the Export command.*

Setting Document Preferences

When it comes to enabling you to assert control over the display and behavior of QuarkXPress documents, the stops have been pulled. Other programs often provide far too many customization options to make life easy. But the options of QuarkXPress are logically organized, neatly presented, and relatively straightforward to select. Options have been organized into seven main areas comprised of General, Measurements, Paragraph, Character, Tools, Trapping, and Layer. This section covers setting General, Measurements, Paragraph, Character, Layer, and Tools preferences.

By setting Document Preferences with no documents opened, you are actually setting the defaults for all newly created QuarkXPress documents. If this isn't your intention, open only the document you want to apply the preferences to first, before opening the Document Preferences dialog.

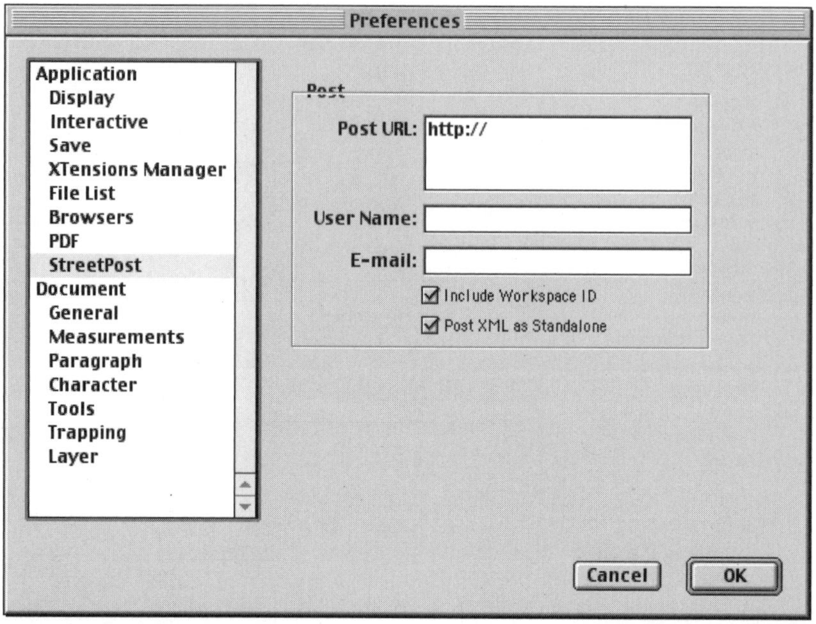

Figure 13-14.   *Street Post preferences enable you to post an Avenue.Quark XML document to a Web application, a server, or other systems capable of reading and interpreting tags in a multipart form post.*

Measurements Preferences

The Measurements Preferences dialog (see Figure 13-15) features all options that relate to how QuarkXPress displays and measures distances and values. The function of options in this dialog is defined as follows:

- **Horizontal and Vertical Measure**   Choose from Inches (Standard or Decimal), Picas, Points, Millimeters, Centimeters, Ciceros, or Agates for display of each ruler measure. The choice you make here also affects the default measurement display of interface elements such as drop-down menus and numeric fields in dialog boxes and palettes. However, you may enter any measurement you want by adding the measure abbreviation after the value. For information on these abbreviations, see the Keyboard Shortcuts guide included with this book.

- **Points/Inch**   This field enables you to enter a conversion setting for your document. Unless you have a specific need for changing this, it should be left at

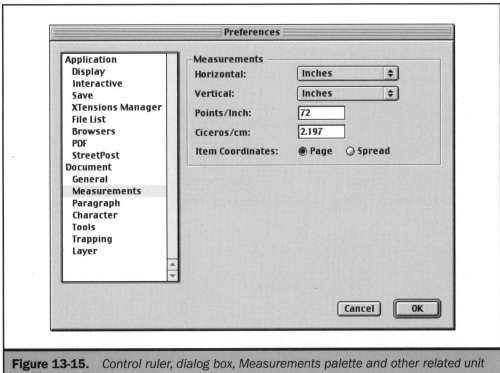

Figure 13-15. *Control ruler, dialog box, Measurements palette and other related unit measure values using options in this dialog.*

72 points per inch, which is the standard used in electronic publishing. Some users may want to adhere to older standards where an inch can be equal to either 72.27 or 72.307 points.

■ **Ciceros/Cm** As with the Points/Inch measure, this field enables you to enter a more exact value for ciceros per centimeter. The standard in electronic publishing has been rounded to 2.197 (the default) and it may be wise to leave this as is. If you have a specific need, you may change this to the more exact traditional value measure of 2.1967.

■ **Item Coordinates** This option enables you to set how item positions are measured and displayed by choosing Page (the default) or Spread. With Page selected, item positions are measured from the ruler zero point of each page. With Spread selected and facing pages in use, item positions are measured continuously across page spreads starting at the ruler zero mark.

General Preferences

General preferences include a mixed bag of options that mainly affect the display of items and interface elements in your document (see Figure 13-16). The default settings for these options are selected by Quark based on user feedback, but the choice to keep them or not is yours:

■ **Greek Below** This option controls when text on your page is greeked. Greeking significantly speeds screen draw time. The higher this setting, the faster your pages will screen draw, but the less you'll be able to read on screen (unless you zoom in). By default, this is set to 7 points.

Increasing your Greek Below size to 12 or 14 points will significantly improve your screen draw speed, without reducing the readability of large or headline-sized text.

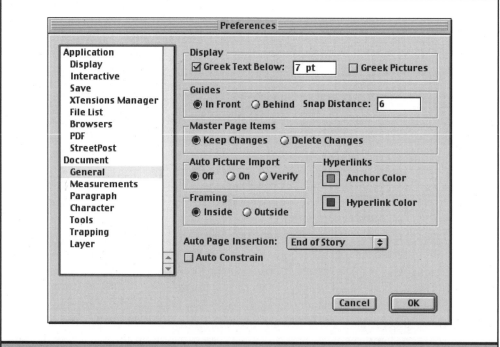

Figure 13-16.   *The General tab offers these assorted options for controlling document display, text, guides, page, import, hyperlink, and framing.*

- **Greek Pictures**   Allowing pictures to be greeked has the same effect as for text, enabling QuarkXPress to fill picture boxes with a gray screen until selected. This is an extremely powerful feature to use if your documents contain pictures. By default, it is not selected, but it may be a wise choice to activate it.

- **Guides**   Set your guides to display In Front or Behind (the default) the items that you see on your screen. Guides include margin, ruler, and grid marks on your screen as well as shapes for clipping paths and runarounds.

- **Snap Distance**   The snap distance determines the distance between which items are magnetically drawn to guides on your page, such as margin, ruler, and grid lines. The snap distance is 6 points by default, but may be changed to any value between 1 and 216 points.

- **Master Page Items**   The Master Page Items option may be set to *Keep Changes* (the default) or *Delete Changes*. If you choose at some point to reapply a new master page to a page that already contains items, QuarkXPress looks here for guidance on whether to keep any previous master page items or not, depending on whether the master page item has been modified or not. With Keep Changes selected, modified master items are kept, and with Delete Changes, selected modified master page items are overwritten with the newly applied master page items.

- **Auto Picture Import**   This option is simply set to *Off* (the default) *On*, or *On (verify)*. Set to On, it has the effect of forcing QuarkXPress to reimport all pictures each time the document is opened. Set to On (verify), it has the effect of reimporting all pictures and then displaying a warning dialog if pictures are missing. It also provides options for updating any missing or modified pictures.

- **Hyperlinks**   Set the color of Anchors and Hyperlinks applied to text in your document using these options. To change the colors of each, click the color buttons to open the Color Picker (Macintosh) or Color Selector (Windows) dialogs, and use the dialog options to select and accept the new color.

- **Framing**   Choose whether the frames (such as dash patterns or stripes) of your text or picture boxes are displayed and printed *Inside* (the default) or *Outside* your text or picture boxes. Choosing Outside framing from the drop-down menu has the effect of enabling solid, dash, or stripe patterns to be applied around the outside of your boxes, which has the effect of making boxes larger in size and is more difficult to work with than the *Inside* option. The difference between these two states (see Figure 13-17) significantly affects the appearance of boxed items with frame properties applied. In this case, two boxes of the same size are created using the two different framing states.

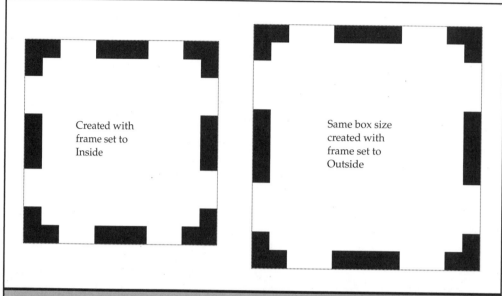

Figure 13-17.   *The Framing option enables you to set how frame styles applied to boxes appear in relation to the box boundaries.*

- **Auto Page Insertion**   When text documents are imported into your QuarkXPress document, the text may not always fit in your selected text box, and overflow will often occur. Select this option *Off* or *On* under three conditions: *End of Story, End of Section*, or *End of Document* from the drop-down menu to tell QuarkXPress when and where to add automatic text boxes to hold the overflow text.

- **Auto Constrain**   Selecting the Auto Constrain option creates an automatic hierarchy among items on your document page. Each item you create is constrained by the borders of a box stacked behind it, so long as the box fully surrounds the newly created items. This option is for users who are accustomed to the way QuarkXPress behaved in earlier versions. In those days, all items on a document page were forced to exist in boxes. In order for a layout to be moved or copied to another page as a single unit, you were forced to keep all items stored in a single box. If this is your favorite way to work in layout, you may select Auto Constrain to return QuarkXPress behavior to these days of old. Otherwise, it may be wise to leave it unselected. For more information on constraining and unconstraining items, refer to "Managing Page Content" in Chapter 11.

Paragraph Preferences

Setting Paragraph preferences enables you to make decisions about how Auto Leading is applied, how baseline grids are set up, and your paragraph text hyphenation method by using options in the Paragraph Preferences dialog (see Figure 13-18). The options specific to paragraph preferences are as follows:

- **Leading**   When leading in your document is set to Auto, the spacing between lines of text is applied based on a percentage of the font size. Auto leading is a powerful feature to use, because of its flexibility in applying spacing between lines based on the line's content and font size. By default, this value is set to 20 percent leading, meaning, for example, that 10-point type will be applied with leading of 12 points, or two extra points added to the leading value. You may set the auto leading percentage to any percentage value between 1 and 100 percent.

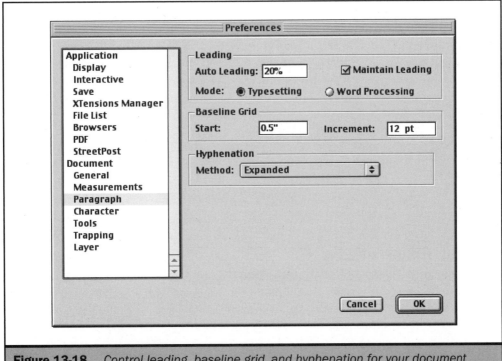

Figure 13-18.   *Control leading, baseline grid, and hyphenation for your document using options in this dialog.*

You may also set the mode used by QuarkXPress for leading to *Typesetting* or *Word-processing*. Choosing Typesetting (the default) enables QuarkXPress to measure leading upward from baseline to baseline, while choosing Word-processing measures leading from downward from ascender to ascender.

> **Tip**   *You may also enter incremental values in the Auto Leading field option. For example, entering +1 pt in the field sets Auto Leading at 1 point more than the largest font size in your line of text. You may also specify Auto Leading in other measurements by appending the value with measure abbreviations such as mm for millimeters and so on. If a measurement unit is not specified, the value entered in the Auto Leading field will be interpreted as a percent value.*

- **Baseline Grid**   Baseline grids are used in high-end publication design and enable you to create underlying grids on which all text and objects align. You may view the baseline grid of your document onscreen by choose View | Baseline Grid (OPTION/CTRL+F7). The start point of the grid is measured in relation to the edge of your document page and the spacing of the grid is usually determined by the leading of your body text. The Baseline Increment value must fall within 1 and 144 points.

- **Hyphenation**   Select *Standard, Enhanced*, or *Expanded* from the Method drop-down menu for a good-better-best scenario for the hyphenation of your paragraph text. Standard hyphenation uses a hyphenation algorithm based on technology implemented prior to QuarkXPress version 3.1, while choosing Enhanced uses an improved hyphenation algorithm implemented in versions developed since then. Choosing Expanded uses the Enhanced algorithm in combination with any Hyphenation Exceptions saved with the document.

> **Note**   *If you open a previous version document, the Standard method of hyphenation is used as the default.*

Character Preferences

The Character Preferences dialog options (see Figure 13-19) will be of significant interest to designers or professional typesetters who need to customize document characters to a specified or established character design.

Character preferences include the following options:

- **Superscript and Subscript**   Superscript characters are usually smaller and are positioned above the baseline of text, while subscript characters are usually smaller, but appear below the baseline of text. You may control superscript and subscript characteristics using the Offset and Scale option here. Offset controls the amount of the baseline shift, while the vertical (VScale) and horizontal

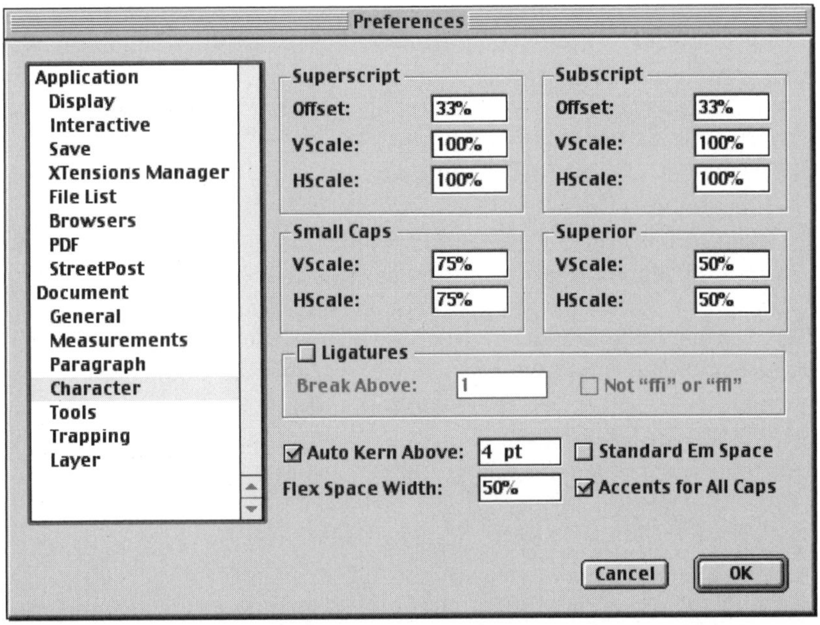

Figure 13-19. *Control how specialized character styles are formatted using options in this dialog.*

(HScale) values set the change in size relative to the font size. By default, both baseline offsets are set to 33 percent and the scaling is left at 100 percent of the font size.

- **Small Caps and Superior**   Small caps and superior caps are hybrids of a font's upper-case character formatting. In essence, applying this style converts upper- and lower-case text to all upper-case characters, leaving upper-case (small caps) characters larger than lower-case (superior) to simulate the shape of upper- and lower-case text. The degree to which the characters are reduced may be set by entering vertical (VScale) an horizontal (HScale) values based on percentage changes from the original font size. By default, small caps are 75 percent of the original font size, while superior caps are 50 percent. Small caps and superior caps are often referred to as Caps and True Caps.

- **Auto Kern Above**   Choosing this option and entering a value enables you to set at which font size the automatic kerning tables kick in. The default is the option selected and a font size of 4 points.

■ **Flex Space Width**   Flex spaces are spaces that you may enter in text manually in an effort to fine-tune the spacing of justified text, or whatever reason you choose. Flexible spaces change size with the justification of your text.

To enter a breaking flexible space in text, press OPTION+SHIFT+SPACEBAR (Macintosh) or CTRL+SHIFT+5 (Windows). To enter a non-breaking flexible space, press CMD+OPTION+SHIFT+SPACEBAR (Macintosh) or CTRL+ALT+SHIFT+5 (Windows).

■ **Standard Em Space**   To use Standard Em Space measures in your text, select this option. Standard em spaces are as wide as the font is tall, meaning a standard 12-point em space is 12-points wide. By default, this option is not selected, enabling QuarkXPress to use its own measure for creating em spaces based on the width of two zeros of a given font size. The QuarkXPress method enables em spaces to change in width if vertical or horizontal scaling is applied to your text.

To enter an en space in your text, press OPTION+SPACE (Mac) or CTRL+SHIFT+6 (Windows) while using the Content tool in a text box.

■ **Accents for All Caps**   Selecting this option (the default) enables QuarkXPress to apply accents to capitol letters in your text. Sometimes accents can adversely affect the appearance of text set with little or no leading, causing the accents to jut into the descenders on the line of text above.

Changing Tool Preferences

Each time you select a tool and create a box, line, or shape in XPress, the resulting item features certain default properties. In cases where you find yourself constantly changing item properties to suit the type of documents you regularly produce, over time this added step can accumulate to more than a little lost productivity. You can change the defaults of properties associated with new items for each and every tool in XPress through the use of tool customization.

Tool preferences are changed via the Tool Preferences dialog (see Figure 13-20). To open this dialog, choose Edit | Preferences | Preferences and click Tools under Document (CMD/CTRL+Y) in the tree directory at the left. As mentioned earlier, you may change these defaults for all new documents or simply the document you are currently working in, depending on when you choose to change them. If you'd like to change tool properties for all new documents, apply your changes while no documents are open. To change them for only a certain document, change them while the document is open.

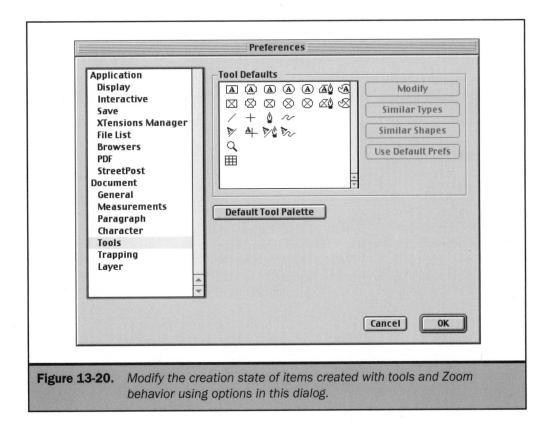

Figure 13-20.   *Modify the creation state of items created with tools and Zoom behavior using options in this dialog.*

The Tool Preferences dialog features a list of all the tools available in the Tool palette of XPress and five command buttons for accessing tool options or applying preference states. The function of these command buttons is defined as follows:

- **Modify**   With one or more tools selected, clicking this button opens the Modify dialog. The tabs that appear indicate the options you may change, specific to the type of item the selected tool creates. In cases where more than one tool is selected when this button is pressed, you may also see a Group tab that features common options for the selected tools being modified.

- **Select Similar Types**   Because XPress includes many tools that perform related functions, such as the various text, picture, and line tools, you may automatically select all related tools by clicking this button.

- **Select Similar Shapes**   Since several tools create similar type shapes in text, picture, or shape conditions, selecting one of these tools and clicking this button selects all the tools that create the same type of shape.

- **Use Default Prefs**   Clicking the Use Default Prefs button with one or more tools selected returns the tools to their original defaults when XPress was first installed.

- **Default Tool Palette**   If your Tool palette display has been changed in any way, clicking this button immediately returns the Tool palette to its original default state.

To open the Document Preferences | Tool tab dialog quickly, double-click the Zoom tool or any Text, Picture, or Line tool.

- **Zoom Tool**   While the Zoom tool is selected, clicking Modify opens the View dialog (shown next), which enables you to set the Minimum, Maximum, and Increment fields. By default, the Zoom tool is set to XPress' maximum and minimum capabilities. If you wish, you may change these limits by entering new settings in the Minimum and Maximum fields. Each time the Zoom tool is clicked on your page your magnification changes by a preset value according to the Increment field. By default, this is set to 25 percent, but you may change this to any increment value within a range between 1 and 400 percent.

The maximum magnification factor of the Zoom tool is set using options in the View dialog and it is accessed by choosing Tools from within the Preferences dialog (CMD/CTRL+OPTION/ALT+SHIFT+Y), clicking the Zoom tool from the tools collection, and clicking the Modify button.

- **Text Box Tools**   While any text box tool is selected, you may modify the Box, Text, Frame, and/or Runaround properties associated with the selected tool(s).

- **Picture Box Tools**   While any picture box tool is selected, you may modify the Box, Picture, Frame, and/or Runaround properties associated with the selected tool(s).

- **Line Tools**   With any line tool selected, you may modify Line and/or Runaround properties.
- **Text-Path Tools**   With any text-path tool selected, you may modify the tool's Line, Text-Path, and/or Runaround properties.
- **Tables Tool**   This new addition to the Tools Preferences dialog enables you to set the default creation state for new tables.

To reset your currently selected tools to their default preferences, click the Use Default Prefs button. To change all the tools in the palette to defaults, select all tools by holding SHIFT while clicking the top-right-most tool (Freehand Text tool) and then the bottom-left tool (Table tool) in the list. Then click the Default Prefs button. To reset only the Tool palette to its default state, click the Default Tool Palette button.

For information on setting Trapping preferences for your document, see "Setting Trapping Preferences" in Chapter 15.

Layer Preferences

The Layer Preferences dialog (see Figure 13-21) features four options for setting the default state of new layers created using the Layers palette. Choose whether new layers are created as visible, locked, printable, or include runaround effects. These options are similar to those that may be changed using the Layer Attributes dialog.

To open the Layers palette and view the current layers in a document, choose View | Layers. To change the attributes of an existing layer, double-click the layer in the Layers palette to open the layer's Attributes dialog. For complete information on working with Layers, refer to "Layering Layout Elements" in Chapter 11.

Setting Web Document Preferences

If you've arrived here in search of a way to control specific Web Document preferences, you may wish to review some of the information covered in previous sections for controlling preferences for your application and/or document. The command for opening the Preferences dialog (see Figure 13-22) while working in a web document is the same as for that of a regular QuarkXPress 5 document: choose Edit | Preferences | Preferences (CMD/CTRL+Y).

If the document you are creating is a web document, you'll notice a few differences in the Preferences dialog from those offered for typical QuarkXPress documents. Although the application-related preferences are identical for any type of document, you'll discover Web-related options in certain Document Preferences dialogs. The following section summarizes the differences.

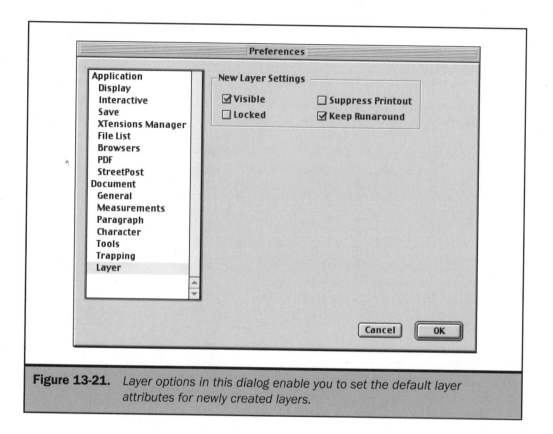

Figure 13-21. *Layer options in this dialog enable you to set the default layer attributes for newly created layers.*

General Web Document Preferences

Two additional options are available in the Preferences dialog while General is selected in the tree directory (shown next). Use the Image Export Directory option to specify a default name for all images necessary to display exported HTML web pages. Enter a folder name in the Site Root Directory box to specify where exported HTML documents will be stored or click the Select/Browse button to open the Select/Browse for Folder dialog to choose a folder interactively.

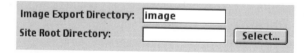

Web Document Measurement and Paragraph Preferences

Since the Web uses pixels in place of any other unit measure, the default Horizontal and Vertical unit values are preset to pixels while Measurements is selected in the tree

Figure 13-22. *The Preferences for a Web document are slightly different from that of a regular document.*

directory (shown next). Although it may not be advisable to deviate from this, you may still choose whichever unit value you wish from either drop-down menu.

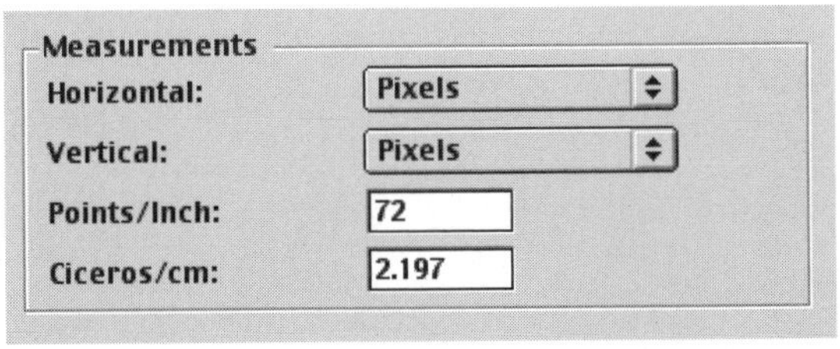

The only significant difference in the Paragraph page of the Preferences dialog between typical QuarkXPress documents is the measurement values controlling baseline grids. In this case, instead of inches being the default unit value, pixels are used as the default values in setting baseline grid Start and Increment values (shown next). For more information on working with baseline grids, see "Working with Baseline Grids in QuarkXPress" in Chapter 12.

Specific Tools for Web Documents

Several new tools are available specifically for creating Web-specific items in web documents. While the Preferences dialog is open, the Tools page features access to options dialogs to set creation preferences for the Oval Image Map, Bézier Image Map, and Form tools. While either the Oval or Bézier image map tools are selected, clicking the Modify button opens the Image Map Properties dialog (shown next) which enables you to set the default Maximum Points limit and the Granularity detail.

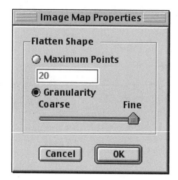

While the Form tool is selected, clicking the Modify button opens the Form Tool Properties dialog (shown next), which enables you to set the default width and height sizes (in pixels) for new form items. For more information on working with web document-specific tools, see "Using Web Tools" in Chapter 19.

Since web documents do not require the color trapping control of typical documents, no Trapping options are offered while viewing preferences if your current document is a Web document.

Creating H&J Styles

The appearance of hyphenation in your document has always been one of the more subtle issues surrounding document design. If you create documents that are short on text but long on pictures, you may not be too concerned with hyphenation. You may merely need to either turn it on or turn it off.

But for many text-heavy or high-end publications, the capability to control hyphenation is extremely critical to controlling the look of text. Hyphenation affects all text, but mostly text set in very large sizes or to very narrow column widths (or both). Hyphenation factors also come into play when creating runaround effects between text boxes and pictures or uneven shapes. The best rule of thumb to follow is that *less is better.* In fact, ideally no hyphenation is the best scenario. But turning hyphenation off in many instances causes the text length to end far short of the margin or it adds distracting spaces between words, especially if your text is justified.

QuarkXPress comes with only one H&J recipe, *Standard,* which serves as the default when applying any paragraph text formatting or when simply entering text into a text box. The options for hyphenation and justification are set in the Edit Hyphenation dialog (shown next), which is accessed by clicking the Edit button in the H&J dialog. To open the H&J dialog, choose Edit | H&Js (Option/Ctrl+Shift+F11 or Cmd/Ctrl+Option/Alt+H).

Edit Hyphenation & Justification

Name:

Standard

☑ **Auto Hyphenation**

Smallest Word: 6

Minimum Before: 3

Minimum After: 2

☐ Break Capitalized Words

Hyphens in a Row: unlimited ⬍

Hyphenation Zone: 0"

Justification Method

	Min.	Opt.	Max.
Space:	85%	110%	250%
Char:	0%	0%	4%

Flush Zone: 0"

☑ Single Word Justify

Cancel   OK

PUTTING IT ALL TOGETHER

The thrust of this feature is to create an H&J recipe that minimizes the number of hyphens that appear at the right margin of your text. The Standard H&J is set to these properties:

- **Standard H&J** Auto Hyphenation Enabled; Smallest Word: 6; Minimum Before: 3; Minimum After: 2; Don't Break Cap Words; Hyphens in a Row: Unlimited; Hyphenation Zone: 0"; Space Minimum: 85%; Optimal: 110%; Maximum: 250%; Character Minimum: 0%; Optimal: 0%; Maximum: 4%; Flush Zone: 0"; Justify Single Word.

  If you're not familiar with the terms used, this H&J feature might seem like secret code. In an effort to demystify these hyphenation options, the following terms may help:

- **Auto Hyphenation** With this option selected, the currently selected hyphenation settings are enabled. While not selected, hyphenation is essentially turned off. Auto Hyphenation is determined by entries in the main dictionary installed with the program and by the QuarkXPress automatic hyphenation algorithm. While enabled, the next three options are available.

- **Smallest Word** Enter the minimum number of characters a word must be comprised of to be eligible for Auto Hyphenation.

- **Minimum Before** When a word is split by an automatic hyphen, portions are left on two different text lines. Enter the smallest number of characters that may precede the hyphen. The higher the value, the easier the text will be to read, and the higher the risk poor word spacing may result in your text.

- **Minimum After** As with Minimum Before, enter the smallest number of characters that may follow a hyphen.

- **Hyphens in a Row** By default in the Standard H&J, this option is set to *Unlimited*, meaning potentially every line could end with a hyphen. Realistically, you may not really want this to happen. Setting this to 2 or 3 hyphens in a row is probably the most you would ever want to see in your text.

- **Hyphenation Zone** The hyphen zone is the area between the right margin of your text column and the space value you enter in this field. Any word in the hyphenation zone is fair game for a hyphen if its length spills over the right margin. Wide hyphenation zones increase the likelihood of hyphens, while shorter distances decrease this. The Standard H&J has a hyphenation zone of 0 inches.

Justification of your text is determined by the settings chosen in this area of the H&J dialog. Justification is divided into two main treatments: character and word spacing. These two properties may be adjusted in order for text to justify. The amount of adjustment to word and character spacing is determined by the settings you enter in the space fields.

- **Space Minimum, Optimal, Maximum**   Every font has its own degree of word spacing as an integral characteristic. The spacing options in these three fields enable you to set limits for the least and most amount of space QuarkXPress may add to or subtract from the original spacing, based on percentage. The Optimum space is used for lines that don't require adjustments to justify, such as left, right, and center alignments.

- **Char. Minimum, Optimal, Maximum**   As with word spacing, every font has its own degree of built-in character spacing. The spacing options here enable you to limit the percentage of space applied between characters. The Optimum value is also used for left, right, and center alignments.

- **Flush Zone:** The flush zone may sound like an uncomfortable place to eat your lunch, but it actually enables you to control whether a line that doesn't completely fill your column width is justified or not. The flush zone is measured from the right margin of your column and by default is set to 0 in the Standard H&J, meaning lines are not justified until they reach all the way to the right margin.

- **Justify Single Word:** Selecting this option (the default) enables QuarkXPress to justify words alone on a single line, or it essentially turns off justification where no word spaces exist. While this option is not selected, lines that contain a single word are left unjustified, even if they reside in the middle of a paragraph.

QuarkXPress users often pride themselves on their software's sophisticated capability to edit or customize kerning and tracking tables while in reality few users know how to do this properly. And if you haven't the need for change or experience in editing kerning and/or tracking tables, it may be best to leave these as is. Existing kerning and tracking tables in QuarkXPress serve many average applications well. Both kerning and tracking are controlled through use of the Kern-Track XTension.

Customizing Kerning

The controls for editing kerning tables are accessed by choosing Utilities, Kerning Edit. After choosing the command, you are presented with a dialog that enables you to select the font you wish to create a custom kerning table for. Once the font is selected, clicking Edit opens the Kerning tables for [*font name*] dialog (shown next).

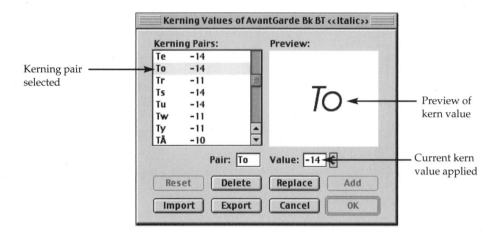

Kerning pair selected

Preview of kern value

Current kern value applied

On one side of the dialog are the available kern pairs to edit, while on the other side is a preview window that reflects the effects of applied values and command buttons for applying your editing changes. To adjust a kern pair, follow these steps:

1. Select the pair in the Kern Pair window or enter the pair in the Pair window. The pair appears in the preview window.

2. With the pair selected, edit the kern spacing by clicking the Value spinners or entering a value. Each time you click a spinner, the value changes the kerning by 1/200 ems within a range between −100/200 to 100/200 ems. Negative values reduce the kern space while positive values increase it.

3. To apply the changes, click the Replace button.

4. To restore the font to its original built-in kerning, click the Reset button.

5. To delete a kerning pair, highlight the pair and click DELETE.

6. Once you are finished editing the kerning table for your font, click OK to return to the first dialog, click Save to save your editing changes to the table, and close the dialog.

Tip *Saved kerning tables are stored in the Preferences folder within your QuarkXPress application folder.*

While the previous steps make kerning table editing seem simple, it is anything but. Kerning a font to appear uniformly kerned across all characters can take hours. But if you have knowledge and expertise in this area, the results can be rewarding. To ease some of the labor involved in creating and applying kerning pair edits, you may use the Import and Export buttons to save your kerning edits and apply them to other fonts. By clicking the Export button, you may save the information in your kerning table as an ASCII text file and reimport it for use with other fonts by clicking the Import button.

Customizing Tracking

The controls for editing the tracking table for a font are accessed by choosing Utilities | Tracking Edit. After choosing the command, you are presented with a dialog that enables you to select the font you wish to edit the tracking table for. Once the font is selected, clicking Edit opens the Tracking Values for [*font name*] dialog (shown next).

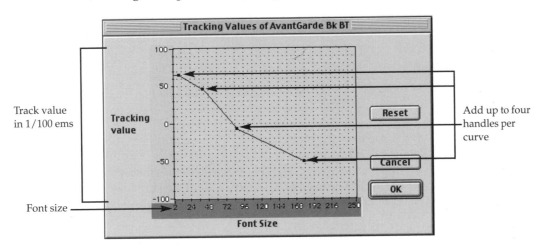

Track value in 1/100 ems

Font size

Add up to four handles per curve

As the graph illustrates, tracking values from 100/200 ems to 100/200 ems may be applied and measured at the left axis to fonts ranging in sizes from 2 to 250 points (measured along the bottom axis). A zero value indicates no tracking is applied to a font at a given size. The tracking curve may be manipulated by adding curve handles to it by clicking your cursor directly on the tracking curve. A curve may include up to four handles. Clicking the Reset button flattens to tracking curve to 0 for all font sizes.

To save edits to the tracking curve, click OK to return to the previous dialog and click Save to exit the Tracking Edit feature. Tracking applies whenever a font is used in QuarkXPress, regardless of whether you edited the tracking with a document open or closed.

To remove a curve handle from a tracking curve, hold OPTION/CTRL *while clicking on the handle.*

Kerning and tracking changes are saved to the Preference settings file of QuarkXPress. If you edit kerning and/or tracking and subsequently open a previously created document, QuarkXPress will warn you of changes to the Kern/Track values with the dialog shown next.

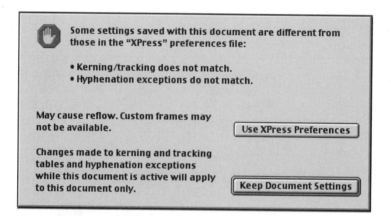

Unfortunately, to really see the results of your tracking, you will need to view text with the tracking in use. There is no preview feature in the dialog. If you edit the tracking for a particular font, be sure to edit the same tracking curve to each of the font's related styles. For example, if you edited Helvetica Plain, be sure to edit tracking for the Bold, Bold Italic, and Italic styles and any other variations you have in use.

The Complete Reference

QuarkXPress 5

Part IV

Beyond QuarkXPress Basics

The Complete Reference

QuarkXPress 5

Chapter 14

Designing in Color

In this chapter, our examination of QuarkXPress 5 moves deeply into the inner workings of color. Whether your QuarkXPress 5 documents are simple or complex, you may eventually be publishing them in one form or another, be it offset printing or online publishing. This chapter examines the higher functions of both QuarkXPress and color publishing. You'll learn to master the available color resources available to you and discover how to measure, apply, and customize color.

How QuarkXPress Displays and Prints Document Color

In the software world there is no shortage of ways in which you can measure and apply color. Color can be as simple or as complex as you need it to be, but before you venture too far into how XPress sees color, it may help to know a few of the limitations involved with working in color.

Although your eyes are able to detect a huge range of colors, your monitor and printer are only capable of reproducing a very small fraction of that range. And in cases where you use devices that record color, the limitations are similar. In an effort to recreate the color seen by input devices and those that you see on your computer and in print, various color standards have been established. If there were only a single application for color, the solutions would be simple. But with the variations that exist in today's publishing industry, each niche area has adopted its own specific brand of color.

For example, each color monitor has its own characteristics and capabilities, directly affecting how you view the colors on your screen, which may be perhaps where the complications begin. In the software world there are system colors, browser palettes, and platform issues to consider. And in the real world, there are various ink colors and reproduction methods. The easy solution is to become completely familiar with the specific color measurement system you deal with regularly and stick with it.

XPress, like other software applications, uses color measurement systems called *models*. Color models are mathematical definitions of color properties and vary in theory from model to model. Ultimately, you will be viewing all of the items on your document page, at least initially, by way of your monitor, which renders only in Red, Green, and Blue (RGB) color. And so, any of the color models you choose to work in will become RGB *interpretations* of those colors.

If your document is destined for offset reproduction, you'll likely be applying either spot or process color to your items. Although the Cyan, Magenta, Yellow, and Black (CMYK) color model enables you to measure, view, and formulate colors to apply to your items, it is merely a color model and not an organized color system. Although the CMYK color model enables you to create nearly any combination of process ink colors, the device you are printing your document to may not be capable of reproducing the complete range of ink percentages. For example, a low-end printing press using paper plates may not be capable of reproducing a 3 percent black screen without the screen dots fading away, nor might it be capable of producing a 97 percent black screen without the holes in the screen plugging up. The correct strategy to follow is either through an organized system of color such as the matching systems included with XPress or through consultation with your printing vendor.

Applying Color in Your Layouts

Colors are easily applied in XPress, but unlike other applications where various colors are immediately available, most colors in QuarkXPress must first be created and named in order for them to be available in dialogs and menus. Once a color exists though, you may apply it to nearly any item you wish using a variety of techniques.

Applying Color Using Menus and Dialogs

The first method we'll look at for applying color to layout items is via menus and dialogs. Applying color through command menus is perhaps the most straightforward method, but only one aspect of color may be applied at any one given time. Using dialogs may be less convenient, but multiple color properties may be defined in a single dialog. Suffice it to say, each has its pros and cons. Ultimately, using either of these techniques will be your own personal choice.

Because colors may be applied in many ways—to text, boxes, frames, lines, and dashes and stripes—there is no one all-encompassing procedure to follow when using menus or dialogs. Most commonly, colors are applied to lines, text, box backgrounds, or the box frames. Options for accomplishing any of these are all contained in various tabs of the Modify dialog, which changes to display tabs specific to the item (or group of items) selected.

As a practical exercise in applying color via the Modify dialog, try these quick steps:

1. In an open document, create a text box and add text to it.

2. Open the Measurements palette (F9) and use it to format your text. Notice the Measurements palette contains no color options.

3. Choose the Item tool (or hold CMD/CTRL) and double-click the text box to open the Modify dialog. Select the Frame tab and choose a width of 6 points. While still in the Frame tab, choose Black as the color and leave the Shade value at 100 percent (shown next).

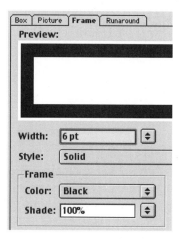

4. Click the Box tab and select Black as the color and 20 percent as the shade (shown next).

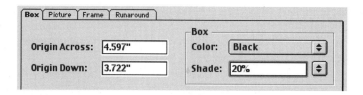

5. Click OK to accept the changes and close the dialog. Notice the text box frame and background colors you selected have been applied to the box, but the text remains unchanged at the default color (usually black).

6. Using the Content tool, click-drag to select a portion of the text you entered in the box. Choose Style | Color and choose White as your color choice. Then click anywhere within the text box to deselect the characters and notice the characters themselves have changed to white (shown next). Notice also that although some wouldn't consider either black or white actual colors, QuarkXPress categorizes them as actual colors.

Using the Colors Palette to Apply Color

The Colors palette in QuarkXPress is perhaps the most convenient resource to use when applying colors to lines, text, box frames, and box backgrounds. For the most part, the Colors palette is context sensitive, meaning options within the palette change to reflect the type of item selected.

Anatomy of the Colors Palette

The key areas to be concerned with when applying color to various parts of a selected item are located at the top of the palette. While a line is selected (be it a straight, curved, freehand, Bézier, orthogonal, or open or closed path line), the palette displays only a single line color option. While text or boxes are selected, the palette displays three mode buttons that, when pressed, display and control the applied color of various parts of the box. These include the Frame, Text, and Background color modes (as shown in Figure 14-1). While a picture box is selected, the options are less comprehensive, offering only options for controlling the frame and background color (since no text exists).

You'll also notice that two new symbols appear adjacent to the defined colors that the palette contains for any open document. These two symbols indicate the model used to define the type of color being displayed. One identifies spot colors, while the other identifies process (CMYK) color. For more information on what color models are and how they define types of colors, see "About Color Models" discussed later in this chapter.

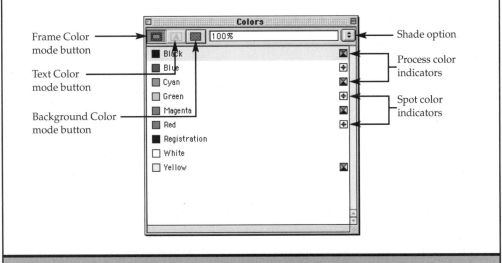

Figure 14-1.   *While a text box is selected, the Colors palette offers three modes of color control.*

While an item is selected, pressing one of the mode buttons displays the selected color in the palette as well as the shade properties applied (except in the case of white). While the Item or Content tools are in use and a box is selected, all three mode buttons are available; however, only while the Content tool is in use and text characters are currently selected does changing the color of text change the color of the text selection.

Applying Color Using the Colors Palette

If you're new to using the Colors palette to specify colors to items in your document, try these steps:

1. In an open document, create three different items on your page: a line, a picture box, and a text box containing a few characters of text. Be sure the text is large enough not to be greeked and that the line features a width large enough to be viewed easily at your current view magnification.

2. Open the Colors palette by choosing View | Colors (F12). The palette opens onto your screen and displays the currently defined default colors for your document.

3. Using the Item tool, click to select the line. Notice the Colors palette now features a Line mode button, which is selected by default (shown next). Click to select different selections in the Colors palette and notice how the line changes color. Choose (or enter) a value from the Shade menu and notice the line takes on a shade of the selected color.

Line mode selected ———→

4. Still using the Item tool, click to select the picture box, which should ideally be empty and contain no imported picture. Notice both the Frame and Background mode buttons in the Colors palette become available (shown next). Click the Frame mode button to display frame colors and click a color and/or shade. Notice the box frame color only changes immediately as you make your color choices.

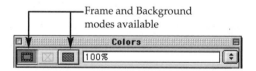

5. Click the Background mode button and click a background color and/or shade for your picture box. Notice that only the inside area of the picture box changes color.

6. Next, choose the Content tool and turn to your text box containing a few sample text characters. Using your cursor, click-drag to select some or all of the characters. Notice the Colors palette now features all three mode buttons available, including the Text mode (shown next). Make a selection in the Colors palette and notice the characters change color. The important thing to remember is that you must first *select* the characters in order for you to control their color. If you wish, follow the previous steps to apply a frame and background color to the text box.

Text mode selected ——

7. Finally, click to place your cursor between or at the end of the sample characters you entered in the text box. In the Colors palette, select a different color from the one currently selected. Notice nothing appears to change. Now type a few additional characters and notice the new characters are colored according to the current Colors palette color.

This is essentially the basic technique of applying colors to various types of items using the Colors palette. It provides a level of convenience over other techniques for applying color such as through the use of the command menus.

Creating New Colors

If you've just followed the previous exercises, you will likely have a colored text box with colored text on your page using colors you probably hadn't intended to use. What happens when you don't see the color you wish to use available in the list? The answer is to edit an existing color or add a completely new one.

Using the Colors Dialog to Create and Edit Colors

Colors may be defined and/or edited using the Colors for [*document name*] dialog, which is opened by choosing Edit | Colors (SHIFT+F12). Once the dialog is opened, you may view specific types of available colors in your document using the Show menu. Although a color is selected in the dialog, a detailed summary of the color's specifications is listed in the lower portion of the dialog. From here, you have the choice of creating a new color, duplicating or editing an existing (and selected) color, or appending color lists from other documents using command buttons found at the bottom of the dialog (see Figure 14-2).

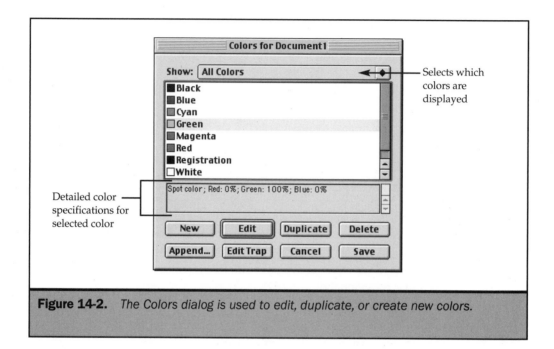

Selects which colors are displayed

Detailed color specifications for selected color

Figure 14-2.   *The Colors dialog is used to edit, duplicate, or create new colors.*

For the most part, the procedures for defining colors using either the Edit, Duplicate, or New command buttons in the dialog are similar. To define color specifications using any of these command buttons, follow these steps:

1. To create a new color, click the New button. The Edit Color dialog opens to reveal RGB color controls by default. To create a screen-only color, choose RGB | LAB | HSB from the Models drop-down menu and click a color in the color wheel. For a specific manufactured ink color, choose from either Pantone, Focoltone, Trumatch, Toyo, or DIC and select an ink color from the electronic catalog that appears by clicking on it once. For a specific browser-compatible color, choose from either Web Safe or Web Named Colors. For the sake of this example though, let's create a custom process color by choosing CMYK from the Models drop-down menu.

2. Pick a purple color from the color picker by clicking near the lower-right corner of the wheel or by entering a value of 20 percent in the C: field and 60 percent in the M: field (these two fields represent cyan and magenta ink colors), leaving 0 as the value in both the remaining Y: and K: fields (representing yellow and black), as shown in Figure 14-3.

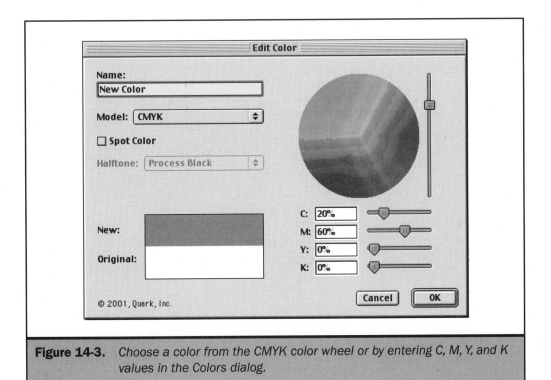

Figure 14-3. *Choose a color from the CMYK color wheel or by entering C, M, Y, and K values in the Colors dialog.*

3. Experiment with the effects of the Brightness slider by moving it up and down. Notice as you move the slider up, the color brightens and the values you entered change, as do the slider positions adjacent to the color fields. If necessary, reenter your C: and M: values after experimenting.

   Enter the name **Medium Purple** for your new color and uncheck the Spot Color option to allow this color to separate to different plates when printed. Leaving the Spot Color option selected forces the color to print as if it were on its own individual printing plate when your document colors are separated during printing.

5. Click OK to accept the properties for your new color and click Save in the Colors for [*document name*] dialog to save your color and to close the dialog.

6. In your open document, select any item and choose Item | Modify to open the Modify dialog and click either the Box or Frame tabs. Notice your new color now appears in the list of available colors from the Colors menu in either dialog (see Figure 14-4). You may now apply this color to items in your document.

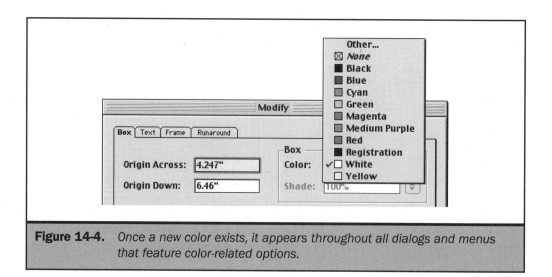

Figure 14-4. *Once a new color exists, it appears throughout all dialogs and menus that feature color-related options.*

> **Tip** *In the past, and still in some other software applications today, the naming scheme you use for your colors was critical to identifying their color type and makeup. Thankfully, QuarkXPress 5 eliminates this need by enabling you to sort and display colors and their details in the Colors for [document name] dialog. To sort and identify colors using this feature, choose Edit | Colors (SHIFT+F12) and use the Show drop-down menu to select All Colors, Spot Colors, Process Colors, Multi-ink Colors, Colors in Use, or Colors Not Used. To view details of a color, select it in the available colors list and read the description listed in the lower section of the dialog. Colors will be listed as Spot or Separated, and the color model and/or associated values will be listed.*

Defining colors associated with specific catalog-type swatch color collections in the Colors dialog is slightly different than defining RGB, HSB, LAB, or CMYK colors. From within the dialog, clicking either the Edit, Duplicate, or New command buttons and choosing either DIC, Focoltone, Pantone Hexachrome, Toyo, or Trumatch displays a listing of color samples categorized by name and/or color number according to how each of these colors is formulated.

In these cases, colors are defined simply by browsing the list and clicking to choose a color. These types of color come prenamed when selected, although you may apply your own custom name if you choose. For more information on choosing colors from these catalogs and the specifications of each, see "Using Matching System Color Swatches" later in this chapter.

Using the Colors Palette to Create and Edit Colors

Although you may open the Colors dialog directly by choosing Edit | Colors (SHIFT+F12), the Colors palette includes a few convenient shortcuts for editing, duplicating, or creating new colors.

As a practical example of creating colors to apply continuing from the exercise in the previous section, follow these steps:

1. To open the Colors dialog from directly within the Colors palette, hold CMD/CTRL while clicking any listed color in the palette. The Colors for [*document name*] dialog opens immediately, enabling you to define colors according to the procedure described in the previous section.

2. You may also create new colors or edit or duplicate selected colors listed in the Colors palette using context-sensitive popup menus from within the Colors palette. To do so, the technique differs slightly between platform versions. Macintosh users hold CTRL while clicking a color, while Windows users perform a right-click on a selected color to open the Colors for [*document name*] dialog and define colors according to the procedure described in the previous section. The popup menu (shown next) that appears also enables you to delete a color or convert its state between process or spot color.

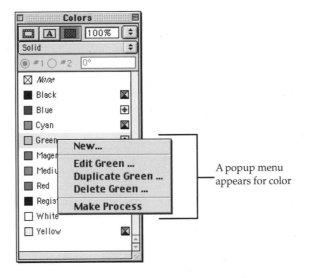

A popup menu appears for color

Tip

If you wish to use colors created in other documents in your current document without recreating them from scratch, use the Append command in the Colors for [document name] dialog to select and append colors. If you wish the colors you have created to be available for all documents and appear in your default available colors list, close all documents and repeat the append process.

Choosing Types of Color

With all these terms identifying spot, process, registration, and multi-ink colors mentioned, it may help to have a primer on exactly what these color types are, what they represent, and how they will affect the items they are applied to. Plus, there are other options you've seen in the dialogs that up to now have remained a mystery. This section explores specific properties you may apply to new or existing colors.

Using the Spot Color Option

When creating or editing a color using the Edit Colors dialog, you may set the color to print as a spot color regardless of whether you have specified a separated process color using one of the process color models such as CMYK, Pantone Process, Trumatch, Focoltone, or Hexachrome. Because of this fact, this option should be chosen with care and attention. For example, if your document is to be eventually reproduced in process colors only, selecting any of your process colors as spot will cause extra color plates to be created when your final CMYK separations are printed. Since the costs associated with printing separations to certain types of printers can be high, this can be a costly mistake if chosen in error.

Tip

You may quickly locate a specific color in any collection by entering its color number in the field below the color collection list.

By default, the Spot Color option is automatically checked when selecting any of the spot colors from Pantone Coated or Uncoated, Toyo, or DIC color collections. So, in this same regard, unchecking the Spot Color option for any of these colors will cause them to print as separated colors in a matching formula of process color percentages. This may also be a costly error if your actual intent is to use these ink colors as spot colors. For example, if your document is destined to be reproduced in two or three spot colors of ink, but one or more of your spot colors has been specified as process by unchecking the Spot Color option, you'll end up with four additional process color separation plates when the document is printed to separations.

If you require, you may quickly convert any color listed in the Colors palette from a spot to a process (or vice versa) using the context-sensitive popup menu by holding CTRL and clicking a color (Macintosh) or right-clicking a color (Windows) and choosing Make Spot or Make Process from the popup menu that appears. The state of the selected color will immediately be changed and indicated as either spot or process by the accompanying color symbol in the palette.

Setting the Halftone Color Option

While the Spot Color option is selected, the Halftone drop-down menu becomes available and contains choices for Process Cyan, Process Magenta, Process Yellow, and

Process Black. But the naming of this option may be slightly misleading or confusing. The real purpose of this option is to specify the *screen angle* of colors when the items in your document have been specified to print as a shade of the selected color. The screen angle is the angle at which dot percentages that compose the shades of ink colors are angled. Screen angles are measured in degrees.

When you select a specific color from the Halftone drop-down menu, you are actually setting screen angles to match process color screen angles, which (by default) print at the following settings:

Process Cyan: **105** degrees

Process Magenta: **75** degrees

Process Yellow: **90** degrees

Process Black: **45** degrees

Screen angles for process or spot colors may be overridden at the printing stage by settings in the printing device in use or through options in the Print dialog. For more information on setting spot and process screen angles, see "Choosing Output Options" in Chapter 17.

Setting Up Multi-ink Colors

If you've been working with desktop software equipped with color printing capabilities for more than a few years, you may be pleased to have access to this next feature. The Multi-ink feature enables you to create a single color composed of two or more different ink colors and apply them to a single item on your document page. When items are applied with a multi-ink color, the individual colors comprising the multi-ink color may be specified to print separately as individual color plates.

The procedure for creating a multi-ink color is slightly different from that of a single spot or process color. Multi-ink colors are selected by choosing them from the available colors list. So, to use a specific color, you must first create it and add it to the list. Once it's available, it may be used in a multi-ink color composition.

As a practical exercise in creating a multi-ink color based on two different spot colors not yet available in your current list of colors, follow these steps:

1. Open the Colors for [*document name*] dialog by choosing Edit | Colors (SHIFT+F12). The dialog opens.

2. For this exercise, you'll create a single multi-ink color based on yellow and blue spot colors, which will in essence enable you to create a shade of green to apply to items in your document. Click the New button to create the first color. The Edit Colors dialog opens.

3. Choose Pantone Coated from the Models drop-down menu and select Pantone CV 106 (a yellow color) from the color collection that appears. Notice the name

automatically appears in the Name field and the Spot Color option is automatically selected.

4. Click OK to add the color to your currently available colors list and close the current dialog.

5. Click New a second time, select Pantone Coated again, choose Pantone 292 CV (a blue color) from the color collection, and click OK to close the dialog and add this second color to your list.

6. Click New a third time, this time to create your final multi-ink color. Choose Multi-ink from the Models drop-down list and notice the colors you just created are both present in the list that appears on the right of the dialog (see Figure 14-5). By default, all colors are currently applied with *no* shade, meaning your current multi-ink color contains no ink colors. Notice the Spot Color option in the dialog is also unavailable while Multi-ink is selected. This indicates the multi-ink color you are specifying may not be printed to a single plate when your document is printed, meaning the colors will separate to their own individual plates and the halftone screen angle will be controlled by the options set for the individual multi-ink colors.

7. Observe that above the colors are two column labels, one for the color name and one for shade.

8. Select Pantone 106 CV in the list and click the Shade button. Set the shade to 100 percent by selecting 100 from the drop-down menu that appears. Notice the New area to the lower-left changes to reflect the change in color, indicating yellow.

9. Select Pantone 292 CV in the list, click the Shade button, and set the shade to 100 percent. Notice the New area to the lower-left changes to reflect the change in color, now indicating green.

10. Enter a name for your new color in the Name field, such as "Multi-ink green."

11. Click OK to add the color to exit the dialog and to add it to your colors list.

12. Before clicking Save to save your new colors, click on the multi-ink color you just created and observe its details at the bottom of the dialog. Notice it describes the color as "Multi-Ink color; Components: 100% PANTONE 106 CV; and 100% PANTONE 292 CV."

Tip   *When combining spot colors from different color models for a multi-ink to create a single color, avoid mixing spot colors from different matching systems such as Pantone, Toyo, and DIC. Because of their different color and ink coverage properties, rarely do print vendors use different brands of ink in a printed job.*

With a multi-ink color created, you may now apply it to various items in your document, such as backgrounds of boxes, frames, lines, dash and stripe patterns, and so

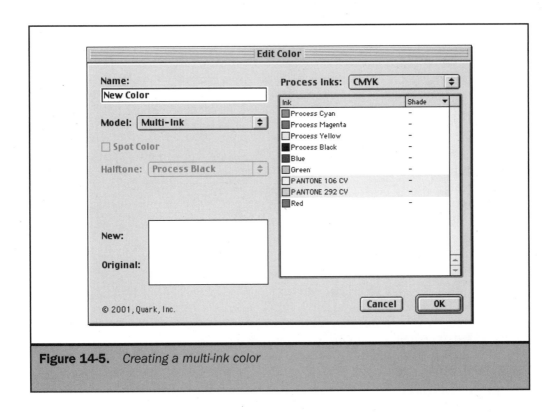

Figure 14-5. *Creating a multi-ink color*

on. Because you are combining two colors of ink, you will now be capable of creating a third color for items in your document without the expense of printing a third ink color. You may even apply the multi-ink color in percentages by specifying shade values.

What Is "Registration" Color?

You may have already noticed in your list of available colors a listing named Registration. The availability of this color is both a blessing and a curse if you aren't aware of its effects. Applying an item with Registration has the effect of forcing the item to appear on all printed plates when your document colors are separated during printing. By default, Registration appears as black on your screen; set to RGB colors 0%, 0%, and 0% respectively.

The purpose of setting items to appear on all plates enables you to use any item as a registration element while still positioned on or close to your page. This definitely has its advantages when printing your document pages to a printing device that cannot include the usual registration marks (which appear by default outside of your page dimensions). Creating registration marks outside your printed page is a method often used when printing to sheet-fed offset printing presses where the final printed product will be physically trimmed to a given size.

High-volume, lower-quality flyers or newspapers use Registration color to enable registration since this type of printing is fed by web-type printing presses where the final printed product isn't trimmed to size.

The curse of using Registration arises if you apply it to an item in error. When an item in your document prints on all separation plates instead of only the one you intended, it often causes a printing puzzle that is difficult to solve, and the mistakes can be costly if your document needs to be reprinted to correct the error.

Note   *The Registration color in QuarkXPress 5 may not be edited or deleted from the list of available colors in your document or from the default list.*

Applying Color Blends to Text and Picture Boxes

The ability to apply color blends to items in your document page certainly opens the doors for more than a little design and creative ingenuity. Blends may be applied to any closed-path item, such as various shapes of text and picture boxes, Bézier shapes, text converted to boxes, and all variations between.

Applying a blend to an item in XPress causes a smooth gradation between two colors. The colors you blend may be any of those you have created in your available colors list. Blends may be applied using either the Modify | Box tab dialog (see Figure 14-6) or the Background mode of the Colors palette. In certain instances, the blend feature may enable you to blend from a spot color to a process color, between two process or spot colors, or from one multi-ink color to another. Blends may also be set with certain angles or rotations depending on the type of blend selected.

Tip   *In order for the entire list of blends discussed here to be available to you, you must have the Cool Blends XTension listed as Active in the XPress XTensions Manager. If the XTension is not listed in the XTensions Manager, install it from the XPress program disc using the Import command. After importing, you will need to quit and relaunch XPress in order for Cool Blends to be available.*

With Cool Blends active in the XTensions Manager, QuarkXPress 5 enables you to formulate and apply six basic styles of blends. Along with the definitions and examples that follow, you'll find color examples of each of these blend styles in the color section of this book.

Linear Blends

The Linear blend style enables you to blend in an even gradation between two colors at any angle. The gradation of color occurs at a steady rate starting at color #1 on one side

Modify

Box | Text | Frame | Runaround

Origin Across: 1.34"

Origin Down: 6.511"

Width: 0.265"

Height: 0.184"

Angle: 0°

Skew: 0°

Corner Radius: 0"

☐ **Suppress Printout**

Box

Color: Cyan

Shade: 100%

Blend

Style: Linear Blend

Angle: 0°

Color: Black

Shade: 100%

[Apply]   [Cancel]   [OK]

Figure 14-6.   *Blend options in the Box tab of the Modify dialog*

of your object and continuing to color #2 on the other side (as shown next). The distance between the two sides determines how much space it takes for one color to gradate to the other. The less space the colors have to blend with each other, the less smooth the blend will appear. Entering a degree value between 0 and 180 or choosing one of the preset angles (0, 45, 90, 135, or 180 degrees) enables you to set an angle for the blend.

When using the Modify | Box tab dialog to apply blends, the box color serves as color #1, while the blend color serves as color #2.

Mid-Linear Blends

The Mid-Linear blend style enables you to create a blend of color where color #1 blends to color #2 at the mid-distance of the box shape and then blends back to color #1 at the far side of the box (shown next). Again, the blend smoothness is determined by the size of the box. Entering a degree value between 0 and 180 or choosing one of the preset angles (0, 45, 90, 135, or 180 degrees) in the Angle menu field enables you to set an angle for the blend.

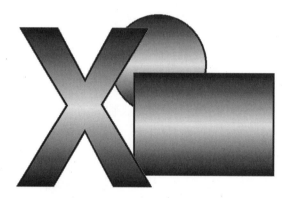

Rectangle Blends

This and the Diamond blend are perhaps the more stylized of the blend styles. The Rectangle blend style begins blending from color #2 to the color at the center of the box shape and blends outwards in a square or rectangular shape to color #1 until reaching the edges of your box shape (shown next). The resulting shape of the blend is determined by the overall proportions of your box shape. Entering a degree value between 0 and 180 or choosing one of the preset angles (0, 45, 90, 135, or 180 degrees) in the Angle menu field enables you to rotate the blend effect within the box shape.

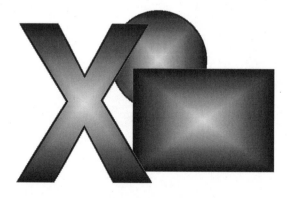

Diamond Blends

The Diamond style creates a blend in a similar way to the Rectangle style, beginning at color #2 in the center and blending to color #1 outward until reaching the outside edges of the box shape (shown next). The shape of the Diamond blend is determined by the overall proportions of the box shape. Entering a degree value between 0 and 180 or choosing one of the preset angles (0, 45, 90, 135, or 180 degrees) in the Angle menu field enables you to rotate the blend effect within the box shape.

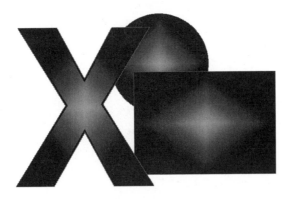

Circular Blends

The Circular blend style creates a circular-shaped blend beginning at color #2 in the center and blending outward to the edges of your box (shown next). Entering a degree value between 0 and 180 or choosing one of the preset angles (0, 45, 90, 135, or 180 degrees) in the Angle menu field enables you to control how quickly the blend effect occurs. Higher values cause the blend to occur more slowly, while lower values cause it to occur more quickly.

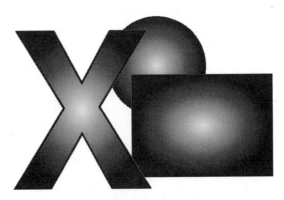

Full-Circular Blends

The Full-Circular blend style behaves nearly identically to the Circular blend style. It creates a circular-shaped blend beginning at color #2 in the center and blending outward to the edges of your box (shown next). But in this case, the blend occurs more naturally and more smoothly (as shown in the following examples) than for that of the Circular style. Entering a degree value between 0 and 180 or choosing one of the preset angles (0, 45, 90, 135, or 180 degrees) in the Angle menu field enables you to control how quickly the blend effect occurs. Higher values cause the blend to occur more slowly, while lower values cause it to occur more quickly.

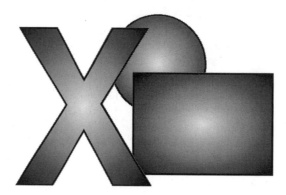

Applying Color Blends Using the Colors Palette

Besides being having the ability to formulate blends in the Modify dialog, you may also use the Colors palette (F12) while a box item is selected and while the palette is selected to display the Background color options (see Figure 14-7).

As a practical exercise in defining a blend using the Colors palette, follow these steps:

1. In an open document, create any box shape using either a text or picture box tool.

2. If you haven't already done so, open the Colors palette by choosing View | Colors (F12).

3. Select the box you just created by clicking it, and click the Background mode button in the Colors palette. By default, the drop-down menu that appears reads Solid.

4. Choose Linear Blend from the drop-down menu. Notice two color option buttons appear below the drop-down menu.

5. Click the #1 button, click a color in the list, and choose a shade for the starting color of the blend.

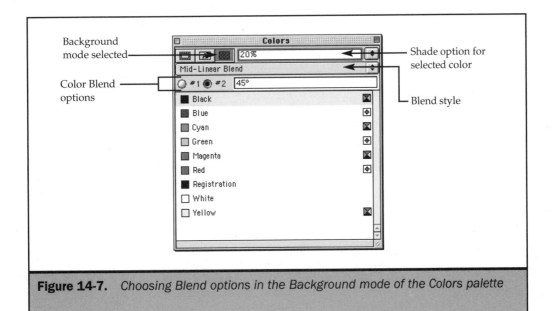

Background mode selected

Shade option for selected color

Color Blend options

Blend style

Figure 14-7. *Choosing Blend options in the Background mode of the Colors palette*

6. Click the #2 button, click a color in the list, and choose a shade for the ending color of the blend. Your box blend appears immediately.

7. By default, your blend angle is set to 0 degrees, meaning it is vertically oriented. Enter a new angle for your blend by entering 180 in the Angle field. Your box is now blended in the opposite direction.

8. Set the blend on an angle now by entering 45 in the Angle field. Your blend now occurs at the specified angle.

9. Apply a new blend style now by selecting Mid-Linear from the drop-down menu. The effect is immediate and your box now features more realistic-looking depth.

10. Choose Diamond from the drop-down menu and observe the effects. Enter a different rotational value by returning the blend to 0 degrees (enter 0 in the Angle field).

11. Next, choose Circular from the drop-down menu and observe the results.

12. Adjust the blend by entering 45 in the degree field and notice the blend now occurs more slowly than before.

Tip   *To remove a blend applied to a box, choose Solid from the drop-down menu in the Colors palette. The applied blend will immediately be changed to a solid color.*

About Color Models

As mentioned earlier, color models (or color spaces as they are sometimes referred) enable you and your software to measure, display, and apply consistent and reproducible color. The most significant point to remember when working with color models is that they merely provide a way to measure color and are not colors collections themselves (except for Multi-ink). To create and apply a color in XPress, you must first create the color as a named color style. This can be done by first selecting Edit | Colors (SHIFT+F12) and clicking either the Edit button (to change the values of an existing color) or New to open the Edit Color dialog, shown in Figure 14-8 with the RGB color model selected.

Earlier on in this chapter, you learned to create new colors according to the needs of your document and reproduction methods, but now let's closely examine the principles of how color in QuarkXPress 5 is measured and displayed. There are four basic color models included in QuarkXPress 5, each accessed from the Models drop-down menu from within the Edit Color dialog. QuarkXPress also features the Multi-ink model, which has its own specialized use. The color models' functions and operations are defined next.

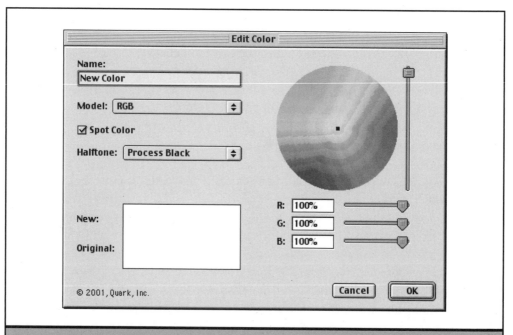

Figure 14-8. *Specifying an RGB color in the Edit Color dialog*

RGB Color

When it comes to your monitor and what you see on your screen, the RGB color model is the master model of all color. Your monitor renders color using the RGB model on a full-time basis, regardless of which color model your items have been formatted with. CRT monitors use an RGB color gun to project color to your screen, while essentially interpreting the particular color model you have selected to use. The RGB color model is based on transmitted or additive color, divided into units of red, green, and blue light in values ranging from 0 to 100 percent.

Combined RGB values of red = 100 percent, green = 100 percent, and blue = 100 percent will produce pure white. All RGB values set to 0 percent will render pure black. Color values may be changed interactively using the three color sliders and the Brightness slider. Raising or lowering the Brightness slider has the effect or raising or lowering the percentage values of all three RGB values simultaneously.

The operations of the RGB color model interface controls are similar to those for HSB, LAB, and CMYK color models with slight variations for the specific colors involved.

HSB Color

The HSB color model measures color in terms of the transmitted color values of hue (the actual color), saturation (the amount of color), and brightness (the intensity or the amount of white) in the color. Hue is measured in degrees according to the color's position on the color wheel, which is divided into 360 degrees, beginning at a value of 0 at the three o'clock position and increasing counterclockwise. Saturation and brightness are measured in color ranging from 0 to 100 percent. In this color model, the Brightness slider is redundant with the brightness percentage value.

LAB Color

The LAB color model is defined by luminance (L) and chromatic components A and B, or color ranges from red to green (A) and blue to yellow (B). LAB color is a standard that first originated with the Commission Internationale d'Eclairage (CIE) in 1931 and is a model designed to render accurate color independent of the device outputting the image (a monitor, printer, or scanner). This color model is perhaps the most widely used model for color translation between software applications and is sometimes referred to as CIELAB. Colors in this model are described numerically, which is critical to the way color mode conversions are calculated during display and printing. Luminance is divided into values ranging from 0 percent (darkest) to 100 percent (lightest), while the A and B components may range in color unit values between -120 and 120. The Brightness slider has the effect of increasing or decreasing the luminance value, while making only slight changes to the A and B color component values.

Reproduction and translation to RGB screen color and CMYK color conversion in XPress 5 are achieved through LAB color space conversion.

CMYK Color

If you work in offset printing, you may already be aware of the importance of the CMYK color model. The abbreviation CMYK represents color based on the four-color ink method used in traditional web and offset printing. The four basic colors measured in this color model are cyan, magenta, yellow, and black. Each color is divided into percentages ranging from 0 to 100. As with other models, cyan, magenta, and yellow values may be selected by manipulating their respective slider controls or by picking a color in the color wheel. In this color model, the Brightness slider has the effect of changing not only the black color component, but it also increases or decreases the values of C, M, and Y ink colors.

 To obtain an equivalent color across color models or the matching systems discussed in the following section, select the original color first from a color model or matching system and then immediately select the color or matching system you wish for the equivalent color. The XPress Color dialog will automatically display the closest or equivalent color.

Multi-ink Colors

Choosing Multi-ink enables you to combine colors created and based on either CMYK or Hexachrome process colors, and then combine them with other process colors or spot colors to create a color that may be applied in various percentages to items in your document. To learn more about the tricky procedure for creating a multi-ink color, refer to "Setting Up Multi-ink Colors."

Using Matching System Color Swatches

You might assume that the remaining selections under the Models drop-down menu measure color, while in fact there is a subtle difference not indicated as such in the dialog. Although the first four selections of RGB, LAB, HSB, and CMYK measure color, these selections are actually called matching systems. A matching system is a collection of colors that displays in RGB on your monitor, but may be set to print as specified ink colors. The term matching system actually stems from the fact that each of these systems is supported by printed hard copy sample books called color swatches to refer to the actual printed inks. Each of these color systems has its own specialized method for identifying specific colors. Using a matching system is more reliable than judging ink colors from how they appear on your monitor.

XPress 5 includes 13 different matching systems, including Multi-ink, Toyo, DIC, Trumatch, Focoltone, Pantone Process, Pantone Process Uncoated, Pantone Matte,

Pantone Coated, Pantone Solid to Process, Pantone Uncoated, Hexachrome Uncoated, and Hexachrome Coated. The matching system you choose depends on how your document will eventually be reproduced. And since these swatches are developed and distributed by different competing companies, their properties vary widely.

Pantone Swatches

The largest and most comprehensive color matching system of them all is offered by Pantone, one of the first internationally recognized color standardization systems to dominate the printing industry. Pantone was on the scene long before digital color fell into the hands of the general public. The Pantone electronic palettes found in programs such as QuarkXPress 5 are supported by a hard-copy collection of high-quality color swatches available in both uncoated and coated paper stock versions. The Pantone electronic process color collection contains more than 3,000 different colors, all of which claim to fall in the printable screen range. Colors are composed of screen percentages ranging from 0 to 100 in 3- and 5-percent increments. The Pantone electronic spot color collection (see Figure 14-9) contains over 220 different colors. Pantone spot colors also display the process color equivalent in the CMYK fields, if you switch to a CMYK color model.

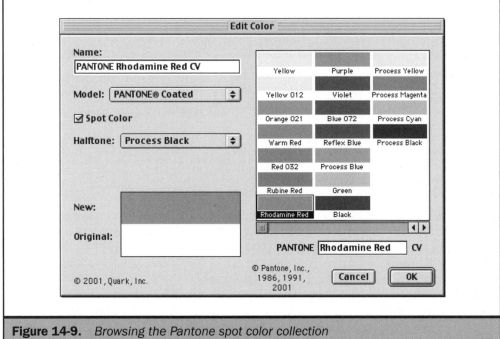

Figure 14-9. *Browsing the Pantone spot color collection*

The Pantone process color palette contains more than 3,000 different printable colors and the Pantone spot color palette contains more than 220 different colors.

Pantone uses its own numbering system for process colors. The coding is geared toward locating the colors on their hard-copy printed swatches. For example, an ink color such as S 97-1 may be recognized first by S, which indicates that SWOP inks were used for print reproduction. The letter is followed by the numeral 97, indicating the page number of the color swatch. The last number, 1, indicates the position counted down from the top of that page. All colors are arranged in chromatic order according to the natural-light spectrum, and each page contains nine tints.

 Pantone's Solid to Process color matching system enables you to select the closest possible process colors based on your choice of spot colors, without the need for purchasing a spot-to-process conversion swatch.

The inclusion of Pantone's electronic spot and process colors in XPress is just the tip of the iceberg when it comes to the full extent of their entire matching system. The complete Pantone matching system includes a line of slickly packaged products, including color formula guides, color selectors, color-specifying chips, color tint selectors, color foil selectors, color papers, markers and inks, transfer systems, and digital color imaging software to name just a few.

 *If you would like to contact Pantone for more information about their products, see their web site at **www.pantone.com** or contact one of their three worldwide offices as follows:*

Pantone, Inc.: 590 Commerce Boulevard, Carlstadt, New Jersey, 07072-3098, Tel: (201) 935-5500, Fax: (201) 896-0242

Pantone UK, Inc.: 115 Sandgate Road, Folkstone, Kent, CT20 2BL, England, Tel: 44-0303-259959, Fax: 0303-259830

Pantone, Asia: Room 904, New World Tower, 16-18 Queen's Road Central, Hong Kong, Tel: (852) 845-8388, Fax: (852) 845-7841

About Toyo and DIC Swatches

The Toyo and Dianippon Ink and Chemicals, Inc. (DIC) color matching systems are widely used in Asia and other Pacific rim countries, especially Japan. Each contains its own numbering system and collection of different process colors. The Toyo collection of colors (see Figure 14-10) has been developed using Toyo's own special process ink colors that vary in density and color from other standard process color inks.

The DIC color system has been developed using DIC's brand of process color inks and is divided into three categories of color, including DIC, DIC Traditional, and DIC Part II. When the DIC color samples are viewed (see Figure 14-11), the DIC category is identified by asterisks accompanying the associated color number. Standard DIC colors

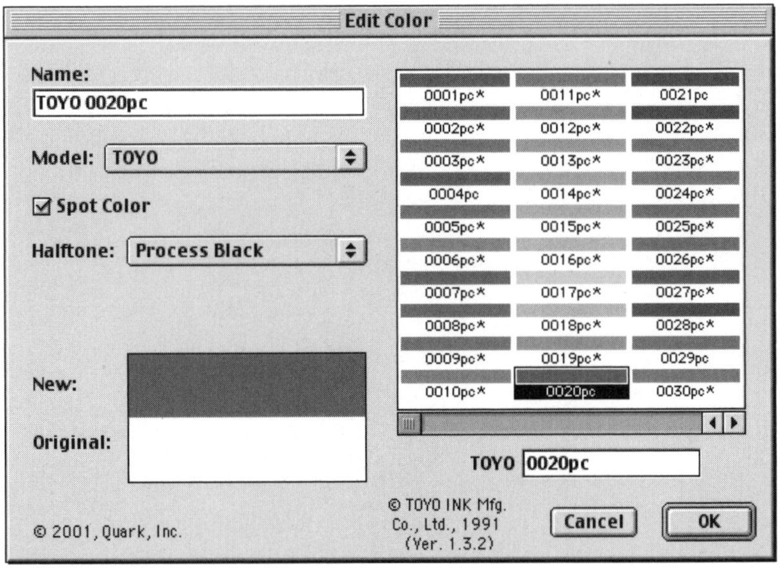

Figure 14-10. *Choosing Toyo from the Models menu displays Toyo's color catalog.*

are identified with no associated asterisk, while DIC Traditional is identified by one asterisk (*) and DIC Part II is identified by two asterisks (**).

Trumatch Swatch

The Trumatch color matching system is composed of over 2,000 easily printable colors. Trumatch has specifically customized their color matching system to suit the digital color industry, using the Computer Electronic Prepress System (CEPS). The collection of colors is comprised of 40 tints and shades of each hue (see Figure 14-12). Black is varied in 6 percent increments.

As with other color matching system vendors, Trumatch has also developed their own numbering system. For example, a green color that is numbered Trumatch 23-C2 can be tracked by its number. The first number indicates a particular hue value. Hues are numbered sequentially around the color wheel of the visible color spectrum. The following letter indicates the tint of the hue graduated from A or 100 percent to H or 5 percent screens. The number following the letter indicates the percentage of black present. Black is divided up into 6 percent increments from a 0 value, indicated by no number, to 42 percent indicated by the number 7.

Edit Color

Name:
DIC 19p*

Model: DIC

☑ Spot Color

Halftone: Process Black

New:

Original:

1p	11p*	21p
2p	12p*	22p
3p	13p*	23p
4p*	14p*	24p
5p*	15p*	25p
6p*	16p*	26p*
7p	17p*	27p
8p	18p*	28p
9p	19p*	29p*
10p	20p	30p*

DIC 19p*

© 2001, Quark, Inc.

© Dainippon Ink &
Chemicals, Inc.,
1991

Cancel   OK

Figure 14-11. *Choosing DIC from the Models menu displays the DIC color ink catalog.*

The Trumatch numbering system may take some time to get used to. Trumatch has designed and printed process color swatches composed of coated and uncoated versions, printed using a standard set of Standard Web Offset Printing (SWOP) inks using a common screen frequency of 150-line. The printed Trumatch colors are broken down into YMCK; they are ordered differently to match the order in which the process inks are printed. Most other color matching systems are broken down into CMYK, which indicates a different printing order.

Although Trumatch is a relative newcomer to the digital color world and new as far as color matching systems go, their system is quite solid and well conceived. Trumatch palettes can be seen in other software products such as CorelDRAW, Photoshop, Illustrator, Freehand, PageMaker, PhotoStyler, and Micrografx Designer. The Trumatch technology has also been adopted by imagesetter manufacturers such as CreoScitex, Linotype-Hell, and Du Pont.

Trumatch can be reached at 50 East 72nd Street, Suite 15B, New York, NY, 10021, Tel: (800) TRU-9100 (800-878-9100), Fax: (212) 517-2237 from within the U.S. or Canada.

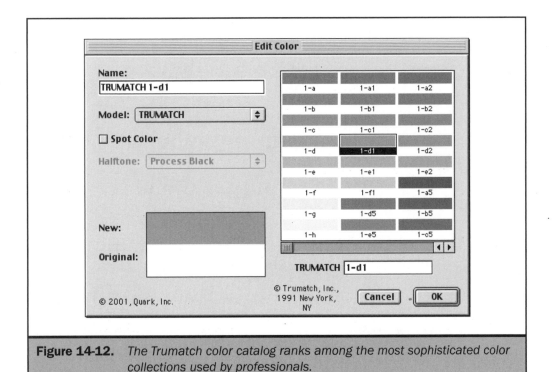

Figure 14-12. *The Trumatch color catalog ranks among the most sophisticated color collections used by professionals.*

Focoltone Swatch

The Focoltone color matching system has been in existence for years. Focoltone, a European-based company, designed this 750-color palette to reduce much of the need for tedious color trapping. The Focoltone color collection shown in Figure 14-13 works by standardizing CMYK screen percentages to 5 percent increments. The thrust of this standardization is to increase the likelihood of common, color screen percentages by reducing the variety of screens used. The Focoltone matching system has been arranged in such a way that a full spectrum of colors is displayed on the palette at any given point.

Focoltone's head offices are located in the United Kingdom. Contact their sales offices by phone at 44-0785-712677 or by fax at 44-0785-714587. Their main office number is 44-0222-810940, and their fax number is 44-0222-810962.

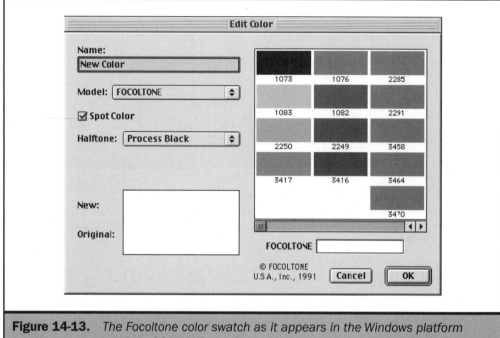

Figure 14-13. *The Focoltone color swatch as it appears in the Windows platform version of QuarkXPress 5*

Hexachrome Swatch

The Hexachrome system has been developed by Pantone and is relatively new in comparison to the others. Hexachrome is based on technology that enables high-fidelity or hi-fi color matching systems that consist of colors printed with six process colors instead of the standard four, hence the name. Orange and green are added to the CMYK plates to create more impact and increase the range of reproducible colors. Hexachrome printing is far more costly than printing ordinary process color, while for many designers, printing to process color is often a luxury in itself. The selection scheme for Hexachrome colors is shown in Figure 14-14.

Because Hexachrome printing requires that six inks overlap each other at various angles, the ink coverage, density, and screening angles are quite different from that of usual process-color printing. Be sure to consult with your printing vendor before applying Hexachrome ink colors to items in your document.

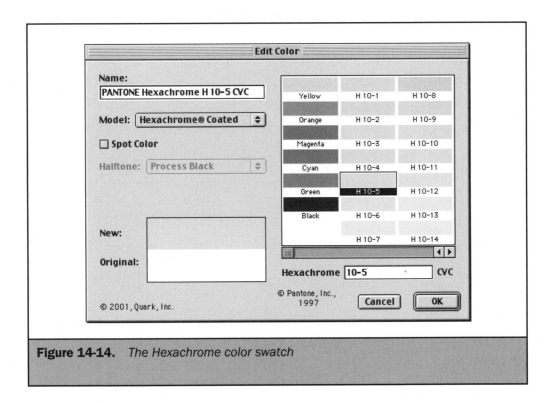

Figure 14-14. *The Hexachrome color swatch*

Color can add dramatic impact to your documents, and if you have the luxury of using it, you'll want to squeeze as much creative freedom as possible from the ability to use it. This chapter has explored both the technical side of color and the creative possibilities of color in XPress. Because QuarkXPress 5 has superior power when it comes to preparing documents destined for offset printing, you've seen how many of the issues surrounding color are directly tied to printing your documents.

The
Complete
Reference

QuarkXPress
5

Chapter 15

Color Trapping Basics

Understanding the concept of trapping is certainly not for the meek. Even tradespeople who have been in the prepress industry for years will stop dead in their tracks and think for a moment when faced with questions regarding color trapping. If you're new to the subject, you'll need a clear head and a quiet spot where you can absorb some of the logistical theory behind trapping and use the tools in XPress to control it.

In early desktop technology, color trapping desktop-created documents was a disaster to put it mildly. Developers neatly avoided the entire issue, opting instead to leave trapping to the user through content workarounds and plenty of grief. In time, the problem was partly overcome through highly specific automated "prepress" software capable of interpreting color desktop files and applying trapping values to color items. What many designers and electronic artists discovered was that trapping was not entirely an automatic process, and rarely could these applications correctly interpret and apply all instances of trapping.

In this chapter, you'll learn what trapping is and whether it's even something you need to be concerned about. If it is a concern, you'll learn about all the automated features and manually applied options in QuarkXPress 5 that enable you to apply trapping to color items in your document. You'll learn the three levels on which trapping may be controlled and some strategies to use when approaching the trapping stage of preparing your document for print.

Exactly What Is Color Trapping?

The terms and phrases involved in describing trapping operations can easily be confusing to newcomers to this prepress science. But believe it or not, although the terms may be foreign, the practical application is relatively straightforward. Perhaps this simple analogy will help.

Imagine placing both your hands side by side to cover an item on the desk or table in front of you. Try to place your hands closely together so that none of the item below is visible between them. Notice if you shift the position of your hands, the chances of the item becoming visible increase. Now overlap the edges of your hands where they meet while still covering the item and shift the position of your hands slightly again. With your hands slightly overlapping, the likelihood of the item below becoming visible is decreased. This is essentially trapping in the most simplistic sense.

If you've ever had the opportunity to see poor-quality printing, you may have experienced firsthand the results of poor press registration and poorly trapped color. Comic books you may have read as a child may come to mind. Imagine the black outline of a comic book character whose various illustrative colors are slightly out of alignment. When inks print out of register, gaps or color shifts appear between objects (see Figure 15-1).

Poor color registration and color trapping are two issues that are interconnected. Color registration is the process of correctly aligning multiple colors of ink on the

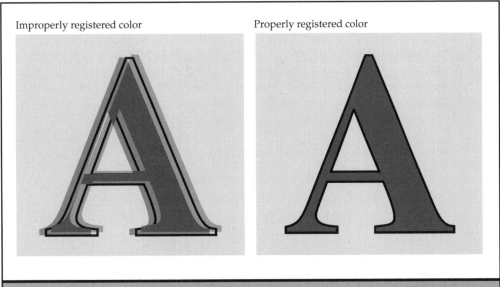

Improperly registered color   Properly registered color

Figure 15-1. *The visual result of both improperly and properly registered inks after printing*

printed page, while color trapping is the process of creating slight overlaps where colors in your document meet. Trapping compensates for misregistration by slightly expanding one adjacent color into another.

Consider for a moment the forces at work against color inks aligning in printing. As the printing press is running at high speeds, it vibrates, causing rollers and guides to misalign and paper to shift position. Temperature and humidity changes in the press room also affect the material your document is being printed onto. The more sophisticated the printing machinery is, the less readily this happens, but these issues are always factors to consider when preparing a multicolor document for print.

Color registration can occur any time a multicolored document is reproduced. Not only is this an issue when reproducing documents on a conventional offset printing press, but also when a document is silk-screened, stamped, or lithographed.

Also, the larger the size of the printed document and the color shapes being printed, the less noticeable misregistration is. And the larger the color shapes in your document are, the more opportunity you will have to build in color traps in order to reduce misregistration. Color shapes may be any item on your document page such as text and picture boxes, lines and shapes, and the various colored parts they are composed of. For example, the trapping values associated with a document such as a postage stamp will be much smaller and more difficult to print than that of a transit bus sign.

Once color trapping has been set up (either manually, automatically, or as a combination of both), the next step is preparing your document for printing by generating color separations. In all likelihood, you'll also need to prepare a color proof of the separations to check color accuracy, registration, and trapping. Color proofing often involves creating color acetate overlays of the separated film output in an effort to create a *match print* or *color key*. Match prints are often preferred over color keys because of the fact that they reflect accurate color.

Is Trapping Really Necessary?

Whether you need to allow for trapping your document depends on your answers to a number of questions you may need to ask yourself:

- Is the document destined to print in more than one color?
- Do different colors meet at any point on your pages?
- Is there a possibility the press will poorly register these colors?

If your answer to all of these questions is *no*, then proceed to the next chapter. If you answer *yes* just once, you'll need to consider applying color traps either throughout your entire document or to individually selected items. How you proceed depends on how extensive the color printing is, how many colors are involved, and the capabilities of the offset press printing your document.

Note *When determining whether you need to do specific trapping beyond Quark's default, it's also important to check with your service bureau where the final product will be output. They may prefer to do the trapping on the file, or they may have guidelines they require you to follow.*

There will, of course, be instances where you don't need to or can't color trap your document. For example, if there is a single process color photograph in the document that does not feature any type of frame, isn't positioned over the top of a color background, or doesn't meet with any other color items on the page, then it won't be possible to trap the process colors, even though the person operating the press would love to have a black frame around the photograph to hide any improper ink registration.

Understanding Traps and Trap Terms

To understand trapping and the terms used to describe certain types of trap situations, you'll need to take a close look at a few simple trap examples using color shapes. The following points define the most common trapping terms you'll encounter with visual examples of each. Since the pages you see here are reproduced in black and white, these examples are repeated in the color section of this book. Try to imagine them in color here or refer to the full-color examples for clarity.

- **Trap**   The term *trap* describes adding a small portion or area to a shape to reduce the hazards of poor color registration. Shapes of different colors are trapped in a direction from the lighter color to the darker color in such a way that the two colors overlap.

- **Spread**   When two colors meet in a situation where the lighter-colored shape is positioned in front of the darker-colored shape, portions are added to the edges of the lighter-colored shape in order to *spread* into the darker color. Figure 15-2 shows an example of a basic color trapping spread.

- **Choke**   When two shapes meet in a situation where the darker-colored shape is positioned in the foreground and the lighter-colored shape is in the background, the lighter background is *choked* where the two colors meet, meaning the lighter background's edges overlap into the darker shape's edges where the two shapes meet, as shown in Figure 15-3.

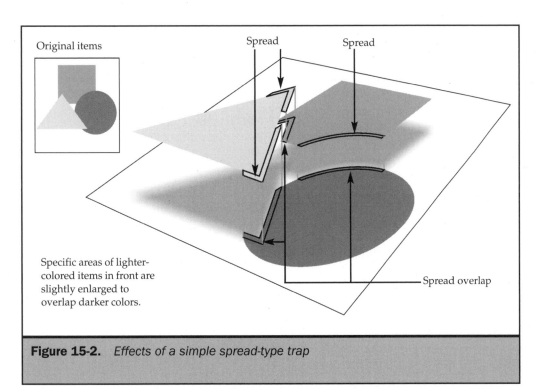

Figure 15-2.   *Effects of a simple spread-type trap*

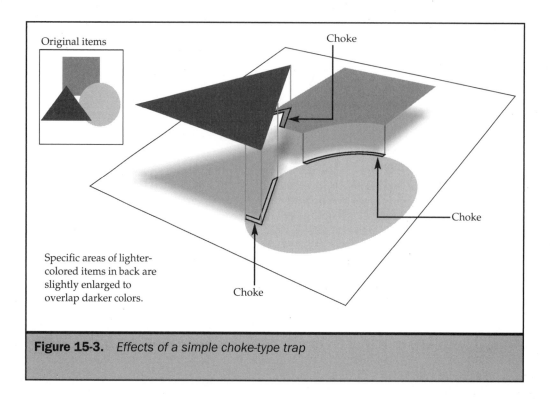

Figure 15-3. *Effects of a simple choke-type trap*

- **Overprint**   As the name implies, when one colored item overlaps and *overprints* another item of a different color, the ink coverage in the areas where the two shapes overlap is combined, as shown in Figure 15-4. In other words, one ink color prints on top of another. Overprinting can cause the two colors to combine to create the illusion of a third ink color, which can cause unexpected results or be manipulated to an advantage.

- **Knockout**   When one colored item overlaps another item of a different color, the usual method of handling this is to remove the portion of the item that lies beneath the frontmost item. This action is called *knocking out* and is illustrated in Figure 15-5.

 Keep in mind the golden rule of trapping: Always trap in a direction from light to dark.

In QuarkXPress 5, there are essentially three levels of trapping control available to you:

- Default trapping controlled by options in the Trap Preferences dialog
- Color trapping controlled by options in the Edit | Color | Edit Trap dialog
- Item trapping controlled by settings in the Trap Information palette

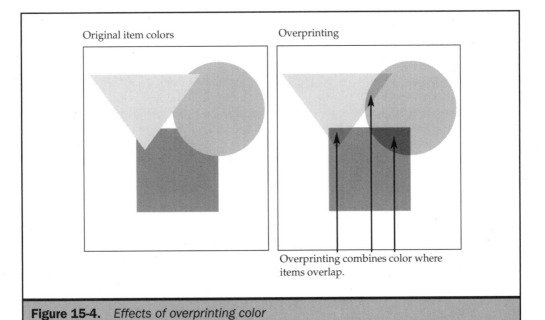

Figure 15-4.   *Effects of overprinting color*

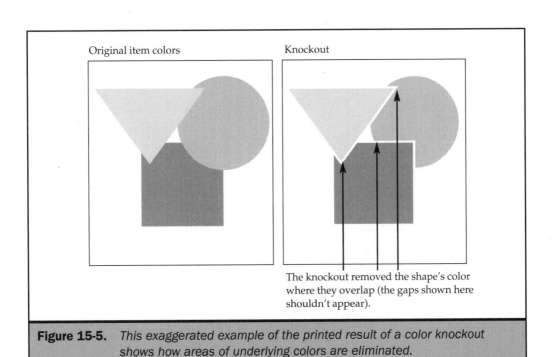

Figure 15-5.   *This exaggerated example of the printed result of a color knockout shows how areas of underlying colors are eliminated.*

Even before XPress prints your document, it examines each item for trapping conditions and looks to these three control areas for information and guidance on how to proceed. Each subsequent level of control supersedes the previous. Trap preferences are followed in a very general sense for all objects not applied with any further trap options. The Color trap options override all preference settings, so if your item contains a color that has specific trapping options applied to it in the Edit Color dialog, these options are used. If trap options have been applied to an item using the Trap Information palette, these settings override all others.

When it comes to trapping text, the same trapping rules apply; only the resulting trap effect is much more complex, especially when dealing in process color. Figures 15-6 through 15-9 demonstrate the effects of applying choke and spread trapping to text characters.

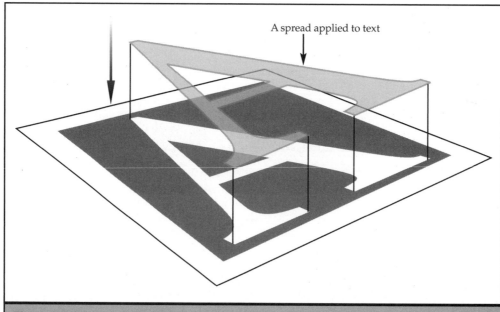

Figure 15-6. *A typical spread-type trap applied to text*

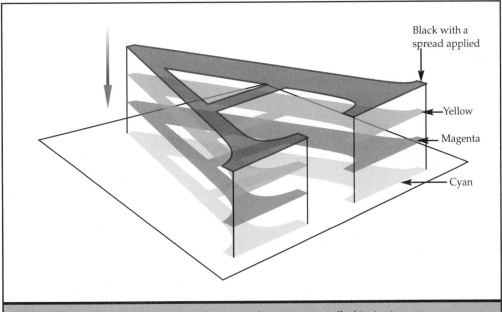

Figure 15-7.   *A typical process color spread-type trap applied to text*

Note

For text up to 24 points and small items (with dimensions up to 10 points), QuarkXPress attempts to preserve the item's shape during process trapping by not allowing automatic spreads or chokes when the item's shape would be compromised. QuarkXPress does this by comparing the darkness of each process component of an item to the darkness of its entire background. A spread is applied only when the process components of an item are less than or equal to half the darkness of its background. A choke is applied only when the process components of a background are less than or equal to half the darkness of the item in front of it.

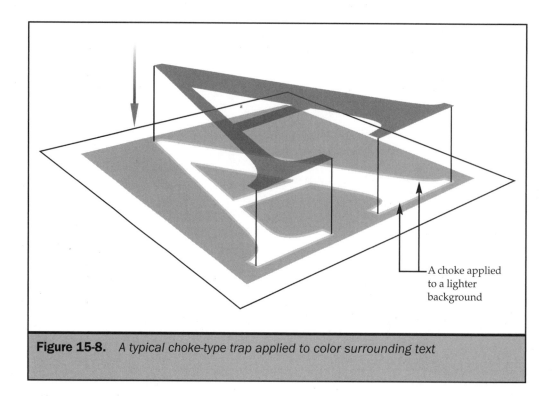

A choke applied to a lighter background

Figure 15-8.   *A typical choke-type trap applied to color surrounding text*

When trapping text or other small items, the chance that your text or item's shape may become distorted or disfigured is high. Fortunately, XPress has a built-in feature that examines any text characters below 24 points and other items less than 10 points in size to determine whether trapping will distort the item's shape when printed. To do this, XPress compares the difference in the luminance value between the text or item and its background or foreground color. Spreads and chokes are then applied only when the difference in color is less than half the color (luminance) of the background or foreground.

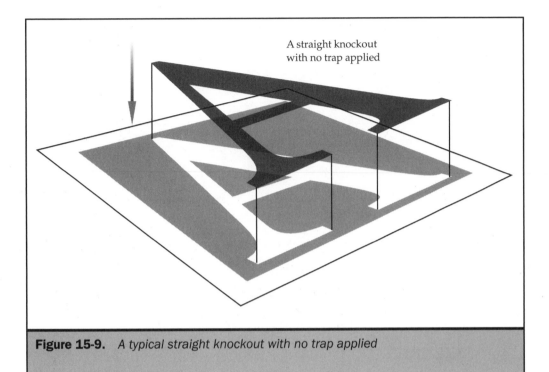

A straight knockout
with no trap applied

Figure 15-9.   *A typical straight knockout with no trap applied*

Setting Trapping Preferences

Since many instances of trapping can be guided by a certain set of rules or principles, much of the labor involved in applying traps may be automated. As you select trapping preference options for your document, you are actually defining specific rules for QuarkXPress to follow when it applies automatic color traps. Automatic trapping is performed according to the basic principles of trapping, meaning lighter colors are spread or choked according to their layering position and color. Colors may also be automatically knocked out or overprinted according to user options set in these preferences.

Tip

Keep in mind that color trapping is only applied when a document is printed, and simply applying a trap value to items in your document will not enable you to actually view the traps. For that, you'll need to examine the resulting printed page.

QuarkXPress 5's document Preferences commands control the top level of color trapping, and as you'll soon discover, XPress has a unique collection of terms all its own for describing and setting these options. The Trapping page of the Preferences dialog, shown in Figure 15-10, features what is essentially the master set of controls for determining the trapping of colored items in your document whenever it is selected to print to a PostScript-compatible printer. To access these dialog options, choose Edit | Preferences | Preferences to open the Preferences dialog and click Trapping under Document from the tree directory to the left of the dialog.

To quickly access the first dialog in the sequence of document-related preference options, press CMD/CTRL+Y.

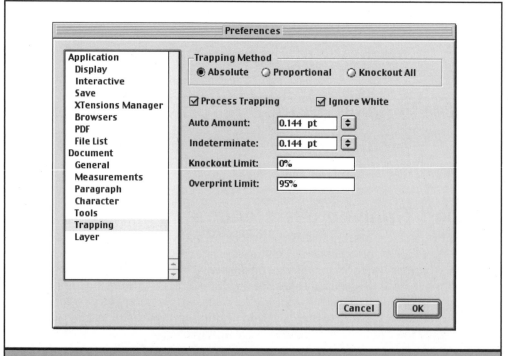

Figure 15-10. *Trapping options in this dialog control trapping globally for your document printing.*

For the most part, trapping options enable you to apply overall trapping in the most common instances. The choices you make in the Trapping dialog will answer questions such as when to trap and how much to trap by, as well as limits on when to knock out and overprint. In an effort to understand these options and how they will affect your document's color, the following definitions identify their capabilities:

- **Trapping Method**   This section contains three choices for controlling trapping and is perhaps the most important of all the options you'll select in this dialog. Select *Knockout All* to turn trapping off and deactivate the remaining options in the Trapping dialog. Select *Absolute* to enable XPress to apply trapping according to the values set in the *Auto Amount* field discussed later. Select *Proportional* to enable XPress to use the most complex option of the three. The Proportional option creates trap values based on the Auto Amount value by multiplying the difference in lightness and darkness (luminance) between the two colors being trapped. Using Proportional is perhaps the most automated and forgiving choice, enabling trap amounts to be larger as the difference in colors increases.

  For example, if your item colors differ only marginally, then the chance of a misregistration gap being noticeable is lessened. If the colors differ greatly, then misregistration gaps will be more noticeable, so the resulting trap value applied is larger.

Tip   *To have your trapping preferences apply to all future documents as default settings, set them while no documents are open. To have them apply to a specific document, set them while the document is open.*

- **Process Trapping**   Process Trapping may be selected on or off from this check box. While Process trapping is off, process color items are not trapped. With Process Trapping on, XPress examines each process color separation individually in relation to other colors being overlapped in your document. The resulting trap is set according to the trapping method selected. With *Absolute* chosen, the trap is applied with half the value set in the Auto Amount field and is applied to the darker component of the color on each plate. With *Proportional* chosen as the trapping method, half the Auto Amount value is multiplied by the difference in lightness and darkness (luminance) between the two colors being trapped. Table 15-1 shows examples of the results of process trapping applied using Absolute and Proportional trapping methods.

Color	Front Item	Back Item	Absolute Trap	Proportional Trap
Cyan (C)	40	10	Spread at half Auto Amount	Auto Amount $(40 - 10) \div 2$
Magenta (M)	50	70	Choke at half Auto Amount	Auto Amount $(50 - 70) \div 2$
Yellow (Y)	60	70	Choke at half Auto Amount	Auto Amount $(60 - 70) \div 2$
Black (K)	40	35	Spread at half Auto Amount	Auto Amount $(40 - 35) \div 2$

NOTE: All values above are percentage values.

Table 15-1. *Absolute and Proportional Trap Values*

- **Auto Amount**   The value entered in the Auto Amount field controls the width of the spread or choke amount XPress applies to items in your document when trapping. By default, Auto Amount is set to 0.144 points, but you may enter any value between 0 and 36 points. Auto Amount is the value used in automatic trapping in general and it is also set for specific colors in the Trap Specifications dialog, discussed later in this chapter. You may also choose Overprint as the Auto Amount, which results in the item overprinting other colors instead of an automatic trap being applied.

- **Indeterminate**   This may be one of the strangest terms you'll encounter in the new XPress trapping dictionary and essentially means "cannot be determined." Indeterminate is a fancy way of describing items with a color that cannot be identified because of its value (such as colors with equal luminance values) or its color composition (such as imported color pictures). In these cases, the Indeterminate trapping value is automatically applied. For example, when XPress encounters an item that is in front of an indeterminate background, the Indeterminate value is used. The indeterminate default is 0.144 points, but you may enter any value between 0 and 36 points. You may also choose Overprint as the Indeterminate value, which results in the item overprinting indeterminate colors instead of an automatic trap being applied.

■ **Knockout Limit** The Knockout Limit value enables you to control whether a color is knocked out or not. It is expressed as the percentage difference between a foreground and a background item color, and Knockout Limit enables you to control the point at which an object color knocks out a background color. If a color is not knocked out, settings in the Auto Amount field apply. The default is 0.

■ **Overprint Limit** All items colored solid black (100 percent) overprint by default. But if the item is less than 100 percent black, XPress checks your preference for how much black should be present before overprinting. By default, Overprint is set to 95 percent, meaning all items between 95 and 100 percent will overprint, and all items below will be trapped according to the remaining trap options and the amount set in the Auto Amount field.

■ **Ignore White** This item is checked by default, enabling XPress to knock out the shape of items colored with white. When left unchecked, all items overprint the white item and the results may be undesirable. For example, if a white item is between two differently colored items, the item on top will be trapped to the item on the bottom, meaning traps could be visible in the white area when the final document is printed. Unchecking Ignore White should only be used when trapping under special printing circumstances.

Setting Ink Color Trap Specifications

The next level of trapping is set according to options applied to ink colors in the Trap Specifications for [*color name*] dialog, shown in Figure 15-11. These options override those set in the Trapping page of the Preferences dialog and are essentially a function of ink color. To access options in the Trap Specifications dialog for a specific ink color, choose Edit | Colors (SHIFT+F12) to open the Colors dialog, click to select an ink color, and click the Edit Trap button. The Trap Specifications dialog opens to display the list of currently available colors in your document.

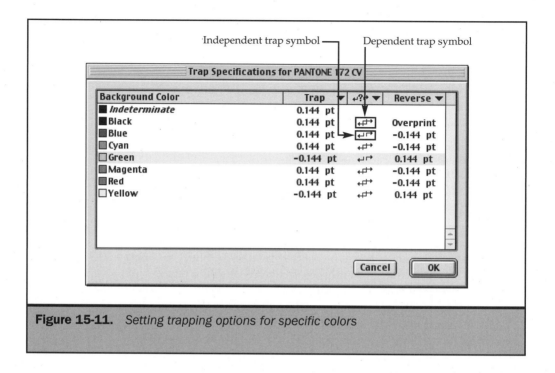

Figure 15-11. *Setting trapping options for specific colors*

Tip *To have your trapping specifications apply to all future documents as default settings, set them while no documents are open. To have them apply to a specific document, set them while the document is open.*

The Trap Specifications dialog includes a number of options for controlling how your selected color traps when it comes in contact with other colors in your document, regardless of which type of item the color has been applied to. The dialog displays three columns of settings according to the colors in your document list. While a color is selected, the following options are available in the form of drop-down menus in the headings of the columns:

- **Trap** This column displays the current trap amount that XPress will automatically create when your selected color overlaps another color, in this case listed as background colors. Choose *Default* to leave the trap amounts to be created at the options selected in the Trapping Preferences dialog or choose *Overprint, Knockout,* or *Auto Amount (-)* for chokes; *Auto Amount (+)* for spreads; or *Custom* to override the preference settings for all instances. While Knockout and Overprint options are selected in this list, the *Knockout* and *Overprint limits* in the Trapping Preferences dialog determine how the color will print.

For quick reference, XPress indicates values other than defaults in the Trap Specifications list with an asterisk (*).

- **Reverse** The concept of reverse trap can be a little confusing. The options in this dialog are geared toward cases where your selected color is applied to an item *in front* of an item applied with one of the colors in this list. In this case, the other colors serve as backgrounds. Reverse enables you to apply a trap value in the opposite situation where your *selected* color serves as the background and the listed colors are applied to the object in front of it. By default, reverse traps are simply negative values of the trap value. If you wish, you may override the defaults by choosing *Overprint, Knockout,* or *Auto Amount (-)* for chokes; *Auto Amount (+)* for spreads; or *Custom* to override the preference settings for all instances. As with the Trap options, Knockout and Overprint options are determined by the *Knockout* and *Overprint limits* in the Trapping Preferences dialog.

- **Dependent/Independent** As discussed previously, trap values and reverse values are essentially the opposite of each other by default. For example, if the trap value for a color is 0.144 points (a positive value), then the reverse value will be -0.144 points (a negative value). The Dependent/Independent option enables you to break this relationship if you choose to, so that the trap and reverse values may be set independently of each other. The unconnected arrow symbol represents a dependent condition, while the overlapping arrow symbol represents an independent condition. To toggle between conditions for any given color, click once on the currently displayed symbol.

The Indeterminate color listing enables you to specify a trap value or printing condition when your selected color comes in contact with an indeterminate color, such as an imported color picture or a color of equal luminosity.

Once you have completed editing the traps for your color, click OK to close the Trap Specifications for [*color name*] dialog (where *color name* represents the name of the color you have selected to edit the trap specifications for), and click Save in the Edit Color dialog to save your trap editing and close the dialog.

Using the Trap Information Palette

The final level of trapping options is set directly in your document and applied to selected items. This is perhaps the most labor-intensive operation when trapping a document, but it is also the most significant of all three levels. Options set at this point override both your document Preference options and the options chosen in the Trap Specifications list. Applying traps directly to items in your document using the Trap

Information palette (see Figure 15-12) is referred to by XPress as *item-specific* trapping. To open this palette, choose View | Trap Information (OPTION/CTRL+F12).

When applying item-specific trapping, you have a number of things to consider. First of all, the items you are applying trap properties to may feature more than one element. For example, a text box could conceivably be composed of text, a background, and a frame dash and stripe, including both the frame and the gap. And each of these elements could be assigned a different color and/or shade.

The Trap Information palette is context sensitive, meaning the available options change depending on the type of item selected. When setting the item-specific trap for various elements of the items in your document, you'll notice the Trap Information palette features the same set of trapping options for each element, composed of selections for Default, Knockout, Overprint, and Auto Amount (-) for applying chokes; Auto Amount (+) for applying spreads; and Custom for entering your own trap value. The effects of selecting these trapping options are identical to those applied in the Document Preferences | Trapping tab and the Trap Specifications dialog:

- **Background**   While a text or picture box item with no frame property applied is selected, the Background option becomes available. Although the background of a text or picture box is the usually the most expansive area, it is the simplest part to identify. The background is the interior portion of any text or picture box.

- **Frame Inside, Frame Outside**   Frames are perhaps one of the most complex elements to trap, especially if a dash or stripe pattern is applied. While a box or line with any frame value is applied, the two frame elements, Frame Inside and Frame Outside, become available. Frame Inside controls the trap properties

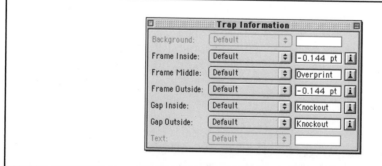

Figure 15-12.   *Viewing assigned trap values in the Trap Specifications dialog*

where the innermost edge of the frame overlaps the background color (or an item beneath this edge while the box background color is set to None). Frame Outside refers to the trap properties where the outermost edge of the frame overlaps a background item's color.

- ■ **Frame Middle** Frame Middle trap options control the edges of colored portions of a frame style. This option becomes available while boxes with complex frame styles containing interior elements such as the default frame styles Double or Dash Dot are applied.

- ■ **Gap Inside, Gap Outside** While a box or line is selected with a patterned frame style applied and the gap set to a color, the Gap Inside and Gap Outside trap property options become available in addition to the three frame trap options discussed previously. Gap Inside controls the edges where the gap color overlaps the interior elements of the box, such as the background (or an item beneath this edge while the box background color is set to None). Gap Outside controls trapping for the edge of the gap that overlaps background items beneath it.

- ■ **Text/Picture** While text in a box is selected, the text color may be set with trap properties using the Text options. While a picture box containing a picture is selected, the Picture trap options are available. In the case of pictures, you may only set trap options to Default, Knockout, or Overprint; otherwise, the process color trapping set in the Document Preferences dialog is used.

- ■ **Line, Line Middle, Gap** While lines are selected, the Line trap option becomes available, enabling you to control the edges of the line where it overlaps other background items. If the line is applied with a pattern, the Line Middle trap option becomes available to control traps for the edges where the frame dash or stripe color overlaps background items. If a gap color has been applied to the line or frame, the Gap option enables you to apply trap properties where the gap color edges contact the line (or frame) dash color, any background colors, or color items beneath.

The Trap Information palette has one last function, that being the capability to actually provide information about the intended trap, as shown in Figure 15-13. While an item is selected and certain elements of the item are available for trap options, XPress is able to display information about the trap properties applied through clicking and holding on the i symbol adjacent to the trapping option.

The information box that appears (see Figure 15-13) lists information about the element's color, the color of elements underneath, the source of trap values in use (Edit Trap or Trap Preferences), and any trap preferences currently in use by the element, such as Proportional, Process Trapping, Rich Black, Overprint Limit, Knockout Limit, and Smallest Trap Value.

 For more information on assigning color to content items, refer to Chapter 14, and for information on calibrating color throughout the publishing process, see Chapter 16.

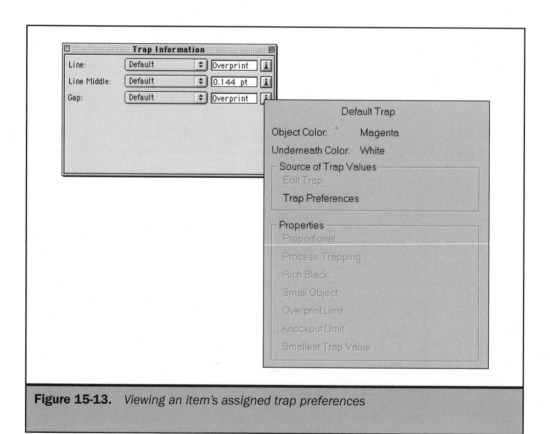

Figure 15-13. *Viewing an item's assigned trap preferences*

The Complete Reference

QuarkXPress 5

Chapter 16

Achieving Accurate Color

Advancing technology and lower pricing has made color scanners, color printers, and even digital cameras increasingly more affordable, making it so that even the most casual users are able to produce full-color documents. Unfortunately, getting consistent color throughout the production process continues to be a challenge. In this chapter, you'll learn some of the pitfalls in striving for accurate color reproduction and discover how QuarkXPress 5 provides built-in color tools for managing, displaying, and printing accurate color.

Of course, the key to achieving proper color lies in mastering the variables and knowing your digital software tools. With color technology changing so quickly, this is no easy feat. Rest assured though, QuarkXPress 5 *does* have advantages over lower-end applications; these are made possible through the implementation of some sophisticated software aimed at achieving color correctness.

Setting Up an Accurate Color System

Many of the factors involved in achieving consistent color have more to do with the hardware you're using than with the software. Each scanner or digital camera model available on the market today is capable of detecting and recording a certain range of color, which in turn can be stored in an image file and displayed on your monitor. Different types of monitors display the same image file differently, depending on the technology used in their manufacture. The same applies to color printers, composite proofing printers, and separations printers. To make matters even more complex, your monitor and printer actually use different methods to produce color, so getting an exact color match between the colors these two devices produce is another challenge. Monitors use *additive* color principles based on light projection, which produce colors in various red, green, and blue (RGB) values to produce a spectrum of color. The higher the RGB color values, the lighter the color. In contrast, many print reproduction processes use *subtractive* color principles—such as the four-color process used in offset printing. In this case, percentages of cyan, yellow, magenta, and black (CMYK) are used to produce colors. Higher percentages of CMYK color result in more color on the printed page—the opposite of how your monitor projects color. Add to this the fact that each color-capable device features a finite range of colors that it can accurately reproduce—something referred to as *gamut*. Each type of color device (monitor, scanner, camera, or printer) has its own unique gamut range. Even among devices of the same type and model, the gamut may vary from one device to another. When your monitor displays a particular shade of color, it's likely to appear much brighter and more saturated than the same color produced by your printer. This is because the color on the monitor is not in the same gamut range as the printer.

The color designs created by even the most professional designers and illustrators can get bad reviews if produced on a color-inaccurate desktop system. Reasons for poor color can result from a poorly calibrated monitor, digital image source, or color-proofing device; from poor print reproduction; or from any of the many processes in between. The trick to identifying and avoiding color errors begins with understanding all the processes involved, many of which are loosely represented in Figure 16-1.

Because of the huge range of color-capable devices available, it's nearly impossible to provide a comprehensive reference for working with all the possible variations of hardware, image types, and printing methods in use today. Instead, the next sections provide a general overview of the color management process and some of the tools involved in producing consistent color.

Monitor (Display) Color

When it comes to what you see on your monitor or display, as it is sometimes referred to, the process begins with your eyes and what they interpret from the screen on your color monitor. It continues down the line to include your color software, color scanner or digital camera, your desktop color-proofing device, imagesetter and printing press, or virtually any reproduction method.

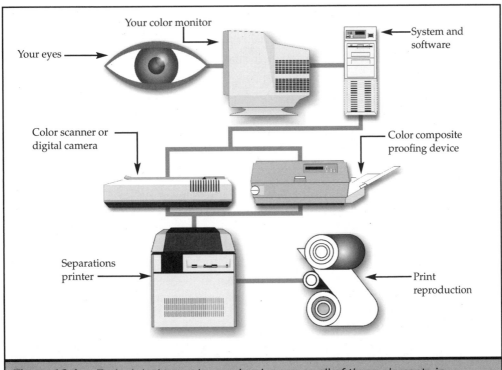

Figure 16-1.   *Typical desktop color can involve any or all of these elements in producing color documents.*

Needless to say, the wisest first step to take on your color accuracy quest is examining what you see on your monitor. Following these steps ensures a controlled environment for viewing colors:

- Begin by obtaining a printed hard copy color reference such as a color swatch. Be sure your swatch is recent; over time swatch colors can fade. If you purchase a new swatch, be sure to mark the date when you purchased it.

- When viewing colors, be sure your monitor is sufficiently warmed up. Waiting roughly half an hour will ensure that the projected color has stabilized.

- Set your work area lighting to your usual working light level. Controlled lighting is ideal; avoid having natural light coming into the room because lighting levels change during the day. Bright light reduces the spectrum of light our eyes let in, and vice versa for low light. This affects how the colors on your monitor appear.

- Take steps to shield your system from power surges. Changing power levels during various times of the day can affect the color produced on your monitor.

- If your monitor is newer, it may feature brightness and contrast controls. Be sure to set these to comfortable levels and avoid changing these settings after you have begun using your system. If you share a system with other users, be sure everyone is warned to leave the settings as they are.

- When adjusting brightness and contrast on your monitor, try matching the colors appearing on your screen as closely as possible to your swatch colors. In QuarkXPress 5, compare the displayed color to the exact color in your reference color swatch. For example, if your printed swatch is Pantone, compare this to the Pantone colors available in XPress. Compare screen colors to printed colors by creating a selection of colored items on a neutral-gray background using the color model you've chosen and compare these colors to your hard-copy color swatch. Be sure to choose a range of color that spans the color spectrum and includes shades of red, green, and blue. Adjust your monitor's contrast and/or brightness settings to match these colors as closely as possible.

This list enables you to begin aligning the color information your monitor is providing with real-life color. If the colors on your monitor look reasonably close to those in your color swatch book, you are well on your way to achieving accurate color.

Accurate Printed Color

A multitude of color printer manufacturers exist in the industry, using various printing technologies such as laserjet, bubblejet, laser, color sublimation, or thermal wax transfer to name just a few. These technologies vary widely in the way they interpret and reproduce color; many recent printers reproduce color based on CMYK models, and others use their own special recipes of spot and/or process colors.

As far as your software is concerned, only two different breeds of printers exist: PostScript and non-PostScript. *PostScript* is a page-description language developed by Adobe, which is a virtual standard in the desktop industry. PostScript-based color printers build color based on information on your PostScript driver. The accuracy of these printers is dependent on how their drivers read the color information from the print engine of your software (that is, QuarkXPress). Non-PostScript printers interpret the color from your software's print engine, but usually have drivers that interpret PostScript color information.

Another determining factor of color proofing is the resolution of your printer. The higher the resolution, the more accurate your color proof is. Printer technology is advancing quickly; most lower-end color proofing devices still commonly print using either 600 or 1200 bits per inch of resolution. Compare that to the final imagesetter film resolution—often between 2,400 to 3,600 dots per inch.

Recording for Color

Desktop image recording technology has revolutionized the ability for most layout artists and designers who produce print or Web documents to use color pictures. What used to be a costly pre-press step in obtaining color images is now digital wizardry, but with this wizardry comes a heaping helping of illiteracy on the part of users. Many users find after scanning an image or downloading a digital picture from a camera that the picture lacks the satisfactory color they wanted to capture. The problem can also be compounded by placing these unrefined images into page layouts. The thing to keep in mind is that a scanner is just a recording device. As with a sound system, you may have to adjust the base and treble a bit to hear all the sounds.

Scanners and digital cameras operate on various optic technologies. Scanners often use a light bar or laser to record the colors in a light-reflective original and subsequently convert the information to data. Digital cameras record color in a similar way—by interpreting the view seen through the camera lens and instantly compressing and processing the color detail to eventually create data. In both cases, the data is then converted into RGB. In many instances, RGB color is the perfect color model for Web document layout. If you're producing a spot or four-color process document for print and want to reproduce your image in the available colors, it helps immensely to have an image editor capable of converting your color picture to a specific color model and/or refining the image.

For process color, convert to CMYK and save the file as a TIF to be compatible with XPress. For duotones using spot colors, convert the picture to grayscale, then to duotone (adding your chosen spot color), and save it as EPS. When in XPress, the file separates at the printing stage.

When you prepare an image using an image editor, you need to make a number of decisions concerning resolution, compression (if any), and file format. Resolution is determined by the print resolution you require for your final publishing process, but compression and format are determined by the image editor or utility you are using to acquire the color image. The TIF file format is widely accepted and importable into most desktop applications, such as QuarkXPress 5, but you may also use a variety of others.

Using Quark's Color Management System

When it comes to managing color in XPress 5, Quark has engineered its own *color management system* (CMS). The role of the CMS is to enable you to specify the properties of your monitor, composite printer, and separations printer in the form of device profiles. Quark's CMS is managed through the use of an XTension component. When activated, CMS enables you to use Quark's *Color Management Module* (CMM), a built-in color engine capable of interpreting and translating colors based on the properties of the device in use. Properties of compatible devices are interpreted by data contained in the *International Color Consortium* (ICC) device profiles, which conform to standards followed by color-capable publishing software developers.

The purpose of the CMS is to control and manage color across devices. The thorny issues surrounding color management can often be complex and confusing, but suffice it to say that the whole thrust of this feature is to be able to view the same color on both your monitor and what you'll eventually hold in printed form in your hands. Quark's CMS works as intermediary between all your devices in an effort to regulate color and provide your eyes with color information, accurately portraying what ends up in your hands when printed. Figure 16-2 loosely shows a graphic representation of the factors involved. When you specify device profiles, you're essentially specifying to the color engine what your device limitations and capabilities are so that it may interpret and reflect the correct color back to you.

About ColorSync

For the sake of discussion, you'll explore color management as it's handled on the Macintosh, using ColorSync components. Although the actual components themselves may differ for Windows users, the underlying principles are the same, and the processes and procedures you'll learn also apply to Windows users.

To simplify the process of translating color between device gamuts, Apple Computer developed ColorSync. *ColorSync* is mostly transparent (meaning that it exists as a feature of your operating system), but it plays a key role in color management throughout all devices connected and installed on your system. Essentially, Apple's ColorSync component acts as a mediator of sorts, using data stored in an ICC profile to translate specific color information regarding your color devices to QuarkXPress 5's CMS. By synchronizing the profiles for your scanner, monitor, and printer, ColorSync

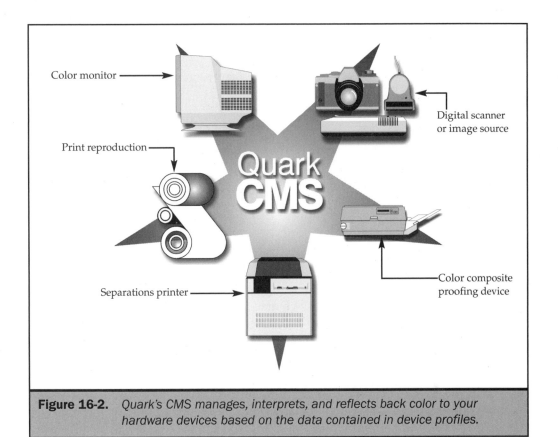

Figure 16-2. *Quark's CMS manages, interprets, and reflects back color to your hardware devices based on the data contained in device profiles.*

matches the color displayed on your monitor to that of your printer. Quark's CMS piggybacks on this technology by providing resources for selecting and managing these profiles.

Using the Quark CMS XTension

The first step in benefiting from color management in QuarkXPress 5 is to ensure that the CMS component of your application is installed and operating properly. The CMS XTension is managed through the use of the XTension Manager. To check if yours is installed and active, open the XTension Manager dialog by choosing Utilities | XTension Manager (shown next).

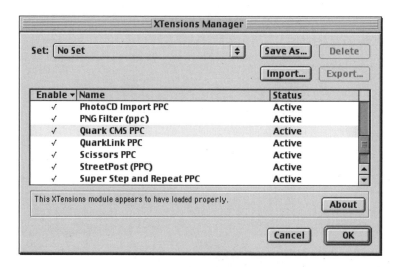

To enable the Quark CMS XTension, highlight the item named Quark CMS PPC, and then select Yes from the Enable drop-down menu; or click in the column to the left of the XTension in the list. After enabling it, you must quit and relaunch QuarkXPress 5 for it to become active and for its components to be added to your application menus. When XPress is relaunched, you'll notice the following CMS XTension color-related items throughout your application:

- Access to the Color Management Preferences dialog is added to the Preferences submenu (shown next) and can be selected by choosing Edit | Preferences | Preferences.

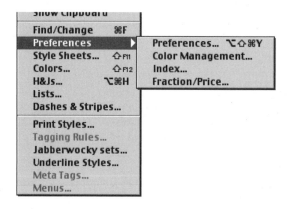

- With Color Management selected and active in the Preferences dialog, access to the Profile Manager is added to the Utilities menu (shown next).

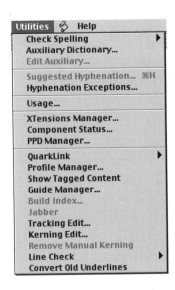

- Access to the Show Profile Information palette has been added to the View menu (shown next).

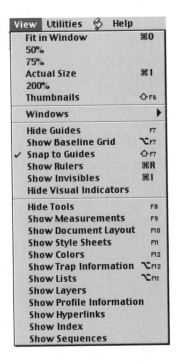

■ A dialog tab named Profiles has been added to the Usage dialog (shown next) and can be opened by choosing Utilities | Usage.

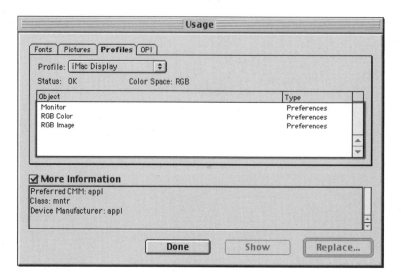

■ Color Correction and Profile options are added to the Get Picture dialog (shown next).

■ A Profiles tab is added to the Print dialog (shown next).

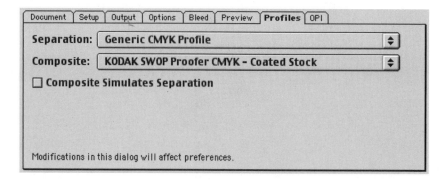

Choosing Color Management Preferences

With your CMS XTension installed and active, choose Edit | Preferences | Color Management to open the Color Management Preferences dialog (shown next). This dialog is the master control for specifying the ICC profiles for the color devices you are using to obtain images, display, and print your document. As you specify device profiles, you're essentially creating an architecture of data files to describe the capabilities and limitations of all the hardware devices you are currently using.

```
┌──────────── Color Management Preferences for Document1 ────────────┐
│  ☑ Color Management Active                                         │
│  ┌─ Destination Profiles ──────────────────────────────────────┐  │
│  │  Monitor:           [ iMac Display                      ] ⇕ │  │
│  │  Composite Output:  [ Canon CLC500/EFI Printer          ] ⇕ │  │
│  │  Separation Output: [ Tektronix Phaser III Pxi          ] ⇕ │  │
│  └──────────────────────────────────────────────────────────────┘  │
│  ┌─ Default Source Profiles ──────────────────────────────────┐    │
│  │ [RGB] CMYK  Hexachrome                                      │    │
│  │  ┌─ Solid Colors: ──────────────────────────────────────┐  │    │
│  │  │  Profile:          [ iMac Display            ] ⇕     │  │    │
│  │  │  Rendering Intent: [ Profile Default         ] ⇕     │  │    │
│  │  └──────────────────────────────────────────────────────┘  │    │
│  │  ┌─ Images: ────────────────────────────────────────────┐  │    │
│  │  │  Profile:          [ iMac Display            ] ⇕     │  │    │
│  │  │  Rendering Intent: [ Profile Default         ] ⇕     │  │    │
│  │  └──────────────────────────────────────────────────────┘  │    │
│  │  ☑ Color Manage RGB Sources to RGB Destinations            │    │
│  └────────────────────────────────────────────────────────────┘    │
│  Display Simulation: [ Monitor Color Space              ] ⇕        │
│                                    [ Cancel ]   [  OK  ]            │
└────────────────────────────────────────────────────────────────────┘
```

As mentioned earlier, these device profiles contain data that describe the color capabilities of your hardware devices—including color monitors, color scanners, color composite printers, and color separation devices. Quark's CMS is then able to reflect back to your monitor a reasonable interpretation of the colors you'd expect in print, based on these properties.

By default, when QuarkXPress is first installed, Color Management features are not active. To activate CMS, click the Color Management Active option at the top of the dialog and choose the profiles that correspond to the various display and printing devices you are using.

To begin the process, choose the devices you are using to view and print your document from the Monitor, Composite Output, and Separations Output drop-down menus in the Destination Profiles area. The purpose of selecting options in the Destination Profiles area is to enable QuarkXPress 5 to display and print your document's color pictures accurately on the selected devices. By default, Macintosh users will see a selection of ICC profiles for the most commonly used Apple- and Macintosh-compatible color devices. Windows users will see a different collection of the most commonly used Windows platform devices.

For the next step in the process, choose the options for device profiles from the Default Source Profiles area. This area includes choices for the Solid Color and Image profiles for conditions where your color picture is in RGB, CMYK, or Hexachrome color. This area also enables you to select the rendering intent for both the Solid Colors and Image profile areas. A rendering intent tells the CMM what color properties it should preserve when it translates a color from the source device gamut to the destination device gamut.

Use the Rendering Intent drop-down menu to choose between Profile Default (the default), Perceptual, Relative Colorimetric, Saturation, and Absolute Colorimetric. Although highly technical (and somewhat advanced), the function of each rendering intent is defined as follows:

- **Profile Default** This option is selected automatically as the default for all solid colors and color images in your document, and it causes no change in the translation of gamut values other than that of the device profile selected.

- **Perceptual** Choosing this rendering intent option causes the CMM to scale down the colors in the source gamut to fit the capabilities of the destination device gamut.

- **Relative Colorimetric** This rendering intent option causes the CMM to retain colors that are in both the source and destination gamuts, changing only those colors that do not fit the color space of either device gamut.

- **Saturation** This option has the effect of evaluating the saturation of source colors and changing them to colors with the same relative saturation as the destination gamut colors.

- **Absolute Colorimetric** As the most advanced and complex of all rendering options, this option retains all colors that fall within both the source and destination gamuts, and it adjusts the colors outside each gamut in relation to how they would look when printed on white paper.

The final option in the Color Management Preferences dialog enables you to choose a Display Simulation for both your solid colors and pictures. Display simulation enables you to specify which color space you want to see solid colors and images in. (This option is only available when you have selected a Monitor profile in the Destination Profiles section.) The available selections are defined as follows:

- **Off/None**   Macintosh users may select Off, and Windows users may select None to deactivate the Display Simulation features entirely.

- **Monitor Color Space**   Choosing this option causes the Color Management feature to show the optimum display based on the ICC profile selected for your monitor in the Destination Profiles area.

- **Composite Output Color Space**   This option forces a simulation of your solid colors and images to display the colors your composite output printer has selected in the Destination Profiles area according to its ICC profile information. The colors you see are limited by the color-rendering capabilities of the monitor you are using.

- **Separation Output Color Space**   Choosing this option forces a simulation of your solid colors and images to display color according to your selected separation output printer as selected in the Destination Profiles area according to its ICC profile information. Again, the colors you see are limited by the color-rendering capabilities of the monitor you are using.

> **Tip**
>
> *As with other preference features, you may apply color management to a single document or to all subsequently created documents. To set these preferences for a specific document, make your selections with the document open. Doing so applies your choices only to that document. To have your profile preferences apply to all subsequently created documents, close all documents before opening the Color Management Preferences dialog and selecting your profiles.*

When CMS is activated, a number of significant color-profile related features spring to life behind the scenes and become available for you to use. These include additional tabs in the Usage and Print dialogs, and a Color Correction option in the Get Picture dialog. If CMS is not selected as active, these items are not available. With CMS inactive, the Profile information palette opens, but remains dormant and the command for viewing the Profile Manager is unavailable in the Utilities menu.

Applying Color Correction to Pictures

When you create a new document and import your first color picture, you'll see an option for color correction in the Get Picture dialog (shown next). Beyond setting overall application and document color management preferences, this is the first step in actively applying color correction while working with imported items on your page. With your color picture selected to be imported in a picture box and the CMS feature active, the Rendering Intent option becomes available, as does the Profile drop-down menu and the Color Manage to CMYK/RGB destinations checkbox. Choosing Color Manage to CMYK/RGB enables you to set the device profile for the color that your imported picture displays.

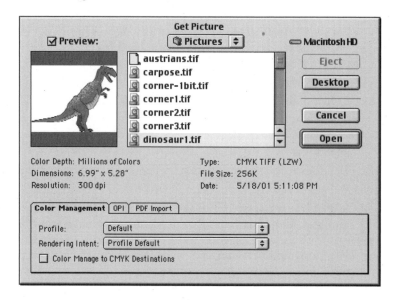

To apply color correction to your imported picture, click Color Manage to CMYK/RGB Destinations and choose the device profile that corresponds to the device used to scan the image from the Profile drop-down menu. After the picture is imported, XPress attempts to reproduce accurate color depending on the printer selected in your Color Management Preferences dialog.

If Quark's CMS feature is not selected as active in the Color Management Preferences dialog, the Color Correction option and Profile drop-down menu do not appear in the Get Picture dialog. To activate CMS, choose Edit | Preferences | Color Management, and click the Color Management Active option at the top of the dialog.

Using the Profile Information Palette

Although your Color Management Preferences dialog enables you to set the overall color profile settings for your document, you may still need to edit or override these settings in some cases. This is the role of the Profile Information palette. After a picture has been imported, you may change its color correction color space (or deactivate it) at any time using the Profile Information palette (shown next). To open the Profile Information palette, choose View | Show Profile Information.

```
┌──────────────────────────────────────────┐
│░░░░░░░░░░░░░░░ Profile Information ░░░░░░░░░│
├──────────────────────────────────────────┤
│ Picture Type:    Color                     │
│ File Type:       TIFF                       │
│ Color Space:     CMYK                       │
│ Profile:       [ 150-Line (Pantone)    ▼]  │
│ Rendering Intent: [ Profile Default    ▼]  │
│ ☐ Color Manage to CMYK Destinations        │
└──────────────────────────────────────────┘
```

The Color Correction and Profile options in the Profile Information palette only become active when color pictures are selected.

Tip *If Quark's CMS feature is not active, the Profile Information palette does not operate. To activate CMS, choose Edit | Preferences | Color Management, and click the Color Management Active option at the top of the dialog.*

The Profile Information palette displays specific information about selected pictures including the Picture Type, the File Type, and the Color Space for your selected picture. The palette also enables you to specify various types of rendering intents. For information on rendering intent selection, see the rendering definitions described in the "Choosing Color Management Preferences" section earlier in this chapter.

The last option in the Profile Information palette enables you to choose whether the color translation between RGB and CMYK pictures is managed by the selected device profiles. When an RGB picture is selected, the Color Manage to RGB Destination option appears at the bottom of the palette. This enables you to specify whether Quark CMS applies color management when the color model used by the image is the same as the Monitor or Composite Output profile gamut selected in the Color Management Preferences dialog.

When a CMYK picture is selected, the Color Manage to CMYK Destination option appears at the bottom of the palette. This enables you to specify whether Quark CMS applies color management when the color model used by the image is the same as the Separation Output profile color space chosen in the Color Management Preferences dialog.

Note *XPress supports color correction only for certain types of picture file formats. If your selected picture cannot be color-corrected, the Profile Information palette displays the Picture Type and Color Space as Unknown, but still indicates the File Type information. Unsupported file types include EPSF (EPS) and desktop color separations (DCS) file formats, both of which feature predetermined color and may not have their color space information altered for printing. For information on using various file format types, see the "Working with Picture Formats" section in Chapter 7.*

Tip
Choices made in the Profile Information palette override those made previously in the Color Management Preferences dialog for a selected picture.

Using the Profile Manager

The Profile Manager is perhaps your master control when working with various types of device color profiles in XPress. It lists all the device profiles currently available and enables you to activate or deactivate them at any time using options in the Profile Manager dialog (shown next). To open the Profile Manager, choose Utilities | Profile Manager.

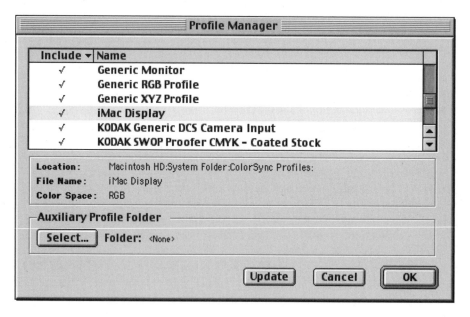

The Profile Manager displays a list of all the profiles available on your system and subsequently to Quark CMS. You may activate or deactivate any of the device profiles listed by clicking to highlight them, and then choosing Yes or No from the Include drop-down menu. You can also do this by clicking the checkmark to the left of the listing, which toggles the active state on and off. You may also define and update an Auxiliary Profile folder by clicking the Browse button to locate alternate profile locations, and then clicking Update.

Note
If Quark's CMS feature is not selected as active in the Color Management Preferences dialog, the Profile Manager is not accessible from the Utilities menu. To activate CMS, choose Edit, Preferences, Color Management, and click Color Management at the top of the dialog to activate it.

Checking Profile Usage

As with other types of usage features, such as fonts and pictures, the Profile Usage command enables you to obtain a quick snapshot of what's going on in your document file in terms of profiles and color correction. To open the dialog (shown next), choose Utilities | Usage | and select the Profiles tab.

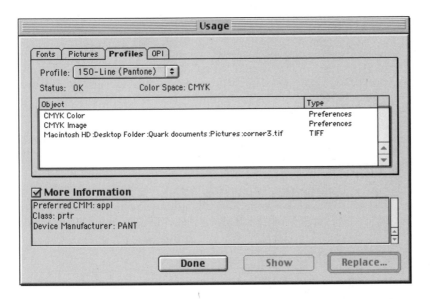

To obtain only the profile used for a given picture file, select the picture before opening the Usage dialog. To obtain information about all the profiles used for pictures in your document, open the dialog while no pictures are selected.

Options in the dialog enable you to select a profile that is in use from the Profile drop-down menu, and to obtain an instant summary of the pictures associated with it in the list. The list itself is comprised of two columns representing the type of item that is using the profile and the type of profile that is assigned to correct the item's color.

If Quark's CMS feature is not selected as active in the Color Management Preferences dialog, the Profiles tab does not appear in the Usage dialog. To activate CMS, choose Edit | Preferences | Color Management, and click the Color Management Active option at the top of the dialog.

You may use the Profiles tab of the Usage dialog to replace the device profile that is in use for a given item. This is done by highlighting the item in the list and clicking the Replace button, which opens the Replace Profile dialog (shown next). Select the new profile by choosing it from the Replace With drop-down menu, and then click OK to close the Replace Profile dialog. Click Close to exit the Usage dialog.

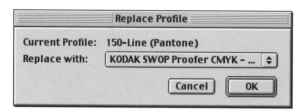

The lower portion of the Usage dialog features an option to view more information about a selected profile. When selected, the dialog expands to reveal profile information such as the CMM, the class of the device, and its manufacturer.

Choosing Profiles at Print Time

The final step in applying device profiles comes into play when you choose to print your document. Quark's CMS feature automatically adds a Profiles tab (shown next) to the Print command (CMD/CTRL+P) dialog. This enables the color engine to interpret the device profiles of your composite and separations printers and send the appropriate color data to your selected printer.

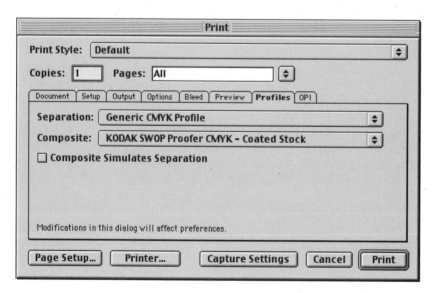

If your selected printer is incapable of producing color, the Profiles tab option is unavailable.

By default, when you first open the Profiles tab, it displays the device profiles you originally specified in the Color Management Preferences dialog, but this is your last chance to change them prior to printing. Choose device profiles for your separations printer and/or composite printer from the Separation and/or Composite drop-down menus. If you are actually proofing the color separations that you eventually intend to print to your separations printer, you may check the Composite Simulates Separation option in the dialog.

If Quark's CMS feature is not selected as active in the Color Management Preferences dialog, the Profiles tab does not appear in the Print dialog. To activate CMS, choose Edit | Preferences | Color Management, and click Color Management Active.

The Complete Reference

QuarkXPress 5

Chapter 17

Tackling Printing Tasks

f there's ever a time when creating a layout actually becomes exciting, printing is definitely it. This is when all your hard work bears fruit. For many desktop designers and layout artists, printing can be a rewarding experience when their creative efforts become tactile, informative, and functional products. But depending on how you've prepared your document, printing can be a time of joy or a frustrating experience.

If your QuarkXPress 5 document is destined for offset reproduction, as many are, there are several stages it has yet to travel through. As it does, you'll be faced with specific decisions to make and options to choose, which may seem unfamiliar. On the other hand, you may also be faced with the prospect of handing your document to a service bureau for remote output. In either case, there is a certain order of steps to follow. This chapter walks you through the sequence involved in printing your document to a desktop printer or imagesetter, and it details what you'll need to know when taking your file to a service bureau for remote output.

Setting Print Options

Because of the multitude of situations involved with printing documents, there are an enormous number of variables that may be set in the Print command dialog (CMD/CTRL+P) of QuarkXPress. The options you choose will depend on your own particular needs and the device you are using to print your document. The main Print dialog (shown next) has been subdivided into eight basic areas taking the form of dialog tabs.

These areas include Document, Setup, Output, Options, Bleed, Preview, and open prepress interface (OPI) tabs, containing myriad options, the functions and detailed purposes of which follow in this chapter. If you are using Quark's Color Management System (CMS) and it is active, another tab for setting your color profiles will also appear. The following section may serve as a guide in choosing these options.

Selecting a Printing Device

Choosing a printer in the Print dialog (shown next) is the very first step in beginning your print procedure. Once selected, the capabilities of your printer are reflected through options available in the various tabbed Print dialogs of QuarkXPress. The most significant factor of your printer's capabilities will be decided by whether it is a PostScript or non-PostScript type. Since QuarkXPress 5 is fully PostScript-compatible and heavily geared toward describing items in your document in this format, PostScript printers feature many more capabilities for printing documents than non-PostScript printers do.

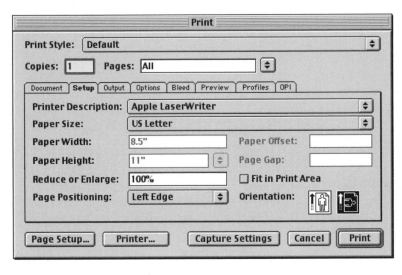

Select a Chooser Printer (Macintosh Only)

In order to print using the capabilities of a specific printer on a Macintosh system, you must first specify a printer in the Chooser window. You may access the Chooser at any time either from the Finder or while QuarkXPress (or any other application) is launched. To open the Chooser window (shown next), click the Apple icon in the upper-left corner of your screen to open the Apple menu and select Chooser.

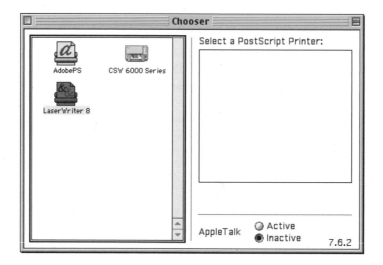

Once a printer is selected in the Chooser, the Page Setup dialog options will be updated to reflect the printer's capabilities. You may access the Page Setup options for your selected printer directly from within QuarkXPress 5 by choosing File | Print (CMD/CTRL+P) to open the Print dialog and clicking the Page Setup button.

In order for a printer to be available in the Chooser, you must first have installed a compatible PostScript printer description (PPD) in the System/Extensions/Printer Descriptions folder on your Macintosh system. For more information on obtaining both Macintosh and Windows printer descriptions, see "Obtaining a PPD File" discussed later in this chapter.

For example, while a PostScript printer is selected, you will be capable of printing color separations for any or all colors, specifying page size options, and using Quark's PostScript Error Handler for print troubleshooting. While a non-PostScript printer is selected, these options are unavailable. To select a printer using Macintosh versions of QuarkXPress 5, click the Printer button, select a printer from the dialog that appears, and click OK to accept your choice. Choosing a printer using Windows versions is slightly simpler; make your selection from the Printer drop-down menu.

Note

If your printer does not appear in the Printer drop-down menu, this may indicate it is unavailable, not operating properly, or not installed on your system. On Macintosh platforms, if your printer is already installed and operating properly, you may only need to select it by opening the Chooser from your Apple drop-down menu. Using Windows versions, this often indicates the printer is not installed. In either case, consult your system documentation and follow the procedures to install and/or select the printer.

Once your printer is selected, its associated printer driver will enable or disable the available options in the remaining tabs of the Print dialog. The printer driver contains data associated with the printer you have chosen and essentially tells QuarkXPress of its capabilities. While using the Windows version, a button to review the properties associated with your chosen printer is available, enabling you to verify the printer's capabilities if you choose to do so. The illustration (shown next) demonstrates the properties associated with a Linotronic 930 imagesetter. The majority of options contained in this dialog is duplicated by options set in the various Print dialog tabs.

Print Dialog Buttons and Options

In the Print dialog, a number of options are available, regardless of which type of printer you have chosen or which dialog tab is selected. These include options for choosing a print style, specifying the number of copies you wish to print, defining which pages to print, and a Capture Settings button. Macintosh users may set printer settings using the Printer button, while Windows users have a Printer Properties button. Macintosh users also have quick access to QuarkXPress 5's Page Setup dialog. The function of each of these is detailed as follows:

- **Print Style**   Choosing a print style enables you to instantly define all of the printing options in all dialog boxes. If you have created print styles as described in the next section, you may select this from the drop-down menu. Print styles must be set in advance of opening the Print dialog in order for a defined print style to be available.

- **Copies**   Use this field to enter the number of copies of the selected page(s) you wish to print. This field accepts a value of up to 999 copies for each printed page.

- **Pages**   Enter the page numbers you wish to print in this field. You may print all the pages in your document (the default) or specify the contiguous or non-contiguous pages you wish to print by using range separators between the page entries. By default, a dash (-) separates contiguous pages, while a comma (,) separates non-contiguous pages. For example, to print pages 1, 4, 5, 6, 7, 8, 21, 22, 23, 24, 25, and 40 of a 40-page document, you would enter 1, 4–8, 21–25, and 40 in the Pages field. Spacebar characters entered in the Pages field are ignored.

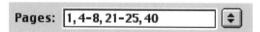

- **Capture Settings**   This button enables you to freeze your currently chosen printing options to be automatically set the next time you open the Print dialog. In essence, after clicking the Capture Settings button, your chosen options become your printing default settings. Use the Capture Settings button as the alternative to the Print button to make your current settings available the next time you open the Print dialog. Captured settings only apply to the document you currently have open.

Using Print Styles

Print styles are more of a productivity tool than anything else and enable you to immediately select printing options that have been previously saved using the Print Styles command. When a print style is created and saved using this feature, it becomes available to all subsequently printed documents, as opposed to being saved to a specific document. If no print styles exist in your Print Style drop-down menu, it indicates none are available. But the use of print styles may be a wise strategy to follow if you routinely print a variety of document types using varied print media.

To create a print style, choose Edit | Print Styles to open the Print Styles dialog (shown next).

Command buttons in the Print Styles dialog are identical to those seen in the Style Sheets, Colors, H&Js, Lists, and Dashes and Stripes commands found under the Edit menu with a slight variation: While a print style is selected in the Print Styles dialog list, a brief description of it appears in the lower area of the dialog, just as with other property style creations. There is no Append command button since print styles are available to all documents, along with the addition of Import and Export command buttons discussed next. The remaining buttons include commands for New, Edit, Duplicate, Delete, Save, and Cancel. To create a new print style, click the New button to open the Edit Print Style dialog (shown next).

The Edit Print Style dialog is subdivided into four tabbed areas, *Document, Setup, Output* and *Options,* which contain options nearly identical to those found in the Print dialog. To create a new style, you merely enter a name for your new style in the Name field, choose the options you wish to apply to your print style, click OK to exit the dialog, and click Save to close the Print Styles dialog and save your print style. The new style will be available the next time you open the Print dialog while a PostScript printing device is selected. See the following sections for information on setting print style options.

Note	*Print styles may only be used when a PostScript-compatible printer is selected from the Printers drop-down menu.*

Import and Export buttons in the Print dialog have the following function:

- **Import**   Click the Import button in the Print Styles dialog to import a style created by another user. Imported styles are data files that store all the options selected by another user. Windows users may identify saved print styles by their three-letter QPJ extension.

- **Export**   If you wish, you may make print styles you have created available to other users through use of the Export button. When a print style is exported, it takes the form of a data file.

Setting Document Printing Options

While the Document tab (shown next) in the Print dialog is selected, the following options will be available, depending on the type of printer you have selected.

- **Separations**   If your document contains more than one color, choosing the Separations option will enable you to separate the colors to a compatible printer type. Separation options may be chosen in the Output tab. For each selected plate of color, a separate sheet of output material will be generated for each of your selected pages.

Tip

For more information on printing and working with desktop color separation (DCS) files, see Chapter 18.

- **Spreads** If your document features left and right pages or pages arranged in a horizontal row in the Layout palette in the form of spreads, choose this option. The Spreads option has the effect of enabling you to print pages across defined page boundaries, provided your chosen printer supports a page size large enough to do so. In cases where it doesn't, you may need to use the Tiling option discussed later on in this section.

- **Collate** If you have chosen to print more than one copy of a selected page(s), the Collate option becomes available. Choosing the Collate option essentially has the effect of duplicating the print data sent to your printer once for each copy you select to print. As a result, choosing the Collate option increases the time it will take to print your pages relative to the number of copies you select.

- **Print Blank Pages** This option is selected off by default due to the fact that few users require blank pages in their documents to print, especially when printing to an imagesetter or any printing device where output material is costly. Choosing Print Blank Pages causes QuarkXPress 5 to print pages that do not include user-created items.

- **Thumbnails** Choosing to print thumbnails has the effect of printing your pages at the smallest possible size (less than 10 percent of the original), even less than the 25 percent minimum that may be set in the Reduce or Enlarge field, discussed further in this section and found in the Options tab. While Thumbnails are selected to print, other options such as the Separations option are unavailable.

- **Back to Front** Choosing this option simply enables you to print a document consisting of more than one page in reverse order, the last page being printed first.

- **Page Sequence** This drop-down menu features three choices for printing all (the default) or the odd- or even-numbered pages of your document.

- **Registration** This option includes three options for printing registration marks with your document. Registration marks consist of trim (corner) marks that define the page edges of your document and registration symbols, sometimes referred to as target dots, which enable film separations to be aligned during the stripping stage of offset printing. Choosing Off (the default) omits registration marks from your printed pages. Choosing Centered has the effect of printing four registration symbols centered at each of the four sides of your document pages. Choosing Off Center also prints four registration symbols at the sides of your document, only they are printed not to align with the center marks of your pages.

■ **Offset**   With registration marks set to print with your document, the Offset option becomes available and enables you to set the distance between your registration marks and the outer edges of your page (shown next). Offset may be set within a range between 0 and 30 points, the default of which is 6 points.

Registration:	Centered ◆	Offset:	6 pt

■ **Tiling**   Choose an option from the Tiling drop-down menu if you need to print your document to a page size that is smaller than your document page without reducing its size. Tiling has the effect of printing your document page(s) in sections with the eventual aim of assembling them manually after printing. Choosing Off (the default) turns the tiling feature off, while choosing either Manual or Automatic activates the feature. While Manual is selected, the origin of your tiles is dependent on your ruler origin (zero) position, beginning each tile at the upper-left corner. Choosing Automatic enables QuarkXPress to set the portion of your document page that appears on each tile and centers the tiles on each page's output page. The number of tiles required to print your entire document is indicated in the Print, Preview tab. Choosing Automatic also enables you to set the two following options.

Tip   *When QuarkXPress prints automatic tiles, tick marks and page information are included with the tiled pages to ease the task of reassembling the printed pages.*

■ **Overlap**   With Automatic tiling selected, you may set the Overlap value of each printed tile (shown next). Setting an Overlap value makes it much easier to assemble individual tiles for transparent output material such as film. Overlap may be set between 0 and 6 inches, the default of which is set to 3 inches.

Tiling:	Automa... ◆	Overlap:	3"	☐ Absolute Overlap

■ **Absolute Overlap**   With Automatic tiling selected, the Absolute Overlap value also becomes available (shown next). When selected, Absolute Overlap enables QuarkXPress to print each tile without centering it on the output material.

Tiling:	Automa... ◆	Overlap:	3"	☑ Absolute Overlap

For more information on tiling, see the section called "Specialized Printing Tasks" later in this chapter.

Choosing Print Setup Options

Setup options enable you to control options for your printer and the output material you will print your document on. While the Setup tab (shown next) in the Print dialog is selected, the following options may be available, depending on the type of printer you have selected:

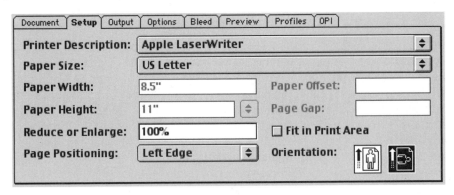

- **Printer Description**   The Printer Description drop-down menu contains the list of all available printer types according to the printers enabled in the PPD Manager. For more information on enabling or disabling the printers in this list, see "Using the PPD Manager" later in this chapter.

- **Paper Size**   For new users, this option may be slightly misleading; it refers to paper when, in fact, the material you are printing your document on may not be paper at all. For instance, you might be printing to a PostScript file in order to create a PDF. Paper size also refers to the size of your *output material,* rather than the page size of your document. Output material is measured in page formats such as *Letter, Legal, Tabloid,* and so on, influenced by your choice of Printer Description. While a specifically defined paper size is selected, Paper Size, Paper Width, and Paper Height options are unavailable.

If you have selected registration marks to print, be sure to select an output page size larger than your document page size to accommodate these marks. Add at least 0.5 inches of space to each of the four sides of your printed page. For example, if your document page is 10 by 15 inches, choose an output material size of 11 by 16 inches. For standard sizes such as Letter, Legal, and Tabloid, preset sizes appended with the term .Extra are often available with your PPD, such as Letter.Extra (which sets an output material size of 9.5 by 12 inches).

■ **Paper Width/Height** To enter your own paper width and height values, choose a paper size of Custom from the Paper Size drop-down menu. Custom is often the last option listed in the Paper Size menu (although occasionally this size may not be available). Once selected, you may enter the width and height for your output material. Both the Custom Paper Width and Height values must fall within 1 and 240 inches. Paper Height may be set to Automatic (the default).

■ **Reduce or Enlarge** If you require your document to change size when printed, enter a reduction or enlargement value in this field based on a percentage of the original size. Values entered below 100 percent reduce the size, while values entered above 100 percent enlarge the size. Reduction or enlargement values must fall within a range between 25 and 400 percent.

■ **Page Positioning** In order for the Page Positioning options to be available, you may need to choose either *Custom, MaxPage,* or *MaxMeasure* as your output material size from the Paper Size drop-down menu. Choosing Custom enables you to enter your own page sizes in the Paper Width and Paper Height fields. Choosing MaxPage has the effect of imaging your document to the largest size your selected printer is capable of. While a paper size of MaxPage is selected, Page Positioning may be set to either *Left Edge, Center, Center Horizontal,* or *Center Vertical* from the available drop-down menu.

■ **Paper Offset/Page Gap** While a Custom paper size is selected, Paper Offset and Page Gap each become available (shown next). Paper Offset enables you to control where the left edge of the document page begins from the left edge of the output material and must be set between 0 and 48 inches. The Page Gap value enables you to control the amount of space between individually printed pages and is useful when printing multiple pages to roll-fed printing devices where the pages are printed one after another. The shorter the distance, the less output material is wasted. Page Gap may be set between 0 and 5 inches. The default values for both options is 0.

Paper Size:	Custom		
Paper Width:	8"	Paper Offset:	0"
Paper Height:	Automatic	Page Gap:	0"

■ **Fit in Print Area** This option becomes available when QuarkXPress detects that the page size you are printing to is smaller than your document page size. Choosing this option has the effect of enabling QuarkXPress to automatically calculate a page reduction size for you. For example, if your document pages are Tabloid size (11 by 17 inches) but your chosen paper size is Letter, choosing

Fit in Print Area enables QuarkXPress to calculate an automatic page reduction size of 70.7 percent. Unchecking the option returns the Reduce or Enlarge option to 100 percent.

- **Orientation**   The term *orientation* describes the manner in which your page is fed into your printer. Orientation of your output material often matches the orientation of your output material. Orientation is directly related to the width and height measures of your chosen paper size such as Letter, Legal, Tabloid, and so on. The term has always been surrounded by confusion since users often mistake orientation of the document with the orientation of their output material. Thankfully, QuarkXPress 5's print feature includes a Preview tab (discussed later in this chapter) that enables you to view both your document orientation and your output material selection at once. If you have any uncertainty about which option is correct for your print setup, check out the Preview tab after making your Orientation selection.

Choosing Output Options

The Output tab options enable you to set virtually all the color, resolution, and line frequency settings for your printed output. While the Output tab (shown next) in the Print dialog is selected, the following options may be available, depending on the type of printer you have selected:

- **Plates**   While the Separations option in the Document tab is checked, the Plates drop-down menu is displayed. This option includes three choices for separations: displaying only the process and spot colors used in your document, changing all colors in your document to a four-color process using the Convert to Process option, or displaying all process and spot colors defined in your document. While Convert to Process is selected, only cyan, magenta, yellow, and black plates appear in the Options tab colors list.

■ **Print Colors**   While the Separations option in the Document tab is unchecked, the Print Colors drop-down menu (shown next) is available in the Output tab instead of the Plates drop-down menu. Choose from *Black and White, Grayscale, Composite CMYK,* or *Composite RGB* printing.

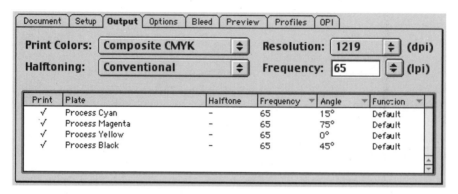

■ **Halftoning**   Halftoning describes the screening method used to reproduce shades of color and digital photographs. Two methods of halftoning may be selected from this drop-down menu: *Conventional* or *Printer*. The Conventional option enables QuarkXPress to include halftoning information with the print data sent to the printer. Choosing Printer enables you to let the default halftoning method for the selected printer be used instead.

■ **Resolution**   Much confusion surrounds this term since resolution may refer to scanning resolution, screen resolution, and so on. In the case of printing resolution, it refers to the amount of detail the imagesetter will build into the printed output. The higher the resolution, the more detailed the output will be. A resolution of roughly 1270 dpi is often the default used for photographic paper output, while photographic film output is often set to roughly 2540 dpi (or higher), depending on the offset reproduction method in use. If you are unsure about which resolution to specify, check with your service bureau or your print vendor for their requirements.

■ **Frequency**   The term frequency is used to describe the number of rows of dots measured in the dot screen halftone of your printed output and is measured in lines per inch (LPI). The LPI Frequency value you choose is dependent on your reproduction method and the quality of the printing press in use. It may also be influenced by the resolution value chosen. The higher the frequency, the finer the detail will be in your final output. Common sheet-fed printing presses may usually accommodate up to 150 LPI, while high-speed Web presses are usually capable of 85 to 100 LPI. If you are unsure which value to choose, consult your print vendor. Setting the Frequency value sets the default value for the frequency associated with each ink color listed in the lower area of this dialog.

The lower area of the Output dialog is fashioned into a list of colors and their associated printing properties. In order for this color list to display more than simply black, you must be printing to a PostScript printer selected in the Printer drop-down menu, and the Separations option in the Document tab must be selected active. Each color in the list represents a separate printing plate, and each may be controlled individually by selecting it and choosing the available options from drop-down menus at the top of the Print, Halftone, Frequency, Angle, and Function columns. Options are defined as follows:

- **Print**   The Print drop-down menu enables you to turn printing for a particular plate on or off, as indicated by a checkmark. To turn printing on or off, choose Yes or No from the drop-down menu or click in this column to the left of the Plate name to toggle the appearance of the checkmark.

- **Plates**   The Plates column lists and identifies the colors actively applied to items in your document.

- **Halftone**   Another repeated option name here, but in this case the Halftone option refers to setting the screen angle of non-process colors for shades, pictures, and digital photographs to match that of a process color ink. Choose either C (cyan), M (magenta), Y (yellow), or K (black, the default) from the drop-down menu to have the angles of shades, pictures, and digital photographs match a process color angle. By default, cyan = 105 degrees, magenta = 75 degrees, yellow = 90 degrees, and black = 45 degrees.

- **Frequency**   Using the Frequency option, you may set LPI frequency for a specific color differently from others if you wish. Choose Default (the default) to have the Frequency match the value selected in the Frequency option in the upper area of the dialog, or choose Other to enter your own value and override the default.

- **Angle**   Using the Angle option, you may set the angle at which the rows of dots describe shades of color, pictures, and digital halftones for a specific color individually. By default, process colors will already be entered, but spot colors will each be set to match black (45 degrees). Choose Other to enter your own value and override the default.

- **Function**   The Function for each printed color may be selected individually from this drop-down menu. Function is the shape of the dot that describes shades of colors, pictures, and digital photographs. It may be set to *Dot, Line, Ellipse, Square,* or *Tri-dot.*

Selecting Printing Options

The Options tab contains a potpourri of options for setting picture output options, page flipping and negative printing options, and EPS overprinting. While the Options tab (shown next) in the Print dialog is selected, the following options may be available, depending on the type of printer you have selected:

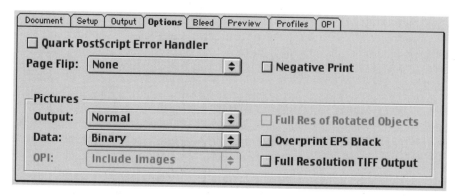

- **Quark PostScript Error Handler** Quark has gone one better when it comes to identifying PostScript errors with an improvement to the usual, and often cryptic, error messages associated with complex page items that may halt printing. Besides the usual error messages that print when a particular page refuses to print, Quark's improvements involve printing a bounding box around the offending item encountered in your document, identifying it with a box featuring a black border and a 50 percent black background. Plus, a message at the top-left corner of the unsuccessfully printed page indicates the cause of the problem. To locate (and usually replace or delete) the offending item, match the position of the bounding box that appears with an object on your page. To activate Quark's Error handler, simply click the check box.

- **Page Flip** The Page Flip drop-down menu enables you to print your page backwards and/or upside down by choosing Horizontal (to print backwards), Vertical (to print upside down), or Horizontal and Vertical (both backwards and upside down). Although these options might seem ridiculous when printing to a laser printer, for high-resolution film output they are invaluable and enable you to control the side on which the film emulsion faces. Emulsion is the photo-sensitive layer adhered to film that enables it to appear either black or clear in order to reflect the items on your page. Flipping your printed page causes the emulsion side to appear on the back side of the film in order for the emulsion side to contact the photosensitive side of the printing plates during plate production. Setting the Page Flip option to None (the default) enables the pages to print normally.

■ **Negative Print**   This option is another function of generating film output and enables you to print your pages as negative images. Where items are usually white on your page, they will appear black on the film.

■ **Pictures**   The purpose of the Output drop-down menu is to give you choices for printing pictures in normal, low-resolution, or very rough conditions. This option is useful when proofing the text of documents that are image-intensive, causing them to take additional time to print. Choosing *Normal* (the default) leaves pictures to print in the usual way. But choosing *Low Resolution* enables QuarkXPress to forego the high-resolution data that describes pictures and instead replaces them with the 72-dpi screen resolution previews. Setting Output to *Rough* completely suppresses the picture printing of pictures in your document, leaving only the picture's frame and background properties to print.

■ **Picture Data**   The ability to choose the data type that describes the pictures in your document enables you flexibility when it comes to printing your document through a print spooler and to a wider range of printer types. Clean 8-bit is similar to Binary, but it omits additional data strings that Binary adds to communicate with parallel port printers. The *ASCII* format is a more versatile format, compatible with a wide range of printers and print-spooling software.

■ **OPI**   The OPI menu is available only while the QuarkXTensions software is not loaded, and it enables you to control the substitution of TIFF and EPS pictures during printing. Choose Include Images (the default) if you are not using an OPI server to prevent high-resolution versions of EPS pictures from being substituted in the final output. If the high-resolution version cannot readily be found during printing, the screen preview of the images is output instead. Choose Omit TIFF to prevent high-resolution TIFF images from being substituted during the printing operation without omitting the printing of EPS images. Choose Omit TIFF and EPS to prevent high-resolution substitutions of both image types.

For information on working with systems that use digital separations, see Digitally Separating Pictures for XPress in Chapter 18.

■ **Overprint EPS Black**   Although other items on your document page may be controlled through automatic or manual trapping properties, EPS pictures may not. For these, you will need to rely on the diligence of the creator of these files to add the proper trapping. But choosing the Overprint EPS Black option has the effect of forcing all black elements in an EPS picture to overprint regardless of their applied internal trapping properties.

■ **Full Res of Rotated Objects**   While Normal is selected as the Output method while printing to a non-PostScript printer, choosing this option enables full-resolution printing (instead of simply the screen image) of TIFF images that have been rotated. A word of warning: Use of this option may significantly burden your system's memory during printing, depending on the speed of your processor and other available operating system resources.

- **Full Resolution TIFF Output** Choose this option if you would like your TIFF pictures to print at the highest line frequency supported by the printer you are using at your selected printer resolution (see the Output tab options). With this option selected, TIFF pictures will automatically be set to print at the highest line frequency (LPI) possible.

  For example, while a resolution of roughly 2540 dpi is selected to print on an imagesetter printer, the line frequency choices range from 100 to 150 LPI for all shades of color, pictures, and digital photographs. With Full Resolution TIFF Output selected, all TIFF images will print at 150 LPI, independent of the LPI setting chosen for the rest of the printed document. Leaving Full Resolution TIFF Output unchecked leaves the Frequency value set in the Options tab as the LPI setting used for TIFFs.

Choosing Bleed Options

The term *bleed* refers to the amount of space between the printed edges of your document and the imaginary border surrounding your page in which items overlapping the edge may appear on the printed page. Bleed is actually a term borrowed from the offset printing industry and is used to describe situations where ink is allowed to overlap into the area of a page that will eventually be trimmed from your final printed document. Color backgrounds and photographs are a popular item type to have bleed off your page. Bleed options are set in the Bleed tab of the Print dialog (shown next). In order for the Bleed tab to appear in the Print dialog, the Custom Bleeds PPC XTension must be selected as active in the XTensions Manager.

Document	Setup	Output	Options	**Bleed**	Preview	Profiles	OPI

Bleed Type: **Asymmetric** ⇕   Top: 0"
☑ Clip at Bleed Edge   Bottom: 0"
Left: 0"
Right: 0"

The Bleed Type drop-down menu in this dialog tab enables you to choose from one of three bleed types: Page Items, Symmetric, or Asymmetric, the result of which is defined as follows:

- **Page Items** While this option is selected (the default), no bleed area is defined, meaning items that overlap the edge of your document page are clipped at the edge of the page.

- **Symmetric** While Symmetric is selected, you may enter a single value as the Bleed amount in the Amount box, resulting in a uniform bleed area around your printed document page. Items that overlap the page edges will be clipped at this point.

- **Asymmetric** While Asymmetric is selected as the Bleed type, you may create a nonuniform bleed area around the edges of your printed page by entering different values in the Top, Bottom, Left, and Right boxes. Again, items that overlap the page edges will be clipped according to the values entered.

Depending on which option you have selected from the Bleed Type drop-down menu, the Amount/Top, Bottom, Left, and Right boxes become available. These boxes enable you to set the Bleed value for each between 0 and 6 inches, the default of which is 0.

- **Clip at Bleed Edge** While Symmetric or Asymmetric is selected as the Bleed type, choosing the Clip at Bleed Edge option (selected by default) enables you to specify that items that extend beyond the specified bleed amount are clipped. If this option is not selected, items extending beyond the bleed amount print to the edges of the imageable area specified for the selected printer.

Previewing Your Print Selections

A critical habit to adopt is to check the Preview tab just prior to pressing the Print button regardless of how simple or complex your document printing session is destined to be. The Preview tab enables you to view certain printing-related options you have set in the Document and Setup tabs, such as page size, output material size, registration mark printing, thumbnail printing, tiled printing seams, bleeds, and so on. The display consists of a statistical display in text form and a viewing window indicating your document, as shown next. The main purpose of the Preview feature is to ensure that your document fits correctly on the output material while Document and Setup options are set.

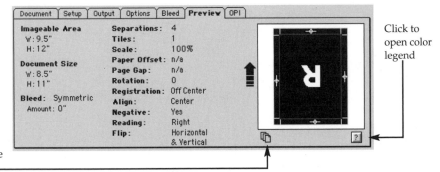

BEYOND QUARKXPRESS BASICS

Unfortunately, the display of your document in the Preview tab has limited capabilities. It does not display any details of your pages' content or any options that may be selected in the Output or Options tabs, including resolution display, the number of pages to print, flipping, negative print, picture handling, and other conveniences found in some applications.

You may also get info on the color indicators displayed in the Preview window by clicking the small ? icon below the bottom-right corner of the window. The legend popup that opens indicates display colors for the imageable area (green), the document page edges (blue), the bleed edges (gray), registration marks (black), and the clipped areas (red). A small icon below the lower-left corner of the Preview window also displays whether the selected device is a sheet-cut (meaning output is printed to single sheets of material) or a roll-fed (meaning the output is printed onto a roll of material) device.

If you are using Quark's Color Management System (CMS) feature, the Profiles tab will also appear in the Print dialog. For information on using CMS and choosing related options at print time, see Chapter 16.

Choosing Color Management Profiles

Although you may specify the color devices you are using in the Color Management Preferences dialog, you may also update or change them prior to printing using options in the Color Management tab of the Print dialog (shown next).

| Document | Setup | Output | Options | Bleed | Preview | **Profiles** | OPI |

Separation: KODAK SWOP Proofer CMYK – Coated Stock ⬍

Composite: Color LW 12/660 PS Profile ⬍

☐ **Composite Simulates Separation**

Modifications in this dialog will affect preferences.

The Color Management tab enables you to specify options that set how QuarkXPress 5's color management module (CMM) handles both CMYK and RGB color items in your document. For more information on using color management features, see Chapter 16.

Using OPI

OPI functions may be controlled using the OPI tab of the Print dialog (shown next). While OPI Active is selected, these options enable you to tune the printing of pictures while printing to OPI servers.

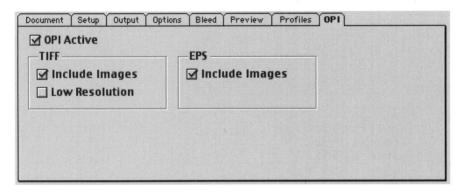

OPI systems have the capability of substituting high-resolution data files that describe picture files in place of the images you have imported onto your pages. High-end OPI systems are used for ultra-high resolution color pictures where importing the enormous picture files associated with such resolution just wouldn't be practical. Before printing, the high-resolution images are substituted for lower-resolution placeholders. Choose Include Images (the default) if you are not using an OPI system to print your document. To add the OPI comments to your low-resolution TIFF picture placeholders at print time, deselect Tiff Include Images, and while using OPI for both TIFF and EPS picture files, deselect both boxes for EPS and Tiff Include Images.

Using the PPD Manager

The purpose of the PPD Manager is to enable you to manage the display and access to printer descriptions. PPD files are needed to describe the properties of your printer and appear in the Printer Description drop-down menu of the Setup tab of the main Print dialog of QuarkXPress. PPD files are often supplied by manufacturers with the purchase of a new printing device.

A single PPD file can contain multiple collections of printer models for a single manufacturer brand, making PPD lists long and time-consuming to navigate. For example, the PPD files describing the list available for AGFA brand printing devices include more than 30 entries, which are displayed in the list numerically and alphabetically. If the PPD you need to select each time you print is at the end of the list, repeatedly searching for and selecting it can be annoying and time-consuming.

Managing your PPD List

The PPD manager enables you to control which printer types appear in the Printer Description drop-down menu (found in the Print, Setup tab dialog) by either checking or unchecking the mark to the left of each listed printer in the PPD Manager (shown next). To open the PPD Manager, choose Utilities, PPD Manager. To change whether a PPD appears in the Printer Description list, select the PPD and choose Yes or No from the Include drop-down menu or click next to the PPD in the list to toggle display of the checkmark. Once your PPD list has been changed, clicking OK saves your changes.

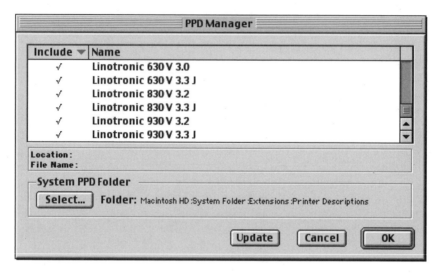

While a PPD is selected, the location and associated file name appear below the PPD list. By default, PPDs are located in your system folder for your operating system. But if you wish, you may set the folder location for your PPDs using the Browse button in the dialog. In fact, it may be wise to keep all of your PPDs in a single folder separate and secluded from system files in order to easily keep track of them. To do this, create a folder named PPDs in your QuarkXPress program folder and store your PPDs there. After changing the folder location, the PPD list is automatically updated, or you may click the Update button to manually update the list.

When choosing which PPDs display in the list, you may select multiple continuous and non-continuous PPDs using CMD/CTRL and SHIFT while making your selection. Once a selection of PPDs is highlighted, you may select Yes or No from the Include drop-down menu to change the display conditions of all of them at once.

Obtaining a PPD File

Usually, PPD files are distributed on disc with new printing hardware. But you may be in a situation where you need to update a current driver or simply can't locate the PPD file for your printer for whatever reason. If you don't have the correct PPD, you simply can't print properly. Obtaining these files is easier than it has been in the past, but it still takes some hunting. Quark does not supply PPD files on the QuarkXPress 5 program disc, so if you've misplaced the disc that came with your printer, you'll have some work to do.

The absolute best source for getting a PPD file is the Internet. If you don't have access, contact your manufacturer by phone, contact the vendor who originally sold you the printer, or locate another user who may own the same printer model as you. If you do have Internet access, you might try visiting Quark's Web site at **www.quark.com**. At the time of this writing though, Quark's collection of downloadable PPDs was somewhat limited.

Tables 17-1 through 17-6 outline the Macintosh PPDs and related files, which are available at **www.adobe.com/support/downloads/pdrvmac.htm.**

File Size	Language	Release Date
2.1MB	Brazilian Portuguese	04/17/2001
2.1MB	Chinese Simplified	04/17/2001
2.1MB	Chinese Traditional	04/17/2001
2.1MB	Danish	04/17/2001
2.1MB	Dutch	04/17/2001
2.1MB	English	04/17/2001
2.1MB	Finnish	04/17/2001
2.1MB	French	04/17/2001
2.1MB	German	04/17/2001
2.1MB	Italian	04/17/2001
2.1MB	Japanese	04/17/2001
2.1MB	Korean	04/17/2001
2.1MB	Norwegian	04/17/2001
2.1MB	Spanish	04/17/2001
2.1MB	Swedish	04/17/2001

Table 17-1.   *Macintosh PPDs (Version 8.7.2)*

File Size	Language	Release Date
1.7MB	Brazilian Portuguese	07/16/99
1.7MB	Danish	07/16/99
1.9MB	Dutch	07/16/99
1.7MB	Finnish	07/16/99
1.7MB	French	07/16/99
1.7MB	German	07/16/99
1.7MB	Japanese	07/16/99
1.7MB	Norwegian	07/16/99
1.7MB	Spanish	07/16/99
1.7MB	Swedish	07/16/99
1.7MB	U.S. English	06/25/99

Table 17-2.   *Macintosh PPDs (Version 8.6)*

File Size	Language	Release Date
2.1MB	Brazilian Portuguese	07/14/2000
2MB	Chinese Simplified	04/28/2000
2MB	Chinese Traditional	04/28/2000
2.1MB	Danish	04/28/2000
2.1MB	Dutch	04/28/2000
2MB	English	04/28/2000
2.1MB	Finnish	04/28/2000
2.1MB	French	04/28/2000

Table 17-3.   *Macintosh PPDs (Version 8.7)*

File Size	Language	Release Date
2.1MB	German	04/28/2000
2.1MB	Italian	04/28/2000
2.1MB	Japanese	04/28/2000
2.2MB	Korean	04/28/2000
2.1MB	Norwegian	04/28/2000
2.1MB	Spanish	04/28/2000
2.1MB	Swedish	04/28/2000

Table 17-3. *Macintosh PPDs (Version 8.7)* (Continued)

File Size	Plugin Name/Version	Language	Release Date
64KB	PDF Printer Driver Plugin (8.5.1)	Japanese	04/10/98
174KB	PDF Printer Driver Plugin (8.5.1)	U.S. English	04/10/98
157KB	Virtual Printer Plugin (v 8.5.1)	U.S. English	01/28/98
293KB	Watermark Plugin (v 8.5)	U.S. English	01/28/98

Table 17-4. *Macintosh PPD-Related Plugins (version 8.5.1)*

File Size	Language	Release Date
1.6MB	Brazilian Portuguese	01/12/98
1.6MB	Chinese Simplified	01/12/98
1.6MB	Chinese Traditional	01/12/98

Table 17-5. *Macintosh PPD(version 8.5.1)*

File Size	Language	Release Date
1.6MB	French	01/12/98
1.6MB	German	01/12/98
1.6MB	International English	01/12/98
1.6MB	Italian	01/12/98
1.6MB	Japanese	01/12/98
1.6MB	Korean	01/12/98
1.6MB	Spanish	01/12/98
1.6MB	U.S. English	12/24/97

Table 17-5. *Macintosh PPD(version 8.5.1)* (Continued)

File Size	Device Manufacturer	Release Date
218KB	SofHa GmbH	08/25/98
403KB	Autologic	07/10/98
484KB	Heidelberg	07/07/98
77KB	Birmy Graphics PowerRIP	07/06/98
663KB	MGI	06/30/98
565KB	Agfa	06/29/98
40KB	Oce Graphics	06/29/98
661KB	Tektronix	06/29/98
639KB	Xerox	06/29/98
479KB	Oki	06/25/98
170KB	Infowave Software/GDT Softworks	06/23/98

Table 17-6. *Macintosh PPDs (All Versions)*

File Size	Device Manufacturer	Release Date
150KB	Ricoh	06/23/98
12KB	Konica	06/22/98
247KB	Apple	06/20/98
31KB	CalComp	06/20/98
117KB	Dataproducts	06/20/98
13KB	ElexTech	06/20/98
429KB	Fuji Xerox (FX)	06/20/98
360KB	Hewlett-Packard	06/20/98
137KB	IBM	06/20/98
69KB	Minolta	06/20/98
95KB	NEC	06/20/98
44KB	TDS	06/20/98
472KB	XANTE	06/20/98
319KB	Imation	06/15/98
100KB	Splash	04/01/98
76KB	ECRM	03/02/98
451KB	EFI	02/02/98
378KB	Canon	01/30/98
303KB	DS	01/16/98
65KB	Mitsubishi Electric	12/13/97
444KB	Epson	12/12/97
143KB	IPT	11/27/97
21KB	Optronics	10/25/97
106KB	FFEI	09/26/97

Table 17-6.   *Macintosh PPDs (All Versions)* (Continued)

File Size	Device Manufacturer	Release Date
35KB	Fuji Photo Film	09/26/97
10KB	NSG	09/23/97
31KB	Cactus	09/12/97
68KB	Hitachi	08/22/97
1.2MB	PrePRESS Solutions	08/06/97
27KB	Nipson	07/29/97
526KB	Linotype-Hell	07/23/97
132KB	Scitex	07/23/97
18KB	Riso	07/09/97
73KB	COLORBUS Software	06/26/97
149KB	Kodak	06/23/97
5KB	Amiable	04/16/97
50KB	3M	04/08/97
13KB	Adobe	04/08/97
7KB	AST PS-R4081	04/08/97
15KB	Bull Italia PageMaster	04/08/97
8KB	C Itoh	04/08/97
9KB	Cascade Software	04/08/97
35KB	Colossal	04/08/97
36KB	Compaq PageMarq	04/08/97
89KB	Crosfield Electronics	04/08/97
487KB	Dainippon	04/08/97
149KB	Digital	04/08/97
7KB	Fujitsu	04/08/97

Table 17-6. *Macintosh PPDs (All Versions)* (Continued)

File Size	Device Manufacturer	Release Date
6KB	IDT	04/08/97
18KB	Laser Graphics	04/08/97
20KB	Laser Press	04/08/97
88KB	Mannesmann Scangraphic	04/08/97
50KB	Monotype Systems	04/08/97
5KB	NeXT	04/08/97
29KB	Panasonic	04/08/97
9KB	Pix Computersysteme	04/08/97
109KB	QMS	04/08/97
7KB	Qume	04/08/97
18KB	Radius	04/08/97
7KB	Schlumberger	04/08/97
239KB	Seiko Instruments	04/08/97
24KB	Shinko	04/08/97
196KB	Sony	04/08/97
9KB	Sun Microsystems	04/08/97
159KB	Texas Instruments	04/08/97
19KB	Unisys	04/08/97
277KB	Varityper	04/08/97
9KB	VerTec Solutions	04/08/97
24KB	Fargo Electronics	02/01/97
15KB	DuPont	06/05/96
26KB	Indigo	06/05/96

Table 17-6.   *Macintosh PPDs (All Versions)* (Continued)

The following Windows PPDs and related files in Tables 17-7 through 17-11 are available from **www.adobe.com/support/downloads/pdrvwin.htm.**

File Size	Language	Release Date
5.8MB	Brazilian Portuguese	06/22/2001
5.7MB	Chinese Simplified	06/22/2001
5.7MB	Chinese Traditional	06/22/2001
5.8MB	Danish	06/22/2001
5.8MB	Dutch	06/22/2001
5.7MB	English	06/22/2001
5.8MB	Finnish	06/22/2001
5.8MB	French	06/22/2001
5.8MB	German	06/22/2001
5.8MB	Italian	06/22/2001
5.8MB	Japanese	06/22/2001
5.7MB	Korean	06/22/2001
5.8MB	Norwegian	06/22/2001
5.8MB	Spanish	06/22/2001

Table 17-7. *Windows PPDs: AdobePS for Windows 95/98/ME/NT/2000, AdobePS 4.5.1 for Windows 95/98/ME, AdobePS 5.2 for Win NT 4.0, and PScript 5 for Windows 2000*

File Size	Language	Release Date
1.1MB	Brazilian Portuguese	04/30/99
1.1MB	Chinese Simplified	04/30/99
1.1MB	Chinese Traditional	04/30/99
1.1MB	French	04/30/99
1.1MB	German	04/30/99
1.1MB	Italian	04/30/99
1.1MB	Japanese	04/30/99
1.1MB	Korean	04/30/99
1.1MB	Spanish	04/30/99
1.1MB	U.S. English	04/30/99

Table 17-8. *Windows PPDs, Adobe PS Version 4.2.6*

File Size	Device Manufacturer	Release Date
162KB	SofHa GmbH	08/25/98
306KB	Autologic	07/10/98
301KB	Heidelberg	07/07/98
101KB	Birmy Graphics	07/06/98
551KB	Management Graphics	06/30/98
455KB	Agfa	06/29/98
57KB	Oce	06/29/98
493KB	Tektronix	06/29/98
349KB	Xerox	06/29/98

Table 17-9. *Windows PPDs (All Versions)*

File Size	Device Manufacturer	Release Date
118KB	Ricoh	06/23/98
156KB	Apple	06/22/98
43KB	CalComp	06/22/98
103KB	Dataproducts	06/22/98
31KB	ElexTech	06/22/98
369KB	Fuji Xerox (FX)	06/22/98
206KB	Hewlett-Packard	06/22/98
120KB	IBM	06/22/98
122KB	Kodak	06/22/98
30KB	Konica	06/22/98
70KB	Minolta	06/22/98
88KB	NEC	06/22/98
272KB	Okidata	06/22/98
51KB	TDS	06/22/98
514KB	XANTE Corporation	06/22/98
35KB	Optronics	06/20/98
131KB	Imation	06/15/98
31KB	Iwatsu	06/04/98
69KB	Fuji Film	04/15/98
92KB	Splash	04/02/98
69KB	ECRM	03/02/98
270KB	Canon	02/12/98
336KB	EFI	12/19/97
63KB	Mitsubishi Electric	12/13/97

Table 17-9.   *Windows PPDs (All Versions)* (Continued)

File Size	Device Manufacturer	Release Date
145KB	Epson	12/12/97
120KB	IPT	12/12/97
70KB	COLORBUS Software	11/25/97
114KB	Scitex	11/25/97
275KB	Sony	10/28/97
95KB	FFEI	09/26/97
28KB	NSG	09/23/97
68KB	Hitachi	08/22/97
908KB	PrePRESS Solutions	08/06/97
427KB	Linotype-Hell	08/04/97
30KB	Riso	08/04/97
40KB	Nipson	07/29/97
61KB	3M	07/21/97
45KB	Fargo Electronics	05/19/97
25KB	Amiable	04/16/97
27KB	C Itoh	03/17/97
27KB	Cascade	02/28/97
35KB	Mutoh	02/13/97
103KB	QMS	02/07/97
30KB	Adobe	01/30/97
131KB	Digital	01/28/97
27KB	Samsung	01/28/97
88KB	Seiko Instruments	01/28/97
38KB	Shinko	01/28/97

Table 17-9. *Windows PPDs (All Versions)* (Continued)

BEYOND QUARKXPRESS
BASICS

File Size	Device Manufacturer	Release Date
219KB	3M, Agfa, and Apple	06/05/96
194KB	Autologic to CalComp	06/05/96
193KB	Canon to Crosfield	06/05/96
219KB	Dainippon and Fuji	06/05/96
219KB	DataProducts to EFI	06/05/96
288KB	Epson to Indigo	06/05/96
219KB	Laser Graphics to Oce Graphics	06/05/96
219KB	Oki, Panasonic, and Pix	06/05/96
219KB	PrePRESS Solutions	06/05/96
219KB	QMS to Sun Microsystems	06/05/96
293KB	Tektronix, Texas Instruments, Unisys	06/05/96
208KB	Varityper	06/05/96
189KB	VerTec Solutions, XANTE, and Xerox	06/05/96

Table 17-10. *Windows Printer Manufacturer INF Files*

File Size	Device Manufacturer	Release Date
27KB	DuPont	10/12/95
133KB	Texas Instruments	09/14/95
151KB	Dainippon	08/10/95
45KB	Colossal	07/17/95
37KB	Mannesmann Scangraphic	07/17/95
53KB	Crosfield Electronics	07/13/95

Table 17-11. *Windows PostScript Printer Descriptions*

File Size	Device Manufacturer	Release Date
34KB	Radius	07/13/95
28KB	Sun Microsystems	04/18/95
39KB	Indigo	03/31/95
34KB	Laser Graphics	03/31/95
27KB	Pix Computersysteme	03/29/95
26KB	AST	02/14/95
27KB	Bull Italia	02/14/95
47KB	Compaq PageMarq	02/14/95
26KB	Fujitsu	02/14/95
35KB	Infowave Software/GDT Softworks	02/14/95
35KB	Laser Press	02/14/95
55KB	Monotype Systems	02/14/95
25KB	NeXT	02/14/95
41KB	Panasonic	02/14/95
26KB	Qume	02/14/95
26KB	Schlumberger	02/14/95
35KB	Unisys	02/14/95
218KB	Varityper	02/14/95
28KB	VerTec Solutions	10/13/94
25KB	IDT	11/19/93

Table 17-11.   *Windows PostScript Printer Descriptions* (Continued)

Requesting Remote Output

In older versions of QuarkXPress, collecting all the files that pertain to your document file was a manual process. For complex documents, this was often a time-consuming task and the files required for remote output could easily be missed. QuarkXPress 5 now includes a more robust *Collect for Output* command, which has the effect of locating and copying all the various elements needed for taking your file to a service bureau.

Streamlining Files for Remote Output

Before you begin the process of collecting your files for output, there are a few things you may want to do yourself before commencing the process. Since file size and complexity may be an issue when transferring your document files to the service bureau, you may streamline the document itself by eliminating unused resources such as stray items and stored attributes your file doesn't need in order to output. Performing the following steps may reduce your document file size, speed printing, and/or reduce the complexity of the document, but before you begin, make a copy of your document by choosing Save As (CMD/CTRL+OPTION/ALT+S):

- *Eliminate all unused items on your pasteboard.* Select them by pressing DELETE/BACKSPACE. The Pasteboard is the area outside your page borders on which items will not print.

- *Delete any unwanted or "spare" pages in the document.* Includes master pages such as those found at the end of the document that are not considered part of your finished document.

- *Remove unused style sheets.* To do this, open your document and choose Edit, Style Sheets (SHIFT+F11), choose Style Sheets Not Used from the Show drop-down menu, select the unused style sheets that display in the list, and click Delete. To save your changes and exit the dialog, click Save.

- *Remove unused colors.* Open your document; choose Edit | Colors (SHIFT+F12); choose Colors Not Used from the Show drop-down menu; select the unused colors that display in the list; and click Delete. Click Save to save your changes and close the dialog.

- *Remove unused H&Js.* Open your document; choose Edit | H&Js (CMD/CTRL+SHIFT+F11); choose H&Js Not Used from the Show drop-down menu; select the unused H&Js that display in the list; and click Delete. To save your changes and exit the dialog, click Save.

- *Remove Dash and Stripe and Lists.* Perform the same operation as above by deleting unused dashes and stripes and lists in your document by choosing the appropriate command from the Edit menu.

Using the Collect for Output Command

The Collect for Output command streamlines the remote output process considerably and enables you to quickly copy your document file, all picture files (including TIFF and EPS), fonts, color profiles, and an optional Report document in the form of an QuarkXPress tags (XTG) document to a specified folder or drive. The Report file may be used to review the fonts and XTensions used in your document, as well as details surrounding picture placements, paragraph and character style sheets, colors, and applied trapping methods.

Tip

Before you use the Collect for Output command, it may be wise to ensure your system has a reasonable amount of free hard drive space available for copying these files and create a new separate folder for QuarkXPress to copy the files into. Copying the files into a folder that already contains other QuarkXPress documents may cause confusion as to which files belong to which output document.

To use the Collect for Output command, follow these steps:

Tip

Before choosing Collect for Output, save your recent changes by choosing File | Save (CMD/CTRL+S).

1. Choose File | Collect for Output. QuarkXPress immediately opens the Collect for Output dialog (shown next), which enables you to create and/or select the folder into which your collected files will be copied. The Collect for Output dialog also features options for selecting which elements you would like collected. Choose from Document, Linked Pictures, Embedded Pictures, Color Profiles, Screen Fonts, and Printer Fonts. You may also choose to generate only the Collect for Output report document (discussed in the next section). Choose the Report Only option and enter a name for the Report document in the Name field. With the Report Only option selected, QuarkXPress will create only a summary of your document that you may then review if you wish. To review the file, open a new QuarkXPress document and import the report as an QuarkXPress Tags file, or open the file in a text editor.

BEYOND QUARKXPRESS BASICS

2. After specifying a folder location and/or choosing your collection options, click OK to proceed with the file collection operation. At this point, QuarkXPress 5 will scan the content of your document to verify the location and modification dates of linked files. If any files are missing or modified, an alert dialog typical of the one (shown next) will appear detailing which linked files are changed or missing from when they were imported.

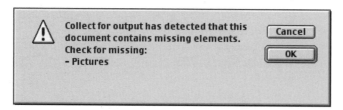

3. If you wish, click Cancel to abort the collection operation and locate and select each of the missing or modified pictures using the Usage, Picture dialog to relink and/or update the missing or modified images. Or click OK in Macintosh or Continue in Windows to ignore the alert and continue with the file collection operation. Doing so will cause only those files that are not missing or modified to be copied during the collection process.

4. If you choose to Cancel and instead review your document picture status, the Picture tab of the Usage dialog (*Macintosh*: OPTION+F13, *Windows*: SHIFT+F2, or choose Utilities | Usage) enables you to update and/or relink your pictures (as shown next). Click any of the missing or modified pictures in the listing and click the More Information option to view the picture details. While a missing or modified picture is selected, clicking the Update button opens a dialog (shown next) that enables you to reestablish the picture link.

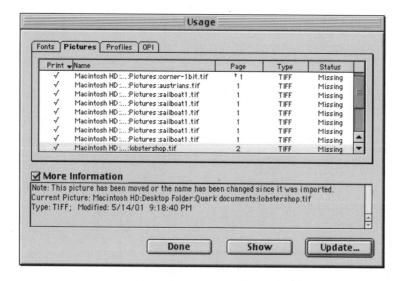

5. Click any of the missing or modified pictures in the listing and click the More Information option to view the picture details. While a missing or modified picture is selected, clicking the Update button opens a dialog (shown next) that enables you to reestablish the picture link.

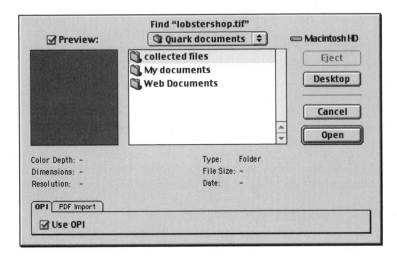

6. After you have reviewed the document picture files, re-established the picture links, and are satisfied your document is ready for output, choose File | Collect for Output and begin the process again. After completing the collection operation, all linked picture files required to print the document will be copied to the folder you specified in the Collect for Output dialog.

Reviewing the Report File

When a report file is created, the following details about your document are summarized in an QuarkXPress Tags file:

- Document name
- Date of the file
- Platform and version(s) of QuarkXPress used to create the file
- Your document file size
- Total pages
- Document width and height
- All required XTensions
- Active XTensions

- Names of the fonts used in the document
- Graphics used, including their file size, box/picture angle, skew, path name, type, fonts in EPS, and their location in the document
- Resolution of pictures
- Paragraph and character style sheets
- H&J specifications used in the document
- Each color created and information to reproduce custom colors
- Trapping information, including the preference methods selected
- Color plates required for each page
- Color profiles

The Report file is quite thorough, as is the entire Collect for Output command, in summarizing and copying all information related to your document output.

Using the Output Template

As a convenience for sending a file for output, you may also use the Output template included with QuarkXPress for actually ordering your output. The purpose of the template is to enable you to print a hard copy and hand-mark your output request. In most cases, you will want to use the output request provided by the service bureau to have an idea of what you will be charged for any services you request. But when that isn't possible or when one doesn't exist, the output template may serve as a guide. Figure 17-1 shows the information included in the Output template. The template is named *Output Request Template* (Macintosh) or *Output.QXT* (Windows) and is located in your QuarkXPress program folder in the Documents folder.

In the case of the Output template, Macintosh users have an advantage over Windows users. Using the Macintosh version of QuarkXPress, you may import the Report file directly into the Output Request template, selecting Include Style Sheets on import. The resulting document may then be included with the collected output files to be sent electronically to the service bureau.

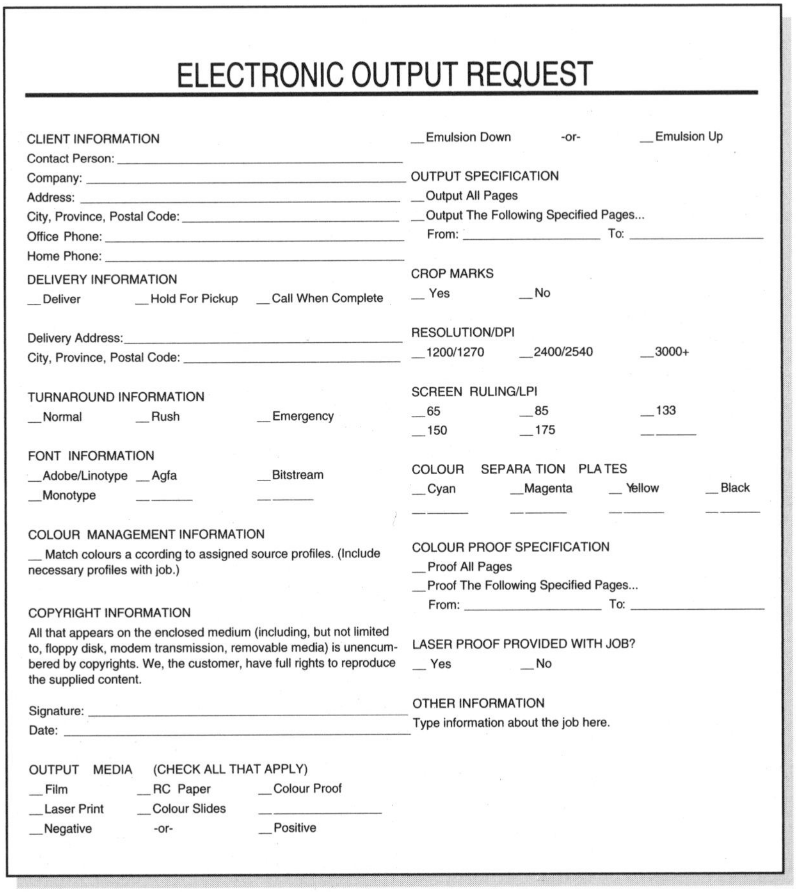

ELECTRONIC OUTPUT REQUEST

CLIENT INFORMATION

Contact Person: _____

Company: _____

Address: _____

City, Province, Postal Code: _____

Office Phone: _____

Home Phone: _____

DELIVERY INFORMATION

__ Deliver   __ Hold For Pickup   __ Call When Complete

Delivery Address: _____

City, Province, Postal Code: _____

TURNAROUND INFORMATION

__ Normal   __ Rush   __ Emergency

FONT INFORMATION

__ Adobe/Linotype __ Agfa   __ Bitstream

__ Monotype   __ _____   __ _____

COLOUR MANAGEMENT INFORMATION

__ Match colours according to assigned source profiles. (Include necessary profiles with job.)

COPYRIGHT INFORMATION

All that appears on the enclosed medium (including, but not limited to, floppy disk, modem transmission, removable media) is unencumbered by copyrights. We, the customer, have full rights to reproduce the supplied content.

Signature: _____

Date: _____

OUTPUT MEDIA   (CHECK ALL THAT APPLY)

__ Film   __ RC Paper   __ Colour Proof

__ Laser Print   __ Colour Slides   _____

__ Negative   -or-   __ Positive

__ Emulsion Down   -or-   __ Emulsion Up

OUTPUT SPECIFICATION

__ Output All Pages

__ Output The Following Specified Pages...

From: _____   To: _____

CROP MARKS

__ Yes   __ No

RESOLUTION/DPI

__ 1200/1270   __ 2400/2540   __ 3000+

SCREEN RULING/LPI

__ 65   __ 85   __ 133

__ 150   __ 175   __ _____

COLOUR   SEPARATION PLATES

__ Cyan   __ Magenta   __ Yellow   __ Black

_____   _____   _____   _____

COLOUR PROOF SPECIFICATION

__ Proof All Pages

__ Proof The Following Specified Pages...

From: _____   To: _____

LASER PROOF PROVIDED WITH JOB?

__ Yes   __ No

OTHER INFORMATION

Type information about the job here.

Figure 17-1. *Quark's supplied output order form*

Specialized Print Tasks

It goes without saying that not all documents are created equal, and certain types of documents or circumstances may require special printing procedures. This section covers cases when you may need to print oversized documents in tiles, a typical imagesetter printing session, and it also covers preparing a portable print file.

Printing Manually Tiled Pages

Tiled printing is often required when your document page size is significantly larger than the largest page size your printer is capable of generating, and you ultimately need a proof printed to actual size. For example, if you are creating a 24-by-18-inch poster but your printer prints only to legal-sized (8.5 by 14 inch) or letter-sized (8.5 by 11 inch) pages, you'll need to tile print it.

The Tiling option of QuarkXPress is found in the Print, Document tab dialog and features two modes besides Off: Manual and Automatic. But the tiling exercise is actually a function of setting several options, including choosing the printer, PPD, page size, and other options you may require. Choosing Automatic tiling is perhaps the safest and easiest method to use, and it has the result of enabling QuarkXPress to determine the portion of your document page, which appears on each tile and centers the section on each page output page. Choosing Automatic also enables you to set Automatic Overlap and Absolute Overlap. For information on using these options, see "Print Dialog Buttons and Options" earlier in this chapter.

The automatic tiling method has little regard for the labor subsequently required in assembling the tiles or for the amount of output material that is used in the process. Manual tiling, although it takes more thought, enables you full control over these two factors. Where the automatic method enables only a single page size and orientation, the manual method enables you to print each tile as you choose. In the previous example, to print a 24-by-18-inch poster in tiles to a printer capable of printing letter or legal-sized pages, the automatic method creates between 6 and 9 tiles, depending on how the output material is oriented (portrait or landscape). Using the Manual method you may use only five: four legal plus one letter sized tile, as shown in Figure 17-3.

To begin your manual tile operation, sketch out a tiling plan based on the size of your document page and your available output sizes. Keep in mind that since each tile will be printed individually, you may toggle the orientation of pages or even change page sizes. Figure 17-2 shows a typical planning sketch.

With this scenario in mind (a landscape-oriented 24-by-18-inch document page), follow these steps in the manual tiling of this page:

1. Open your document and display the Rulers (CMD/CTRL+R) of QuarkXPress. Double-click on the ruler origin (the point at which the vertical and horizontal ruler bars meet) to set them to align exactly with the upper-left corner of your page. Manual tiling has the effect of printing a tile of the area that falls below and to the right of the ruler origin.

2. With your tiling sketch in hand, drag the vertical and horizontal guide lines to the points at which your tiles will meet. In this case, it should be two vertical guidelines at 8.5 and 17 inches and a horizontal guideline at 14 inches, as shown next.

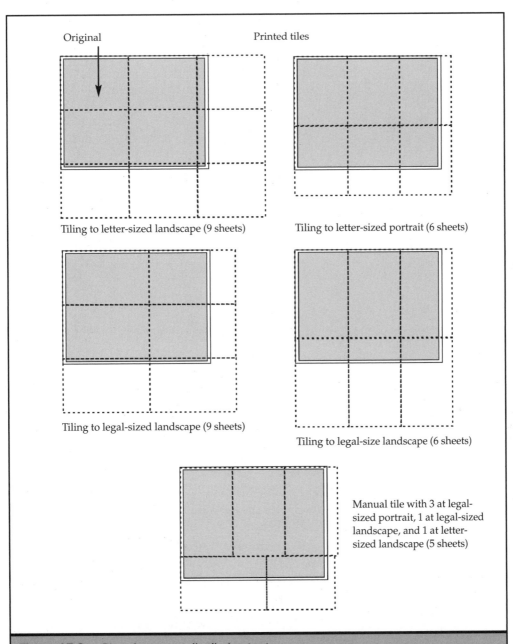

Original

Printed tiles

Tiling to letter-sized landscape (9 sheets)

Tiling to letter-sized portrait (6 sheets)

Tiling to legal-sized landscape (9 sheets)

Tiling to legal-size landscape (6 sheets)

Manual tile with 3 at legal-sized portrait, 1 at legal-sized landscape, and 1 at letter-sized landscape (5 sheets)

Figure 17-2.   *Planning manually tiled output*

BEYOND QUARKXPRESS
BASICS

3. Choose File | Print (CMD/CTRL+P) to open the Print dialog, and select your printer and its corresponding PPD file from the Printer Description drop-down menu in the Setup tab. Then enter your page number and the number of copies of your tiles you would like to print.

4. Choose Legal as the paper size, and Portrait as the orientation.

5. Click the Document tab and choose Manual from the Tiling drop-down menu. At this point, your first tile is in position, but you may want to choose other options from the Setup or Options tabs.

6. Click the Preview tab to verify that the position of the first tile is in the upper-left corner of your document page.

7. Click the Capture Settings button to save your current settings, click Print to print the first tile, and close the Print dialog. The first tile prints.

8. Drag your ruler origin to print the next tile, in this case to a point at the upper edge and 8.5 inches to the right.

9. Choose File | Print (CMD/CTRL+P) and notice your settings are saved from the previous session. Click the Print button to print the second tile and close the dialog. The second tile prints.

10. Repeat the previous procedure to print the third tile, moving right to left, top to bottom. When you reach the fourth tile, be sure to change the orientation of your output material to Landscape in the Document tab.

11. When you reach the fifth tile, be sure the page size is set to Letter and the orientation is set to Landscape, and print the last tile.

12. Assemble the tiles as you would normally.

If your printer is not capable of printing to the edges of your output pages, you will need to make allowances when planning your tiling and subsequently positioning your ruler origin.

Printing to Imagesetter Devices

Printing to an imagesetter can be a tricky exercise since most imagesetters are fed by rolls of film instead of precut sheets. The Setup tab features controls specifically for printing to imagesetters. As a practical exercise in printing to an imagesetter, follow these steps:

1. With your document open, choose File | Print to open the Print dialog.

2. Choose the imagesetter you wish to use from the Printer drop-down menu and enter your page number(s) and copies to print.

3. Enter your specific printing specifications in the Document tab.

4. Click the Setup tab and choose your imagesetter PPD from the Printer Description drop-down menu. Notice the Paper Size is automatically set to Custom and the Paper Height is set to Automatic.

5. In the Paper Width field, enter the maximum imageable width your imagesetter supports.

6. In the Paper Height field, enter the width or height of your document (depending on whether you are printing in portrait or landscape orientation), and add enough space to accommodate registration marks if this option is selected. An extra inch is usually enough.

7. Choose Center from the Page Positioning drop-down menu. This has the effect of centering your page vertically and horizontally within the imageable output material size you have specified. If you decide to choose any of the other options, you may wish to specify a value in the Paper Offset field described in the next step.

8. For Page Positioning options other than Center, specify a Paper Offset value. The Paper Offset option enables you to control where the left edge of the document page begins from the left edge of the output material.

BEYOND QUARKXPRESS BASICS

9. Enter a value in the Page Gap field. Page Gap enables you to control the space between printed pages when printing onto a continuous roll of output material. A gap of 6 points is often enough space to separate pages so that they may be cut apart.

10. Choose your orientation by selecting either Portrait (the default) or Landscape. If your document page is wider than the output material size you have chosen, Landscape is chosen automatically.

11. Click Print to print your pages to the imagesetter.

Creating Print Files

Print files are used as an alternative to printing to a connected printer. Normally when you print a file, a collection of data describing your document is sent directly to an online printer. When a print file is created, the data used to print the document is temporarily stored in a data file that may be stored indefinitely until downloaded to a printer. Print files enable you to create a complete and self-contained representation of your printed page (meaning it contains all necessary font and image information needed to print), which is usually transferred by some means to the destination or target printer. Creating a print file, sometimes referred to as a PostScript file, is not a complex operation and is very similar to printing to your desktop printer. As long as you have the correct drivers installed and a basic understanding of the way the target printer operates, creating the file is a relatively straightforward operation.

Print files essentially contain text in the form of PostScript commands, which your target printer will interpret in order to reproduce the page. Having the correct printer driver installed on your system before you print to file is perhaps the only requirement; the rest of the setup may be done on your desktop. To install a printer driver, obtain the latest version from your hardware manufacturer or service bureau and consult your system documentation for exact procedures on installing the driver.

While the correct driver is installed, create a print file using a Macintosh system by following these steps:

1. Open your QuarkXPress 5 document file and choose File, Print. Set your printing requirements in the usual way or according to your target printer's capabilities and your current printing needs.

2. Within the main Print dialog, click the Printer button to open the driver dialog capabilities for your printer (shown next). In the upper-right corner of this dialog, choose File from the Destination drop-down menu. Click Save to secure the settings and close the dialog.

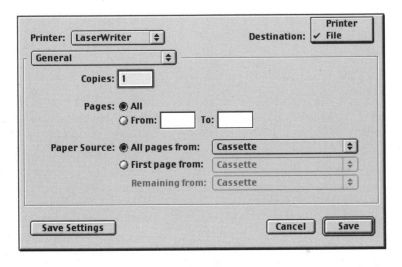

3. A dialog will open automatically (shown next), enabling you to name your new
    Print file and set its file location. Once you have named the print file and
    specified a folder location, click the Save button to close the dialog and return
    to the QuarkXPress Print dialog. PostScript print files are automatically
    appended with a .PS extension on the Macintosh platform.

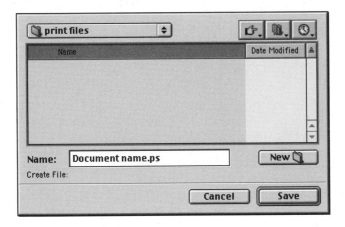

4. Clicking the Print button next creates the print file and saves it to the location you specified.

While the correct driver is installed, create a print file using a Windows system by following these steps:

1. Open your QuarkXPress 5 file and choose File | Print. Set your printing requirements in the usual way or according to your target printer's capabilities.

2. From your Windows taskbar, click the Start button and choose Settings, Printers to open the Printers window. Right-click on the printer name representing the printer you wish to use to open the popup menu and choose Properties. The [*printer name*] Printer Properties dialog opens (shown next) to the General tab.

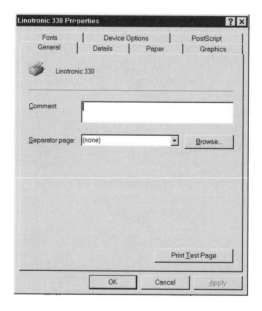

3. Click the Details tab in the Printer Properties dialog. The Details tab contains specific port communications options, including a drop-down menu with the label Print to the Following Port. Choose the option named FILE (creates a file on disk) from the list (as shown next) and click OK to accept the changes.

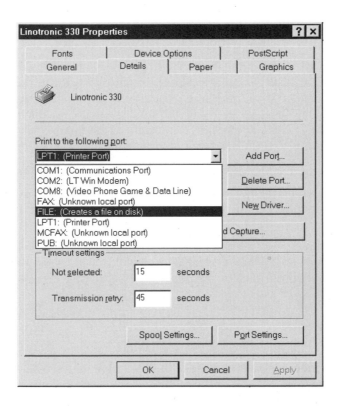

4. The next time you print to this printer, it will create a print file; as the file is being created, the printer's driver will prompt you for a name and a location to save the file using a dialog alert. Print files on the Windows platform are applied with the three-letter extension PRN.

Once you have set up your printer to create a print file, be sure to change it back again to print normally once again (if this is your need). If you regularly create print files, you may wish to create a specific print style just for this purpose.

5. Name and save your print file in the Print to File dialog box.

After your computer has finished writing the file to disk, you may send it to the service bureau (or whomever will be printing it) a number of different ways. Compressing the file first before you send it is always a wise choice. A common Windows compression utility is PKZip, while Stuffit is popular on Macintosh platforms.

A Remote Output Checklist

When sending your document files and the files collected by the Collect for Output command to the service bureau, it may be wise as a precaution to review a checklist to ensure you haven't left anything out. For example, you always want to include any fonts used in your document if your document uses fonts the service bureau may not already have. Or you may deal regularly with the service bureau, in which case you may be storing commonly used picture files for documents on their system. In any case, the following may serve as a checklist when purchasing output from a remote service:

- Provide all electronic files copied by the Collect for Output command.

- Include a printed hard-copy (or fax) summary of the document. For this you may want to simply print the report created by the Collect for Output command.

- Include a hard copy (or fax) of the pages you would like to have output, so that the service bureau may cross-check against the output to ensure the output is satisfactory. In the case of color separations, include a hard copy proof of the separations along with a composite printout.

- Include a hard copy (or fax) of your ordering information either through use of the Output template or an order form supplied by the service bureau operator.

- In the case of requesting color output in film separation form and/or color matching, include a color composite of the document pages to be printed. The color composite should be at least a reduction of the original document, clear enough to demonstrate reasonably accurate color and legible enough to identify fonts, font styles, and characters.

Using a Service Bureau

Before the advent of desktop publishing, there were (and still are) businesses dedicated solely to word processing, typesetting, and prepress, employing experts in these particular areas. Preparing text, artwork, or photographs for any of these traditional processes was usually a practical task. But things have changed quickly in the last dozen years or so, and procedures are not exactly what they used to be. Now much of the expertise involved is falling on the shoulders of the electronic artists using a personal computer and/or a layout program.

Using QuarkXPress 5, virtually anyone can have the necessary tools needed to create professional layouts and designs. With version 4, the tools have been developed to a point where even the most demanding professional can achieve sophisticated results. But in certain cases, layout artists who may not be familiar with remote output from a service bureau may find themselves forced into unfamiliar territory.

While using QuarkXPress 5 to create documents destined for offset printing, you may be faced with the prospect of using a service bureau for film output, scanning, and/or color-matched proofing, as is usually their core business. High-resolution film, used to produce offset-press printing plates, is often a common requirement. Film output can range from simple single-color output to complicated process color separations employing the use of process and spot color. With process color, four separate pieces of film are needed to print the cyan, magenta, yellow, and black plates. With each additional spot color, an additional piece of film is required.

Most professional service bureaus are familiar with QuarkXPress since it has become a near-standard for professionals in the publishing industry. You'll find many pride themselves on their expertise in handling, troubleshooting, and outputting client files. If you're a first-time client, you may find yourself being carefully eyed by the operators as they try to determine if you really know what you're doing. And you may also be eyeing them from the other side of the counter as you try to determine if *they* know what they're doing. Both of you are justified in doing so, since service bureau output can often be a complex exercise in "information coordination."

It's often been said that giving three different people the same document to create will result in three completely different documents, even if they appear to be identical onscreen. The first may create a document that looks and prints just fine. The second will look fine, but take forever to print, and the third will simply won't print at all.

With inexperienced layout artists, problems can often be encountered. Files may be created in strange ways, causing grief for all involved. This is the type of thing everyone tries to avoid. If you are fully prepared for the experience of buying output, you can substantially reduce your chance of having output problems. Whether you are a first-time purchaser of output or a seasoned professional, you'll find that printing your files at a service bureau *can* be a pleasant experience as long as you have slowly and carefully reviewed the information in previous sections of this chapter, and have open communication with your service bureau.

Understanding Imagesetters

This section provides some background on what an imagesetter is and the acrobatics it performs to image your file. Whether you ask for a single page of output or high-resolution film for a 100-page book, your data will likely go through the same channels.

All imaged files must first be downloaded through a raster image processor (RIP) according to the specific directions you provide. In the case of print files, the files may download directly to the imagesetter. If you provide a source file, the file may be imaged directly out of QuarkXPress 5. In most cases, the service bureau uses a spooler to hold the data until the imagesetter is ready for it. A healthy service bureau business likely has its imagesetters running 24 hours a day and uses dedicated print spoolers to handle the flow of traffic between the operators' computers and the actual imagesetters.

Next, after your data starts feeding to the imagesetter, the image is burned onto a layer of photographically sensitive film. From there, the film is fed into a chemical processor that develops, fixes, washes, and dries the film much the way your local one-hour film processor handles your vacation photos. After processing, the finished output is cut into separate film pages and packaged.

Two principle models of imagesetters are currently used. First, a *capstan* imagesetter uses a 200-foot roll of film that is loaded much like an ordinary camera. The film enters the imagesetter and is fed by rollers to a laser device that exposes the film. From there, it's fed into a light-tight cassette that may be easily removed from the imagesetter without exposing the contents. The service bureau operator removes the cassette for processing, just like a regular camera.

The second type of imagesetter is the *drum model* imagesetter. Drum model imagesetters image film that has been cut into large sheets and vacuum-mounted to the inside of a light-tight, half-barrel-shaped housing. An imaging laser moves back and forth inside the drum to expose the film. The exposed film then is track-fed into a take-up cassette, and a new sheet of film is fed into its place.

Imaging Output Material

You likely will order two types of film output from the service bureau: paper and/or film. These materials may be confusing because both are photographically sensitive and considered to be *film*, even though one is paper-based. Once the film has been imaged by the imagesetter, film processors are used to automatically process, fix, wash, and dry both types of output. A properly maintained processing system is fed by a filtered, constant water supply that is temperature-controlled. Like imagesetters, processors require regular maintenance to provide constant results. The professional service bureau constantly monitors both imagesetters and processors for such things as dust, dirt, static, and film density.

If you have prepared your files properly and provided the service bureau with everything they need, you won't have any surprises when your film comes back. If a problem occurs and your output is not satisfactory, the first thing to do is check your output order form to ensure your order is correct.

If your files are complex, the service bureau may charge you for additional processing time in the form of surcharges. Most service bureaus follow a rule of thumb that allows 15 minutes for each letter-sized page to be imaged and processed. Beyond that, you may be charged up to a dollar per minute for the additional time needed to image the page. This practice is not uncommon, but keep in mind that good customers are rarely charged.

Chapter 18

Preparing Digital Color Separations

In a strictly digital publishing environment where virtually all content exists on a computer in one form or another, there are certain production techniques that those "in-the-know" use often for increasing productivity or as solutions to difficult problems. This chapter demonstrates one such technique. In the coming pages, you'll learn the ideal way of preparing color picture files from other applications for use in QuarkXPress 5 by utilizing efficient separation technology pioneered by Quark's own engineers. It enables you to digitally preseparate pictures in PostScript format for import in QuarkXPress 5 and still make use of high-end pictures without substantially increasing your document file size. It also enables you to export content from your QuarkXPress document pages in a preseparated format for use in other documents or other applications using export functions.

As you'll discover, the technology we'll explore here, coined *Desktop Color Separations*, or simply DCS, is engineered into QuarkXPress 5 and other applications as a standard file format. One of the most popular applications for producing preseparated color PostScript files is Adobe Photoshop. You'll not only learn the typical procedure to follow from within Photoshop, but also why you're choosing it and what it does, so you'll be able to employ the same procedure for use with other applications equipped with DCS export features.

Color Separating Typical Pictures

First, let's examine exactly what DCS is and how it works. In typical situations, importing a color picture file into XPress is a straightforward operation. Create a picture box and import the file using the Get Picture command to locate and open a compatible picture format, typically EPS or TIFF. After importing your picture file, a preview of the image is displayed on your document window, but the actual data representing the picture is stored externally outside of QuarkXPress.

Using Pictures Prepared with Process Color

When using typical picture color such as a four-color offset printing process, the file you import must be prepared in a specific color format, namely Cyan, Magenta, Yellow, and Black (CMYK). Some picture files you import may originate in Red, Green, and Blue (RGB) color, which is great for the Web, but not for print. Most popular image-editing applications such as Photoshop or Photo-Paint enable you to perform simple color mode changes or use export filters to create new copies in CMYK color.

Once the picture is imported into XPress in CMYK format, the exact colors required to print or export it are prepared and ready. When the file is printed, the process colors in the picture end up separating to the corresponding CMYK plates along with other color items in your document.

Using Pictures with Process and Spot Colors Combined

Not all digital separations are necessarily prepared using typical color. Some may contain two or three spot ink colors, possibly even in *addition* to the process colors they contain depending on the complexity of the picture and reproduction. Graphic illustrations can often contain multiple spot ink colors, which is commonplace in limited-run or low-budget printing. These pictures may also contain elements destined to be reproduced in all standard process colors as well as additional spot colors, making the film separation and printing processes even more complex.

Digital pictures that include more than just four process ink colors must either be specially edited and/or intentionally prepared this way using software capable of preparing the file to support the extra color. For this specialized type of work, encapsulated PostScript (EPS) is the only compatible format, as must be the printer separating the color output. Illustrations prepared using spot ink colors may also include spot ink colors, but again EPS is the only format and the pictures themselves must also contain some type of CMYK composition.

> **Note**
>
> *Two-, three-, or four-color digital photographs (referred to as duotones, tritones, and quadtones respectively) are the most common digital picture types containing spot colors. They may be created in an image editor or by using specialized high-fidelity color-editing software. Duotones, tritones (even quadtones), and high-fidelity color pictures essentially enable your pictures to appear richer in tone and depth than simply using a single color of ink. However, pictures containing spot colors alone are not compatible with DCS technology; the picture file being saved to DCS (discussed in the section to follow) must contain elements in the CMYK color space. Picture files containing spot ink colors alone may not be exported or saved to the DCS format.*

Quark's DCS Technology

The DCS concept involves digitally separating picture files into PostScript files before they're imported into XPress. Saving a picture to EPS format and digitally separating it may be done using a full-featured desktop image-editing application such as Photoshop or Photo-Paint. The process often begins with a picture containing multiple colors saved to TIFF format and it involves exporting or saving the picture file to EPS. During the save or export operation, full-featured image editors usually offer options to save in either DCS 1.0 or DCS 2.0 with a host of additional options for controlling the condition of the saved EPS separations.

After choosing your preferred preview and separation file options and saving the picture to DCS format, one or more files will result. Where single files are created, all image data will be digitally separated, but remain in a single file. Where multiple files are created, one file will be what is referred to as a master, containing a preview image of the picture in RGB format. The remaining files contain the actual separation data needed to reproduce the picture when printed or exported. Each will be named automatically by default according to the picture's filename.

The master is the picture you'll import into your QuarkXPress document as a placeholder of sorts and contains only a preview of the picture at a fixed low resolution. Since it contains no color separation data and a low resolution, its file size will be relatively small and will require much less storage space than a typical picture file. This enables you to perform quicker Save commands and demands less memory space for the QuarkXPress document it is imported into, without compromising output quality when performing print tasks. The master preview also contains embedded links to the remaining separation data files needed to reproduce it in its original state.

A DCS picture file set is sometimes referred to as a *five-file* picture since five actual files are typically created from a single color picture file, as shown in Figure 18-1. One master preview EPS file is created for use as the picture preview for importing into your XPress document page, and four supporting EPS files representing cyan, magenta, yellow, and black are created. The preview file is the only file that may be used for importing into your XPress document. The resulting digitally separated EPS files take the form of PostScript and do not contain any image to preview.

When using a DCS image, the master is the one imported onto your document page. During printing, the digital separations contained in the data file are substituted for the master, a process that is repeated for each color plate being printed. Figure 18-2 illustrates the picture data-swapping action during the printing of a typical color document containing a CMYK picture prepared using the DCS format.

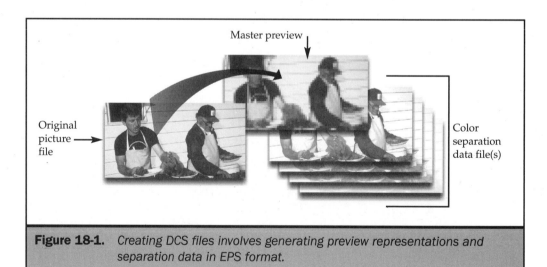

Figure 18-1.   *Creating DCS files involves generating preview representations and separation data in EPS format.*

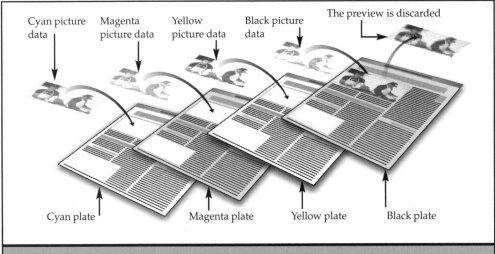

Cyan picture data

Magenta picture data

Yellow picture data

Black picture data

The preview is discarded

Cyan plate

Magenta plate

Yellow plate

Black plate

Figure 18-2.   *Using digitally separated DCS files to print process color pictures*

Digitally Separating Pictures for XPress

The quality of the master DCS preview and the state of color data composing the picture vary depending on the options selected when the file was created. Different applications and platform versions offer differing options and how you prepare the files is completely dependent on your own workflow preferences and the size of the resulting files. Preview quality may be varied in resolution and color depth, while the accompanying data may be composed of a single composite file containing all color data, or a collection of separate files, each containing a separate color.

As mentioned earlier, there are also two versions of DCS you may be required to choose from. The original version, DCS 1.0, supports only CMYK color separations as well as limited preview quality options and file structures. This means if the file you are creating contains spot color in addition to process color, or if you'd like more control over how the preview or separation data files are prepared, this may not be the best format to choose. For pictures containing spot color inks, you'll need to select DCS 2.0, which is capable of separating both spot and process ink colors from a single image file. It also offers expanded preview and separation file options.

For any process- or spot-color-equipped picture to be eligible for the DCS workflow process though, it must be in a final condition and ready to go. This means that all image editing changes such as image manipulation, filter effects, and/or image adjustments must be complete. No matter which format or color depth the picture file currently exists in, it may need to be changed to CMYK color mode. It may also need to have any desired spot color inks added and saved to TIFF and eventually also to the DCS EPS format.

For a somewhat generic-type guide for using either platform version of Photoshop 5.0 or 6.0 to save a picture file prepared in CMYK color, follow these steps to create a digitally separated DCS file set:

1. If you haven't already done so, complete your picture editing and save the file.

2. Convert color pictures destined only for process color to CMYK by choosing Image Mode | CMYK Color. If the option is unavailable, the image is likely already in this color mode.

3. Once your color mode conversion has been applied, choose File | Save As, choose TIFF as the format, and provide a name. This picture file will serve as your safe copy.

4. After creating a safe copy, choose File | Save As and choose Photoshop DCS 2.0 (EPS). Specify a name and location for the DCS files to be created and click OK to proceed to the next dialog containing further options (see Figure 18-3).

5. For the maximum quality preview image (meaning the placeholder image you'll see on your QuarkXPress document page), choose TIFF (8 bit/pixel) from the Preview drop-down menu. Macintosh users will also have JPEG as a preview picture format to select, but TIFF is the best option for cross-platform uses.

6. From the DCS drop-down menu, choose carefully from the available list. The options vary between multiple files or single files and they refer to whether the separation files are saved separately or not. You'll also have the choice of controlling whether the preview (referred to as the composite) will be prepared in grayscale, color, or not at all. For the maximum quality with separate files for each ink color, choose Multiple File with Color Composite.

7. From the Encoding drop-down menu, choose between Binary, ASCII, or JPEG, the safest of which is Binary. Choosing ASCII may be required for certain specialized uses. Choosing JPEG features several levels of compression (selected by the quality rendered) and offers you a degree of control over the required memory size of the resulting composite preview.

8. For specialized halftoning or transfer functions applied to your picture in Photoshop, you may wish to choose Include Halftone Screen or Include Transfer Function as options that will override any equivalent image controls applied in QuarkXPress. Otherwise, these options should be as is and unselected.

9. Click OK to close and exit the dialog, and your DCS files will be created according to the options you've selected.

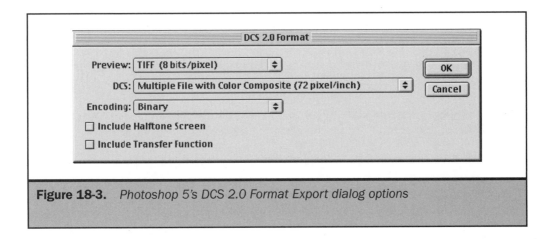

Figure 18-3. *Photoshop 5's DCS 2.0 Format Export dialog options*

Creating typical process color EPS separation files from Photoshop using DCS options specifying multiple files and a composite preview will result in the following files being created:

- *Filename*.**EPS**   The master preview or composite picture file
- *Filename*.**c**   The cyan EPS separation
- *Filename*.**m**   The magenta EPS separation
- *Filename*.**y**   The yellow EPS separation
- *Filename*.**k**   The black EPS separation

The previous example merely uses Photoshop as an example. Other image-editing applications may be used to create DCS files while the specific options may differ and the resulting EPS files may feature different naming conventions. For example, Corel's Photo-Paint uses the file extensions 01, 02, 03, and 04 to represent the four process colors, cyan, magenta, yellow, and black, respectively.

Importing DCS Files into XPress

Once your digital separations have been created, the master preview EPS file may be imported into your XPress document using the EPS filter in the Get Picture (CMD/CTRL+E) dialog. At this point only *you* will know it is a master preview representing a digital separation. Since the file is in EPS format, you will not be able to determine its color depth using the Usage | Pictures tab.

However, when the Collect for Output command is used to prepare your document for transferring to a service bureau or remote output service, QuarkXPress will automatically collect the required digital separations. To verify this, use the Report

BEYOND QUARKXPRESS BASICS

Only option in the Collect for Output dialog to create a report of the files that will be collected.

For more information on using the Collect for Output command, refer to "Requesting Remote Output" in Chapter 17.

In the case of preparing a picture in DCS using Photoshop, a typical report will identify the digital separations in the following way:
@picture items:
Driveletter:\folder\filename.eps
Cyan plate *filename: Driveletter:\folder\filename*.C
Magenta plate *filename: Driveletter:\folder\filename*.M
Yellow plate *filename: Driveletter:\folder\filename*.Y
Black plate *filename: Driveletter:\folder\filename*.K

Screening Hazards for Duotones, Tritones, and Quadtones

Regardless of whether you use the DCS technique for preparing your files or not, one hazard exists for users who may not be familiar with preparing pictures that contain multiple spot ink colors for printing. The hazard involves screening angles and arises when printing the individual separations associated with spot color shapes in a graphic illustration or the overall applied colors in a duotone, tritone, or quadtone. When a multi-ink color picture is imported into QuarkXPress as an EPS image, the colors it contains are automatically added to your XPress document colors list. When the document is printed to color separations, the additional colors are automatically available for printing. Of course, this is the good news though.

The bad news involves screens, the tiny rows of dots that compose a printed picture. In process color printing, overlapping rows of dots are automatically angled to standard degree measures to avoid unsightly moiré patterns caused by dots overlapping at odd screen angles. But although there are standard angles for overlapping process screen angles, there are no standards for spot colors, only defaults. This means that the screen for each spot color in a document is destined to print at the same angle, which happens to be 45 degrees, the same standard angle used by the process color black. If the multi-ink picture you're printing includes black as one of the colors (as many often do), it may not produce satisfactory results when your document is reproduced in offset printing.

This is especially a concern in instances when color screens in your imported picture combine or overprint color screens for other items in your document. It is also a concern in cases where pictures have been prepared as multi-ink pictures such as duotones, tritones, or quadtones. By their nature, the ink colors in a multi-ink picture overprint each other. Ideally though, the screen angles for each color should be different in the same respect that process colors are angled differently.

To improve the appearance of these multi-ink color pictures, it may be necessary to change the screening angles of overlapping spot ink color screens. One solution is to angle the screens to match those for process colors (see Figure 18-4), but ultimately you'd be well advised to contact your printing vendor for the ideal angles to set for overlapping spot color screens.

To change color screening angle options for spot colors, follow these steps:

1. With your QuarkXPress document containing the imported multi-ink pictures open, choose File | Print (CMD/CTRL+P) to open the Print dialog.

2. Choose a PostScript printer as your printer type from the top of the dialog. This will indicate to QuarkXPress that you intend to print the PostScript image data contained in the linked EPS picture files.

3. Click the Document tab and click to activate the Separations option. This will enable XPress to examine your document and its linked picture files for multiple ink colors.

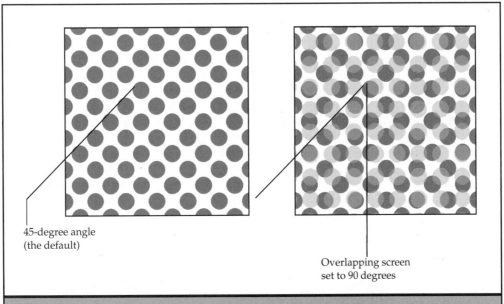

45-degree angle
(the default)

Overlapping screen
set to 90 degrees

Figure 18-4.   *This default screen (left) features an angle of 45 degrees, while the overlapping screen (right) has been altered to 90 degrees.*

4. Click to select the Output tab (shown in Figure 18-5) and view the list of separations destined to print. A check mark beside the color indicates it is selected to print. Color names are listed under the Plate heading. Halftone, Frequency, Angle, and Function settings are also displayed.

5. Click to select the spot ink color you wish to change the angle for, click the button adjacent to the Angle heading, and choose Other from the pop-up menu that opens. This will open the Other dialog. Notice (by default) the angle is preset to 45 degrees.

6. Enter a new angle value and click OK to close the dialog. Your new screening angle value is applied and will now alter the screening angle for the selected spot color when the document is printed. When ready, proceed with printing your document.

For more information on changing the screen angles for printed ink colors, refer to "Choosing Output Options" in Chapter 17.

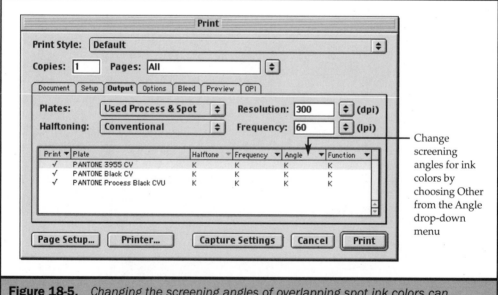

Figure 18-5. *Changing the screening angles of overlapping spot ink colors can significantly improve the printed appearance of multi-ink pictures.*

Digitally Separating QuarkXPress 5 Documents

If you've been following along in this chapter, you may already be aware of the advantages of digitally separating picture files before they reach your QuarkXPress document. It's certainly a great resource to have available should you need to use it.

But QuarkXPress also enables you to create your own document layout pages as EPS files in DCS format using the Save Page as EPS command. This is especially useful when a layout you may be creating requires a picture of an existing QuarkXPress page in a different document. This is a common requirement in publications that feature pictures of other publications such as publisher catalogs or an advertising promotion for virtually any printed document. It also provides a unique solution to resizing completed layouts where none existed before; an imported EPS file may be resized much more easily than resizing an entire page of individual content layout items.

The Save Page as EPS command (CMD/CTRL+OPTION/ALT+SHIFT+S) provides options for saving your page to either DCS (meaning version 1.0) or DCS 2.0 (see Figure 18-6). The DCS format you choose will depend on whether your document contains strictly process color or combined spot and process items, but choosing DCS 2 over DCS will guarantee that any additional spot colors your document content has been prepared in will be included.

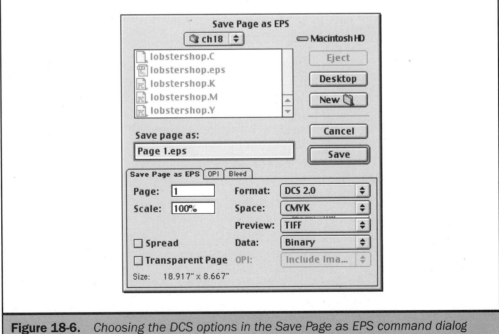

Figure 18-6.   *Choosing the DCS options in the Save Page as EPS command dialog*

BEYOND QUARKXPRESS BASICS

The files created by QuarkXPress 5's Save as EPS command while using the DCS option are similar to those created by other DCS-compatible applications, but these files do feature their own different twist and file naming scheme. While DCS is selected as the format, multiple files are created, but the format only supports CMYK process color. While DCS 2.0 is selected, a single file is created containing a preview master image, all four process colors, and any additional spot colors specified to print items in your document. By default, these DCS files are created in the same folder as your original document and use the following naming scheme:

- *Filename.EPS*   For DCS master previews or composite DCS 2.0 files
- *Filename_C.EPS*   Cyan plate only
- *Filename_M.EPS*   Magenta plate only
- *Filename_Y.EPS*   Yellow plate only
- *Filename_K.EPS*   Black plate only

These DCS files may then be imported back into XPress or imported in other applications and output independent of QuarkXPress 5.

Note   *The Save Page as EPS command does not include an option for embedding the fonts in an EPS file. If the file you are preparing is destined for use in another application, a service bureau, or a different user's system, include the necessary fonts with the file. If you do not include the fonts, font substitution may occur when the EPS files are printed.*

This chapter has exposed you to a slightly higher-end focus on working in color pictures and printing tasks within XPress. For basic color layout techniques, separating for digital color may be slightly ahead of its time, but at some point you may find yourself considering it. It's also not a technique you'll find very well documented, since it essentially falls somewhere between XPress and the other applications you may use.

Tip   *For more information on using the Save Page as EPS feature, see "Saving Pages in EPS Format" in Chapter 20.*

Chapter 19

Creating Web Documents

T he introduction of a full and comprehensive set of Web Document tools and resources is a leap ahead for QuarkXPress. Although it may be the beginning of a vast extension to the life of the documents you create, the Web can also be an intimidating place if you're not familiar with this design-challenging arena.

In this chapter, you'll examine the similarities and differences between publishing typical QuarkXPress 5 documents and look closely at the unique set of tools and capabilities of Web documents. You'll learn to create both simple and complex Web Document design elements and open avenues for more exploration. As you'll soon discover, QuarkXPress 5 enables you to create Web documents ranging from basic to sophisticated.

Anatomy of the Web Document Window

The key to quickly grasping QuarkXPress 5's Web concept is in understanding what you're seeing onscreen as you work with your Web content. The Web documents you create in QuarkXPress are merely the construction area for the HTML page you eventually create. As you build your Web document, you'll see many of the hidden aspects of the content you're working with. Many of the elements you're creating won't appear and behave onscreen as you intend them to in your final Web page. QuarkXPress can't display elements as they would appear in a Web browser. For this, the page must be viewed in a browser, which can be done using XPress 5's HTML Preview feature. Before we delve too far into the various Web elements that you can add to your Web document though, let's explore the various parts of a QuarkXPress Web Document window, and how they differ from typical QuarkXPress Document windows.

As you can see in Figure 19-1, Web documents have their own supplemental collection of tools found in the Web Tool palette—available only while working in a Web document. You can also see that Web documents have no margins, but instead have a single right-page border to indicate the page width limit. An HTML Preview button at the bottom of the document window enables you to view how your current Web page appears in a browser window. Otherwise, mostly all of QuarkXPress 5's tools and features are available for composing content.

Beginning a New Web Document

The first thing you might notice when beginning a new Web document is that the document itself must be started from scratch as a Web document. Although you might be able to copy content from other QuarkXPress documents, the initial step must always be to choose File | New | Web Document (CMD/CTRL+OPTION/ALT+SHIFT+N). Doing so opens the New Web Document dialog (see Figure 19-2), which enables you to establish a basic foundation for certain aspects of the document including setting Web page, color, and layout properties. As with typical QuarkXPress documents, choosing

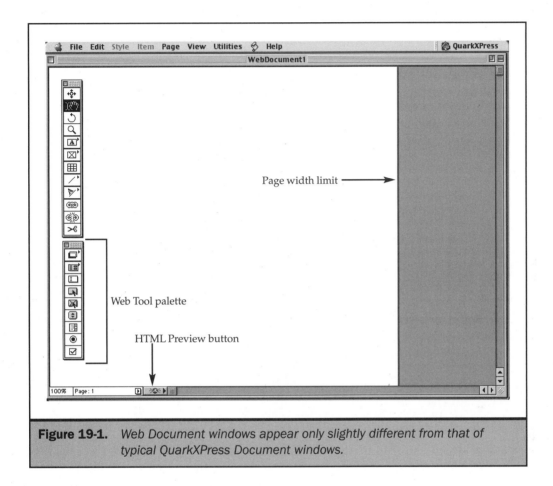

Figure 19-1.   *Web Document windows appear only slightly different from that of typical QuarkXPress Document windows.*

options in this dialog acts as a basis for default settings, but actual content may be modified to any properties you want.

Choosing Color Options

Web documents use their own special type of color—a pared-down, somewhat standardized collection of red, green, blue (RGB) colors. The purpose of these Web color collections is to provide a wide selection without going beyond the colors that typical browsers are capable of properly displaying. In QuarkXPress 5, you may choose colors from one of two basic palette types: Web Named or Web Safe. Both types are discussed in detail later in this chapter in the section "Working with Web Color." Web color defaults may be specified for the following items:

■ **Text**   Choosing a text color using this option sets the default color for all text entered in typical text boxes; initially the default is Blue. Text color may be changed later using the Colors palette.

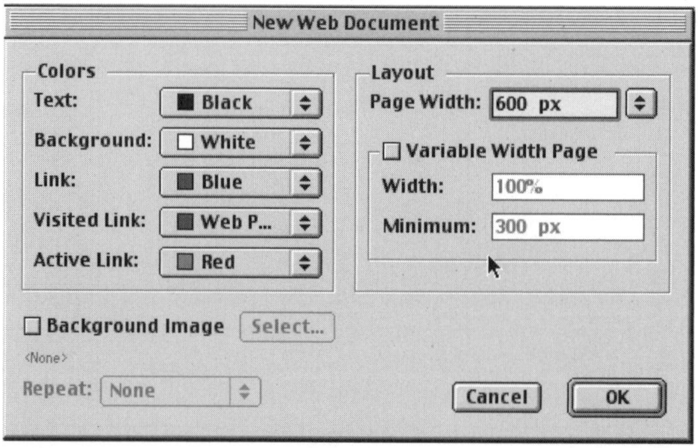

Figure 19-2. *Choosing options in the Web Document dialog is always the first step.*

■ **Background**   Choosing a background color sets the default page color for all pages in your Web document; initially, the default is White. The page background color may be customized later for each page using the Page Properties command (discussed in the "Setting Page Properties" section later in this chapter).

■ **Link**   The color chosen using this option sets the default color for text applied with hyperlinks, as it appears on your Web Document page and in the final Web page.

■ **Visited Link**   This option sets the color of hyperlinks that your Web page audience has already visited, as they appear in the Web browser used to view the final Web page.

■ **Active Link**   This option sets the color for items that are currently being clicked—an action referred to as a *mouse down* in interactive terms. When text is applied with a hyperlink, it changes color as it is being clicked, according to the color chosen here.

Defining Layout Options

Your page width may be set to nearly any width you want, but is always measured in pixels (px)—the Web's universal unit of measure. Choose a value from the Page Width drop-down menu (shown next) to set the fixed width for your Web document, or enter a value of your own. Preset widths include 600 px (the default), 800 px, 1,024 px, and 1,268 px. The range for custom pixel values is between 10 and 3,455 px. Because Web pages may be virtually unlimited in length, no page length value needs to be set.

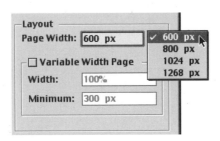

Unlike typical print documents, which have a constant and fixed physical page size, the width of the browser window used to view your Web page can, and often *does*, vary within an audience. With respect to page layout, the width may be set to two basic types: Fixed or Variable. When set to Fixed (the default), your Web Document page width remains at a constant width, no matter how wide the browser window used to view it is. The Fixed width state is often the most desirable for design work because the layout can remain constant.

A Variable page condition presents completely different design requirements than those of fixed width layouts. When a page is set to Variable width, the page content is allowed to flow from left-to-right and top-to-bottom according to the available width of the browser window being used to view it.

Using Web Page Backgrounds

A Web page background may also be set to an image if you want. To do so, choose the Background Image option (shown next) and click the Browse button to locate and select an image file. Choose Joint Photographers Expert Group (JPEG), Graphical Interchange Format (GIF), or Portable Network Graphic (PNG), each of which is ideal for Web display. When an image file is specified, you may also choose an image tiling option from the Repeat drop-down menu.

For more information on choosing a Web picture format, see the "Choosing a Web Picture Export Format" section later in this chapter.

The purpose of these Repeat options is to enable you to control how tiled images appear in the background of your Web page in the following ways:

- **Tile**   Choosing this option enables your background image to tile both vertically and horizontally to completely fill the background of your Web page.

- **Horizontal**   Choosing this option causes the selected background image to be tiled only horizontally in a single row to completely fill the width of your Web page.

- **Vertical**   Choosing this option causes the selected background image to be tiled only vertically in a single row to completely fill the length of your Web page.

- **None**   Choosing this option deactivates the tiling function, but still allows your Web page background image to appear once in the upper-left corner of the Web page.

> **Tip**   *Although you may add new pages to your Web document, the pages may not be fashioned into spreads, and you may not be able to view more than one page at a time. To insert pages, choose Page | Insert, and use options in the Insert Pages dialog. For more information on inserting, deleting, and otherwise managing pages in QuarkXPress 5, see the "Using the Menu Command to Add, Remove, or Move Pages" section in Chapter 2.*

Setting Page Properties

When you first chose to begin a brand new Web document, you were likely faced with making choices for certain page properties such as text and hyperlink colors, page layout sizes, and page background image. Since you first created the document, you may have changed your design or added additional pages. If your design requires it, you may apply different page properties for each page using options in the Page Properties dialog (see Figure 19-3), which can be opened by choosing Page | Properties (CMD/CTRL+OPTION/ALT+SHIFT+A).

For the most part, options available in the Page Properties dialog are identical to those available in the New Web Document dialog (see the "Beginning a New Web Document" section earlier in this chapter). One key difference exists: This dialog enables you to apply properties to each individual Web page, including entering a specific page title and export file name, and assigning a saved meta tag set. The following list details the purpose of the additional page property options available in this dialog:

- **Page Title**   Entering a name in the Page Title box enables you to apply a unique name for your Web page. This is the text that appears in the title bar of

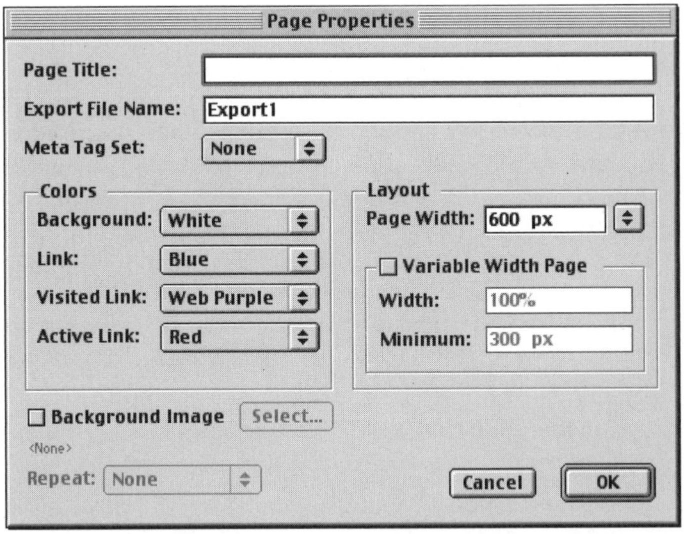

Figure 19-3.   *You may change page property defaults using options in this dialog.*

the browser that is being used to view your page. It is also used as the default
page name if your Web audience bookmarks the page using the browser
bookmark command.

- **Export File Name**   The Export File Name option enables you to apply a
  unique name to the exported HTML page for a specific Web Document page.
  The default name is automatically set to ExportX.htm (where X represents the
  order of the page in your QuarkXPress Web document). The HTML export file
  name also identifies the specific page on the Web server that is hosting the
  page, and is used as the unique URL path when the page is displayed in your
  Web audience's browser.

- **Meta Tag Set**   This option enables you to assign a meta tag to your Web
  Document page. Meta tags are invisible text that enables Web search engines to
  index Web pages more easily. In order for a meta tag to be available for
  selection, you must first create a list of meta tag text. By default, the only meta
  tag set available from the Meta Tag Set drop-down menu is the generic Set1 set.
  For more information on creating and using meta tags, see the "Using Meta
  Tags in Web Documents" section later in this chapter.

Using the HTML Solid 3D Style
for Frames, Lines, and Tables

One of the most significant differences you'll discover when applying line and frame styles in Web documents with QuarkXPress 5 is the availability of a specialized Solid 3D style. This style enables you to take advantage of a style that is traditionally available to HTML. It may be applied to rectangular text, picture boxes, straight lines, or the grid lines separating and surrounding table cells—provided that they have not been rotated from their original orientation.

The Solid 3D style is available from the Style menu in either the Measurements palette or the Frame tab of the Modify dialog (while any of these items are selected). To apply the 3D Solid style to a selected box frame, line, or table, follow these brief steps:

1. Use the Item tool from the Tool palette and click to select the rectangular text box, picture box, line, or table.

2. Open the Modify dialog by choosing Item | Modify (CMD/CTRL+M) or double-clicking the selected item.

3. Click the Frame tab within the Modify dialog and choose Solid Shade (HR) for lines, or Solid 3D for rectangular boxes (shown next).

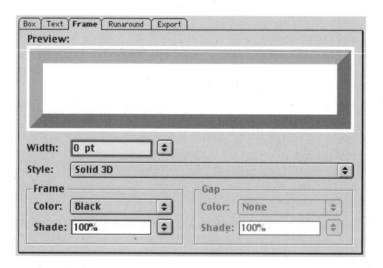

4. If the item you have selected is a table, click the Grid tab in the Modify dialog and choose Solid Shade(HR) from the Style menu. Notice that

the Grid preview displays the appearance of your new table grid style (shown next).

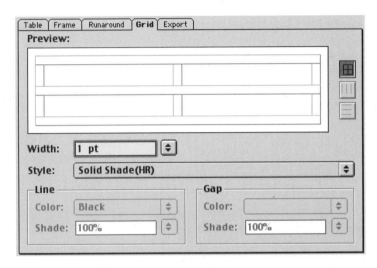

5. Choose any other options for the properties of your box frame, line, or table grid, and click OK to close the dialog. Your Solid 3D style is applied.

After the 3D Solid style has been applied to boxes, lines, or tables, the items may not be rotated using the Rotation tool.

Creating Interactive Elements

Interactive elements are what distinguish Web documents from typical QuarkXPress documents. Interactive elements (such as forms, rollovers, hyperlinks, and anchors) enable your Web audience to interact in certain ways with the content on the Web page(s) you are creating. Interactive elements are those that enable users to navigate to different Web pages (or points on a Web page), enter and upload data, or to perform various other actions.

Creating a Rollover

One of the most sought-after effects of any new Web page designer is the rollover effect. Rollovers enable you to create a simple two-step animated effect whenever your Web audience's pointer is positioned over a specific picture on your Web page. While the picture is being viewed, the first image is visible and while the cursor is held over this picture, a different picture is displayed.

To create a rollover effect, you must have two images prepared in advance using a compatible Web picture format (such as JPEG, GIF, or PNG). Most popular image-editing applications enable you to create pictures in these Web picture formats. Ideally, the two images you use should be similar in size (if not exactly the same).

Creating a rollover effect in QuarkXPress 5 is done using the Rollover command, which is available while building a Web document and while a picture box is selected. To create a rollover effect, follow these steps:

1. In an active Web document, use any of the picture box tools to create a picture box that defines the size and location for your rollover picture. With either the Item or Content tools selected, import a picture using the Get Picture dialog, which is opened by choosing File | Get Picture (CMD/CTRL+E). Initially, the imported picture should appear in a non-rollover state (before the rollover effect takes place).

2. With a picture imported, choose the Item tool, and then choose Item | Rollover | Create Rollover, or CTRL/RIGHT-click the picture and choose Create Rollover from the popup menu to open the Rollover dialog (shown next). Notice that the picture you imported into the picture box is automatically listed as the Default Image. If you want, you may change the picture by clicking the Select/Browse button to open the Select Image dialog and select a picture.

3. In the Rollover dialog, click the Select/Browse button adjacent to the Rollover Image box and select the picture you want to use as the secondary picture of the rollover effect. When selected, the picture file name appears in the Rollover Image box.

4. If the picture is to be used as a hyperlink or mailto (email address), enter the URL or email address in the Hyperlink box. As a convenience, you may automatically apply http://, https://, ftp://, or mailto: prefixes by making a selection from the Hyperlink drop-down menu. Macintosh users may click the Select button to open a dialog that enables them to select an HTML page to link to.

5. Click OK to complete the rollover effect operation. To preview the effect, click the HTML Preview button. Notice that as the cursor is held over the picture in the browser window, the secondary image you specified appears. If a hyperlink is applied, the page view changes to display the linked page.

6. To edit an existing rollover effect, the operation is quite similar. Simply use the Item or Content tools and click to select the existing rollover effect. Then, choose Edit Rollover from the Item | Rollover submenu, or CTRL/RIGHT-click the picture to open the popup menu. To delete an existing rollover effect, choose Item | Rollover | Delete Rollover. The rollover effect is removed without affecting the imported picture in the picture box.

Defining Hyperlinks and Anchors

Hyperlinks and anchors are perhaps the most commonly applied types of interactive element in Web design. Hyperlinks are designed to navigate to different pages within your Web document or to other Web sites, and anchors enable your Web page audience to navigate to specific points within a Web page.

Essentially, two basic types of hyperlinks exist that you should be familiar with: absolute and relative. Absolute hyperlinks specify a Web site URL (such as **www.abc_company.com**), but relative hyperlinks link to pages within your own Web site relative to the folder containing the exported Web page. A typical relative hyperlink should be specified using the prefix ../, which tells the browser to look for the page in a specific folder—within the folder containing the current page.

For example, a typical relative hyperlink might appear like this: ../index/products.html. This means that the destination page being linked to (products.html) resides within a folder named index that is located in the folder containing the current Web page (signified by ../). When a hyperlink is applied to text, the text appears using typical hyperlink underlining, as it appears in the final HTML Web page. When a hyperlink is applied to a picture, a hyperlink icon appears in the upper-right corner of the picture box (see Figure 19-4). The hyperlink symbol accompanying a picture box does not appear in the final HTML Web page.

Using relative hyperlinks has a significant advantage over using absolute hyperlinks. When an absolute hyperlink is applied, the browser must navigate the Web to locate the server containing the specified page, which often takes more time. When a relative hyperlink is used, you enable the browser to simply switch folders within the server it has already found, without navigating the Web.

Use of relative hyperlinks also makes it considerably easier to move the complete contents of a Web site (containing multiple pages and folders) between servers without breaking the page links. It's also easier to change the unique URL of your Web site (for example, changing the URL from **www.abc_company.com** to **www.english.abc_company.com**). Moving a site that uses absolute hyperlinks would

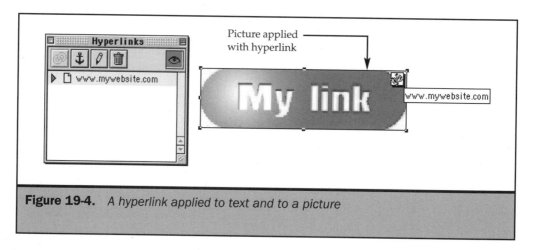

Figure 19-4.   *A hyperlink applied to text and to a picture*

require updating all the links you've applied. Because relative hyperlinks do not reference the server, the site may be moved without breaking the links.

An anchor is a marker applied to a specific point in a document (such as text or a picture). When a hyperlink points to an anchor, clicking the anchor causes the browser to display the point where the anchor has been applied, rather than simply displaying the top of the page. When an anchor is applied to text, a colored arrow appears beside the text it is applied to in your Web document (shown next). When an anchor is applied to a picture, the hyperlink chain symbol is used. This anchor symbol does not appear in the exported Web page.

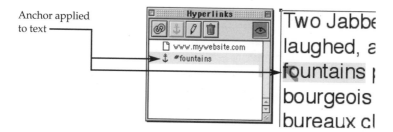

Using the Hyperlinks Palette

Hyperlinks may be applied to either text within a text box or pictures in picture boxes. The most efficient technique for applying hyperlinks and anchors is through the Hyperlinks palette. (Although you may also apply them using menu commands, which are available by choosing commands from Style | Hyperlinks or Style | Anchors submenus, or by using the context-sensitive popup menu). To open the Hyperlinks palette (shown next), choose View | Show Hyperlinks.

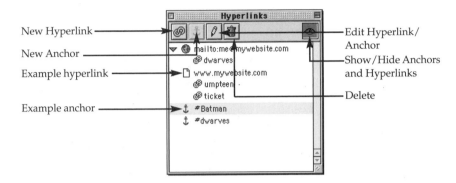

New Hyperlink

New Anchor

Example hyperlink

Example anchor

Edit Hyperlink/
Anchor

Show/Hide Anchors
and Hyperlinks

Delete

The Hyperlinks palette lists any available hyperlinks and anchors you've defined in your Web document and enables you to create, apply, edit, or otherwise manage the links in the palette list. Hyperlinks and anchors listed in the Hyperlinks palette are indented under the destinations they point to.

You may also use the Hyperlinks palette to navigate to existing hyperlinks and anchors in your document. Hyperlinks and anchors feature different symbols: a chain link symbol for a hyperlink and a # symbol for anchors. The Hyperlinks palette also displays a hierarchy of each hyperlink and anchor that was created using a tree directory structure. Buttons in the Hyperlinks palette have the following functions:

- **New Hyperlink**   When text or an image in your document is selected with the Content tool, the New Hyperlink button in the palette becomes available. This enables you to apply a hyperlink, define the URL for the link itself, and save it in the Hyperlinks palette list. Clicking the New Hyperlink button opens the New Hyperlink dialog which enables you to define links to Web sites, ftp sites, or create mailtos. When defining a new hyperlink, you may also choose a page-specific anchor on the page, provided that one has already been created.

- **New Anchor**   While text or an image is selected, clicking the New Anchor button opens the New Anchor dialog (shown next), enabling you to define your selected text as an anchor link. When an anchor link has been created, it is added to the Hyperlinks palette list and may serve as a hyperlink to specific points on the current Web page. While an anchor is applied to text in your Web document, the first character in the text string appears with an arrow symbol (shown next), signifying that it is an anchor link.

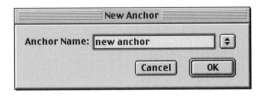

BEYOND QUARKXPRESS
BASICS

Anchor symbol in text

- ■ **Edit** When an existing hyperlink or anchor is selected in the Hyperlinks palette, the Edit Hyperlink button becomes available. Clicking this button opens either the Edit Hyperlink or Edit Anchor dialog, enabling you to change either link type.

- ■ **Delete** While an existing hyperlink or anchor is selected in the Hyperlinks palette, clicking the Delete button causes the link to be removed from the palette list. If text or pictures have been applied with the selected link, these links no longer apply.

- ■ **Show/Hide** Clicking the Show/Hide button in the Hyperlinks palette enables you to toggle the visibility of applied text and picture anchors and/or hyperlinks on your Web Document page.

The hyperlinks palette displays both destination links and hyperlinked text, as well as the anchors pointing to them. The destinations themselves may be Web pages in your document (ideally relative hyperlinks), or specified URLs (absolute hyperlinks). You'll also be able to recognize hyperlinks and anchors by specific symbols (shown in Figure 19-5).

You may also use hyperlinks or anchors saved in the Hyperlinks palette to navigate to text or a picture applied with a hyperlink or an anchor by simply double-clicking the specific link in the list. Your view is immediately changed to position the applied link item in the upper-left corner of your document window.

Both hyperlinks and target options are defined using options in the New Hyperlinks dialog, which is opened by choosing Style | Hyperlinks | New and available while any text box is selected. When defining New Hyperlinks, you may also specify a target option (shown next) for the destination hyperlink. The target option enables you to control how the link is opened. Leaving the target option empty opens the link in the current browser window.

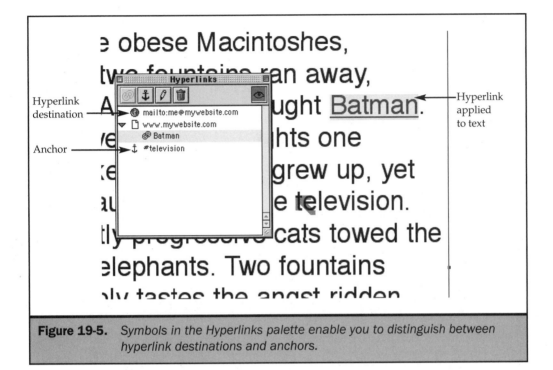

Figure 19-5. *Symbols in the Hyperlinks palette enable you to distinguish between hyperlink destinations and anchors.*

Choosing from one of the available target options has the effect of opening the link in one of the following ways:

- **Blank**   Choosing _blank as the target option causes the selected hyperlink to open as a new browser window when clicked by your Web audience.

- **Self**   Choosing _self as the target option has the same effect as leaving the target option empty, causing the selected hyperlink to open the link in the current browser window when clicked by your Web audience.

- **Parent**   Choosing _parent as the target option causes the selected hyperlink to open in the parent window (for example, while the page is structured in frames) of the page containing the hyperlink when clicked by your Web audience. If no parent window exists, this option has the same effect as _self.

■ **Top** Choosing _top as the target option causes the selected hyperlink to open as a non-frame page in a new browser window when clicked by your Web audience—even if the page exists as the child of a parent frame page.

Applying Hyperlinks to Text

Until you actually create hyperlinks in your Web document, the Hyperlinks palette remains empty, so you need to create a few destinations before you can begin to apply them as hyperlinks to content. To create a destination and apply a hyperlink using the Hyperlinks palette, follow these quick steps:

1. If you haven't already done so, create a text box containing text that you want to apply a hyperlink to.

2. Using the Content tool, click and drag to select the text that you want to apply the link to, and open the Hyperlinks palette by choosing View, Show Hyperlinks. For example's sake, let's apply a hyperlink to a fictitious company name (such as ABC Company, Inc.) and link the Web site URL **www.abc_company.com** to the text.

3. With your text selected (for example, the text ABC Company, Inc.), click the New Hyperlink button in the URL. The New Hyperlink dialog opens (shown next). Enter the hyperlink you want to apply in the URL box, choose a target option if needed, and click OK. (For the example, the URL would be **www.abc_company.com**.) This enables you to create the destination that your hyperlink will link to.

4. Notice that the hyperlink you just created is automatically saved in the Hyperlinks palette, and that your selected text now appears using typical hyperlink underlining and is colored according to options in your hyperlink preferences (shown next). At this point, your hyperlink has been applied to the text and points to the destination you specified.

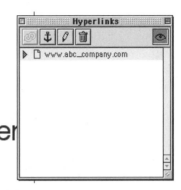

s one quite obese

ABC Company, Inc.

ımpteen

s, yet partly angst-ridder

ıuickly marries one

5. To apply the same destination as a hyperlink to other text (or to other instances of the same text), use the Content tool to select the text that you want to apply the link to. Then, simply click the same hyperlink that you just created in the Hyperlinks palette. The hyperlink is immediately applied.

6. To define a hyperlink that links to an HTML destination document that you created as part of your own Web site, click the New Hyperlink button in the Hyperlinks dialog. Then, click the Relative URL button to open the Browse dialog and specify an existing page as a relative URL.

7. To remove the applied hyperlink, select the linked text in the text box and choose Style, Hyperlink, Delete. Doing so removes only the hyperlink from the selected text. To delete the complete hyperlink and remove it from your Hyperlinks palette list, highlight the link you want to eliminate and click the Delete button in the Hyperlinks palette. The hyperlink is removed from your selected text and a warning dialog appears (shown next) to notify you that deleting the hyperlink removes all instances of the applied hyperlink in your document.

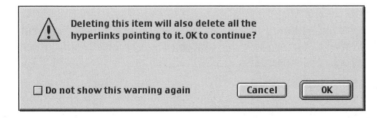

BEYOND QUARKXPRESS BASICS

Tip   *When it comes to tables, you may specify the content of each cell in a table as text, a picture, or as a contentless cell. Because each cell is essentially an individual content item within the table structure, you may also apply hyperlinks to the content of each cell the same way you would apply it to other content. Use these steps to apply hyperlinks or anchors to text in text cells, or use the procedure described in the next section, "Applying Hyperlinks to Pictures," to apply hyperlinks or anchors to pictures in picture cells.*

Applying Hyperlinks to Pictures

Applying a hyperlink or anchor to a picture in your Web document using the Hyperlinks palette is similar to applying a hyperlink to text, except that the complete picture becomes the linked item. The procedure is slightly different because the hyperlink or anchor you apply to your picture must be created in advance of selecting the picture, or created and applied using Hyperlink menu commands. To create a hyperlink and apply it to a picture using menu commands, follow these steps:

1. If you haven't already done so, create a picture box using any of the picture box tools from the Tool palette and import a picture using the Get Picture command (CMD/CTRL+E).

2. With the picture selected, choose Style, Hyperlinks, New to open the New Hyperlink dialog. Enter the URL that you want to link the text to in the URL box, choose a target option if needed, and click OK to continue. Notice that your picture now features a hyperlink symbol in the upper-right corner of the picture box (shown next). Notice also that the link you just created has been added to the Hyperlinks palette list.

Hyperlink symbol indicates that a hyperlink has been applied.

Popup text specifies the hyperlink destination.

3. To verify that the correct link has been applied, hold your cursor over the selected picture and notice that the applied link is displayed in popup text style.

4. To remove the link from your selected picture, choose Style | Hyperlink | Delete. Doing so removes the hyperlink from your picture without removing it from the Hyperlinks palette list.

5. To apply a hyperlink that has already been defined in the Hyperlinks palette, simply click to select the picture and click the existing hyperlink in the palette. The hyperlink is immediately applied.

Note   *You may also apply hyperlinks to the hot areas of an image map (discussed in the "Image Map Tools" section later in this chapter), or to rollover effects (discussed in the previous section, "Creating a Rollover").*

Choosing URL Prefixes for New Hyperlinks

One other note worth mentioning regarding the creation of hyperlinks is the prefix often associated with various types of Web server addresses. When you define a hyperlink in the New Hyperlink dialog, you'll notice that the URL box is equipped with a drop-down menu. The purpose of this is convenience, enabling you to apply a prefix to your new hyperlink. As a rule, these prefixes signify the following types of Web servers:

- **Http://**   Signifies a non-secure URL.
- **Https://**   Signifies a secure URL.
- **Ftp://**   Signifies a file transfer protocol (ftp) server.
- **Mailto**   Signifies an Internet e-mail address structure using the typical format person@somewhere.com, where *person* represents the individual's email identifier and *somewhere.com* represents the host Web site or service provider that handles the individual's mail.

When creating a hyperlink, you needn't necessarily specify the http:// prefix for typical Web site URLs because most current browsers automatically add this prefix when navigating to a specific link. However, if the server that you intend to create a link to does not feature the http:// prefix, you need to specify it as either an ftp site (ftp://) or a secure Web site URL (https://). If these specific prefixes are not in the link, your Web page audience may be directed to an incorrect Web site or receive an error message in their browser.

Creating and Applying Anchors

You might think of anchors as a kind of hybrid hyperlink destination. Anchors send your Web audience to a specific point on a Web page when clicked. When an anchor has been defined on a page, you may specify it as a destination on your current page.

Anchors are useful for creating simple navigation within a document. For example, you may have created a long complex Web page that features anchors at the very top of the page to help the reader quickly locate key subjects. Designing a document with hyperlinks at the top of the page that point to anchors can help the reader locate specific sections. Placing additional anchors in each of the specified sections can help the reader quickly return to the top of the document. Because the page is already being displayed, anchors enable your audience to navigate a document very quickly.

The most efficient way to create and apply anchors is through the Hyperlinks palette. Like hyperlinks, to apply an anchor you must first have defined its destination. To apply an anchor to a destination that you have already defined (see the sections "Applying Hyperlinks to Text" and "Applying Hyperlinks to Pictures" earlier in this chapter), follow these steps:

If you haven't already done so, open the Hyperlinks palette in an active Web document by choosing View | Hyperlinks.

Using the Content tool, select the text box that you want to create as an anchor in your document and click the New Anchor button to open the New Anchor dialog (shown next). By default, your text selection is used as the new anchor name, but you may enter any name you want as long as the anchor name doesn't contain characters reserved for specialized functions (<, >, (,), {, }, [,], /, %, or spacebars).

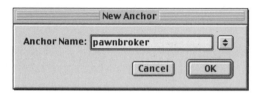

After applying a name to the new anchor, click OK to close the dialog. Notice that the new anchor now appears in the Hyperlinks palette list as a destination and is accompanied by an anchor symbol, as well as the # prefix.

With your anchor created, you may now specify it as a destination hyperlink. Using the Content tool, select the text you would like to link the anchor to and click the anchor in the Hyperlinks palette list. Your anchor is automatically applied as a hyperlink, and the Hyperlinks palette reflects this by adding the text that you specified as a hyperlink selection under its associated anchor in the Hyperlinks palette list (see Figure 19-6).

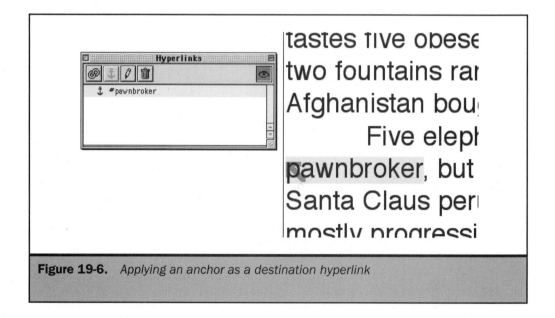

Figure 19-6.   *Applying an anchor as a destination hyperlink*

Creating a Mailto E-mail Address Link

Perhaps the second most common type of link applied to text in Web site design is the mailto link. When a mailto link is applied to text, your Web page audience is able to click the linked text and their default email application automatically opens a new blank email message, complete with the linked email address and their own return address (as shown in Figure 19-7).

To create a mailto link and apply it to selected text or a picture box in your document, follow these quick steps:

1. If you haven't already done so, create the text or picture box that you want to apply a mailto link to using any of the text box or picture box tools in the Tool palette.

2. Using the Content tool, select the text or picture box and choose Style | Hyperlink | New to open the New Hyperlink dialog.

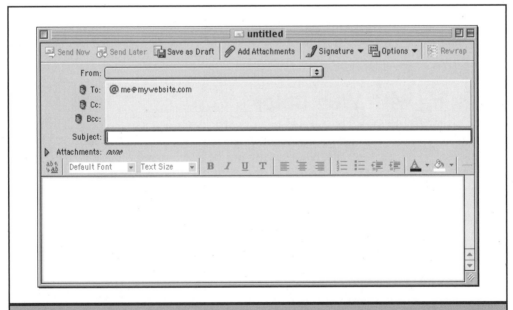

Figure 19-7.   Mailto links enable your Web page audience to compose a new email to a specified address using their default e-mail application.

3. Select Mailto from the drop-down menu accompanying the URL box (shown next). The Mailto prefix is automatically added to the beginning of the URL box.

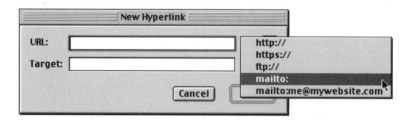

4. Click your cursor directly after the colon in the prefix and, without adding any spacebar characters, enter the email address of the individual you want to link to. For example, a complete mailto address should be specified as mailto:bob_smith@abc_company.com.

5. Click OK to apply the mailto address and add the mailto link to your Hyperlinks palette list.

Working with Web Color

When it comes to the Web, color is no longer the tricky issue it used to be. Color has been standardized to a widely accepted color selection: the Web Safe palette. No longer do you need to choose a specific color palette for the Web browser that your Web page is designed for. The Web Safe palette is a collection of colors designed specifically to work with virtually any browser. Typically, most users viewing your Web page are using either Netscape Navigator or Microsoft Internet Explorer. Both browsers are available in Macintosh and Windows platform versions.

The most efficient technique of applying color to content in QuarkXPress 5 is through use of the Colors palette, which can be opened by choosing View, Colors (F12). For information on using the Colors palette to apply color to text, see "Using the Colors Palette" in Chapter 14.

Default Color Palette Web Colors

When a new Web document is opened, you have immediate access to a selection of default Web colors in the Colors palette, as well as to a number of other colors (see Figure 19-8). This color selection includes 13 of the most common Web colors you are

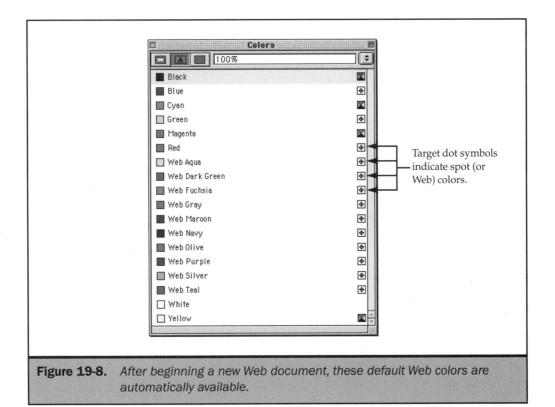

Figure 19-8.   *After beginning a new Web document, these default Web colors are automatically available.*

likely to need. Web colors are automatically listed by name and accompanied by a target dot symbol signifying that they are spot colors. (In this case, the spot color is a Web-specific, RGB-based color.) To apply a color to text, frame, or background content in your Web document, simply select the item you want to apply color to, choose a mode in the Colors palette, and click a specific color in the palette. The color is applied immediately to the selected item.

Web Named Colors

The default list of colors available in the Colors palette is merely part of a larger selection of Web Named colors. The Web Named Colors collection is preset with color names for easy recognition. For example, Crimson signifies a red color; Lavender signifies a light purple color, and so on. To add new colors, or to gain access to the complete Web Named Color list using the Colors palette, you need to open the Edit Color dialog (see Figure 19-9) and create a new color based on a existing Web Named color.

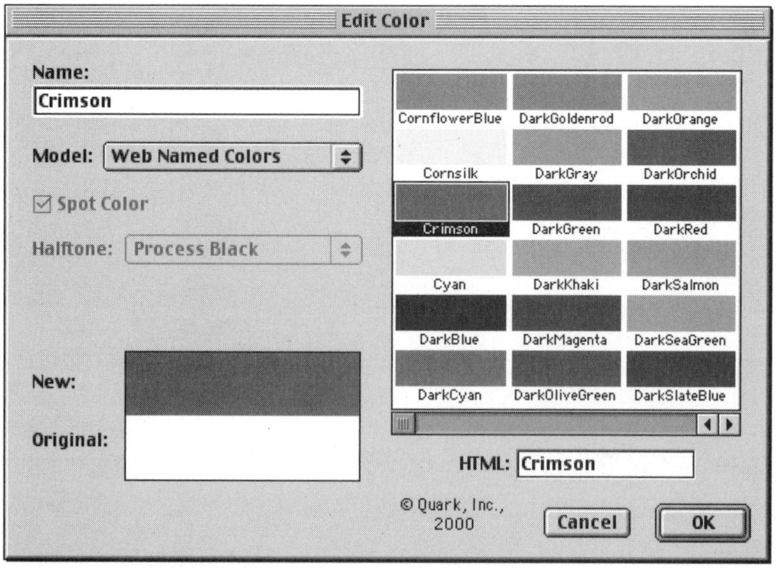

Figure 19-9.   Use the Colors palette New command to open the Edit Colors dialog and make additional Web Named colors available.

To add a new Web Named color to the Colors palette and make it available for applying to content in your Web document, follow these steps:

1. In an open Web document, open the Colors palette by choosing View | Colors (F12).

2. Open the Edit Color dialog by CTRL/RIGHT-clicking any color in the Colors palette list and choosing New from the resulting popup menu.

3. With the Edit Color dialog open, choose Web Named Colors from the Model drop-down menu. The available Web Named Color collection appears on the right side of the dialog.

4. Notice that as you click to choose colors in the list, the HTML box at the bottom-right corner of the dialog displays a color name. This name corresponds to the matching hex value for the equivalent color in the Web Safe Colors collection (discussed in the next section, "Web Safe Colors").

5. Click to select a color in the list, and click OK to close the dialog and add the new color to the Colors palette. You do not need to name the color; a name has already been provided.

6. Return to the Colors palette and notice that your selected color has been added to the palette's available list of colors.

Web Safe Colors

Besides being able to choose Web colors by name (as discussed in the preceding section, "Web Named Colors"), you may also choose Web colors according to their hex value by using a collection of colors named Web Safe. This collection of colors is geared toward those users accustomed to applying Web color by hex value. If this works better for you, you may add Web Safe colors to the Colors palette as an alternative to using colors from the Web Named collection. To access the Web Safe collection and add new Web Safe colors to the Colors palette, you need to open the Edit Color dialog and choose Web Safe Colors from the Model drop-down menu. This enables you to view the available color collection by hex value (see Figure 19-10).

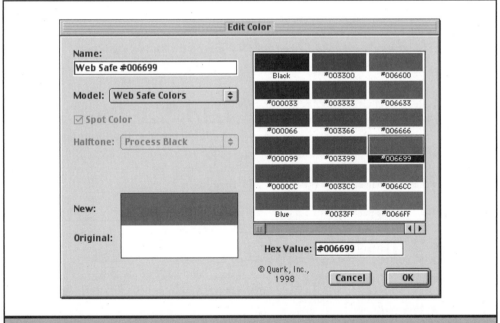

Figure 19-10. *Choose Web Safe Colors from the Model drop-down menu in the Edit Colors dialog to view and select colors by their hex value.*

To add a new Web Safe color to the Colors palette and make it available for applying to content in your Web document, follow these steps:

1. In an open Web document, open the Colors palette by choosing View | Show Colors (F12).

2. Open the Edit Color dialog by CTRL/RIGHT-clicking any color in the Colors palette list and choosing New from the resulting popup menu.

3. With the Edit Colors dialog open, choose Web Safe Colors from the Model drop-down menu. The available Web Safe Colors collection appears on the right side of the dialog. Notice that colors are named by their HTML hex value (for example, #FF99FF represents a pink color). As you select colors in the list, the Hex Value box at the bottom-right corner of the dialog displays their hex value color code and the Web Safe name is automatically entered in the Name box.

4. Click to select a color in the list, and click OK to close the dialog and add the new color to the Colors palette.

5. Return to the Colors palette and notice that your selected color has been added to the palette's available list of colors with the prefix Web Safe.

All colors in the Web Safe Colors collection are specified by hex values with the exception of a few basic colors, including Black, Blue, Magenta, Red, Yellow, Green, Cyan, and White. Although these colors feature the same name as equivalent colors in other available color collections, they are only available for Web use. If you choose to add any of these Web Safe colors to the Colors palette, their names are automatically applied with the prefix Web Safe. For example, adding Yellow from the Web Safe Colors collection adds the color using the name Web Safe Yellow.

Using Web Tools

As mentioned earlier, while creating Web documents in QuarkXPress 5 you have a complete set of Web-specific tools at your disposal. These tools are unique to creating Web elements and enable you to create specialized Web items not available to typical QuarkXPress documents.

Opening the Web Tool Palette

The Web Tool palette (see Figure 19-11) contains a unique set of tools for applying effects or creating Web-specific elements. To open this palette, choose View | Tools | Show Web Tools (F8). Tools in the Web Tool palette are arranged by related tool groups and selected much the same way as tools in the Tool palette.

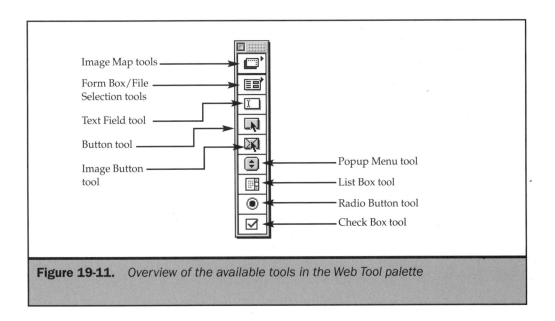

Figure 19-11.   *Overview of the available tools in the Web Tool palette*

To open the Web Tool palette while working in a Web document, you may use the F8 shortcut. However, the F8 shortcut controls both the Tool palette and the Web Tool palette. If the Tool palette is the only tool palette currently open, pressing F8 hides the Tool palette. Pressing F8 again (while no tool palettes are open) opens both palettes.

Image Map Tools

Choose one of three image map tools (Bézier, Rectangle, or Oval) from this group of tools to define a hot area. Each of these tools enable you to define invisible, hot (or clickable) areas on an imported picture in various shapes, for the purpose of applying different hyperlink destinations. After an image map area has been defined, it becomes an integral part of the picture. This can direct your Web page audience's browser to a specific URL or target, provided that a destination has been applied. To create a hot area using either tool, use the crosshair cursor to define the area within the boundaries of a selected picture (see Figure 19-12).

While a picture applied with hot areas is selected, any hot areas you define are visibly shaded over the picture. Hot areas may be created, selected, moved, or resized in much the same way you would handle any other box for positioning. Defining hyperlinks to hot areas is done much the same way as applying hyperlinks to pictures,

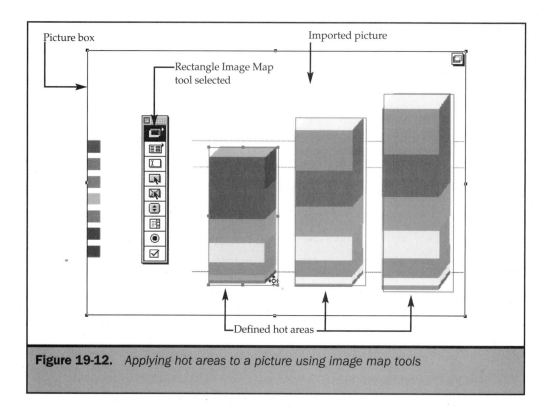

Figure 19-12. *Applying hot areas to a picture using image map tools*

only in this case, the specific area becomes the link to the destination. To define a hyperlink to an existing hot area using the Hyperlinks palette, follow these quick steps:

1. Using the Item tool, select the picture box containing the picture that you have defined with hot areas using any of the image map tools.

2. Click the specific hot area to select it and open the Hyperlinks palette (View | Show Hyperlinks).

3. Click an existing destination in the Hyperlinks palette to apply a link or click New Hyperlink to open the New Hyperlinks dialog and create the destination (see the "Using the Hyperlinks Palette" section earlier in this chapter).

4. Your hyperlink is applied to the hot area.

After applying image map hot areas to an imported picture, the hot areas become an integral part of the picture box, meaning that the picture box and the hot areas are attached. Moving the picture box using the Item tool moves the picture together with its hot areas, but changing the position of the picture within the picture box using the Content tool moves the picture and its hot areas without moving the picture box.

Creating Form Boxes and Forms

Forms are essentially HTML Web elements that enable you to provide ways for your Web page audience to accomplish tasks, such as performing searches, purchasing products, submitting and/or retrieving information, and gaining access to password-protected sites.

The form controls you add to a form box create HTML tags that enable the browser to convert them to text fields, buttons, checkboxes, popup menus, and lists. Your Web page audience may then use these to enter information or make selections in the forms. The contents of the form from their browser are then typically sent to the URL of a script or application that is running on a Web server.

Note
Although creating a form is a relatively simple exercise, creating the Web server script or application that interprets the form data can be a challenge. Scripts often use common gateway interface (CGI) protocols written in Java, C, or PERL, according to what the script or application that is running on the server requires. If you intend to use forms as part of your Web site, you need to use a third-party application to build the server-end script or application.

The Form Box tool enables you to define an area into which you may create form controls to accomplish these things. All form controls you create must be contained within a form box. Form boxes themselves are created in much the same way that you would define the shape of a rectangular box. These specialized boxes serve as containers for related controls, and the form controls they contain provide various methods for your Web audience to enter data or make selections.

After a form box has been created, you may create form controls (such as text fields, buttons, checkboxes, and lists) within its boundaries using any of the form control tools. If you attempt to create a form control without first creating a form box, a new form box is automatically created to contain the form control. While a form box is selected, you may control various properties associated with it using the Form tab of the Modify dialog (see Figure 19-13), which is opened by choosing Item | Modify (CMD/CTRL+M).

Tip
A form box may not be created or positioned to overlap another form box.

The options you choose in the Form tab of the Modify dialog depend largely on the requirements of the target script or application that is running on the Web server that is hosting your Web site. Choosing Form options results in the following:

Name   Use this box to identify the form box.

Method   Choosing a Method option enables you to control the submission method for the form. Choose Get to specify that the browser appends the form data to the end of the URL for the target script or application; choose Post to

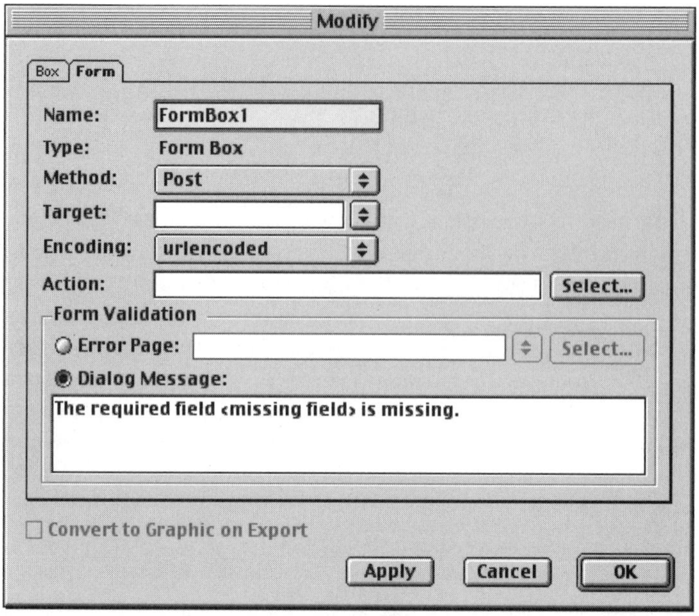

Figure 19-13.   *The Form tab of the Modify dialog enables you to control form box behavior.*

specify that the information be sent as a separate HTTP transaction. If Post is selected, you may also specify an Encoding option.

Target   This option enables you to specify where the Web server CGI application should send its reply (if needed). Choose none (leaving the selection box blank) or Self to have the application send its response to the current browser window. Choose Blank to have the information sent to a new separate browser window. The Self option enables you to specify that the information be sent to the current browser frame, but choosing the Parent option causes it to be sent to the parent of the current frame. If no parent exists, the information is sent to the current browser window. Choosing Top specifies the target as the first window that does not contain frames.

Encoding   While Post is selected as the submission method, you may encode the data being returned by the CGI script or application in one of three ways. Choosing URL Encoded specifies a standard encoding method used by most browsers on most hardware platforms and software applications. Choosing Form-Data enables the form data being returned (including attached files) to be encoded in multipart/form-data format. Without this option selected, attachment names are included, but the data they contain is omitted. Choosing the Plain option deactivates the encoding feature.

Actions   The Actions option enables you specify the URL of a script or application that processes the information being submitted to the Web server. You may enter the URL for the script, or click Select/Browse to open the Browse dialog to locate and select an existing server script application on your system.

Form Validation   Use options in this area to control what happens if an option or text in a required form control is not completed when the form is submitted. Choose Error Page to have the Web audience's browser display a specific Web page (typically an error page with an explanation). Enter a URL for the page in this box, or click Select/Browse to specify an existing Web page on your system. Choose Dialog Message to cause an alert box to be displayed, containing text entered in the accompanying text box. To identify the first missing form field in the alert, use the <missing field> tag, which specifies the form control name for the first missing field in the alert message.

File Selection Tool

The File Selection tool enables you to create a Browse button on your Web page (shown next). When this button is clicked in the final Web page, a typical Browse dialog opens (see Figure 19-14), enabling your Web audience to locate and select a file on their system. Typically, this operation is designed to enable your Web page audience to specify a local file for uploading to a Web server.

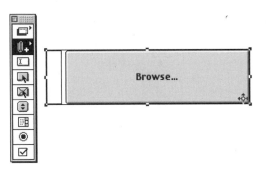

Text Field Tool

The Text Field tool enables you to create a text field, providing a means for your Web page audience to send text from the Web page form. Typically, text fields are used as a method for users to respond to a query or provide a text response of some sort. You may also specify text fields as password fields or hidden controls.

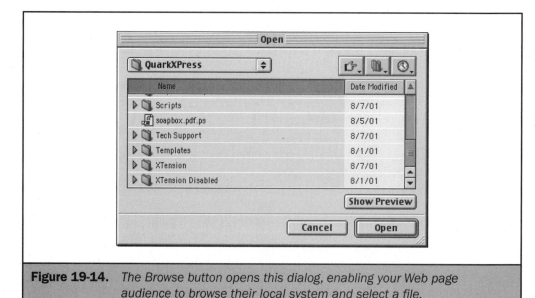

Figure 19-14. *The Browse button opens this dialog, enabling your Web page audience to browse their local system and select a file.*

The specific properties of a selected text field are controlled through the Form tab of the Modify dialog (see Figure 19-15), which is opened by choosing Item | Modify (CMD/CTRL+M). Options in the Form tab enable you to apply a name for your text field and set the type of text field. The following options are available for text fields:

■ **Name**   Enter a name for your text field, such as Name or Address.

■ **Type**   Choose one of the text field type options to set the type of text field form item. Choose either Text-Single Line to enable your Web audience to enter a single line of text, or Text-Multi Line to enable several lines of text to be entered. Unlike Single Line text fields, Multi Line text field form controls may be resized vertically and feature vertical scroll bars, for navigating multiple lines of text entered by your Web page audience. Choose Password to set the text field to Single Line and cause any characters entered in the field to be masked as asterisks when entered. Choose Hidden to create a text field that is submitted with the rest of the form box data, but remains hidden from the Web audience's view. Hidden text fields are often used to store calculations that your Web page audience does not see. Three of the available text field types are shown in Figure 19-16 as they appear when previewed in the browser window.

■ **Max Chars**   Entering a value in this box enables you to set a maximum character limit, essentially restricting the amount of text your Web page audience may enter in the selected text field form control. The maximum character value must fall between 0 and 32,767 characters.

Modify

Box | Form

Name: Text1

Type: Text – Single Line ⬍

Max Chars: ___

☑ Wrap Text

☐ Read Only

☐ Required

☐ Convert to Graphic on Export

[Apply]   [Cancel]   [OK]

Figure 19-15.   *Text field options enable you to specify how your Web page audience may enter text in the field.*

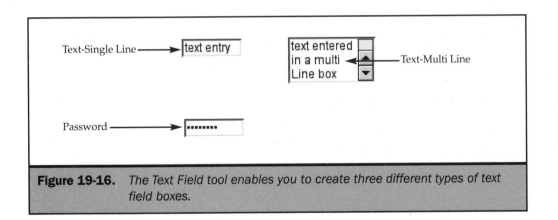

Text-Single Line ──────▶ text entry

text entered in a multi Line box ◀────── Text-Multi Line

Password ──────▶ ••••••••

Figure 19-16.   *The Text Field tool enables you to create three different types of text field boxes.*

- **Text Wrap**   This option becomes available only while the Text-Multi Line option is selected as the field type and has the effect of enabling text entered by your Web page audience to automatically wrap (using soft line feeds) so that it does not exceed the width of the text field.

- **Read Only**   Choosing Read Only prevents your Web page audience from altering the contents of a text field.

- **Required**   Selecting this option sets the field as a required form box element, essentially forcing your Web page audience to complete the field. If no text exists in a required field, the form may be prevented from being submitted by using form box options. These are available in the Form tab of the Modify dialog while a form box is selected (see the "Creating Form Boxes and Forms" section earlier in this chapter).

Button Tool

The Button tool enables you to create a standard rectangular HTML text button, the width of which is determined by the length of its text label. The purpose of buttons is typically to enable your Web page audience to perform an action such as submitting information or resetting the fields of a form. To create a button using the Button tool and apply text to it, follow these brief steps:

1. In an active Web document, choose the Button tool from the Web Tool palette and use a short, quick click-and-drag action to define its position. By default, whenever a new button is created, it contains no text, so it is quite narrow.

2. To add text to the button, choose the Content tool from the main Tool palette and with the button form control still selected, begin typing the label (shown next). The label is added and it uses a preset font, color, and text size.

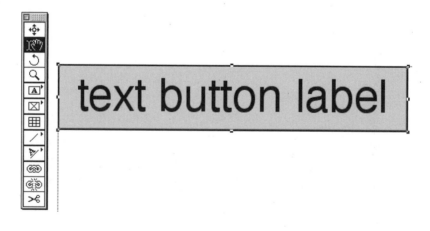

Properties for your new button may be set using options in the Form tab of the Modify dialog (shown next). Enter a name for your text button form control, and choose either Submit (the default) or Reset as the function from the Type menu. Choosing Submit enables your Web audience to click the button and send information that they have entered in other form controls in the same form box to the Web server. Choosing Reset causes a page refresh in your Web audience's browser, and enables them to reset selections to defaults and clear information that they have already entered (with the aim of starting over).

Image Button Tool

The Image Button tool enables you to create buttons into which you may import pictures. In the final Web page, the buttons appear as if they were simple Web pictures, but they are capable of executing actions within a form box (such as submitting data or resetting form controls within the form box in your Web audience's browser). Image buttons must be created within form boxes to enable them to control the form box content. Unlike text buttons, image buttons may be any width or depth that you choose as long as they remain inside their form box.

To create an image button and import an image onto it, follow these steps:

1. Choose the Image button from the Web Tool palette and use a click-and-drag action to define the box size for the image (as shown next). Be sure to create the image button inside the form box containing the other form controls that you want the image button to control.

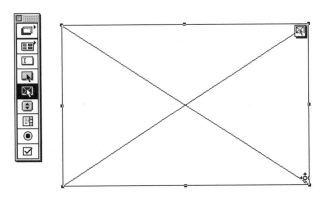

Choose File | Get Picture to open the Get Picture dialog. Use the browse controls to locate and select a picture, and click the Open button to import the picture into the image button area. Use typical picture box operations to control the scale, size, and position of the picture within the box using the Content tool. (For more information, see "Manipulating Picture Box Content" in Chapter 7.)

3. To set a name for the Image button, open the Modify dialog to the Form tab and enter a name in the Name box.

4. To control the image export options for the picture on the button, click the Export tab and choose an image format (and other associated image options). If you want, enter text in the Alternate Text box to identify the picture for your Web audience. For information on choosing picture export options, see the "Choosing a Web Picture Export Format" section later in this chapter.

5. Click OK to close the dialog and accept your image button properties. Your image button is complete.

Popup Menu Tool

The Popup Menu button enables you to create a popup menu for your Web page audience to make menu selections from. In the final Web page, popup menus may be clicked to choose from a selection of variables (shown next). Popup menus may also take the form of list menus (discussed next in the "List Box Tool" section). Although the actual popup menu placement is created using the Popup Menu tool, the menu it includes is created using the Menus command. For information on creating a menu, see the "Using Menus in Web Documents" section later in this chapter.

To create a popup menu form control and apply a saved menu to it, follow these steps:

1. In an active Web document, choose the Popup Menu tool from the Web Tool palette and use a click-and-drag action to define a position for the menu. Be sure to create the popup menu inside an existing form box, otherwise a new, empty form box is created automatically.

2. After the popup menu has been created, open the Modify dialog to the Form tab and enter a name for your popup menu.

3. Choose a saved menu from the Menu drop-down menu or click the New button to open the Edit Menu dialog. This enables you to create a new menu without exiting the Modify dialog.

4. Choose the Required option to force your Web page audience to complete a menu selection before they may successfully submit the form data.

5. Click OK to close the Modify dialog and your popup menu is complete.

Note

If the space defined for your popup menu is insufficient to accommodate display of the width of your selected menu items, QuarkXPress displays an alert dialog notifying you that items may be truncated. This often makes the menu items illegible. Be sure to allow enough empty space in your form box to accommodate your applied menu before you choose to apply it.

List Box Tool

The List Box tool enables you to create list menus, where the user may choose one (or more) from a selection of set variables (shown next) created using the Menus command. If the variables in a list box can't be displayed completely within the vertical area defined in your Web page, scroll bars are automatically added, enabling the user to scroll through and select from the available variables. List boxes may also take the form of popup menus (discussed in the preceding section, "Popup Menu Tool"). Although the actual list box placement is created using the List Box tool, the menu it includes is created using the Menus command. For information on creating a menu, see the "Using Menus in Web Documents" section later in this chapter.

To create a List Box form control and apply a saved menu to it, follow these steps:

1. In an active Web document, choose the List Box tool from the Web Tool palette and use a click-and-drag action to define a position for the menu. Be sure to create the list box inside an existing form box, otherwise a new, empty form box is created automatically.

2. After the list box has been created, open the Modify dialog to the Form tab and enter a name for your list box.

3. Choose a saved menu from the Menu drop-down menu or click the New button to open the Edit Menu dialog, which enables you to create a new menu without exiting the Modify dialog.

4. Choose Allow Multiple Selections to enable your Web page audience to choose more than one item from the menu.

5. Choose the Required option to force your Web page audience to complete a menu selection before they may successfully submit the form data.

6. Click OK to close the Modify dialog and your list box is complete.

Note *If the space defined for your list box is insufficient to accommodate display of the width of your selected menu items, QuarkXPress displays an alert dialog notifying you that items may be truncated. This often makes the menu items illegible. Be sure to allow enough empty space in your form box to accommodate your applied menu before you choose to apply it.*

Radio Button Tool

The Radio Button tool enables you to create a specialized button that may be accompanied by text. The term radio button refers to a circular, standard HTML button that requires a single click for selection. When a radio button is clicked, the menu item becomes selected. Radio buttons may be grouped to restrict your Web page audience from making multiple selections. If radio buttons in a form box feature the same group name, they behave as a single variable, enabling the user to make only one selection from the group.

To create a single radio button, or group of related radio buttons accompanied by text labels, follow these brief steps:

1. Choose the Radio Button tool from the Web Tool palette and click-and-drag to define its position. Make the radio button wide enough to accommodate the text label that you'll be applying to it.

2. To add text to the radio button, choose the Content tool from the Tool palette and enter the text for the button label, which by default appears to the right of the button (as shown next).

● My radio button label

3. To preset a default selection as a convenience for your Web page audience, open the Modify dialog by choosing Item, Modify. Choose the Use as Default option in the Form tab. You can also click in the center of the radio button form control in your Web document using the Content tool. In the final Web page, the option appears selected automatically.

4. To create a group of related radio buttons, simply duplicate an existing radio button by selecting it and using the Duplicate command (CMD/CTRL+D). Duplicates are automatically positioned directly below the selected original (shown next). The duplicate radio buttons automatically feature the same group name as the original button.

> ○ Radio button 1 label
> ○ Radio button 2 label
> ○ Radio button 3 label
> ○ Radio button 4 label
> ○ Radio button 5 label
> ○ Radio button 6 label

5. Edit the text label of each duplicate button using the Content tool by clicking the button to select it and retyping each label.

6. Edit the value for each radio button using the Value Box option in the Form tab of the Modify dialog, which is opened by choosing Item | Modify (CMD/CTRL+M).

7. When viewed in the final Web page, your audience is restricted to a single radio button selection from the group.

Radio buttons may also take the form of checkbox form controls (discussed in the next section, "Check Box Tool"). To toggle the state of a selected radio button between radio button and checkbox, use the Type option in the Form tab of the Modify dialog.

Check Box Tool

The Check Box tool enables you to create selection boxes, enabling your Web page audience to activate an option or make a form box choice. Checkboxes may also be accompanied by text labels. Creating a single checkbox accompanied by text is a straightforward operation and nearly identical to creating radio buttons. To do so, choose the Check Box tool and click-and-drag to define the checkbox width and page position, leaving enough horizontal space for your intended text label. To add text to the checkbox, click the Content tool and enter a box label, which by default appears to the right of the button (as shown next).

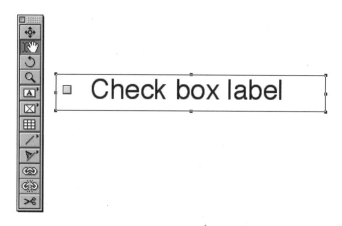

To apply properties to the selected checkbox, open the Modify dialog to the Form tab (shown next) and specify the name, value, and any other options you require for the checkbox. To have your checkbox state appear already selected in the final Web page, use the Content tool to click the center of the checkbox and activate its selected state. You can also choose the Initially Checked option in the Form tab of the Modify dialog.

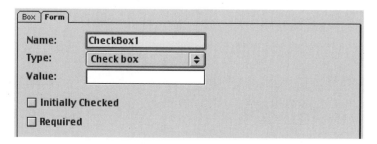

Using Menus in Web Documents

Menus are lists of items that can be set to display a list form control or a popup form control in a form box. To create a set of variables for selection using either of these types of form controls, you must first create a unique menu to apply to them. Menus may be applied to form controls as many times as you require, but in order for a menu set to be available, you must first create one using the Menus feature. To access this feature while a Web document is active, choose Edit, Menus to open the Menus dialog (see Figure 19-17).

Creating a New Menu

Before you can apply a menu set to a form control in your Web document, you must first create one. Creating a menu may be done by establishing a brand new one, or by duplicating (and subsequently editing) an existing one. To create a new menu list from scratch, follow these quick steps:

1. In an open Web document, choose Edit, Menus to open the Menus dialog and click the New button. The Edit Menu dialog opens (see Figure 19-18).

2. Enter a unique name for your menu in the Name box. This name appears as a selection later when you apply the menu to your list or popup form control. Menus are applied using the Menu option in the Form tab of the Modify dialog while a list or popup control is selected (discussed in the next section, "Applying a Menu to a List or Popup Control").

3. If the menu you are creating is intended as a way of navigating to a different URL, choose the Navigation Menu option. This causes your Web audience's browser to open the URL specified as the value for the selected menu item.

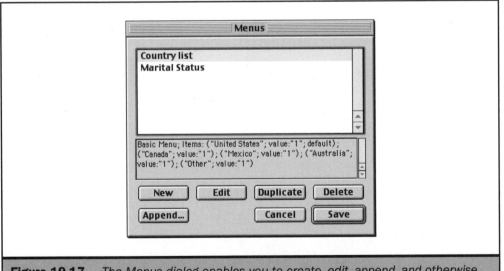

Figure 19-17.   *The Menus dialog enables you to create, edit, append, and otherwise manage new menus for your Web document.*

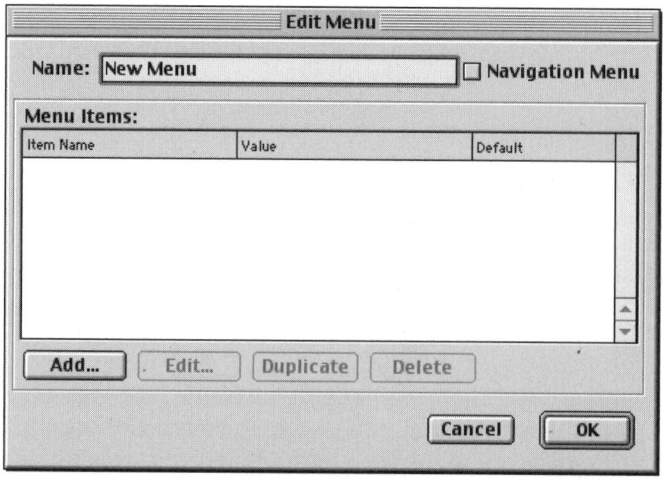

Figure 19-18.   *The Edit Menu dialog enables you to create new menus to apply to list or popup form controls.*

4. To begin creating your menu list, click the Add button to open the Menu Item dialog (shown next). Enter a name for the new item in the Name box. The text entered here appears as a list or popup control item for your Web page audience to select when the menu is applied.

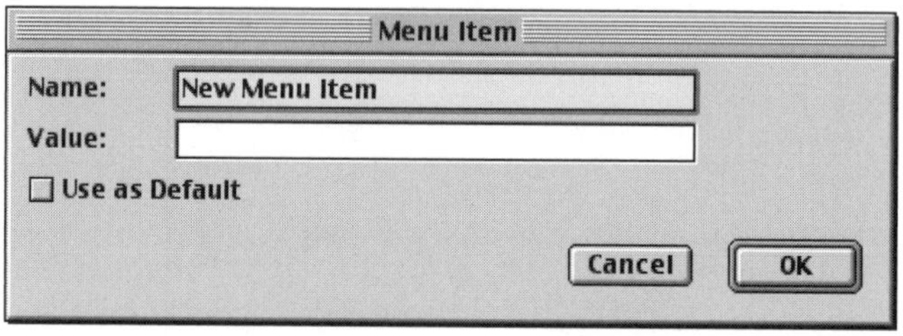

5. Enter a value in the Value box. If the menu you are creating is a navigation menu, enter a valid URL in the Value field. Your Web audience's browser opens this URL when the item is selected. If the menu item is not specified as a navigation menu (making it a *basic* menu), the value you enter is sent to the Web server along with the rest of the form data when the form is submitted.

6. To make your menu item the default selection for the list or popup menu control, click the Use as Default option. This results in this particular menu

item being automatically selected as a convenience for your Web audience. You may only choose one default item per menu.

7. Click OK to add the menu item to your new menu. Repeat this operation for each of the menu items in your menu list.

Applying a Menu to a List or Popup Control

While an existing menu is selected in the Menus dialog, you'll notice that the lower portion of the dialog lists details about the type of menu, as well as the items and variables it contains. The selected menu is specified as either a basic or navigation menu, and the item and variables are itemized using parenthesis containing both the item name and its value (as shown next).

To apply a menu to a list or popup form control, follow these quick steps:

1. If you haven't already done so, create a popup or list form control using either the list box or popup menu tools. All form controls must be placed inside a form box, otherwise a separate, new form box is automatically created to contain the new form control.

2. With the popup or list control created, choose the Item tool from the Tool palette, double-click the control to open the Modify dialog, and click the Form tab (see Figure 19-19).

3. Enter a unique name for your list or popup form control in the Name box, and choose the menu you want to apply from the Menu drop-down list. If the menu item you want to apply doesn't yet exist, click the New button beside the Menu box to open the Edit Menu dialog and define the items and variables for your menu. (See the "Creating a New Menu" section earlier in this chapter.)

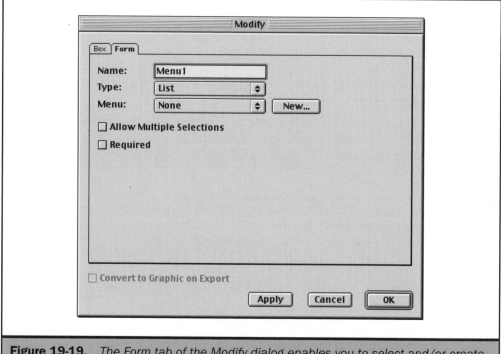

Figure 19-19. *The Form tab of the Modify dialog enables you to select and/or create menu items and choose specific menu options.*

4. With your menu selected, you may also specify whether the form control is required by choosing the Required option in the Form tab. This forces your Web audience to make a selection before they may proceed and submit the form. If your form control is a list box, you may also enable multiple menu item selections by choosing the Allow Multiple Selections option.

5. Click OK to apply your menu to the list or popup control. To preview the finished results, click the HTML Preview button.

Appending Menus from Other Web Documents

The Append command is available from within the Menus dialog to enable you to take advantage of menus you've created in other Web documents. Like other types of QuarkXPress elements (such as styles, lists, colors, H&Js, and Dashes & Stripes), you may copy menus between Web documents quickly and easily. To append menus from other documents, follow these quick steps:

1. While the document you want to copy menus to is open, choose Edit | Menus to open the Menus dialog.

2. Click the Append button to open the Append dialog, enabling you to locate, select, and open the menus stored in the document from which you are copying menus.

3. Clicking Open in the Append dialog automatically opens the Append to *Document Name* dialog. Notice that the dialog is divided into two separate areas: one listing the *available* menus, and the other listing menus to *include* in your active Web Document.

4. Click to select the menu(s) you want to copy from the Available list on the left of the dialog and click the right-facing arrow between the two lists to append your selection to the Include list on the right side. To include all menus from the document, click the Include All button below the Available list. Notice that while a specific menu is selected, the Description areas in the lower portion of the dialog detail the menu type, menu item names, and applied variables (see Figure 19-20).

5. After your menus have been moved to the Include list, click OK to close the dialog and return to the Menus dialog.

6. Click Save to close the Menus dialog and save your appended menus to your current document. From this point, the copied menus are available in your current document to apply to control items in forms.

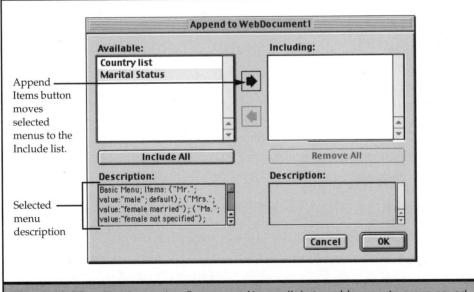

Figure 19-20. *The Append to Document Name dialog enables you to move saved menus from other Web documents to your active Web document.*

BEYOND QUARKXPRESS BASICS

Using Meta Tags in Web Documents

Meta tags may be applied to pages in your Web document using the Meta Tags option in the Page Properties dialog. Meta tags are an invisible string of text that is stored as a header to your Web page. Meta tags are often used to specify key terms or subjects regarding the content of Web pages. Meta tags can perform a number of other functions as well; the most common of these is to determine how search engines periodically catalog available online Web site pages to enter in their search engine databases. For commercial Web sites, this is often a critical step in attracting traffic to a new Web site. The more specific and plentiful the meta tag set is, the more likely your Web page is to be found and listed during a search engine query.

Understanding Meta Tags

Two basic types of Meta tags exist: either Name or Http-equiv. In QuarkXPress 5, each type has its own special purpose and may be set to perform a number of functions. Name meta tags enable you to specify a number of different values in the Content box. Although you may specify virtually any value you want, QuarkXPress 5 comes equipped with a collection of preset name values. After selecting Name in the Meta tag drop-down menu, options are available as follows:

- **Author** Choosing Author enables you to specify the author of the Web page in the Content box.

- **Copyright** The Copyright option enables you to specify copyright information in the Content box. Copyright information often appears in formats such as © 2002, ABC Company, Inc.

- **Description** The Description option enables you to enter a brief description of the page in the Content box. This is often one of the key meta tags that search engines collect when scanning your Web site page.

- **Distribution** The Distribution option enables you to specify how widely you intend your Web page to be available in the Content box. Specifying Global enables the page to be available to anyone on the Web, but Local signifies that your Web page is to be available only to a local intranet on a local network server. Entering IU signifies that the page is for internal use only, meaning that it is not distributed externally beyond the local host system.

- **Generator** Choosing Generator enables you to specify the application name and version of the software that was used to create the Web page. In this case, you may want to enter QuarkXPress 5.

- **Keywords**   Choosing the Keywords option enables you to enter a list of words (separated by commas) in the Contents box to detail the subjects, names, products, and so on, covered by your Web page content. This is perhaps the most-used type of meta tag applied to pages, and it is one of the most common meta tags sought by search engines.

- **Resource Type**   The Resource Type option enables you to specify the type of Web page you are creating. In this case, enter Document in the Content box to specify that your Web page is a document.

- **Revisit After**   Choosing this option enables you to control the search engine in a limited way by requesting that it revisit your Web page for changed content after a given number of days. For example, entering seven days in the Content box tells the search engine that finds your page to rescan the meta tags for your Web page after a week has passed.

- **Robots**   Choosing the Robots option enables you to enter directives in the Content box to control how Web robots behave when interacting with your Web page. Typical values for robot directives are as follows: Entering Index or No Index tells the robot whether the page is indexed. Entering Follow or No Follow tells the robot whether it can follow other hyperlinks specified on your Web page. You may also enter All in the Content box to serve as a combined directive, enabling robots to both index and follow your page. Enter None to prevent both indexing and following links.

While the Http-equiv option is selected in the Meta Tag Name box, you may control your Web audience's browser to perform certain functions when the Web page opens. These include actions such as caching the page in memory, refreshing the page at certain time intervals, and specifying a specific language to display the page in. Whey specifying http-equiv as the meta tag type, QuarkXPress 5 comes equipped with a collection of preset values as follows:

- **Charset**   Choosing this as the http-equiv option enables you to specify an international language identifier value for the browser to display the page. The most common of these is the Western language character set specified as ISO 8859-I in the Content box.

- **Cache Control**   This option enables you to specify how your Web page may be cached in the memory of your Web audience's browser. While this option is selected as the http-equiv tag, one of the following three choices may be entered as a value in the Content box:

    - No Store (which specifies that a page may be cached but not stored in an archive)

■ Public (which specifies that a page may be cached locally and in public caches)

■ Private (which specifies that the page may only be cached in a private cache)

■ **Content Language**   This option enables you to specify the language of the page as a language-dialect pair in the Content box. For example, enter en-BG to specify the Web page's language as British English.

■ **Content Script Type**   Use this option to specify a default scripting language for your page. Values entered in the Content field must be a valid multimedia Internet Mail extension (MIME) type, such as text/javascript.

■ **Content Style Type**   Choose Content Style Type to specify the default style sheet language for your page. Again, the value entered in the Content box must be a valid MIME type, such as text/css.

■ **Content Type**   Use this option to specify the type of content in your Web page. Typically, a value entered in the Content box while using this option would appear with the following structure: text/html;charset=ISO-20220-JP.

■ **Expires**   The Expires option enables you to set the expiry date and time for the cache control. After expiring, your Web audience's browser automatically requests the page again for refreshing the content. The value that you enter in the Content box for the expiry time should be formatted in the following way: Thurs, 29 March 2001 11:30:00 GMT. This specifies the page expiry as Thursday, March 29, 2001 at exactly 11:30 Greenwich Mean Time.

■ **PICS Label**   The PICS label option enables you to set a platform for Internet content selection (PICS) rating for the content of your Web page. The format for the PICS label should be entered using the following structure: 1994.11.05T08:15-0500 until 1995.12.31T23:59-ooo for http://w3.org/PICS/Overview.html ratings (suds 0.5 density 0 color/hue 1).

*For more information on PICS ratings, see the World Wide Web Consortium Web site at **http://w3.org/PICS/Overview.html**.*

■ **Pragma**   This option enables you to prevent Netscape Navigator from caching your page in memory. The value entered in the Content box should be No-Cache.

■ **Refresh**   Choose the Refresh option to control how often your Web audience's browser refreshes your page content. The value entered specifies the number of seconds between refresh and the specific URL to direct the browser to. For example, this option is useful for content that changes often, such as stock quotes or weather information. You may want to force the browser to refresh in situations when different content (such as advertising banners) is set to appear. The Refresh option is also often used for redirect controls to force the redirect of a browser to view a different page at specific time intervals. The value entered in the Content box should appear in the following way: 10 (to refresh after ten seconds) or 10, **www.abc_company.com/index** (to direct the browser to display a new page after 10 seconds has elapsed).

■ **Reply To**   Choosing this option enables you to specify an email address as the value in the Content box. Typically, this option is used for the address of the creator of the page or the Webmaster of the site. The value in the Content box should take the form of a typical e-mail address.

■ **Set Cookie**   Choosing Set Cookie enables you to specify whether an Internet cookie is sent to your Web page audience's browser, and to specify its expiry date and time (provided that their browser is set to accept cookies). The value entered in the Content box should take the following format: xxx;expires Thursday, 30-Dec-01 23:59:59 BMT; path-/ (where xxx represents the cookie data).

Creating a New Meta Tag Set

Before you actually create a meta tag set, you may want to spend a few minutes thinking about how you would like your Web page to be found and cataloged, and what other actions and information you would like to add. Make a brief list according to the subject matter, key names, key definitions, products, and procedures that your Web page content discusses. The accuracy of the list you create helps increase traffic to your Web site by making it more easily found and determining how your Web page is viewed.

Meta tag sets are created using the Meta Tags for *Document Name* dialog, which is opened by choosing Edit, Meta Tags (see Figure 19-21). Command buttons in this dialog are similar to those seen in other dialogs for creating things like menus. While in this dialog, you'll see a listing of the meta tags currently saved and available in your active Web document. To create a new meta tag, follow these steps:

1. Click the New button to open the Edit Meta Tag Set dialog. The dialog opens with an empty list by default. Enter a name for your new meta tag in the Name box.

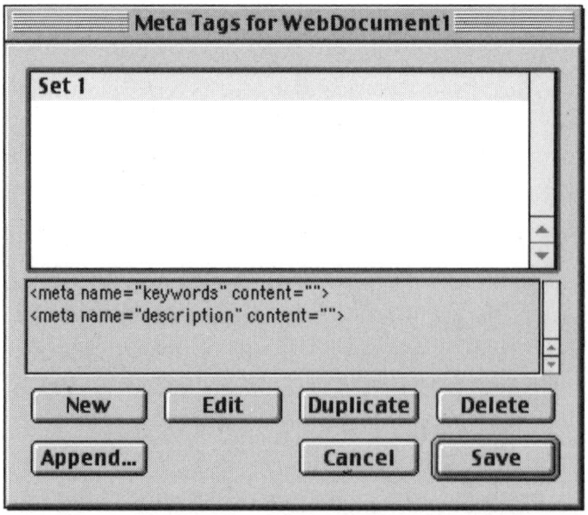

Figure 19-21. *Use the Meta Tags dialog to create new meta tags to apply to your Web page.*

2. Click the Add button to open the New Meta Tag dialog (shown next). Choose a meta tag for your new tag from the Meta Tag drop-down menu (either Name or Http-equiv).

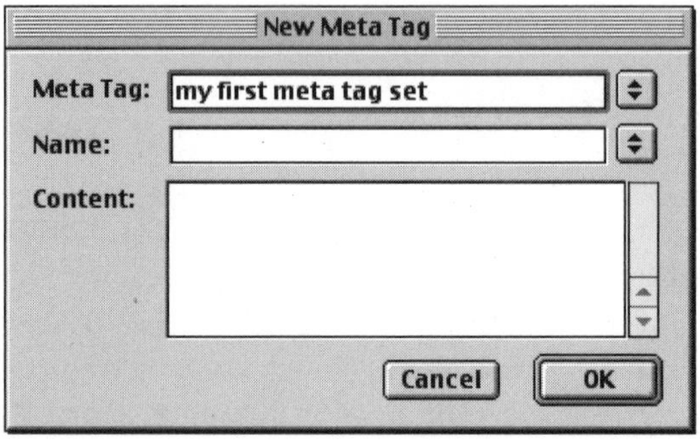

3. Depending on which meta tag type you have selected, you may choose from a collection of specific tags from the Name drop-down menu. (See the preceding sidebar, "Understanding Meta Tags.")

4. With your tag name selected, enter a value in the Content box to specify the tag value.

5. Click OK to close the dialog and return to the New Meta Tag dialog. Repeat this operation to add additional tags to your meta tag list, and click OK to return to the Meta Tags for *Document Name* dialog. Click Save to save the meta tag list and close the dialog. Your meta tag is now saved, but not yet applied to your page.

To edit an existing meta tag, choose Edit, Meta Tags to open the Meta Tags for Document Name dialog and click to select the tag set you want to edit from the listing in the dialog. Click Edit to open the Edit Meta Tags Set dialog and follow the previous procedure to add or change each individual tag in the set. After editing, be sure to click Save in the first dialog that appears to save any editing changes.

Applying a Meta Tag Set to a Web Page

After a meta tag set has been created and saved, the next logical step is to apply it to the corresponding page in your Web document. Doing this is a quick operation using an option in the Page Properties dialog (shown next).

To apply a meta tag to a specific page, follow these quick steps:

1. With your Web document open, turn to the specific page you would like to apply the saved meta tag set to.

2. Choose Page | Page Properties (CMD/CTRL+OPTION/ALT+SHIFT+A) to open the Page Properties dialog.

3. Choose your saved meta tag from the Meta Tag Set drop-down menu and click OK to close the dialog. Your meta tag set is applied to the page and is embedded as invisible coding in the header of your exported Web page.

Appending Meta Tags from Other Web Documents

The Append command is available from within the Meta Tags dialog to enable you to take advantage of the meta tags you've created in other Web documents. Like other types of QuarkXPress elements (such as styles, lists, colors, H&Js, and Dashes &

Stripes), you may copy meta tags between Web documents quickly and easily. To append meta tags from other documents, follow these quick steps:

1. While the document that you want to copy menus to is open, choose Edit | Meta Tags to open the Meta Tags for *Document Name* dialog.

2. Click the Append button in the dialog to open the Append dialog, enabling you to locate, select, and open the meta tags stored in the document you want to copy meta tags from.

3. Clicking Open in the Append dialog automatically opens the Append to *Document Name* dialog. Notice that the dialog is divided into two separate areas: one listing the available meta tags, and the other listing meta tags to include in your active Web document.

4. Select the meta tag set(s) that you want to copy from the Available list on the left of the dialog, and click the right-facing arrow between the two lists to append your selection to the Include list on the right. To include all meta tags from the document, click the Include All button below the Available list. Notice that while a specific meta tag set is selected, the Description areas in the lower portion of the dialog detail the meta tag set name, the meta tag type, and content values (see Figure 19-22).

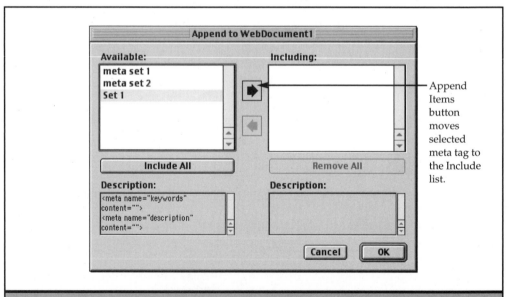

Figure 19-22.   *The Append to Document Name dialog enables you to move saved meta tags from other Web documents to your active Web document.*

5. After your meta tag has been moved to the Include list, click OK to close the dialog and return to the Meta Tag Main dialog.

6. Click Save to close the Meta Tag Main dialog and save your appended menus to your current document. From this point, the copied meta tag is available in your current document to apply to specific pages.

Controlling Web Content
Export Options for Text and Tables

You may control how each of the content items in your Web document is exported to your final Web page in HTML format. This can be done on an individual basis by selecting the item and choosing options in the Export tab of the Modify dialog.

   When it comes to exporting the text items in your Web document, QuarkXPress 5 automatically exports all text as just that—text (with all the specific properties you've applied). However if you'd prefer, you may export the entire contents of a text box as a graphic, meaning that the text box and all text content takes the form of a bitmap. This includes the text cells in tables that you may want to convert.

Note   *Because HTML does not support content that has been altered to be incompatible with typical HTML standards, items that cannot be reproduced using HTML are automatically converted to graphics on export. This includes rotated items, non-rectangular items (such as oval, Bézier, rounded-corner, and freehand text and picture boxes), freehand lines, and text applied to paths. To set the image type to be used for any of these items created in your Web document, use options in the Export dialog to choose a specific bitmap format. For these types of items, the default is automatically set to GIF.*

To convert a selected text box to a graphic on export, follow these brief steps:

1. Choose the Item tool from the Tool palette, and click to select the text or complete table that you want to be converted to a graphic on export.

2. Choose Item | Modify to open the Modify dialog and click the Convert to Graphic on Export option at the bottom of the dialog (shown next).

3. Click the Export tab in the dialog to view the export options that enable you to specify a bitmap format for QuarkXPress to use. By default, GIF is selected as the format, but you may choose GIF, JPEG, or PNG from the Export As drop-down menu.

4. Choose any other image export options and/or enter text to identify the resulting graphic in the Alternate Text box. Click OK to close the dialog. When your page is exported to HTML, your selected text box or complete table is converted to a bitmap, according to your selection. For more information on choosing which format to use, see the following section, "Choosing a Web Picture Export Format."

Note *Converting text to a graphic on export increases the memory size (and display and download time) that is required for your Web audience to view your Web page in the browser. The slower the Internet connection, the more time it takes to display the page. Wherever possible, you may want to leave text as text, or use this option only for small amounts of text.*

Choosing a Web Picture Export Format

Controlling how pictures are exported is likely going to be your main concern when preparing your Web document for the final HTML export process. If you want, you may control the export characteristics of pictures on an individual basis by using options in the Export tab of the Modify dialog while a picture box is selected. To open the Export options for an individual picture, use the Item tool from the Tool palette to select the picture box and use a double-click action to open the Modify dialog. Click the Export tab to gain access to specific picture export options (see Figure 19-23).

Depending on which format you select, various other options become available in the dialog. Regardless of which picture you select, you may also apply a text label to the selected picture by entering text in the Alternate Text box. This text appears as popup text while your Web audience's cursor is held over the picture. The Export As option enables you to set which Web picture format to use for the selected picture when exporting your document as an HTML Web page. Choose between JPEG, GIF, or PNG for your image type; the unique options and properties of which are detailed next.

JPEG Format

One of the most commonly used export file formats is the popular Web image format known as JPEG. The JPEG format, pronounced jay-peg, was a bitmap standard adapted for use with Web page images, due to its variable compression capabilities. The JPEG file compression technique is a *lossy* compression standard, meaning that quality may be compromised to achieve smaller image file sizes. However, the amount of

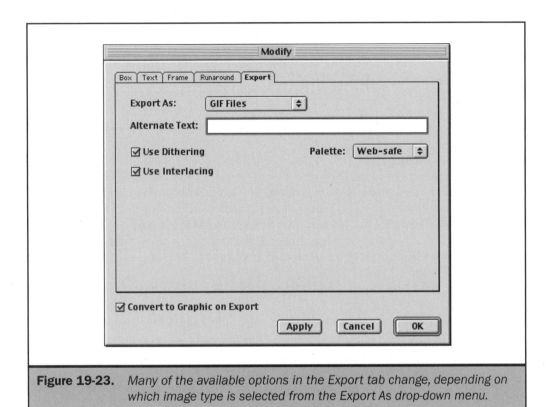

Figure 19-23.   *Many of the available options in the Export tab change, depending on which image type is selected from the Export As drop-down menu.*

compression used is variable (set by the user), enabling you to retain some control over the size of the file and weigh that against the quality of the image. Because Web page display seldom exceeds 72 dpi, compression may be increased significantly before image quality is compromised.

Compression in the Export tab while JPEG is selected may be controlled by making a selection from the Image Quality drop-down menu (shown next). Choose one of five slightly ambiguous compression settings, comprised of Highest (the least compression and default), High, Medium, Low, and Lowest (the most compression). While JPEG is selected as the file format type, you may also choose to have it display progressively by choosing the Progressive option. Normally, JPEG images load in an even linear fashion from the top of the image dimensions to the bottom. Unfortunately, this often takes some time to complete, depending on the inherent JPEG image resolution. Selecting Progressive enables you to set the image to load in a style similar to a camera lens being turned to focus. As the image displays, the focus becomes progressively sharper, enabling the viewer to get an idea of what the image is before it completely loads.

Box	Text	Frame	Runaround	**Export**

Export As: JPEG ⬍

Alternate Text: picture text

Image Quality: Highest ⬍   ☐ **Progressive**

If the image you are exporting is already in the JPEG format, and has been prepared using the final compression and quality that you want to use for your Web page, it may be wise to leave the compression setting at Highest (the default). Changing to a lower-image-quality setting (and subsequently increasing the compression applied to the picture) may result in over-compression, which occurs when an image that already features compression is additionally compressed.

GIF Format

The GIF file format is another that has been widely adapted for Web use. Like JPEG formats, the GIF standard features significant fixed compression saving, but without the loss in quality associated with JPEG files. The GIF format uses run length encoding (RLE), a lossless compression technique, meaning that the image file is compressed without any visible quality loss. However, GIF was likely adapted for its other strengths—namely transparency, animation, and palette color controls. If the picture you are exporting is uneven in shape, QuarkXPress automatically creates a transparency mask (referred to as a softmask) to mask out the areas surrounding the uneven boundaries around the image. As a result, items seen layered below the picture in your Web document (such as the page background) are allowed to show through the transparency mask.

While GIF is selected as the image type in the Export tab of the Modify dialog (shown next), you may choose a variety of options to set dithering, interlacing, and color palette characteristics defined in the following list:

Box	Picture	Frame	Runaround	**Export**

Export As: GIF Files ⬍

Alternate Text: picture text

☑ **Use Dithering**   **Palette:** Web-safe ⬍
☑ **Use Interlacing**

- **Use Dithering** Choosing this option (selected by default) causes the pixels in the selected picture to be exported in a patterned arrangement using error diffusion based on the tones and color in the image. Ordered dithering has the effect of applying a smoothing effect, and is often used to eliminate unwanted pixelation.

- **Use Interlacing** Choosing this option (selected by default) enables you to prepare your resulting GIF image to display in "venetian blind" style as it loads into a Web page browser window. This display method is similar to the progressive loading of JPEG images, but has the visual effect of the image being viewed through horizontal blinds as they are opened.

- **Palette** The Palette menu enables you to control the type of embedded color palette used by the resulting GIF picture. Choose from Web-safe (the default), Adaptive, Windows, or Mac OS. Choosing Web-safe is perhaps the ideal option because it embeds a palette that matches the Web Safe Colors palette available in the Edit Color dialog and the primary color collection used by QuarkXPress 5. Choosing Adaptive embeds a color palette in the GIF image and uses up 256 colors to create a unique color palette for the image. Choosing either Windows or Mac OS embeds color palettes that are optimized for the respective operating systems. Use either of these options if the Web page you are creating is destined to be used on a Windows-only or Mac-only closed intranet environment.

PNG Format

The PNG file format is another image format that is being adopted by Web page designers. Its strengths lie in its ability to offer *lossless* compression, while supporting up to 24-bit color (more colors than are supported by the GIF format). This format also supports transparency colors, but it uses a compatible image editor such as Corel PhotoPaint or Adobe Photoshop to do so.

While PNG is selected as the image type in the Export tab of the Modify dialog (shown next) for a selected picture, several other options become available for controlling the picture's color and display method. Choosing True Color (the default) uses a 24-bit color palette similar to that used by JPEG images and more than that of the GIF format. Choosing Indexed Color enables you to apply smoothing with the Use Dithering option, or control specific color palette options by choosing an option from the Palette menu (comprised of Web-safe, Adaptive, Windows, and Mac OS). For information on the results of choosing Dithering or Palette options, see the previous section, "GIF Format."

Box | Picture | Frame | Runaround | **Export**

Export As: PNG

Alternate Text:

○ True Color
● Indexed Color   ☐ Use dithering   Palette: Web-safe

☐ Use Interlacing

If you want, you may automatically convert specific nonbitmap picture items (such as text boxes) into bitmap-based graphic images during the file export process, when your Web page is exported to HTML. To do so, select the item you want to convert using the Item tool and open the Modify dialog by choosing Item | Modify (CMD/CTRL+M). At the bottom of the dialog, choose the Convert to Graphic on Export option that causes options in the Export tab to become available. This enables you to select an image type, enter alternate text, and choose image-specific options for the item.

Exporting Your Web Document to HTML

After you've spent time proofing and previewing your Web Document text, and then double-checking the content, you are ready for the final operation—preparing your document in a format readable by your Web audience's browser. If the entire process becomes exciting at any time, this is certainly it.

Before you begin though, you may want to set your image folder and root directory options in the Preferences dialog. To access and specify these options, follow these steps:

1. With your Web document open, choose Edit | Preferences | Preferences (CMD/CTRL+OPTION/ALT+SHIFT+Y) to open the Preferences dialog and click to select General under Web Document in the tree directory on the left of the dialog.

2. At the bottom of the dialog, specify a folder name to store your Web page images in the Image Export Directory box. By default, the folder is named Image (shown next).

Image Export Directory: image
Site Root Directory: [   ] Select...

Cancel   OK

3. Specify a Site Root directory (the folder name for all the pages of your Web site) using the box provided; the default is the same folder where your QuarkXPress 5 Web document is stored. To specify a different folder, use the Browse button to open a dialog that enables you to browse your system for a different folder.

4. Click OK to accept your new Web Document preferences and close the dialog.

The HTML export operation is controlled by a number of application components, namely the HTML Export, GIF, and JPEG filters. If you want, you may verify that these components are active and functioning normally by choosing Utilities | Component Status to open the Component Status dialog (see Figure 19-24).

To export your document in HTML, follow these brief steps:

1. With the Web document you want to export to HTML open, choose File | Export | HTML to open the HTML Export dialog (shown next).

Export HTML
- Web Documents — Macintosh HD
  - button1a.jpg
  - button1b.jpg
  - form1.qwd
  - form2.qwd
  - my forms
  - my web site
  - Web elements.qwd

Eject | Desktop | New | Cancel | Export

Pages: All | □ External CSS File
☑ Launch Browser

2. Use options in the dialog to specify a location for your new HTML document. The default folder is the folder that you originally specified in the Preferences dialog as your Site Root directory, but you may change this to a different folder if you want. All images and HTML files are saved in the folder that you specify here.

3. Enter the page numbers you want to export in the Pages box using the format 1, 2, 3 or 1 through 3 to specify document pages, or choose All from the drop-down menu. Because the Web Document page you are exporting uses the Export File name assigned to each page in the Page Properties dialog, no page names need to be entered.

4. If your Web document uses styles to apply text formatting, you may want to choose the External CSS file to have the style sheet information exported as a

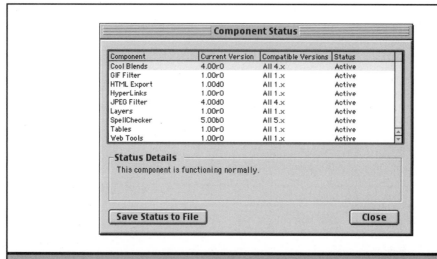

Figure 19-24. *Export to HTML functions are controlled by installed components, as seen in this dialog.*

CSS file during the HTML export operation. This enables your Web audience's browser to open and use the CSS to display the exported HTML files.

5. To have your default browser launch and display the first page in the sequence of HTML files that you are exporting, choose the Launch Browser option.

6. Click OK to create the HTML files. If you choose to launch the browser after the export process is complete, the first page of your document is opened in your browser window.

About Media Independent Workflow and XML

One of the key demands of many QuarkXPress users is to repurpose their existing QuarkXPress documents for the Web. With the introduction of the capability to create new Web documents from QuarkXPress 5, much of this demand has been answered to meet future document needs. But what about all those existing documents that users have archived and in storage? Unfortunately, many of the features and effects available to typical QuarkXPress documents are geared toward printing and creating portable PDF documents, which makes converting older documents to new Web documents a laborious, tedious process.

Quark's solution to this problem is Avenue.Quark, a separate application that enables users to create documents that are *media independent*, meaning that the content in a document may be prepared with tags and then extracted to XML format. Avenue.Quark version 1.1 is included as part of the QuarkXPress 5 suite, but the most recent version is available as a separately purchased application.

The acronym XML stands for extensible markup language—a standardized tagging format that enables you to label different types of content. When a document has been tagged, the content may be extracted automatically for a variety of uses. For example, you may place the content in a database and make it available on the Web, or use HTML templates to automate the formatting of each tagged item to create new HTML documents. The XML tags determine the appearance of the content, but the order and structure of the content is created using a document type definition (DTD). The DTD maps the element types, or labels, that you may apply to the various parts of the document.

Avenue.Quark is an application that enables you to use a DTD to extract structured content from a QuarkXPress document and store that content in XML format. Avenue.Quark operates on tagging rules, which enable you to associate styles and structures in QuarkXPress documents with element types in a DTD. For example, you might associate a style named Body Text with an element type named <bodytext>.

After defining your tagging rules and associating styles with element type names, you may use Avenue.Quark to automate the tagging process. For example, all text applied with a style name Body Text may be tagged automatically with the element type name <bodytext>. This automation enables you to quickly prepare your QuarkXPress document for extraction to XML format.

For more information on XML and Avenue.Quark, visit Quark's Web site at ***www.quark.com/products/avenue*** *and follow the Product Tour link under About Avenue.Quark.*

BEYOND QUARKXPRESS BASICS

Chapter 20

Importing and
Exporting Content

This chapter explores a potpourri of issues surrounding working with XPress in the real world. It explores importing and exporting content to and from your QuarkXPress 5 documents and it takes a close look at issues involved when moving files between platforms. It also details the import and export features of QuarkXPress 5.

Importing Text and Pictures

If you've been working in other chapters covering the use of text and pictures, you likely already have some idea of the basic operations involved in creating text and picture boxes. In this section, you'll learn about specific formats compatible with each of these types of content on both the Macintosh and Windows platforms.

Compatible Text Import Formats

When it comes to text, QuarkXPress 5 is capable of importing nearly any type of text file. This includes text prepared in specific formats independent of native application formats. For the most part, these text file types are interpreted by text import filters available to the XTensions Manager. To view the list of loaded and active filters, choose Utilities, XTensions Manager. In order for a specific filter to be available, the corresponding Xtension must be enabled in the list. Table 20-1 lists the text format's names, details, and corresponding filter XTension.

QuarkXPress 5 also enables you to import text files that have been saved in certain popular word processing application formats. Table 20-2 lists the native word processing text format names, details, and the corresponding filter XTension that must be enabled in the XTensions Manager in order for the import to be successful.

Text File Type XTension	Description	Controlled by Filter
ASCII	American Standard Code for Information Interchange text	N/A
ASCII	Text prepared in ASCII format with QuarkXPress tags	XPress Tags Filter
HTML	Hypertext markup language text	HTML Text Import
RTF	Rich text format (Windows only)	RTF Filter
XML	Xtensible Markup Language	XML Import

Table 20-1.   *Text Formats Available for Importing into QuarkXPress 5*

File Type XTension	Native Application	Controlled by Filter
DOC	Microsoft Word 97/98/2000	MS-Word 6-2000 Filter
DOC	Microsoft Word 6.0/95	MS-Word 6-2000 Filter
WP, WPD, DOC, WPT	WordPerfect 6.x/5.x/3.x	WordPerfect Filter

Table 20-2. *Native Word Processing Applications Supported by QuarkXPress 5*

The Get Text command essentially imports text files into a selected text box. To use this command, follow these steps:

1. Create a text box with any of QuarkXPress 5's text box tools using a click-drag action. Once you finish defining the box size, the Content tool is automatically selected and a blinking I-beam cursor indicates the insertion point.

2. If you're importing text into an existing text box, choose the Content tool and click in the existing text (or highlight text to replace it) to define the insertion point for the imported text.

3. Choose File | Get Text (CMD/CTRL+E). The Get Text dialog appears, as shown in Figure 20-1.

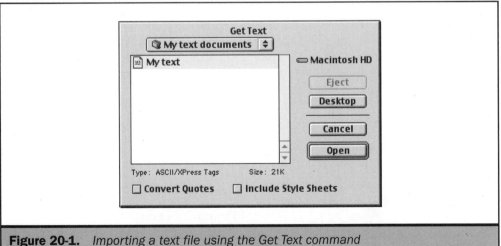

Figure 20-1. *Importing a text file using the Get Text command*

4. Locate the folder containing the text file you wish to import and click on the file to select it. (Windows users: be sure the Files of Type drop-down menu reads All Text Files). Notice certain information about the file appears in the bottom-left corner of the dialog and two options for quote and style sheet handling are available. Leave these at their defaults for now. Choose any import options you require before proceeding.

5. Click Open to import the text into your text box and your import operation is complete.

When choosing import options in the Get Text dialog, the Convert Quotes option (selected by default) converts straight quotes (') to curly open and close quotes (" "). The Include Style Sheets option enables QuarkXPress to interpret, load, and apply any styles that have been saved and applied to your text file. This option enables the styles applied to text to be preserved when importing ASCII text files with embedded XPress tags code, RTF files (Windows only), or native word processing application files supported by QuarkXPress 5, discussed previously in this section. On import, styles are automatically appended to your document's style sheets list.

When importing text into a text box, the text being imported is automatically inserted at the I-beam insertion point or it replaces a selection of text. During the import and/or conversion of large amounts of text, the Page Indicator field at the lower-left corner of your document window temporarily changes to a progress meter indicating the percentage of the file that is being imported.

Compatible Picture Formats

The assortment of compatible picture file formats in QuarkXPress 5 has been greatly expanded to include many vector and bitmap formats as well as specific image formats used in Web document layouts. Table 20-3 lists the types of picture formats compatible for importing into QuarkXPress 5 and lists the required XTensions that must be enabled in the XTensions Manager in order for the picture import operation to be successful.

Importing a picture into your QuarkXPress 5 document requires that you have a picture box created and selected with the Content tool. Pictures must reside in picture boxes in order to exist on your page. Once a picture box is selected with the Content tool, the Get Picture command becomes available and is essentially your picture import command. To import a picture into a selected picture box, follow these quick steps:

1. With the Content tool selected, choose File | Get Picture (CMD/CTRL+E) to open the Get Picture dialog (see Figure 20-2).

2. Locate the folder containing your picture and click once on the file representing your picture to select it. (Windows users may use the Files of Type drop-down menu to limit the display of picture formats to the specific file format of your picture. Or leave the selection at the default All Picture Files selection.)

File Type	Description	Required Xtension Filter
BMP, RLE, DIB	Bitmap, Run Length Encoding	N/A
EPS, AI	Combined bitmap/vector in Adobe EPS format or native Adobe Illustrator EPS format	N/A
GIF	Graphics Interchange Format	N/A
JPEG	Joint Photographic Experts Group	N/A
Mac PICT	Combined bitmap/vector from Mac OS	N/A
PCD	Kodak PhotoCD format	PhotoCD Import
PCX	Bitmap	N/A
PDF	Adobe Portable Document File format	PDF Filter
PNG	Portable Network Graphics	PNG Filter
PRF	Hyperlinks image map file	Image Map Filter
Scitex	Proprietary CREO/Scitex image files	N/A
TIFF	Tagged image file format	N/A
TIFF (LZW)	TIFF images compressed using Lempel-Ziv-Welch	LZW Import
WMF	Windows Metafile	N/A

Table 20-3.   *Picture Formats Compatible with QuarkXPress 5*

3. If the Preview option isn't already selected, choose it now. Notice a small representation of the image appears in the preview window. Using the Preview option is a quick way to visually check that you are selecting the correct picture.

4. Click Open to import the picture and close the dialog.

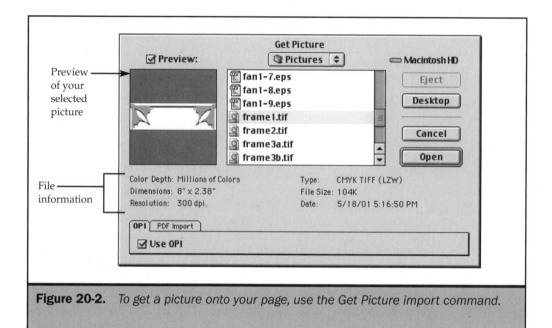

Figure 20-2. *To get a picture onto your page, use the Get Picture import command.*

   To replace a picture box's content with a different picture, repeat the import process by selecting the picture box, choosing the Get Picture (CMD/CTRL+E) command, and open another picture. The new picture simply replaces the previous one.

Exporting Text

If you need to prepare the text you've created in your QuarkXPress 5 document for use in a different application, you may export selected text to various word processing applications' native formats using the Save Text command. While a picture box is selected and/or text in the box is highlighted using the Content Tool, the Save Text command (CMD/CTRL+OPTION/ALT+E) becomes available. Choosing this command opens the Save Text dialog (see Figure 20-3), which features the Format (Macintosh) or Save as Type (Windows) drop-down menu options for saving your exported text to the file formats listed in Table 20-4.

While a text box is selected, options in the Save Text dialog enable you to export text in the following ways:

■ **Entire Story**   While a text box is simply selected and no text has been highlighted using the Content tool cursor, this becomes the default function and has the effect of exporting all text in the selected text box, including text in

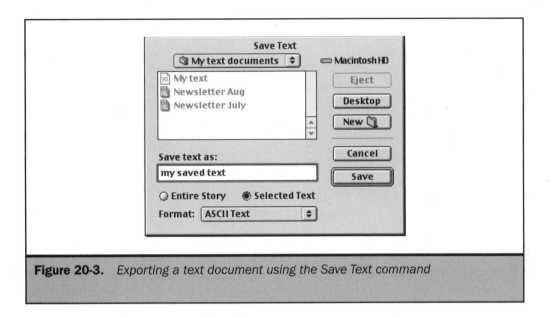

Figure 20-3.   *Exporting a text document using the Save Text command*

File Format	File Type/Windows Extension
ASCII Text	TXT
HTML	HTM
Microsoft Word 97/98/2000	DOC
Microsoft Word 6.0/95	DOC
XPress Tags	XTG
WordPerfect 6.0	WPD
Rich Text Format (Windows only)	RTF

Table 20-4.   *File Formats Compatible with the Save Text Command*

any linked text boxes. This also becomes an option while text is highlighted in addition to the next option.

■ **Selected Text**   While text is highlighted in a text box using the Content tool cursor, this is the default selected option and has the effect of exporting only the selected text (and not the entire story).

■ **Mac OS Line Endings** (Windows only)   Windows users may choose this
option (shown next) to prepare text specifically for the Macintosh platform. On
the Mac OS, standard line breaks are specified using only a return character,
which is different from the Windows operating systems. Macintosh users may
choose ASCII from the Format drop-down menu to prepare files for the
Windows platform, which has the effect of using Return characters plus Line
Feed to describe line breaks.

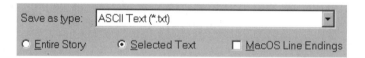

Exporting to HTML

If you've created a Web document (as opposed to a typical QuarkXPress document),
you'll no doubt eventually be exporting it to Hypertext Markup Language (HTML)
format. To do so, you'll need to use the Export HTML dialog (see Figure 20-4) opened
by choosing File | Export | HTML.

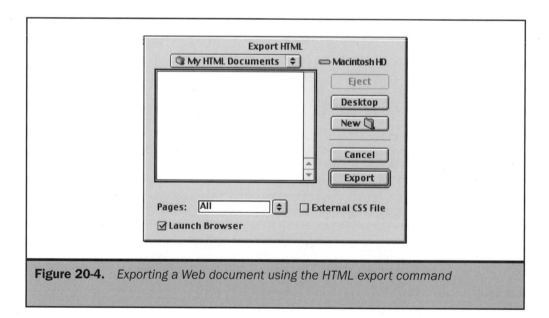

Figure 20-4.   *Exporting a Web document using the HTML export command*

The HTML dialog features no option to name your new HTML document. Instead, your document name is used automatically and appended with numerals for each of the pages in the document. While the HTML is opened, you have two key options to select for controlling how your HTML file is created:

- **External CSS**   The External CSS (cascading style sheet) option enables you to specify that the style information for the exported HTML file will be stored as a CSS file in the export folder you specify. CSS files contain style information used by a Web browser being used to view the HTML Web document.

- **Launch Browser**   This option (selected by default) causes your exported HTML file to immediately be opened for viewing in your selected Web browser.

Saving Pages in EPS Format

The Save Page as EPS (encapsulated PostScript) command enables you to save whole pages in encapsulated PostScript page description language. The capability to save whole pages and/or page spreads as EPS files enables you to use your layouts in other QuarkXPress documents or save them for import into other applications.

PostScript pages are much more versatile than bitmap images since the vector objects they contain may be infinitely resized and printed at the maximum resolution of the printer in use. When pages are saved, all information, including fills, Bézier lines and so on, are self-contained in the EPS file, so that they may be transferred through networks, ported across platforms, or archived without the need for QuarkXPress to be available on a host system in order to be viewed. If the page contains high-resolution picture files linked to the document, the data representing these images may be included in the EPS file using open prepress interface (OPI) options.

Note   *The Save Page as EPS command does not embed fonts into the EPS file when it is created. In order for fonts used in the document being saved as EPS to print correctly, the same fonts must be available on the host system being used to print the document or resident in memory on the printer in use.*

To save a page in EPS format, open your completed QuarkXPress document and choose File | Save Page as EPS (CMD/CTRL+OPTION/ALT+SHIFT+S) to open the Save Page as EPS dialog (see Figure 20-5). The lower portion of the dialog consists of several tabbed areas for choosing export options. Specifically, the Save Page as EPS tab provides access to the available EPS options, while options in the Profiles | Bleed | and OPI tabbed areas may also be set.

Once the options in the Save Page as EPS dialog have been selected, clicking OK immediately exports the page using the name and location you specify and prepares the file according to the options you choose. This results in the following effect on the condition of your exported EPS page:

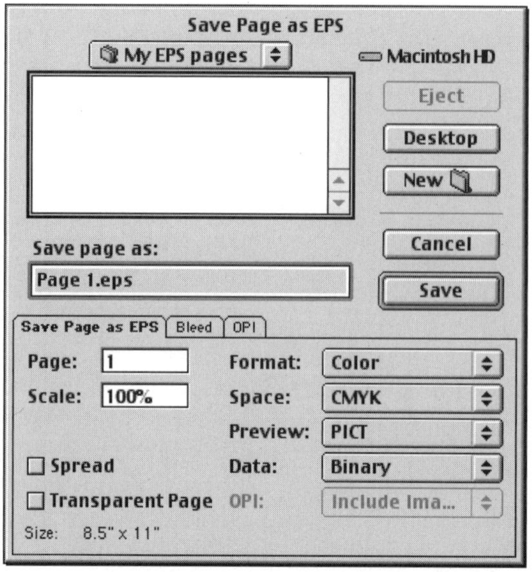

Figure 20-5. *Choosing options for pages saved in EPS format*

■ **Save Page As/File name**   Enter a file name for XPress to assign to the new EPS file in this box. By default, the file name is set to Page X.eps, where X represents the page number currently being displayed on your screen.

■ **Save as Type** (Windows only)   Windows users will see this drop-down menu, which is set to EPS by default, and is the only option available.

■ **Page**   In this field, enter the document page number you wish to save in the EPS format. You may also enter an absolute page number, which corresponds to the page's actual sequence in your document, by entering a + to precede the page number.

■ **Scale**   Enter a scaling reduction for the document page being saved to EPS. Scaling must fall between 10 and 100 percent. The term scale may be slightly misleading since you may only *reduce* the document page's overall size. The default is 100 percent.

■ **Format**   The next four options enable you to set the treatment of header, color, and data formats for your exported EPS file. The Format drop-down menu enables you to choose either *Color, B&W* (black and white/grayscale), *DCS* (desktop color separations), or *DCS 2.0*. These options are vastly different in their formats and you'll need to choose them carefully in order for your EPS file to be prepared correctly. Choose Color to enable the EPS to be created with a color preview, or choose B&W to set the preview to a single color of black. In both cases, the items contained in the EPS will also be created to include color or black and white (or grayscale). Choose DCS to create an EPS file containing process color, or DCS 2.0 to include process color and spot colors.

■ **Space**   This option enables you to control the color space used by all items in your exported EPS file. Choose between Cyan, Magenta, Yellow, and Black (CMYK) to specify a process color space, or Red, Green, and Blue (RGB) to specify screen colors only.

■ **Preview**   The Preview drop-down menu enables you to include a preview header in the EPS file by selecting TIFF format, PICT, or None. Choosing TIFF (the default) sets the preview in a tagged image file format (TIFF), while choosing None leaves the EPS without any preview at all. Omitting the preview is sometimes useful for reducing the resulting EPS file size.

■ **Data**   Three choices are available from this drop-down menu: ASCII, Binary, and Clean 8-bit. The capability to choose the Data type that describes the EPS file enables you a certain degree of flexibility when in comes to printing a document containing the EPS file through a print spooler and with a wider range of printer types. Clean 8-bit (the default) is similar to Binary, but omits additional data strings that Binary adds to communicate with parallel port printers. The ASCII format is a more versatile format, compatible with a wide range of printers and print spooling software.

Tip   *If you are saving an EPS file for use on QuarkXPress Windows versions, choose either Clean 8-bit or ASCII rather than Binary as the Data format.*

■ **OPI**   The OPI tab of the Save Page as EPS dialog enables you to determine whether picture information is included in the EPS file. OPI options enable you to print using only the preview contained in the EPS file or substitute this with the original data file representing the picture. Before printing, the high-resolution images are substituted for lower-resolution placeholders. Choose Include Images (the default) to include all TIFF and EPS picture information in the EPS file being created. Choose Omit TIFF to leave out all TIFF picture data and insert OPI comments to link to these files externally when the EPS file is printed. Or choose Omit TIFF and EPS to leave out both TIFF and EPS data and insert OPI comments to link to these files externally. When choosing either of the latter two options, the omitted picture files will need to accompany the EPS file in order for them to print correctly.

■ **Spread**   Choose this option to create an EPS file of the complete spread. While selected, the Spread option will include whichever page is facing the page entered in the Page field.

- **Transparent Page** This option enables you to control whether your exported EPS page features a transparent or standard white page background. While selected, the background of your exported EPS file will enable items in the destination document layered beneath it to be visible.

- **Profiles** If Color Management is enabled for your document, the Profiles tab appears in the Save Page as EPS dialog and includes color profile options for choosing the Composite and Separation profile information to be inserted as comments in the EPS file. Choose the profiles that correspond to the type of composite- and separations-printing hardware your EPS file is destined to be printed to. While a separations profile is selected, the Composite Simulates Separation option also becomes available. Profile information will only apply if the EPS file you are creating is destined to be imported into a QuarkXPress document supporting Quark's color management system and will only become useful if the destination document is actively using CMS. For more information on using Quark's CMS, see Chapter 16.

Tip *The Separations drop-down menu will only be available as an option if either DCS or DCS 2.0 is selected in the Format drop-down menu of the Save Page as EPS tab.*

- **Bleed** The Bleed tab enables you to include items that overlap the edges of your document page to a certain extent, and include them in your EPS file. Choose between Symmetric (the default) and specify a value in the Amount box, or choose Asymmetric and enter values in the Top, Bottom, Left, and/or Right boxes. In either case, Bleed values may range between 0 and 6 inches. While left at the default setting of 0 inches, portions of items that extend beyond the edge of the document borders of your exported EPS page will be clipped at the document page boundaries.

Tip *For more information on choosing Bleed options, see "Choosing Bleed Options" in Chapter 17.*

Creating Portable Documents from QuarkXPress 5

Shortly after the release of XPress 4, a new portable document file (PDF) export filter XTension was released to enable QuarkXPress users to generate PDFs of their pages. The PDF Export Filter for QuarkXPress (now integrated into version 5) enables you to save one or more pages from your QuarkXPress 5 document as a PDF file. Adobe's PDF format has become popular for many applications since the files may be viewed with the Adobe Acrobat viewer, which is distributed free of charge. PDFs display and print independently of the host program used to create the document and need no supporting files such as pictures or fonts. The filter saves the pages in PostScript format and employs the use of Adobe Acrobat Distiller software in order to create the file.

You must have the Adobe Acrobat Distiller PPD present in your list of PPDs available in the PPD Manager. To make this PPD available, use the PPD Manager opened by choosing Utilities | PPD Manager. For more information on managing printer descriptions, see "Using the PPD Manager" in Chapter 17.

Beginning the PDF Export Process

In order to successfully create a PDF using QuarkXPress 5, you must specify a printer description in the PDF Preferences dialog before you can begin. If one is not selected, an alert dialog will prompt you to do just that. To do so, choose Edit | Preferences | Preferences (CMD/CTRL+OPTION/ALT+SHIFT+Y) to open the Preferences dialog and click PDF in the tree directory in the list. This dialog (see Figure 20-6) enables you to

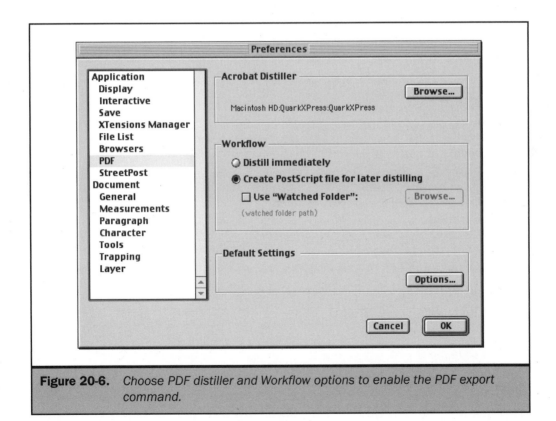

Figure 20-6.   *Choose PDF distiller and Workflow options to enable the PDF export command.*

specify Acrobat Distiller and WorkFlow settings (see "Controlling PDF Workflow Options" later in this chapter). Click the Browse button to open the Locate Acrobat Distiller dialog and specify the folder location of the Adobe Acrobat Distiller.

With the distiller specified and any Workflow options selected, follow these steps to create a PDF:

1. Choose File | Export | Document as PDF to open the Export as PDF dialog (shown next).

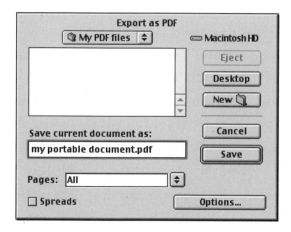

2. Enter a name for your new PDF. By default, your QuarkXPress 5 document file name is used.

3. Enter the starting page number in the Page(s) field. By default, this is set to your currently displayed page.

4. Enter the last page in the series of pages you wish to create the PDF for, or choose All from the drop-down menu.

Note *You may not create a PDF of noncontinuous pages as you are able to do in the Print dialog of XPress. Instead, the pages you use must be in sequence.*

5. To export one spread per page, click the Spread option.

6. To set specific PDF properties, click the Options button to open a tabbed dialog containing Document Info, Hyperlinks, Job Options, and Output options as required (see the following illustration). (These options are detailed in the next section.)

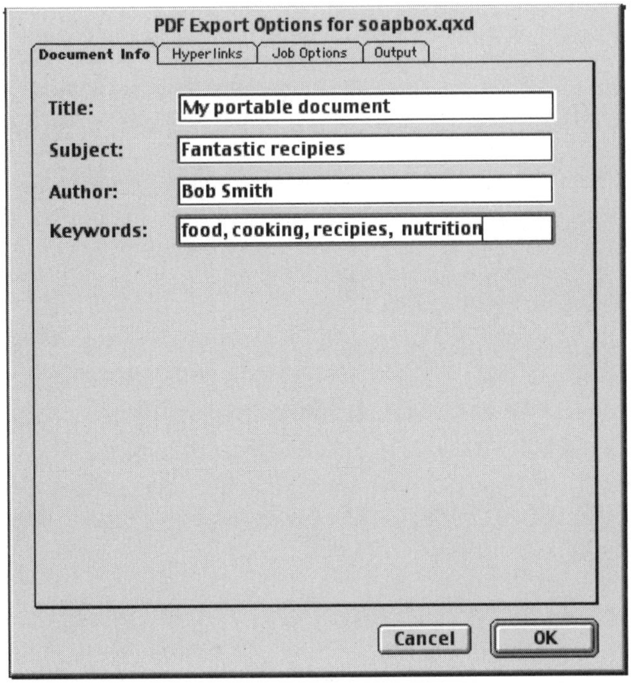

PDF Export Options for soapbox.qxd

| Document Info | Hyperlinks | Job Options | Output |

Title: My portable document

Subject: Fantastic recipies

Author: Bob Smith

Keywords: food, cooking, recipies, nutrition

Cancel   OK

7. Once your options have been chosen, click OK to close the PDF Export Options dialog and click Save to create the PDF and close the Export as PDF dialog. To view the PDF, open it in Adobe Acrobat Reader to ensure the file has been created according to your needs.

Installing Acrobat Distiller and the PDF Filter

In order to successfully create a PDF file, you must first have two key elements installed in specific places on your system: Adobe Acrobat Distiller and the PDF filter Xtension. Both are pivotal in creating PDF files from your QuarkXPress 5 document. Adobe Acrobat Distiller is a utility that converts PostScript page information into a portable document format that may be read by Adobe Acrobat Reader. Acrobat Reader is available free of charge, but recent versions of Adobe Acrobat Distiller are available as a purchase from Adobe. Adobe Acrobat Distiller is bundled with several Adobe products. If you already own an Adobe product such as PhotoShop, Illustrator, or Pagemaker, you may already own the distiller. For information on purchasing Acrobat Distiller Software, visit Adobe's Web site (**www.adobe.com/products/main.html**).

The PDF filter for QuarkXPress 5 is automatically copied onto your system during a Complete installation. If you require, you may install the filter as a Custom installation or manually by following the step sequences that follow.

Macintosh Users May Install the PDF Filter Using These Brief Steps:

1. If QuarkXPress 5 is currently running, choose File | Quit (CMD+Q) to close the program.

2. Insert your QuarkXPress 5 application disc into your CD-ROM drive. Locate and copy the file named PDF Filter from the disc into the XTensions folder in the QuarkXPress folder on your hard drive.

3. Also locate and copy the three files named PDFL40.LIB, CoolTypeLib, and AGMLib from your QuarkXPress application disc to the Extensions subfolder in the System folder on your hard drive, or into the XTensions folder in your Quark application folder.

Windows Users May Install the PDF Filter Using These Brief Steps:

1. If QuarkXPress 5 is currently running, choose File | Quit (CTRL+Q) to close the program.

2. Insert your QuarkXPress 5 application disc into your CD-ROM drive. Locate and copy the file named PDF Filter.xnt from the disc into the XTensions folder in the QuarkXPress folder on your hard drive.

3. Also locate and copy the three files named PDFL40.DLL, Cooltype.DLL, and AGM.DLL from your QuarkXPress application disc into the Windows/System folder on your hard drive, or into the Xtensions subfolder in your Quark application folder. (Windows 2000/NT users should copy these files into the Windows/System32 folder.)

Once these steps are complete for either platform version, relaunch QuarkXPress 5 and verify that Acrobat Distiller is available as a selection in the PPD Manager, which can be opened by choosing Utilities | PPD. Once the PPD is available and selected, proceed with your PDF export operation.

Setting PDF Document Info Options

While exporting a page in EPS format using options in the Export as PDF dialog, clicking the Options button provides access to a number of options for controlling specific properties of the PDF file you are creating. The PDF Export Options dialog is subdivided into four main option areas in a tab arrangement. The first tabbed area you'll encounter is Document Info (shown next), which provides areas for adding a title, a subject, an author's name, and keywords to your new PDF.

```
              PDF Export Options for Document1
  [ Document Info ] [ Hyperlinks ] [ Job Options ] [ Output ]

       Title:     [Document1                    ]

     Subject:     [                             ]

      Author:     [                             ]

   Keywords:      [                             ]




                                      [ Cancel ]  [  OK  ]
```

Entering text in these boxes enables you to provide information that appears in the PDF file while being viewed using Adobe Acrobat Reader. Information entered in these boxes will eventually be available to those viewing the PDF file you create. Choosing File | Document Info | General while viewing the PDF file in the Reader application enables this information to be viewed in the General Info dialog (see Figure 20-7).

Choosing PDF Hyperlink Options

Adobe's portable document files support hyperlink functions in specific ways. Hyperlinks may be created automatically to help the reader navigate between points within the document. Hyperlinks may be created automatically based on lists and

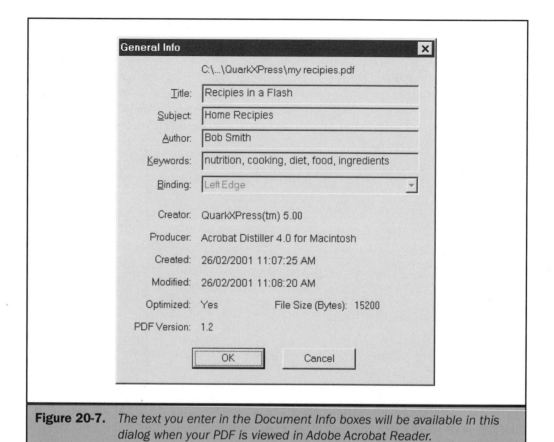

Figure 20-7.   *The text you enter in the Document Info boxes will be available in this dialog when your PDF is viewed in Adobe Acrobat Reader.*

indexes you've created in your document. To enable these features in the PDF file you're creating, click the Options button in the Export as PDF dialog to open the PDF Export Options dialog and click the Hyperlinks tab. In the Hyperlinks tab (shown next), you'll find a series of options that enable you to set whether hyperlinks are included, how they are generated, and how they'll appear in your exported PDF.

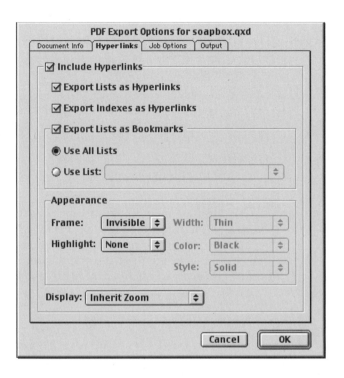

Once the Include Hyperlinks option is selected, the remainder of the dialog options become available. Choosing these options enables you to control the following properties of your PDF hyperlinks:

- **Export Lists as Hyperlinks**   When this option is selected, the resulting PDF will include hyperlinks to pages that relate to each list item in your document, such as a hyperlinked table of contents. For information on creating and working with lists in XPress, see "Working with Style Lists" in Chapter 12.

- **Export Indexes as Hyperlinks**   When this option is selected, the resulting PDF will include hyperlinks to pages from an index of their contents. This feature operates in a similar way to QuarkXpress 5's Index palette feature. For more information on using the Index palette and creating indexes, see "Working with Indexes" in Chapter 12.

- **Export Lists as Bookmarks**   When this option is selected, the resulting PDF will automatically include bookmarks to the pages that each of the list items refers to. Bookmarks is a built-in feature of Adobe Acrobat Reader.

- **Use All Lists**   Choose this option to create all lists in your document as hyperlinks.

- **Use List** Choose this option instead of the Use All Lists option to specify specific lists as hyperlinks. While selected, the drop-down menu to the right becomes available, enabling you to specify which lists to use. Only lists saved to your current document are eligible as hyperlinks.

- **Frame Appearance** This option enables you to control how text applied with hyperlinks appears on the PDF pages, regardless of whether they were created by lists or indexes. If needed, you may have frames of different widths, colors, or styles appear around the hyperlinks in your document. By default, frames are invisible, but you may choose Visible to have the frames appear and specify Width, Color, and Shade options that become available once the Visible option is selected.

- **Highlight Appearance** To control how hyperlinks appear when clicked, use options available from the Highlight drop-down menu. Choosing None applies no highlighting, while the three remaining options create highlighting effects. Choose Invert to have the hyperlink change color according to its complimentary or "opposite" color according to standard color wheel position. Choose Outline to have a black outline appear around the link. Or choose Inset to create a three-dimensional button effect.

- **Display** This option enables you to control how the linked PDF page linked to the hyperlink will appear when opened. Choose Inherent Zoom (the default) to leave the view magnification as is or choose from one of three remaining options in the menu. Choosing Fit Window opens the selected linked page to fit vertically and horizontally within the current window. Choosing Fit Width or Fit Length automatically applies a scale factor to open the linked PDF page to fit either horizontally or vertically (respectively).

Note *To successfully include lists as hyperlinks during the export process, they must actually be used as an integral part of the content of your document. Lists that are simply defined but not built (or that are built but not within document page area) will not be included during the export process.*

Choosing PDF Job Options

The Job Options tab of the PDF Export Options dialog (shown next) enables you to override font options and picture compression options set in your Adobe Acrobat Distiller software. Choose either or both of the Override Distiller's Font options and Compression options to enable the related options.

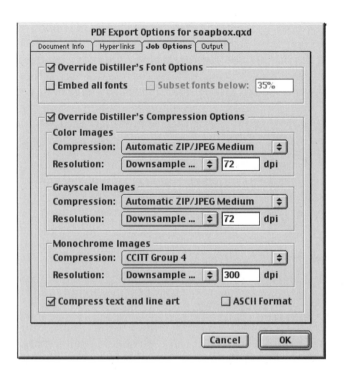

It's worth mentioning at this point that overriding Adobe Acrobat Distiller's Font options can often result in overly large PostScript files being created prior to the software distilling the file into PDF format. If you're encountering large PostScript files during file distilling, you may wish to leave the Font options as is and concentrate only on the Image Compression options (discussed next) as your primary strategy for reducing the size of your exported PDF file.

While the Override Distiller's Font options are selected, the following font-related options become available:

- **Embed All Fonts**   Embedding the fonts used in your PDF document is the ideal way of preparing your portable document since the fonts used on your own host system may not necessarily match those available on the system being used to view the PDF. To be sure your PDF is viewed the way you prepared it, choosing this option is always recommended and has the effect of embedding all fonts in the PDF file.

■ **Subset Fonts Below**   While the Embed All Fonts option is selected, this font
subset option becomes available. While selected, it enables you to embed only
the font characters that are used in your original QuarkXPress document into
the PDF file (instead of embedding all sizes for the font used). This option is
accompanied by a threshold setting that is preset at 35 percent. At this setting,
the Adobe Acrobat Distiller software will make a subset of font character
thresholds below 35 percent. If more than 35 percent of the font characters are
used in your exported PDF, the distiller will embed the entire font.

While the Override Distiller's Compression options are selected, you may set the
Compression and Resolution properties, which are divided into three separate areas for
controlling color, grayscale, and/or monochrome (1-bit) images independently of each
other in the following ways.

Image Compression

In each of the image type areas, you may control how images are compressed.
Compression options enable you to reduce the physical memory size of bitmap images
in your exported PDF file. Color and grayscale bitmap images may be prepared using
various combinations of Automatic or Manual methods using either ZIP or JPEG
compression at varying degrees. The default value is preset to Automatic ZIP/JPEG
Medium, which leaves the compression method up to the Distiller software and is
suitable for compressing images to a satisfactory size without compromising display
quality. However, you may also choose from a variety of Automatic ZIP/JPEG
compression levels ranging from High to Low compression, which represents the image
quality of the exported image. For example, a selection of High applies the least
compression, but maintains the maximum image quality, while a selection of Low has
the opposite effect. Choosing one of the Manual compression methods enables you to
choose whether images are compressed using ZIP or JPEG compression methods.
Compression options for monochrome (1-bit) images are an exception to this rule.
Monochrome images may be compressed using a variety of specialized compression
methods comprised of CCITT Group 4 (the default), CCITT Group 3, ZIP, Run Length
(also known as Run Length Encoding [RLE]), or None.

Image Resolution

With regards to this option, resolution represents the dpi value the images in your
exported PDF will be prepared using. The lower the resolution, the less detailed your
images will be. The Resolution option in each of the color areas may be set to either
Downsample To (the default), Keep Resolution, or Subsample To.
Choosing Keep Resolution leaves the resolution of your exported images as is,
without resampling their resolution in any way. Downsampling and Subsampling
options both cause the respective images in your exported PDF to be reduced in
resolution according to the accompanying dpi value, but in different ways. Choosing

Downsample To causes the distiller to reduce the resolution using pixel color averaging, while Subsample To uses a center pixel color method.

While either the Downsample or Subsample To options are selected, you may enter a specific resolution value in the dpi box. By default, color and grayscale image resolution is preset to 72 dpi, while monochrome images are preset to 300 dpi, each of which are suitable for typical screen display. However, if the PDF you are preparing is destined for print reproduction, you may wish to increase this value. A dpi value of 300 is often enough for typical offset reproduction, but you may wish to check with your print vendor for the ideal value. Resolution may range between 9 and 2400 dpi.

In addition to the image compression options, you may also control compression using two final options in the Job Options dialog as follows:

- **Compress Text and Line Art**   Choosing Compress Text and Line Art enables you to reduce the information associated with displaying fonts, lines, and shapes created in your document using ZIP compression.

- **ASCII Format**   This option enables you to export your PDF file in ASCII format instead of the default binary format. Choose ASCII if you intend on opening the file in a text editor for viewing or editing, or if you intend on sending your new PDF across networks or mail gateways that don't support binary files.

Setting PDF Output Options

If the PDF document you are preparing is destined for print reproduction, the Output tab of the PDF Export Options dialog (shown next) enables you to specify printing-related options. These options enable you to set which device will be used to print the document, how color is handled, and control other print-related conveniences.

- **Printer Description** Choose a printer description based on the PPDs available to your Adobe Acrobat Distiller software.

- **Composite/Separations** This option enables you to control whether your PDF will be prepared as a composite color PDF document or as PDF separations. While Composite is selected, the next option becomes the Print Colors option, enabling you to specify a color model for all color elements in the resulting file. While Separations is selected, the next option becomes the Plates option, enabling you to control the color included on each of the resulting separation plates.

- **Print Colors/Plates** Depending on which type of color document you are creating (composite or separations), this next drop-down menu changes to offer relevant options for controlling how color elements in the resulting PDF are prepared. While Composite is selected, you may specify elements to be reproduced in grayscale (the default), RGB, CMYK, or black and white (monochrome). While Separations is selected, the selection changes to separation-specific color. Choose Used Spot and Process to generate PDF color separations only for those colors that have been used in your document. Choose Convert to Process to change all colors (including spot colors) to process color and print only PDF separations representing CMYK color. Choose All Spot and Process to print PDF separations for all colors specified in your document's color list, regardless of whether they include color elements or not.

- **Produce Blank Pages** Choose this option (not selected by default) to create pages in your PDF document that do not include either text or picture content.

- **Use OPI** Choose this option to use OPI functions for your PDF. OPI enables you to embed picture comments for high-resolution picture substitution during printing of the exported PDF. While selected, the Images drop-down menu becomes available and enables you to choose which types of picture formats in your document are included in the resulting PDF. Choose Include Images (the default) to embed OPI comments for both TIFF and EPS pictures. If a high-resolution file cannot be found for printing, the screen preview in the PDF will be used in its place. Choose Omit TIFF to embed OPI comments to high-resolution TIFF pictures only, but embed all EPS picture information. Choose Omit TIFF and EPS to embed OPI comments for both TIFF and EPS pictures. In both cases, if the pictures cannot be found during printing, screen previews are used instead.

- **Registration** The Registration option enables you to specify whether registration marks (the crosshair marks used to align separations during film separation and printing) are included in the resulting PDF file. Choose Off (the default) to omit registration marks entirely, or choose Centered or Off Center to specify the placement of marks around each page. While Off Center is selected, you may specify the Offset amount, the default of which is 6 points.

■ **Bleed**   Choosing the Bleed option enables you to include portions of items overlapping your document page to be included in the resulting PDF file to varying degrees up to 6 inches beyond the boundaries of your document page. While Page Items Only (the default) is selected, the bleed area is extended to include items extending beyond your page boundaries. To specify a given amount, choose either Symmetric or Asymmetric. Choosing Symmetric causes an Amount box to appear, enabling you to specify an exact bleed measure uniformly around all pages in your resulting PDF file. Choosing Asymmetric causes Top, Left, Right, and Bottom boxes to appear, enabling you to specify non-uniform bleed boundaries.

For more information on separation printing techniques, see Chapter 18.

Controlling PDF Workflow Options

Besides being able to specify your Acrobat Distiller application in the PDF page of the Preferences dialog, you may also set Workflow and document info defaults. Under the heading Workflow, choose between immediate distillation of the file or postponing the distillation of individual files by saving them in PostScript format to a folder that is periodically polled by the Adobe Distiller. This folder is referred to as the "Watched" folder. To define the Watched folder, click the Use Watched Directory option and click the Browse button to locate the folder.

Dragging Pages Between Documents

Chances are there will be times when you'd like to copy an entire page layout or a sequence of pages from one document to another. The easiest way to do so is to simply drag and drop them from one file to the other, but to pull this off, you'll need to do a little preliminary setup work. In the discussion to follow, let's refer to the file that content is coming from as the source document and the document that the content is being moved to as the destination document.

1. Start by opening a document (the source document) and taking note of the document setup. The best strategy to follow is to drag thumbnails only between documents with similar setups for such things as page size, margins, facing/nonfacing page spreads, and the number of columns.

2. Create or open another document (the destination document) with the same setup as the source document.

3. At this point, you'll need to display both documents in Thumbnails view and position them so they're both visible onscreen at the same time. Hold

OPTION/ALT and choose View | Windows | Tile Documents (Macintosh) or Window | Tile Vertically or Tile Horizontally (Windows). QuarkXPress will automatically switch both documents to Thumbnails view and tile each of them so they're both visible. Or press OPTION+SHIFT, click on either document's title bar to view the Windows popup menu options, and perform the same operation (Macintosh only).

As an alternative to changing to Thumbnail view, press CTRL+V to highlight the View Percent field in the lower-left corner of your document window and enter a T followed by pressing ENTER.

4. Click the title bar of the source document window to make it active, choose the Item tool from the Tools palette, and select the page(s) you want to copy. To select a complete page, click once to select it. To select a range of pages, click on the first page, hold down SHIFT and click on the last page in the range. To select noncontiguous pages, hold down CMD/CTRL and click to select each page.

5. With your page(s) selected in the source document, drag the pages across the document windows to a new location in the destination document. When you position the pages at a compatible point in the destination document, your cursor will change to provide a number of feedback states. For example, if the newly added pages will not cause the existing page order to change, your cursor will show either a single-sided, left-facing, or right-facing page icon symbol. If placing the new pages *will* cause existing pages to move, your cursor will show either a force-left, force-right, or force-down icon symbol.

6. Depending on the layout of the destination document and the number and placement of pages you've moved, it may be necessary to rearrange the pages in your destination document or even to delete blank pages. To move pages, simply drag them (in Thumbnail view) into place. To delete a page, select it and choose Delete from the Page menu.

It's worth keeping in mind that when you perform a thumbnail drag operation between documents, your style sheets, colors, dashes and stripes, and H&Js used in items dragged, saved, and applied to items in the source document will automatically be added to the destination document. If a conflict arises during the drag operation (meaning the destination document already contains elements that have the same name as elements in the source document), the destination document's specifications will be preserved.

> **Tip** *When you drag pages between documents, the layout applied by the related master page is also copied. If a conflict arises during the drag operation (meaning the master page being copied in the destination document already has the same name as the master page from the source document), the master page from the source document will be renamed. For example, if both documents already contain Master A and Master B, and you drag a page based on the source document's Master A, it will be renamed Master C in the destination document.*

Moving Files Between Versions and Platforms

In today's versatile digital publishing world, moving files from one computer to another is a common practice. It goes without saying that not all users employ the same type of computer or publishing setup. Moving your QuarkXPress files between platforms is often a requirement for such operations as film output or even production. With all of its complex functionality, QuarkXPress 5 enables you to "port" files between platforms. The term porting is used to describe this operation whereby document files originating on one platform version may be opened on another, such as Windows to Macintosh or vice versa. For instance, you may port a QuarkXPress version 5 file from Macintosh to version 5 on the Windows platform. You may also port files that have been created or saved in previous versions across platforms, in essence porting and updating the files simultaneously.

There are certain details you may want to familiarize yourself with before attempting file-porting operations. Since each platform has its own special characteristics, so too do the creative devices you may have placed or created as you produced your artistic undertaking. When moving QuarkXPress document files between platforms in either direction, consider the following limitations of the porting capabilities of XPress:

- **Font compatibility**   Perhaps the most significant anomaly you may encounter when porting files across platforms is the ever-present problem with font compatibility. Windows users often employ the use of TrueType fonts, while Macintosh users tend to avoid them. In the opposing direction, Macintosh platform users often use Adobe Type 1 fonts, which may not be available on the Windows platform.

> **Tip** *When porting a file between platforms, be sure to also port all supporting files that may have been imported into your document file. In some cases, files may need to be reimported to display or print properly. You don't need to create new picture boxes to accomplish this; when the file is ported, QuarkXPress will retain all scaling, color, picture*

box specifications, and so on. Using the Pictures tab of the Utilities, Usage dialog box enables you to reestablish the links between your XPress document and the imported files. If your pictures don't display properly because they feature PICT previews, you may need to reopen the file in your image editor or illustration application, resave it with a TIFF preview, and then update the link.

■ **Incompatible application preferences**   Your QuarkXPress preferences application file (located in your QuarkXPress folder) won't port successfully across platforms. The XPress preferences file controls application preferences for your version of QuarkXPress and stores user settings, custom kerning and tracking information, hyphenation exceptions, other customized preferences, and so on. However, the preferences you've set in your document for such things as style sheets, colors, H&Js, lists, and Dashes & Stripes will open seamlessly on the platform to which your file is ported.

■ **Incompatible Library files**   QuarkXPress 5 Library files and auxiliary dictionaries will not be ported across platforms.

■ **Incompatible picture files**   Certain picture file formats may not port between platforms, and even if successfully ported, some pictures may not appear or print as they should. For example, the popular PICT format on the Macintosh operating system may not properly port to Windows. Likewise, pictures prepared in the Windows Metafile format on Windows versions of QuarkXPress 5 may not display or print correctly when ported to the Macintosh. Instead, use the application used to create the picture to save the file in a Macintosh-compatible format such as TIFF or EPS and reimport the picture after your document has been ported to the other platform.

■ **Macintosh file-linking issues**   Likewise, the Publish and Subscribe features unique to the Macintosh operating system aren't supported on Windows versions of XPress 5.

■ **File updating isn't automatic**   When opening a ported XPress document on a different platform version, you may discover that the file isn't automatically saved in the current platform version. To save (and update) the file, use the Save (CMD/CTRL+S) or Save As (CMD/CTRL+OPTION/ALT+S) commands. After being saved, the file will be compatible with your current platform version.

■ **Porting ligature characters**   When moving files from Macintosh to Windows, you may also encounter problems associated with the use of ligatures. A ligature is a single character that incorporates the shape of two joined characters and is often used in certain instances by professional desktop publishers. In these cases, there simply is no equivalent on Windows. Character spacing and size may also differ slightly between platform versions of a certain font. If your document uses fonts where these differences exist, you may encounter text reflow problems due to the difference in spacing or size. Again, there's simply no quick or easy workaround for this without closely examining text in the ported file against an original hard-copy proof of the document file being ported. Spacing and line breaks may then be corrected manually. If you're going to produce a variety of documents in a cross-platform environment, take the time to locate fonts that are available in the same version for both platforms. Then test the fonts to see if they reflow.

- **Sharing Book files**   Although more than one user on a network may open Book files, all users must be working on the same platform. Book files can't be opened on two different platforms at the same time.

- **Windows file-linking issues**   Object linking and embedding (OLE) objects imported into Windows versions of QuarkXPress 5 won't be supported when the file is ported to a Macintosh version of QuarkXPress 5.

Getting Alert Messages

If you're faced with the challenge of porting files, QuarkXPress may display a series of alert messages as the files are opened, depending on the contents of the document and how it's been prepared. Alert messages are designed to warn you of undesirable circumstances while working with your XPress document, and the Quark engineers have spared no effort in implementing the most commonly encountered of these.

As noted earlier, ligature characters available to certain fonts on the Macintosh platform in many cases aren't supported by Windows. So, this warning simply informs you of this fact. When you see the ligatures warning, you may want to check your ported document against hard copies of the original document file to determine whether text reflow has occurred (and whether incorrect characters have been substituted for ligatures). Also note that if you subsequently reopen the document in the Macintosh version of QuarkXPress 5, the Ligatures feature remains off. If you want ligatures, you'll need to turn the feature back on by checking the Ligatures option in the Character tab of the Document Preferences dialog box.

The next dialog box to appear during the porting process is likely the Preferences alert (see Figure 20-8). A variety of preferences saved with the original document may not be compatible with the alternate platform version you're currently using to open the file. In the case of preference warnings, clicking the Keep Document Settings button is often the safest route to follow. The Preference alert also provides information regarding the incompatibility of the preferences compared to your document and your application preference file.

Updating Font and Picture Usage

Following this preferences warning, you'll likely encounter the most significant warning of all: the Fonts Warning dialog box (see Figure 20-9). As mentioned earlier, unless the system being ported *to* has the same fonts installed, this warning will no doubt appear. If fonts aren't a concern, you may click the Continue button and your fonts will automatically be substituted with your system's default font (which is

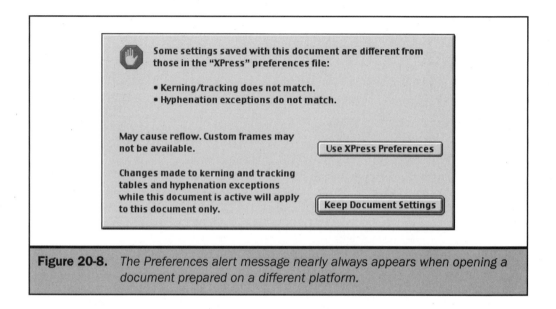

Figure 20-8.   *The Preferences alert message nearly always appears when opening a document prepared on a different platform.*

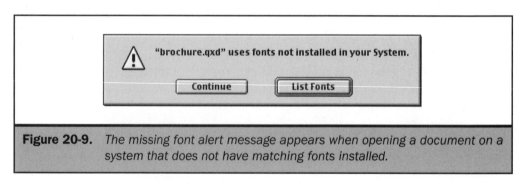

Figure 20-9.   *The missing font alert message appears when opening a document on a system that does not have matching fonts installed.*

usually not desirable). Unfortunately, this usually results in overflowing text boxes, making it difficult to salvage the layout or read all the text in the document.

Most digital layout artists experienced with using QuarkXPress between platforms will likely find themselves feeling a little uneasy about seeing this message, and rightly so. Font substitution problems can often require hours of corrective work. To avoid this, if you have access to the document's missing fonts, close the file without saving any changes and install the font(s) on the host system. To set substitutes for the missing font(s) before opening your file, click the List Fonts button to view a list and set the substitutes as shown in Figure 20-10. For each missing font in the list, select the font, click Replace to access a list of your currently installed fonts, and choose a replacement.

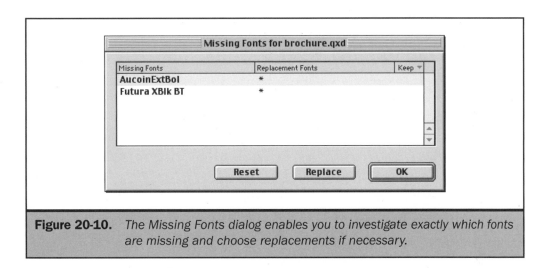

Figure 20-10. *The Missing Fonts dialog enables you to investigate exactly which fonts are missing and choose replacements if necessary.*

Tip   *When porting QuarkXPress 5 document files from Macintosh to Windows program versions, adding the three-letter file extension .QXD (including the period) will make opening the file less problematic. Adding this extension will enable you to view the document in the Open dialog box, since the Windows default Files of Type drop-down menu is set to automatically display files with this extension. For QuarkXPress template documents, add the .QXT extension. Macintosh document files don't normally use file extensions, unless added by the user.*

If you choose to open the document without setting replacements, you may still view the missing fonts by using the Usage command's Fonts tab, which should perhaps be the first dialog box you visit after opening any ported file. Missing fonts are indicated in the list by curly braces ({ and }), while the weight and style are indicated inside less than/greater than symbols, < and >. Clicking the More information option will expand the dialog box to reveal further comments regarding the font. To open the Usage dialog box (see Figure 20-11), choose Utilities, Usage.

The Usage dialog box also enables you to view a list of the missing or modified pictures that the document requires to print properly. Clicking the Pictures tab of the Usage command will list all pictures in the document (see Figure 20-12) and will enable you to reimport them, a step that's always necessary to reestablish a picture's location and linking information.

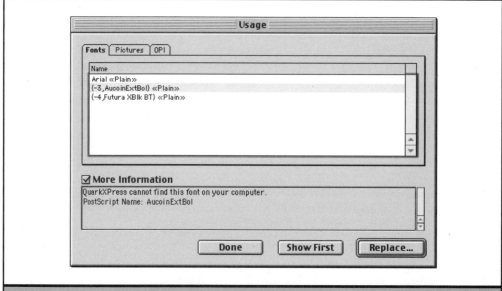

Figure 20-11. *After opening your ported file, you may still choose substitutes for missing fonts by opening the Usage dialog.*

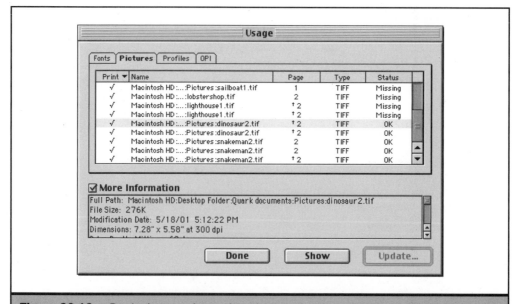

Figure 20-12. *Replacing or reimporting pictures that have become unlinked is a common practice when opening files from other platforms.*

Tip

Updating your QuarkXPress document files from previous versions of XPress can be a tricky operation. When you open a version 4 document in version 5, the first time you save, the Save As dialog box will open and force you to choose a new format: 4 or 5. Quark implemented this as a safeguard against users accidentally converting all their documents to version 5 files. You'll need to rename the document and save it over your existing document file to update it for version 5. To save your XPress 5 document as an XPress 4 document, use the Save As (CMD/CTRL+OPTION/ALT+S) command and choose 4 from the Version drop-down menu.

With these somewhat delicate issues in mind, your XPress files may be successfully ported between Macintosh and Windows platforms (or vice versa). But, as you might have gathered, the process is far from being completely seamless. In certain cases, you may want to plan or structure your document with these issues taken into consideration, especially if you work in a complex, multiplatform publishing environment.

Glossary

In the discussion of commands, procedures, and QuarkXPress-specific features in this book, you're undoubtedly going to encounter terms you may be unfamiliar with. Although a good portion of these mysterious terms originate from the use of QuarkXPress itself, many are specific industry terms that are referred to occasionally. The aim of this glossary is to define these terms in an easy-to-understand language. Although it is by no means a comprehensive dictionary of all the terms you may encounter, it will provide you with an understanding of those that are most commonly used.

1-bit   A color format consisting of black (or any color) paired with white, it usually refers to color schemes associated with line art.

8-bit   A color format consisting of 256 colors.

Agates   A unit of measure used to describe vertical column length in advertising when calculating the depth (and cost) of the ad space used. The QuarkXPress ruler increments may be set to agates in the General tab of the Edit | Preferences | Document (CMD/CTRL+Y) command.

Alert   A dialog that may appear if QuarkXPress (or your operating system) detects a problem with your application, your system, or your system drives. Alerts also appear when you are about to perform an operation that can't be undone using Edit commands.

Alt (alternate) text   Text commonly used to identify visual elements and that may be added to picture files in web documents.

Anchor   The term given to any item that is pasted between characters or paragraphs in a text box. Since anchors become part of the text in your text box, they may move freely with the flow of text in your document. While creating web documents, the term anchor can also refer to a hyperlink destination, which refers to a specific point on a web page.

Ascender   The portion of a text character that extends above the character's x-height.

ASCII   The acronym for American Standards Code Information Interchange, it has long been a standard for data representing digital files.

Auto leading   The term used to describe the vertical spacing between lines of text in your document while Auto is selected as the leading value. By default, the QuarkXPress Auto Leading feature is set to 20 percent of the character height, but this value may be customized in the Paragraph section of the Preferences dialog accessed by choosing Edit | Preferences | Preferences (CMD/CTRL+Y) and clicking Paragraph under Document in the tree directory.

Baseline   The imaginary line on which all type rests.

Baseline grid   This term describes the vertical spacing measurement associated with your document's layout and/or design. When text and items in your document are made to align with the baseline grid, the result may often be a more professional-looking document. Baseline grids in QuarkXPress underlie all items on your document page and are invisible and nonprinting. The spacing of the baseline grid may be set using the Paragraph tab of the Preferences dialog accessed by choosing Edit | Preferences | Preferences (CMD/CTRL+Y). Baseline Grid display may be toggled using the View | Show/Hide Baseline Grid command (OPTION/CTRL+F7).

Baseline shift   The amount of space that a character is offset above or below its original baseline.

Bézier   This term is named after mathematician Pierre Bézier and it describes curves using two points, each controlled by a curve handle. The shape of a Bézier curve is defined by the relative position of the two points and the relative position of the curve handles associated with those points.

Bitmap   This term is used to describe graphic images (which QuarkXPress considers pictures) that are composed of a pattern of pixels. The term bitmap is often interchangeable with the term *raster*, which describes a file format containing dot patterns measured in resolution values. Bitmaps may contain 1-bit, 2-bit, 8-bit, 24-bit, or 32-bit information and feature color depths such as black and white, grayscale, or color.

Bleed   This term is used to describe the procedure where images are intentionally left to overlap the document page edges, leaving the ink to figuratively bleed off the edge of the trimmed and finished page.

Blend   In QuarkXPress, this refers to a smooth transition between two colors within the background of a box shape.

Body text   The term used to describe text characteristics or the style of the main textual content of a document.

Book   In QuarkXPress, this refers to a specific type of file used in tracking, accessing, and managing the various sections (such as chapters) of a large publication. When these sections are part of a book file, their styles, colors, and hyphenation and justifications (H&Js) may be defined and managed globally.

Box   In QuarkXPress, a box may be any closed path that is capable of supporting pictures or text.

Browser   An application used to view web pages prepared in HTML format.

Check box   An HTML form control element that you may create in a web document. Check boxes are typically used to enable your web page audience to make a selection based on choices such as Yes/No, On/Off, or Select/Deselect.

Choke   In offset printing, this refers to the action or state caused by enlarging the edges of an item applied with a lighter color of ink to overlap the edges of another item applied with a darker color of ink. Choking is performed on different colored items in order to avoid registration problems when the document is reproduced in offset printing.

Cicero   A European measure of font sizes. One cicero is equivalent to 4.55 millimeters.

Columns   The vertical division of text within a text box.

Comp   This is the short term for comprehensive, which is essentially a sketched-out layout plan or design of a document. A comprehensive may be anything from a simply drawn marker sketch to a full-color exact duplicate of the finished printed document.

Composite   A printout where all colors and overlays are printed.

Compound path   A compound path is a shape composed of two or more open or closed paths. In the case of compound paths, the individual paths are referred to as *subpaths*.

Compression   A mathematical process for reducing the amount of memory space used to fully describe a collection of data. A compression package is the software program that uses this process.

Compression software   A program that compresses file size, often used to make it easier to archive, transfer, or transmit files.

Constrain   In QuarkXPress, this term is used to describe three states—moving, rotating, and drawing. When items are moved or rotated, they may be constrained to vertical, horizontal, or angular rotational movement. While shapes are being drawn, the state of the various segments that compose the shape may be constrained vertically, horizontally, or at given angles.

Content tool   This is perhaps one of the most critical tools to be aware of when creating or editing pictures or text in QuarkXPress. While the Content tool is used to edit text, it transforms to an I-beam cursor, and while used for picture manipulation, it becomes a grabber hand.

Crop marks   Corner marks indicating the edges of a printed page.

Crosshairs   Used in ink and printing registration, crosshairs describe marks (also known as registration marks) that printers use to line up separate color film overlays.

CT scan   Continuous tone scan.

Dashes   In QuarkXPress, dashes are essentially the various on/off line patterns you may apply to the borders of boxes or lines.

Default   A predetermined setting for any attribute or property associated with newly created items. In QuarkXPress, nearly all default values or properties may be customized.

Density   Service bureaus refer to density as the value or measure given to the relative opaqueness of a developed film negative.

Descender   The portion of a character that falls below the baseline.

Deselect   For lack of a better term, deselect is used to describe the action of turning an option off, deactivating a feature, or generally changing the state of an object to be *not selected.*

Device profile   A date file representing the color capabilities of a display, printing, or image recording device.

DIC   Stands for Dainippon Ink and Chemicals, Inc., and refers to a Japanese conglomerate that manufactures and catalogs ink colors. The letters DIC are a prefix to their cataloged ink colors.

Didot   A didot is a European unit of measure subdivided into smaller units called *ciceros*. It is equivalent to 1.07 times a U.S. point; 67.567 didots equals one inch.

Digital halftone   A printed digital image composed of various sized dots of resolution and arranged in rows to simulate a continuous tone, photographic, or graphic image. A digital halftone is usually produced from scanning hardware or from a digital-image manipulation software program.

Digital image   An image that is described by way of data, or ones and zeros. More specifically, a digital image is a term that usually refers to a photographic-type image.

Dot gain   This term refers to the phenomena of ink soaking into dry paper (absorption rate). The image becomes slightly larger and may be distorted. You can compensate for the gain at the film stage by adjusting the size of the dots.

Download   The action of transferring a file between a local computer system to a remote computer system.

Dpi   Stands for dots per inch, which refers to a measure of dots in scanning or imagesetter resolution. Dpi also may refer to the detail an imagesetter renders on a film negative or positive.

Driver   A file composed of machine programming commands that communicates between software and hardware.

Drop cap   The term given to applying the first letter in a paragraph with character properties larger and more pronounced than the text to follow.

Drum scanner   A type of scanner in which the original is mounted on a drum-style holder and spun at high speeds while a laser digitally records the image.

DTP   An abbreviation for desktop publishing.

Em dash   A dash the width of two zeros of a given font.

Em space   Traditional typesetting defines an em space as a space with a width equal to the height of a given font. Defaults in QuarkXPress set an em space's width equal to two zeros of a given font.

Emulsion   A photosensitive, silver-based coating applied to one side of a sheet of a polyester carrier. You can recognize the emulsion side of the film by its dull, non-reflective appearance.

En dash   The size of an en dash is exactly half the width of an em dash and slightly larger than a hyphen. To create an en dash, enter the keyboard shortcut OPTION/ALT+- (hyphen).

En space   The size of an en space is exactly half the width of an em space. To enter an en space, use the keyboard shortcut OPTION/ALT+SPACE.

EPS   Stands for Encapsulated PostScript and refers to textual data representing a complete page or image. EPS files are based on PostScript, a page description language invented by Adobe that has become a standard in the desktop industry for describing vector-based pages and images that may be printed independently of the resolution limitations of the device in use.

Extension   In Windows-platform applications, this term typically refers to the three characters following a file's name after a separating dot. The extension often indicates which program the file originated from or which program is capable of editing it. On the Windows platform, typical QuarkXPress document files are given the extension QXD.

Filter   A fibrous, paper-thin material featuring minute perforations that enable particle-laden liquids to pass through it. Such bean-based liquid beverages are often used to stimulate the brains of writers who largely ignore their health and sanity in order to meet deadlines and fulfill contractual agreements.

Flatbed   A type of scanner in which the original is placed face down on a flat document glass and a reflection-sensitive light bar passes below it, recording the image data.

Font conflict   This is a state that occurs when one font has the same font identification number as another. This problem is essentially a thing of the past, but font conflict plagued service bureaus in the early days before font identification standards were set.

Fonts   The digital description of a typeface. The term originates from early typesetting systems that used large metal or nylon discs with images of letters cut out of them to represent typefaces.

Form   One or more HTML control elements that may be created in web documents to enable text entry, menu selection, or variable selection in order for a web audience to upload to a web server from a web page.

Frame   In QuarkXPress, this term is used to describe the properties of the outer border of a box.

GCR   Gray Component Replacement, which is the process of replacing Red, Green, or Blue (RGB) color with gray values.

Grayscale   A term from the days of camera work where a small strip of photographic paper graduated in steps of gray was photographed and developed along with artwork, acting as a benchmark for film density and image quality. Digitally speaking, a grayscale describes density values.

Greek   In QuarkXPress, to greek a picture or text is to enable it to display without any detail. Instead, a gray color appears in picture boxes, or gray stripes appear to roughly represent the text shape.

Halftone   The term given to a picture that will eventually be reproduced in dots of varying sizes to simulate varying degrees of gray or color.

Header   In QuarkXPress, this may actually be two different things. A header may be the text appearing at the top of a page to identify the subsection of a larger document. It may also be the information contained in a picture file used to describe the image it contains. Picture headers may be in various resolutions, color conditions, or color levels.

Highlight   This may be either a state or action. When an item or text is highlighted, it is immediately available for editing. To highlight text or an item is to *select* it, causing it to be available for editing.

HQS   High-quality screening, a screening algorithm developed by Linotype, makers of Linotronic imagesetters. The purpose of HQS technology is to optimize the screen angle when imaging process color separations in order to reduce the frequency of undesirable moirés.

HTML   Stands for Hypertext Markup Language, a standardized tagging language used to format web page content.

Hyperlink destination   Hyperlinks are designed to navigate to different pages within a web page or to pages of other web sites. Both text and pictures may be applied with hyperlinks.

I-beam   The style of cursor used by QuarkXPress while working in text boxes using the Content tool.

Image Map   Invisible "hot" or clickable areas on a picture that (when clicked from a browser window) enable web page viewers to change to different hyperlink destinations.

Imagesetter   A PostScript or non-PostScript printer that generates a hard-copy printout.

Insertion point   The point at which your I-beam cursor has been or will be clicked, indicating a point for text entry.

Invisible characters   In QuarkXPress, the term invisible refers to non-printing characters such as paragraph returns, spaces, line feeds, and tab characters. In QuarkXPress, you may control the display of invisibles in a text box by choosing View | Show/Hide Invisibles (CMD/CTRL+I).

Item   This is a highly generic term used to describe any element that may exist on your document page. In QuarkXPress, there are four typical types of items—lines, text boxes, picture boxes, and text paths.

Justify   The state of a column of text that aligns on both the right and left margins.

Kerning   The action of editing or altering the space between specific combinations of characters in text with the aim of improving the text's readability.

Knockout   A term that refers to eliminating the shape of a colored area below another shape on a higher layer. The term knockout is the opposite of *overprinting*.

Laminate   Colored layers of a microthin, carrier-film-bonding process that produces a highly accurate color sample of the finished printed film.

Landscape   Represents page orientation and describes both document orientation and print orientation. Document orientation is set in the New Document dialog when your document is first created, while print orientation is set in the Setup tab of the Print dialog box. In QuarkXPress 5, landscape describes a page that has greater width than height.

Leading   The vertical space between lines of text in a column. Leading is often measured in points and measures the distance between baselines of text.

Library   In QuarkXPress, a library is a specific file format that may be used to store pictures, text, or entire QuarkXPress layouts independently of the documents from which the items originate. Library items may be moved between libraries or to document pages and may be exchanged between users.

Ligature   Specialized characters that combine two characters into one. Ligatures are often used to add flair and design to text in artistic documents.

Linear   In QuarkXPress, this refers to a style of color blending. When two color backgrounds are blended in a linear, the transitions occur evenly between the colors.

Line art   Any artwork composed of solid black or solid white images, digital or otherwise.

Linen tester   A small magnifying glass used to closely examine film.

Linotronic   A line of imagesetters manufactured in Germany by a company named Linotype-Hell.

List box   An HTML form control element that you may create in a web document. List boxes are typically used to enable your web page audience to make a choice or selection based on a number of variables.

Loop   A small magnifier used to closely examine film.

LPI   An acronym for lines per inch, this refers to the number of rows of dots counted in one linear inch of a color tint or halftone screen in printed output.

Mailto   An HTML element that may be created in a web document to enable your web audience to automatically launch their email application to compose new email to a specific recipient.

Master items   These are items that automatically appear on your document pages and originate and are controlled by master pages. Master page items may be manipulated like other items on your document page.

Master page   One of the key features of QuarkXPress is the capability to create and apply master pages with commonly used page elements and properties. Master pages are nonprinting pages that automatically create page properties and items when applied.

Menu list   Lists of items that may be set to display in a list form control or a pop-up form control in a form box.

Meta tag   Meta tags are invisible text that precedes HTML tagging in an HTML document and enables you to specify how web search engines catalog the content of a web page.

Moiré Pronounced more-aye, this is an effect whereby a blurry checkerboard pattern appears when screening angles are improperly aligned. Moirés are most commonly seen on final printed documents or scanned images that have been previously screened.

Nested fonts Caused by performing unwise procedures such as importing EPS files containing fonts into a drawing in QuarkXPress, and then exporting the file in the same or a different file format.

Nesting files Like nested fonts, this is an unwise practice caused by importing files into a drawing in QuarkXPress, and then exporting the file in the same or a different file format.

Nudge This term refers to the action of moving items or pictures in boxes in one-point increments using the left, right, up, or down arrow keys on your keyboard. You may also nudge items or pictures in boxes $1/10$ of a point by holding the OPTION/ALT key in combination with the arrow keys.

Overprint In offset printing, the term overprint refers to the action of layering the color of one item on top of another differently colored item. An overprint is the opposite of a knockout.

Palette In QuarkXPress, this is a term given to an interface element that may "float" on your document window and represent a specific collection of properties or feature options. Palettes may be minimized or maximized by double-clicking their title bars.

Pica A unit of measure unique to the printing industry and widely adopted in desktop publishing to measure fonts, page coordinates, sizes, or distances. Six picas are equivalent to one inch and are subdivided into a smaller measure called points. Each pica is subdivided into 12 points, so an inch is equivalent to 72 points.

PICT A file format commonly available on the Macintosh platform that supports both vector and bitmap.

Pixel A measure of display resolution.

Plate Interchangeable with the term separation, this refers to the paper or metal sheets installed onto an offset printing press or a color separation or film overlay representing an ink color.

PMS Stands for Pantone Matching System and is widely used for specifying colors in the printing industry.

Point A unit of measure unique to the printing industry and widely adopted in the desktop publishing field to measure fonts, page coordinates, sizes, or distances. One point is equal to $1/72$ of an inch, while 12 points are equal to 1 pica.

Point size   A measure of the size of a character.

Pop-up menu   An HTML form control element that you may create in a web document. Pop-up menus are typically used to enable your web page audience to make a choice or selection based on a number of variables in a pop-up-style selection.

Portrait   This represents page orientation and describes both document orientation and print orientation. Document orientation is set in the New Document dialog when your document is first created, while print orientation is set in the Setup tab of the Print dialog box. In QuarkXPress 5, portrait describes a page that has greater height than width.

PPD   This is the acronym for PostScript Printer Description and is a file representing the specific properties of an output or printing device.

Preview   In QuarkXPress, this term refers to the low-resolution image QuarkXPress uses to represent picture files placed on your document page.

Print file   A PostScript text file created when printing a document. On the Windows platform, print files are usually recognized by the file extension PRN. A print file may contain all the information necessary for imaging a file to a particular printer.

Processing   This term means either film processing or image (data) processing. Film processing is the task of developing, fixing, and washing exposed film; data processing refers to computer calculations that the raster image processor (RIP) of an imagesetter performs.

Processor   This term refers to either the machine that physically develops, stops, fixes, washes, and dries the actual imagesetter film, or the main computer chip that drives your computer.

Proof   The term given to a printed document used for reviewing the text, composition, and/or color of a document before it is reproduced in offset printing.

Property   This is a generic term given to describe the characteristics of items or elements on your document page. Properties include variables such as style, position, color, condition, and so on.

Radio button   An HTML form control element that you may create in a web document. Radio buttons are typically used to enable your web page audience to make a selection based on choices such as Yes/No, On/Off, or Select/Deselect.

Raster graphic   This term is used to describe graphic images (which QuarkXPress considers pictures) that are composed of a pattern of pixels. The term raster graphic is often interchangeable with the term *bitmap*.

Registration   The procedure of matching several film overlays by alignment markings imaged onto the film and the images on the film itself.

Resident scans   Digital images stored at the service bureau for the convenience of imaging linked client files.

Resolution   The measure of detail contained in a displayed or printed image. Resolution may also refer to the level of detail an imagesetter records on film. The higher the resolution, the more detail displayed, printed, or recorded.

Reverse   The term reverse refers to the action of applying white to an area in order to reproduce a shape.

Rich black   This is a formulated process color that appears and prints as black, but may appear more saturated and intense than simply printing 100 percent black alone. Rich black may be composed of 100 percent black ink, plus an additional color or colors, such as cyan and/or magenta.

RIP   Raster image processor, which is a term that refers to the data-crunching engine in many imagesetters. Commonly referred to as a RIP, which can be interchanged as a noun or a verb. For example, a file is RIPped before it is imaged.

Rollover   A two-step animated picture effect designed to react to a cursor positioned over a specific point on a web page being viewed in a web page browser. While the picture is visible on the web page, the first image is visible, and while the cursor is held over the picture, a different picture is displayed.

RRED   Right reading emulsion down, which describes the condition of imaged film. RRED describes film that, when held up with the emulsion side facing away, contains images and type that are read from left to right.

RREU   Right reading emulsion up, which describes the condition of imaged film. RREU describes film that, when held up with the emulsion side facing toward you, contains images and type that are read from left to right.

Runaround   This term describes text that is set to follow the contours of a picture or another item's shape. In QuarkXPress, you may apply runaround effects automatically by using the Runaround tab of the Modify dialog box (CMD/CTRL+T).

Screen frequency   Describes the LPI or number of rows of dots measured in one linear inch.

Segment   This term refers to a line or curve created between two Bézier points.

SelectSet   A line of imagesetters developed by AGFA, Inc.

Separation   In QuarkXPress, the term separation refers to the dissection of various layers of ink color onto film with the purpose of printing colors on an offset printing press.

Solid   When a color is solid, its shade has been set to 100 percent. When referring to leading, the term solid refers to a leading space of none, meaning no additional space (besides the vertical height of the characters) has been applied between lines of text.

Source file   The original or native file created by a program.

Spooler   A type of software program or dedicated computer that handles the print traffic between one or several computers and one or several imagesetters. Files may be held in the spooler indefinitely or until it is necessary to image them.

Spread   Two or more pages positioned beside each other. In QuarkXPress, pages may be viewed, printed, or exported as spreads.

Text chain   This refers to text boxes that have been linked together using linking tools. When text boxes are linked, text may flow from one text box in the chain to another as the text changes size or content is added or removed.

Tiles   The individual sections that may be printed when the dimensions of a document exceed the maximum size of the output material.

Title bar   The portion of an interface element, such as the QuarkXPress application window, a document window, or a palette, that identifies the element. A title bar may also contain command buttons that offer control over the window or palette it belongs to.

Track   The state of the spacing between words and characters in a string of text.

Trap   A condition where one color item has been expanded to overlap the edges of another differently colored item in order to compensate for press misregistration.

Uncheck   The state or action where a feature or option is deselected or *turned off*.

URL   Stands for Uniform Resource Locator and typically identifies a web site as its site address.

Web Safe   The Web Safe palette is a collection of colors designed specifically to work with virtually any browser used on either Macintosh or Windows platforms.

X-Height   The height of a lower-case character minus the height of ascenders and descenders.

XML   Stands for Extensible Markup Language, a standardized tagging format that enables you to label different types of content.

Index

Q

INTERNATIONAL CONTACT INFORMATION

AUSTRALIA
McGraw-Hill Book Company Australia Pty. Ltd.
TEL +61-2-9417-9899
FAX +61-2-9417-5687
http://www.mcgraw-hill.com.au
books-it_sydney@mcgraw-hill.com

CANADA
McGraw-Hill Ryerson Ltd.
TEL +905-430-5000
FAX +905-430-5020
http://www.mcgrawhill.ca

GREECE, MIDDLE EAST,
NORTHERN AFRICA
McGraw-Hill Hellas
TEL +30-1-656-0990-3-4
FAX +30-1-654-5525

MEXICO (Also serving Latin America)
McGraw-Hill Interamericana Editores S.A. de C.V.
TEL +525-117-1583
FAX +525-117-1589
http://www.mcgraw-hill.com.mx
fernando_castellanos@mcgraw-hill.com

SINGAPORE (Serving Asia)
McGraw-Hill Book Company
TEL +65-863-1580
FAX +65-862-3354
http://www.mcgraw-hill.com.sg
mghasia@mcgraw-hill.com

SOUTH AFRICA
McGraw-Hill South Africa
TEL +27-11-622-7512
FAX +27-11-622-9045
robyn_swanepoel@mcgraw-hill.com

UNITED KINGDOM & EUROPE
(Excluding Southern Europe)
McGraw-Hill Publishing Company
TEL +44-1-628-502500
FAX +44-1-628-770224
http://www.mcgraw-hill.co.uk
computing_neurope@mcgraw-hill.com

ALL OTHER INQUIRIES Contact:
Osborne/McGraw-Hill
TEL +1-510-549-6600
FAX +1-510-883-7600
http://www.osborne.com
omg_international@mcgraw-hill.com

New Solutions for QuarkXPress™

Printools™ XT
The Ultimate in Printing Assistance

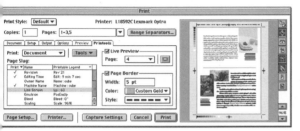

Discover how easy printing can be – streamlined, intuitive and amazingly error-free. Let Printools XT simplify and shorten your daily printing tasks. You'll wonder how you ever managed to print without it before.

Interactive Print Previews
Preflighting
Batch Printing
Interactive Manual Tiling
Rename At Print

• **Create Print Styles**
• **Print/Save Usage Reports**
• **Additional Page Tags**
• **Print Selected Items**
• **Add Page Border**

FullColor™ XT
The Art of Color Control

Experience exceptional freedom in working with colors and blends. FullColor's interactive controls will help you achieve color workflow with an elegance and efficiency you haven't found until now.

• **Create, Edit and Manage Colors and Blends Instantly**
• **Save Blends as Color Swatches**
• **Search for Colors and Blends**
• **Options for Filtering the Color List**
• **Drag and Drop Colors Between Panels**
• **View Color Usage**
• **Mixer with CMYK, RGB, Web Safe Models**
• **Color Inheritance**
• **Dockable Palette**

FullMeasure™ XT
Full Power to the Measurements Palette

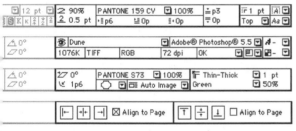

Save endless trips to menus and dialogs with the supercharged FullMeasure XT strip. All the essential controls, plus valuable time-saving tools, are now at your fingertips – without cluttering your screen space.

Text and Paragraph Attributes
Complete Picture Information
Box and Frame Attributes
Word Count and Change Case
Add Guides Precisely

• **View Imported Fonts and Colors**
• **Fit Picture/Text to Box**
• **Preferences and Units**
• **Item Alignments**

LiveKeys™ XT
The Key to Productivity

LiveKeys XT gives you the freedom you need to make QuarkXPress shortcuts work just the way you want. With this new ability to assign and change all program shortcuts, you are no longer limited to the standard keyboard equivalents.

• **Fully Customize All Menu Shortcuts**
• **Assign Shortcuts to Tools**
• **View and Redefine Hidden Shortcuts**
• **Change Style Sheet Keystrokes Easily**
• **Check for Shortcut Conflicts**
• **Load and Save Custom Sets**

www.badiaxt.com

badia
software™

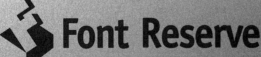

About the CD-Rom

What's on the CD

The CD included with this book contains a variety of QuarkXPress XTensions for your use from the following companies:

Badia Software

Imhof/EDV

DiamondSoft, Inc

Xpedient Corporation

Koyosha Graphics of America, Inc

Please note that at press time, a few of the vendors were still perfecting their XTensions for the new version of QuarkXPress, so they have included a late beta version of their product along with a link to the updated version. Please see the ReadMe files for each vendor for specifics on the different products.

 There are XTensions for Macintosh and for PC users, and you'll find these in separate folders.

To Use the CD

Load the CD into your machine's CD drive. Use Windows Explorer or your favorite method to locate the contents of the CD, and double click the CD icon to view the contents. You can browse through each of the vendor's folders and pick which products you'd like to explore.

THIS PRODUCT (THE "PRODUCT") CON   AND INFORMATION (INCLUDING DOCUMENTATION) OWNED BY THE McGRAW-HILL COMPANIES, INC. ("McGRAW-HILL") AND ITS LICENSORS. YOUR RIGHT TO USE THE PRODUCT IS GOVERNED BY THE TERMS AND CONDITIONS OF THIS AGREEMENT.

LICENSE: Throughout this License Agreement, "you" shall mean either the individual or the entity whose agent opens this package. You are granted a non-exclusive and non-transferable license to use the Product subject to the following terms:

(i) If you have licensed a single user version of the Product, the Product may only be used on a single computer (i.e., a single CPU). If you licensed and paid the fee applicable to a local area network or wide area network version of the Product, you are subject to the terms of the following subparagraph (ii).

(ii) If you have licensed a local area network version, you may use the Product on unlimited workstations located in one single building selected by you that is served by such local area network. If you have licensed a wide area network version, you may use the Product on unlimited workstations located in multiple buildings on the same site selected by you that is served by such wide area network; provided, however, that any building will not be considered located in the same site if it is more than five (5) miles away from any building included in such site. In addition, you may only use a local area or wide area network version of the Product on one single server. If you wish to use the Product on more than one server, you must obtain written authorization from McGraw-Hill and pay additional fees.

(iii) You may make one copy of the Product for back-up purposes only and you must maintain an accurate record as to the location of the back-up at all times.

COPYRIGHT; RESTRICTIONS ON USE AND TRANSFER: All rights (including copyright) in and to the Product are owned by McGraw-Hill and its licensors. You are the owner of the enclosed disc on which the Product is recorded. You may not use, copy, decompile, disassemble, reverse engineer, modify, reproduce, create derivative works, transmit, distribute, sublicense, store in a database or retrieval system of any kind, rent or transfer the Product, or any portion thereof, in any form or by any means (including electronically or otherwise) except as expressly provided for in this License Agreement. You must reproduce the copyright notices, trademark notices, legends and logos of McGraw-Hill and its licensors that appear on the Product on the back-up copy of the Product which you are permitted to make hereunder. All rights in the Product not expressly granted herein are reserved by McGraw-Hill and its licensors.

TERM: This License Agreement is effective until terminated. It will terminate if you fail to comply with any term or condition of this License Agreement. Upon termination, you are obligated to return to McGraw-Hill the Product together with all copies thereof and to purge all copies of the Product included in any and all servers and computer facilities.

DISCLAIMER OF WARRANTY: THE PRODUCT AND THE BACK-UP COPY ARE LICENSED "AS IS." McGRAW-HILL, ITS LICENSORS AND THE AUTHORS MAKE NO WARRANTIES, EXPRESS OR IMPLIED, AS TO THE RESULTS TO BE OBTAINED BY ANY PERSON OR ENTITY FROM USE OF THE PRODUCT, ANY INFORMATION OR DATA INCLUDED THEREIN AND/OR ANY TECHNICAL SUPPORT SERVICES PROVIDED HEREUNDER, IF ANY ("TECHNICAL SUPPORT SERVICES"). McGRAW-HILL, ITS LICENSORS AND THE AUTHORS MAKE NO EXPRESS OR IMPLIED WARRANTIES OF MERCHANTABILITY OR FITNESS FOR A PARTICULAR PURPOSE OR USE WITH RESPECT TO THE PRODUCT. McGRAW-HILL, ITS LICENSORS, AND THE AUTHORS MAKE NO GUARANTEE THAT YOU WILL PASS ANY CERTIFICATION EXAM WHATSOEVER BY USING THIS PRODUCT. NEITHER McGRAW-HILL, ANY OF ITS LICENSORS NOR THE AUTHORS WARRANT THAT THE FUNCTIONS CONTAINED IN THE PRODUCT WILL MEET YOUR REQUIREMENTS OR THAT THE OPERATION OF THE PRODUCT WILL BE UNINTERRUPTED OR ERROR FREE. YOU ASSUME THE ENTIRE RISK WITH RESPECT TO THE QUALITY AND PERFORMANCE OF THE PRODUCT.

LIMITED WARRANTY FOR DISC: To the original licensee only, McGraw-Hill warrants that the enclosed disc on which the Product is recorded is free from defects in materials and workmanship under normal use and service for a period of ninety (90) days from the date of purchase. In the event of a defect in the disc covered by the foregoing warranty, McGraw-Hill will replace the disc.

LIMITATION OF LIABILITY: NEITHER McGRAW-HILL, ITS LICENSORS NOR THE AUTHORS SHALL BE LIABLE FOR ANY INDIRECT, SPECIAL OR CONSEQUENTIAL DAMAGES, SUCH AS BUT NOT LIMITED TO, LOSS OF ANTICIPATED PROFITS OR BENEFITS, RESULTING FROM THE USE OR INABILITY TO USE THE PRODUCT EVEN IF ANY OF THEM HAS BEEN ADVISED OF THE POSSIBILITY OF SUCH DAMAGES. THIS LIMITATION OF LIABILITY SHALL APPLY TO ANY CLAIM OR CAUSE WHATSOEVER WHETHER SUCH CLAIM OR CAUSE ARISES IN CONTRACT, TORT, OR OTHERWISE. Some states do not allow the exclusion or limitation of indirect, special or consequential damages, so the above limitation may not apply to you.

U.S. GOVERNMENT RESTRICTED RIGHTS: Any software included in the Product is provided with restricted rights subject to subparagraphs (c), (1) and (2) of the Commercial Computer Software-Restricted Rights clause at 48 C.F.R. 52.227-19. The terms of this Agreement applicable to the use of the data in the Product are those under which the data are generally made available to the general public by McGraw-Hill. Except as provided herein, no reproduction, use, or disclosure rights are granted with respect to the data included in the Product and no right to modify or create derivative works from any such data is hereby granted.

GENERAL: This License Agreement constitutes the entire agreement between the parties relating to the Product. The terms of any Purchase Order shall have no effect on the terms of this License Agreement. Failure of McGraw-Hill to insist at any time on strict compliance with this License Agreement shall not constitute a waiver of any rights under this License Agreement. This License Agreement shall be construed and governed in accordance with the laws of the State of New York. If any provision of this License Agreement is held to be contrary to law, that provision will be enforced to the maximum extent permissible and the remaining provisions will remain in full force and effect.